Japanese/Korean Linguistics

Volume 20

edited by
Bjarke Frellesvig
&
Peter Sells

Published for the Stanford Linguistics Association by

CSLI PUBLICATIONS
Center for the Study of Language and Information
Stanford, California

CSLI Publications
Center for the Study of Language and Information
Leland Stanford Junior University
Printed in the United States
17 16 15 14 13   1 2 3 4 5

Library of Congress Cataloging-in-Publication Data

Conference on Japanese/Korean Linguistics (1st : 1989 : University of Southern California)

Japanese/Korean Linguistics / edited by Hajime Hoji.

Volume 20 / edited by Bjarke Frellesvig and Peter Sells

p.   cm.

Includes bibliographical references and index.
ISBN-13: 978-1-57586-639-0
ISBN-13: 978-1-57586-638-3 (pbk.)

1. Japanese language—Congresses. 2. Korean language—Congresses. 3. Japanese language—Grammar, Comparative—Korean—Congresses. 4. Korean language—Grammar, Comparative—Japanese—Congresses. 5. Linguistics—Congresses. I. Hoji, Hajime. II. Stanford Linguistics Association. III. Center for the Study of Language and Information (U.S.) IV. Title.
PL503.C6 1989
495.6–dc20   90-2550
CIP

∞ The acid-free paper used in this book meets the minimum requirements of the American National Standard for Information Sciences—Permanence of Paper for Printed Library Materials, ANSI Z39.48-1984.

For a list of volumes in this series, along with a cumulative table of contents, please visit

http://cslipublications.stanford.edu/site/JAKO.shtml

CSLI was founded in 1983 by researchers from Stanford University, SRI International, and Xerox PARC to further the research and development of integrated theories of language, information, and computation. CSLI headquarters and CSLI Publications are located on the campus of Stanford University.

CSLI Publications reports new developments in the study of language, information, and computation. Please visit our web site at
http://cslipublications.stanford.edu/
for comments on this and other titles, as well as for changes and corrections by the author and publisher.

Japanese/Korean Linguistics

Volume 20

Contents

Part III
Phonology and Phonetics

Part IV
Experimental Linguistics

Acknowledgments

The 20th Japanese/Korean Linguistics conference was hosted by the University of Oxford, and took place 1-3 October 2010. It was jointly organized by the Research Centre for Japanese Language and Linguistics in the Faculty of Oriental Studies, University of Oxford, and the Department of Linguistics at the School of Oriental and African Studies, University of London. This was the second time that the conference took place outside the U.S. and its first time in Europe. The Research Centre for Japanese Language and Linguistics, which was established by the University of Oxford in March 2009, was particularly pleased to host the conference in Oxford.

Thanks to the British Academy, funds were available to provide bursaries for graduate students working on Japanese and/or Korean linguistics in universities in Europe in order for them to attend the conference. Several students were awarded grants. The conference was also generously supported by the Japan Foundation, the Arts and Humanities Research Council, Hertford College, the Young-Bin Min/Korea Foundation Endowment Fund, and the Oxford University Sasakawa Fund.

The keynote speakers for the conference were: Professor Taro Kageyama (Director, the National Institute for Japanese Language and Linguistics, Tokyo); Professor Young-Key Kim-Renaud (Chair, Department of East Asian Languages and Literatures, George Washington University); and Professor Beth Levin (Department of Linguistics, Stanford University). The majority of the papers presented at the conference are collected here.

We would like to thank Cecily Nowell-Smith who efficiently coordinated and organized the practicalities of the conference in Oxford. The preparation of the volume for publication required the invaluable assistance of Minkoo Kim, Becky Taylor, Carly Collier, and in particular Kerri Russell, and we gratefully acknowledge all their hard work.

Bjarke Frellesvig, Oxford
Peter Sells, York
April 2013

Part I

Discourse

Sequential Context of *-canh-a(yo)*: Hearers' Perspective

HEE JU & SUNG-OCK SOHN
University of California, Los Angeles

1. Introduction

This study examines the sequential contexts of *-canh-a(yo)* 'you know' and its equivalent forms. While previous studies have demonstrated that a speaker invites hearers' alignment through the form, this study investigates the hearers' responses to and with *-canh-a(yo)* utterances. The findings indicate that the form is used both in aligning and disaligning responses—with the latter occurring at a slightly higher frequency. A major function of the form in both types of responses is to provide accounts for participants' explicit or implicit claim. That is, by pointing to what is presumed to be common ground between interlocutors through *-canh-a(yo)* utterances, hearers modulate any stance differential displayed by a prior speaker. Moreover, we investigate how other concurrent resources such as prosody and facial expressions contextualize participants' stance in conjunction with

Japanese/Korean Linguistics 20.
Edited by Bjarke Frellesvig and Peter Sells.

-canh-a(yo). Our findings suggest the reflexivity of grammar and interaction in Korean conversation.

2. Background

Earlier studies have demonstrated that Korean sentence ending *-canh-a(yo)* 'you know' or its equivalent forms[1] indexes speakers' epistemic, affective, and/or moral stance toward a statement (Kawanishi, 1993; Kawanishi & Sohn, 1993, Kim & Suh, 2004; Lo, 2006). Kawanishi and Sohn (1993) discuss how speakers display affective and epistemic stance through the use of the form during conversational story-telling. Lo (2006) shows how *-canh-a(yo)* utterances index speaker's moral stance by showing how afterschool teachers use the form to socialize children. Kang (2009) describes that speakers use *-canh-a(yo)* utterances during complaints or critiques. Park's (2003) analysis of prosodic features of *-canh-a(yo)* shows that high boundary tone accompanied by the form signals speakers' monitoring of hearers' reaction while low boundary tone conveys speakers' assumption of shared information.

Speakers' use of *-canh-a(yo)* utterances not only display their stance but also indicate their expectation of hearers' alignment (Kawanishi & Sohn, 1993). According to Lee (1999), particle *-ci-* consists of the original form of *-canh-a(yo),* i.e., *ci+anh-a(yo),* and indicates a speaker's commitment to stated information. Utterances with *-canh-a(yo)* may signal the speaker's assumption of hearers' agreement toward his/her statement. However, hearers may not necessarily agree with the speaker's *-canh-a(yo)* utterance as Lee (1999) argues.

In so far as previous studies analyzed speakers' use of *-canh-a(yo)*, very few studies have examined how hearers display their stance with respect to prior speaker's *-canh-a(yo)* utterances. This study explores the following issues: (1) How hearers respond to speakers' *-canh-a(yo)* utterances; (2) How hearers use the form to display their stance; (3) How hearers display stance using other concurrent features in conjunction with the form?

The organization of this paper is as follows: Section 3 introduces the data and analytic methods used for this study, including the definition of alignment; Section 4 introduces findings on hearers' responses through *-canh-a(yo)* utterances; Section 5 discusses implication of the findings. Section 6 concludes this study.

[1] Our database indicates that the use of*–canh-* co-occurs predominantly with the polite ending *–yo*. We found very rare cases of formal sentence ending, i.e., *(su)pnita*. The authors appreciate Jieun Kiaer for bringing up this issue.

3. Data And Methods

The data for this study is drawn from Call-Friend Korean corpus of 100 telephone calls (Han et al., 2003) and 10 hour-videotaped face-to-face interaction collected by the authors. First of all, *-canh-a(yo)* utterances were collected from telephone conversation data using AntConc concordance program[2] and categorized into two groups, i.e., 'first position' and 'second position' (see Table 1). The categories are based on the notion of adjacency pairs in conversation, e.g., a speaker's question followed by a recipient's answer or alternative response, or a speaker's assertion followed by a recipient's agreement or disagreement (Heritage 1984; Sacks, 1995; Schegloff 2007; Schegloff and Sacks, 1973). The distribution of *-canh-a(yo)* utterances based on their sequential positions are as follows.

Table 1. Telephone Conversation Data

	First Position	Second Position	Total
LDC	1114	366	1480

Secondly, we compiled a collection of *-canh-a(yo)* utterances produced in response to a prior speaker's talk (totaling 420 segments) by combining 54 examples drawn from video-taped data (see Table 2).

Table 2. Distribution of *-canh-a(yo)* In Second Positions

LDC	366
Face-to-face Conversation	54
Total	420

Responses to and with *-canh-a(yo)* utterances were categorized in terms of recipients' procedural and attitudinal alignment to speakers. The procedural alignment is defined by Stivers (2008:34) as follows:

> When a recipient *aligns* with a telling, he or she supports the structural asymmetry of the storytelling activity: that a storytelling is in progress and the teller has the floor until story completion. *Disaligned* actions undermine this asymmetry by competing for the floor or failing to treat a story as either in progress or—at story completion—as over. Thus, *alignment* is with respect to the activity in progress.

2 Anthony, Lawrence (2007). AntConc 3.1, Waseda University, Japan.

On the other hand, a recipient's attitudinal alignment refers to 'affiliation,' which Stivers (2008:36) describes in the following:

> In contrast to *alignment*, with the term *affiliation* I mean that the hearer displays support of and endorses the teller's conveyed stance. ... in the environment of story completion in which what is due is for the recipient to display his or her stance toward the reported event, preferred and affiliative uptake involves taking a stance that matches the teller's stance toward the event(s) being described as, for example, funny, sad, horrible, or exciting.

Our notion of attitudinal alignment further includes recipients' alignment to a speaker's explicit assertion, which is beyond Stiver's definition described above. Finally, based on our definition of alignment, i.e., procedural and attitudinal, we examined hearers' alignment or disalignment with respect to a prior speaker's talk.

The following section will introduce the distribution of hearers' aligning and disaligning responses within the sequential contexts of *-canh-a(yo)* and discuss the implication of the results.

4. Data Analysis[3]

4.1. Responses To *-canh-a(yo)* Utterances

Our analysis of telephone conversation data indicates responses to prior speakers' *-canh-a(yo)* utterances predominantly display alignment (95%). The result confirms the previous studies' claim that speakers' use of *-canh-a(yo)* tends to invite hearers' alignment (Kawanishi & Sohn 1993).

Table 3. Responses to *-canh-a(yo)* utterances

	Alignment	Disalignment	Total
LDC	1055	59	1114

4.1.1. Alignment

Hearers' aligning responses to *-canh-a(yo)* overwhelmingly occur in story-telling contexts. Many of these responses are in the form of minimal responses, e.g., *uh* 'yes, uh huh,' which occur in response to a speaker's topic initiation (line 2 in Example 1) and/or continuation of a story in progress.

[3] This study uses the following abbreviations: NM: Nominative, AC: Accusative, COMM: Commital, TC: Topic/contrast, POL: Polite, INT: Intimate, INTJ: Interjection, HON: Honorific, MOD: Modality, PST: Past, REP: Reported speech, SH: Subject honorific, Q: Question.

(1) [LDC 4328]

1	A:	iss-canha i cenhwa-iss-ci?
		exist-you know this phone/call-exist-COMM
		'you know, speaking of this phone call?'
2->	B:	ung
		'yes'

Alternative responses include hearers' news receipt, i.e., *kulay* 'really?' in response to speakers' announcement. While minimal responses are the most common response to a speaker's *-canh-a(yo)* utterance, it is evident that hearers produce explicit agreement with the speaker's claim (line 2 in Example 2).

(2) [LDC 5997]

1	B:	kuliko local-un toy-canha
		and local-TC become/work-canha
		'and local connections are ok, right?'
2-->	A:	kuleh-ci
		so-COMM-INT
		'that's right.'

4.1.2. Disalignment

Hearers' disaligning response to a speaker's *-canh-a(yo)* utterance is displayed through rejection of a speaker's conveyed stance, e.g., by not providing an answer or by correcting the prior speaker's talk. In Example (3), B produces negative assessment of a third party using *-canh-a(yo)*. In response, A produces a repair initiator *mwe* 'what' (line 2), which indicates A's trouble with understanding B's talk (Schegloff, 2007). As a result, A disaligns with B's stance.[4]

(3) [LDC 6614]

1	B:	samonim kulekey yeppuci-anh-canha.
		pastor's wife like that pretty-not-you know
		'the pastor's wife is not that pretty, you know.'
2->	A:	mwe. ((laugh))
		'what.'

Alternatively, a hearer may disalign with a speaker's talk by initiating other-correction (Example 4).

(4) [LDC 6559]

4 A's laughter also indicates the inappropriateness of B's comment.

1	A:	twu sal	pan	cengto-myen	ka-canha
		two years	half	about-if	go-canha
		'(kids) go (to preschool) at age two and a half, right?'			
2-->	B:	twu sal	toy-myen-un		
		two years old	become-if-TC		
		'when (they) become two years old'			

In the example above, B corrects A's talk by replacing 'two and a half' with 'two years old' (line 2) and disagrees with A, as a result.

4.2. Responses With *-canh-a(yo)* Utterances

In the earlier section, we have seen that hearers' responses to *-canh-a(yo)* utterances mostly display alignment to a prior speaker's talk. To the contrary, our analysis of hearers' responses with *-canh-a(yo)* indicates that the form is used both in alignment and disalignment, with slightly higher frequency in disalignment, i.e., 167/420 (40%) vs. 253/420 (60%).

Table 4. Responses with -c*anh-a(yo)* utterances

	Alignment	Disalignment	Total
LDC	152	214	366
Video Data	15	39	54
Total	167	253	420

The smaller number of *-canh-a(yo)* utterances in second position compared to first position is attributed to the fact that prior speakers mainly hold the floor in telephone conversation. Overall, the result shows that *-canh-a(yo)* is not always associated with hearers' alignment.

4.2.1. Alignment

As mentioned above, hearers may display alignment to a prior speaker by supporting the speaker's floor and/or endorsing his/her conveyed stance during storytelling. Excerpt (5) in the following is a telephone conversation between two friends. K told S that she had purchased bikini swimwear and continues her story as follows.

(5) [LDC 4012: Swimsuit][5]

7	K:	((smiling voice)) ↑ small	size-lul	sa-ss-ey,	tto::,
		small	size-AC	buy-PST:INT	besides
		'(I) bought small size, besides::,'			

[5] We use following transcript symbols: ? Rising Intonation . Falling Intonation , Continuing Intonation :: Sound stretch - Cut-off ↑ Rising shift in intonation

8-> S: extra small sa-yatoy-canh-a caki-
buy-MOD-COMM-INT yourself
'(you) should buy extra small, right? you-'

In the excerpt, K's smiling voice in line 7 implies that the 'small' size swimsuit does not fit her. Subsequently, S demonstrates her understanding of K's stance by inferring that the swimsuit might be too big for her (line 8)[6]. This example illustrates how a hearer shows her alignment with the speaker's stance through *-canh-a(yo)* utterance immediately following the prior speaker's talk.

However, our data also show that hearers' alignment with the form may not necessarily occur immediately. The prior speaker may have to provide additional information to support his/her stance until the hearer acquiesces to the speaker's stance. In Excerpt (6), J has complained that her room is too small to have a desk and implied that she might have to move out of her parents' house. E suggests that J should use the dining table (line 8).

(6) [LDC 5937: desk]

8 E: ya, chayksang-eps-umyen sikthak ka-se kongpwuha-y.
hey desk-not exist-if table go-and study-INT
'hey, if there is no desk, study at the dining table.'

9 J: **ah hah hah hah**

10 E: uh, apenim ilccik cwumwu-si-lthey-ntey
INTJ father:HON. early sleep:HON-SH-MOD-CIR
'uh, (your) father must be going to bed early.'

((lines 11-13 omitted: J requests clarification and E repeats her utterance))

14-> J: hhh kulay kulayse maynnal
right so everyday
'hhh right. that's why everyday'

15-> J: chayk pottali tul-ko wa-ssta ka-ssta ha-canh-ayo::,
book bag carry-and came and went do-COMM-POL
'(I) move around carrying (my) backpack::,'

16 J: cip-eyse-nun:::,
home-at-TC
'at home:::,'

17 E: ta kulen-ke-ya:::
all so-thing-be:INT
'everyone's like that:::'

---

[6] Through their conversation, it was revealed that K is known to be 'skinny.' S's inference, therefore, is drawn from shared knowledge between the interlocutors.

In the excerpt, J's response with laughter indicates that she does not accept E's suggestion that J should use the dining table (line 9). E provides additional information to justify E's position (line 10). Then, J aligns with E's stance (lines 14-15). This example illustrates how a hearer uses a *-canh-a(yo)* utterance to display alignment with a prior speaker after negotiation of stance.

4.2.2 Disalignment

Hearers display disalignment through competition for floors and/or disaffiliative responses to a prior speaker's talk. Our data demonstrate that hearers often confront a prior speaker by countering his/her statement with a *-canh-a(yo)* utterance, especially when the topic involves shared experiences. In Example (7), SH complains that AR doesn't always finish her food.

(7) [AR & SH]

6	SH:	ku: hangsang ne-ka namki-nikka kulehci
		that always you-NM leave-because so
		'the- it's because you always leave (the food)'
7	AR:	onul-un pyello an namky-ess-canha.
		today-TC much not leave-PST-COMM
		'(I) didn't leave much (food) today, you know.'

In line 7, AR challenges SH (prior speaker) by calling attention to the fact that she did not leave much food on this occasion (line 7). In this example, a recipient uses shared experience to challenge the prior speaker's statement using *-canh-a(yo)* utterance.

When a recipient invokes shared experience between interlocutors to challenge the prior speaker's talk, the prior speaker may not necessarily acknowledge the experience. In Example (8), SEI states that he could be a singer if he keeps on practicing. In response, Lee counters SEI's statement by bringing up a past event in which SEI was negatively critiqued of his vocals.

(8) [Bryan & Maiko]

1	SEI:	ah nay-ka nolay-lul yay- yay-mankhum-man
		INTJ I-NM song-AC this kid this kid-as well as-only
2		pwull-ess-umyen elmana coh-ulkka.
		sing-PST-if how good-Q
		'how wonderful it would be if I could sing just as well as this guy'

3 LEE: kkum kkay.
dream break:INT
'stop dreaming!'
4-> SEI: ya nolay-nun, yensupha-myen ta tway.
hey song-TC practice-if all alright:INT
'hey, as long as (I) practice, (I) can sing.'
5-> LEE: kulay?
so:INT
'really?'
6-> LEE: akka Korean-pan-eyse ku sengak sensayngnim-i
earlier Korean-class-in that voice teacher-NM
7-> LEE: oppa moshanta-ko mak kulay-ss-canha.
older brother not good-QT just say-PST-COMM
'earlier in the Korean class, that voice teacher said that you were no good (at singing), right?'
8-> SEI: nay-ka encey?
I-NM when
'(to) me, when?'

In the example, LEE refutes SEI's claim that he can improve his singing. LEE brings upon past experience where a teacher gives a poor evaluation of SEI's singing performance (lines 4-7). The prior speaker, SEI, however, does not acknowledge the past experience. This example illustrates how disaligning responses may occur in a circular pattern. That is, a recipient disaligns with a prior speaker's stance using a *-canh-a(yo)* utterance, which in turn may be opposed by the prior speaker.

4.2.3 Concurrent Features

The examination of grammatical and lexical forms that co-occur with *-canh-a(yo)* utterances demonstrate that recipients often use a preface to disagreement, e.g., *kuntey* 'but' or *ani* 'no' among others. Moreover, disaligning responses often occur with a topic-contrast marker, i.e., *-(n)un*. These grammatical forms frequently co-occur with *-canh-a(yo)* as a recipient counters prior speakers' utterance to display disalignment.

Excerpt (9) is drawn from a telephone conversation between E and J. E is older than J by six years. In the example, J challenges E's self-deprecation of her own age.

(9) [LDC 5937: age]
9 E: i naimanhun enni-to::, huh huh huh huh
this old older sister-even
'even if I am old::, huh huh huh huh'

10->	J:	kulayto	enni-nun::	↑master-ha-canh-a::↑
		nevertheless	older sister-TC	master-do-COMM-INT
		'but you are working on your ↑Master's (degree), ri::ght ↑'		

11->	J:	na-nun	incey	↑under-canh-a↑
		I-TC	now	undergraduate-COMM-INT
		'(I) am just an ↑under(graduate)↑'		

In the example above, J contrasts E's higher academic standing with her own by employing a parallel structure, i.e., 'I am … (but) you are…,' and topic-contrast marker *–(n)un* in her utterances with *-canh-a(yo)* (lines 10-11). Moreover, the turn-initial marker *kulayto* 'nevertheless, still' signals her disaligning response to E's prior talk.

In conjunction with grammatical resources, the recipient's disalignment is also displayed through prosody. In Example (9) above, the recipient's disalignment is displayed through high pitch, as shown by an upward arrow (line 10). The analysis of the Praat program[7] indicates how J produces sentence final *-canh-a* with drastic pitch contour (see Figure 1).

10->	J:	kulayto	enni-nun::	↑master-ha-canh-a::↑
		nevertheless	older sister-TC	master-do-COMM-INT
		'but you are working on your ↑Master's (degree), ri::ght ↑'		

7 Paul Boersma and David Weenink (2010). Praat 5.2.06. University of Amsterdam.

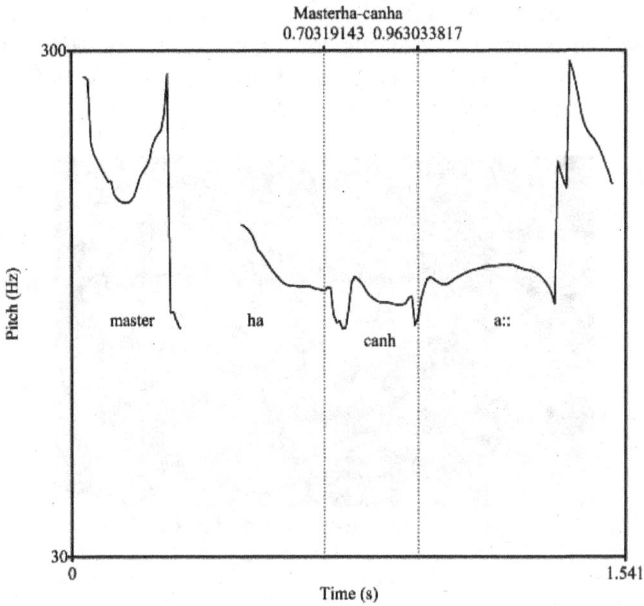

Figure 1. Pitch Contour of *-canh-a(yo)*

According to Park's (2003) prosodic analysis of *-canh-a(yo),* high boundary tone of the form signals that a speaker's monitoring of hearers' reaction. That is, hearers are expected to demonstrate their understanding or recognition of a referent. While Park's study mainly focuses on *-canh-a(yo)* utterances in first position, our analysis indicates that the prosodic features of *-canh-a(yo)* utterances in second position may function differently from those in first position.

In addition to grammatical features and prosody, a recipient's body movements may also display disaligning stance in conjunction with *-canh-a(yo)* utterance. In Excerpt (10), SH complains that AR orders too much food, which has caused him to eat too much. In response, AR denies SH's claim with a *-canh-a(yo)* utterance.

(10) [AR & SH: Food]

1 SH: kulenikka AR-ka com cektanghi sikhi-ko:
so name-NM a little properly order-and
'so, you should order a moderate portion of food'

2-> AR: onul ha(h)na-pakkey an si(h)ky-ess(h)-can(h)ha: ah hah
today one-only not order-PST-canha
'(I) only o(h)rdered o(h)ne dish, you know(h): ah hah'

In the example above, AR's facial expressions including widening eyes and raised eye brows display her disalignment with respect to SH's prior claim (see Figure 2). Moreover, her laughter tokens—as indicated as (h) and 'ah hah'—indicate her stance toward SH's statement.

Figure 2. Facial Expression of AR (left)

5. Discussion

Previous studies claim that hearers' agreement is assumed when speakers use *-canh-a(yo)* utterances (Kawanishi & Sohn 1993; Lee 1999). Our data analysis confirms that hearers' responses to *-canh-a(yo)* utterances are predominantly aligning to a prior speaker's talk. Moreover, our analysis showed that responses with *-canh-a(yo)* utterances display both alignment and disalignment toward a prior speaker's talk. Disaligning responses were slightly more frequent than its counterpart. Furthermore, the results indicate that recipients display disalignment through the use of multimodal resources including prosody and body display in conjunction with the linguistic form *-canh-a(yo)*. The examples illustrated that hearers' disalignment with *-canh-a(yo)* tend to point to what is assumed to be common ground between interlocutors, i.e. shared experiences. Consequently, *-canh-a(yo)* may modulate stance differential displayed among participants.

5.1. Establishing Common Ground[8]

According to our data analysis, it was shown that alignment is not the default context of the form *-canh-a(yo)* in its sequential contexts, e.g., first and second positions. It was also illustrated that interlocutors presume common ground, which may provide or undermine accountability of a prior speaker's claim. Hearers' utterances with *-canh-a(yo)* seem tied to prior speakers' talk in that they provide reasons to accept or reject the prior speakers' claim.

[8] The authors thank Hye Ri Kim for her valuable comments on this point.

That is, *-canh-a(yo)* utterances produced by hearers present accounts to support or undermine a prior speaker's claim. However, the common ground does not necessarily refer to shared experiences between participants (see Kawanishi, 1993; Kawanishi & Sohn, 1993). Regardless of interlocutors' actual awareness or experience, recipients present a fact as if interlocutors should have been aware of it. By pointing out a 'fact' which the other party presumably knows, the *-canh-a(yo)* utterances are effectively used to rule out the other speaker's claim.

5.2 Modulating Stance Differential

We have shown that hearers' *-canh-a(yo)* utterances not only indicate their alignment with a prior speaker's talk but also display their disalignment. Commonly, *-canh-a(yo)* utterances provide accounts for hearers' stance, for example, by invoking some shared experiences that support or undermine the prior speaker's talk. The finding is in line with previous studies' claim that *-canh-a(yo)* utterances index the hearers' assumption of the other party's agreement regardless of its actual realization (see Lee 1999).

In the case of dialigning responses, we argue that hearers use *-canh-a(yo)* as a way of modulating stance differential by invoking common ground between participants. That is, the form provides an interactional resource for hearers to negotiate stance effectively. In so doing, we have seen that hearers employ grammatical resources, e.g., topic-contrast marker *–un/nun*, etc., as well as prosody and facial expression to display disalignment. Accordingly, these multimodal resources contextualize the meaning of *-canh-a(yo)* utterances and the hearer's stance. The findings suggest that the meaning of a form is shaped through contexts rather than predetermined.

6. Conclusion

In this study, we have examined the use of *-canh-a(yo)* by considering sequential contexts of the form and hearers' stance with respect to a prior speaker's talk. We found that the form is used to display not only alignment but also disalignment. Simultaneously-used resources including grammar, prosody, and nonverbal behavior contextualize an interlocutor's stance in the use of the form. Moreover, we found that *-canh-a(yo)* utterances invoke common ground between interlocutors, thus modulating stance differential between interlouctors. Finally, we conclude that the analysis of *-canh-a(yo)* indicates the reflexive relationship between grammar and context: Grammar not only indexes participants' stance in interaction but also may be better understood through contexts (Duranti & Goodwin, 1992; Ochs et al., 1996).

References

Duranti, A. & Goodwin, C. (1992). *Rethinking Context.* Cambridge University Press: Cambridge.

Han, N.-R., Graff, D., & Kim, M. (2003). *Korean Telephone Conversations Lexicon.* Linguistic Data Consortium: Philadelphia.

Heritage, J. (1984). *Garfinkel and ethnomethodology.* Cambridge, UK: Polity Press.

Jefferson, G., Sacks, H., & Schegloff, E. (1987). Notes on laughter in the pursuit of intimacy. In G. Button, & J. Lee, *Talk and social organization* (pp. 152-205). Philadelphia: Multilingual matters.

Kang, H.-H. (2009). A study on teaching method of discourse function of '*-canhta*'. *Korean Semantics , 28*, 1-27.

Kawanishi, Y. (1993). An Analysis of Non-Challengeable Modals: Korean -*canha(yo)* and Japanese -janai. *Japanese/ Korean Linguistics* 3, 95-111.

Kawanishi, Y., & Sohn, S.-O. (1993). Grammaticization of Korean negation: a semantic-pragmatic analysis of *-canh-a(yo).* In S. Kuno, J. Whitman, I.-H. Lee, J. Mailing, & Y.-J. Kim, *The Fifth Harvard International Symposium of Korean Linguistics* (pp. 552-561). Cambridge, MA: The Harvard ISOKL Committee.

Kim, K.-H., & Suh, K.-H. (2004). An analysis of Korean sentence-ending suffixes in caregiver-child interaction. *Ohak Yonku (Language Research)* 40 (4), 923-950.

Lee, H.-S. (1999). A discourse-pragmatic analysis of the committal *-ci* in Korean: a synthetic approach to the form-meaning relation. *Journal of Pragmatics* 31, 243-275.

Lo, A. S.-M. (2006). *Socializing morality: a linguistic anthropological study of Korean American Educatonal Institutions*. Unpublished doctoral dissertation. UCLA.

Ochs, E., Schegloff, E. A., & Thompson, S. A. (1996). *Interaction and Grammar*. Cambridge University Press: Cambridge.

Park, M.-J. (2003). *The meaning of Korean prosodic boundary tones.* Unpublished PhD Dissertation. University of California, Los Angeles.

Sacks, H. (1995 [1992]). *Lectures on conversation: Volumes I & II.* (G. Jefferson, Ed.) Oxford.

Schegloff, E. A. (2007). *Sequence organization in interaction: A primer in conversation analysis.* Cambridge: Cambridge U.P.

Schegloff, E. A., & Sacks, H. (1973). Opening up closings. *Semiotica, 8, 289-327.*

Stivers, T. (2008). Stance, Alignment, and Affiliation During Storytelling: When Nodding Is a Token of Affiliation. *Research on Language and Social Interaction, 41*(1), 31–57.

The Korean Adverb *kunyang* in Spoken Discourse

MARY SHIN KIM & JIEUN KIM
University of Hawai'i & University of Chicago

This study examines the use of the Korean adverb *kunyang* as a stance marker in spoken discourse. *Kunyang* has traditionally been viewed as a manner adverb which can be translated into 'as it is', 'continuously', or 'just', depending on the context, as shown in (1)-(3). [1]

(1) cepsi **kunyang** twe.
dish as:it:is leave:IE
Leave the dish as it is.

(2) pi-ka congil **kunyang** wa.
rain-NOM all:day continuously come:IE
It is raining continuously all day.

[1] For abbreviations and transcript conventions, see the end of the chapter

Japanese/Korean Linguistics 20.
Edited by Bjarke Frellesvig and Peter Sells.

(3) wuli-nun **kunyang** chinkwu sai-ya.
we-TOP just friend relationship-to:be:IE
We are just friends.

An examination of *kunyang* in spoken discourse reveals that it frequently functions as a stance marker, as seen in (4)-(6), which differs considerably from its function as a manner adverb.

(4) KTCS 6626[2]
A:Hwu yeki-n pissa-ki-man ha-ko
oh here-TOP expensive-NML-only do-and
seysangey koki han pack-ey **kunyang** sip pwul ton-i-ya.
my:gosh meat one pack-for ten dollar money-to:be-IE
Oh! It's expensive here. My gosh, one package of meat is kunyang ten dollars!

(5) KTCS 6528
ani eccemyen tto kulehkey **kunya::ng** cal sala kaciko,
oh:my how again like:that well live and
Oh my, how can she be that kunya::ng rich,

nemwu **kunyang** cengmal, awu, awu
so really ah ah
so kunyang really, ah, ah

(6) KTCS 4548
hhhh > yo kicipay **kunyang** acwu **kunyang** < hhh
this girl very
Hhhh you are kunyang, so kunynang hhh

As a stance marker, *kunyang* embeds the speaker's attitude, evaluation, or emotion concerning the proposition, rather than adding any propositional content. In (4) and (5), *kunyang* expresses the speaker's stance toward the price of meat and someone's wealth, which s/he views as excessive or extreme. In (6), *kunyang* conveys the speaker's negative attitude toward an individual without verbalizing much of her actual criticism. Accordingly, as a stance marker, *kunyang* often appears in affectively loaded evaluative utterances with interjections (e.g. *seysangey* 'my gosh!', *awu* 'ah!'), as seen in these segments.

---

2 The catalogue number from the *Korean Telephone Conversations Speech* corpus is provided for each example.

Nevertheless, the different uses of *kunyang* as a manner adverb and as a stance marker are not always easy to separate. Multiple meanings and functions of *kunyang* frequently overlap and coincide in spoken discourse data, as do many other discourse markers (Brinton 1996, Erman 2001, Aijmer 2002). Taking *kunyang*'s etymology as a point of departure, this study will explicate how the different functions coexist and are interrelated under the core meaning.

No prior studies have analyzed *kunyang*'s discoursal pragmatic functions despite its multifunctionality in spoken discourse. [3] This study aims to uncover the syntactic, pragmatic, and prosodic features of *kunyang* as a stance marker.

The following section 2 describes the data for this study. Section 3 discusses the etymology of *kunyang*, which provides an understanding for the multiple meanings and functions of *kunyang*. The core meaning of *kunyang* will reveal how changes in its semantic meaning and discoursal pragmatic functions arise through a subjectification process (Traugott 1995). Section 4 analyzes the syntactic, pragmatic, and prosodic features of *kunyang* as a stance marker.

2. Data

This study used the *Korean Telephone Conversations Speech* corpus data from the Linguistic Data Consortium (Ko *et al.*, 2003). The corpus consists of 100 telephone conversations recorded between native speakers of Korean. Each conversation lasts 30 minutes, of which 15 to 18 minutes were transcribed.

In 100 transcribed conversations, totaling approximately 190K words, *kunyang* occurs a total of 1407 times. [4] 254 tokens of *kunyang* are found to solely function as a stance marker. However, the distribution of the different uses of *kunyang* can be best depicted as a continuum of subjectivity, from less subjective to more subjective, which will be further discussed in the following section.

---

[3] Lee (2007)'s study of the discourse functions of the Korean adverb *kuce* is the only similar study to this examination of *kunyang*, as *kuce* and *kunyang* adverbs share semantic similarities, both of which can be translated as 'just' or 'continuously'. Lee analyzes *kuce*'s discourse and pragmatic meaning in four categories, 'nothing but', 'emphatic', 'negative implication', and 'elaboration'. Despite their similarities, *kuce* and *kunyang* have different original meanings and development paths. Lee's study explicates that the discourse functions of *kuce* developed primarily in certain dialects, such as *Yangyang* dialect, *Jeju* dialect, and *Goryeo* dialect of Central Asia.

[4] The high occurrence rate of *kunyang* is not an anomaly of the *Korean Telephone Conversations Speech* corpus. According to the Korean vocabulary frequency list by the National Institute of the Korean Language, *kunyang* is the 7th most frequently used adverb in Korean spoken discourse.

3. The Etymology of *kunyang* and its Semantic Changes

According to the *Korean Etymology Dictionary*, the original meaning of *kunyang* is 'as it is shaped', as shown below in Figure 1 (Kim *et al*., 1997). This original meaning provides an essential clue for understanding how the different functions of *kunyang* as an adverb and as a stance marker are interrelated.

ku [其]	+ n +	yang [樣]
that	epenthetic phoneme	shape

Figure 1. The etymology of *kunyang*

Because *kunyang*'s original meaning is elusive and not concrete, its interpretation can vary depending on its context, as shown in the following examples. *Kunyang* in example (7) can be translated either 'as it is' or 'continuously'. Furthermore, with a high pitch elongation, *kunyang* can serve to embed the speaker's negative attitude toward a man's continuous drinking.

(7) **kunyang** masye.
drink:IE
(He) drinks it kunyang.

The ambiguity of *kunynang*'s meaning in example (7) becomes clarified in examples (8) and (9) when other contextual clues are provided.

(8) (selthang neh-ci anh-ko) **kunyang** masye.
sugar put-NML not-and as:it:is drink:IE
(He) drinks it as it is (without adding sugar).

(9) (congil) **kunyang** masye.
all:day continuously drink:IE
(He) drinks it continuously (all day).

In (8), the preceding clause ('without adding sugar') restricts the interpretation of *kunyang* to '(just) as it is'; not making any changes to the action. In (9), the temporal adverb *congil* 'all day' narrows down the interpretation of *kunyang* as 'continuously'; highlighting the continuing state of the action.

Nonetheless, in natural conversational data, numerous examples of *kunyang* display vagueness and overlap in their meanings and functions, as shown below.

(10) KTCS 4314

awu ce salam-un cenhye **kunyang kunyang** kulenikka
ah that person-TOP at:all so
selsa-lul talko sal-a-yo.
diarrhea-ACC live:with-IE-POL
Ah, he (my husband), kunyang, kunyang, lives with diarrhea.

(11) KTCS 6704

kunyang cheum-pwuthe kyeysok yethay-kkaci nol-taka
beginning-from continuously now-until play-and:then
(I) have been playing kunyang from the beginning until now continuously.

mwe myechil cen-ey incey sicakhay-ss-ci mwe.
well a:few:days before-at now to:begin-PST-COMM well
(I) started (to work) just a few days ago.

(12) KTCS 6452

pamsaytolok kichimha-ko khosmwul-i
all:night cough-and runny:nose-NOM
mak **kunyang** cwulcwul cwulcwul nawa-ss--
much dripping dripping come:out-PST
(I) coughed all night and had kunyang a runny nose.

Each example in (10)-(12) describes a continuing state of a certain event (constant diarrhea, playing for a long time, a runny nose), wherein *kunyang* can be semantically interpreted as 'continuously'. However, it is difficult to simply restrict the meaning of *kunyang* as 'continuously', when there are other expressions in each of the utterance which explicitly expresses the same meaning (e.g. *talko sal-ta* 'live with', *kyeysok* 'continuously', *pamsaytolok* 'all night', *cwulcwul cwulcwul* onomatopoeic expression depicting liquid running through).

Moreover, compared to other expressions which convey a more concrete timeline of the continuing state, such as, *cheum-pwuthe yethay-kkaci* 'from the beginning until now', *pamsaytolok* 'all night', the meaning of *kunyang* is based more on the speaker's subjective interpretation: how the speaker perceives the length of the continuing state. In all of these examples, the speaker construes the prolonged event to be excessive or extreme. Accordingly, *kunyang* imprints the speaker's perspective in representing the proposition.

As seen in these examples, because the original meaning of *kunyang* is inexplicit, its basic meaning becomes easily bleached in certain contexts, and the interpretation of *kunyang* becomes increasingly based on the speaker's subjective construal of the proposition. As Traugott (1989, 1995) notes, the development of subjective meaning occurs at the last stage in semantic change. Many examples in spoken discourse data, like the segments in (10)-(12) provide evidence for the semantic change in *kunyang* as they retain traces of its basic meaning of 'continuously' and at the same time reveal the speaker's attitudinal involvement with the proposition.

In contrast to examples in (10)-(12), the following segments show examples of *kunyang* functioning exclusively to mark the speaker's stance toward a proposition.

(4) KTĆS 6626
A:Hwu yeki-n pissa-ki-man ha-ko
oh here-TOP expensive-NML-only do-and
seysangey koki han pack-ey **kunyang** sip pwul ton-i-ya.
my:gosh meat one pack-for ten dollar money-to:be-IE
Oh! It's expensive here. My gosh, one package of meat is kunyang ten dollars!

(13) KTCS 6002
kulssey mal-iey-yo acwu **kunyang** koyngcanghi malu-sy-e kaciko
well word-to:be-POL very really be:thin-SH-and
You're right. (She) is so kunyang really thin.

(14) KTCS 6173
kamki kellye kaciko sikkwu-taylo
cold catch because family-each
sikkwu-taylo na:llina-ss-e **kunyang**.
family-each freak:out-PST-IE
All family members, all family members are freaking out because they caught colds kunyang.

In examples (4), (13), (14), *kunyang* does not add anything to the propositional content, but instead conveys the speaker's stance toward the state or action being described; how the speaker perceived the meat price to be too high (1), how the speaker felt the person was too thin (13), and how the speaker perceived the family members' extreme suffering from colds (14).

In sum, the different meanings and functions of *kunyang* from example (1) to example (14) can be best shown as a continuum of subjectivity, from less subjective to more subjective, as in the following figure 2. *Kunyang* is another example of how changes in semantic meaning and pragmatic and discourse functions arise through a subjectification process (Traugott 1995).

Less subjective — More subjective

----------------------------►

Adverb *kunyang* — Stance marker *kunyang*

Figure 2. The subjectification process of *kunyang*

4. The Syntactic, Pragmatic, and Prosodic Features of *kunyang*

Based on an understanding of how *kunyang* has developed into a stance marker, this section will discuss the discoursal pragmatic functions of *kunyang* as a stance marker. A close investigation of the use of *kunyang* in spoken discourse reveals the syntactic, pragmatic, and prosodic differences of *kunyang*, depending on whether it is used as a stance marker or as a manner adverb.

4.1. *Kunyang*'s Syntactic Features as a Stance Marker

The syntactic position of *kunyang* as a manner adverb is tied to the predicate or clause which it modifies. On the other hand, *kunyang* as a stance marker appears in variable syntactic positions, in particular, often in post-predicate position where an emotive, subjective voice readily emerges, as shown in (14)-(16).

(14) KTCS 6173
kamki kellye kaciko sikkwu-taylo
cold catch because family-each
sikkwu-taylo na:llina-ss-e **kunyang**.
family-each freak:out-PST-IE
All family members, all family members are
freaking out because they caught colds kunyang.

(15) KTCS 6528
seysangey: ya acwu unkyengi nemwu cal tway-ss-ney **kunyang.**
good:heavens wow very Eunkyung very well become-PST-FR
Good heavens! Wow! It really turned out well for Eunkyung, kunyang.

(16) KTCS 5074
> oywe-to ice mek-ko oywe-to ice mek-ko <
memorize-even:if forget-and memorize-even:if forget-and
(.5) CCAcungna-n-ta acwu **kunyang.**
be:annoyed-IMPFV-DC very
(I) forget and forget even if I memorize it again and again. (I) am annoyed so kunyang.

In examples (14)-(16), the speaker promptly embeds her attitude toward the proposition as soon as she finishes her description of the proposition.

It is also interesting to note that most co-occurrences of *kunyang* with emphatic adverbials (e.g. *acwu* 'very', *wancenhi* 'completely', *mak* 'much, hard') occur as stance markers, not as manner adverbs. The following table shows the distribution of *kunyang* with emphatic adverbials.

Table 1. Distribution of *kunyang* with other emphatic adverbials

	Manner adverb /stance marker [5]	Stance marker	Total
acwu 'very'	0	31	31
mak 'much, hard'	4	30	34
wancenhi 'completely'	0	23	23
kulehkey 'like that'	0	13	13
Total	4	97	101

As a manner adverb, *kunyang* cannot co-occur semantically with emphatic adverbials, as seen in (17) and (18).

(17) ***acwu kunyang** chinkwu sai-ya.
very just friend relation-to:be:IE
**(We) are very just friends.*

(18) *cepsi **acwu kunyang** twe.
dish very as:it:is leave:IE
**Leave the dish very as it is.*

Nonetheless, as a stance marker, *kunyang* can appear with emphatic adverbials because its primary meaning is bleached. The emphatic adverbials function to intensify the speaker's attitude or emotion, as seen in (6), (16) and (19).

[5] This category represents cases where *kunyang* carries its basic meaning and at the same time embeds the speaker's stance.

(6) KTCS 4548

hhhh > yo kicipay kunyang **acwu kunyang** < hhh
this girl very
Hhhh you are kunyang, so kunynang hhh

(16) KTCS 5074

EHYU: cincca meli thecye **acwu kunyang** kuke.
egh really head explode:IE very that:thing
EGH: that makes (my) head really explode so kunyang.

> oywe-to ice mek-ko oywe-to ice mek-ko <
memorize-even:if forget-and memorize-even:if forget-and
(.5) CCAcungna-n-ta **acwu kunyang.**
be:annoyed-IMPFV-DC very
(I) forget and forget even if I memorize it again and again. (I) am annoyed so kunyang.

(19) KTCS 6528

cekes com pwa. khun saepka-kwuna, **acwu kunyang**.
that:thing little see:IE big businessman-UNASSIM very
See that, (he) is a big businessman, so kunyang.

As shown in Table 1 and in these examples, *acwu* and *kunyang* frequently co-occur together as a chunk and function as a stance marker.

Furthermore, as seen in example (20), the speaker combines more than one emphatic adverbial, *acwu* 'very' and *wancenhi* 'completely', to maximize the attitudinal or emotional effect.

(20) KTCS 6773

mal-ul **acwu kunyang wancenhi**.
word-ACC very completely
(She) speaks so kunyang completely.

EWU ku mal cal ha-n-ta wancenhi.
wow that word well speak-IMPFV-DC completely
WOW, (she) really speaks well.

As the examples above clearly show, semantic, syntactic, functional transformations correlate and coincide in language change. As *kunyang* goes through semantic changes, it develops a new function as a stance marker, and its syntactic position and collocation pattern change as well.

4.2. *Kunyang*'s Pragmatic Features as a Stance Marker

As prior segments demonstrated, *kunyang* as a stance marker conveys the speaker's view of an action or state being described as excessive or extreme (e.g. (4) too expensive, (5) too wealthy, (13) too thin, (14) too sick, (16) too annoying). By highlighting the excessiveness or extremity of an action or state, the speaker further displays his/her discontent or sarcastic attitude.

The following segment, wherein two friends exchange sarcastic remarks, demonstrates this discoursal pragmatic use of *kunyang* for displaying a speaker's negative attitude toward another speaker.

(6) KTCS 4548

01 A: ne-nun *soho* an-- an tolatani-llay kulemyen?
you-TOP SoHo not not go:around-want:to then
You're not-, you don't want to go to SoHo (with us) then?

02 B: *soho* cohaha-ko iss-[ney
SoHo like-and exist-FR
SoHo, Are you kidding me?

03 A: [hhhhh

04 > yo kicipay **kunyang** acwu **kunyang** < hhhh
this girl very
HHH you are kunyang, so kunynang hhhh

05 B: *paper* twu:: kay ssu-nun cwung-i-ya cikum.
paper two CL write-in:the:middle:of-to:be-IE now
(I) am in the middle of writing two:: papers (right) now.

In response to A's invitation to visit SoHo together, B declines A's invitation with sarcasm toward A (lines 1-2). B's response in line 2, *cohaha-ko iss-ney*, which can be roughly translated into English as 'Are you kidding me?', puts down A. Note how A takes offense toward B in lines 3-4. B names A *yo kicipay* 'this girl', a playful put down between two females, and then utters *kunyang* twice. *Kunyang* sufficiently conveys B's negative stance toward A without fully verbalizing her actual criticism. In response to A's negative stance, B defends herself as to why she cannot accept A's invitation (line 5).

The following provides another example where *kunyang* sufficiently manifests the speaker's negative stance toward a person without explicit criticism.

(21) KTCS 5941

01 A: ku salam mith-ey iss-ess-te-n kel
that person under-at exist-PST-RT-ATTR fact:ACC
02 ekswu calang-ulo iyakiha-tey. Hhhhh
heavily boasting-as talk-RT:IE
(He) boasts so heavily about the fact that he was under that person. hhhhh

03 B: hhh he-- cham michin saykki-ya.
hah really crazy guy-to:be:IE
hhh hah Really, (he) is a crazy guy.

04 A: kuntey (cikum-to) ku wuli pocwakwan-i kuttay
but now-also that our aide-NOM that:time
05 ci kwangcwu kasstawass-ta kule-te-la-ko.
his Kwangju come:and:go-DC like:that-RT-INTROS-QT
He, the (general's) aide at the time, used to come and go to Kwangju.

06 B: e
Uh huh

07 A: kulemyense nay-ka ku cangkwun mith-eyse
and:then I-NOM that general under-at
08 ecce-ko cecce-ko hay saah-tey.
like:this-and like:that-and say repeatedly-RT:IE
And, (he) keeps telling (us) this and that how he (worked) under the general.

09 aiko **kunyang**. Ei ssi. Hhh
oh:my darn:it
Oh my, kunyang, darn it. Hhh

10 B: ike ettehkey tolaka-nun-ci-lul molu-keyss-ney.
this how happen-ATTR-whether-ACC not:know-DCT:RE-FR
(I) don't know what's going on (with the politics).

Here, A describes a person who used to constantly boast that he was an aide to a general in the military (lines 1-2, 4-5, 7-8). After the description of the person's action, note how A provides his overall assessment of the man's irritable behavior. In line 9, he exclaims an interjection (*aiko* 'oh my'), a stance marker (*kunyang*), and a curse (*ei ssi* 'darn it'), displaying his critical stance toward the protagonist of the story.

As shown in these examples, *kunyang* frequently occurs in affectively loaded evaluative utterances and complements the speaker's action of taking a negative stance concerning the proposition.

4.3. *Kunyang*'s Prosodic Features as a Stance Marker

As *kunyang* serves to embed the speaker's attitude or emotion, it often has distinct prosodic features in spoken discourse data, as shown in the following examples.

(5) KTCS 6528

ani eccemyen tto kulehkey **kunya::ng** cal sala kaciko,
oh:my how again like:that well live and
Oh my, how can she be that kunya::ng rich,

nemwu **kunyang** cengmal, awu, awu
so really ah ah
so kunyang, really, ah, ah

In segment (5), the speaker makes an exclamation and at the same time indicates her envy toward her friend's daughter who became wealthy after her marriage. The speaker accentuates her sarcastic attitude by elongating and stressing the stance marker *kunyang*. [6]

(22) KTCS 6452

ecekkey-to halwu congil pamsaytolok kho ttaymwun-ey=
yesterday-also all:day all:night nose because:of
= **kunya::ng** cam-ul mos ca-n-ta-nikka
sleep-ACC cannot sleep-IMPFV-DC-you:see
Yesterday also, all day, all night, because of my (runny) nose, (I) kunya::ng could not sleep.

In segment (22) as well, the speaker stresses and elongates the word *kunyang* as she makes a complaint about her lack of sleep due to a runny nose. As shown in these segments, when *kunyang* functions as a stance marker, it is, in general, markedly elongated and/or stressed than the talk around it.

---

[6] The underline below *kunyang* indicates stress or emphasis, either by increased loudness or higher pitch (e.g. *kunyang*). The colon displays stretching of the sound (e.g. *kunya::ng*).

5. Conclusion

This paper explicates how the Korean adverb *kunyang* has been extended from its original function to serve as a stance marker in spoken discourse. *Kunyang* is primarily known as a manner adverb, which has the basic meaning of 'as it is', 'continuously', or 'just'. However, in natural conversational data, *kunyang* shows distinct syntactic, pragmatic, and prosodic features which are quite distinct from its use as an adverb. Instead of adding any propositional content, *kunyang*, expresses the speaker's attitude or evaluation of the action or state being described as excessive or extreme. Unlike its use as a manner adverb, *kunyang* as a stance marker shows variable syntactic position, in particular, in post-predicate position where an emotive, subjective voice frequently emerges. It also routinely co-occurs with emphatic adverbials as a chunk, intensifying the speaker's attitude or emotion. *Kunyang* also shows distinct prosodic features, such as prolongation and stress, which manifests the speaker's attitudinal involvement with the proposition.

Moreover, by tracing the etymology of *kunyang*, this paper explains how its different meanings and functions as an adverb and as a stance marker coexist and are interrelated under its core meaning. Because the original meaning of *kunyang*, 'as it is shaped', is inexplicit and vague, its primary meaning becomes readily bleached in certain contexts, and instead its meaning becomes increasingly based on the speaker's subjective construal (i.e. highlighting the excessiveness or extremity of an action or state). Accordingly, *kunyang* begins to function solely as a stance marker displaying the speaker's negative or sarcastic attitude concerning the proposition. *Kunyang* is an example of how changes in semantic meaning and discoursal pragmatic functions arise through a subjectification process (Traugott 1995).

This paper not only points out the function of *kunyang* as a stance marker, but it also broadens the scope of research of Korean stance markers to include stance adverbials, whereas previous studies have focused on Korean sentence-endings. Adverbials with high frequency in spoken discourse, such as *kunyang,* need further investigation on their variant functions and uses in interactions.

Abbreviations

ACC accusative
ATTR attributive
CL classifier
COMM committal
DC declarative suffix
DCT:RE deductive reasoning
FR factual realization
IE informal ending
IMPFV imperfective
INTROS introspective
NML nominalizer
NOM nominative

POL polite suffix
PST past suffix
QT quotative particle
RT retrospective
SH subjective honorific
TOP topic marker
UNASSIM unassimilated

Transcript Conventions

[ ]	simultaneous talk
=	contiguous utterances
(0.0)	length of silence in tenths of a second
--	cut-off
.	falling intonation
,	continuing intonation
?	rising intonation : sound stretch
::	the prolongation or stretching of the sound just preceding them
word	underlining indicates some form of stress or emphasis, either by increased loudness or higher pitch
WOrd	upper case indicates especially loud talk
> <	a stretch of talk is compressed or rushed
hhh	hearable aspiration, laughter, etc.
(word)	uncertainty on the transcriber's part

References

Aijmer, K. 2002. *English Discourse Particles. Evidence From a Corpus*. Amsterdam: John Benjamins.

Brinton, L. J. 1996. *Pragmatic Markers in English*. Berlin: Mouton de Gruyter.

Erman, B. 2001. Pragmatic Markers Revisited with a Focus on *you know* in Adult and Adolescent Talk. *Journal of Pragmatics* 33: 1337-1359.

Kim, M., H. Choi, and Kim M. 1997. *Wulimal Ewon Sajeon* [Korean Etymology Dictionary]. Seoul: Tayhaksa.

Ko, E., N. Han, A. Caravan, G. Zipperlen. 2003. *Korean Telephone Conversations Speech*. Philadelphia: Linguistic Data Consortium.

Lee, K. 2007. Discourse Function of Geujeo in Discourse. *Discourse and Cognition* 14(3): 105-130.

Traugott, E. 1989. On the Rise of Epistemic Meaning in English: An Example of Sub-jectificatioin in Semantic Change. *Language* 65 (1): 31-55.

Traugott, E. 1995. Subjectification in Grammaticalization. *Subjectivity and Subjectivisation: Linguistic Perspective*, eds. D. Stein and S. Wright, 31-54. Cambridge: Cambridge University Press.

The Formulaic Expressions of 'Thing' in Spoken and Written Registers: A Corpus Study of Bound Nouns *kes* and *ke* in Korean

SUNG-OCK SOHN & KILIM NAM
University of California, Los Angeles & Kyungpook National University

1. Introduction*

Formulaicity describes a phenomenon that includes various types of multi-word units and collocations, idioms, lexical bundles/phrases, and wordstrings which appear to be prefabricated. Research indicates that formulaic expressions are so widespread in natural discourse and at least one-third to one-half of language is composed of formulaic elements (Biber et al.1999, 2004; Conklin & Schmitt 2008).[1] With the availability of a large-scale corpus, recent studies show that formulaic expressions play an im-

* This work was supported by the Korea Research Foundation Grant (KRF-2009-013-A00027).
[1] Formulaic sequences constitute 58.6% of spoken discourse and 52.3% of written discourse (Erman & Warren 2000).

Japanese/Korean Linguistics 20.
Edited by Bjarke Frellesvig and Peter Sells.

portant role in both spoken and written discourse (Biber & Barbieri 2007).[2] By using computational technologies, researchers have provided empirical evidence for the most common recurrent sequences and their discourse functions in a given register. A growing body of research has been conducted on the multi-word sequences using different approaches and criteria. For instance, in Biber's phenomenal work (Biber, Conrad & Cortes 2004; Biber & Barbieri 2007; Biber et al. 2010), the multi-word sequences ('lexical bundles' in his term) are identified using a frequency-driven approach. Lexical bundles are defined simply as the most frequently occurring sequences of words. Only uninterrupted sequences of words were treated as lexical bundles.[3] As discussed in Biber & Barbieri (2007), multi-word lexical bundles tend to be structurally not complete and not idiomatic in meaning (e.g., *I don't know if, I just wanted to*), but serve important discourse functions in both spoken and written texts. It is also noted that in identifying lexical bundles, Biber and his colleagues relied on orthographic word units. For example, *into, cannot, self-control*, and *don't* are all regarded as single words in Biber's analysis of English bundles.

Previous studies on formulaic expressions are mainly based on languages with isolating morphology, where grammatical morphemes are realized as separate words (e.g. prepositions). Few studies have explored formulaic sequences in agglutinative languages, such as Korean, where grammatical morphemes are attached to a root in the form of a string of affixes.

In recent work, Kim (2009) and Biber et al. (2010) describe the distribution and functions of lexical bundles in Korean. Based on the spoken discourse and academic texts drawn from the Sejong corpus, Kim (2009) shows that, compared to English, Korean has few recurrent sequences of words: there were only six recurrent 4-word lexical bundles in the Korean corpus. Since there were very few lexical bundles in Korean which contain a sequence of four words, Biber et al. (2010) focused on 3-word bundles. The frequency cut-off used to identify lexical bundles is based on 20 times per million words in at least five different texts. Even after adjusting the size of the sequences to three words, the authors still found far fewer lexical bundles in Korean than in English (and Spanish). As pointed out by Biber et al. (2010), the overall rarity of lexical bundles in Korean is due to the highly inflected agglutinative morphology.

Since the number of Korean bundles in Biber et al. (2010) is based on orthographic words, it does not represent the morphological characteristics

---

[2] There are at least 40 different terms used in the area of formulaicity, such as fossilized forms, routine formulae, multiword units, lexical bundles, prefabricated expressions and preconstructed phrases that constitute single choices (Wray & Perkins 2000).

[3] Lexical sequences that spanned a turn boundary or a punctuation mark were excluded in Biber's study.

of Korean. (Words are separated by spaces in Hangul orthography.) For instance, many verbal suffixes in Korean which are expressed in words in English (e.g., *-myen*, 'if', *-nikka* 'because') are excluded from the bundles.[4]

As a typical agglutinative language, Korean has over 600 suffixes. These suffixes (and particles) do not have counterparts in English. The stem of all Korean predicates (verbs or adjectives) are bound in that they do not occur without one or more inflectional suffixes (Sohn 1999:216). For instance, the verb stem *ka-* 'go' cannot stand alone. It becomes a free word only with a sentence-ending suffix. A formulaic expression like *swu iss-ul kes-i-ta* (수 있을 것이다) 'it would be probably' which is identified as a 3-word bundle in Biber et al. (2010) can be further analyzed into 6 morphemes. Each of these morphemes has a unique meaning as follows:

swu 'possibility' *iss* 'be'-*ul* (prospective) *kes* 'thing'- *i* 'be'-*ta* (declarative)

Given the rich inflectional morphology in Korean, it is vital to incorporate grammatical morphemes into formulaic sequences. The present study attempts to fill the gap between word-based lexical bundles and morpheme-based bundles (i.e. formulaic expressions) by investigating the use of formulaic sequences of the bound noun *kes* 'thing' and its reduced form *ke* in spoken and written registers in Korean. The bound noun, *kes/ke* 'thing' is considered the most frequent lexical item in Korean according to the statistical research conducted by *The National Institute of the Korean Language*. The frequency is based on the 21st Century Sejong corpus which comprises both spoken (naturally occurring discourse) and written texts. In spite of the high frequency, very little empirical research has been conducted on the morpho-syntactic distribution of the bound noun.

Syntactically, *kes/ke* is defective (bound) noun in that it does not occur without being preceded by a demonstrative, or a modifying clause, or another noun (Sohn 1999:205).[5] In example (1) below, drawn from natural discourse, the defective noun *kes/ke* (marked in bold) occurs in two different positions: in one condition, it is preceded by a demonstrative and in the second it is preceded by an adnominal clause (marked in brackets).[6]

---

[4] Space is placed in Korean before all words whereas all affixes are attached to the respective stems.

[5] There is a large of number of defective nouns (e.g., *swu* 'possibility', *kes* 'thing', *tey* 'place') in modern Korean (cf. Rhee 2008).

[6] The Yale Romanization is used to transcribe the Korean data. In addition, the following abbreviations are used for morpheme glossary. ACC: Accusative; DEC: Declarative; MOD: Modifier; NOM: Nominative; NOML: Nominalizer; POL: Polite; PSV: Passive; TOP: Topic

(1) A: i **ke** Mexican umsik katha po-i-nta.
this thing Mexican food seem look-PSV-DEC
'This looks like Mexican food.'
B: Mexican umsik i-yeyyo.
Mexican food be-POL
[Mexican-i pha-nun] **ke**-yey-yo.
Mexican-NOM sell-NOML thing-be-POL
'It is Mexican food. It is what Mexicans sell.'

When preceded by a clause, the bound noun serves as head noun of the nominalized construction, as in (1) above. The nominalized clause syntactically has the same structure as a noun modifying construction such as a relative clause, and the head noun (*kes/ke*) functions as a nominalizer.

Using a morpheme-based n-gram analysis, the present study examines the distribution and the use of formulaic sequences of bound nouns *kes* 'thing' and the reduced form *ke*.[7] Specifically, we raise the following two research questions: (i) What are the distribution and functions of formulaic expressions of the bound nouns (*kes* and *ke*) in Korean? (ii) To what extent do different registers influence the development of formulaic expressions of *kes* and *ke*? By exploring these research questions, we hope to understand the mechanism for the development of formulaic expressions in agglutinative languages like Korean.

2. Data and methodology

The corpus for this study consists of one million words of written academic texts, 290,000 words of spoken academic corpus (e.g. lectures, public speech), and 220,000 words of conversation (natural discourse). Each corpus is sampled from across 48 texts drawn from a sub-component of the 21st C. Sejong corpus.[8]

A normalization is used to compare formulaic expressions across corpora of different size. The frequency cut-off used to identify formulaic expressions for this study is based on 5-morpheme sequences (e.g. *iss-ul kes-i-ta*) occurring more than 30 times per million words drawn from at least five different texts to avoid idiosyncratic uses by individual speakers or writers.

To define a 5-morpheme sequence, we adopted the method of an n-gram model which is widely used to identify an uninterrupted common sequence of words, syllables, morphemes or phonemes in natural languages. For ex-

---

7 The bound noun *kes*, the most frequent lexical item in Korean, is considered as the most flexible one among all bound nouns in terms of syntactic constructions (Hong 2006).

8 The data adopted for this study are drawn from the 2006 release.

ample, lexical bundles in Biber et al. (1999, 2010) are identified using an n-gram model. While lexical bundles (e.g. *do you want to, I don't know what*) are based on the most frequently occurring sequences of words, considering the morphological characteristics of Korean, the present study adopted a morpheme-based n-gram model.

Here are examples of most common 5-grams incorporating *ke* from the Sejong spoken corpus in Korean.

(2) *ha* 'do'-*nun ke* 'thing' (*i* 'be')-*ya* (sentence ender) 하는 거야
toy 'become' -*nun ke* 'thing' (*i*)-*ya* (sentence ender) 되는 거야
nun-ke 'thing' (*i*) *ani* 'not'-*la* (sentence ender) 는 게 아니라
nun-ke 'thing' (*i* 'be') *canh-a* (sentence ender) 는 거잖아
kulu 'to be so'-*nun ke* 'thing' (*i* 'be')-*ya* (sentence ender) 그러는 거야

As shown above, morpheme-based formulaic sequences are different from word-based lexical bundles in that the meanings of the formulaic expressions are not transparent from the individual components. Unlike lexical bundles, formulaic expressions in (2) are mainly comprised of grammatical morphemes such as the noun modifying suffix (-*nun*) and sentence ender. This reflects the rich inflectional morphology in Korean. In addition, most morpheme-based bundles are not a complete syntactic unit (e.g. phrase or clause). For example, the formulaic expressions like -*nun ke ani-la* or -*nun ke-canh-a* (sentence ender) in (2) do not represent a complete structural unit. However, morpheme-based formulaic expressions reveal important information for the development and functions of recurrent morpheme sequences in agglutinative languages like Korean. For example, it is interesting in (2) that the most common 5-grams of *ke* in spoken discourse have systematic patterns in that they are modified by the non-past suffix (-*nun*) and tend to occur with the informal ending suffix (-*ya*).

In identifying 5-morpheme sequences, we analyzed a portmanteau form (i.e. a combination of two morphemes) into two separate morphemes. For example, the intimate sentence ending suffix -*ya* as in *ha-nun ke-ya* in (2) is analyzed into two morphemes: copula *i* 'be' and the informal suffix -*a*. Thus, the formulaic expression like *ha-nun ke-ya* is considered a 5-morpheme sequence. Similarly, *toy-nun ke-ya* and *kulu-nun ke-ya* above are analyzed as 5-morpheme sequences.

In analyzing a reduced form, we followed the method of a morpheme analysis adopted in the Sejong corpus. Each reduced form in the Sejong corpus is analyzed as a combination of a full form and an accompanying morpheme. Following this method, the reduced form, such as *kel* as in *mek-ul kel* 'things to eat' is analyzed into a sequence of the full form *kes* 'thing' and the accusative marker *-(u)l*.

While morpheme sequences of any length can be analyzed, the analysis here is based on the 5-morpheme sequences. The rationale for only 5-morpheme sequences is based on the empirical evidence discussed in Choi et al. (2010). Using a morpheme-based n-gram method, Choi et al. compared the frequency results of 4-gram, 5-gram, and 6-gram sequences in Korean academic written texts (corpus size: one million words). The result indicates that among the three types of sequences, the selection of 4-gram sequences is more effective for frequency research, as illustrated in Table 1.

Table 1 summarizes the most frequent 4-, 5-, and 6-morpheme sequences in the million word corpus of academic written texts. As discussed in Choi et al, while a 4-gram bundle allows more types, the bundles are limited to grammatical morphemes and do not show a variety of formulaic expressions. The frequencies of bundles drop drastically as the sequences are extended to 5- and 6-gram bundles. There are very few recurrent sequences in 6-gram bundles.

Table 1. Most frequent 4-gram, 5-gram, and 6-gram bundles (top 6 list) (occurring more than 5 times per 100,000 words, from Choi et al. 2010)[9]

4-gram	freq	5-gram	freq	6-gram	freq
l swu iss-ta ㄹ 수 있다	250	*ha-l ssu iss-nun* 할 수 있는	57	*l swu iss-ul kes-i* ㄹ 수 있을 것이	25
ha-l swu iss 할 수 있	202	*ha-l swu iss-ta* 할 수 있다	57	*ul al-l swu iss-ta* 을 알 수 있다	24
nun kes-i-ta 는 것이다	148	*ha-l swu iss-ta* 할 수 있다	50	*ila-ko ha-l swu iss-ta* 이라고 할 수 있다	22
l swu iss-nun ㄹ 수 있는	147	*al-l swu iss-ta* 알 수 있다	33	*swu iss-ul kes-i-ta* 수 있을 것이다	22
n kes-i-ta ㄴ 것이다	117	*ul al-l swu iss-* 을 알 수 있	30	*ila-ko ha-l swu iss* 이라고 할 수 있	18
l kes-i-ta ㄹ 것이다	108	*iss-ul kes-i-ta* 있을 것이다	29	*la-ko ha-l swu iss-ta* 라고 할 수 있다	15

In addition, Table 1 indicates that most bundles consist of mainly grammatical morphemes (e.g. particles, verbal suffixes) and bound nouns (e.g. *swu* 'possibility, *kes* 'thing'). There are very few content words in the most common sequences in Table 1.[10]

[9] To be included in each n-gram, sequences had to occur in at least 5 different texts.

[10] In Table 1 that *ha-l swu iss-ta* is listed twice. The first one (with frequency 57) incorporates *ha-* 'to do' as verb like *kongpwu-lul ha-* 'to do study', and the other one (with frequency 50) refers to a noun-incorporated *ha-* as in *kongpwuha-* 'to study'.

3. Findings

In the present study, we applied a computer program which identifies every 5-morpheme sequence incorporating *kes* and *ke* in the 1 million word corpus. We compared the lexical and grammatical collocations of the two bound nouns across three registers consisting of academic written, academic spoken and conversation. Table 2 displays the distribution of the formulaic sequence types (i.e. the frequency of different formulaic types) of *kes* and *ke* in each register. The overall frequency of formulaic expressions in each register is much higher, because each formulaic expression recurs at least 30 times per million words.

Table 2 shows that the formulaic expressions of *kes* and *ke* are strikingly different in terms of their distribution and functions across registers. First, as illustrated in Table 2, *kes* bundles are predominantly used in academic discourse, which is comprised of both written and spoken registers. There is only a single *kes* bundle type (i.e. *-nun kes-to aniko*) in face-to-face conversation.[11] In contrast, *ke* bundles are prevalent in spoken discourse, including conversation and spoken academic discourse. There is not even a single token of *ke* bundle in written registers. Second, the overall frequency of *ke* bundles is much higher than *kes* bundles (260 versus 201 types). This finding suggests that *ke* bundles have more diverse lexico-grammatical collocations than that of *kes* bundles.

Table 2. Distribution of formulaic expressions of *kes* and *ke*

	kes	*ke*	Total
Academic written	160	0	160
Academic spoken	40	99	139
Conversation	1	161	162
Total	201	260	461

Previous studies have shown that the spoken vs. written difference influences the distribution and functions of bundles (Biber, Conrad & Cortes 2004; Biber et al. 1999, 2010). However, the finding in Table 2 indicates that the dimension of the written vs. spoken discourse is not enough to explain the distinctive distribution of *kes* and *ke* bundles across registers. As displayed in Table 2, *kes* bundles are predominantly used in academic discourse, which comprises both spoken and written texts. This finding indicates that we need to consider another dimension of register in addition to

[11] The use of *kes* in this case appears to be morphologically conditioned. When followed by particles like *to* 'also', *chelem* 'like', and *tul* (plural marker), only the full form (*kes*), not the reduced form is used.

the spoken vs. written distinction. According to Celce-Murcia & Olshtain (2000:5-6), both spoken and written texts are further distinguished according to the level of formality or genre (i.e. communicative purpose). We can have written language which is intended to be spoken, and spoken language that is designed to be read. These distinctions further interact with register (level of formality) and genre as shown in Figure 1.

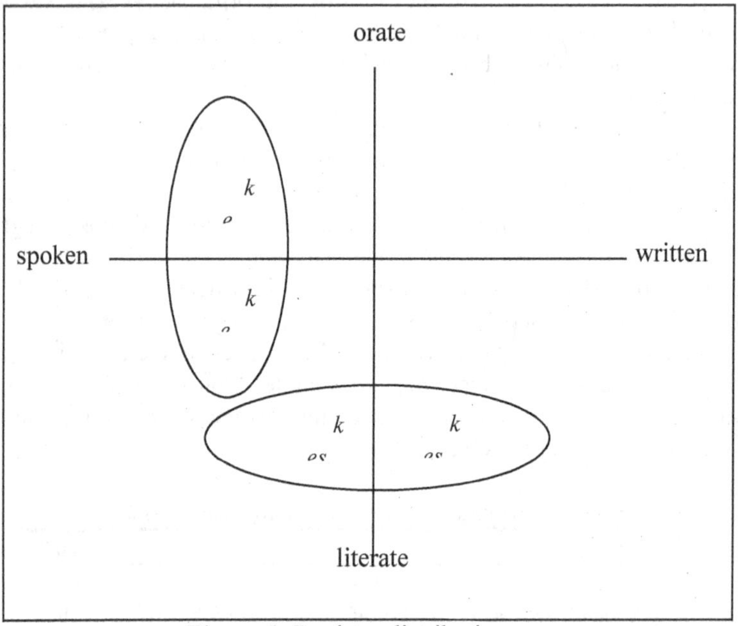

Figure 1. Register distribution

As illustrated in Figure 1, *kes* bundles are generally used in formal register (e.g. academic discourse), whereas *ke* bundles are dominant in orate/spoken (conversation, lectures, public speech). While both *kes* and *ke* bundles are used in academic spoken discourse, the frequency of *ke* bundles is more than twice of *kes* bundles (44 vs. 99 types). The asymmetrical distribution of the bundle types reflects the characteristics of each register. The high frequency of *kes* bundles in academic discourse indicates the formality of the literate/written discourse which is usually planned and context-reduced (Celce-Murcia & Olshtain 2000). In contrast, the extremely high frequency of *ke* bundles in spoken discourse supports the informal nature of the reduced form (*ke*) in orate/spoken discourse.

Table 3 shows a normalized frequency of top 20 most frequently occurring sequences of *kes* and *ke* across 3 registers. As displayed in the Table, the majority of formulaic sequences incorporating *kes* and *ke* appear in sentence-final position. For instance, 17 out of the 20 most common formulaic expressions in conversation occur in sentence-final position, as demonstrated by the occurrence with sentence-ending suffixes like *-ya/a* and *-ci*, as in *ha-nun ke-ya* and *nun ke-canh-a*. Similarly, 15 out of the 20 most frequent bundles in academic written texts occur in sentence-final position, as illustrated by the sentence-ending suffix *-ta* (declarative plain style) such as *iss-ul kes-i-ta, ha-l kes-i-ta,* and *iss-nun kes-i-ta*. Many other 5-gram bundles in Table 3 which are not marked with a sentence-ending suffix (e.g. *swu iss-ul kes-i* and *-l swu iss-ul ke*) are followed by sentence-ending suffixes in the expanded sequences. Considering that the last morphemes of the 5-gram bundles can be the beginning elements of another bundle (Biber et al. 2010), the overall frequency of *kes/ke* bundles in sentence-final position might be much larger. (This will be discussed in more detail in section 4.)

Table 3. Most frequent 5-gram bundles across three registers

Academic written		Academic spoken		Conversation	
Form	Freq	Form	Freq	Form	Freq
iss-ul kes-i-ta	293	*l swu iss-nun ke*	311	*ha-nun ke-ya*	323
l swu iss-nun kes	291	*i-lako ha-nun kes*	204	*toy-nun ke-ya*	242
l swu iss-ul kes	290	*lako ha-nun-kes*	178	*nun-key ani-la*	211
swu iss-ul kes-i	267	*nun-key ani-la*	169	*nun ke-canh-a*	191
ess-ten kes-i-ta	253	*toy-nun ke-yey-yo*	160	*kulu-nun ke-ya*	184
ha-nun kes-i-ta	241	*ila-ko ha-nun kes*	155	*ha-nun ke-ya*	163
i-n kes-i-ta	229	*toy-nun ke-cyo*	142	*l swu iss-nun ke*	156
nun-kes-i ani-la	228	*ha-nun ke-yey-yo*	137	*ha-nun ke-ya*	129
ha-lkes-i-ta	212	*ha-nun ke-yey-yo*	137	*eps-nun ke-ya*	129
iss-nun kes-i-ta	209	*l swu iss-nun kes*	133	*iss-nun ke-ya*	126
ass-ten kes-i-ta	202	*nun ke-yeyyo kulayse*	129	*ha-nun ke-ya*	123
iss-nun kes-i-ta	184	*iss-nun ke-cyo*	124	*kule-n ke-ya*	116
ko iss-nun kes-i-ta	182	*ha-nun ke-cyo*	124	*n key ani-la*	112
toy-nkes-i-ta	177	*swu iss-nun key*	120	*kulen ke kathay*	112
ha-n kes-i-ta	169	*l swu iss-ul ke*	111	*toy-l ke kathay*	109
i-l kes-i-ta	157	*swu iss-nun key*	107	*iss-nun ke-ya*	109
a-ya ha-l kes-i	151	*toy-n-ta-nun ke-cyo*	107	*toy-nun ke-ci*	106
toy-n kes-i-ta	149	*ha-nun ke-cyo*	107	*nun-ke-ya kulayse*	106
nun kes-un ani-ta	147	*nun-key ani-la*	102	*ilu-nun ke-ya*	92
ess-ul kes-i-ta	131	*nun-ke cyo kulayse*	98	*iss-nun ke kathay*	89

In addition, it should be noted in Table 3 that the most dominant structure in academic written discourse incorporates the VP-based bundle, that is, [noun modifying suffix + *kes* + copula (*i*)]. The VP-based bundle is also prevalent in conversation. When used in naturally-occurring discourse, the VP-based [-*n ke-ya*] which incorporates the noun modifying suffix (-*n*) and the colloquial ending suffix (-*ya*) is most prevalent.

Furthermore, note that the most frequent bundle type (i.e. noun modifying suffix + *kes/ke* + copula (*i*) + sentence ender) occur in sentence-final position and hold the structural characteristics of nominal predicates. The nominal predicate (lit. 'it is the thing that') refers to the predication that consists of an adnominal suffix such as *-nun* (non-past)/*-(u)n* (past/perfect)/-*(u)l* (prospective) + the head noun *kes/ke* + copula (*i*) + sentence ending suffix (e.g. *-ta, -ya, -a,* or *-yo*) (Sohn 2010). Research indicates that nominal predicates function as a discourse cohesive marker which foregrounds the speaker's or writer's stance (cf. Iwasaki 1985, Rhee 2008, Sohn 2010). We will return to the discourse functions of the most common *kes/ke* bundles in section 4.

The nominal predicates in Table 3 display a distinctive pattern across registers with respect to a speech style. Specifically, in academic written discourse the nominal predicate occurs with the plain speech style (-*ta*), whereas it occurs with the informal polite suffix (-*yo*) in academic spoken discourse and with the intimate/causal suffix (-*ya*) in conversation. This indicates that there is a tight relationship between the types of formulaic expressions and register/genre.

Thus far, we have discussed that the majority of formulaic expressions of *kes* and *ke* are used in the form of VP-based bundles in sentence-final position. In particular, the extremely high frequency of -*n kes-i-ta* in academic written discourse and -*n ke-ya* in conversation indicates that they become fossilized as a single unit of a sentence ender.[12] In the next section, we will examine the structural types of all formulaic expressions (total 461 types) across registers. We will compare and contrast the distribution and functions of *kes* and *ke* bundles across registers.

4. Structural types

The formulaic expressions of *kes/ke* are classified into two types: VP-based and NP-based bundles according to the syntactic feature of the head of the formulaic sequence.[13] VP-based bundles are further analyzed into two subtypes: sentence-final and non-final VP bundles. While sentence-final bundles occur with sentence-ending suffixes (e.g. *-ta* and *-a*), the non-final VP bundles consist of either VP-clausal (e.g. *-nun kes-i anila*) or VP fragments (e.g. *swu iss-ul kes-i, nun-kes-un ani-*). The non-final VP bundles incorporate clause suffixes (e.g. *-myen* 'if', *-ko* 'and') or fragments as in (3).

---

[12] The noun modifying suffix -*n* here refers to both -*nun* (nonpast) and -(*u*)n (past/perfect).

[13] See Choi et al. (2010) for more details of the classification of syntactic types.

Here are some examples of each type.

(3) VP-based bundles

1) Sentence-final:

iss-ul kes-i-ta/ess-ten kes-i-ta/ha-nun kes-i-ta (Academic written)
있을 것이다/었던 것이다/하는 것이다
ha-nun ke-ya/toy-nun ke-ya/coh-un ke kath-ay (Conversation)
하는 거야/되는 거야/좋은 거 같애

2) Non-final:

nun kes-i anila/nun kes-kwa kathun (Academic written)
는 것이 아니라/는 것과 같은
nun key mwe-nya-myen/nun-key anila (Academic spoken)
는 게 뭐냐면/는 게 아니라

(4) NP-based bundles:

l swu iss-nun kes/hako iss-nun kes (Academic written)
ㄹ 수 있는 것/하고 있는 것
cwungyo-han-kes-un/swu iss-nun kes-un (Academic spoken)
중요한 것은/수 있는 것은
l swu iss-nun ke/ha-ko siph-un-ke (Conversation)
ㄹ 수 있는 거/하고 싶은 거

NP-based bundles incorporate noun phrase fragments. Most NP-based bundles incorporate bound nouns such as *swu* 'possibility' and *kes* 'thing as illustrated in (4).

Table 4 shows structural types of *kes* bundles in academic discourse. The result indicates that there are more VP-based bundles than NP-based bundles (139 vs. 61 types). Nearly 50% of these VP-based bundles (69 out of 139 types) appear in sentence-final position, indicating that many *kes* bundles are used as nominal predicates, in particular in written academic texts. In addition, there are more NP-based *kes* bundles in written academic discourse than in spoken academic discourse (39 vs. 22). This pattern can be explained by the frequent omission of nominals (e.g. nouns, noun phrases) in spoken discourse. In particular, there is a strong tendency in Korean that contextually understood nominals are left unexpressed in spoken discourse (Sohn 1999:15).

Table 4. Structural types of *kes* bundles in academic discourse[14]

kes bundles		Spoken academic		Written academic	
		Type	Token	Type	Token
NP-based		22	147	39	232
VP-based	S-final	5	23	64	582
	Non-final	13	60	57	359
Total		40	230	160	1173

Table 5 shows that the distribution *ke* bundles are quite different from that of *kes* bundles. While there are more VP-based bundles in both *kes* and *ke* than NP-based bundles, the percentage of VP-based bundles in *ke* is higher than that of *kes* bundles. Nearly 88% of *ke* bundles (230 out of total 260 tokens) belong to VP-based bundles, and 57% (131 out of 230) of these bundles appear in sentence-final position. Considering that non-final VP bundles are often followed by sentence-ending suffixes in expanded sequences, the actual percentage of sentence-final VP-based bundles can be higher. The extremely high frequency of VP-based bundles in sentence-final position indicates that the formulaic expressions incorporating *ke* are developing into a fossilized sentence ender in spoken discourse. In other words, *ke* formulaic expressions become grammaticalized into sentence-final suffixes. This is illustrated in example (5) drawn from the spoken discourse in the Sejong corpus.

Table 5. Structural types of *ke* bundles s in spoken discourse

ke bundles		Spoken academic		Conversation	
		Type	Token	Type	Token
NP-based		20	134	10	59
VP-based	S-final	42	281	89	576
	Non-final	37	184	62	296
Total		99	599	161	931

(5) tape-lul sa-nikka yeki mwenka pwuthi-ko siph-un ke-ya.
tape-ACC buy-since here something stick-and want-N KE-YA
etita pwuthi-l tey-ka eps-nun ke-ya.
somewhere stick-MOD place-NOM not exist-N KE-YA
(테이프를 사니까 여기 뭔가 붙이고 싶은 거야. 어디다 붙일 데가 없는 거야.)
'Since I bought a tape, I wanted to stick something on here-N KE YA. There was no place to put it-N KE-YA.'

[14] There was a single type frequency (with four tokens) of *kes* bundle in conversation. Due to the low frequency, we did not include it in Table 4.)

In (5) *ke* does not express its erstwhile meaning of 'thing' any longer. Attached to the adnominal suffix, *-n ke-ya* functions like a single syntactic unit which is no longer analyzable into individual morphemes. The adnominal suffix loses its grammatical status as a noun modifying suffix, and the syntactic boundary between the adnominal suffix and the head noun '*ke'* disappears.

The fossilization of *-n keya* as a single unit is further supported by the statistical analysis of morpheme sequences incorporating *ke* in conversation Specifically, we analyzed the distribution of the most common 4-gram bundles occurring after a predicate stem, such as *-nun ke kath-ay* 'it seems' of the 5-gram sequence [*ka-* 'go' *-nun ke kath-ay* '(he) seems to go']. The 4-gram bundles begin with a noun modifying suffix (*-nun/ul/un*) + *ke*. The result shows that the nominal predicate (i.e. *-nun/ul/un ke-ya*) is by far the most common 4-gram sequence. Nearly 22% of *ke* tokens hold the nominal predicate (i.e., *-nun/ul/un ke-ya*), and among the three types of adnominal suffixes, the non-past form (*-nun ke-ya*) is the most frequent. As much as 80% of the nominal predicates occur with the adnominal suffix (*-nun*). The extremely high frequency supports the grammaticalization of *-n ke-ya* into a sentence ender.

Research on natural discourse shows that *-n ke-ya* appears in recurrent interactional contexts, such as clarification, dispute or argument to display the speaker's epistemic authority (Sohn 2010). The epistemic stance-marking of *-n ke-ya* can be explained by the syntactic nature of nominalization. Being derived from a noun modifying construction, the information expressed by the adnominal clause is non-challengeable (i.e., not open for questioning) information (Iwasaki 1985). Combined with the sentence ender *-ya* which expresses new information, *-n ke-ya* allows the speaker to express epistemic authority.

Moreover, the distribution of most frequent 4-gram bundles indicates that *ke* bundles in spoken discourse are mainly used for stance-marking function which expresses the speaker's attitude or assessment of certainty. For instance, in addition to the most common bundle of nominal predicates (22%), the next frequent 4-gram bundle (*-nun/ul/ ke kath-ay*) incorporates a stance-marking predicate (*kath-ay* 'it seems') and the third frequent bundle incorporates the committal suffix *-ci* as in *-n/nun ke-ci*.

While the formulaic expressions of *ke* are dominant in stance bundles in spoken discourse, *kes* bundles are predominantly used in academic discourse. The analysis of the most common 4-gram bundles indicates that the nominal predicate (*-n/nun kes-i-ta*) is by far the most common sequence. A large portion (27%) of *kes* tokens is used in sentence-final position with copula (*i*) + declarative ending (*-ta*). For example,

(6) kamhwa-nun kamtongha-ko tongsiey mwuesinka-lul
influence-TOP be touched-and while something-ACC
paywun-ta-nun kes-i-ta.
learn-DEC-N KES-I-TA
(감화는 감동하고 동시에 무엇인가를 배운다는 것이다.)
'Influence means that you learn something while being inspired.'

The nominal predicates with a plain speech style (*-n/nun kes-i-ta*) relate the current proposition to other segments of the discourse. That is, they function as discourse cohesive markers. As discussed in Rhee (2008), the nominalized clause with *kes* signifies objectification or reification due to the erstwhile lexical meaning of *kes* 'thing'. Rhee contends that through the act of regarding a proposition as a concrete entity 'thing', an emphatic meaning of the nominalizer *kes* is obtained. As such, the nominal predicate (*-n kes-i-ta*) is frequently used to foreground the validity of the propositional contents and to achieve discourse cohesiveness in academic discourse.

Finally, the findings in Tables 4 and 5 indicate that there are more NP-based bundles in *kes* than in *ke* (61 vs. 30 types). This can be explained by the salient features of Korean. Due to the flexibility of word order in Korean grammar, contextually understood elements such as subject and object are frequently omitted in spoken discourse. The infrequency of NP-based *ke* bundles is thus related to the high frequency of *ke* bundles in conversation.

5. Summary and conclusion

In contrast to earlier research on word-based lexical bundles, we adopted a morpheme-based approach to formulaic expressions in order to accommodate the inflectional morphology in Korean. The findings show that morpheme-based bundles of the full form *kes* and the reduced from *ke* have a distinctive distribution across registers. Overall, there are more bundle types in the reduced form than in the full form, indicating that *ke* has more diverse collocation patterns than the full form.

In addition, the research result shows that not only the distribution but the structural types of bundles (NP- vs. VP-based) are influenced by registers and communicative goals. The finding shows that there are more VP-based bundles than NP-based bundles in both the full and reduced forms. This pattern of finding is consistent with the salient features of Korean grammar which allows frequent ellipsis of noun phrases.

The sub-classification of bundles shows that NP-based bundles are predominant in academic discourse than in conversation. Academic registers focus on informational communication. As such, *kes* bundles, prevalent in academic discourse, are often used for a referential framing in NP-based bundles and function to foreground the validity of propositional contents. In sharp contrast, *ke* bundles, predominant in spoken registers are mainly used for speaker's stance. The vast majority of *ke* bundles appear in VP-based bundles in sentence-final position and become grammaticalized into stance markers along with the loss of a referential meaning and a phonetic reduction. This study indicates that the formulaic expressions of *kes* and *ke* develop to serve the most important communicative needs of a register.

In sum, morpheme-based bundles provide a more detailed account of the distribution and functions of formulaic expressions in languages with an inflectional morphology.

References

Biber, D. & F. Barbieri. 2007. Lexical bundles in university spoken and written registers. *English for Special Purposes* 26:263-286.

Biber, D., Conrad, S. & Cortes, V. 2004. If you look at …: lexical bundles in university teaching and textbooks. *Applied Linguistics* 25:371–405.

Biber, D., Johansson, S., Leech, G., Conrad, S., & Finegan, E. 1999. *The Longma-grammar of spoken and written English*. London: Longman.

Biber, D., Y.-J. Kim, & N. Tracy-Ventura. 2010. A Corpus-driven approach to comparative phraseology: lexical bundles in English, Spanish, and Korean. Iwasaki et al (eds.) *Japanes/Korean Linguistics* 17:75-94, CSLI Publication.

Celce-Murcia, M. & E. Olshtain. 2000. *Discourse and context in language teaching*. Cambridge: Cambridge University Press.

Choi, J., H. Song, & K. Nam. 2010. *Hankwuke-uy cenghyenghwa-toyn yenkwu. Phyohyen* (Formulaic expressions in Korean). *Discourse and Cognition* 27 (2):163-189. Seoul: Korea.

Conklin, K. & N. Schmitt. 2008. Formulaic sequences: Are they processed more quickly than nonformulaic language by native and nonnative speaker? *Applied Linguistics* 29(1):72-89.

Erman, B. & Warren, B. 2000. The idiom principle and the open choice principle. *Text* 20(1): 29-62.

Hong, S.-M. 2006. *Uycon myengsa 'kes'-uy sacek yenkwu* (A Diachronic study of the bound noun *kes*). *Emwunlonchong* 44:101-144. Seoul: Korea.

Iwasaki, Shoichi. 1985. Cohesion, nonchallengeability and the *-n desu* clause in Japanese spoken discourse. *Journal of Asian Culture*. Graduate Students in Asian Studies at UCLA, 9:125-142.

Kim, Y.J. 2009. Korean lexical bundles in conversation and academic texts. *Corpora* 4(2):135-165.

Rhee, S. 2008. On the rise and fall of Korean nominalizers. In J. Lopez-Couso & Seoane, E. (eds.) *Rethinking Grammaticalization: New Perspectives*. TSL 76, 239-264, Amsterdam: John Benjamins.

Sejong Corpus. 2006. The 21st Century Sejong corpus. The National Institute of the Korean Language. (www.sejong.or.kr)

Sohn, H. 1999. *The Korean Language*. Cambridge: Cambridge University Press.

Sohn, S. 2010. Nominalization in Korean conversation: A case study of *-nun ke-ya* In S. Lee (ed.), *Contemporary Korean Linguistics: International Perspectives*. Seoul: Korea. Thayhaksa. 320-347.

Wray, A., & Perkins, M. 2000. The functions of formulaic language: An integrated model. *Language and Communication* 20:1-28.

Part II

Historical Linguistics

Analysis and Value of *Hentai Kanbun* as Japanese

EDITH ALDRIDGE
University of Washington

1. Introduction

This paper proposes a generative syntactic analysis of word order patterns in *hentai kanbun* (変体漢文). *Hentai kanbun* is an early Japanese writing system for recording Japanese using Chinese characters for their semantic and morphosyntactic value rather than their phonetic value. Consequently, *hentai kanbun* texts bear surface resemblance to Classical or Middle Chinese, due to the lack of Japanese syllabic symbols for functional categories and the tendency for VPs and PPs to be head-initial, as they are in Chinese. This paper primarily considers the 8th century historical chronicle *Kojiki* (古事記). (1) shows SVO word order, which is a consistent feature of Chinese from classical to modern times. Japanese, on the other hand, has been an SOV language throughout its attested history. When the sentence is read (indicated by '=>'), the word order is translated into head-final Japanese order.

Japanese/Korean Linguistics 20.
Edited by Bjarke Frellesvig and Peter Sells.

(1)	採	其	地	之	青菜	(*Kojiki*, Nintoku)
	pick	[DEM[1]	place	GEN		vegetable]
=>	[soko=no		awona]=wo			**tumu**[2]
	there=GEN		vegetable=ACC		pick	
	'pick the vegetables of that place'					

Adpositional phrases are likewise head-initial, with the adposition preceding its complement DP.

(2)	自	其	地	(*Kojiki*, Jimmu)
	from	[DEM	place]	
=>	soko	ywori		
	there	from		
	'from there'			

However, not all word orders found in the *Kojiki* are of a type attested in Chinese. In ditransitive clauses in which both internal arguments are overtly expressed, the verb appears between the two objects.

(3)	名	賜	曙立	王		(*Kojiki*, Suinin)
	name	**give**	Aketatu	prince		
=>	na=wo		Aketatu=no		Opokimi=ni	**tamapi**-te
	name=ACC		Aketatu=GEN		prince=DAT	give-CNJ
	'(He) gave a name to Prince Aketatu, and....'					

At least since Motoori (1798), there has been an awareness in the field that *hentai kanbun* texts were intended to be read in Japanese. As for the composition of the texts themselves, the general assumption seems to be that *hentai kanbun* is some sort of hybrid, containing elements of both Chinese and Japanese (Miller 1967; Minegishi 1986; Feng 1995; Uchida 1995; Rabinovitch 1996). Others treat *hentai kanbun* texts as primarily Japanese (Tsukishima 1963; Nishimiya 1993; Yamaguchi 1995; Sema 1999). However, systematic analysis of the word order in these texts has by and large remained elusive, Nakagawa (1995) and Aldridge (2001) being the only exceptions that I am aware of.

In this paper, I propose a syntactic analysis which accounts for both the Chinese type orders as in (1) and (2) and unexpected word order types like (3). The word order derivation I propose consists of a two-step encoding process from surface Japanese word order to the word order of the text. The first step simply reverses the order of head and complement within a phrase, turning head-final order in Japanese into the head-initial order in

[1] Glosses conform to the Leipzig MPI rules with the following exceptions: ADN ('adnominal'), C ('complementizer'), CNJ ('conjunction'), HON ('honorific'), MOD ('modal'), STAT ('staive').

[2] Transcriptions for Old Japanese are based on reconstructions in Frellesvig & Whitman (2008).

the text. This process suffices to derive cases like (1) and (2). For less straightforward cases, I propose the addition of a second step. After the head-complement order has been set, part of the complement can be raised into the specifier of the head. I further suggest that the availability of this second step to the author of the text relies on the existence of an object raising transformation which was commonly employed in natural Japanese of the time. Consequently, we can conclude not only that *hentai kanbun* texts are Japanese (and not Chinese), but also that their apparent deviation from both languages offers clues to the syntax of natural Japanese of the time.

2. Reordering

The orders in (1) and (2) can be straightforwardly accounted for by reversing head-final Japanese order to produce head-initial Chinese type word order.[3]

(4) *<u>Hentai Kanbun</u>* <u>Word Order Derivation</u> (general)
Hentai kanbun word order is derived from surface Japanese by reversing head and complement order within every XP whose head position in Chinese differs from Japanese.

In the case of a verb and its complement direct object like in (1), the verb is reordered from its Japanese position following the object to a position immediately to the left of the object. The arrow in this example indicates the order in the text.

(5) [$_{VP}$	[$_{V'}$	[soko=no	awona]=wo		**tumu**]]
		there=GEN	vegetable=ACC		pick
=>	採	其	地	之	青菜
	pick	[DEM	place	GEN	vegetable]
	'pick the vegetables of that place'				

The same process applies to the PP in (2), with the result that a postposition in Japanese is reordered as a preposition in the text.

Ditransitive clauses, however, are not quite so easily dispensed with. As shown in (3) above, the verb appears between its two internal arguments in ditransitive clauses. Additional examples are given in (6). Regardless of the relative order or the dative and accusative objects, the verb surfaces between the two internal arguments.

---

[3] The reversal only applies to XPs whose head position is different in Japanese and Chinese. Hence, nominal categories, which are head-final in both Japanese and Chinese, do not undergo the word order reversal.

(6) a. 於 其 隼人 賜 大臣 位。(*Kojiki*, Richū)
to DEM Payabito **give** minister rank
=> Sono Payabito=ni opomayetukimi=no kurawi=wo
DEM Payabito=DAT minister=GEN rank=ACC
tamapi....
give
'(He) gave the Payabito the rank of minister....'

b. 多 禄 給 其 老 女 (*Kojiki*, Ōryaku)
many thing **give** Dem old woman
=> Amatano mono=wo sono omina=ni tamapi-te
many thing=ACC DEM old.woman=DAT give-CNJ
'He gave many things to the old woman, and….'

This order is unexpected in Old, Middle, or Modern Chinese. The corresponding Chinese ditransitives are schematized in (7). In both the dative construction (7a) and the double object construction (7b), the verb precedes both of its internal arguments.

(7)	<u>Chinese</u>	*<u>Kojiki</u>*
a.	**V** DP PP(*give something to someone*)	DP_{Acc} **V** DP_{Dat}
b.	**V** DP DP(*give someone something*)	DP_{Dat} **V** DP_{Acc}

The two types of ditransitive can be observed in the following Classical Chinese example. The first of the two conjoined clauses employs a dative construction and packages the goal as a PP. The second clause is a double object construction in which the goal appears as a DP in immediate post-verbal position.

(8) 天子 能 薦 人 於 天，
Tianzi neng **[jian** ren yu tian]
ruler can recommend person to heaven
不 能 使 天 與 之 天下。
bu neng shi tian **[yu** zhi tianxia]
not can make heaven give 3.OBJ world
'The ruler can recommend someone to heaven, but (he) cannot make heaven give him the world.' (*Mencius* 9)

Aldridge (2001) accounts for the medial positioning of the verb in *Kojiki* ditransitives by claiming that word order in this text reflects underlying head-initial word order in which the verb surfaces in its base position in VP. Following Miyagawa (1997), Aldridge assumes that the two objects can be base merged in either order, one as the verb's complement and the other in the specifier position.

(9) a.

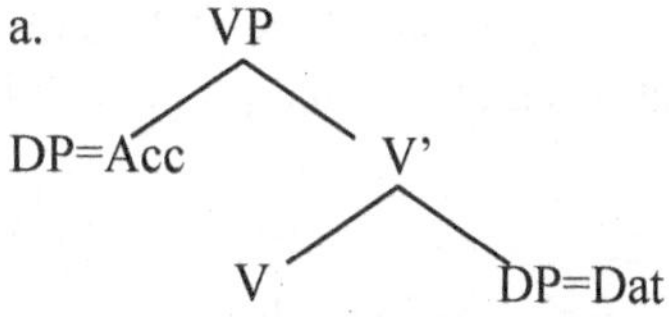

b.

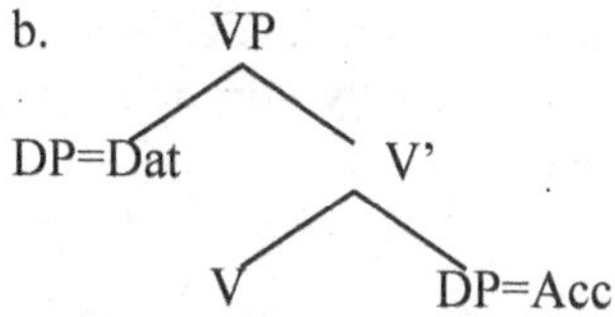

We can avoid the controversial position of assuming underlying head-initial order for Japanese and still easily derive the verb-medial order with the linearization rule in (4) by switching the order of head and complement within VP. However, this approach still relies on the assumption that the input to the reordering process is underlying Japanese structure, in which the verb is in V and has not moved to *v* or higher. This is a problematic assumption, because there is in fact evidence in the text that verb-movement has taken place. Specifically, verbs appear fully inflected in the text. (10) shows an example of the modal suffix *–mu*, which is written with the Classical Chinese character expressing future modality 将.

(10) 将 入 海 時 (*Kojiki*, Keikō)
MOD enter sea time
=> umi=ni iri-tamapa-**mu-to-su-ru** toki=ni
sea=DAT enter-HON-MOD-C-do-ADN time=DAT
'when (she) was about to enter the sea'

(11) shows an example of this modal in Classical Chinese. As in the *Kojiki* example in (10), the modal immediately precedes the VP.

(11) 吾 將 問 之。 (*Analects* 1)
Wu **jiang** wen zhi.
I MOD ask 3.OBJ
'I will ask him.'

However, in the *Kojiki*, this modal always appears in immediate preverbal position and is never separated from the verb.

(12) 自 出雲 將 上坐 倭國 而
from Idumo **MOD** go.HON Yamato CONJ
=> Idumo=ywori Yamato=no kuni=ni
Izumo=from Yamato=GEN country=DAT
nobori-masa-mu to si-te (*Kojiki*, Ōkuninushi)
go-HON-MOD COMP do-CONJ
'As (he) was about to go to Yamato from Izumo, ….'

Note in particular that the modal follows a PP in (12). (13) shows an early Middle Chinese example with a similar type of PP. In both Middle and Classical Chinese, this modal was a free morpheme and occupied a specific syntactic position high within the TP structure (Wei 1999 and Aldridge 2010). Crucially, for the purposes at hand, this modal precedes a PP of the type seen in (12).

(13) 公 將 自 東 征 備。
Gong **jiang** zi dong zheng Bei.
lord MOD from east attack Liu Bei
'Our lord was about to attack Liu Bei from the east.'
(*Sanguozhi* 1.1)

The contrast between (12) and (13) can be accounted for if we assume that the verb appears in the *hentai kanbun* texts with inflections like the modal suffix attached to it. This entails that the verb has moved at least high enough in the structure where it is visible to the probe which can value inflectional features. I assume, then, that verbs in the *Kojiki* have moved to *v*, where they are located in the edge of the *v*P phase and are therefore accessible to probes in the inflectional domain immediately dominating *v*P.

However, this presents a problem for deriving word order in ditransitive construction by means of the encoding process in (4). On the assumption that both internal arguments in a ditransitive construction reside within VP, it cannot be the case that the word order in the text is the result of merely reordering the verbal complex in *v* around its complement VP. This is because reordering V+*v* around its complement VP would result in the verb preceding both internal arguments. This problem is eliminated, however, if one of the objects moves into the edge of *v*P, as I show in the next section.

3. Raising

Yanagida (2006) and Yanagida and Whitman (2009) argue that definite or specific objects and raise obligatorily to the edge of *v*P in Old Japanese. A bare object with a nonspecific interpretation appears in immediate preverbal position. Examining (14), it can be seen that the object follows the genitive subject in (14a), while the definite object raises to a position preceding the genitive subject in (14b). Yanagida and Whitman (2009) point out that unraised objects are always bare X^0-level categories and never appear with the case-marker *wo*. They propose that these objects are incorporated to the verb. Dislocated objects can be phrasal and generally take the case-marker *wo*. These are analyzed as undergoing object shift to the edge of *v*P.

(14) a. 佐欲比賣能 故何 比列 布利斯 夜麻
Sayopimye=no *kwo=ga* **pire** puri-si yama
Sayohime=GEN child=GEN scarf wave-PST.ADN hill
'the hill where the girl Sayohime waved her scarf' (MYS 5:868)

b. 蜻野叩[4] 人之 懸者
[$_{vP}$ Akidu nwo=wo [$_{v'}$ pito=no [$_{VP}$ t_{Obj} kakure-ba]]]
Akizu field=ACC man=GEN speak.of-when
'When a man speaks of the moorland of Akizu…'
(MYS 7:1405)

Given the above considerations, ditransitives in the *Kojiki* in which the accusative object precedes the dative can easily be incorporated into the analysis developed so far. Given the evidence that Japanese surface strings provide input to the encoding process, I assume that the verbal complex resides in *v*. The encoding process in (4) will result in V+*v* being linearized to the left of VP. In an example like (15a), which has a phrasal direct object, this object will have undergone object shift to the edge of *v*P. Since it is located in a specifier of *v*P, its position in the text will be just to the left of the reordered verb.

(15) a. 多 禄 給 其 老 女 (*Kojiki*, Ōryaku)
many thing **give** DEM old woman
=> Amatano mono=wo sono omina=ni tamapi-te
many thing=ACC DEM old.woman=DAT give-CNJ
'He gave many things to the old woman, and….'

b.

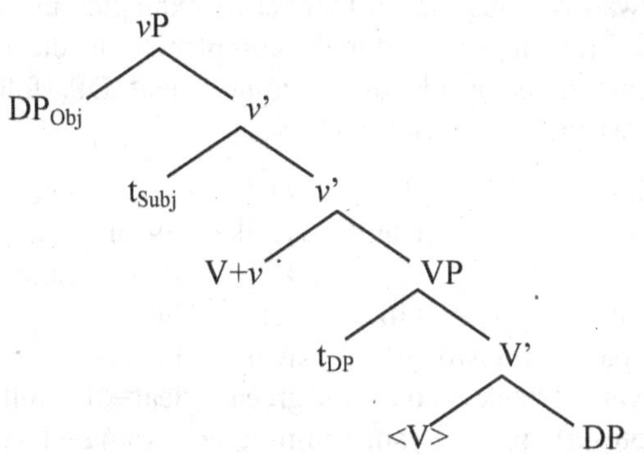

Another possible source for verb-medial ditransitive order in the text is incorporation of bare objects. This is a possible derivation of the following, in which the preverbal object appears to be just a bare noun. If we analyze this as incorporation, the preverbal position is still accounted for, since the object will move with the verb to *v*.

---

4 The character in the text is slightly different, composed of a mouth and a blade.

(16) a. 名 賜 曙立 王 (*Kojiki*, Suinin)
name **give** Aketatu prince]]
=> na=wo Aketatu=no Opokimi=ni **tamapi**-te
name=ACC Aketatu=GEN prince=DAT give-CNJ
'(He) gave a name to Prince Aketatu, and….'

b.

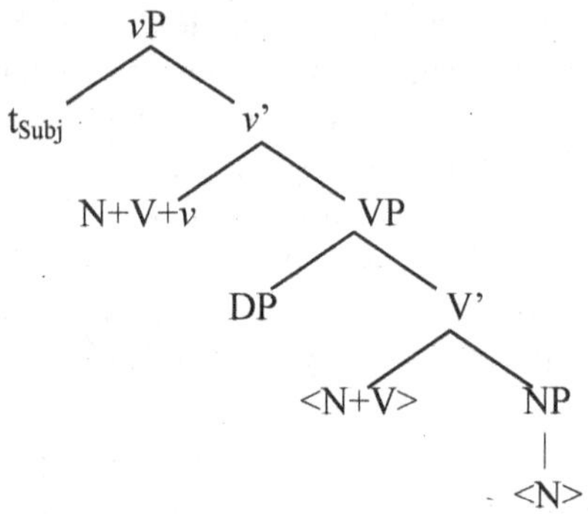

Given the restrictions on object position in Old Japanese, word order in ditransitive clauses in the *Kojiki* falls out naturally from the encoding process in (4). However, there are some anomalous orders which are not derived so straightforwardly. There are a number of examples in the text in which a verb or adposition appears within the complement it selects. In (17), an adposition appears to be inside of its complement DP, following a demonstrative in (17a) and a possessor in (17b).

(17)a. 是 於 河 下 如 青 葉 山
[DEM **on** river bank] be.like green leaf hill
者 見 山 非 山。 (*Kojiki*, Suinin)
TOP appear hill not.be hill
=> [kono kapa shimwo **ni**] awo ba=no yama=no
this river bank on green leaf=GEN hill=GEN
goto-ki]=pa yama=to miye-te yama=ni ara-zu.
be.like-ADN=TOP hill=C seem=CNJ hill=DAT be-NEG
'What looks like a hill of green leaves on this river bank is not a hill.'

b. 所殺 迦具土 神 之 於 頭
[[[PASS.kill K god] GEN] **from** head]
所成 神 名 正鹿山津見 神
PASS.make god name Masakayamatumi god

=> [[[Korosa-ye-si Kagututi=no kamwi]=no] kasira]=**ni**
kill-PASS-PST.ADN K=GEN god=GEN head=DAT
nar-er-u kamwi=no na=pa
bear-STAT-ADN god=GEN name=TOP
masaka yamatumi=no kamwi.
M=GEN god

'The name of the god born [from the head of the slain Kagutsuchi god] was Masakayamatsumi.' (*Kojiki*, Izanagi)

What I propose here is that there was a second step in the encoding process for the *Kojiki* which borrowed from the object shift transformation. Specifically, in addition to the reversal of head and complement order in the relevant XPs, part of the complement in the XP could be raised to the specifier of that XP.

(18) Hentai Kanbun Word Order Derivation (*Kojiki* only)
Word order in the *Kojiki* is derived from surface Japanese by:

1. Reversing head and complement order within every XP whose head position in Chinese differs from Japanese.
2. Optionally raising a specifier or adjunct in the complement to the specifier of the head.

The anomalous orders seen in (17) can be accounted for with this two-step process, as shown in (19). The order of P and DP is reversed. Then the specifier or adjunct in the complement DP is moved into the specifier of the PP. This will be the demonstrative in (17a) and the possessor in (17b).

(19)

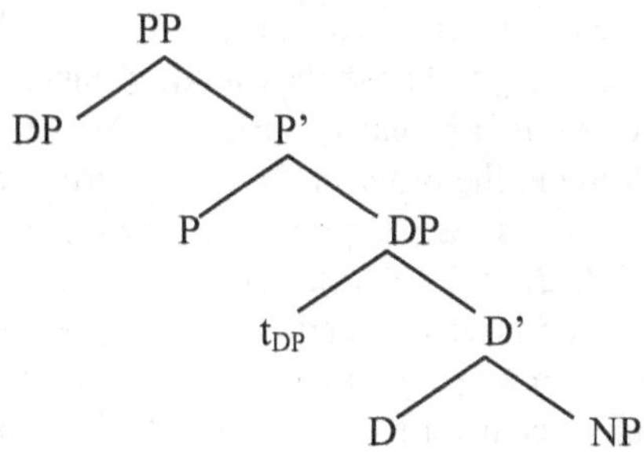

This proposal goes beyond Nakagawa's (1995) analysis of word order in the *Kojiki*. Nakagawa accounts for verb-medial order in ditransitives by claiming that verbs are placed between the two objects in order to distinguish them. However, this approach has nothing to say about cases like (17), in which adpositions appear inside their complements.

An alternative analysis of the placement of the adpositions in (17) might be to claim that the P is a bound form which simply reorders around the noun it attaches to. However, this is not a possible explanation for the examples in (20). In these examples, we see the verb in a higher clause appearing inside a relative clause modifying the complement of the higher verb. The relative clause in (20a) contains a coordinate structure. The first of these conjuncts appears before the matrix verb. In (20b), the subject of a relative clause precedes the matrix verb.

(20) a. 作 筌 有 取 魚 人。 (*Kojiki*, Jimmu)
[[set trap **exist** take fish] person]
=> [[Upe=wo puse-te, uwo=wo tor-u]
trap=ACC make-CNJ fish=ACC take-ADN
pito] **ari-ki.**
person exist-PST
'There was a person laying fish traps and fishing.'

b. 天下 者 汝 非 應 知 國。
world TOP [[you **not.be** should govern] realm]
=> Ame=no sita=pa [[imasi=no sirasu
Heaven=GEN below=TOP you=GEN govern
be-ki] kuni]=ni **ara-zu**. (*Kojiki*, Chūai)
should-ADM realm=COP be-NEG
'The world below is not a realm which you should govern.'

The placement of these verbs cannot be accounted for in terms of reordering within an X^0-level category, since the reordering does not target morphemes within a single word. These orders can, however, be accounted for on the current proposal if we assume that the preverbal constituent can be raised into the edge of the *v*P where the matrix verb resides. First note that relative clauses appear in the text preceding the head they modify. Since relatives in both Chinese and Japanese are prenominal in surface order, the reordering process will not apply in deriving the order in the text. I further assume the raising analysis of relative clauses, as proposed and developed by (Kayne 1994, Bianchi 1999, Bhatt 2002, and others). (21) is Honda's (2002) proposal for modern Japanese. The head nominal is located (base merged for Honda, but raised for Kayne) in a specifier in the CP layer of the clause. The TP portion of the relative clause raises to [Spec, DP], with the result that the head nominal follows it in surface order.

(21) [$_{DP}$ [$_{TP}$ Taroo-ga tabeta *pro$_i$*] [$_{D'}$ [$_{CP}$ ringo t_{TP}]]]
Taro-Nom ate apple
'the apple that Tarō ate'

The raising approach to relative clause structure allows a straightforward analysis of the aberrant word orders in the *Kojiki*. In (20a), the embedded TP, which is a coordinate structure, has been raised to [Spec, DP]. The specifier within this constituent can subsequently be raised to [Spec, *v*P] in the matrix clause, according to the second step in the *Kojiki* word order derivation process in (18).

(22)

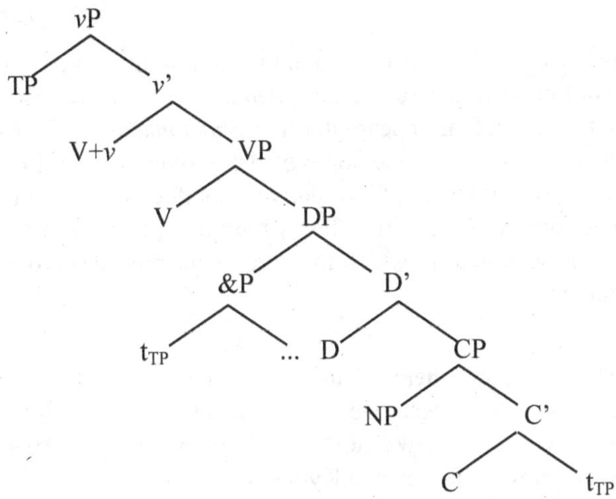

In (20b), it is the embedded subject which raises to the edge of matrix *v*P. Admittedly, these movements violate the ban on extraction from moved categories proposed by Wexler and Culicover (1980), Nunes and Uriagereka (2000), and others. However, note that in both cases, it is the specifier of a specifier which moves, which has been argued to take place in cases of possessor raising (Szabolcsi 1984, Landau 1999, and others). I assume, then, that this type of movement is an option made available by Universal Grammar.

Another crucial assumption I make is that the raising step in the *hentai kanbun* encoding process was the result of co-opting an existing transformation in spoken Japanese of the time. In the next section, I show that the loss of that transformation in the natural language correlates with the unavailability of the raising process in *hentai kanbun* word order derivation.

4. Loss of Raising

By Early Middle Japanese of the 10th century, specific objects were no longer required to move to [Spec, *v*P]. In (23), an object marked with the case-marker *wo* follows a subject marked with *ga*.

(23) Kaguyapime tepu *opo* *nusupito=no* *yatu=ga*
Kaguyahime be.calledbig villain=GEN bitch=GEN
hito=wo korosa-mu to suru nari-keri.
person=ACC kill-MOD C do COP-PST
'That bitch of a villain Kaguyahime was trying to kill people.'
(*Taketori*)

I argue in this section that this change in the natural language is also reflected in the word order of the 10th century *hentai kanbun* text *Shōmonki* 『将門記』. At first glance, it appears that the *Shōmonki* is not a fully *hentai kanbun* text. It seems to include some of the anomalous word order types found in the *Kojiki*, in which a PP or dative constituent follows the verb but a direct object precedes the verb. This is reminiscent of the word order of ditransitives in the *Kojiki*, in which the verb never precedes more than one internal argument.

(24) 具 由 聞 於 京都。 (*Shōmonki*)
all *news* **hear** in Kyōto
=> Tubusani yosi=wo Kyōto=ni kiku.
all news=ACC Kyōto=DAT hear
'(He) heard all the news in Kyōto.'

On the other hand, there are also orders like (25) which appear to follow the Chinese model. In other words, the verb precedes both the direct object and the PP.

(25) 玄明 試 聞 此 由 於 將門。 (*Shōmonki*)
Paruaki try **ask** *this* *matter* P Masakado
=> Paruaki kokoromini kono yosi=wo Masakado=ni
Paruaki tentatively this matter=ACC Masakado=DAT
kiku.
ask
'Haruaki tentatively put this matter to Masakado.'

This apparent inconsistency is easily resolved, however, in light of the word order change which has taken place from Old to Early Middle Japanese. Specific objects were no longer required to undergo object shift. Likewise, bare nonspecific objects were presumably also not required to incorporate to the verb. In short, the positioning of objects was much freer in Middle Japanese, as it is in Modern Japanese. I assume then that the preverbal object in (24) has achieved its position by scrambling to the edge of *v*P. Thus, when V+*v* is reordered to the left of VP, the verb will follow an object which has been scrambled. But it will precede a constituent which remains in VP. Note further that the difference between DP-V-PP and V-DP-PP orders in the *Shōmonki* cannot be due to definiteness or specificity. The object in both (24) and (25) is definite and refers to a situation described in the immediately preceding context.

I would further like to suggest here that the loss of object shift in the spoken language correlates with the loss of the raising step in *hentai kanbun* word order derivation. Interestingly, I have found no examples of argument taking heads appearing inside their complements. For example, the adposition in a PP always precedes its entire complement DP. This suggests that the raising step is not applied in deriving word order in the *Shōmonki* text.

Another asymmetry between the *Kojiki* and the *Shōmonki* is in passive constructions. In the *Kojiki*, agents in passive constructions always precede the verb.

(26) 汝 者 我 見欺。 (*Kojiki*, Ōkuninushi)
you TOP *me* **PASS.deceive**
=> Na=pa ware=ni azamuka-ye-tu.
you=TOP me=DAT deceive-PASS-PRF
'You have been deceived by me.'

Classical and Middle Chinese also formed passives with the morpheme 見 *jian*. But in Chinese, the agent always follows verb.

(27) 吾 長 見 笑 於 大方 之 家 。
Wu chang **jian** xiao *yu dafang zhi jia.*
I MOD PASS laugh by enlightened GEN person
'I would have been laughed at by an enlightened person.'
(*Zhuangzi*, Qiushui)

In the *Shōmonki*, the passive agent also follows the verb.

(28) 將門 被 摺 度度 之 敵
Masakado **PASS** [break [many GEN enemy]]
=> Masakado=pa tabi-tabi=no teki=ni kujik-are
Masakado=TOP many=GEN enemy=DAT break-PASS.CNJ
'Masakado was broken by enemies on many occasions....'
(*Shōmonki*)

The difference between the *Kojiki* and *Shōmonki* derivations can be accounted for as follows. In the *Kojiki*, the passive agent is raised into the *v*P layer, as per the second step in the encoding process in (18). In the *Shōmon-*

ki, on the other hand, this raising does not take place and the PP agent remains in VP. In the text, the PP will precede the verb in the *Kojiki* but follow the verb in the *Shōmonki*.

(29) a. $[_{TP}$ DP $[_{vP}$ PP V+v $[_{VP}$ t_{PP} $[_{VP}$ t_V t_{DP}]]]] (*Kojiki*)

b. $[_{TP}$ DP $[_{vP}$ V+v $[_{VP}$ PP $[_{VP}$ t_V t_{DP}]]]] (*Shōmonki*)

In short, word order in the *Shōmonki* text is derived only by head-final to head-initial linearization. There is no subsequent step of raising.

5. Conclusion

In this paper, I have proposed a syntactic analysis of how *hentai kanbun* word order is encoded from Japanese. I have argued for a single head-complement linearization process which is common to both the 8th century *Kojiki* and the 10th century *Shōmonki*. I have argued for an additional step for the *Kojiki* which involves raising. I have further suggested that the raising step was co-opted by the author of the text from a raising transformation in his native Japanese. If this analysis is on the right track, it indicates not only that *hentai kanbun* texts can be used in an analysis of Japanese but that the rules which derive the peculiar characteristics of their word order also provide a window into syntactic processes of the language of the time.

Primary Sources (Japanese)

Hayashi, Rokuro (annotator). 1975. *Shinsen Nihon Koten Bunko* [New Compilation of Classical Japanese Literature] (vol. 2): *Shōmonki*. Tokyo: Gendai Shichosha.

Nakagawa, Yoichi (annotator). *Taketori Monogatari*. Tokyo: Kadokawa.

Nakanishi, Susumu. 1978. *Manyooshu Zenyakuchuu Genbunzuki* [*Manyoshu* Complete Translation and Annotation with Original Text] 1. Tokyo: Koodansha.

Nakanishi, Susumu. 1980. *Manyooshu Zenyakuchuu Genbunzuki* [*Manyoshu* Complete Translation and Annotation with Original Text] 2. Tokyo: Koodansha.

Nomura, Kenji and Yukichi Takeda (annotators). 1958. *Nihon Koten Bungaku Taikei* [Compendium of Classical Japanese Literature] (vol. 1): *Kojiki, Shukuji*. Tokyo: Iwanami (reprinted in 1972).

Primary Source (Chinese)

Hanji Dianzi Wenxian [Electronic Corpus of Chinese Texts]
http://hanji.sinica.edu.tw/index.html?
Institute of Linguistics, Academia Sinica, Taipei, Taiwan

References

Aldridge, E. 2001. *Hentai Kanbun* Perspective on Short Scrambling. *Journal of East Asian Linguistics* 10:169-200.

Aldridge, E. 2010. Clause-internal *Wh*-movement in Archaic Chinese. *Journal of East Asian Linguistics* 19.1:1-36.

Bhatt, R. 2002. The Raising Analysis of Relative Clauses: Evidence from Adjectival Modification. *Natural Language Semantics* 10:43-90.

Bianchi, V. 1999. *Consequences of Antisymmetry*. Berlin: Mouton de Gruyter.

Frellesvig, B. and J. Whitman. 2008. Introduction. *Proto-Japanese*, ed. B. Frellesvig and J. Whitman, 1-9. John Benjamins.

Feng, L. 1995. Gudai Hanyu he Gudai Riyu de Jiaorong: *Gushiji* de Yuyan Tese [Fusion of Old Chinese and Old Japanese: Linguistic Characteristics of the *Kojiki*]. *Zhongguo Yuyanxue Bao* 1994.7:114-120.

Honda, K. 2002. An Antisymmetric Approach to Japanese Syntax [in Japanese]. In *Jisedai no Gengo Kenkyu* I, ed. Tsukuba Daigaku Gendai Gengogaku Kenkyukai, 175-224. Tsukuba, Japan.

Kayne, R. 1994. *The Antisymmetry of Syntax*. Cambridge, MA: MIT Press.

Landau, I. Possessor Raising and the Structure of VP. *Lingua* 107:1-37.

Miller, R. A. 1967. *The Japanese Language*. Tokyo: Tuttle.

Minegishi, A. 1986. *Hentai Kanbun*. Tokyo: Tokyo-do Press.

Miyagawa, S. 1997. Against Optional Scrambling. *Linguistic Inquiry* 28.1:1-25.

Motoori, N. 1798. *Kojiki-den*, translated by Ann Wehmeyer, published by Cornell University East Asia Program, 1997.

Nakagawa, Y. 1995. Kojiki no Kufuu: Mokutekigo (o-kaku) o Meiji Suru Tame ni [Innovation in the Kojiki -- to Clarify the Direct Object (Accusative Case)]. *Buntaishi, Gengo Seikatsushi*, Kooza Kokugoshi, vol. 6. Tokyo: Taishuukan.

Nishimiya, K. 1993. Kojiki *no Kenkyu* [Research on the *Kojiki*]. Tokyo: Oofuusha.

Nunes, J. and J. Uriagereka. 2000. Cyclicity and Extraction Domains. *Syntax* 3:20-43.

Rabinovitch, J. N. 1996. An Introduction to *Hentai Kanbun* (Variant Chinese). *Journal of Chinese Linguistics* 24.1:98-127.

Sema, M. 1999. Kanji de Kakareta Kotoba: Kundokuteki Shiso o Megutte [Words Written in Chinese Characters: On the Thought of *Kundoku*]. *Kokugo to Kokubungaku* 76.5:36-36.

Szabolcsi, Anna. 1984. The Possessor that Ran Away from Home. *The Linguistic Review* 3:89-102.

Tsukishima, H. 1963. *Heian Jidai no Kanbun Kundokugo nituite no Kenkyu* [Research on reading *kanbun* in the Heian Period]. Tokyo University Press.

Uchida, K. 1995. *Kojiki* no 'Bun' ['Sentence' in the *Kojiki*]. Kojiki *Kenkyu Taikei:* Kojiki *no Kotoba* [*Kojiki* Research Series: Language], ed. *Kojiki* Gakkai, 47-67. Tokyo: Takashina.

Wei, P. 1999. Lun Xian-Qin Hanyu Yunfu de Weizhi [On the Position of Operators in Pre-Qin Chinese]. *Linguistic Essays in Honor of Mei Tsu-lin: Studies in Chinese Historical Syntax*, ed. A. Peyaube and C. Sun, 259-297. Paris: Center de Recherches Linguistiques sur l Asie Orientale.

Wexler, K. and P. Culicover. 1980. *Formal Principles of Language Acquisition.* Cambridge MA: MIT Press.

Yamaguchi, Y. 1995. Kojiki *no Hyoki to Kundodu* [Orthography and Translation of the *Kojiki*]. Tokyo: Yuseido.

Yanagida, Y. 2006. Word Order and Clause Structure in Early Old Japanese *Journal of East Asian Linguistics* 15:37-67.

Yanagida, Y. and J. Whitman. 2009. Alignment and Word Order in Old Japanese. *Journal of East Asian Linguistics* 18.2:101-144.

The Split of the Tōkyō type tone system into a number of subtypes, and what this can tell us about the tone system of proto-Japanese

ELISABETH M. DE BOER
Leiden University

1. Introduction

Japanese historical linguistics has failed to produce a convincing account of the historical developments from the tone system of proto-Japanese to the tone systems of the various modern dialects. The problems stem from the fact that the reconstructed tone system of proto-Japanese does not fit in well with the modern dialect data. This is because it is based on the reconstruction of the tone system of Middle Japanese by Kindaichi (1951).

It is known what the tonal distinctions of Middle Japanese were like, because of so-called tone dots that were added to texts from this period (11th to 14th century). These dots were added around the *kana* graphs and indicated which syllables or moras of the language had /H/, /L/, /F/ or /R/ tone.[1]

[1] As the tonal behavior of subsyllabic moras differs from dialect to dialect in modern Japanese,

Japanese/Korean Linguistics 20.
Edited by Bjarke Frellesvig and Peter Sells.

The tonal oppositions of Middle Japanese were far more numerous than those of any of the modern dialects. The number of oppositions overall agrees however, with the number that has to be reconstructed for the proto-system, based on a comparison of the modern dialects.[2] This indicates that the tone system of Middle Japanese and the tone system of proto-Japanese must have been close, and so it makes sense to give great weight to the tone system of Middle Japanese.

But while the oppositions of Middle Japanese are clear, the phonetic realization of these oppositions is not: As the tone marks fell out of use in the 14th century, the tonal value that is assigned to them is a matter of interpretation. The most reliable source on the phonetic realization of the distinctions of Middle Japanese are therefore the tone systems of the modern dialects.

Based on these, S.R. Ramsey (1979) argued that the tone system of Middle Japanese had been reconstructed 'upside down' by Kindaichi. If the tones were exactly reversed, the tone system of Middle Japanese looked like a more complicated version of the Tōkyō type tone system. The Kyōto type tone system was the result of a leftward tone shift that occurred in central Japan after the Middle Japanese period. Although this theory explained a range of puzzling phenomena (among which the fact that the Kyōto type tone system is limited to central Japan, surrounded on all sides by the Tōkyō type), the traditional interpretation of the Middle Japanese material was not changed.[3]

In this article I will show that – taking Ramsey's reconstruction of the Middle Japanese tone system as the starting point of the historical developments – it is possible to explain the origin behind the split of the Tōkyō type tone system into a number of subtypes in a natural way. In addition it is possible to explain the phonetic background behind the tone reduction that later generated the modern restricted or 'accentual' tone systems.

---

the cross dialect reflexes are complex. I will therefore limit myself to the developments in syllables (i.e. syllabic moras). I will also limit myself to a discussion of the tonal developments in nouns.

[2] There is a split in the merged tone classes 2.4/5 and 3.4/5 in the Ryūkyūs that cannot be found in Middle Japanese or the dialects of mainland Japan. This split does not necessarily have to go back to an extra tonal distinction in proto-Japanese. (For an overview of possible explanations, see De Boer 2010: 232-237.)

[3] In earlier research (2008a, 2010) I have shown that various arguments that have been brought up against Ramsey's theory lack foundation, while on the other hand, descriptions of the tones by Buddhist monks from the Middle Japanese period support Ramsey's reconstruction.

2. Ramsey's theory

The most famous split between the tone systems of the Japanese dialects is the split between is dialects with a Tōkyō type tone system and dialects with a Kyōto type tone system. It is usually thought that the Tōkyō type tone systems developed out of the Kyōto type, by shifting the tones one syllable to the right, towards the end of the word.

Based on evidence from internal reconstruction and dialect geography, Ramsey argued that it was the other way around: The Kyōto type tone systems developed out of the Tōkyō type, by shifting the tones one syllable to the left, towards the beginning of the word.

2.1. The geographical distribution of the tone systems

The Kyōto type tone system can be found in the center of Japan, surrounded by the different Tōkyō type tone systems. Tōkyō type tone has three major subtypes: Nairin, Chūrin and Gairin. The Gairin type is again divided into two subtypes, Gairin A and Gairin B.[4]

The Nairin or 'inner circle' type is located in the most central part, closest around the Kyōto type. (There are also a number of villages with a Nairin type tone system in the mountainous and inaccessible Totsukawa region, right in the middle of the area with Kyōto type tone.) Surrounding the Nairin type there is the Chūrin or 'middle circle' type. The last type is called Gairin or 'outer circle' type. It is distributed in four blocks: northeast Kyūshū, Izumo and surrounding area, the Tōhoku region and finally the Tōkai area around Hamamatsu in the center of Honshū.[5]

If one follows the standard theory, the Tōkyō type tone systems developed out of the Kyōto type. This means that all dialects that surround Kyōto, which are separated from each other by Kyōto type tone in the middle, shifted the tones one syllable to the right, independently. This theory goes against one of the central assumptions of dialect geography: People that are geographically widely separated from each other cannot influence each other's speech, and so it is usually thought that features that agree with each other in the periphery must be old.

As the peripheral regions agree with each other in that they have Tōkyō type tone, Ramsey's idea that the Kyōto type tone system is the result of an

---

[4] The original Gairin system is Gairin A, Gairin B is an innovation. I will only discuss Gairin A in this article.

[5] A third type, the Kagoshima word-tone system, is located in the southwest of Kyūshū. This type can be regarded as a simplification of the Gairin Tōkyō type tone system that can also be found on the island. There are also a number areas without lexical tone. As these can most often be found in areas where – formerly – two different tone systems met, a number of them are most likely the result of confusion.

innovation makes sense, especially as Kyōto type tone has not been preserved anywhere outside of the central Japanese area.

2.1. Ramsey's reversed interpretation of the tone dots

According to Ramsey, the value given to the Middle Japanese tone dots should be reversed: What is usually reconstructed as /H/ was actually /L/. What is usually reconstructed as /L/ was actually /H/, and the same reversal applies to the two contour tones of Middle Japanese.

When the Middle Japanese tone system is reconstructed in accordance with Ramsey's theory, it agrees with the Tōkyō type tone system on a fundamental point: Whenever there is a transition from [H] to [L] in Middle Japanese, such a transition can be found in the Tōkyō type dialects in the same location. When the Middle Japanese tone system is reconstructed in accordance with the standard theory on the other hand, it resembles the tone system of Kyōto. In some of the tone classes the resemblance is almost perfect, but in others it is completely absent. Although at first sight the resemblance between standard Middle Japanese and Kyōto may seem larger, the agreement between Ramsey's Middle Japanese and Tōkyō is much more systematic.

The question of which tonal type is older (Kyōto or Tōkyō) and the interpretation of the Middle Japanese material can therefore not be separated: In the standard interpretation, Middle Japanese – and by extension proto-Japanese – was Kyōto-like, and the Tōkyō type tone systems developed later. In Ramsey's interpretation, Middle Japanese – and by extension proto-Japanese – was Tōkyō-like, and the Kyōto type tone systems developed later (after the 14th century, when the use of tone dots was abandoned).

So far, I have recounted the rather famous controversy concerning the split between the Tōkyō type and the Kyōto type tone systems, and the question of which type is older. Another problem, which is usually given much less attention, is the following: How did all the different Tōkyō type tone systems develop? And is it possible to say which one of these is most archaic?

In the following sections I will show how the split into three different Tōkyō subtypes can be explained if one follows Ramsey's reconstruction of the Middle Japanese tone system. I will also show that the Nairin type (and within the Nairin type the dialect of Nozaki) is most archaic, and that the Gairin and Chūrin types are the result of innovations.

3. The tone system of Middle Japanese

Table 1 shows the tone of nouns of one, two and three syllables in Middle Japanese (in Ramsey's reconstruction) and in the modern (but archaic) Japanese dialect of Nozaki. The left-hand column shows the different tone classes of nouns, represented by an example word and a number. The number before the dot indicates the number of syllables, and the number after the dot is the number that is conventionally assigned to the tone class. (1.3b does not have its own number as this class – although distinguished in Middle Japanese – has left no clear reflex in the modern dialects.)

From the Middle-Japanese material, it is clear that almost every syllable had its own tone, /H/ or /L/, including the particles. All examples have been indicated followed by the case particle *ga*, but *ha, wo* and *ni* had the same tone. In the oldest material (for instance in the *Tosho-ryō-bon* (1142) and *Maeda-ke-bon* (1150) of *Nihon shoki)* the tone of these particles is always /L/, and this is the type of Middle Japanese that I have shown here.

There were contour tones but these were most likely the result of contractions. The basic opposition was between two level tones of a different register, /H/ versus /L/. The only pattern that is missing is /LHL/, but some members of class 3.3, which is usually /LHH/, have been attested with /LHL/ tone markings (cf. *kasiko* 'that place', *tikara* 'strength', *mohara* 'exclusively', *ahabi* 'abalone'). This indicates that part of the words with a /LHH/ tone pattern in Middle Japanese may go back to earlier /LHL/. The final /L/ tone apparently assimilated to the preceding /LH/ contour and became /H/.

The division in classes goes back to Kindaichi, who is the founder of the standard theory. Because the reflexes of class 3.3 are very irregular, Kindaichi later removed this class from his set of proto-Japanese tone classes. I think the irregularity goes back to the fact that this class may have two separate origins, and that some dialects went through the assimilation I have just mentioned, while other dialects did not.

Apart from the fact that within the word stem, /L/ was no longer allowed after /LH/, Middle-Japanese had a relatively unrestricted tone system. The tone systems of the modern dialects are much simpler. Nowadays most dialects for instance, allow no more than one phonological /H/ tone per word. This single remaining /H/ tone is usually called 'the accent' when Japanese is analyzed in terms of pitch-accent. The pitches of the other syllables in the word or phrase are governed by automatic pitch assignment rules. These syllables can therefore be analyzed as having Ø tone. They are usually called 'unaccented' when Japanese is analyzed in terms of pitch-accent.

4. The tone system of Nozaki

The dialect of Nozaki was spoken (at least until the early nineteen fifties, when it was recorded by Kindaichi) in Nozaki and a number of other villages on Noto Island (Kindaichi, 1954). The underlying phonology of the Nozaki tone system can be analyzed primarily in terms of /H/ and Ø tone.

The pitch assignment rules are as follows: Ø tones that precede /H/ tone have [H] pitch (except in case of the phrase initial syllable). If they follow /H/ tone they have [L] pitch. If there is no /H/ tone, there is an automatic rise in pitch after the phrase-initial syllable.[6]

When Middle Japanese and the tone system of Nozaki are compared, we see how the tonal oppositions of Middle Japanese were reduced: /H/ tones that were followed by another /H/ tone in Middle Japanese were lost in the modern dialect. But whenever there was a /H/ tone followed by a /L/ tone in Middle-Japanese (or [H] pitch followed by [L] pitch as in /F/, or /R/ followed by /L/), this /H/ tone was preserved as a phonological /H/ tone or accent in the modern dialect.

Table 1. Reduction of the tonal oppositions of Middle Japanese resulting in a Nairin merger pattern

Tone class	Middle Japanese	Nozaki (Archaic Nairin type)	
1.1 *ko-ga* 'child'	/L-L/	> [L:-H]	/Ø-Ø/
1.2 *na-ga* 'name'	/R-L/	> [H:-L]	/H-Ø/
1.3a *te-ga* 'hand'	/H-L/	> [H:-L]	/H-Ø/
1.3b *hi-ga* 'fire'	/F-L/	> [H:-L]	/H-Ø/
2.1 *tori-ga* 'bird'	/LL-L/	> [LH-H]	/ØØ-Ø/
2.2 *mura-ga* 'village'	/LH-L/	> [LH-L]	/ØH-Ø/
2.3 *yama-ga* 'mountain'	/HH-L/	> [LH-L]	/ØH-Ø/
2.4 *umi-ga* 'sea'	/HL-L/	> [HL-L]	/HØ-Ø/
2.5 *saru-ga* 'monkey'	/HR-L/	> [HL-H]	/HR-Ø/
3.1 *katati-ga* 'shape'	/LLL-L/	> [LHH-H]	/ØØØ-Ø/
3.2 *aduki-ga* 'azuki bean'	/LLH-L/	> [LHH-L]	/ØØH-Ø/
3.4 *kagami-ga* 'mirror'	/HHH-L/	> [LHH-L]	/ØØH-Ø/
3.3 *tikara-ga* 'strength'[7]	/LHH-L/	> [LHL-L]	/ØHØ-Ø/
3.5 *kokoro-ga* 'heart'	/HHL-L/	> [LHL-L]	/ØHØ-Ø/
3.6 *suzume-ga* 'sparrow'	/HLL-L/	> [HLL-L]	/HØØ-Ø/
3.7 *kabuto-ga* 'helmet'	/HLH-L/	> [HLH-L]	/HØH-Ø/

[6] For an extensive discussion of this tone system, including the influence of voiced consonants and close vowels on the realization of the tones, see De Boer 2010: 165-177.

[7] The reflex of *tikara* 3.3 in Nozaki seems to have developed from the /LHL/ tone attested in part of the Middle Japanese material. For the sake of simplicity I will follow Kindaichi's example and leave class 3.3 out of the discussion from now on.

As the tone of the monosyllabic case particles in the type of Middle Japanese shown in Table 1 was always /L/, all Middle Japanese nouns ending in /H/ tone were followed by /L/ tone. As a result, all /H/ tones occurring on the final syllable of Middle Japanese nouns were preserved in Nozaki.

In Nozaki the two non-consecutive /H/ tones of class 3.7 in Middle Japanese have been preserved as well. We see that these tones occur in the same location, and in the same tone class as in Ramsey's reconstruction of the Middle-Japanese tone system. If one follows the standard theory, this agreement has to be regarded as a coincidence.

4.1. The reflexes of Middle Japanese /R/ and /F/ tone in Nozaki

When tone classes 2.4 and 2.5 in Nozaki are compared, it can be seen that the particle after class 2.5 in Nozaki has [H] pitch while it has [L] pitch after class 2.4. As the particle is the same, there has to be something special about the final syllable of class 2.5. I think that this is the presence of a phonological /R/ tone, which is realized as [L] pitch with the rise to [H] pitch shifted onto the enclitic case particle. The location of the /R/ tone in Nozaki, and the noun class in which it occurs, agree exactly with Middle-Japanese in Ramsey's reconstruction. If one follows the standard theory, this must be another coincidence.

The reason why the final /R/ tone of class 2.5 was preserved (at least phonologically) is most likely as follows: By the time the contour tones of Middle Japanese were being simplified, the rise to [H] of the /R/ tone in class 2.5 had already been shifted onto the attached case particle (as it still is today). In this way the /R/ tone had already been lost phonetically: [HR-L] > [HL-H]. As there was thus no immediate need for further phonetic simplification, the /R/ tone was preserved phonologically.

In case of class 1.2 on the other hand, the rise to [H] pitch caused by the presence of the /R/ tone had most likely not yet shifted onto the attached case particle at the time when the contour tones of Japanese were simplified. I think this delay is related to the fact that the area where Nairin type tone is found in Japan is also the area where monosyllables are automatically lengthened. It will be clear that it is easier to accommodate a contour tone on a long vowel. As there was thus less need to shift the rise to [H] pitch onto the attached case particle, class 1.2 was still characterized by a rising contour on the noun, followed by a drop to the /L/ tone of the case particle. As a result the /R/ tone of class 1.2 – although phonetically preserved for a longer time – was eventually simplified to /H/ tone: /R-L/ > /H-L/.

The /F/ tone of class 1.3b, which included a transition from [H] to [L] as well, was likewise simplified to /H/ tone in Nozaki.

5. The modern Japanese prosodic systems as 'restricted tone'

A similar development from a relatively unrestricted register tone language to a language in which the number of /H/ tones is severely reduced, is known from a number of east African Bantu languages. The idea is that, as the number of /H/ tones per word becomes reduced, the remaining /H/ tones stand out more and more and become accent-like. Their location in the word starts to determine the pitches of the other syllables in the word. These languages are known under different names: restricted tone languages, /H/ vs. Ø tone languages, or accentual tone languages.

An analysis of the modern Japanese prosodic systems in terms of restricted tone has the advantage that it can be applied to all modern Japanese tone systems, including the tone system of a dialect like Nozaki, where multiple (non-consecutive) /H/ tones per word, as well as /R/ tone have been preserved. An analysis of the tone system of a dialect like Nozaki in terms of pitch-accent would be forced and extremely complicated.

6. The mechanism behind the /H/ tone reduction

The reason why only /H/ before /L/ in Middle Japanese was preserved as /H/ tone is most likely as follows: Both phonetic and phonological studies have shown that a [HL] interval is subject to polarization, or exaggeration. A /H/ tone will often be significantly greater in height when followed by /L/ tone, and such a pre-L /H/ tone may be raised to a contrastive /S/ or super-H toneme (Hyman, 2007:3).

I assume that this is how the /H/ tone reduction in Middle Japanese started out: Pre-L /H/ tones became greater in height than other /H/ tones. We can also analyze this as a gradual lowering of all /H/ tones that did not precede /L/ tone. In this way /H/ before /H/ was lost, but /H/ before /L/ was preserved.

7. Further simplification in the other Nairin dialects

The dialect of Nozaki is archaic. In most other Nairin dialects the simplification of the tone system went further: In these dialects the phonological rising tone of class 2.5 was lost, and class 2.5 merged with class 2.4. Likewise the second of the two non-consecutive /H/ tones of class 3.7 was lost, and this class merged with class 3.6.

Modern Kyōto has preserved the separate tone classes 2.5 and 3.7, but is surrounded by Nairin type dialects that have not. This means that the leftward tone shift in Kyōto must have occurred before this simplification took place, at a stage of the language that was still more like Nozaki.[8]

---

[8] In restricted /H/ vs. Ø tone systems, the /H/ tones stand out so much that they can be anticipated, and leftward tone shift is not uncommon. The fact that modern Kyōto has distinctive /L/

It also means that the simplification in a number of Nairin areas that surround Kyōto must have happened independently. However, independent parallel developments are less problematic when they concern simplifications, and the overall move towards an accentual system was a conducive factor: In an accentual system, /R/ tone has no place, and it is normal for accents (or accent-like /H/ tones) to be restricted to one per word.

8. The origin of the different merger patterns in the Nairin, Chūrin and Gairin dialects

In the previous section I have shown how the modern Nairin tone systems can be derived from Middle Japanese. In Table 2, I give an overview of the differences between the three Tōkyō subtypes.

Table 2. Overview of the Nairin-Chūrin-Gairin merger patterns

	Totsukawa (Nairin)		Tōkyō (Chūrin)	Ōita (Gairin)	
1.1 *ko-ga*	[L:-H]	/Ø-Ø/	as Gairin	[L-H]	/Ø-Ø/
1.2 *na-ga*	[H:-L]	/H-Ø/		[L-H]	/Ø-Ø/
1.3a *te-ga*	[H:-L]	/H-Ø/		[H-L]	/H-Ø/
1.3b *hi-ga*	[H:-L]	/H-Ø/		[H-L]	/H-Ø/
2.1 *tori-ga*	[LH-H]	/ØØ-Ø/	as Nairin	[LH-H]	/ØØ-Ø/
2.2 *mura-ga*	[LH-L]	/ØH-Ø/		[LH-H]	/ØØ-Ø/
2.3 *yama-ga*	[LH-L]	/ØH-Ø/		[LH-L]	/ØH-Ø/
2.4 *umi-ga*	[HL-L]	/HØ-Ø/		[HL-L]	/HØ-Ø/
2.5 *saru-ga*	[HL-L]	/HØ-Ø/		[HL-L]	/HØ-Ø/
3.1 *katati-ga*	[LHH-H]	/ØØØ-Ø/	as Nairin	[LHH-H]	/ØØØ-Ø/
3.2 *aduki-ga*	[LHH-L]	/ØØH-Ø/		[LHH-H]	/ØØØ-Ø/
3.4 *kagami-ga*	[LHH-L]	/ØØH-Ø/		[LHH-L]	/ØØH-Ø/
3.5 *kokoro-ga*	[LHL-L]	/ØHØ-Ø/		[LHL-L]	/ØHØ-Ø/
3.6 *suzume-ga*	[HLL-L]	/HØØ-Ø/		[HLL-L]	/HØØ-Ø/
3.7 *kabuto-ga*	[HLL-L]	/HØØ-Ø/		[HLL-L]	/HØØ-Ø/

It can be seen that if there is a /H/ tone in the word it will be in the same location in all three Tōkyō subtypes. However, compared to the Nairin type,

tone which the modern Tōkyō type dialects (including Nozaki) lack, seems to argue against the idea that the leftward shift occurred at the restricted tone language stage. However, the redevelopment of distinctive /L/ tone (which is limited to the initial syllable of the word in modern Kyōto) can be explained as a result of the leftward tone shift. (See De Boer 2010:108-109.)

in the other two types certain word-final /H/ tones are missing, which leads to different mergers between the tone classes.

In the Gairin type for instance, tone classes 1.2, 2.2 and 3.2 have lost the word-final /H/ tone. As a result, class 1.2 has merged with class 1.1, class 2.2 has merged with class 2.1, and class 3.2 has merged with class 3.1. The Chūrin type on the other hand, largely agrees with the Nairin type, with the exception of the reflexes of tone class 1.2. Just as in the Gairin dialects this class has lost the /H/ tone and merged with class 1.1.

As the Gairin type differs most profoundly from the Nairin type, I will start by discussing the /H/ tone loss that can be found in this subtype. An interesting point is that it is possible to recognize the first stage of the word-final /H/ tone loss in classes 1.2, 2.2 and 3.2 already in the Middle Japanese material itself.

The tone systems represented in the Middle Japanese material do not agree with each other in every detail. Although the old documents usually agree with each other as to the tones of the nouns themselves, depending on the text, the tone of the attached case particles (*ha, ga, wo, ni*) differs. What I have shown so far is the type with the oldest attestations, in which the tone of the case particles was always /L/. I have also shown how the modern Nairin type tone systems derived from this type.

In other material however, such as *Kokin kunten-shō (1305),* and the *Date-ke-bon (1226) of Kokin waka-shū,* it can be seen that the tone of attached case particles was influenced by the tone of the preceding noun. In such texts the pitch of the particle is suddenly [H] when attached to nouns that end in /R/ or /LH/ tone (classes 1.2, 2.2 and 3.2).[9] In other words; in case of these tone classes, the drop from the final [H] of the noun, to the [L] of the particle was lost.

As shown in Table 3, those tone classes that lost the drop to [L] pitch after the final [H] of the noun are exactly those classes that have lost word-final /H/ tone in the modern Gairin type dialects. As the presence of a transition from [H] to [L] played a key role in the reduction of the tonal contrasts of Middle Japanese, I do not consider this agreement a coincidence: The modern Gairin type dialects must have developed from a type of Middle Japanese in which the case particles behaved as in texts like *Kokin kunten-shō.* As only pre-L /H/ tones were preserved, the word-final /H/ tones in classes 1.2, 2.2 and 3.2 were lost at the time of the tone reduction.

---

[9] We have seen in Section 3 that /L/ after /LH/ was no longer allowed within the word stem in most dialects of Middle Japanese. We now see that in certain types of Middle Japanese a similar rule applied across the word boundary. For simplicity's sake I have not divided the Middle Japanese reflexes in Table 3 into a phonetical and a phonological representation. However, as the case particles had lost their independent tone, in a more precise phonological representation they should be marked with Ø tone.

Table 3. Reduction of the tonal oppositions of Middle Japanese (cf. Kokin kunten-shō (1305), Date-ke-bon (1226) of Kokin waka-shū) resulting in a Gairin merger pattern

	Middle Japanese	Ōita (Gairin)	
1.1 *ko-ga*	/L-L/	> [L-H]	/Ø-Ø/
1.2 *na-ga*	/R-H/	> [L-H]	/Ø-Ø/
1.3a *te-ga*	/H-L/	> [H-L]	/H-Ø/
1.3b *hi-ga*	/F-L/	> [H-L]	/H-Ø/
2.1 *tori-ga*	/LL-L/	> [LH-H]	/ØØ-Ø/
2.2 *mura-ga*	/LH-H/	> [LH-H]	/ØØ-Ø/
2.3 *yama-ga*	/HH-L/	> [LH-L]	/ØH-Ø/
2.4 *umi-ga*	/HL-L/	> [HL-L]	/HØ-Ø/
2.5 *saru-ga*	/HR-H/	> [HL-L]	/HØ-Ø/
3.1 *katati-ga*	/LLL-L/	> [LHH-H]	/ØØØ-Ø/
3.2 *aduki-ga*	/LLH-H/	> [LHH-H]	/ØØØ-Ø/
3.4 *kagami-ga*	/HHH-L/	> [LHH-L]	/ØØH-Ø/
3.5 *kokoro-ga*	/HHL-L/	> [LHL-L]	/ØHØ-Ø/
3.6 *suzume-ga*	/HLL-L/	> [HLL-L]	/HØØ-Ø/
3.7 *kabuto-ga*	/HLH-H/	> [HLL-L]	/HØØ-Ø/

As to the split between the Nairin and Chūrin tone systems: Table 2 shows that the Chūrin dialects agree with the Nairin dialects except in case of class 1.2, the monosyllables with /R/ tone in Middle Japanese. In the Chūrin dialects this class has no /H/ tone, while in the Nairin dialects it does.

As I already briefly mentioned in Section 4.1, I think it is no coincidence that the Nairin type tone systems are found in central Japan, the area that has automatic vowel length in monosyllables. This vowel length helped to preserve the phonetic [R:] tone in class 1.2, and the drop to [L] pitch on the attached case particle for a longer time. Eventually this resulted in a simplification to /H/ tone, and a merger with class 1.3.

In the Chūrin areas on the other hand, where there was no vowel length, [R-L] became [L-H]. As there was no longer a drop to [L] pitch, this resulted in a simplification to Ø tone, and a merger with class 1.1.

9. The attestation of different dialects of Middle Japanese in the written record

In the oldest attestations of Middle Japanese, the tone of the particles is /L/, but apart from that, there is no clear chronological development in the documents from no assimilation, to assimilation only after /R/, to assimilation after /LH/ as well as /R/. This indicates that the differences were dialectal, and do not represent different historical stages of one and the same dialect.

The archaic type with no assimilation, which can be regarded as the ancestor of the Nairin type tone systems, is still attested in the 14th century (cf. *Maedake-bon* of *Jōben shūi waka-shū,* 1333), so it does not disappear from the written record after the more innovative types have been attested.

Another example are the *Mikanagi-bon* and *Ōei-bon* of *Nihon shoki-shiki* (1278-1293). These manuscripts have assimilation after class 1.2, but not yet after classes 2.2 and 3.2 (which is why they would qualify as ancestors of the Chūrin type tone systems). This is despite the fact that they are of later date than the *Date-ke-bon* (1226) of *Kokin waka-shū,* which has assimilation after all of these tone classes. As shown in Table 3, the *Date-ke-bon* is an example of the kind of tone system that later developed a Gairin merger pattern.[10]

The non-assimilating Nairin type may have the earliest attestations primarily because this type was located in the area that formed the cultural and political center of Japan at the time. It does not necessarily mean that the other types did not yet exist. After 1185 political power shifted to military rulers from eastern Japan (the Minamoto, the Hōjō and the Ashikaga). This may explain the appearance of the other types in the written record. The modern Gairin dialect area that is located closest to the center of Japan is the area in the Tōkai region around Hamamatsu. Texts like the *Date-ke-bon* of *Kokin waka-shū* may reflect the Middle Japanese tone system of this region.

10. Conclusions

What I have shown so far, is that the three modern Tōkyō type tone systems can be derived from Ramsey-style Middle Japanese if we assume two dif-

10 Kindaichi (1964:338) attributes the lack of assimilation after 2.2 and 3.2 in *Nihon shoki shi-ki* (1278-1293), which are commentaries to the *Nihon shoki*, to influence of the tone dots added to old manuscripts of the *Nihon shoki* itself. However, the fact that *Nihon shoki shi-ki* does show assimilation after classes 1.2 and 2.5, while most manuscripts of *Nihon shoki* do not, argues against this theory: Why would there be adherence to archaic norms in case of classes 2.2 and 3.2 but not in case of classes 1.2 and 2.5? *Nihon shoki shi-ki* is also innovative in that the tone dots added to *yodan* verbs show that the *shūshi-kei* was already being replaced by the *rentai-kei* (Sakurai, 1975:203). All of this argues against adherence to archaic norms as an explanation for the lack (or relative lack) of assimilation of the tone of the particles in this text.

ferent stages in the developments: First, some of the dialects went through a number of tonal assimilations (which have actually been attested in the written record). Later, all dialects went through a major reduction in the number of tonal oppositions in that only /H/ before /L/ remained as an active tone. (This change was caused by the heightening effect that /L/ tone has on a preceding /H/ tone.) The tone reduction caused the merger of many Middle Japanese tone classes, but as not all dialects had previously gone through the same assimilations, the mergers were different in each of the three Tōkyō subtypes.

The above is the first account to provide a natural explanation for the split of the Tōkyō type tone system into a number of subtypes. For the first time also, the mechanism behind the transformation of the full register tone system of Middle Japanese into the severely restricted tone systems of the modern dialects has a sound basis in phonology.

The fact that the modern tone systems of the mainland Japanese dialects can be traced back to Middle Japanese, and that there is no need to go back further in time, is in line with similar outcomes from research on segmental phonology and grammar.

These points, and the striking regularity of the correspondences between the modern tone systems and their Middle Japanese ancestors offers strong support for the reversed reconstruction of the tones of Middle Japanese.

Finally, many dialects in the Ryūkyūs still have word-tones that phonetically resemble the pitches of a Tōkyō type tone system. This is another indication that the Tōkyō-like reconstruction of the tone system of Middle Japanese is phonetically correct. It also gives us good reason to trust that the tone system of proto-Japanese was not radically different from the tone system of Middle Japanese: Just like Middle Japanese, the tone system of proto-Japanese must have been Tōkyō-like.

References

Akinaga, K. 1974. *Kokin waka-shū shōten-bon no kenkyū, Kenkyū-hen*. 1972. *Sakuin-hen*. Tōkyō: Azekura shobō.

De Boer, E. 2008a. The Middle Chinese tones through Japanese eyes. *Chinese linguistics in Leipzig (CLÉ 2)*, ed. R. Djamouri and R. Sybesma, 71-86. Paris: EHESS-CRLAO .

De Boer, E. 2008b. The origin of alternations in initial pitch in the verbal paradigms of the central Japanese (Kyōto type) accent systems. *Evidence and Counter-evidence. Festschrift Frederik Kortlandt* 2. (SSGL, 33.) 35-50. Amsterdam-New York: Rodopi.

De Boer, E. 2010. *The historical development of Japanese tone. Part I: From proto-Japanese to the modern dialects. Part II: The introduction and adaptation of the*

Middle Chinese tones in Japan (Veröffentlichungen des Ostasien-Instituts der Ruhr-Universität Bochum, 59.) Wiesbaden: Harrassowitz Verlag.

Frellesvig, B. 1994. Morphemic tone and word tone in central Japanese. *Acta Linguistica Hafniensia* 27: 147-161.

Hattori, S. 1951. Genshi Nihongo no akusento. *Kokugo akusento ronsō*, ed. K. Terakawa et al, 45-65. Tōkyō: Hōsei daigaku shuppan-kyoku.

Hattori, S. 1978–1979. Nihon sogo ni tsuite 1–22. *Gengo* 7(1)–7(3), 7(6)–8(12).

Hayata, T. 1984. Ko-shahon Nihon shoki no joshi no akusento. *Kyūdai gengo-gaku kenkyū-shitsu hōkoku* 5:15-49.

Hayata, T. 1999. Accent and tone: Towards a general theory of prosody. *Cross-linguistic studies of tonal phenomena: tonogenesis, typology and related topics*, ed. S. Kaji, 221-234. Tōkyō: Institute for the study of languages and cultures of Asia and Africa (ILCAA).

Hirayama, T. 1960. *Zenkoku akusento jiten*, Tōkyō: Tōkyō-dō.

Hirayama, T. 1979. Gengo-tō Nara-ken Totsukawa hōgen no seikaku. *Gengo kenkyū* 76:29-73.

Hiroto, A. & Ōhara T. 1953. *San'in chihō no akusento*. Matsue: Hōkō-sha.

Hyman, L. & Schuh, R. 1974. Universals of tone rules: Evidence from West Africa. *Linguistic Inquiry* 5:81-115.

Hyman, L. 1978. Historical tonology. *Tone, a linguistic survey*, ed. V. Fromkin, 257-269. New York: Academic Press.

Hyman, L. 2001. Privative tone in Bantu. *Cross-linguistic studies of tonal phenomena: tonogenesis, Japanese accentology, and other topics*, ed. S. Kaji, 237-257. Tōkyō: Institute for the study of languages and cultures of Asia and Africa (ILCAA).

Hyman, L. 2007. Universals of tone rules: 30 years later. *Tones and tunes: Studies in word and sentence prosody*, ed. C. Gussenhoven & T. Riad, 1-34. Berlin: Mouton de Gruyter.

Ikuta, S. 1951. Kinki akusento-ken henkyō-chiku no sho-akusento. *Kokugo akusento ronsō*, ed. K. Terakawa et al, 257-346. Tōkyō: Hōsei daigaku shuppan-kyoku.

Ishizuka, H. 1977. Maeda-bon Nihon shoki Insei-ki ten (honbun henpo). *Hokkaidō-daigaku bungaku-bu kiyō* 26-1: 69-136.

Kindaichi, H. 1951. Nihon shisei kogi. *Kokugo akusento ronsō*, ed. K. Terakawa et al, 629-708. Tōkyō: Hōsei daigaku shuppan-kyoku.

Kindaichi, H. 1954. Tōzai ryō-akusento no chigai ga dekiru made. *Bungaku* 22-8:63-84.

Kindaichi, H. 1955. Kodai akusento kara kindai akusento e. Kokugo-gaku 22:15-29.

Kobayashi, Ch. 1975. Japanese dialects: Phonology and reconstruction of the proto-accentual system. Doctoral dissertation, Cornell University.

Martin, S. 1987. *The Japanese language through time*. New Haven/London: Yale University Press.

Masamune, A. ed. 1970. *Ruiju myōgi-shō (hensan, kōtei)*. Tōkyō: Kazama Shobō.

Matsumori, A. 1998. Nihon-sogo no akusento. *Nihongo-gaku (tokushū: akusento kenkyū no genzai)* 3:34-44.

Matsumori, A. 2001. Historical tonology of Japanese dialects. *Cross-linguistic studies of tonal phenomena: tonogenesis, Japanese accentology, and other topics*, ed. S. Kaji, 93-122. Tōkyō: Institute for the study of languages and cultures of Asia and Africa (ILCAA).

Matsumori, A. 2008. On the reconstruction of the proto-accentual system of Japanese. *Proto Japanese: Issues and Prospects*, ed. B. Frellesvig & J. Whitman, 103-124. Amsterdam-Philadelphia: John Benjamins Publishing Company.

Meeussen, A. 1972. Japanese accentuation as a restricted tone system. *Papers in Japanese linguistics* 1:267-270.

Mochizuki, I. 1974. *Ruiju myōgi-shō yonshu shōten-tsuki wakun shūsei*. Tōkyō: Kasama shoin.

Odden, D. 1999. Typological issues in tone and stress in Bantu, *Cross-linguistic studies of tonal phenomena: tonogenesis, typology and related topics*, ed. S. Kaji, 187-215. Tōkyō: Institute for the study of languages and cultures of Asia and Africa (ILCAA).

Okada S. 1956. Nihon shoki ko-shahon no akusento to Kokin kunten-shō no akusento ni tsuite. *Joshidai bungaku* 8:51-69.

Ramsey, S. 1979. The Old Kyōto dialect and the historical development of Japanese accent. *Harvard Journal of Asiatic Studies* 39:157-175.

Ramsey, S. 1980. Nihongo akusento no rekishiteki henka. *Gengo* 9-2:64-76.

Ramsey, S. 1982. Language change in Japan and the Odyssey of a Teisetsu. *Journal of Japanese studies* 8-1:97-131.

Sakurai, S. 1975. Joshi akusento no shi-teki kōsatsu. *Kodai kokugo akusento-shi ronkō*. 183-225. Kyōto: Ōfūsha.

Shimabukuro, M. 1997. Word-initial low register in Proto-Japanese. *Japanese/Korean Linguistics* 6, ed. H. Sohn & J. Haig, 135-141. Stanford: CSLI Publishing.

Shimabukuro, M. 2007. *The accentual history of the Japanese and Ryukyuan languages: A reconstruction.* (The languages of Asia series.) Folkestone: Global Oriental.

Tsukishima, H. 1951. Jōben-bon shūi waka-shū shosai no akusento ni tsuite. *Kokugo akusento ronsō*, ed. K. Terakawa et al, 107-178. Tōkyō: Hōsei daigaku shuppankyoku.

Uwano, Z. 1981. Article accompanying the dialect map in: *Language atlas of the Pacific area*, ed. S. Wurm & S. Hattori, Canberra: Australian Academy of the Humanities/Japan Academy.

Uwano, Z. 2006. Nihon-go akusento no saiken. *Gengo-kenkyū* 130:1-42.

Vovin, A. 2008. Proto-Japanese beyond the accent system. *Proto Japanese: Issues and Prospects*, ed. B. Frellesvig & J. Whitman, 141–156. Amsterdam-Philadelphia: John Benjamins Publishing Company.

Yamana, K. 1951. Totsukawa onchō. *Onsei no kenkyū* 7:191-201.

Ryukyuan perspectives on the Proto-Japonic vowel system

THOMAS PELLARD
JSPS / Kyoto University

1. Introduction

The Ryukyuan languages are a family of (at least) five endangered languages spoken in the Ryūkyū Islands, an archipelago stretched between Kyūshū and Taiwan and naturally delimited by the Kuroshio current (Figure 1). They form a sister branch to Japanese, and both derive from a common ancestor, Proto-Japonic (PJ). Ryukyuan can be divided into a Northern branch that includes Amami and Okinawan, and a Southern branch comprising Miyako, Yaeyama and Yonaguni (Pellard 2009).

Traditionally, Japanese historical linguistics has been virtually synonymous with philology, and the reconstruction of PJ has thus exclusively relied on the evidence from the Old Japanese (OJ) texts of the 8th c. CE. Comparative data from the Ryukyuan languages is nevertheless of great importance for this topic, though this importance is still too often underestimated.

In particular, it is known since Hattori (1932, 1978–1979) that the Ryukyuan vowels do not straightforwardly correspond to the Old Japanese ones,

Japanese/Korean Linguistics 20.
Edited by Bjarke Frellesvig and Peter Sells.

and a careful comparison of Ryukyuan and OJ requires reconstructing more vowels in Proto-Japonic than usually posited.

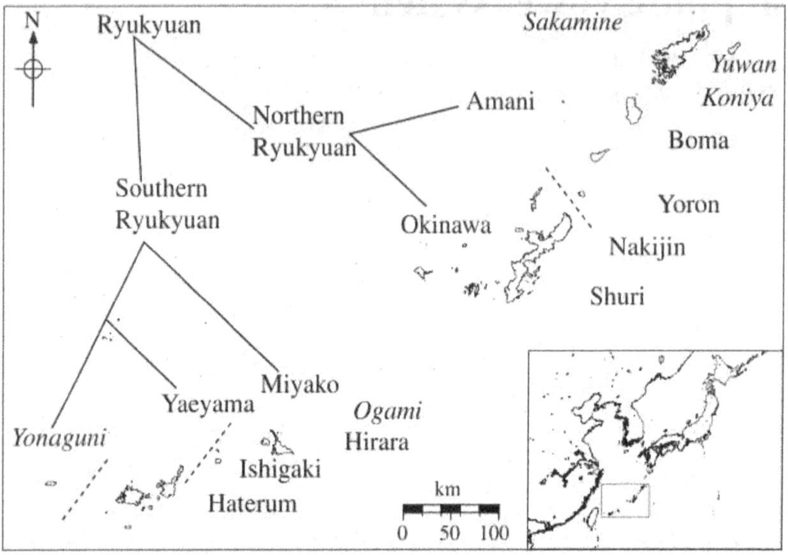

Figure 1. The Ryukyuan languages

Based on data I collected in the field and from existing sources,[1] I adduce new comparative evidence from several Ryukyuan languages that add further support to the reconstruction of six vowels in Proto-Japonic, and I propose to reconstruct a new diphthong, namely *oi.

2. The reconstruction of the PJ vowel system

2.1. The four-vowel hypothesis (4VH)

The application of the method of internal reconstruction to the vowel alternations and vowel crasis phenomena of OJ has led many scholars to reconstruct, more or less independently, only four vowels in PJ (Miller 1967, Matsumoto 1975, Ōno 1977, Whitman 1985, Martin 1987), represented in Figure 2. The other vowels of OJ and later Japanese are said to be later de-

[1] The map in Figure 1 gives the location of the different dialects mentioned in this study. Varieties for which I have first-hand data coming from my own fieldwork (Sakamine, Yuwan, Koniya, Ōgami, Yonaguni) are indicated in italics. In addition, I have used the following sources: Koniya: Uchima and Arakaki (2000), Yoron: Kiku and Takahashi (2005); Boma: Nakama (1992); Nakijin: Nakasone (1983); Shuri: Kokuritsu kokugo kenkyūjo (1963); Hirara: Nevskij (1922–1928 [2005]); Ishigaki: Miyagi (2003); Hateruma: Miyanaga (1930); Yonaguni: Ikema (2003).

velopments of diphthongs constituted of the above four primary vowels: i_2 < PJ *ui, *əi; e_1 <*ia, *iə; e_2< *ai, *əi; o_1 < *ua, *au, *uə.

i u

ə

a

Figure 2. The four-vowel hypothesis

This reconstruction is however problematic since it does not take into consideration any comparative data from the Ryukyuan languages, and in fact is not able to account for it, as will be shown below.

2.2. The PJ six-vowel hypothesis (6VH)

Previous works on the comparative reconstruction of Ryukyuan and Japanese (Hattori 1978–1979, Thorpe 1983, Serafim 1999, 2008, Pellard 2008, 2009) have led to the the addition of two mid vowels, *e and *o, to the 4VH (Figure 3).

i u

e ə o

a

Figure 3. The 6-vowel hypothesis

For several decades, this hypothesis has been mostly rejected, and the 4VH has remained, and still does for some scholars, the common *doxa* in Japanese historical linguistics. It is only recently, more than thirty years after Hattori's (1978–1979) commanding comparative study of Ryukyuan and Japanese, that it has begun to gain general acceptance.[2]

The fact few examples were given in support of this hypothesis, with Proto-Ryukyuan (PR) and PJ reconstructions and correspondences sometimes given without clear explanation, probably explains why the 6VH has been rejected so far. The following sections will propose new and straight-

[2] See Frellesvig and Whitman (2008a), Vovin (2010).

forward Ryukyuan evidence[3] for the 6VH and counter-evidence to Whitman (1985)'s criticisms.[4]

3. The PJ mid vowels *e and *o

3.1. PJ *e

The reconstruction of PJ *e has been the most controversial one. There are indeed few examples, and further examples of *e can only be discovered by a minutious examination of the Ryukyuan data. The supporting correspondences are summarized in Table 1.

Table 1. Reflexes of PJ *i and *e

OJ <	PJ >	PR >	Amami ::	Okinawa ::	Miyako ::	Yaeyama ::	Yonaguni
i_1	*i >	*i >	ˀi, N ::	ˀi, ʲi, N ::	ɿ, ɯ, s, N, ∅ ::	ɿ, N, ∅ ::	i, N, ∅
	*e >	*e >	ʰɨ, i ::	ʰi, i ::	i ::	i ::	i

Whitman (1985) made the important remark that in all the examples proposed by Hattori (1978–1979) and Thorpe (1983)[5], *e always appears before a sonorant or a voiced/prenasalized obstruent followed by a high vowel, while * ə never does. He thus proposed to account for *e by the following fronting rule:

(1) PJ *ə > PR *e, OJ i_1 / __$C_{[+voiced]}V_{[+high]}$

There are nevertheless counter-examples to Whitman's (1985) fronting hypothesis, such as *to*$_2$*ri* 'bird' or *no*$_2$*ri* 'seaweed', which do not have alternating shapes and thus should simply be reconstructed as *təri and *nəri (Miyake 2003:94). Such words cannot be reconstructed with a final *əi, as shown by their Ryukyuan reflexes (ex: Miyako-Ōgami *tuɯ*, *su-nuɯ*, see section 4). Moreover, Arisaka's (1934b) second law states *ə and *u do not coexist in a disyllabic root, so there is little chance these words come from *tərui and *nərui. Anyway, *tərui and *nərui would have shifted to ˣtiri and

[3] This reconstruction is also partly supported by data from Eastern Old Japanese (EOJ, *Azuma uta, Sakimori uta*) and some archaic dialects like Hachijō (Hino 2003, Pellard 2008). See also Miyake (2003) for a summary of the subject.

[4] Whitman has since accepted the reconstruction of *e and *o (Frellesvig and Whitman 2008a).

[5] PJ *eNtu 'which', *keNtu 'wound', *memeNsu 'earthworm', *meNtu 'water', *peru 'garlic', *peNsi 'elbow'. Serafim (1999), quoted in Miyake (2003), proposed several examples of *e appearing in other environments, but the comparative data underlying his reconstructions remains unkwnown, and my own data do not agree with most of his reconstructions.

ˣniri in OJ according to Whitman's fronting rule. Hattori's (1978–1979) and Thorpe's (1983) examples thus remain valid.

Table 2 illustrates a minimal pair PJ *piru 'daytime' vs. *peru 'garlic', which are homophoneous in OJ but are distinguished in most varieties of Ryukyuan. Other examples where I propose to reconstruct *e include PJ *erə 'color', which can be reconstructed from the correspondence OJ iro_2 :: Ōgami *iɾu* (cf. 'put in' OJ *ire* :: Ōgami *ɯɾi* < PJ *irV), and PJ *neNkə 'get muddy', from the correspondence OJ $nigo_2r$- :: Yuwan *nɨguɾɨɾ-* (cf. 'grasp' OJ $nigi_1$ :: Yuwan *nigij-* < PJ *niNkir-).

Table 2. PJ *i vs. *e: PJ *peru 'garlic'

		'daytime'	'garlic'
OJ		pi_1ru	pi_1ru
Amami	Koniya	çiɾ	ɸɨɾ
Amami	Yoron	pjuː	pʰiɾuː
Miyako	Ōgami	psː-ma	piɯ
Yaeyama	Ishigaki	pɿːɽ	piŋ
Yonaguni		tsˀuː	çiɾu
PR		*piru	*peru

3.2. PJ *o

The reconstruction of *o is less problematic and is supported by many examples of a correspondence OJ *u* :: PR *o. As listed in Table 3, PJ *u tends to drop or assimilate to a contiguous nasal, contrary to *o, whose reflex is regularly u. These two different reflexes are exemplified by PJ *mukap- 'to face' vs. *moNki 'wheat' (Table 4), *mukaNtV 'centipede' vs. *moko 'bridegroom' (Table 5), *uma 'horse' vs. *omi 'sea' (Table 6).[6]

Table 3. Reflexes of PJ *u and *o

OJ	< PJ	> PR	> Amami	:: Okinawan	:: Miyako	:: Yaeyama	:: Yonaguni
u	*u	> *u	> ˀu, N	:: u, N	:: u, N, Ø	:: u, N, Ø	:: u, N, Ø
	*o	> *o	> ʰu	:: u̧	:: u	:: u	:: u

PJ *u also has a special fronted reflex after coronals in most Ryukyuan varieties, which can be seen in the reflexes of PJ *usu 'mortar', while *o is always u, as in *kusori 'medicine' (Table 7).

Another example is PJ *ori 'melon', which can be reconstructed from the comparison 'melon' OJ *uri* :: Ōgami *uɯ* (cf. 'sell' OJ ur-i :: Ōgami *vv*).

[6] See Pellard (2008) for more details on this last reconstruction.

4. PJ diphthongs: Where have all the *oi gone?

From morphophonemic alternations occuring in OJ, it is possible to reconstruct two different PJ sources of OJ i_2:

- *ui, for OJ cases where OJ i_2 alternates with *u*, e.g. *tuku-yo*$_1$ 'moon(light)' ~ *tuki*$_2$ 'moon' or *sugus-* 'pass (transitive)' ~ *sugi*$_2$ 'pass (intransitive)';
- *əi, where i_2 alternates with o_2, like in *ko*$_2$*dati* 'stand of trees' ~ *ki*$_2$ 'tree' or *oko*$_2$*s-* 'raise' ~ *oki*$_2$ 'rise'.

Table 4. PJ *u vs. *o (1): PJ *moNki 'wheat'

		'to face'	'wheat'
OJ		*pi*$_1$*ru*	*pi*$_1$*ru*
Amami	Sakamine	mutɕui	muɲi
Okinawa	Shuri	ŋke:	mudʑi
Miyako	Ōgami	ŋkai	mukɯ
Yaeyama	Ishigaki	ŋkai	muŋ
Yonaguni		ŋkai	muŋ
PR		*mukae	*mogi

Table 5. PJ *u vs. *o (2): PJ *moko 'bridegroom'

		'centipede'	'bridegroom'
OJ		*mukade* (MJ)	*mo*$_1$*ko*$_1$ > *muko*
Amami	Sakamine	mukadʑi	muku, mukka
Okinawa	Shuri	ŋkadʑi	mu:ku
Miyako	Ōgami	ŋkati	muku
Yaeyama	Ishigaki	ŋkadza	muku
Yonaguni		ŋkadi	mugu
PR		*mukade	*moko

Table 6. PJ *u vs. *o (3): PJ *omi 'sea'

		'horse'	'sea'
OJ		*(m)uma*	*umi*$_1$
Amami	Sakamine	ma	ʔumi
Amami	Yuwan	mˀa	ʔuŋ
Amami	Yoron	uma	uŋ
Okinawa	Nakijin	mˀa:	ʔumi
Yaeyama	Ishigaki	mma	iŋ ~ umɿ
Yonaguni		mma	iŋ ~ unnaga
PR		*uma	*omi

Table 7. PJ *u vs. *o (4): PJ *kusori 'medicine'

		'mortar'	'medicine'
OJ		*usu*	*kusuri*
Amami	Yuwan	ʔusɨ	kˀusui
Amami	Koniya	ʔusɨ	kusuɾ
Amami	Sakamine	usu	sui
Okinawa	Nakijin	ʔuɕi	kʰusui
Miyako	Ōgami	us	ffuɯ
Yaeyama	Ishigaki	usɿ	ɸuɕiɾɿ
Yonaguni		utɕi	tsˀuɾi
PR		*Usu	*kusori

As first noticed by Arisaka (1934a), and then fully demonstrated by Hattori (1932),[7] the Shuri dialect preserves this distinction, but this is also the case with many other Ryukyuan varieties[8] (Table 8). The fact that Ryukyuan faithfully preserves a distinction already lost in Japanese in the 8th c. and only recoverable through internal reconstruction suffices to establish beyond reasonable doubt the two have split *at least* before the beginnings of Japanese history.

Table 8. PJ *ui and *əi in Ryukyuan

		*ui		*əi	
		'moon'	'pass'	'tree'	'rise'
OJ		*tuki*$_2$ (~tuku-)	*sugi*$_2$ (~sugus-)	*ki*$_2$ (~ko$_2$)	*oki*$_2$ (~oko$_2$s-)
Amami	Yuwan	tsɨki	sɨgi-	kʰɨ:	xɨ:ɾ-
Okinawa	Nakijin	ɕitɕi:	ɕidʑi:ɾuŋ	ki:	ɸukiɾuŋ
Okinawa	Shuri	tsitɕi	sidʑijuŋ	ki:	ʔukijuŋ
Miyako	Ōgami	ksks	sɯki	ki:	uki
Yaeyama	Ishigaki	tsɿkɿ	sɿgiɾuŋ	ki:	ukiɾuŋ
PR		*tuki	*sugi	*ke	*oke

In Ryukyuan, PJ *ui and *i merge as PR *i but stay distinct from the merged reflexes of PJ *əi and *e (as well as *ai and *ia, PR *e). On the other hand, in OJ, the primary vowels *i and *e generally merge as i_1 (see

[7] Arisaka's paper appeared *after* Hattori's, but Hattori acknowledged it was Arisaka's discovery.

[8] In Southern Ryukyuan, *ui-ending polysyllabic verb stems have been reshaped by analogy with the *əi-ending ones, and the *ui/*əi distinction is thus well-preserved in nominals only.

however subsection 5.2) and stay distinct from i_2, the merged reflex of the diphthongs *ui and *əi. These evolutions are summarized in Figure 4.

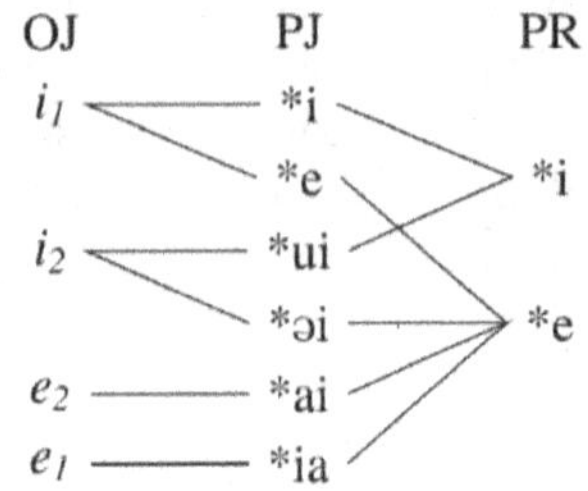

Figure 4. OJ and PR reflexes of the PJ diphthongs

The PJ system however surprisingly lacks a diphthong *oi. I propose that in fact some of the *ui and *əi usually posited should rather be reconstructed as *oi, and that *oi merges with *ui and not *əi in Ryukyuan to give PR *i.

4.1. From *ui to *oi

OJ u ~ i_2 apophonic stems usually have Ryukyuan cognates that exhibit a similar *u ~ *i alternation, and are thus reconstructed as *ui in PJ. See for instance *padui 'shame' (Table 9) or *mui 'body, flesh' (Table 10).

However, some *u* ~ i_2 apophonic nouns, traditionally reconstructed as *ui, have an alternating shape (*hifukukei*) that should be reconstructed with a stem-final *o rather than *u, as is clear from their Ryukyuan reflexes. They should thus be reconstructed with a diphthong *oi in PJ.

This is the case of 'yellow' (Table 11), which appears in OJ as *ku-* ~ *ki*$_2$ but has a reflex *ko- in PR. This *ko- is reconstructed on the basis of the aspiration or lenition of the velar in Northern Ryukyuan, and the *lack* of fricativization in Southern Ryukyuan, to be compared with the reflexes of *ku exemplified by PJ *kumo 'cloud'. This reconstruction is further confirmed by the existence of the later Japanese form *kogane*, the standard form since the Middle Japanese period.

The verb 'exhaust' (OJ *tukus-* ~ *tuki*$_2$-) should be reconstructed as *tukos- for the same reasons as 'yellow'. The cognate of OJ *tukus-* in Miyako-Hirara is *tsɿkus-*, which implies *tukos- since *ku > *f(u)* (cf. 'make' *tsɿfuɿ* :: OJ *tukur-*). Moreover, the Amami-Boma (Tokunoshima) form *tsɨkijuŋ* confirms the PR reconstruction *tuki for the transitive form, which ultimately derives from PJ *tukoi (cf. Boma *uɨjuŋ* 'rise' < PR *oke < PJ *əkəi).

The reconstruction of 'moon' (OJ *tuku-* ~ *tuki*$_2$) as PJ *tukoi proposed by Thorpe (1983:355) is less secure. Though Thorpe is very confident[9] about his proposal, he doesn't clearly explain his reasoning, and the Yaeyama-Hateruma form *sɿkeŋ* is the only evidence he adduces. This is perhaps based on the fact that Hateruma *e* comes from *oe ('burn' PJ *mojai > PR *moe > *me:*) or *ae ('front' PJ *mape > PR *mae > *me:*), but never *ue. The evolution of the Hateruma form might then be reconstructed as follows:

(2) PJ *tuko-jo > *tuko-je > *tsɿkoe > sɿkeŋ (with prothetic -*ŋ*)
(cf. Ishigaki *tuko-jo > *tuko-je > tsɿkui)

Table 9. PJ *hadui 'shame'

		'shameful'	'shame'	'corner'	'arm'
OJ		*padukasi*	*hadi* (MJ)	*kado* (MJ)	*ude*
Amami	Yuwan	hatsɨkaɕa	hadʑi	kadu	ʔudɨ
Amami	Yoron	pantɕikaɕaŋ	padʑi	hadu	udi
Okinawa	Nakijin	padʑikaɕeŋ	padʑi:	hadu:	ʔudɨ:
Miyako	Ōgami	pakskaskam		katu	uti
Yaeyama	Ishigaki	patsɿkaha-	padzɿ	kadu	udi
Yaeyama	Hateruma	pasɿkahaŋ		kadu	udʑi
PR		*pazu	*pazi	*kado	*Ude

Table 10. PJ *mui 'body, flesh'

		'chest'	'flesh'	'thing'	'eye'
OJ		*mune*	*mi*$_2$	*mono*$_2$	*me*$_2$
Amami	Sakamine	munɪ		muŋ	mi:
Amami	Yoron	ni:	mi:	munu	mi:
Okinawa	Nakijin	ni:	mi:	munu:	mi:
Miyako	Ōgami	mmi-fkɯ	miɯ	munu	mi:
Yaeyama	Ishigaki	nni	mɿ:	munu	mi:
Yonaguni		nni	mi:	munu	mi:
PR		*mune	*mi	*mono	*me

[9] "This is why one can legitimately pick out a word like sïkeN 'moon' in the remote Hateruma language as convincing evidence for *ko in JR *tukojo 'moon(night)' millenia earlier" (Thorpe 1983:355)

Table 11. PJ *koi 'yellow'

		'yellow'	'tree'	'gold'	'cloud'
OJ		*ki₂ (~ ku)*	*ki₂ (~ ko₂)*	*kugane*	*kumo₁*
Amami	Koniya	k[?]i:	k[h]i:	k[h]ugani	k[?]umu
Amami	Yoron	kinsaŋ	ɕi: ~ çi:	hugani	kumu
Okinawa	Nakijin	tɕ[?]i:ru:	ki:	ɸuga:ni	k[?]umu:
Miyako	Ōgami	ks:-	ki:	kukani	fumu
Yaeyama	Ishigaki	kɿ:	ki:	kugani	ɸumu
Yaeyama	Hateruma	kɿŋkɿ:	ki:	kugani	ɸumoŋ
PR		*ki	*ke	*kogane	*kumo

4.2. From *əi to *oi and *ə to *o

Traditionally, all instances of OJ i_2 ~ *o* alternations have been interpreted as involving an o_2 < *ə, and thus automatically reconstructed as *əi. However, several problems arise from this mechanistic reconstruction. First, cases where no $o_{1/2}$ distinction is attested could theoretically go back to an earlier *o rather than *ə. Moreover, in some cases this *o* coexists with *a* in the same root, which, according to Arisaka's (1934b) third law, is almost never possible for an o_2. But the most conclusive piece of evidence comes from Ryukyuan: some examples have reflexes with PR *i, while OJ i_2 ~ o_2 < PJ *əi usually corresponds to PR *e, like 'tree' OJ ki_2 ~ ko_2- :: PR *ke. Reconstructing these exceptional cases not as *əi but *oi permits to solve all these problems.

Such examples include 'be, sit', 'fire', 'get drained' and 'indigo', which I respectively reconstruct as PJ *woi, *poi, *poi and *awoi (instead of the traditional *wəi, *pəi, *pəi and *awəi, cf. Martin 1987) on the basis that these have a vowel *i in PR. OJ makes no distinction between o_1 and o_2 after *w* and *p*, and there is thus nothing that could prevent us from reconstructing an *o instead of an *ə in these. Tables 12 to 15 give the reflexes of the above words in Ryukyuan and contrast them with examples of PR *e in similar environments.

I must admit that all the examples where I propose to correct the reconstruction from *əi to *oi contain a labial consonant before the vowel. It could thus be the case that PJ *əi merges with *ui after a labial to give PR *i rather than the usual PR *e:

(3) PJ *əi > PR *i / $C_{[LABIAL]}$__

There is however at least one counter-example to this generalization: the PR *o(p)pe 'big' form (Yuwan *xɨ:* :: Koniya *ɸɨ:* :: Nakijin *ɸupi* :: Shuri *ʔuɸi*) is undoubtedly related to OJ *opo* 'big' ~ *opi₂* 'grow'. Since this form has a reflex with *e in PR and that nearly every *(C)oCo* form in OJ have an o_2 in both syllables, it can be safely reconstructed as PJ *əpəi. This form thus exemplifies a case where PJ *əi corresponds to PR *e and not *i after a labial.

The distributional constraint observed might also be just a coincidence: *o usually gets raised to *u* in OJ, which leaves few possibilities for $i_2 \sim o_1$ alternations. There are not so many cases of $i_2 \sim o$ alternations anyway, and only a handful of examples remain after all cases clearly involving an o_2 are eliminated. Not surprisingly, most remaining examples involve syllables where OJ has no $o_{1/2}$ distinction: *po*, *bo*, *mo*, *wo*, which all have a labial initial. Some examples with unclear $o_{1/2}$ attestation after a non-labial consonant are found, but they seem to have no cognates in Ryukyuan.

Anyway, 'blue' should be reconstructed as *awo in order to comply with Arisaka's (1934b) third law, which states OJ *a* and o_2 (< *ə) seldom co-exist in the same morpheme.

Table 12. PJ *woi 'sit'

		'sit'	'be'	'get drunk'
OJ		*wi-*	*wor-*	*wep-*
Okinawa	Shuri	jijuŋ	wuŋ	wiːjuŋ
Miyako	Ōgami	pɯɾ-	uɾ-	piː
Yaeyama	Ishigaki	bɿɾuŋ	uŋ	biŋ
PR		*wir-	*wor-	*we-

Table 13. PJ *poi 'fire'

		'fire'	'moldboard, spatula'
OJ		pi_2	pe_1ra
Okinawa	Nakijin	pˀiː	pʰiraː
Yaeyama	Ishigaki	pɿː	piɾa
Yaeyama	Hateruma	pɿː	piɾa
Yonaguni		tɕˀiː	çiɾa
PR		*pi	*pera

Table 14. PJ *poi 'get drained'

		'get drained'	'moldboard, spatula'
OJ		*pi$_2$*	*pe$_1$ra*
Amami	Koniya	çiɾ	ɸɨɾa
Okinawa	Nakijin	pˀjuŋ	pʰiɾaː
Miyako	Ōgami	psː	piɾa
Yaeyama	Ishigaki	pɿsuŋ	piɾa
Yaeyama	Hateruma	pɿsuŋ	piɾa
PR		*pi	*pera

Table 15. PJ *awoi 'indigo'

		'blue'	'indigo'	'front'
OJ		*awo*	*awi*	*mape$_1$*
Amami	Koniya	ʔoːsa	ʔeː	məː
Amami	Yoron	oːsaŋ	ai	məː
Miyako	Hirara	oːkaɿ	aɿ	mai
PR		*aU	*ai	*mae

5. Further developments and remaining issues

5.1. A seventh PJ vowel?

Evidence for a seventh vowel in PJ remains scarce. Two proposals for a seventh, high central vowel exist, but they have been made on the basis of completely different kinds of evidence.

Hattori (1978–1979) reconstructs *ü in a handful of words only, most of which are problematic. First, the reconstruction of 'all' as *müina ~ *mürə is only valid if the two OJ words *mi$_2$na* and *mo$_2$ro$_2$* are indeed etymologically related, which remains unsure. Then, 'finger' (Hattori's *əjübəi) is a word with a complex history, and Hattori didn't clearly explain his motivations for this reconstruction (Hattori 1978–1979:(9)116). Finally, Hattori's *püi 'fire' and *pü-dai/*pü-dee 'lightning' are reconstructed with *ü since they have a reflex *i in PR instead of the expected *e, but this can be explained by my own hypothesis as cases of *oi.

On the other hand, Frellesvig and Whitman's (2008a) *ɨ is reconstructed on the main basis of OJ-internal evidence, and there seems to be no supporting comparative evidence from Ryukyuan, EOJ or Hachijō (Table 16). While this hypothesis is interesting, well-founded, and aims at explaining a few otherwise irregular vowel alternations, I feel there are still too few good examples. There is little merit in reconstructing an extra vowel in PJ over recognizing a small number of irregular forms.

Table 16. F & W's PJ *ə and *ɨ

		'seaweed'	'this'
F&W's PJ		**mə*	**kɨ*
OJ		*mo*	*ko₂*
Amami	Koniya	muː	kʰuɾ
Okinawa	Shuri	muː	kuɾi
Miyako	Ōgami	muː	kuɾi
PR		*mU	*kuri

5.2. Vowel raising in OJ

There are several cases of $e_{(1)}$ and o_1 in OJ that cannot be explained away as originating in earlier diphthongs, and these thus constitute exceptions to the vowel raising process that affected OJ. Examples of unraised $e_{(1)}$ in OJ include for example *pe₁ra* 'moldboard, spatula', *ke₁pu* 'today', *pe₁ta* 'near the shore', *sake₁b-* 'shout', *kape₁r/s-* 'return', *uke₁ra* 'Atractylodes japonica', *ter-* 'shine', etc. Instances of unraised o_1 can be seen in *ko₁pi₂* 'love', *ko₁ga-* 'burn', *to₁ma* 'woven rain-cover', *so₁ra* 'sky', *to₁ra* 'tiger', *yo₁wa-* 'weak', *mo₁zu* 'shrike', *ko₁mo* 'eelgrass', etc.

Several explanations have been proposed to account for such cases of unraised *e and *o in OJ. One of these states a phonotactic constraint stipulating final position blocks raising (Frellesvig and Whitman 2008a). This hypothesis does not however explain the cases where an unraised vowel is found in a non-final syllable, such as those quoted above. Hattori (1978–1979) proposed on the other hand it is vowel length that blocks raising, and that unraised *e and *o should be reconstructed as long *ee and *oo in PJ. This is however at odds with the general trend of vowel changes, since long vowels generally tend to rise (Labov 1994:116). If vowel length is to be reconstructed, Hattori's hypothesis should be reversed and raised vowels reconstructed as long (this might account for their relative paucity). Other solutions could include reconstructing those unraised vowels as diphthongs (*ia and *ua or *uə), but the lack of alternating shapes for these deprives us of a solid basis to do so. Reconstructing still extra vowels (*ɛ, *ɔ?) would be quite unparsimonious. The explanation could lie into a combination of two or more of the above hypotheses.

6. Conclusions

A detailed examination of the correspondences between Old Japanese and the different Ryukyuan languages leads to a revision of earlier hypotheses about the Proto-Japonic vowel system. The most important improvements are the reconstruction of the two mid vowels *e and *i and of the diphthong *oi, as well as the reinterpretation of several cases of *ə as *o. The Ryukyuan vowel systems are in a way more archaic than the OJ system, since they preserve a distinction between the vowels *i/*e, *u/*o, *ui/*əi as well as *oi/*əi, which had already merged by the time of the first OJ texts. This is not to say we can dispense with the OJ data, which reveals several distinctions absent from Ryukyuan (*i vs. *ui/*oi, *e/*ia/*iə vs. *ai/*əi).

Though the Ryukyuan data supports the reconstruction of a six-vowel system for PJ, it offers no solid evidence for a seventh vowel, which is anyway supported by too few examples. The reconstruction of the PJ vocalism however still suffers from several problems to be solved by future research. The most important question to be answered concerns the details of the evolution of the PJ vowels in OJ, namely the exact conditions of mid vowel raising. Further work is also needed in order to find more examples of PJ *e, which are still not very numerous, and more evidence for a distinction between *oi and *əi after labials in Ryukyuan. Many other details of the PJ vocalism are still obscure, like the distributional constraints described by Arisaka's laws.

A large-scale comparison of Ryukyuan and Japanese, followed by the application of the methods of internal reconstruction, is without doubt the key to a better understanding of the PJ vowel system.

Note on transcriptions

Old Japanese syllable distinctions are marked with subscript numbers, with 1 indicating the *kō-rui* series and 2 indicating the *otsu-rui*. PR *U indicates it is not possible to decide whether the vowel should be reconstructed as *u or *o, and *N stands for an unknown nasal.

The various Ryukyuan data taken from existing sources have been converted to a broad phonetic notation, that mostly follows the principles of the IPA, except for the symbol [ɿ], that marks a sound rather freely alternating between an alveolar approximant and a fricative, and for [ˀ], which marks non-ejective glottalization. Contextual devoicing and tones are left unmarked.

Acknowledgements

I express my gratitude to all the Ryukyuan speakers whose help made this study possible. This study was supported by a *Grant-in-Aid for Scientific Research* (22·01000) from the Japanese Society for the Promotion of Science.

References

Arisaka, H. 1934a. Boin kōtai no hōsoku ni tsuite. *Onsei gakkai kaihō* 34.

Arisaka, H. 1934b. Kodai nihongo ni okeru onsetsu ketsugō no hōsoku. *Kokugo to kokubungaku* 22.1.

Frellesvig, B. and Whitman, J. 2008a. Evidence for seven vowels in proto-Japanese. In Frellesvig and Whitman (2008b), 15–41.

Frellesvig, B. and Whitman, J. (eds.). 2008b. *Proto-Japanese: Issues and prospects*. Amsterdam; Philadelphia: John Benjamins.

Hattori, S. 1932. Ryūkyū to kokugo no on'in hōsoku. *Hōgen* 2.7, 8, 9, 10, 12.

Hattori, S. 1978–1979. Nihon sogo ni tsuite 1–22. *Gengo* 7(1)–7(3), 7(6)–8(12).

Hino, S. 2003. Nihon sogo no boin taikei: Jōdai Tōgoku hōgen shiryō ni yoru saikō. *Nihongo keitōron no genzai/Perspectives on the origins of the Japanese language, eds.* A. Vovin and T. Osada, 187–206. Kyoto: Kokusai Nihon bunka sentā.

Ikema, N. 2003. *Yonagunigo jiten*. Yonaguni.

Kiku, C. and Takahashi, T. 2005. *Yoron hōgen jiten*. Tokyo: Musashino shoin.

Kokuritsu kokugo kenkyūjo (ed.). 1963. *Okinawago jiten*. Tokyo: Ōkurashō insatsukyoku.

Labov, W. 1994. *Principles of linguistic change v. 1: Internal factors*. Oxford; Cambridge: Blackwell.

Martin, S.E. 1987. *The Japanese language through time*. New Haven; London: Yale University Press.

Matsumoto, K. 1975. Kodai nihongo boin soshiki kō: Naiteki saiken no kokoromi. *Kanazawa daigaku hōbungakubu ronshū* 22: 83–152.

Miller, R.A. 1967. *The Japanese language*. Chicago: University of Chicago Press.

Miyagi, S. 2003. *Ishigaki hōgen jiten*. Naha: Okinawa taimusu. 2 vols.

Miyake, M.H. 2003. Philological evidence for *e and *o in pre-old Japanese. *Diachronica* 20.1: 83–137.

Miyanaga, M. 1930. *Yaeyama goi (kōhen, otsuhen), Miyanaga Masamori zenshū*, vol. 8, 9. Tokyo: Daiichi shobō, 1980–1981 edn.

Nakama, M. 1992. *Ryūkyū hōgen no kosō*. Tokyo: Daiichi shobō.

Nakasone, S. 1983. *Okinawa Nakijin hōgen jiten*. Tokyo: Kadokawa shoten.

Nevskij, N.A. 1922–1928 [2005]. *Miyako hōgen nōto*. Hirara: Okinawa-ken Hirara-shi kyōiku iinkai.

Ōno, S. 1977. On'in no hensen. *Iwanami Nihongo kōza*: On'in, 147–220. Tokyo: Iwanami shoten.

Pellard, T. 2008. Proto-Japonic *e and *o in Eastern Old Japanese. *Cahiers de linguistique – Asie orientale* 37.2: 133–158.

Pellard, T. 2009. Ōgami — *Éléments de description d'un parler du Sud des Ryūkyū*. Ph.D. thesis, École des hautes études en sciences sociales.

Serafim, L.A. 1999. Reflexes of proto-Korea-Japonic mid vowels in Japonic and Korean. Paper presented at the *XVI*[th] *International Conference on Historical Linguistics*. Vancouver.

Serafim, L.A. 2008. The uses of Ryukyuan in understanding Japanese language history. Frellesvig and Whitman (2008b), 79–99.

Thorpe, M.L. 1983. *Ryūkyūan language history*. Ph.D. thesis, University of Southern California.

Uchima, C. and Arakaki, K. 2000. *Okinawa hokubu nanbu hōgen no kijutsuteki kenkyū*. Tokyo: Kazama shobō.

Vovin, A. 2010. *Koreo-Japonica: A critical study in the proposed language relationship*. University of Hawai'i Press.

Whitman, J.B. 1985. *The Phonological basis for the comparison of Japanese and Korean*. Ph.D. thesis, Harvard University.

Agreement and the restructuring of the Japanese pronominal system[*]

YUKO YANAGIDA
University of Tsukuba

1. Introduction

In English, demonstratives bear number agreement with the noun that follows, i.e. *these books/*these book, this book/*this books*. Modern Japanese is said to be a language which lacks number agreement; plurality is specified either on demonstrative or noun. When the noun is [+human], plurality is specified on the noun with the plural suffix *tati* (1b). When the noun is [-human], it is specified on the demonstrative with the suffix *-ra* (2b).

(1) a. sono gakusei
that student
'that student'

b. sono gakusei-tati
that student-Pl
'those students'

[*] I am grateful to Bjarke Frellesvig and Peter Sells for their careful reading of the manuscript and their invaluable comments and suggestions. Thanks also go to John Whitman for discussions of the issues and suggestions on various versions of the manuscript.

Japanese/Korean Linguistics 20.
Edited by Bjarke Frellesvig and Peter Sells.

(2) a. sono hon
that book
'that book'

b. sore-ra-no hon
that-Pl-Gen book
'those books'

The demonstrative *sono* 'that' and *sore-ra-no* 'that-Pl-Gen' as shown in (1)-(2) function as modifiers with genitive *no*. This paper motivates both synchronic and diachronic analyses of demonstratives/pronouns in construction with an appositive NP, parallel to English [*we/these students*] as in (3).

(3) a. *[$_{DP}$ ware gakusei]
I student

b. [$_{DP}$ ware-ra gakusei (-tati)]
we-Pl student-Pl

Under the DP hypothesis, Abney (1987) analyzes determiners and pronouns as the functional head D, selecting a complement NP as in [$_{DP}$ we/the [$_{NP}$ linguists]]. This paper argues that Japanese demonstratives project up to DP, and that there is number agreement inside DP. It also presents evidence that personal pronouns in Old Japanese (8th century) contain an Agreement projection (AgrP) inside an extended nominal projection. Loss of AgrP leads to the result that personal pronouns have an internal structure similar to demonstratives.[1]

2. Demonstratives in Modern Japanese

2.1. Split DP Hypothesis

Whitman (1981) and Fukui (1995) point out a striking difference between demonstratives in Japanese and English: As shown in (4)-(5), Japanese demonstratives can occur after an adjective or a genitive modifier, but English counterparts are unacceptable.

(4) a. [Akai **kono/sono** huku] o karita.
red this/that Gen clothes Acc borrowed
'*I borrowed red this/that clothes.'

b. [John no **kono/sono** huku] o karita
John Gen this/that Gen clothes Acc borrowed
'*I borrowed John's this/that clothes.'

(5) a. [Akai **kore/sore**] o karita.
red this/that Acc borrowed
'*I borrowed this/that.'

---

1 The periodization for Japanese: Old Japanese (abbreviated 'OJ,' approximately 700–800), Early Middle Japanese ('EMJ' 800–1200), Late Middle Japanese ('LMJ' 1200–1600), Early Modern Japanese ('EModJ' 1600–1800).

b. [John no **kore/sore**] o karita.
John Gen this/that Acc borrowed
'*I borrowed John's this/that.'

These differences can be explained by positing an extended structure for demonstratives. In recent research, it has been proposed that demonstratives are not unanalyzable categories, but rather decompose into three morphological elements: definite, deictic and noun, as shown in (6) (cf. Kayne and Pollock (2009), Giusti (2001) among others):

(6) a. that book: *th-* (definite) *-at* (deictic) book (noun)
b. this book: *th-* (definite) *-is* (deictic) book (noun)
c. this/that: th-(definite) –is/at (deictic) THING (noun)

Kayne and Pollock (2009) decompose the bare English demonstratives *that* and *this* into *th* (definite), *at/is* (deictic), and an unpronounced noun labeled THING. Giusti (2001) suggests that both pronouns and demonstratives in Romance and Germanic languages project up to the maximal projection: they originate in AgrP and move to Spec, DP in the extended nominal projection to check the definite feature. This is shown in (7).

(7) $[_{DP}$ DP(Dem)$_i$ $[_{D}$ +def $[_{AgrP}$ t_i $[_{Agr}$ $[_{NP}$ …]]]]]
$[_{DP}$ DP(Pron)$_i$ $[_{D}$ +def $[_{AgrP}$ t_i $[_{Agr}$ $[_{NP}$ …]]]]]

Roberts and Roussou (2003) propose a similar analysis, where demonstratives originate in the Number projection and move to Spec. DP.

(8) $[_{DP}$ that/those$_i$ $[_{NumP}$ t_i $[_{NP}$ …]]]

I will show that the NumberP analysis is particularly suited to Modern Japanese (ModJ). Fukui's data in (4)-(5) indicate a basic difference between Japanese and English: Japanese demonstratives need not move to Spec, DP, suggesting the structure in (9).

(9) a. $[_{DemP}$ *so* $[_{Dem}$ *no*]]
b. $[_{DemP}$ so $[_{Dem}$ re]]
c. $[_{DP}$ Ø [*akai* $[_{NumP}$ $[_{DemP}$ *sono*] $[_{NP}$ *huku*]]]]

I hypothesize that as in (9a)-(b) both *no* and *re* are heads of DemP and thus are in complementary distribution; that is, *sore-no* is unacceptable. As we have seen, unlike their English counterparts, Japanese demonstratives can appear lower than adjectival or genitive modifiers. This fact is explained by the structure in (9c), where the demonstrative remains to the right of modifiers, below DP.

Failure to raise to Spec, DP correlates with an interesting semantic property of Japanese demonstratives. In Giusti's (2001) system, the demonstrative must raise to check a definite feature on D. Thus they allow only a definite reading in Germanic and Romance languages. However in certain contexts, Japanese demonstratives appear not to be specified for definiteness. The idea that *sono/sore*, unlike English *that*, have no specification of definiteness is supported by the fact that *sono/sore* can have a non-referential, specifically a bound variable interpretation (10a)-(b), as pointed out by Hoji (1991).

(10) a. ?Daremo$_i$-ga **sono** hito$_i$-no hon-o sute-ta
everyone-Nom that person-Gen book-Acc throw away-Past
'Everyone$_i$ threw away that person$_i$'s book.'

b. Nanimo$_i$ [[[**sore**$_i$-o tyuumon-sita] hito]-no uti]-ni(-wa)
nothing that-Acc order-Past person-Gen house-to(-Cont)
todokanakatta
did not arrive
'Nothing$_i$ arrived at the house of the person who had ordered that$_i$.'

The English demonstrative *that* is inherently specified for the features [definite] and [deictic], and hence a non-referential/indefinite reading is not allowed. Japanese *sono/sore* 'that,' on the other hand, is specified only for the feature [deictic], which may be interpreted as meaning "derivable from the discourse context."

The structure of demonstratives becomes relevant to the analysis of pronouns in ModJ when we consider the arguments of Hoji (1991) regarding *kare*. Hoji shows that unlike *so*-type demonstratives, the *a*-type demonstratives, *are/ano* 'that' and third person *kare* 'he' cannot be construed as bound variables. The examples in (11) are taken from Hoji (1991).

(11) a. *Daremo$_i$-ga [$_{NP}$ [$_S$ **kare**$_i$ ga tukut-ta] omotya] o kowasi-ta
everyone-Nom he Nom make-Past toy Acc break-Past
'Everyone$_i$ broke the toy that he$_i$ had made.'

b. *Daremo ga$_i$ **ano** hito$_i$ no hon o sute-ta
everyone Nom that person Gen book Acc throw away-Past
'Everyone$_i$ threw away that person$_i$'s book.'

c. *Nanimo$_i$ [[[**are**$_i$-o tyuumon-sita] hito]-no uti]-ni(-wa)
nothing that-Acc order-Past person-Gen house-to(-Cont)
todoka-nakatta
arrive-not-Past
'Nothing$_i$ arrived at the house of the person who ordered that$_i$.'

Given that *kare* 'he' behaves like the demonstrative *are/ano* 'that,' Hoji proposes that *kare* is not a pronoun but a demonstrative.

Ueyama (1998) and Hoji, Kinsui, Takubo and Ueyama (2003) propose that *a*-type demonstratives are strictly 'referential' in the sense that they must denote a specific individual known to the speaker, whereas *so*-type demonstratives can refer to an individual that the speaker does not know at all. But in such cases *so*-type demonstratives require a linguistic antecedent. Thus in (12), *a-itu* can be used without a linguistic antecedent, but *so-itu* cannot.

(12) (Situation: The detective is looking for a man. He somehow believes that the man should be hiding in a certain room. He breaks into the room and asks the people in the room.)

[**A-itu/#So-itu**]-*wa do-ko-da?*
that-guy -Top which-place-Copula
'Where is [**he**]?'

The difference between *so*-NPs and *a*-NPs is formally analyzed in terms of the notion "D-indexing" (13) by Ueyama (1998).

(13) a. *So*-NPs cannot be D-indexed (at least when the target object is not visible at the scene).
b. *A*-NPs must be D-indexed, and marked as [Distal].

The fact that *a*-type demonstratives disallow an indefinite reading (11) and are inherently referential (12) suggests that *a*-type demonstratives, but not *so*-type demonstratives, have a [D] feature.

Cardinaletti and Starke (1999) argue that Romance languages possess two types of pronouns; strong pronouns and deficient pronouns (see Section 3.1.). They claim that strong pronouns, but not deficient pronouns, are inherently referential, and are licensed at a different position within the extended nominal projection. Under the split DP hypothesis, *a*-type demonstratives and *so*-type demonstratives have structures (14a-b) in parallel with strong and deficient pronouns in Romance languages.

(14) a. [$_{DP}$ [$_{DemP}$ ka-re] [+Def [$_{NumP}$ t [$_{NP}$ …]]]] (strong)
b. [$_{NumP}$ [$_{DemP}$ so-re] [$_{NP}$ …]] (deficient)

A-type demonstratives originate in Spec, NumP and move to Spec, DP to check their referential feature, while *so*-type demonstratives that lack referential features stay in Spec, NumP.

2.2. Plural *-ra*

The view that DPs in Japanese may contain a NumberP projection is not new (cf. Kawashima 1994 and Watanabe 2006). The existence of NumberP is evidenced by the behavior of the plural suffix *-ra*. The plural *-ra* is used in so-called associative plural constructions:

(15) [$_{DP}$ **Hiroko ra** gakusei 3nin/tati] no kiboo
Hiroko Pl student 3 Cl/Pl Gen hope
'the hope of Hiroko and the three/other students'

Associative plurals are nominal expressions that designate a group by naming its most salient member, meaning 'X and other people associated with X'. Vassilieva (2008) argues that the *protagonist* X in an associative construction is a referential modifier and has a [D] feature. It starts out in a modifier projection and moves to the specifier of DP, as illustrated in (16).

(16) [$_{DP}$ [$_{DP2}$ **X**]$_i$ D° [$_{NumP}$ Num° [**+Pl**] [$_{NP}$ t$_i$ [$_{NP}$ N° [**+Hum**]]]]]

Following Vassilieva (2008), I assume that the functional features [+hum], [+pl] and [+D] are spelled out by the morphological component as the suffix *-ra*. The claim that elements X preceding *-ra* are in Spec, DP is supported by the fact that they must be either names or pronouns which are inherently referential; common nouns do not appear with *-ra*, as shown in (17).

(17) *?[**gakusei ra** (waka-mono)] no kiboo
student-Pl young-people Gen hope
'the hope of the young students'

The protagonist X and *-ra* always appear in the left peripheral position within the extended nominal projection:

(18) a. *gakusei 3nin/tati Hanako ra no kiboo
student 3 Cl/Pl Hanako Pl Gen hope
'the hope of Hanako and the three students'
b. *Hanako tati gakusei ra no kiboo
Hanako Pl student Pl Gen hope

As discussed below, I assume with Whitman (2001) that the functional head within DP invariably takes its complement on the right. (15) is then derived by movement of the entire NP to Spec, NumP (19).

(19) [$_{DP}$ Hanako [$_{D}$ ra] [$_{NumP}$ [$_{NP}$ gakusei]$_i$ [$_{Num}$ 3nin/tati] t$_{NPi}$]]

The protagonist *Hanako* appears in Spec, DP whose head is spelled out as -*ra*. The D head *-ra* selects NumP whose head can either be morphologically null or spelled out by the numeral or the plural form *tati*.

Demonstratives plus *-ra* have the same structure as associative plurals except that they require the following nominal not to be a [+count] singular. The following nominal can be a mass noun (20a)-(b), or, if it is [+count], plurality must be overtly specified by adding a numeral classifier (20c).

(20) a. [$_{DP}$ kore/sore ra sigen gomi] no haiki basyo
this/that Pl recyclable trash Gen dispose place
'the place to dispose these recyclable trash'

b. $[_{DP}$ kore/sore ra hon-rui] no oki basyo
this/that Pl book-kind Gen put place
'the place to put these kinds of books'

c. $[_{DP}$ kore/sore ra hon *(san-satu)] no oki basyo
this/that Pl book three-Class Gen put-place
'the place to put these three books'

In section 2, we saw Hoji's (1991) argument that third person *kare* is not a pronoun but a demonstrative. Interestingly, *kare* behaves exactly like demonstratives in that the appositive NP without the overt plural suffix *tati* is deviant (21).[2]

(21) a. ??$[_{DP}$ kare ra gakusei] no kiboo
he Pl student Gen hope
'The hope of them students'

b. $[_{DP}$ kare ra gakusei-tati] no kiboo
he Pl student Pl Gen hope
'The hope of them students'

Unlike English, Japanese is said to be a language which lacks agreement. The (un)acceptability of (20-21), however, clearly indicates that demonstratives trigger number agreement between the D head *-ra* and the NP that it selects.

In parallel to the associative plural construction (19), I argue that demonstratives contain NumP. The D head *-ra* selects NumP specified for [+Plural]. The NP (Mass/Plural) moves to Spec, NumP: [3]

(22) $[_{DP}$ $[_{DemP}$ *kore/sore/kare*] $[_{D}$ *ra*] $[_{NumP}$ NP_i $[_{Num}$+Mass/*tati*] t_i]]

Examples (20) then have a structure in which the entire DP appears in Spec, DP(GenP), as represented in (23).

(23)

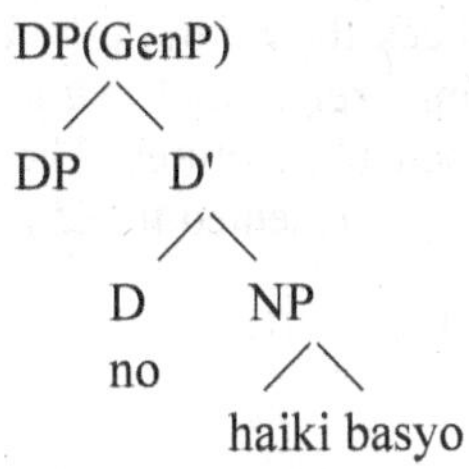

Assuming the split DP hypothesis, this section has argued that demonstratives, including third person *kare* in ModJ, have a structure in which DP is

---

[2] I owe this observation to Atsuro Tsubomoto (p.c.).

[3] Recall that *kore/sore* 'this' decompose into two elements*;* *ko/so* (deictic) in Spec(DemP) and *-re* the head of DemP (see (9)).

made up of two layers; the higher layer is specified for definiteness, and the lower layer is specified for number.

3. Personal Pronouns in the History of Japanese

3.1. Cardinaletti and Starke (1999)

Romance languages possess three classes of pronouns: strong, weak and clitic pronouns. The latter two are classified together by Cardinaletti and Starke (1999) as "deficient." Cardinaletti and Starke propose that the three classes of pronouns are associated with distinct heads inside the extended nominal projection. CP, ∑P and IP are common to nominal and clause structure (24).

(24) $[_{CPL}$ Strong $[_{\Sigma PL}$ Weak $[_{IPL}$ Clitic $[_{LP}\ldots]]]]$,
where LP= Lexical Projection (NP/VP) (Cardinaletti and Starke 1999)

Strong pronouns are licensed at the highest functional projection, which hosts case and referential features. Weak pronouns have a polarity feature which is licensed at what Cardinaletti and Starke call ∑P. Clitic pronouns are licensed at the lowest functional projection, IP, which contains agreement features. Deficient pronouns, both weak and clitic, lack the highest functional projection, and thus, according to Cardinaletti and Starke (1999:192), they appear in a derived position in the clause to recover these features.

Recall that demonstratives have a number specification and Number projects to an independent projection, NumP. Personal pronouns differ from demonstratives in that they are specified for language-specific phi-features, including person, number and gender features. In order to incorporate Cardinaletti and Starke's basic insight into the two layered split DP structure of demonstratives proposed in section 2, I assume with Guisti (2001) that personal pronouns contain AgrP. Strong pronouns are compositionally derived by movement of Agr to D to check their definite/referential features. Deficient pronouns, which lack definite/referential features, originate inside NP and move up to Agr to check their phi-features. The structural positions of strong and deficient pronouns are represented in (25).

(25) $[_{DP}$ Strong $[_{AgrP}$ Deficient $[_{NP}\ldots]]]$

3.2 A Tripartite Pronominal System in Old Japanese[4]

ModJ pronouns are distinctive compared to their Indo-European counterparts in that there is a large inventory of pronominal forms which originate as nouns: e.g. *watakusi* 'I'< 'private,' *boku* 'I' < 'servant,' *kimi* 'you'< 'lord'. It has been pointed out by a number of researchers that these pronouns behave like nouns: they can be coordinated with nouns such as *kimi to Taroo* 'you and Taroo', and modified by adjectives as in *kawaii kimi* 'cute you' (cf. Fukui 1995). Cardinaletti and Starke indicate that strong pronouns in Romance languages can be coordinated with nouns, but they cannot be modified by adjectives. The noun-like properties of *watakusi* 'I' and *kimi* 'you' indicate that the syntactic status of these pronouns remains that of a noun.

In contrast to ModJ pronouns, Whitman and Yanagida (2009) and Yanagida (2010) argue that OJ (8th century) has three classes of pronouns equivalent to those in Romance languages, as illustrated in (26):[5]

(26) Tripartite Pronominal Systems in OJ (8th century)

	clitics	weak pronouns	strong pronouns
1st person	*(w)a*		*(w)a-re*
2nd person	*na*		*na-re*
demonstrative	*si*	*so/ko*	*so-re/ko-re*

The full forms with *-re* such as *(w)a-re* 'I' and *na-re* 'you' are strong pronouns. Examples (27a, b) are taken from the *Man'yôshû* (MYS):

(27) a. Koromo no pimo wo **are** tokame yamo (MYS 3585)
clothes Gen string Acc I untie Q
'Would I untie the string of the garment?'

b. **Nare** waga te pure-nana...oti kamo (MYS 4418)
you I.Gen hand touch-not fall Q
'Will you fall... though my hand never touches you?'

Strong pronouns often appear morphologically unmarked as in (27). Importantly, strong pronouns never appear with genitive *no* or *ga*; that is, (*w*)*are-ga* and (*w*)*are-no* are not found in the OJ corpus.[6] As explained later

---

4 The current study of pronouns is based on three electronic text corpora: the *Nihon Koten Bungaku Honbun* database (National Institute of Japanese Literature), *Man'yôshû Kensaku* (Yamaguchi University), and the Oxford Corpus of Old Japanese, as well as the editions by Nakanishi (1978-1983), Kojima et al. (1995) and Ogihara et al. (1979). This paper follows in general the transcription and glossing conventions for Old Japanese in Frellesvig and Whitman (2008)

5 Yanagida (2007) and Whitman and Yanagida (2009) argue that Old Japanese was a split active language. These three classes of Old Japanese pronouns correlate with active alignment.

6 This fact is also pointed out by Frellesvig (2010).

in detail, I suggest that strong pronouns and genitive may not co-occur because they occupy the same functional head position in the extended nominal projection.

(W)a and *na*, which are the deficient counterparts of *ware* and *nare*, on the other hand, must be accompanied by genitive *ga*, as in (28), when they appear in subject position within a clause or DP.

(28) a. Kwopwi wo **wa ga** suru (MYS 2311)
Love Obj I Gen do
'I am in love.'

b. **Na ga** nake-ba... (MYS 3785)
you Gen cry-Cond
'when you cry...'

Unlike strong pronouns, deficient pronouns cannot be left morphologically unmarked. The case feature of deficient pronouns must be overtly realized by a case particle. This may be attributed to the general properties of deficient pronouns proposed by Cardinaletti and Starke: "deficient elements are necessarily in a case-assigning position at S structure (to recover case) (1999:192)." Like their clitic counterparts in Romance, *wa* and *na* only appear as core arguments of a clause.

According to Cardinaletti and Starke, while strong pronouns must have referential features, deficient pronouns lack these features; thus they can be interpreted as referential only if they are associated with a (non-deficient) antecedent, through coreference. OJ *so/ko*, the deficient counterparts of *sore/kore*, are weak pronouns. As Hashimoto (1966) points out, they only appear in contexts where a specific antecedent is present in the preceding discourse:

(29) Uwe-si ta mo maki-si patake mo asagoto ni sibomi
planted paddy too sowed field too morning.each Loc wither
kare yuku **so wo** mi-reba kokoro wo itami (MYS 4122)
dry.up go that Obj see-when heart Obj hurt
'The paddy that I planted and the fields that I sowed wither and dry up morning by morning. When I see that, my heart aches.'

The demonstrative *ko* may be used deictically, but as Hashimoto points out, *ko* tends to refer to the previously mentioned element in a given discourse. In (30) *ko* refers to the moment or situation when the speaker sitting alone, thinks:

(30) Pitori wite mono omopu yopi ni pototogisu **ko yu** naki wataru
alone sit thing think evening Loc cuckoo this from cry pass
'In the evening as I think of things sitting all alone, a cuckoo passes by (through this scene) crying.' (MYS 1476)

3.3. The DP Structure of OJ Pronouns

In OJ strong pronouns never appear with genitive *ga*, while deficient pronouns must be marked by genitive *ga*. Assuming with Kayne (1994) that *ga* is a functional head that takes a complement to its right (see also Whitman (2001)), Yanagida (2005) argues that *ga* in OJ is the head of AgrP, and that pronominal clitics are directly left-adjoined to *ga*. This is represented in (31) (head adjunction is represented by "=," as in *wa=ga*).

(31) $[_{AgrP} [_{Agr}$ ga$] [_{NP/VP}$ (w)a …$]] \rightarrow [_{AgrP} [_{Agr}$ (w)a_i=ga$] [_{NP/VP} t_i$ …$]]]$

Evidence for the view that *ga* appears in the lowest functional category within DP is that *wa/na* accompanied by genitive *ga* must appear immediately adjacent to both the nominalized (*rentai*) verb (28a), repeated in (32a) and to the head noun as in (32b):

(32) a. Kwopi wo **wa=ga** suru (MYS 2311)
love Obj I Gen do
'I am in love.'

b. Ayu no **si=ga** pata (MYS 4191)
sweetfish Gen it Gen fin
'the sweetfish, their fins'

The idea that OJ genitive *ga* is the head of AgrP captures the word order restriction. The structure (31) is also consistent with Cardinaletti and Starke's approach: under their analysis, clitics appear in the functional category specified for agreement, which appears immediately above NP or VP.

I suggest that strong pronouns are not unanalyzable categories but compositionally derived by movement within the extended nominal projection. The spellout of agreement, *wa/na* moves from inside NP/VP to Agr-head and subsequently to D to check the definite feature.

(33) Strong Pronouns
$[_{DP}$ re $[_{AgrP} [_{Agr}$ wa_i $] [_{NP} t_i$…$]]]$ -> $[_{DP}$ wa_i=re $[_{AgrP} [_{Agr} t_i] [_{NP} t_i$…$]]]$

The fact that OJ *ware* does not appear with genitive *ga* is accounted for by the assumption that *ga* originates in Agr. The presence of genitive *ga* in Agr blocks the movement of *wa/na* to the D-head, possibly due to the Head Movement Constraint (HMC).

The tripartite pronominal system of OJ almost completely disappeared in Early Middle Japanese (EMJ), after 800. Deficient pronouns - both weak and clitic pronouns - were lost and replaced by their strong counterparts (*ware/kore/sore/kare)*. The clitic *wa* came to be used only in the conventionalized form *waga* 'my'.

Recall that in OJ *ware* and *ga* do not co-occur; this is not attested until LMJ. Yanagida (2010) argues that the emergence of *ware-ga* is due to the loss of Agr in DP. Once *ware* surfaces in D and its deficient counterpart is lost, learners are no longer presented with evidence that *ware* contains an agreement projection. AgrP is consequently lost. The loss of AgrP then leads to the categorial reanalysis of *ware* as demonstrative (DemP). This involves a reanalysis of the left peripheral head as Spec, DP, as represented in (34).

(34)

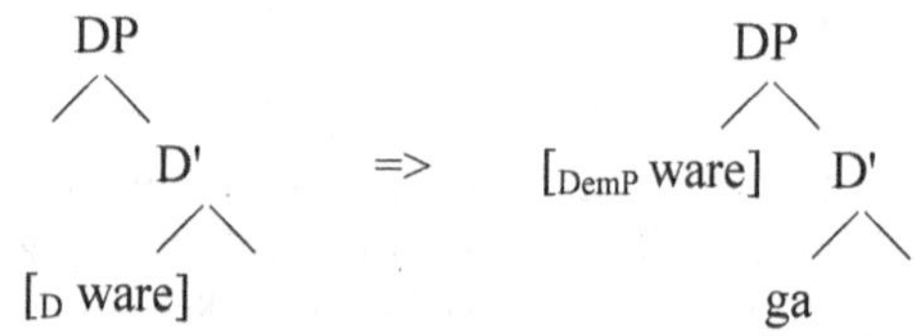

In OJ through MJ, the syntactic status of *ware* is D. Once *ware* appears in Spec, DP, it comes to be able to co-occur with *ga.* The reanalysis of (34) may be motivated by the fact that Japanese is overwhelmingly a head final language. When no overt specifier is realized, the preponderance of head final structures may lead learners to reanalyze phrase-initial heads as specifiers. We see below that the relevant categorial change leads to an increase in semantic/pragmatic significance.

3.4. Intrapersonal Pronoun Shift

OJ *ware/waga* underwent what Whitman (1999) calls "intrapersonal pronoun shift" whereby first person pronoun came to refer to second person (i.e. the hearer). According to Whitman (1999), intrapersonal pronoun shift is widely observed in East Asian languages that lack agreement, and in the case of shift from first to second person, it is always mediated by a diachronic stage where the pronoun has a reflexive function SELF. This may, in fact, be the case in Japanese. *Ware* is used as reflexive comparable to *zibun* 'self'. (35) is from the EMJ text *Ise-Monogatari.*

(35) Iyasikara-nu wotoko **ware**-yori pa masari taru pito wo
low rank-not man self-than Top higher Imper person Acc
omopikakete tosi pe-keru
adore time pass-Past
'A man not of low rank fell in love with a person of rank higher than himself, and time went by.'

In OJ *ware* simply appears as a neutral first person pronoun. But *ware* started to be used in a reflexive function, not limited to first person, in EMJ.

Once *ware* could be used to refer to the second person, it came to convey various stylistic and sociolinguistic implicatures. In LMJ *ware* (second person) is used towards people ranking lower on the social scale. Ultimately, as in (36), it came to carry a derogatory implicature (cf. Nakamura et al. 1982).

(36) Itu **ware** ga ore ni sake o kureta zo (Kyôgen, *Kofi muko*)
when you Nom me Dat sake Acc give Past Foc
'When did you give me sake?'

I propose that intrapersonal shift is a byproduct of the diachronic process by which a pronoun loses its agreement features (i.e. is depersonalized). Attainment of a reflexive meaning is a result of losing the specific person features borne by Agr.

3.5. Pronoun/Demonstrative Plus *-ra*

In OJ the suffix-*ra* functions as a diminutive. (For OJ diminutive *-ra*, see Nakamura et al. 1982.)

(37) a. **Kwo-ra** ga ipyedi yaya ma dopoki wo (MYS 302)
Dim-Pl Gen home-road a little far Excl
'The road where the maid goes home is still far'

b. **pata kwo-ra** ga yoru piru to ipa-zu yuku miti (MYS 193)
field Dim-Pl Gen night day that say-not go road
'the road where farmers go day and night'

The plural denotation of *-ra* is not fully developed in OJ; thus, NP-*ra* can have either singular (37a) or plural (37b) reference. Importantly, the suffix-*ra* never appears with pronouns or demonstratives; that is, *ware/nare-ra* and *kore/sore-ra* are not found in the OJ corpus (cf. Frellesvig 2010). This is due to the fact that pronouns/demonstratives are Ds in OJ. Given that *-ra* is the head of DP, as discussed in section 2, they cannot be followed by *-ra*. The pronoun/demonstrative with the plural *-ra* begins to appear in Middle Japanese (MJ) texts. (38) is from *Utsubo monogatari* (c. 980):

(38) [**Ware-ra** ga ko] wa oya ni masaru nasi
I-Pl Gen child Top ancestor Dat surpass not
'My children do not surpass their ancestors.'

Ware-ra has the same structure as ModJ demonstratives *sore-ra* 'that-Pl' or *kare-ra* 'he-Pl' in that it has a full DP structure throughout its history. While the strong pronoun *ware* and *ga* do not co-occur in OJ through MJ, (38) shows that the plural form *ware-ra* can appear with *ga* in MJ. The entire DP structure of (38) is represented in (39), parallel to ModJ (23).

(39)

```
            DP(GenP)
             /  \
           DP     D'
      ware-ra_i   / \
       'I-Pl'    D   NP
                 ga  ko
                     'child'
```

Ware-ra projects to DP and appears in Spec, DP headed by *ga*. In OJ, the genitive *ga* heads AgrP, but it appears in D in EMJ after Agr is lost.

4. Summary

In this paper, I have argued that ModJ demonstratives, including third person *kare*, have a structure in which D selects NumberP, and that demonstratives trigger number agreement with the NP they select. Following the split DP hypothesis, this paper also argues that D in the projection containing OJ strong pronouns selects AgrP. I have discussed the loss of AgrP in terms of evidence provided by the demise of deficient pronouns, intrapersonal shift from first person to second person, mediated by a reflexive function, and the emergence of *ware* with the D head *ga* and the corresponding plural form *ware-ra*.

Primary Texts

Kojima, N., M. Kinosita and H. Tono 1995. *Man'yôshû* (1-4). *Nihon Koten Bungaku Zenshû* (The Collected Works of Classical Japanese Literature), Tokyo: Shogakukan.

Nakanishi, S. 1978-1983. *Man'yôshû* (1-4). Tokyo: Kodansha Bunko.

Ogihara, A. and H. Konosu 1979. *Kojiki Jôdai Kayô* (Poetry from the *Kojiki* and Other Old Japanese Texts). Tokyo: Shogakukan.

Electronic Corpora

Man'yôshû Kensaku (http://infux03.inf.edu.yamaguchi-u.ac.jp/~manyou/ver2_2/manyou.php)

Nihon Koten Bungaku Honbun (Premodern Japanese Texts), National Institute of Japanese Literature (http://www.nijl.ac.jp/contents/ d_library/ index.html)

The Oxford Corpus of Old Japanese (http://vsarpj.orinst.ox.ac.uk/corpus/)

References

Abney, S. 1987. *The English Noun Phrase in Its Sentential Aspect*. Doctoral dissertation, MIT.

Cardinaletti, A. and M. Starke. 1999. The Typology of Structural Deficiency: A Case Study of the Three Classes of Pronouns. *Clitics in the Languages of Europe*, ed. Henk van Riemsdijk, 145-233. Berlin: Mouton de Gruyter.

Frellesvig, B. 2010. *A History of the Japanese Language*. Cambridge: Cambridge University Press.

Frellesvig, B. and J. Whitman. 2008. *Proto-Japanese*. Amsterdam: John Benjamins.

Fukui, N. 1995. *Theory of Projection in Syntax*. CSLI Publications, Stanford, CA.

Giusti, G. 2001. The Birth of a Functional Category: From Latin *ILLE* to the Romance Article and Personal Pronoun. *Current Studies in Italian syntax: Essays offered to Lorenzo Renzi*, ed. Guglielmo Cinque and Giampaolo Salvi, 157-171. Amsterdam: North Holland.

Hashimoto, S. 1966. Kodaigo no Shiji Taikei: Jôdai o Chûsin ni (Demonstratives in Old Japanese). *Kokugo Kokubun* 35:329-341.

Hoji, H. 1991. Kare. *Interdisciplinary Approaches to Language: Essays in Honor of Prof. S.-Y. Kuroda*, ed. C. Georgopoulos and R. Ishihara, 287-304. Reidel: Dordrecht.

Hoji, H., S. Kinsui, Y. Takubo and A. Ueyama 2003. Demonstratives in Japanese. *Functional Structure(s), Form and Interpretation: Perspectives from East Asian Languages,* ed. A. Li, and A. Simpson, 97-128. London: Routledge.

Kawashima, R. 1994. *The Structure of Noun Phrases and the Interpretation of Quantificational NPs in Japanese*. Doctoral dissertation, Cornell University.

Kayne, R. 1994. *The Antisymmetry of Syntax.* Cambridge, MA.: MIT Press.

Kayne, R. and J.-Y. Pollock 2009. Notes on French and English Demonstratives. ms., New York University and Université de Paris Est, EA 4120.

Nakamura, Y., M. Okami and A. Sakakura 1982. *Kadokawa Kogo Daijiten* (The Kadokawa Dictionary of Premodern Japanese). Tokyo: Kadokawa Shoten.

Roberts, I. and A. Roussou 2003. *Syntactic Change: A Minimalist Approach to Grammaticalization*. Cambridge: Cambridge University Press.

Ueyama, A. 1998. *Two Types of Dependency.* Doctoral dissertation, University of Southern California, USC, Los Angeles.

Vassilieva, M. 2008. A Syntactic Analysis of Nominal and Pronominal Associative Plurals. *University of Pennsylvania Working Papers in Linguistics* 14:339-352.

Whitman, J. 1981. The Internal Structure of NP in Verb Final Languages. *Papers from the Seventeenth Regional Meeting of the Chicago Linguistic Society*, 411-418. Chicago Linguistic Society, Chicago.

Whitman, J. 1999. Personal Pronoun Shift in Japanese: A Case Study in Lexical Change and Point of View. *Function and Structure: In Honor of Susumu Kuno*, ed. Akio Kamio and Ken-ichi Takami, 357-386. Amsterdam: John Benjamins.

Whitman, J. 2001. Kayne 1994: p. 143, fn. 3. *The Minimalist Parameter*, ed. by Galia Alexandrova, 77-100. Amsterdam: John Benjamins.

Whitman, J. and Y. Yanagida 2009. Ninsho to Kakkaku Ruikei: Jôdai Nihongo no Daimeishi Taikei no Kanten kara (Person and Active Alignment: From the Perspective of the Pronominal System in Old Japanese). *Uchi to Soto no Gengogaku* (Linguistics Inside and Outside), ed. A. Tsubomoto, N. Hayase and N.Wada, 175-214. Tokyo: Kaitakusha.

Watanabe A. 2006. Functional Projections of Nominals in Japanese: Syntax of Classifiers. *Natural Language & Linguistic Theory* 24: 241-306.

Yanagida, Y. 2005. Case/Focus Particles and Clause Structure Change. In *The Syntax of Focus and Wh-questions in Japanese: A Cross-Linguistic Perspective*. Tokyo: Hituzi Syobo.

Yanagida, Y. 2006. Word Order and Clause Structure in Early Old Japanese. *Journal of East Asian Linguistics* 15:37-68.

Yanagida, Y. 2007. Jôdaigo no Nôkakusei ni tsuite. [On Ergativity in Old Japanese. In *Nihongo no Shubun Genshô* [Main Clause Phenomena in Japanese], ed. by Nobuko Hasegawa, 147-188. Tokyo: Hituzi Shobo.

Yanagida, Y. 2010. Syntactic Reanalysis of Pronouns as Demonstratives: A Case of Degrammaticalization. *English Linguistics* 27.2: 399-422.

Part III

Phonology and Phonetics

Mimetic Vowel Harmony*

KIMI AKITA
University of California, Berkeley and the University of Tokyo
MUTSUMI IMAI, NOBURO SAJI
Keio University
KATERINA KANTARTZIS, SOTARO KITA
University of Birmingham

1. Introduction

Vowel harmony (VH) is often found in sound-symbolic words (aka mimetics, ideophones). This is more or less true not only in Korean but also in

* We thank the audience of the JK 20 Conference for their insightful comments. We are also grateful to Bjarke Frellesvig, Shigeto Kawahara, Haruo Kubozono, and Kazutaka Kurisu, whose advice helped us to develop this paper. Our gratitude also goes to Farzana Bhaiyat and Alicia Griffiths, who contributed to our experiment as coders. This study was partly supported by Grant-in-Aid for JSPS Fellows (#21-2238) and a grant for Proyectos de Investigación Fundamental no Orientado (Typo A, #FEI2010-14903) to Akita, whose current affiliation is Osaka University (correspondence:akitambo@gmail.com).

Japanese/Korean Linguistics 20.
Edited by Bjarke Frellesvig and Peter Sells.

Japanese, as illustrated by *koro* of *korokoro* 'rolling' and *pata* of *patapata* 'pattering'. Due to the peculiarity of their consonantal distribution, however, this obvious tendency of Japanese mimetic roots has not been seriously investigated in the literature. This study is thus intended to present some basic description of mimetic vowel patterns, which will be interpreted from a general perspective of phonosemantics.

The adjective *mimetic* in the title has dual meaning—'sound-symbolic' and 'seeming'—to mean that the harmonic vowel patterns of mimetics are not instances of VH in a strict sense (or the Altaic sense). Based on an experiment and some additional data, we will instead propose that mimetic vowel harmony (MVH) is a default state of sound-symbolic roots in general.

The organization of this paper is as follows. Section 2 goes through some previous studies on mimetic phoneme patterns. Section 3 presents the vowel patterns of Japanese mimetic roots by means of a dictionary-based statistics. Section 4 reports the vowel patterns of mimetics generated by Japanese and English speakers in a video-based experiment. On the basis of these two types of data, Section 5 discusses the default and primitive nature of MVH, which is reinforced by some related phenomena in the mimetic phonology of other languages. Section 6 concludes this paper.

2. Previous Studies

MVH has been repeatedly discussed for Korean. Korean has VH in its mimetic sublexicon, and it is different from the VH in its verbal morphology (Kim-Renaud 1976, this volume; McCarthy 1983; Finley 2006). As cited in (1), many Korean mimetics form a semantic minimal pair that is based on the 'dark' vs. 'light' vowel distinction. Within a mimetic, a dark vowel only appears with a dark vowel, whereas a light vowel only appears with a light vowel.

(1) MVH in Korean (Cho 1994: 439):

Dark:	i	ü	ɨ	u	e.g.	*tüluk*	*k'ɨtək*	*əlluk*
	e	ö	ə	o		*tölok*	*k'atak*	*allok*
Light:	æ		a			'obese'	'nodding'	'mottled'

Although some parallels have been pointed out for mimetics in Korean and Japanese (Garrigues 1995; Shibasaki 2002; Akita 2009), the existence of a similar but milder vocalic tendency of Japanese mimetics has never attracted previous linguists' serious attention.

The absence of relevant research seems to stem from the striking distributional characteristics of Japanese mimetic consonants. For example, Hamano (1998: 40–45) observes that mimetic roots are subject to strong

OCP (Obligatory Contour Principle) effects, which allow only five exceptions with identical consonants (e.g. *kuki* of *kuQkiri* 'distinct') (cf. Kawahara et al. 2006 for consonant patterns of nonmimetic Yamato (native Japanese) roots).[1] Also, it is well-known that mimetics prefer /p/- and voiced initials (e.g. *poN* 'tossing', *dosaQ* 'thud'), which are banned in the nonmimetic native vocabulary (Hamano 1998: 7). Regarding vowels, only the rarity of /e/ and its negative connotation have often been discussed (e.g. *geQsori* 'haggard', *nebaneba* 'sticky') (Hamano 1998: 40, 47).

VH has been a controversial issue among scholars of Old Japanese (OJ) since Arisaka 1934 (see Frellesvig and Whitman 2004, 2008 for a recent discussion on the vowel system of Old and proto-Japanese). Several proposals have been made for or against the existence of VH in OJ, especially in relation to the alleged Altaic origin of Japanese, for VH is one of the main features of Altaic languages. For example, in the end of his years of research, Ohno (2000) concluded that OJ did not have VH.

Some studies point out a VH-like tendency for some parts of the New Japanese (NJ) lexicon. First, Tamaoka et al. (2004) investigate the tendency for trimoraic Yamato nouns to have identical vowels in their three vowel positions (e.g. *karada* 'body', *kokoro* 'heart'). This tendency is also observed for bimoraic Yamato nouns (e.g. *mimi* 'ear', *siri* 'hips'). Second, Kasuga (1956) argues that the backness VH-like trend of Yamato causative verbs with *-os-* (e.g. *horobos-* 'destroy', *sugos-* spend') is in fact a case of vowel assimilation, which is also instantiated by some old compound nouns, such as *kutu̲-wa* 'bit (for a horse's mouth)' (< *kuti̲* 'mouth' + *wa* 'ring'). Third, Tateishi (1990) discusses a backness VH-like vowel distribution in Sino-Japanese morphemes whose second consonant is /k/ (e.g. *koku* 'nation' (back), *teki* 'enemy' (front)) (see also Kurisu, to appear).

However, these tendencies, except the last one, have not been examined quantitatively in the context of VH. Therefore, this paper will also present numerical data of the vowel patterns of Yamato nouns, which are assumed to minimally contrast with mimetics in the native Japanese lexicon (at least among the lexical classes mentioned here).

3. Dictionary Analysis

3.1. Method

In order to show the harmony orientation of Japanese mimetic vowels, we counted bimoraic mimetic roots with each vowel pattern in Kakehi et al. 1996. Japanese mimetic roots are either monomoraic ((C)V; e.g. *tyu* of *tyuQ* 'smacking') or bimoraic ($((C_1)V_1C_2V_2$; e.g. *huwa* of *huwahuwa*, *huwaQ*,

[1] The symbols N (moraic nasal) and Q (the first half of a geminate cluster) will be used only for mimetics.

huwaN, *huwari*, *huNwari* 'fluffy'). The 524 bimoraic mimetic roots abstracted from the mimetic dictionary were semantically classified into three: phonomimic (N = 165), phenomimic (N = 307), and psychomimic (N = 52). Phonomimes (onomatopoeic, sound-imitative mimetics; e.g. *piyopiyo* 'tweet-tweet', *tyariN* 'clink') are said to be more iconic than phenomimes (mimetics for visual/tactile information; e.g. *kirari* 'twinkling', *subesube* 'smooth and dry'), for they mimic sound by means of sound (Hamano 1998: 9). Some studies argue that phenomimes are in turn more iconic than psychomimes (mimetics for emotional/bodily feelings; e.g. *wakuwaku* 'excited', *zukiN* 'throbbing'), for they represent physical eventualities by means of a physical medium of communication (i.e. linguistic sound) (Akita 2009). In accord with Saussurean arbitrariness, nonmimetic words (e.g. *ringo* 'apple') are basically not iconic.

For the purpose of comparison, we also considered the vowel patterns of bimoraic Yamato morphemes. As we touched upon in Section 2, not only are they assumed to be located 'closest' to bimoraic mimetic roots in the lexicon, but seem to be similar to them in vowel patterns. We used the raw numerical data given in Yoshida (2005: 3) for this purpose.

As a criterion for the overall VH strength of each morpheme class, we adopted Cohen's kappa concordance coefficient, ranging from 0 to 1, which is calculated by the following formula (see Altmann 2005: 195–197):

$$\kappa = \frac{\text{observed concordance rate (OCR)} - \text{expected concordance rate}}{1 - \text{expected concordance rate (ECR)}}$$

The strength of each V_1-V_2 association was judged by means of a collocational t-test (Church et al. 1991):[2]

$$t = \frac{\text{freq of } V_1\text{-}V_2 \text{ colloc} - \text{freq of } V_1 \times \text{freq of } V_2 \,/\, \text{total freq of all Vs}}{\sqrt{\text{freq of } V_1\text{-}V_2 \text{ colloc}}}$$

Both criteria yield a positive value for harmony and a negative value for disharmony. These scores allow us to compare even different languages with different vowel inventory sizes, as in Section 4.

Two kinds of VH were considered in this manner: namely, total (e.g. *poro*) and featural identity/harmony. For the latter, we considered VH based on backness (front (/i, e/) vs. back (/a, o, u/); e.g. *hoku*) and height (high (/i, u/) vs. mid (/e, o/) vs. low (/a/); e.g. *buri*). Roundedness was not considered because it only discriminates /o/ from the rest in NJ. Total identity cases were excluded from the calculation of featural identity, for the strength of featural identity is blurred by the presence of total identity (Haruo Kubozono, personal communication).

---

[2] Mutual information scores, which are dependent on sample size, were also calculated (see Goldsmith and Riggle, to appear), but made no remarkable difference.

We made a twofold prediction based on our preliminary informal survey, which observed the commonness of mimetics with totally identical vowels, such as *harahara* 'thrilled and uneasy', *tiriN* 'ting', and *puQkuri* 'swollen'. First, mimetics were expected to show stronger VH than nonmimetic morphemes. Second, mimetic roots, as well as Yamato nouns, were expected to show strong total vowel identity. We had no obvious clue about the featural identity of mimetic vowels.

3.2. Results

The prediction was mildly borne out. First, Table 1 gives the vowel patterns of bimoraic Yamato nouns, such as *mimi* 'ear'. Their OCR in total identity (27.85%; i.e. shadowed cells) turned out to be significantly higher than their ECR (22.27%) ($\kappa = .07, p < .001$).[3]

Table 1. Vowel patterns of bimoraic Yamato nouns[4]

$V_1 \backslash V_2$	i	e	a	o	u
i	42	37	53	24	24
e	22	4	17	10	9
a	96	76	146*	27	49
o	49	14	49	59***	24
u	50	41	47	28	37

Next, Table 2 presents the vowel patterns of bimoraic mimetic roots, whose OCR (31.68%) also showed a significant divergence from their ECR (21.77%) ($\kappa = .13, p < .001$).[5] Some example mimetics with such roots are given in (2).

Table 2. Vowel patterns of Japanese mimetic roots

$V_1 \backslash V_2$	i	e	a	o	u
i	23	2	29	18	8
e	5	1	26	17	3
a	28	2	48	9	24
o	27	12	35	53**	21
u	14	10	55	13	41*

3 Adjacent two vowels of trimoraic Yamato nouns were also considered using Irie's (1996: 101) raw data. However, they turned out to prefer vowel disharmony (V_1-V_2: 17.15%, $\kappa = -.04, p = .15$ (*n.s.*); V_2-V_3: 9.59%, $\kappa = -.37, p < .001$) (cf. Tamaoka et al. 2004).

4 Hereafter, statistical significance of each V_1-V_2 association, which is based on its *t*-score, will be indicated by the following convention: $*p < .05$, $**p < .01$, $***p < .001$.

5 Hamano (1998: 40, 47) provides similar tables, which are based on subparts of a smaller corpus (i.e. Asano 1978), without a close look.

(2) Japanese mimetics with totally identical vowels:
baQsari 'cutting drastically', *bokoboko* 'beating', *gayagaya* 'making a fuss', *guruN* 'circling', *gyorori* 'glaring', *kibikibi* 'working briskly', *musuQ* 'sullen', *piriQ* 'pungent', *zorozoro* 'standing in line'

The numerical trend in the kappa scores suggests that VH is particularly strong in mimetic roots. A comparison of the OCRs of mimetic and nominal vowels yielded a slight difference (χ^2 (1) = 2.47, p = .12).

What is more important is featural VH. When the above results were re-analyzed in terms of featural identity, neither backness (OCR = 45.81%, κ = –.31) nor height (OCR = 14.25%, κ = –.26) exhibited significant harmony. This means that "VH" of Japanese mimetics is ascribable to their preference for totally identical vowels. Based on the fact that Altaic VHs are based on vowel features, such as backness and roundedness (Aoki 1968; Vago 1973; van der Hulst and van de Weijer 1995; Krämer 2003), it is unlikely that Japanese MVH is a reliable trace of OJ as an Altaic language.[6]

Then, where does it come from? One possible interpretation is that, in a sound-symbolic system, '$V_1 = V_2$' is a default pattern, which takes place unless a special phonosemantic factor motivates a disharmonic pattern. The first piece of evidence for this hypothesis comes from the degrees of MVH differing across the three semantic subtypes of mimetics. Specifically, the MVH strength showed a proportional relationship to the degree of iconicity: phonomimic (OCR = 39.39%, κ = .22, p < .001) > phenomimic (OCR = 28.01%, κ = .10, p < .001) > psychomimic (OCR = 28.85%, κ = .10, p = .16 (*n.s.*)) (> bimoraic Yamato nouns). Under the general assumption that phonomimes instantiate the prototype of mimetics, VH could be conceived of as a fundamental (or primitive) vowel pattern of Japanese mimetics (see Kita 2008 for an evolutionary view of mimetics).

4. Word Generation Experiment

4.1. Method

To demonstrate the default/primitive nature of MVH more clearly, we conducted a word production experiment. 93 native Japanese speakers and 27 native British English speakers were asked to generate mimetics for a hu-

[6] Haruo Kubozono (personal communication) pointed out that MVH is more like a copy phenomenon than VH. In this view, it might be possible to think that mimetic roots with VH are underlyingly monosyllabic (CVC) and that the vowel is copied to avoid the violation of the NoCoda constraint (cf. Hyman 2002; Ribeiro 2002; Nelson 2003: 174–193; Kawahara 2007; Yamaguchi 2010; see Kawahara et al. 2008 for the sound-symbolic importance of the initial part of words). (Copy can also be found in other parts of the mimetic lexicon (e.g. *ahaha, ehehe, ohoho, uhuhu* (laughter); Nasu 2003).) This view seems especially applicable to the CVCV-words coined by speakers of English (Section 4), whose default syllable structure is CVC. We leave this issue open for future research.

man locomotion displayed in each of seventy short video clips. English participants were instructed to create CVCV-words that intuitively (to mean 'sound-symbolically') matched the human motions, for they were assumed not to be as familiar with the notion of mimetics or sound symbolism. Also, assuming the spelling-pronunciation mismatch in English, they were asked to pronounce their words after spelling them. The audio recordings were transcribed by one native speaker of British English.

We excluded Japanese speakers' mimetics with a monomoraic root (e.g. *toQtoQ*) and English speakers' 'mimetics' that did not have a CVCV shape (e.g. *numpi*), those that were obviously made on the analogy of an existent motion-related word (e.g. *jogo* < *jog*), and those that were pronounced ambiguously or as one syllable. As a result of these exclusion criteria, 1,396 and 1,242 'mimetics' from Japanese and English speakers, respectively, were considered for analysis. 77.13% (958) of the English data contained one or two diphthongs or long vowels, whose first half (e.g. /e/ for /eɪ/, /u/ for /u:/) was considered.

English has neither an established mimetic lexicon nor a VH system. Based on these facts, we made the following prediction: If total VH is a default pattern in sound symbolism, it should be preferred by not only Japanese but also English speakers in their generation of mimetics.

4.2. Results

The prediction was clearly borne out. Tables 3 and 4 give the results for Japanese and English speakers, respectively. The strength of total MVH was statistically significant for both Japanese (OCR = 37.89%, $\kappa = .19$, $p < .001$) and English speakers (OCR = 37.28%, $\kappa = .28$, $p < .001$).[7, 8] Some examples are cited in (3) and (4).[9]

---

[7] The English result was quite similar when diphthongs and long vowels were counted separately from short monothongs (OCR = 36.96%, $\kappa = .28$, $p < .001$) or when diphthongs were excluded from the data (OCR = 38.34%, $\kappa = .28$, $p < .001$). The total VH of spelled CVCVs was still more striking (OCR = 48.91%, $\kappa = .32$, $p < .001$).

[8] When we limited ourselves to the 294 (21.06%) mimetics that have no apparent analogical relation to an existent mimetic (e.g. *byotabyota*, *huruuN*), the OCR of Japanese speakers' mimetic vowels was only 22.79% ($\kappa = .01$, $p = .75$ (*n.s.*)). One possible interpretation of this somewhat surprising result in favor of the current discussion would be that the VH of existent mimetics is so remarkable that novel mimetics, which were intended to avoid the conventional phoneme patterns of mimetics, resulted in restricted VH (cf. Nasu 2004).

[9] The VH rate was significantly higher in mimetic roots with a sonorant C_2 (e.g. *gara*) than in those with an obstruent C_2 (e.g. *gasa*) in both dictionary (45.85% vs. 33.70%; χ^2 (1) = 4.14, $p < .05$) and production data (37.72% vs. 28.85%; χ^2 (1) = 19.80, $p < .001$) of Japanese, but not in the English production data (39.63% vs. 39.30%; χ^2 (1) = .01, $p = .91$ (*n.s.*)). We thank Nobutaka Takara for suggesting the relevance of intervening consonants (see Kurisu (to appear) for a related phonological discussion; see also fn. 6).

Table 3. Mimetic vowels generated by Japanese speakers

$V_1 \backslash V_2$	i	e	a	o	u
i	18	2	18	33	1
e	8	26**	25	41	25
a	39	6	136***	16	36
o	117	31	72	292***	67
u	57	36	207***	30	57

(3) Example mimetics with total VH generated by Japanese speakers: *gisigisi* 'clumsy', *noronoro* 'sluggish', *syobooN* 'depressed'; *bikibiki, dosyoNdosyoN, gyaragyara, hyotohyoto, monyomonyo*

Table 4. Mimetic vowels generated by English speakers

$V_1 \backslash V_2$	i	ɪ	e	ɛ	æ	a	ə	ɜ	ɒ	ɑ	ɔ	o	ʊ	u	ʌ
i	111***	0	1	0	10	2	23	0	0	19	0	31	1	15	6
ɪ	32*	1	0	1	7	1	14	0	0	1	0	10	0	9	6
e	12	0	4	0	0	0	4	0	0	2	0	5	0	3	4
ɛ	14	1	0	0	4	0	5	0	0	1	0	9	0	7	6
æ	26	2	0	2	44***	0	9	0	1	2	0	22	0	24	9
a	8	0	0	0	2	12**	2	0	0	2	0	11	0	2	6
ə	0	0	0	0	0	0	1	0	0	0	0	0	0	0	0
ɜ	0	0	0	0	0	0	1	0	0	0	0	0	0	0	0
ɒ	20	0	0	3	3	0	2	0	1	0	0	24	0	7	8
ɑ	28	0	1	1	2	0	1	0	0	69***	0	5	0	8	1
ɔ	3	0	0	2	1	0	3	0	0	0	0	0	0	1	1
o	32	1	0	0	5	4	33	0	0	10	0	152***	0	17	13
ʊ	4	1	0	0	0	0	2	0	0	0	0	2	0	0	0
u	10	2	0	0	9	1	17	0	0	19	0	13	0	64***	10
ʌ	11	3	0	0	10	1	6	0	0	3	0	9	0	9	4

(4) Example mimetics with total VH generated by English speakers: *bælæ, beɪkeɪ, goʊloʊ, mi:hi:, nu:wu:, rada, sumu, toʊpoʊ*

Importantly, featural VH was obtained in neither Japanese (backness: OCR = 50.42%, $\kappa = -.25$; height: OCR = 14.99%, $\kappa = -.25$) nor English speakers' mimetics (backness: OCR = 29.53%, $\kappa = -.12$; height: OCR =

17.97%, $\kappa = -.14$; roundedness: OCR = 48.65%, $\kappa = -.14$). Therefore, MVH is again attributable to the prevalence of totally identical vowels.

Total MVH was equally strong in Japanese and English speakers' mimetics (χ^2 (1) = .11, p = .74 (*n.s.*)). Both of them turned out to be more vowel-harmonic than dictionary mimetics in Section 3 (Japanese: χ^2 (1) = 6.37, $p < .05$; English: χ^2 (1) = 5.04, $p < .05$). These results are consistent with our hypothesis that MVH is a default pattern, which should be preferred in spontaneous word production like the current one. Thus, the present experiment leads us to conclude that MVH in Japanese is an instance of the default vocalic feature in sound symbolism in general.

5. General Discussion

In the previous two sections, MVH in total identity, which was observed both in a dictionary of Japanese mimetics and in Japanese and English speakers' mimetic generation, has been considered to be an unmarked pattern in mimetics. This idea gains further support from four more phenomena in Japanese and other languages.

First, MVH is reported in some languages other than Japanese and Korean. Some examples are cited in (5). Interestingly enough, most of these are instances of total VH.[10] For example, according to Dingemanse (2011: 131), more than 80% of mimetics in Siwu (a Niger-Congo language) are monovocalic (see also (6)).

(5) MVH in other languages:
- a. Ciluba (Kabuta 2001: 142–143):
  batàà 'quiet', *kabakaba* 'embarrassed'
- b. Didinga (de Jong 2001: 122):
  puɾuθ (sound of sth coming out), *k^{w}aɣak* 'striking hard'
- c. Guaraní (Langdon 1994: 95–96):
  sororo 'splitting open', *tyryry* 'dragging, shuffling'
- d. Kisi (Childs 1994: 183):
  bílílí 'heavily flowing', *téŋgéŋ* 'erect like a cobra'
- e. Mundang (Elders 2001: 101):
  tɛ̀yɛ̀y 'open-mouthed in surprise', *hàràŋ* 'in good health, content'
- f. Siwu (Dingemanse 2011: 131):
  kananaa 'silent', *nyagbalaa* 'pungent'
- g. Yoruba (Fordyce 1988: 52):
  réderède 'useless, miserable', *wúruwùru* 'untidy'

[10] de Jong (2001: 122) remarks that MVH in Didinga is based on vowel height and ATR.

h. Zulu (Childs 1994: 183):
gelekeqe 'complete', *khumu* 'stopping'

Second, mimetics often illustrate other types of phonological harmony, such as tonal agreement within morphemes in (6).

(6) Mimetic tonal harmony:
a. Dagaare (Bodomo 2006: 205):
gàrmànà 'lying', *gbàngbàlàng* 'long pole falling down'
b. Hausa (Newman 2001: 252–253):
búzúubùzùu 'long, unkempt (of hair)', *kàzàRkàzàR* 'energetic'
c. Siwu (Dingemanse 2011: 131):
gbràgbràgbrà 'hailstones pouring down', *pɔlɔpɔlɔ* 'smooth'

Tonal harmony is also reported for mimetics in Kanuri, Toura, and Kisi (Childs 1994: 183–184), and the commonness of the flat tone in Mandarin Chinese onomatopoeia (e.g. *chāchā* 'whispering', *pīng* 'bang'; Noguchi 1995: xiv–xv) may be counted as another such case.[11]

Third, our unmarkedness account seems to be compatible with the putative phonosemantics of MVH. According to Hamano (1998: 104), V_1 and V_2 of Japanese bimoraic mimetic roots respectively refer to the initial and resultant phases of an eventuality. In this view, total MVH would be phonosemantically linked with stable eventualities whose internal structure is consistent over time. In fact, the light and small rolling object (e.g. tennis ball) depicted by the VH mimetic *korokoro* remains light and small throughout its rolling motion. On the other hand, the crunchy food (e.g. jellyfish) represented by the non-VH mimetic *korikori* becomes smaller by the chewing activity involved. More generally, as suggested by Childs (1994: 184) and Dingemanse (2011: 132), phonological disharmony can be sound-symbolically associated with irregularity. For example, the ablaut/blend mimetic *karaNkoroN*, as well as its parent VH mimetics *karaNkaraN* and *koroNkoroN*, mimics a clanging sound (e.g. of a bell). Among the three mimetics, however, only *karaNkoroN* depicts an irregular clang. It would be reasonable to speculate that this generalization is more or less applicable to the roots of mimetics as well.[12]

---

[11] In the current view, even reduplication, which is quite common in mimetics across languages (Hinton et al. 1994), might be regarded as a morphological operation for producing phonological consistency.

[12] The participants in our experiment were also asked to rate the 'orderliness' of the locomotion in each video on an eleven-point scale (–5 to 5). The phonosemantic discussion here would expect a positive correlation between orderliness and the strength of VH. However, this was true for neither Japanese ($r_s = -.49$, $p = .33$ (*n.s.*)) nor English data ($r_s = -.38$, $p = .46$ (*n.s.*)). This result suggests that the phonosemantic motivation for MVH, if any, does not regulate the whole mimetic system and competes with other factors in its phoneme distribution.

Fourth, some studies point out the early acquisition of VH. For example, Gósy (1989) and Toivainen (1997) suggest two-year-olds' correct production of VH in Hungarian and Finnish, respectively (see also Ross 1937; Leiwo et al. 2006). These reports suggest the primitive nature of VH. Since MVH is mostly based on total identity, which is the simplest in that it involves only one vowel, its primitiveness is expected to be especially high.

Thus, there is a good reason to think that MVH is a default/primitive vowel pattern of mimetics, which instantiates their general preference for phonological harmony. Since phonological harmony is reasonably associated with a stable, regular eventuality contour, it is thought to constitute the basis for a sound-symbolic system.

6. Conclusion

In this paper, we have argued that MVH in total identity is a default/primitive pattern of Japanese mimetic vowels. In addition to a dictionary analysis, a sound-symbolic word generation experiment provided some evidence for this view. From a phonosemantic point of view, MVH was concluded to be an instance of the general orientation of mimetics to phonological harmony, whose stability symbolism serves as a foundation of a sound-symbolic system. This conclusion is consistent with the fact that Korean 'retains' VH in its mimetic sublexicon.[13]

We have some specific future directions in mind. First, according to the previous and present findings, consonants and vowels have opposite distributional tendencies in Japanese mimetics (cf. Walter 2010). Their consonants strongly prefer disharmony, whereas their vowels are inclined toward harmony. Both tendencies are likely to be stronger than nonmimetic native Japanese morphemes.[14] In our phonosemantic view, it seems that, in the sound-symbolic system of Japanese mimetics, vowels are responsible for rough classification of referent eventualities (e.g. size, shape), which is further specified by consonants.

Beyond this consideration, there will lie a broader typology of the division of labor of different types of segmental sound symbolism, including consonantal, vocalic, and tonal symbolism. On the one hand, the axis of the NJ sound-symbolic system is obviously the voicedness of first consonants in that it creates semantic minimal pairs of mimetic lexical items (e.g. *korokoro* 'a light and small object rolling' vs. *gorogoro* 'a heavy and large ob-

---

[13] Since featural VH divides a vowel space into two or more, it would not be surprising, in terms of phonosemantics, that those subspaces are linked with contrastive sound-symbolic values like 'dark' vs. 'light'.

[14] According to our data based on Kakehi et al. 1996, the strong OCP effects in mimetic consonants are significant in both total (OCR = 1.72%, $\kappa = -.05$, $p < .001$) and featural identity (OCR = 6.25%, $\kappa = -.20$, $p < .001$) (cf. Kawahara et al. 2006).

ject rolling'). In contrast, vocalic contrasts do not bear such a function: exceptional vowel-based mimetic pairs, such as *karakara* 'laughing pleasantly' and *korokoro* 'laughing gracefully', have old-fashioned tones. (This fact may have to do with the relatively restricted MVH in NJ. In this respect, it may be fruitful to compare NJ and OJ in the context of MVH.) On the other hand, as Diffloth 1976: 260 discusses, mimetics in Semai (an Austronesian language) have a well-established paradigm of vocalic symbolism. For example, this language makes a fine-grained distinction of sounds of chewing: *grĩ:p* (small, brittle thing), *grʉ̃:p* (large, somewhat soft thing), *grã:p* (large, hard thing), and *grɔ:p* (large, crispy thing). Korean seems to be located between these two extremes. This language makes great use of vocalic symbolism (e.g. *ttak* 'tick-tick' vs. *ttok* 'knock-knock'), but minimal mimetic pairs based on tripartite consonantal symbolism are also found (e.g. *ttak* vs. *thakthak* 'whack-whack'). Explorations along these lines will lead to some specific suggestions about the universal and language-specific aspects of sound symbolism (see Kilian-Hatz 2001).

Next, perception and articulation experiments, as well as production experiments using different visual stimuli or different morphological restrictions (e.g. CVC(VC), which is more common in English), may help us to clarify the primitive nature of MVH in a more direct fashion. Primitive phonological elements are reasonably expected to be easier to perceive and articulate (cf. Hayes et al. 2009).

Finally, a word generation experiment with children may reveal something more crucial for the evolutional relevance of sound-symbolic VH. The last two directions will also contribute to the phonological study of VH and OCP, whose acquisition and psychological reality remain to be elucidated.

References

Akita, K. 2009. Gradient Integration of Sound Symbolism in Language: Toward a Crosslinguistic Generalization. *Japanese/Korean Linguistics,* Vol. 17, ed. S. Iwasaki, H. Hoji, P. M. Clancy, and S.-O. Sohn, 217–230. Stanford, CA: CSLI.

Altmann, G. 2005. Phonic Word Structure. *Quantitative Linguistik: Ein internationales Handbuch,* ed. R. Köhler, 191–208. Berlin/New York: Mouton.

Aoki, H. 1968. Toward a Typology of Vowel Harmony. *International Journal of American Linguistics* 34: 142–145.

Arisaka, H. 1934. *Kodai-nihongo-ni okeru onsetu-ketugoo-no hoosoku* [Syllable combination rules in Old Japanese]. Bachelor's thesis, the Imperial University of Tokyo.

Asano, T. 1978. *Giongo/gitaigo ziten* [A dictionary of mimetics]. Tokyo: Kadokawa.

Bodomo, A. B. 2006. The Structure of Ideophones in African and Asian Languages: The Case of Dagaare and Cantonese. *Selected Proceedings of the 35th Annual*

Conference on African Linguistics: African Languages and Linguistics in Broad Perspectives, ed. J. Mugane et al., 203–213. Somerville, MA: Cascadilla.

Childs, G. T. 1994. African Ideophones. *Sound Symbolism,* ed. L. Hinton, J. Nichols, and J. J. Ohala, 178–204. Cambridge: Cambridge University Press.

Cho, M.-H. 1994. Vowel Harmony in Korean: A Grounded Phonology Approach. *Japanese/Korean Linguistics,* Vol. 4, ed. N. Akatsuka, 431–445. Stanford, CA: CSLI.

Church, K., W. Gale, P. Hanks, and D. Hindle. 1991. Using Statistics in Lexical Analysis. *Lexical Acquisition: Exploring Online Resources to Build a Lexicon,* ed. U. Zernik, 115–164. Hillsdale, NJ: Lawrence Erlbaum.

de Jong, N. 2001. The Ideophone in Didinga. *Ideophones,* ed. F. K. E. Voeltz and C. Kilian-Hatz, 121–138. Amsterdam/Philadelphia: John Benjamins.

Diffloth, G. 1976. Expressives in Semai. *Austroasiatic Studies, Part I,* ed. P. N. Lenner, L. C. Thompson, and S. Starosta, 249–264. Honolulu: The University of Hawaii Press.

Dingemanse, M. 2011. *The Meaning and Use of Ideophones in Siwu.* Doctoral dissertation, Max Planck Institute for Psycholinguistics/Radboud University.

Elders, S. 2001. Defining Ideophones in Mundang. *Ideophones,* ed. F. K. E. Voeltz and C. Kilian-Hatz, 97–110. Amsterdam/Philadelphia: John Benjamins.

Finley, S. 2006. Morpheme Correspondence and Vowel Harmony in Korean. *Harvard Studies in Korean Linguistics* 11: 131–144.

Fordyce, J. F. 1988. *Studies in Sound Symbolism with Special Reference to English.* Doctoral dissertation, UCLA.

Frellesvig, B. and J. Whitman. 2004. The Vowels of Proto-Japanese. *Japanese Language and Literature* 38: 281–299.

Frellesvig, B. and J. Whitman. 2008. The Japanese/Korean Vowel Correspondences. *Japanese/Korean Linguistics,* Vol. 13, ed. M. E. Hudson, P. Sells, and S.-A. Jun, 15–28. Stanford, CA: CSLI.

Garrigues, S. L. 1995. Mimetic Parallels in Korean and Japanese. *Studies in Linguistics* 19: 359–398.

Goldsmith, J. and J. Riggle. To appear. Information Theoretic Approaches to Phonological Structure: The Case of Finnish Vowel Harmony. *Natural Language & Linguistic Theory.*

Gósy, M. 1989. Vowel Harmony: Interrelations of Speech Production, Speech Perception, and the Phonological Rules. *Acta Linguistica Hungarica* 39: 93–118.

Hamano, S. 1998. *The Sound-Symbolic System of Japanese.* Stanford, CA: CSLI.

Hayes, B., K. Zuraw, P. Siptár, and Z. Londe. 2009. Natural and Unnatural Constraints in Hungarian Vowel Harmony. *Language* 85: 822–863.

Hinton, L., J. Nichols, and J. J. Ohala, eds. 1994. *Sound Symbolism.* Cambridge: Cambridge University Press.

Hyman, L. M. 2002. Is There a Right-to-Left Bias in Vowel Harmony? Paper presented at the 9th International Phonology Meeting, Vienna, 1 November 2002.

Irie, S. 1996. Gendai-nihongo-ni okeru wago 3-paku-meisi-ni tuite: Syutugen-iti-betu-ni mita onso-bunpu-no bunseki-to koosatu [On 3-mora Yamato nouns in Modern Japanese: An analysis and discussion of phoneme distribution in terms of occurrence positions]. *Doosisya kokubungaku* 43: 97–108.

Kabuta, N. S. 2001. Ideophones in Ciluba. *Ideophones,* ed. F. K. E. Voeltz and C. Kilian-Hatz, 139–154. Amsterdam/Philadelphia: John Benjamins.

Kakehi, H., I. Tamori, and L. Schourup. 1996. *Dictionary of Iconic Expressions in Japanese.* Berlin/New York: Mouton.

Kasuga, M. 1956. Kokugo-no boin-dooka [Vowel assimilation in Japanese]. *Gobun-kenkyuu* 4/5: 1–7.

Kawahara, S. 2007. Copying and Spreading in Phonological Theory: Evidence from Echo Epenthesis. *University of Massachusetts Occasional Papers in Linguistics* 32: *Papers in Optimality Theory III,* 113–143. Amherst, MA: GLSA.

Kawahara, S., H. Ono, and K. Sudo. 2006. Consonant Co-Occurrence Restrictions in Yamato Japanese. *Japanese/Korean Linguistics,* Vol. 14, ed. T. J. Vance and K. Jones, 27–38. Stanford, CA: CSLI.

Kawahara, S., K. Shinohara, and Y. Uchimoto. 2008. A Positional Effect in Sound Symbolism: An Experimental Study. *Proceedings of the Eighth Annual Meeting of the Japan Cognitive Linguistics Association,* 417–427.

Kilian-Hatz, C. 2001. Universality and Diversity: Ideophones from Baka and Kxoe. *Ideophones,* ed. F. K. E. Voeltz and C. Kilian-Hatz, 155–164. Amsterdam/Philadelphia: John Benjamins.

Kim-Renaud, Y.-K. 1976. Semantic Features in Phonology: Evidence from Vowel Harmony in Korean. *Papers from the 12th Regional Meeting, Chicago Linguistic Society,* 397–412.

Kim-Renaud, Y.-K. This volume. The Vowel System and Vowel Harmony in 15th Century Korean: “alay-a” Revisited.

Kita, S. 2008. World-View of Protolanguage Speakers as Inferred from Semantics of Sound Symbolic Words: A Case of Japanese Mimetics. *The Origins of Language: Unraveling Evolutionary Forces,* ed. N. Masataka, 25–38. Tokyo: Springer.

Krämer, M. 2003. *Vowel Harmony and Correspondence Theory.* Berlin/New York: Mouton.

Kurisu, K. To appear. Cophonology in Sino-Japanese Vowel Harmony. *Proceedings of the 29th Annual Meeting of the North East Linguistic Society.*

Langdon, M. 1994. Noise words in Guaraní. *Sound Symbolism,* ed. L. Hinton, J. Nichols, and J. J. Ohala, 94–103. Cambridge: Cambridge University Press.

Leiwo, M., P. Kulju, and K. Aoyama. 2006. The Acquisition of Finnish Vowel Harmony. *A Man of Measure: Festschrift in Honour of Fred Karlsson on his 60th Birthday: SKY Journal of Linguistics* 19: 149–161.

McCarthy, J. J. 1983. Phonological Features and Morphological Structure. *Papers from the 19th Regional Meeting, Chicago Linguistic Society,* 135–161.

Nasu, A. 2003. Reduplicants and Prefixes in Japanese Onomatopoeia. *A New Century of Phonology and Phonological Theory,* ed. T. Honma, M. Okazaki, T. Tabata, and S. Tanaka, 210–221. Tokyo: Kaitakusha.

Nasu, A. 2004. Sinzoo-onomatope-no on'in-koozoo-to bunsetu-no muhyoosei [Phonological structure of mimetic neologisms and segmental unmarkedness]. *Japanese Linguistics* 16: 69–91.

Nelson, N. A. 2003. *Asymmetric Anchoring.* Doctoral dissertation, SUNJ Rutgers.

Newman, P. 2001. Are Ideophones Really as Weird and Extra-Systematic as Linguists Make Them out to Be? *Ideophones,* ed. F. K. E. Voeltz and C. Kilian-Hatz, 215–258. Amsterdam/Philadelphia: John Benjamins.

Noguchi, M. 1995. *Tyuugokugo giongo ziten* [A dictionary of Chinese phonomimes]. Tokyo: Toho.

Ohno, S. 2000. *Nihongo-no keisei* [The formation of Japanese]. Tokyo: Iwanami.

Ribeiro, E. R. 2002. Directionality in Vowel Harmony: The Case of Karajá (Macro-Jê). *Proceedings of the Twenty-Eighth Annual Meeting of the Berkeley Linguistics Society,* 475–485.

Ross, A. S. C. 1937. An Example of Vowel-Harmony in a Young Child. *Modern Language Notes* 52: 508–509.

Shibasaki, R. 2002. On Sound Symbolism in Japanese and Korean. *Japanese/Korean Linguistics,* Vol. 10, ed. N. Akatsuka, S. Strauss, and B. Comrie, 76–89. Stanford, CA: CSLI.

Tamaoka, K., S. Makioka, and T. Maruta. 2004. Are the Effects of Vowel Repetition Influenced by Frequencies? A Corpus Study on CVCVCV-Structured Nouns with and without Vowel Repetition. *Glottometrics* 8: 1–11.

Tateishi, K. 1990. Phonology of Sino-Japanese Morphemes. *University of Massachusetts Occasional Papers in Linguistics* 13, ed. G. Lamontagne and A. Taub, 209–235. Amherst, MA: GLSA.

Tovainen, J. 1997. Kysymysliitteen vokaalisointuun mukautumattomuus Oulun aluekielessä. *Virittäjä* 101: 438–440.

Vago, R. M. 1973. Abstract Vowel Harmony Systems in Uralic and Altaic Languages. *Language* 49: 579–605.

van der Hulst, H. and J. van de Weijer. 1995. Vowel Harmony. *The Handbook of Phonological Theory,* 495–534. Cambridge, MA/Oxford: Blackwell.

Walter, M. A. 2010. Harmony versus the OCP: Vowel and Consonant Cooccurrence in the Lexicon. *Laboratory Phonology* 1: 395–413.

Yamaguchi, K. 2010. Partial Reduplication in Japanese Mimetics. Paper presented at Phonology Forum 2010, University of Shizuoka, 23 August 2010.

Yoshida, Y. 2005. Goi-bumon-no inritu-zyoohoo-syori [Processing prosodic information in the lexicon]. *Inritu-ni tyakumoku sita onsei-gengo-zyoohoo-syori-no koodoka* [Advancement of information processing of spoken language focusing on prosody], ed. K. Hirose. The University of Tokyo.

The Vowel System and Vowel Harmony in 15th-Century Korean: '*Alay-a*' (·) Revisited

YOUNG-KEY KIM-RENAUD
The George Washington University

In Middle Korean (MK), which extends from the tenth century to the end of the sixteenth century, the vowel harmony (VH) phenomenon was clearly observable within the boundary of a word, unlike in contemporary Korean where VH applies mainly in sound-symbolic (SS) words and some affix-initial vowel alternations. Long regarded as one of the distinguishing characteristics of Altaic languages, VH in Korean has been the subject of inquiry by numerous linguists. In particular, the dividing line of the two harmonic groups has been the issue that has received the most attention, because the members of the same harmonic group do not seem to form a natural class and because basic vowels are thought not to have changed in their sound values over time. Scholars thus have proposed considerably divergent

Japanese/Korean Linguistics 20.
Edited by Bjarke Frellesvig and Peter Sells.

interpretations vis-à-vis positions of articulation of various MK vowels and principles governing VH.[1]

This paper will show that some of the features used by fifteenth-century scholars in describing various characteristics of MK vowels were borne out by recent phonological and phonetic research well over 500 years later. The MK vowel chart, representing the original depiction of each vowel sound, will make it clear that the vowel letters did not represent the same phonetic value as in contemporary Korean and that the vowel harmony process was phonetically conditioned in MK, unlike in contemporary Korean.

Koreans tried to write their language using Literary Chinese for more than a millennium, but due to the complexity of the Korean syllable structure, no such attempts—neither *itwu* 吏讀 'clerk readings,' *hyangchal* 鄕札 'local letters,' nor *kwukyel* 口訣 'oral formulae/grammatical markers,'[2]—proved an adequate fit for the Korean language. Therefore, plausible reconstruction of ancient forms of the language is too much to hope for.

King Sejong's invention of a new alphabet, originally called *Hwunmin Ceng'um* 訓民正音 ('Correct Sounds for the Instruction of the People,' *HC* hereinafter) but now *Hankul* 한글 ('the Han [Korean/great] script'), was suddenly announced in the twelfth lunar month of the 25th year of his reign (December 1443–January 1444), and the Korean language, which had been hidden in obscurity, suddenly entered the limelight. That is why scholars like Lee and Ramsey (2000:282) say 'the history of the Korean language begins with Late Middle Korean.' But what a beginning it was! With the new writing system, which has a close fit to the spoken language, we can reconstruct linguistic patterns of fifteenth-century Korean, generally called the Late Middle Korean (called Middle Korean or simply MK hereinafter) with relative confidence, as noted by many linguists including Martin (1992:42).

Students of the history of the Korean language are doubly blessed, because of the existence of a scholarly text that clarifies the theoretical underpinnings behind the newly invented alphabet. The promulgation document of 1446, also called *Hwunmin ceng'um* 訓民正音 (*HC*), was a handbook for learning the alphabet with explanatory treatises and examples called *Hwunmin ceng'um haylye* 訓民正音解例 (Explanations and Examples of the Correct Sounds for the Instruction of the People, *HCH* hereinafter).

---

[1] An earlier version of this paper was presented at the SCRIPTA 2008, the First International Conference of the Hunminjeongeum Society, October 9~10, 2008, Seoul National University. Yale Romanization is used except for some well-known spellings such as 'Seoul,' 'Pyongyang,' and 'Sejong,' individual romanizations of people's names that are known to me. Angled brackets < > contain written forms.

[2] For a brief description of how these writing systems worked, see Lee and Ramsey 2000:46-55; Nam 1994:420-421.

A close reading of *HCH* allows us to identify specific phonological characteristics of each letter of the alphabet at the time of its invention, because the design principles of all letter shapes, their sound values, and their usage are succinctly presented in the publication. Thanks to this document, we know that the consonantal forms of the Korean alphabet are iconic, or 'motivated' (Haas 1976), as they are either a depiction of articulatory activity, or the symbolic representation of the place of articulation (C.-W. Kim 1980/88, 1997, Sampson 1985, Kim-Renaud 1997). For example, all apical sounds (sounds pronounced at the tip of the tongue) contain the basic graphic shape <ㄴ>, representing the image of the tongue touching the alveolar ridge, as can be seen in the letters, <ㄴ> /n/, <ㄷ> /t/, <ㅌ> /t^h/, <ㄸ> /tt/, and <ㄹ> /l/.

Once the basic letterforms were designed, related sounds were created expanding on each basic form. A given distinctive feature can be represented in a sound with varying degrees of strength, as noted by Stevens and Keyser (1989:81), and the Korean writing system captures this fact elegantly. For example, the principle of *kahoyk* 'stroke addition' is used in designing graphic shapes for related sounds. The five basic letters, chosen from the gentlest/softest or unmarked series among the consonants, were thus expanded with a set of systematically added strokes so that members of a natural class share a common graphic component, phonologically stronger consonants showing more complex shapes. *HCH*'s description and explanation of how this system works, memorably called "the crown jewel of Sejong's alphabetic theory" by Ledyard (1997:40), is given in (1).

(1) From *Ceycahay* (Explanation of the Design of the Letters) of *HCH*

For the initial consonants there are seventeen letters in all.
The molar sound ㄱ [k] depicts the outline of the root of the tongue blocking the throat.
The lingual sound ㄴ [n] depicts the outline of the tongue touching the upper palate.
The labial sound ㅁ [m] depicts the outline of the mouth.
The incisor sound ㅅ [s] depicts the outline of the incisor.
The laryngeal sound ㅇ [ɦ] depicts the outline of the throat.
The pronunciation of ㅋ [k^h] is a little more severe than that of ㄱ [k]; therefore a stroke is added.

ㄴ [n]	then	ㄷ [t],	ㄷ	then	ㅌ [t^h];
ㅁ [m]	then	ㅂ [p],	ㅂ	then	ㅍ [p^h];

ㅅ [s]	then	ㅈ [c],	ㅈ	then	ㅊ [cʰ];
ㅇ [ɦ]	then	ㆆ [ʔ],	ㆆ	then	ㅎ [x].

Vowel articulation is not as easy to depict with an iconic design as is consonantal articulation. The crucial strategy in designing vowel letters, just as in the case of consonants, was to devise core symbols out of which various contrasting forms could be developed by extension. The three basic vowel letters, extremely simple and clearly distinguishable from consonantal forms, were linked to the concept of *sancai* 三才 (Kor. 삼재 samcay [samjɛ]) 'Three Powers or Talents' in East Asian cosmology, with which Koreans of the fifteenth century were very familiar. These basic forms represented the three vowels that were phonologically the least marked. The phonologically neutral front vowel /i/ was schematically depicted with a vertical line (ㅣ) representing Man. This neutral vowel stood between the yang back vowel (・) representing Heaven, and the central yin vowel with the horizontal line (ㅡ) representing Earth.

The inventor of the alphabet opted to create vowel letters in such a way that one of the most salient phonological phenomena in Korean, VH, is clearly captured. For this purpose mirror-image figures were used to capture the counterparts easily, as well as labeling them according to the age-old East Asian philosophical concept of yin and yang. The position of the dots (currently written as short strokes) in relation to the horizontal or vertical line would determine the membership of vowels within one harmonic group or the other.[3] Thus, in yang vowels (ㅏ, ㅗ, ㅘ, etc.) the dots appear above the Earth (ㅡ) or to the right of the Man (ㅣ) and in yin vowels (ㅓ, ㅜ, ㅝ, etc.) they would be placed at the opposite sides of the horizontal or vertical lines.[4]

In spite of the rich, specific information contained in *HCH*, linguists have not come to an agreement on the MK vowel system—nor, as a consequence, on the VH phenomenon which necessarily has to be explained with reference to the vowel system it operates on.

The VH principle and the posited vowel system have received divergent analyses, especially in contemporary Korean, because neither of the two

[3]These and the other philosophical concepts used in designing and explaining all the letter-forms caused some linguists to see mainly the philosophical basis of the creation of the alphabet (e.g., J. H. Yi 1972, Pak 1988, and S. Yi 2008).

[4]Unlike today's standard dialect, Korean was a tone/pitch-accent language at the time of the alphabet's invention in the fifteenth century. *HC* included special symbols to mark pitch accents- called *pangcem* 방점 傍點 '[left-]side dots': one dot (·) for high pitch *keseng* 거성 去聲 'Going Tone'; two dots (:) for rising pitch sangseng 상성 上聲 'Rising Tone'; and no mark for low or plain 평성 平聲 'Plain Tone.' (Kim-Renaud 1997: 175). In this paper, accent marks are omitted from the texts, as they are not directly relevant to the current research topic.

harmonic groups forms a natural class. Various efforts to explain the unusual VH phenomenon resulted in diverse featural analyses of Korean vowels (e.g., Kōno 1945, S.-N. Lee 1949, Huh 1965, W. Kim 1963, K.-M. Lee 1972, K.-O. Kim 1978, Kim-Renaud 1976, C.-W. Kim 1978, J. Kim 1993, H.-H. Lee 1990, C. W. Chung 2000, Choy 2005, Ko 2010). A significant number of linguists propose that MK vowel letters actually represent a deeper, abstract level and phonetic values of the vowel system of earlier Korean (e.g., K.-M. Lee 1972:133).

Three common but erroneous assumptions about the MK vowel system, which seem to have influenced many linguists' thinking and affected their analyses, are summarized in (2):

(2) a. The expressions or the features describing various sounds of vowel letters in *HCH* are esoteric and may not be universally applicable.
b. The vowel letters have the same phonological features today as they did in the MK era.
c. The disappeared vowel phoneme written with the letter < ㆍ >, called *alay-a*,[5] was an unrounded low-mid back vowel /ʌ/.

In MK, unlike contemporary Korean, VH applied fairly consistently to all word units.[6] Vowels were categorized into three groups: *yin* (Dark, *um* in Korean), *yang* (Bright), and neutral. The seven basic vowels therefore were categorized as shown in (3).

(3) Three Harmonic Groups of Vowels

neutral	ㅣ		
yin	ㅜ	ㅡ	ㅓ
yang	ㅗ	ㆍ	ㅏ

Within the same morpheme, a *yin* vowel occurred with *yin* vowels, and a *yang* vowel occurred with *yang* vowels. VH also worked between the stem and the suffix. The neutral vowel < ㅣ > could occur with either of the groups, as shown in (4):

(4) Examples of MK Vowel Harmony (from Yu 1964/71)

---

[5] *alay-a* literally means 'low a' and got its name from the fact that the vowel always is written below a consonant or a zero, but perhaps more important, it changed to /a/ in a word-initial position. From the eighteenth to the twentieth centuries, it was even used as an alternative form of < ㅏ >, and today people use < ㆍ > in a lively, archaic-sounding spelling of /a/ (Song 1991:79).

[6] VH did not apply across stems, in Chinese loanwords, or in Sino-Korean-based stems.

a. *yin*
구름/구룸 'cloud', 굴헝 'hole', ᄭᅮᆷ을 'dream-Obj', 두껍'be thick', 둥굴 'roll', 벌거벗 'go naked', 부들업 'be soft', 브르 'call', 수울 'tassel', 어듭 'be dark', 우케 'unhulled rice', 웃브 'be laughable', 주먹 'fist', 허믈/허물 fault'.

b. *yang*
골모 'thimble', 나모 'tree', 다ᄅᆞ'be different', 도로 'again', 도ᄌᆞᆨ 'thief', ᄆᆞᅀᆞᆷ 'heart/mind', 방올 'bead', 손가락 'fingernail', 사ᄅᆞᆷ'person', 사ᄅᆞᄆᆞᆯ 'person-Obj', 아모 'anyone', 올창 'tadpole', 조곰 'a little', 하ᄂᆞᆯ'sky, heaven'.

c. *neutral*
(with *yin*) 그저긔 'at that time', 너구리 'raccoon', 도모지 'by all means', 두더쥐 'a mole', 두드리 'knock', 멀거니 'blankly', 버러지 'worm', 슬긔 'wisdom', 어드니 'as one receives',주우리 'starve'.
(with *yang*) 갈고리 'hook', 고사리 'fernshoots', 도토리 'acorn', 마조치 'bump into', 모조리 'all', 바고니 'basket', ᄇᆞᇫ아디 'be broken', 오로디 'solely', 죠고마치 'a little', 바디로이 'by coincidence'.

It was S.-N. Lee (1949) who first observed that in the fifteenth century the complex vowel forms containing more than one vowel within a syllable nucleus—such as ㅐ, ㅔ, ㅚ, ㅟ, which are monophthongs in contemporary Korean—actually represented diphthongs in MK. He thus contributed in a major way to freeing researchers from the contemporary glasses they were wearing in analyzing MK sounds. However, he did not hesitate to reconstruct the lost vowel < • > *alay-a* as /ʌ/, based on the impressionistic observation of how he thought contemporary Ceycwu speakers still pronounced it. He then hypothesized a seven-vowel system for MK as in (5):

(5) The MK Vowel System according to S.-N. Lee (1949)[7]

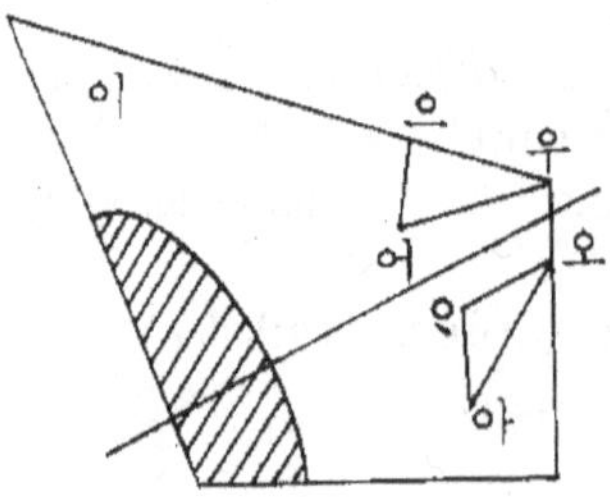

---

[7]For the sake of clarity an empty circle with zero phonetic value is drawn in where the first consonant of a syllable would have been placed—to the left of a vertical stroke and above a horizontal stroke.

The chart for this posited vowel system, however, does not show the changes the lost vowel underwent as plausible and natural processes. It is well known that *alay-a* < • > became <—> in a non-initial syllable and <ㅏ> in a word-initial syllable.

Staying closer to the descriptions provided in *HCH*, W. Kim (1963/71) proposed the vowel chart in (6):

(6) The MK Vowel System according to W. Kim (1963/71)

ㅣ	ㅜ	ㅗ
	ㅡ	ㆍ
	ㅓ	ㅏ

W. Kim hypothesized that the vowel chart given in (6) was an abstract system, and the actual pronunciation of non-high vowels would have been more front, as shown in (7):

(7) The Actual MK Vowel Space according to W. Kim (1963/71)

ㅣ		ㅜ	ㅗ
		ㅡ	ㆍ
	ㅓ		ㅏ

W. Kim (1965) then posited a push-chain type of vowel shift occurring between the 17th and 18th centuries, schematized as in (8).

(8) The Great Vowel Shift of the Seventeenth and Eighteenth Centuries, according to W. Kim (1963/71)

i	ʉ	→	u
	↑		↓
	ə		ʌ
	↑		↓
	e	←	a

Regardless of the period when the hypothesized Great Vowel Shift is thought to have taken place, these are certainly unexpected and incomprehensible vowels in the places indicated, and therefore, this type of push-chain change can hardly be justified. This fact was not obvious when only the Korean vowel symbols were entered in the chart. Although lined up in the same column, the front rounded vowel /ʉ/, /ə/, and /e/ hardly form a natural class together. A similar problem exists with the grouping of /u/, /ʌ/, and /a/.

Many linguists believe that the Great Vowel Shift had already taken place by the fifteenth century and that MK vowels were not much different from today's. Assuming the two vowel systems are very similar to each other, in both systems the line separating the two different harmonic groups would seem diagonal. C.-W. Kim (1978) thus calls Korean VH "diagonal harmony," in the manner of Aoki (1966), inspired by the diagonal line separating the two harmonic groups, as shown in (9):

(9) Diagonal Vowel Harmony

(i)

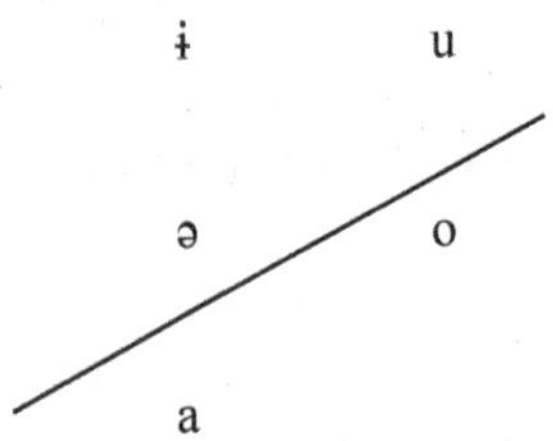

W. Kim (1978) adopts the same analysis. However, the diagonal analysis is not phonetically motivated in spite of its appearance of exhibiting a clear demarcation line.

The misidentification of the vowel positions is mainly based on the persisting preconception that the letters of the Korean alphabet have had the same phonetic values at the time of its promulgation as in their current pronunciation. For example, the seven basic vowels of Middle Korean are commonly posited as shown in (10):

(10) Basic Vowel System showing a Vertical VH in MK (Huh 1965, K.-M. Lee 1972, T.-C. Yi1988:35, Lee and Ramsey 2000:364, Ahn and Iverson 2006)

i	ɨ	u
	ə	o
	a	ʌ

The vowel letters that represent these sounds are the same as those of today except for the lost vowel < • >, as shown in (11).

(11) Korean Orthographic Representation for the MK Vowel System of (10)

ㅣ	ㅡ	ㅜ
	ㅓ	ㅗ
	ㅏ	·

The problem with the orthographic representation given in (11) for the vowel system hypothesized in (10) is that the letter shapes do not match their phonetic description provided in *HCH*. Furthermore, the dividing lines between different harmonic groups are not obvious. One of the most common approaches has been to consider relative tongue height as the force underlying vowel groupings (Lyu 2005:234). The problem with this kind of analysis is having to accommodate such a long distance relationship as the one between the vowels < • > and <—>. That is, how did < • > become <—> in a non-initial position?

In order to account for VH operating on such a vowel system, a vertical VH hypothesis has been put forward, but researchers have often had to reconstruct abstract vowels for late Middle Korean (e.g., K.-M. Lee 1972: 141–42, Cho 2002:280).

The vowel system I hypothesize for MK is shown in (12), which is similar to the one presented in (10).

(12) Basic Vowel System Showing a Vertical/Palatal VH in MK

i	ɨ	u
	ə	o
	a	ɑ

However, the orthographic representation for the MK vowel system differs significantly from the commonly accepted view that the vowel shapes have essentially continued to maintain their original value today. *HCH* makes it clear that the MK vowel symbols did not have the same value as those of contemporary Korean vowels, but in fact they occupied the positions shown in (13):

(13) *HC* Representation for the MK Vowel System of (12)

ㅣ	ㅜ	ㅗ
	ㅡ	ㆍ
	ㅏ	ㅓ

This vowel chart neatly demonstrates that the VH phenomenon in MK was indeed phonetically conditioned. The main phonological feature that distinguished one harmonic group from the other was the combined dynamic of lip rounding [RD] and retracted tongue root [RTR]. The best supporting evidence comes from the specific description of each of the seven basic vowel symbols of *HC*, along with examples and explanations of vowel groups contained in *HCH*. Additional evidence comes from comparative work and internal reconstruction. The comparative material and dialectal data give added evidence for this vowel system.

In *HCH* the three basic vowels are described with simple, well-defined features. The articulatory and perceptual (acoustic) features used not only in describing individual sounds but their relationship to other, related phonemes make them remarkably modern, as shown in (14):

(14) Feature Specifications of the Three Basic Vowels as Described in *HCH*

> ・舌縮而聲深, ㅗ與・同而口蹙, ㅏ與・同而口張
> [・ has retracted tongue, deep sound. ㅗ is like ・ but with pursed mouth. ㅏ is like ・ but with spread mouth]
>
> ㅡ舌小縮而聲不深不淺, ㅜ與ㅡ同而口蹙, ㅓ與ㅡ同而口張
> [ㅡ has partially retracted tongue, neither deep nor acute sound. ㅜ is like ㅡ but with pursed mouth. ㅓ is like ㅡ but with spread mouth]
>
> ㅣ舌不縮而聲淺
> [ㅣ has no retracted tongue and sounds shallow]

The key to understanding the nature of the MK vowel system lies in linguistically significant and plausible reading of the features that *HCH* adopts in describing various vowels. Here it is important to observe that in *Ceycahay* (Explanation of the Designing of the Letters) of *HCH* Chinese character pair "淺" (Kor. 천 *chen*) 'shallow' and "深" (Kor. 심 *sim*) 'deep' are used to contrast front-backness; "縮" (Kor. 축 *chwuk*) 'retract' and "不縮" (Kor. 불축 *pulchwuk*) 'not retract' the presence or absence of tongue body retraction; and "蹙" (Kor. *chwuk*) 'tightly closed' and "張" (Kor. *cang*) 'open' degree of mouth aperture.

Phonetic characteristics of vowels are thus viewed from three different angles. The Chinese characters 淺 and 深 describe acoustic features, 'acute' and 'grave' respectively, which are related to perception by the listener, rather than from the point of view of a person articulating the sounds. However, the features acute or grave are, of course, directly related to the frontness or backness of the tongue position. On the other hand, the Chinese character pair 舌縮 (Kor. 설축 *selchwuk*) and 舌不縮 (Kor. 설불축 *selpulchwuk*) express retraction of the tongue felt by the speaker or the absence of it. And finally the rather uncommon character 蹙 can be translated for linguistic purposes as 'closed, but not completely,' or rather 'pursed,' 'puckered,' etc. In other words, 口蹙 (Kor. 구축 *kwuchwuk*) could mean 'lips tightened in such a manner that the mouth-opening is held tensely as small as possible, i.e., round.' Conversely 口張 (Kor. 구장 kwucang) describes spread lips. Many linguists (e.g., Ledyard 1966/98:235, Y.-S. Kim 1987, J. Kim 1993:102) have opted to interpret this mainly to mean 'rounded,' although the fact that the lips are 'close in but not actually shut' is mentioned by some including Ledyard (ibid.). W. Kim (1963/71) had a similar analysis of the MK vowel system and VH as discussed earlier in this paper, but his revised analysis (W. Kim 1978) adopted an entirely different vowel system, which is similar to that proposed by Huh (1965:376).

The genius of this vowel feature described and employed in *HCH* is its ability to catch simultaneously both the lip rounding and the jaw height associated with each vowel, as shown in (15):

(15) Vowels Categorized by 口蹙 and 口張 Features[8]

ㅜ	ㅗ	口蹙
ㅡ	ㆍ	
ㅓ	ㅏ	口張

Another common but crucial error has been in identifying the articulatory positions of two of the basic vowels, < • > and <—> in the vowel chart. A great majority of linguists have interpreted their tongue frontness and backness, while not considering their jaw height (or the closedness or openness of the lips). Furthermore, the vowel < • > was often placed too low on the chart, and the <—> too high, when they both needed to be placed in the mid position. Once their position has become misplaced, the other related vowel positions could not be identified properly.

Ever since S.-N. Lee, in his influential article (1949), claimed the lost vowel < • > was an unrounded low-mid back vowel [ʌ], this assertion has rarely been challenged. Even Huh (1965), although he himself noticed definite lip-rounding in the pronunciation of the vowel in Ceycwu dialect and quoted Ogura (1944) and K.-L. Yi (1948) who also had observed lip rounding, did not place < • > in the mid height of the vowel chart.

I should like to propose that the lost vowel < • > actually was at least phonologically /o/, with actual pronunciation that could have been a bit lower, i.e., something like [ɔ], which is very close to [ɑ]. This explains, then, how in the strongest word- or stem-initial position, the vowel < • > became <ㅏ>, since their space would have easily overlapped in the narrow space of the back of the mouth.

Although this analysis may sound surprising under the current situation, I am not the first to have proposed this idea. Some time ago, Ogura (1940:20-22) hypothesized the vowel < • > to have represented the /o/ vowel after studying the Ceycwu dialect, which is well recognized as the only dialect that has preserved the disappeared < • >. He repeatedly said there is definitely lip-rounding. Huh also quotes K.-L. Yi (1948:17) who said this

[8]This vowel chart is similar to the one by Singhang Kang (1987:71), but in his analysis the two features 口蹙 and 口張 express only 'closed mouth' and 'spread mouth' respectively.

vowel was pronounced in the low back area, with slight lip-rounding (Reported in Huh 1965:315). Even today, there are testimonies by native speakers of Ceycwu dialect who blog about how the vowel is pronounced, either by themselves or by older speakers. For example, Hon says that the *alay-a* his grandmother pronounces is somewhere between [o] and [a] (http://gall.dcinside.com/list.php?id=language&no=4270). The first vowel /o/ in the famous Ceycwu greeting, 혼저옵서예 honceopseye, is actually the pronunciation of *alay-a* according to what a visitor found and reported in a blog of November 17, 2009 (http://codebuzz.net/10).

Much earlier, Ramstedt (1928/39:27) made a similar observation, giving both internal and comparative evidence. In Korean dialect studies, he discovered [o] as a sound corresponding to < · >. Ramstedt also observed that, in loanwords from various Altaic languages including Mongolian, and also in the Japanese transcription of Korean words, the vowel < · > systematically corresponded to /o/ (Kwak 1990:87). K.-M. Lee (1991:125–35) also notes that the Mongolian word for 'a horse' *mori* is transcribed in Korean as 몰.

How, then would <ㅗ> have been pronounced? There is fairly good evidence this represented a higher vowel, close to [u] in the fifteenth century, although it is pronounced [o] in contemporary Korean. For example, the Mongolian loanword 구렁 'dark brown, maroon' came from Mongolian *küreng*, indicating the <ㅜ> vowel was pronounced in a more frontal area than <ㅗ> (K.-M. Lee 1991:127). K.-M. Lee compares transcriptions of Mongol loanwords of the 13th century and those of the 18th century, and concludes the vowel shift of [u] > [o] and [ɨ] > [u] occurred something between the two centuries (1991:137).

S.-H. Chung (2009:38, 42, 45) also notes that in *Ilopha* 伊路波 (1492), the earliest primer for teaching Japanese to Koreans produced by the Bureau of Interpreters, the vowel [o] in Japanese ほ is transcribed either as <ㅜ> or <ㅗ> in Korean. On the other hand, W. Kim (1963/71:13) notes that when transcribing Chinese [u], the letter <ㅜ> was used systematically. However, it is clear that there was a great deal of change going on in the MK period. So, in actual pronunciation this vowel was already pronounced more commonly as [u]. The ongoing change is evidenced by variation between the two vowels <ㅜ> and <ㅗ>, as both of these were transcribed as [u] in Chinese. For example, the vowels in the two Chinese characters 烏 and 蘇 were used for transcribing both <ㅜ> and <ㅗ>, as shown in (16) (from K.-M. Lee 1972:114):

(16) a. 來曰烏羅 (오라)
井曰烏沒 (우믈)
b. 鹽曰蘇甘 (소곰)
炭曰蘇成 (슷)

Another piece of evidence for the RD value of the *alay-a* < • > vowel can be found in the transcriptions of the Ryukyuan vowel [u]. W. Kim (1963/71:13) expresses his surprise at finding many examples of the Ryukyuan [u] vowel transcribed with *alay-a* in *Eumpenyek* 語音飜譯 (Phonetic Interpretations), an appendix to *Haytongceykwukki* 海東諸國記 (Record of the Various Eastern Nations) by Sin Swukcwu (1471), the earliest transcription of Japanese written in *HC*, for example:

(17) Ryukyuan [u] Vowel Transcribed with *alay-a*

ᄉᆞ미	sumi	墨	'ink'
ᄉᆞ우	suu	醋	'vinegar'
ᄌᆞ기	tsuki	月	'moon'
타ᄌᆞ	tatsu	龍	'dragon'
낟ᄌᆞ	natsu	夏	'summer'
ᄎᆞ라	tsura	面	'face'
ᄉᆞᄌᆞ리	sutsuri	硯	'inkstone'

W. Kim (ibid.) rightly reflects that if the letter <—> had the same phonetic value as today, the post-sibilant [u]s should have been transcribed with <—>, rather than with *alay-a* < • >, just as contemporary Koreans transcribe post-sibilant Japanese high back vowel as an unrounded high back vowel <—>. In MK clearly, then, *alay-a* < • > was more appropriate to express the back vowel, as the symbol <—> represented a nonback mid vowel /ə/. That the <—> vowel had the nonback value is also supported by the fact that the Ryukyuan vowel エ [e] was often transcribed as <ㅢ> in Korean, which did not have the /e/ vowel in its inventory.

One is struck by the rarity of <ㅓ> in foreign-language transcriptions. When it does, it is usually used in transcribing front vowels, for which there was no vowel phoneme other than <ㅣ> in MK. For example, 구렁 'dark brown, maroon' came from Mongolian *küreng*, indicating the <ㅓ> vowel was the closest Korean adaptation for the Mongolian [e] sound (K.-Moon Lee 1991:127). So, it would not be unreasonable to posit that the mid low vowel <ㅓ>, while phonemically /a/, was pronounced more in the front, i.e., as something like [ɜ], which is close to [ɛ]. The strategy to arrive at the mid front vowel position was to add <ㅣ> to <ㅓ>. So, [e] in loanwords are often transcribed in MK, either as <ㅔ> /ay/ [ɛy] , <ㅕ> /ya/ [yɛ], or <ㅖ> /yay/

[yεy]. All three varieties occur in transcriptions of Japanese Kana in *Ilopha* (1492), as shown in (18):

(18) HC Transcriptions of Japanese Kana in *Ilopha* (Data from Chung 2009:37, based on K. Lee 1965:7–8)

エ	ケ	セ	テ	ネ	ヘ	メ	レ	ヱ
예	계	셔	뎨,뎌	녀	ㅸㅖ	몌,며	례	에

Other examples of the use of <ㅓ>, <ㅔ>, or <ㅕ> to transcribe an [e] sound are found in Mongolian loanwords, as well, e.g., 더그레 *degelei* 'jacket, camisole, short fur garment', 털릭 terlig 'military uniform', 구렁 *küreng* 'chestnut brown' (from K.-M. Lee 1991b:127, 129, 134). As K.-M. Lee (1991:137) notes, these are pieces of evidence that the MK vowel <ㅓ> had a different sound value from today's and was a fairly front vowel, close to [e].

Some variational evidence from dialects today also shows us the close relationship between <ㅔ>, pronounced [e] today, and <ㅕ> [yə], too, as shown in such variant forms as in 며느리 myenuli ~ 메느리 meynuli 'daughter-in-law', 몇살 myechsal ~ 멫살 meychsal 'how old', 벼개 pyekay ~ 베개 peykay 'pillow'.

Various kinds of evidence seem to suggest that many preconceived ideas are wrong and unintuitive analyses could be avoided. The basic vowel chart for Late Middle Korean we obtain after these various factors are considered is that shown in (19):

(19) The Middle Korean Vowel System:

Tongue / Mouth	Front/Neutral	Central/Dark	Back/Bright
Close	ㅣ/i/	ㅜ/ɨ/	ㅗ/u/
Mid		ㅡ/ə/	ㆍ/o/
Open		ㅓ/a/	ㅏ/ɑ/

The vowel positions in this chart fit their descriptions in *HCH*. This vowel system allows a linguistically significant, plausible analysis of MK VH. The dividing features between the two harmonic groups were roundness and tongue retraction. This analysis not only helps to explain VH elegantly, but also some other phonological phenomena such as the < ㆍ > /o/ vowel changing to neighboring vowels <ㅏ> /ɑ/ or <ㅡ> /ə/, and <ㅓ> /a/ being raised to <ㅡ> /ə/ in certain circumstances.

The generally accepted hypothesis is that the Great Korean Vowel Shift was caused by the merger of < ㆍ > /o/ with <ㅡ> /ə/. The merger of these two centrally located vowels and other related vowels in the weak, non-initial position is quite natural, as we can see in some ongoing merging of <ㅗ> and <ㅜ> in non-initial syllables today. Furthermore, this vowel chart also illustrates how the vowel < ㆍ > /o/ took the direction of <ㅡ> /ə/ or <ㅏ> /ɑ/ and lost its own distinct identity. The two vowels are articulatorily very close to the vowel < ㆍ > /o/.

My own hypothesis is that the Korean vowel shift was of the push-chain type. The two very closely located low vowels <ㅓ> /a/ and <ㅏ> /ɑ/ created an unstable situation, which caused the low back vowel to take the central position, forcing the low central vowel to raise, thus starting a chain reaction.

The fifteenth century in Korea saw many significant sound changes occur. Thanks to the invention of the wonderful phonetic writing system and detailed description of each sound at the opportune moment, many variant forms at the time of the invention of the Korean alphabet have been captured.

Ceng Inci, head of the royally commissioned scholars who compiled *HCH*, said in his concluding essay in utter awe and admiration of the newly invented writing system:

(20) From Ceng Inci's Concluding Essay in *HCH*

> Insofar as the phonology of characters is concerned, clear and muddy can be distinguished. In matters of music and singing, the twelve semitones may be successfully harmonized. There is no usage not provided for, no destination they do not reach. Even the sound of the winds, the cry of the crane, the cackle of fowl and the barking of dogs—all may be put into writing.
>
> – Transl. by Gari Ledyard (Ledyard 1966/98:320)

This statement is not even accurate, for *HC* was an alphabet and not a phonetic transcription device. Nevertheless, the availability of such rich data thanks to the new writing system, which had a good linguistic fit, not only makes it possible for linguists to study the Korean language change with confidence but could also open ways for us to study linguistic past of the neighboring countries.

However, for the same reason, the direction of language change could be misunderstood, too. It is noteworthy that some of the changes like the demise of < • > did not occur abruptly but lasted for a long time after it lost its distinctive phonemic status. The conservative writing practice certainly contributed to this phenomenon.

Korean language history is still shrouded in enigma. We still badly need clues to what the earlier Korean language was like. It is very encouraging that more and more *kwukyel* data are becoming available and we know more about the language of the pre-*HC* era. Surely the hypotheses presented in this paper on the MK vowel system and VH should be re-examined in the broader context.

References

Ahn, S.-C. and G. I. 2006 (MS). Structured Imbalances in the Emergence of the Korean Vowel System.

Aoki, H. 1966. Nez Perce Vowel Harmony and Proto-Sahaptian Vowels. *Language* 42:759-767.

Cho, S.-M. 2002. An Optimality-theoretic Account of Two Sound Values in Korean Vowel /i/. *Studies in Phonetics, Phonology and Morphology* 8.2:279-293.

Choy, C.-H. 2005. *Cosene Lyeksa Eumlon* (Historical Phonology of Korean). Pyongyang: Sahoykwahak Chulphansa (Social Science Publishing Co.).

Chung, C. W. 2000. An Optimality-theoretic Account of Vowel Harmony in Korean Ideophones. *Studies in Phonetics, Phonology and Morphology* 6.2:431-450.

Chung, S.-H. 2009. Hwunmin Ceng'umkwa Ilpone Phyoki: Sayekwen Yekhakselul Cwungsimulo (Hwunmin Ceng'um and its Transcriptions of Japanese: Focusing on the Foreign Language Studies Material Used by the Bureau of Interpreters) in the *Proceedings of Scripta 2010*:33-50.

Haas, W. 1976. *Writing without Letters*. Manchester, UK: Manchester University Press.

Hon, S.-K. (downloaded, Dec. 2010) Ceycwutouy *alay-a* Parum (Pronunciation of Ceycwu Island's *alay-a*), a personal blog (http://gall.dcinside.com/list.php?id=language&no=4270).

Huh, W. 1965. *Kwuke Umunhak* (Korean phonology). Seoul: Ceng'umsa.

Kang, S. 1987. *Hwunmin Ceng'um Yenkwu* (Study of Hwunmin Ceng'um).

Kim, C.-W. 1978. Diagonal Vowel Harmony?: Some Implications for Historical Phonology. *Recent Developments in Historical Phonology*, ed. J. Fisiak, 221-235. The Hague: Mouton Publishers.

_____ . 1980/88. On the Origin and Structure of the Korean Script. Lecture delivered on October 9, 1980, at the University of Illinois. *Korean language II*. Chin-W. Kim, 721-734. Seoul: Tower Press.

_____. 1997. The Structure of Phonological Units in Han'gŭl. *The Korean Alphabet: Its history and Structure*, ed. Young-Key Kim-Renaud, 145-160. Honolulu: University of Hawai'i Press.

Kim, J. 1993. *Moum Cohwauy Yenkwu* (A Study of Vowel Harmony). Taykwu, Korea: Yeungnam University Press.

Kim, K.-O. 1978. Vowel System of Korean Revisited, *Papers in Korean Linguistics*, ed. Chin-W. Kim, 75-83. Columbia, SC: Hornbeam Press.

Kim, W. 1963/71. Kwuke Moum Cheykyeuy Sinkochal (The Korean Vowel System Revisited). *Cintanhakpo* 24:475-511, 1963. Reprinted in *Kwuke Moum Cheykyeuy Sinkochal* (The Korean Vowel System Revisited), Seoul: Ilchokak, 1971:2-44.

_____. 1965. Wensikwuke Moumloney Kwankyetoyn Susamuy Muncey (Some Problems concerning the Ancient Korean Vowel Theory). *Cintanhakpo* 28:75-97.

_____. 1978. Moum Cheykyewa Moum Cohwaey tayhan Panseng (Reflections on the Vowel System and Vowel Harmony). *Language Research* 14.2:127-139.

Kim, Y.-S. 1987. Articulatory Characteristics and the Vowel System in Hun-min Jeong-um. *Korea Journal* 27.2:18-29.

Kim-Renaud, Y.-K. 1976. Semantic Features in Phonology: Evidence from Vowel Harmony in Korean. *Papers from the Twelfth Regional Meeting of the Chicago Linguistic Society*, ed. S. A. Mufwene, C. A. Walker, and S. B. Steever, 397-412. Reprinted in *Studies in Korean Linguistics*, Y.-K. Kim-Renaud. Seoul: Hanshin Publishing Co. (1986:63-76)

_____. 1997. The Phonological Analysis Reflected in the Korean Writing System. *The Korean Alphabet*: *Its History and Structure*, ed. Y.-K. Kim-Renaud, 161-192. Honolulu: University of Hawai'i Press.

Ko, S. 2010. A Contrastivist View on the Evolution of the Korean Vowel System." *MIT Working Papers in Linguistics* (MITWPL) 61: *Proceedings of the Sixth Workshop on Altaic Formal Linguistics* (WAFL 6), ed. Hiroki Maezawa and Azusa Yokogoshi, 181-196.

Kōno, R. 1945. *Chōsen Hōgengaku Sshikō*: *'Hasami' Gokō* (A Study in Korean Dialectology: A Study of the Word for 'scissors'). Keijō (Seoul): Tōto Shoseki.

Kwak, C.-k. 1990. Moum Cohwa wa Moum Cheykye (Vowel Harmony and the Vowel System). *Kwuke Yenkwu Etikkaci Wassna* (Current Status of Korean Language Research), comp. Kim Hyensik, 84-94. Seoul: Tong'a Chulphansa.

Ledyard, G. 1966/98. *The Korean Language Reform of 1446*: *The Origin, Background, and Early History of the Korean Alphabet*. Doctoral dissertation, University of California, Berkeley, 1966. Slightly revised edition published as *The Korean Language Reform of 1446*, 1998. (Academy of the Korean Language Special Publications series, No. 2) Seoul: Sinkwu Munhwasa.

_____. 1997. The International Linguistic Background of the Correct Sounds for the Instruction of the People. *The Korean Alphabet: Its History and Structure*, ed. Kim-Renaud, 31-87. Honolulu: University of Hawai'i Press.

Lee, H.-H. 1990. Hwunmin Ceng'um. *Kwuke Yenkwu Etikkaci Wassna* (Current Status of Korean Language Research), comp. Kim Hyensik, 615-631. Seoul: Tong'a Chulphansa.

Lee, I. and S. R. Ramsey. 2000. *The Korean Language*. Albany, NY: State University of New York Press.

Lee, K.-M. 1965. Sengcongphan "iropha"eytayhaye. *Tose* 7:3-36. Seoul: Eulyoo Chulphansa.

_____. 1972. *Kwukesa Kaysel* (An Introduction to the History of Korean), Revised edition. Seoul: Mincwung Sekwan.

_____. 1991. *Kwuke Ehwisa Yenkwu* (History of Korean Lexicon). Seoul: Donga Publishing Co.

Lee, S.-N. 1949. *Cosene Umunlon Yenkwu* (Korean Phonology), Vol.1: " · " um Ko (Study on the Korean Letter " · "). *Cosen Munhwa Chongse* (Korean Cultural Anthology), Vol. 7.

Lyu, L. 2005. *Cosenmal Lyeksa* (History of the Korean Language) *I*. Pyongyang: Sahoykwahak Chwulphansa (Social Sciences Publishing Co.).

Martin, S. E. 1992. *A Reference Grammar of Korean*. Hong Kong, Rutland, VT, and Singapore: Tuttle Publishing.

Nam, P. 1994. On the Relations Between Hyangchal and Kwukyel. *Theoretical Issues in Korean Linguistics*, ed. Y.-K. Kim-Renaud, 419-423. Stanford: CSLI.

Ogura, S.小倉進平. 1940. *The Outline of the Korean Dialects*. Tokyo: The Toyo Bunko.

_____. 1944. 朝鮮方言語の研究上·下. *Chōsenhōgengo no Kenkyûjōge* (Study of Korean Dialects), Vol. I, II. Tokyo: Iwanami Shoten (岩波書店).

Pak, C.-H. 1988. 'Hwunminceng'umey Nathananun Yekhakcek Paekyeng (Cosmological Philosophical Background.of Hwunminceng'um). *Hwunminceng'umuy Ihay* (Understanding Hwunminceng'um), ed. Sin Sang-sun, Yi Ton-cwu, and Yi Hwan-muk. Seoul: Hanshin Publishing Co, 239-60.

Ramstedt, G. J. 1928/39. *A Korean Grammar*. Mémoires de la Société Finno-Ougrienne LXXXII. Helsinki.

Sampson, G. 1985. *Writing Systems*. Stanford: Stanford University Press.

Stevens, K. N. & S. J. Keyser. 1989. Primary Features and Their Enhancement in Consonants. *Language* 65.1: 81-106.

Song, K.-J. 1991. Iloncek Chukmyeneyse Pon 15seyki Kwukeuy / · / um, Moumcheykyey, Moumcohwa (The / · / phoneme in 15th century Korean, Viewed from a Theoretical Point of View). *Kwukehak* (Korean Linguistics) 9.4:79-101.

Yi, J. H. 1972. *The Korean Alphabet: Explanation in Korean and English*. Seoul: Po Cin Chay Printing Co., Ltd.

Yi, K.-L. 1948. *Kwukehaknonchong* (國語學論叢, Studies in Korean Linguistics). Seoul: Ceng'umsa.

Yi, S. 2008. Hwunminceng'um kwa Yekhaksasang (Hwunminceng'um and Ideology of *the Book of Changes*), presented at the 42nd academic conference by the Research Institute of Korean Philosophy, May 24.

Yi, T.-C. 1988. Hwunminceng'umuy Haysel. *Hwunminceng'umuy Ihay* (Understanding Hwunminceng'um), ed. Shin Sang-sun, Yi T.-C. and Yi H.-M. Seoul: Hanshin Publishing Co.

Yu, C.-T. 1964/second ed. 1971. Yicoe Sacen (Dictionary of the Cosen-dynasty Language). Seoul: Yonsei Univeristy Press.

Constraint Inviolability in Japanese Mimetic Palatalization*

KAZUTAKA KURISU
Kobe College

1. Introduction

In generative linguistics, an input is usually mapped onto a certain output, but there are cases where this mapping relation does not hold. One is when a given input exhibits variation such that more than one output emerges from one input. The other is cases where an input has no grammatical output.

This paper is a contribution to the second type of cases where one-to-one input-output mapping does not hold. They are often called absolute ungrammaticality or ineffability. There is a growing body of research on how a failure in generation of tangible output is to be accounted for. There are several competing models for explaining absolute ungrammaticality within the framework of Optimality Theory (OT; Prince and Smolensky

*I am grateful to Peter Sells and Bjarke Frellesvig for useful discussion. I also thank an anonymous abstract reviewer for invaluable comments.

Japanese/Korean Linguistics 20.
Edited by Bjarke Frellesvig and Peter Sells.

2004). They include Control Theory, an MPARSE approach, and a paradigmatic approach.

Japanese has a rich repertoire of mimetic items, and palatalization is one of their outstanding characteristics. Palatalization denotes so-called uncontroledness, which is associated with a vast range of meanings such as childishness, inelegance, noisiness, and uncoordinated movement. In disyllabic mimetic roots, there is a systematic gap with respect to palatalization: a sequence of a palatal(ized) consonant and [e]. Earlier studies handle such examples as arising from underparsing of the palatalization feature of the uncontroledness morpheme. Scrutiny reveals, however, that the systematic gap results from ineffability.

Among the three approaches to ineffability stated above, only the one appealing to Control Theory is able to capture the systematic gap in Japanese mimetic palatalization. According to this model originally articulated by Orgun and Sprouse (1999), *EVAL* always emits the optimal candidate, and it is in turn sent to the component called *CONTROL*. *CONTROL* consists of a set of inviolable constraints, and the candidate is evaluated there again. The candidate surfaces if it violates none of the inviolable constraints, but it is eliminated if it breaches at least one of the constraints in *CONTROL*. In effect, the input fails to be mapped onto a successful output in this case, and absolute ungrammaticality follows.

The MPARSE and paradigmatic approaches are competitive possibilities. I show that these analyses encounter ranking paradoxes. This means that these alternative accounts are not feasible, and only Control Theory is able to cope with the systematic gap in the Japanese mimetic vocabulary.

The rest of this paper is organized as follows. In section 2, I present data of Japanese mimetic palatalization. In the same section, they are analyzed within the framework of OT. Section 3 presents examples of absolute ungrammaticality. Earlier literature does not treat them as cases of absolute ungrammaticality, but I argue that they should be viewed as instances of absolute ungrammaticality. Section 4 is devoted to my analysis based on Control Theory. In section 5, I discuss two alternatives: MPARSE and paradigmatic approaches. In section 6, I argue for the need of relativized markedness constraints. Finally, this paper is concluded in section 7.

2. Basic Data and Analysis

In this section, I present data and an OT analysis of mimetic palatalization without absolute ungrammaticality. The analysis presented below is the one proposed in my earlier work (Kurisu 2009).

Japanese mimetic roots are either monosyllabic or disyllabic (Hamano 1998). Of our interest are disyllabic (C)VCV roots. The locus of palatalization is phonologically predictable (Mester and Itô 1989; Zoll 1996, 1997; Hamano 1998; Kurisu 2009; cf. Alderete and Kochetov 2009).

First, coronal consonants are more harmonic hosts of palatalization than non-coronals, as exemplified in (1). The syntagmatic positions of a coronal and a non-coronal do not affect the locus of palatalization in this case.

(1)	*Base forms*	*Palatalized forms*	*Gloss*
	zabu-zabu	ʒabu-ʒabu	splashing indiscriminately
	toko-toko	tʃoko-tʃoko	moving around restlessly
	kasa-kasa	kaʃa-kaʃa	dry rustling sound
	gasa-gasa	gaʃa-gaʃa	noisy rustling sound

Second, a second consonant undergoes palatalization when two root consonants are both coronals. Some examples are given in (2).

(2)	*Base forms*	*Palatalized forms*	*Gloss*
	dosa-dosa	doʃa-doʃa	flowing in large amounts
	nuta-nuta	nutʃa-nutʃa	very clammy
	nuto-nuto	nutʃo-nutʃo	very sticky

Third, palatalization targets the initial consonant when both consonants are non-coronals, as in (3a). However, palatalization targets the root-medial non-coronal in VCV roots, as shown in (3b), where palatalization is lexical.

(3)		*Base forms*	*Palatalized forms*	*Gloss*
	a.	poko-poko	p^{j}oko-p^{j}oko	jumping around
		gaha-gaha	g^{j}aha-g^{j}aha	laughing loudly
	b.		og^{j}a-og^{j}a	crying (baby)

In order to account for the set of data presented above, I start by assuming the three constraints provided in (4). As seen from (4a), I assume in this paper that [–ant] is the phonological feature responsible for palatalization.

(4)			
	a.	MAX[–ant]:	[–ant] must be realized in the output.
	b.	*[–COR]^j:	Palatalized non-coronals are prohibited.
	c.	*COR^j:	Palatalized coronals are prohibited.

The examples in (1) indicate that palatalized coronals are preferred to palatalized non-coronals, so *[–COR]^j should outrank *COR^j. In anticipation, the fact that non-coronals may be palatalized shows that MAX[–ant] dominates *[–COR]^j. The analysis of (1) is provided in (5). In (5) and below, candidates are presented in non-reduplicated forms.

(5)

	/zabu,[–ant]/	MAX[–ant]	*[–COR]ʲ	*CORʲ
a.	zabu	*!		
b. ☞	ʒabu			*
c.	zabʲu		*!	

The current analysis does not predict the correct locus of palatalization in cases where two root consonants are both coronals or non-coronals. The right-edge orientation in (2) is elucidated with interaction of alignment constraints. (6a) requires that the [–ant] feature be realized at the right periphery of a root whereas (6b) calls for palatalization on the opposite side.

(6) a. ALIGN-R([–ant],Rt): [–ant] must be right-aligned to a root.
b. ALIGN-L([–ant],Rt): [–ant] must be left-aligned to a root.

The examples in (2) suggest that (6a) outranks (6b), as illustrated in (7). Alignment violations are counted in segments.

(7)

	/dosa,[–ant]/	MAX[–ant]	ALIGN-R	ALIGN-L
a.	dosa	*!		
b.	dʒosa		**!*	
c. ☞	doʃa		*	**

The coronal dominance effect takes precedence over the right-edge orientation, so *[–COR]ʲ is ranked over ALIGN-R([–ant],Rt), as illustrated in (8).

(8)

	/zabu,[–ant]/	*[–COR]ʲ	ALIGN-R	ALIGN-L
a. ☞	ʒabu		***	
b.	zabʲu	*!	*	**

The analysis presented above predicts root-medial palatalization in (3a) as well, contrary to fact. The conjoined constraint in (9) is operative here.

(9) ALIGN-L([–ant],Rt) & *[–COR]ʲ:
Palatalized non-coronals are licensed root-initially.

This markedness constraint restricts non-coronal palatalization to a root-initial position. The examples in (3a) are analyzed as in (10).

(10)

	/poko,[–ant]/	ALIGN-L & *[–COR]^{j}	ALIGN-R	ALIGN-L
a. ☞	p^{j}oko		***	
b.	pok^{j}o	*!	*	**

The conjoined constraint is not undominated. The example in (3b) suggests that a root-internal non-coronal consonant sponsors [–ant] in the absence of a root-initial consonant. This fact reveals that MAX[–ant] should be ranked over the conjoined constraint, as presented in (11). [oga-oga] does not exist, so palatalization is lexical in [og^{j}a-og^{j}a]. The palatalization feature is retained because of high ranked MAX[–ant].

(11)

	/og^{j}a/	MAX[–ant]	ALIGN-L & *[–COR]^{j}
a.	oga	*!	
b. ☞	og^{j}a		*

Summarizing the analysis in this section, the overall constraint ranking is provided in (12).

(12)

MAX[–ant]
|
ALIGN-L([–ant],Rt) & *[–Cor]^{j}
|
*[–Cor]^{j}
|
*Cor^{j} ALIGN-R([–ant],Rt)
|
ALIGN-L([–ant],Rt)

3. Systematic Gap

The mimetic vocabulary obeys several phonotactic restrictions. Of our interest here is the one in (13).

(13) *[C^{j}e]: [e] must not follow a palatal(ized) consonant.

This phonotactic restriction has important repercussions on the overall paradigm of palatalized forms. The examples in (14) demonstrate the fact that two types of mimetic forms are absent.

(14)	*Base forms*	*Gloss*	*Palatalized forms*	
a.	keba-keba	gaudy	*k^{j}eba-k^{j}eba	*keb^{j}a-keb^{j}a
	neba-neba	sticky	*ɲeba-ɲeba	*neb^{j}a-neb^{j}a
	teka-teka	shining	*tʃeka-tʃeka	*tek^{j}a-tek^{j}a
b.	kune-kune	wriggly	*k^{j}une-k^{j}une	*kuɲe-kuɲe
	kote-kote	thick	*k^{j}ote-k^{j}ote	*kotʃe-kotʃe
	gote-gote	thick	*g^{j}ote-g^{j}ote	*gotʃe-gotʃe
	bote-bote	bulky	*b^{j}ote-b^{j}ote	*botʃe-botʃe

In (14a), the second consonants are not coronals, so [–ant] is predicted to lodge at a root-initial consonant. In (14b), the second consonants are coronals, so they are the expected hosts of [–ant]. The alleged hosts precede [e] in these examples, and no palatalized form emerges.

Zoll (1996, 1997) analyzes the absence of palatalized forms in (14) as arising from underparsing of the [–ant] feature. This view entails that the non-palatalized forms are ambiguous because inputs with and without [–ant] converge upon the same output, as depicted in (15). Contrary to this expectation, the examples in (14) are not ambiguous.

(15) /keba-keba/   /keba-keba,[–ant]/

↘ ↙

[keba-keba]

The lack of ambiguity indicates that palatalized forms in (14) are ineffable. In other words, they are instances of absolute ungrammaticality.

4. Control Analysis

The analysis that I espouse here is built on Control Theory originally proposed by Orgun and Sprouse (1999) and later supported by Bye (2007) and Orgun and Sprouse (2009). It is beneficial to outline the gist of this theory.

In Control Theory, *EVAL* always emits the best candidate relative to a given constraint hierarchy, as shown in (16a). The novel aspect of the theory is the addition of a subsequent component called *CONTROL*. *CONTROL* contains inviolable constraints. The candidate selected by *EVAL* is assessed in *CONTROL* again. If the candidate respects all the constraints contained in *CONTROL*, it surfaces. If the candidate breaches at least one constraint in *CONTROL*, however, it crashes. In other words, the original input fails to be mapped onto a phonologically tangible output, resulting in absolute ungrammaticality. This is illustrated in (16b).

(16) a. b.

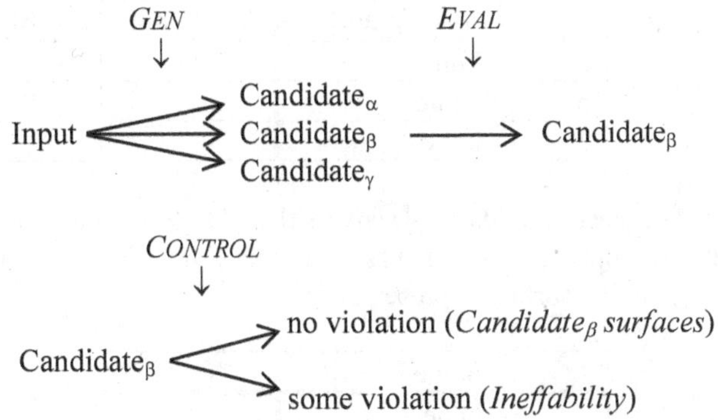

Let us now apply this idea to the examples in (14). First, potential candidates are assessed against the constraint ranking in (12). In (14a), the second consonants are non-coronals, so the candidate with initial palatalization is submitted as the optimal form, as demonstrated in (17). This is essentially the same as what happens to the forms as in (3a).

(17)

	/keba,[–ant]/	MAX[–ant]	ALIGN-L & *[–Cor]^j
a.	keba	*!	
b. ☞	k^{j}eba		
c.	keb^{j}a		*!

In Control Theory, this is not the end of candidate assessment. As mentioned above, the candidate selected by *EVAL* is sent to the *CONTROL* component that comprises a set of inviolable constraints. Such inviolable constraints are determined on the language-specific basis.

Let us assume that *[C^{j}e] is one of the constraints in *CONTROL* in Japanese. This markedness constraint militates against a cluster of a palatal(ized) consonant and [e]. As shown in (18), [k^{j}eba-k^{j}eba] breaches the markedness constraint, so it is eliminated in the *CONTROL* component.

(18)

	/keba,[–ant]/	*[C^{j}e]
x	k^{j}eba	*

The lack of palatalized forms in (14b) is explained in the same fashion. Given the constraint hierarchy in (12), a coronal consonant is preferred to a non-coronal as the docking site of [–ant]. In the same way as in (1), therefore, the coronal consonant undergoes palatalization irrespective of its syntagmatic position within the root, as presented in (19).

(19)

	/kune,[–ant]/	MAX[–ant]	*[–COR]^j	*COR^j
a.	kune	*!		
b.	k^{j}une		*!	
c. ☞	kuɲe			*

The best candidate is sent to the *CONTROL* component. As shown in (20), the optimal form incurs a violation of *[C^{j}e], so it is not allowed to appear in the surface representation.

(20)

	/kune,[–ant]/	*[C^{j}e]
×	kuɲe	*

Control Theory offers a consistent analysis of absolute ungrammaticality in (14). Note that *[C^{j}e] plays no eliminating role in examples in (1), (2), and (3). The actual outputs do not contain a sequence of a palatalized consonant and [e], so they pass the *CONTROL* component.

Wolf and McCarthy (2009) argue that Control Theory is problematic because it is indiscernible where undominated constraints are to be placed. An undominated constraint is affiliated with either *EVAL* or *CONTROL*. It is in *CONTROL* if violation of it is not repaired. If the violation is repaired at the cost of a lower faithfulness constraint violation, the undominated constraint is in *EVAL*. This difference is surely available to language speakers, so they can place undominated constraints in an appropriate component. It is not a problem that there are two positions for undominated constraints.

5. Alternatives

In OT literature, there are two other major approaches to absolute ungrammaticality. One appeals to the MPARSE constraint and the other is based on paradigmatic consideration. In this section, I argue that these alternatives do not succeed in accounting for the data in (14) because they result in ranking paradoxes. First, I discuss an analysis that makes use of MPARSE in section 5.1. In section 5.2, I discuss a paradigmatic approach.

5.1. MPARSE Approach

In the approach appealing to the MPARSE constraint, *GEN* produces a null parse candidate [⊙] as well as candidates with phonological substance. The input has a corresponding output if a candidate other than [⊙] wins, as illustrated in (21a). On the other hand, absolute ungrammaticality arises when [⊙] is the most harmonic, as shown in (21b) (Prince and Smolensky 2004; Raffelsiefen 2004; Wolf and McCarthy 2009). In this case, the input fails to be mapped onto a phonologically tangible output, indicating that the input has no output.

(21) a.

	GEN ↓		*EVAL* ↓	
Input	⟶	Candidate_α		
	⟶	Candidate_β	⟶	Candidate_β
	⟶	$[\odot]$		

b.

	GEN ↓		*EVAL* ↓	
Input	⟶	Candidate_α		
	⟶	Candidate_β		
	⟶	$[\odot]$	⟶	$[\odot]$

$[\odot]$ has no morphological structure, so it violates MPARSE that requires morphological parsing. The nature of $[\odot]$ becomes clearer by comparing the two situations in (22a) and (22b). They are similar in that nothing is uttered. (22a) has no phonological substance since all underlying segments are deleted. As a result, the output in (22a) violates MAX. Crucially, the input is still mapped onto a morphological form even though it is not spelled out phonetically. By contrast, (22b) invokes no segmental deletion, so MAX is respected. No faithfulness violation is incurred by $[\odot]$, indeed. Furthermore, $[\odot]$ vacuously satisfies all phonological markedness constraints because it has no phonological representation. $[\odot]$ breaches only MPARSE, so $[\odot]$ is the most harmonic when violation of MPARSE is the least expensive choice.

(22) a. $/a_1b_2c_3d_4/$ → $[\emptyset_1\emptyset_2\emptyset_3\emptyset_4]$
b. $/a_1b_2c_3d_4/$ → $[\odot]$

In order to explain absolute ungrammaticality in (14a), MPARSE and $[\odot]$ are incorporated in the analysis. In addition, $*[C^je]$ is assumed to occupy the undominated position in the constraint hierarchy. As demonstrated in (23), $*[C^je]$ rules out palatalization of the initial non-coronal consonant, and medial palatalization is penalized by the conjoined constraint. In effect, all candidates other than $[\odot]$ are eliminated by a constraint ranked over MPARSE.

(23)

	/keba,[–ant]/	*[Cʲe]	MAX [–ant]	ALIGN-L & *[–Cor]ʲ	MPARSE
a.	keba		*!		
b.	kʲeba	*!			
c.	kebʲa			*!	
d. ☞	⊙				*

The examples in (14b) are analyzed in the same way. As demonstrated in (24), the null parse candidate incurs the least violation, so the failure in the input-output mapping performs the best. The comparison of (24b) and (24d) reveals that *[–Cor]ʲ outranks MPARSE.

(24)

	/kune,[–ant]/	*[Cʲe]	MAX [–ant]	*[–Cor]ʲ	MPARSE
a.	kune		*!		
b.	kʲune			*!	
c.	kuɲe	*!			
d. ☞	⊙				*

(23) and (24) seem to suggest the success of the MPARSE approach, but this analysis encounters ranking paradoxes. First, (23) shows that the conjoined constraint needs to be ranked over MPARSE. However, the example in (3b) requires the opposite ranking. In the absence of a root-initial consonant, a root-internal non-coronal consonant may be palatalized. As shown in (25), this fact indicates that the conjoined constraint in (9) is ranked lower than MPARSE. This ranking is incompatible with the opposite ranking required for (14a).

(25)

	/ogʲa/	MPARSE	ALIGN-L & *[–COR]ʲ
a. ☞	ogʲa		*
b.	⊙	*!	

Another ranking paradox has to do with the relation between *[–Cor]ʲ and MPARSE. In (24), *[–Cor]ʲ is ranked over MPARSE, indicating that palatalization cannot target non-coronals. However, these two constraints should be ranked the other way round in (3). Palatalization can target a non-coronal consonant when a CVCV root has no coronal consonant as in (3a) and when a medial non-coronal is the sole consonant as in (3b). As illustrated in (26), MPARSE must be ranked over *[–COR]ʲ to accommodate examples as in (3).

(26)

		/poko,[–ant]/	MPARSE	*[–COR]^j
a.	☞	p^joko		*
b.		⊙	*!	

In summary, the MPARSE alternative is rejected for the empirical reason that it comes across ranking paradoxes. The absence of [C^je] is not elucidated with the MPARSE approach.

5.2. Paradigmatic Approach

This section is devoted to discussing an alternative account based upon paradigmatic consideration. The paradigmatic analysis presented below is built upon Rice (2003, 2005, 2007). The gist of the idea is schematically depicted in (27), where α and β denote morphemes and [pf] stands for a phonological form. Unlike in Control Theory and the MPARSE approach, each candidate is paradigmatic, so candidate assessment is necessarily systemic. On the one hand, no gap appears if the winning candidate has phonological forms for the entire paradigm, as illustrated in (27a). On the other hand, absolute ungrammaticality is obtained when the winner has a gap at the expense of a violation of morpheme-specific MAX. This is illustrated in (27b), where the phonological form for β is a gap.

(27) a.

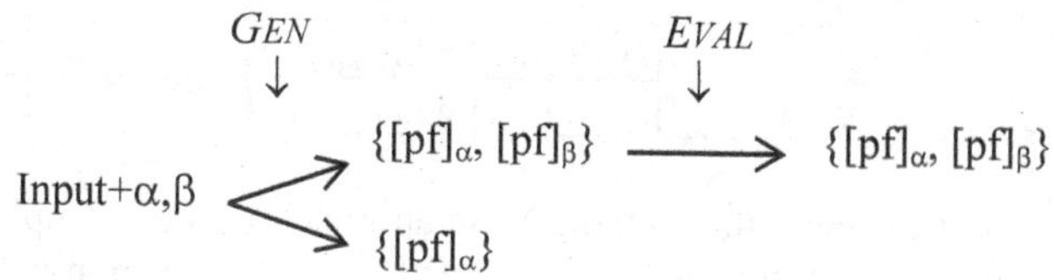

b.

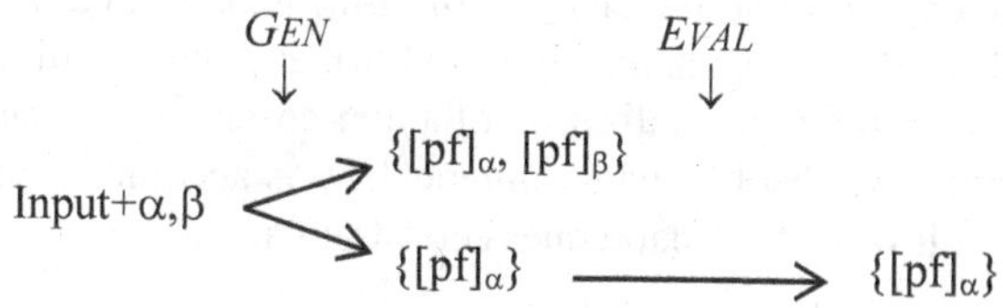

This idea is instantiated below with Norwegian imperatives analyzed by Rice (2003, 2005, 2007). Norwegian imperative forms are usually the same as bare roots (i.e., infinitives minus a final vowel), as demonstrated in (28a). No imperative form is possible, however, when the bare root has a complex coda with increasing sonority. This is shown in (28b).

(28)

	Roots	Infinitives	Imperatives	Gloss
a.	spis	spise	spis	eat
	snakk	snakke	snakk	talk
	løft	løfte	løft	lift
b.	sykl	sykle	*sykl	bike
	åpn	åpne	*åpn	open
	padl	padle	*padl	paddle

Rice assumes the three constraints in (29).

(29) a. SONSEQ: Complex codas with rising sonority are inhibited.
b. DEP: Epenthesis is forbidden.
c. $\text{MAX}_{\text{Imp.}}$: An imperative form must exist in a paradigm.

Equipped with these three constraints, the absence of imperative forms in (28b) is analyzed in (30). SONSEQ is undominated, so the offending consonantal cluster is not realized faithfully. Given that DEP outranks $\text{MAX}_{\text{Imp.}}$, however, epenthesis fares worse than making a gap in the paradigm.

(30)

	/sykl+{Inf., Imp.}/	SONSEQ	DEP	$\text{MAX}_{\text{Imp.}}$
a. ☞	$\{[\text{sykle}]_{\text{Inf.}}\}$			*
b.	$\{[\text{sykle}]_{\text{Inf.}}, [\text{sykl}]_{\text{Imp.}}\}$	*!		
c.	$\{[\text{sykle}]_{\text{Inf.}}, [\text{sykəl}]_{\text{Imp.}}\}$		*!	

Let us apply this paradigmatic approach to the examples in (14). In the following tableaux in this section, the input for a non-palatalized form is indicated by Ø. First, the analysis of (14a) is presented in (31). $*[\text{C}^{\text{j}}\text{e}]$ militates against initial palatalization in (14a), and the conjoined constraint prohibits root-internal palatalization of a non-coronal consonant. The gap in the paradigm (i.e., absolute ungrammaticality) is accounted for if MAX[–ant] is ranked below the two markedness constraints.

(31)

	/keba+{Ø,[–ant]}/	$*[\text{C}^{\text{j}}\text{e}]$	ALIGN-L & $*[\text{–COR}]^{\text{j}}$	MAX [–ant]
a. ☞	{[keba]}			*
b.	$\{[\text{keba}], [\text{k}^{\text{j}}\text{eba}]\}$	*!		
c.	$\{[\text{keba}], [\text{keb}^{\text{j}}\text{a}]\}$		*!	

The data in (14b) are explained in the same way. In this case, $*[\text{C}^{\text{j}}\text{e}]$ and $*[\text{–COR}]^{\text{j}}$ dominate MAX[–ant]. (32b) and (32c), where an uncontroled form is present in the paradigm, are ruled out by the two constraints ranked higher than MAX[–ant].

(32)

	/kune+{Ø, [–ant]}/	*[C^{j}e]	*[–COR]^j	MAX[–ant]
a. ☞	{[kune]}			*
b.	{[kune], [k^{j}une]}		*!	
c.	{[kune], [kuɲe]}	*!		

This alternative analysis is similar to the MPARSE approach in the sense that a constraint antagonistic to ineffability is ranked low in order to account for (14). Hence, the paradigmatic analysis suffers from ranking paradoxes, the same problem as the one discussed in the last section.

First, it is crucial in (31) that the conjoined constraint is ranked above MAX[–ant]. This constraint ranking implies the lack of root-internal palatalization of non-coronal consonants. This is incorrect, given the example in (3b). In order to rule in [og^{j}a-og^{j}a], MAX[–ant] should be ranked over the conjoined constraint, as already demonstrated in (11).

Second, *[–COR]^j must dominate MAX[–ant] in (32), meaning that non-coronal consonants would be never palatalized. This prediction is falsified by the fact that they are actually palatalized unless the second root consonant is a coronal (3a) or if the medial non-coronal is the only consonant (3b). This suggests that MAX[–ant] must be ranked over *[–COR]^j, as shown in (12).

In summary, the difficulty with the MPARSE and paradigmatic analyses is parallel. They encounter precisely the same ranking paradoxes.

6. Markedness Relativization

The mimetic vocabulary does not permit a sequence of a palatal(ized) consonant and [e]. However, this inhibition is not a general restriction imposed on the whole Japanese lexicon. [e] may be preceded by a palatalized consonant in the loanword stratum, as exemplified in (33).

(33)

Loanwords	*Gloss*
tʃeeN	chain
tʃekku	check
ʃeeku	shake
ʃeru	shell

This observation implies that *[C^{j}e] in the *CONTROL* component must be assigned a lexical class index such that rampant elimination of [C^{j}e] is prevented. This finding supports recent studies asserting the need of relativized markedness constraints in OT (Flack 2007; Gouskova 2007; Kurisu 2007; Pater 2007).

The necessity of relativized markedness constraints in the realm of ineffability is independently supported by data from Norwegian. As exemplified in (28b), no imperative form appears when the bare root contains a complex coda with rising sonority. As shown in (34), Norwegian singular nouns do not involve any overt affixation, as in imperatives. Unlike in imperatives, however, a complex coda with rising sonority is repaired with schwa epenthesis. SONSEQ is respected both in imperatives and singular nouns, but they behave differently when SONSEQ would be violated by the fully faithful output.

(34)	*Roots*	*Singular*	*Gloss*
	sykl	sykəl	bike
	adl	adəl	nobility
	hindr	hindər	hinder
	ordn	ordən	arrange

The difference between imperatives and singular nouns is explained by deploying markedness relativization such that SONSEQ is rendered sensitive to distinct morphosyntactic categories. On the one hand, $\text{SONSEQ}_{\text{Imp.}}$ is in *CONTROL* since violation of it immediately leads to ineffability (see (28b)). Following the analysis by Rice presented in (30), I assume that SONSEQ outranks DEP, but SONSEQ has a singular index. As shown in (35), *EVAL* chooses the faithful candidate as the best form. [sykl] is subsequently sent to the *CONTROL* component.

(35)

	$/\text{sykl}/_{\text{Imp.}}$	$\text{SONSEQ}_{\text{Sg.}}$	DEP
a. ☞	sykl	N/A	
b.	sykəl	N/A	*!

The *CONTROL* component contains SONSEQ specialized to imperatives. In (36), the output emitted by *EVAL* incurs a violation of $\text{SONSEQ}_{\text{Imp.}}$, so it is abandoned, resulting in absolute ungrammaticality.

(36)

	$/\text{sykl}/_{\text{Imp.}}$	$\text{SONSEQ}_{\text{Imp.}}$
X	sykl	*

On the other hand, epenthesis is more harmonic than faithfulness to the input in singular nouns because $\text{SONSEQ}_{\text{Sg.}}$ outranks DEP, as in (37).

(37)

	/sykl/$_{Sg.}$	SONSEQ$_{Sg.}$	DEP
a.	sykl	*!	
b. ☞	sykəl		*

The contrastive behavior of Norwegian imperatives and singular nouns thus lends support to the necessity of relativized markedness constraints in absolute ungrammaticality.

7. Conclusion

The absence of [C^{j}e] is a systematic gap in the mimetic vocabulary of Japanese. I argued in this paper that this fact should be interpreted as an instance of absolute ungrammaticality. Among the three approaches to absolute ungrammaticality proposed in OT literature, only Control Theory is capable of handling the phonotactic fact in Japanese. The *CONTROL* component is separated from *EVAL*. This means that OT is not a fully parallel framework.

Besides the necessity of relativized markedness constraints discussed in the previous section, the lack of [C^{j}e] in the Japanese mimetic vocabulary is of interest in showing that absolute ungrammaticality is not a phenomenon special to inflectional morphology even though earlier literature has discussed issues of ineffability in contexts of inflectional paradigms.

References

Alderete, J. and A. Kochetov 2009. Japanese Mimetic Palatalisation Revisited: Implications for Conflicting Directionality. Phonology 26:369-388.

Bye, P. 2007. Allomorphy – Selection, not Optimization. Freedom of Analysis?, ed. S. Blaho, P. Bye, and M. Krämer, 63-91. Berlin and New York: Mouton de Gruyter.

Flack, K. 2007. Templatic Morphology and Indexed Markedness Constraints. Linguistic Inquiry 38:749-758.

Gouskova, M. 2007. The Reduplicative Template in Tonkawa. Phonology 24:367-396.

Hamano, S. 1998. The Sound-symbolic System of Japanese. Stanford, California: CSLI.

Kurisu, K. 2007. Asymmetric Voicing and Relativized Markedness. Proceedings of the Formal Approaches to Japanese Linguistics 4:161-172.

Kurisu, K. 2009. Palatalisability via Feature Compatibility. Phonology 26:437-475.

Mester, A. and J. Itô 1989. Feature Predictability and Underspecification: Palatal Prosody in Japanese Mimetics. Language 65:258-293.

Orgun, O. and R. Sprouse 1999. From MPARSE to CONTROL: Deriving Ungrammaticality. Phonology 16:191-224.

Orgun, O. and R. Sprouse 2009. Hard Constraints in Optimality Theory. Modeling Ungrammaticality in Optimality Theory, ed. C. Rice and S. Blaho, 97-114. London: Equinox.

Pater, J. 2007. The Locus of Exceptionality: Morpheme-specific Phonology as Constraint Indexation. University of Massachusetts Occasional Papers 32: Papers in Optimality Theory III, ed. L. Bateman, M. O'keefe, E. Reilly, and A. Werle, 259-296. Amherst, Massachusetts: GLSA.

Prince, A. and P. Smolensky 2004. Optimality Theory: Constraint Interaction in Generative Grammar. Malden, Massachusetts: Blackwell.

Raffelsiefen, R. 2004. Absolute Ill-formedness and other Morphophonological Effects. Phonology 21:91-142.

Rice, C. 2003. Dialectal Variation in Norwegian Imperatives. Nordlyd 31:372-384.

Rice, C. 2005. Optimal Gaps in Optimal Paradigms. Catalan Journal of Linguistics 4:155-170.

Rice, C. 2007. Gaps and Repairs at the Phonology-Morphology Interface. Journal of Linguistics 43:197-221.

Wolf, M. and J. McCarthy 2009. Less than Zero: Correspondence and the Null Output. Modeling Ungrammaticality in Optimality Theory. ed. C. Rice and S. Blaho, 17-66. London: Equinox.

Zoll, C. 1996. Parsing below the Segment in a Constraint-based Framework. Doctoral dissertation. University of California, Berkeley.

Zoll, C. 1997. Conflicting Directionality. Phonology 14:263-286.

Tone System in Itoman[1]

NOBUTAKA TAKARA
University of California, Santa Barbara

1. Introduction

Itoman Okinawan (for short, Itoman) is one of the varieties of Ryukyuan languages. Genetically, Itoman is subclassified as a variety under Okinawan. The number of speakers of Itoman has been decreasing; most of them are in their sixties or older and are bilingual in Japanese. Hence, it can be considered that Itoman is an endangered language.

Several outstanding characteristics are observed in Itoman. One of them is that Itoman has no glottal stop as a phoneme, unlike many of the other Ryukyuan languages in which it is observed as a phoneme. Therefore, in Itoman the words for 'house' and 'you' are realized as *yaa* [ja:], which correspond to the minimal pair [ja:] 'house' vs. [ʔja:] 'you' in Shuri. Another interesting feature of Itoman is its lack of velar palatalization before/after a

[1] I would like to thank Suzy Cincone, Rose Freeman, and Matthew Gordon. Particularly, I wish to thank Matthew Gordon for helpful suggestions and comments in the phonological analysis of the tone system. My special thanks are due to the speakers of Itoman for their participating in my research. Finally, my special thanks are due to the editors of JK 20 for valuable advice. All errors are mine.

Japanese/Korean Linguistics 20.
Edited by Bjarke Frellesvig and Peter Sells.

high front vowel /i/. Therefore, the word for 'clothes,' which is pronounced as [tɕiŋ] in Shuri, is pronounced as [kiŋ] in Itoman.

One focus of linguistic research regarding Japanese and Ryukyuan languages is the tone (or 'pitch accent') system. There are four studies addressing the tone system in Itoman. However, as I will discuss in Section 2 below, all of them are either impressionistic phonetic accounts or touch on certain patterns only briefly; they give no systematic phonological account of the phonetic realization of the tones. In this paper, I will investigate the tone system in Itoman and give both phonetic and phonological explanations for this system. The structure of this paper is as follows: in Section 2, I will summarize four previous studies and discuss some limitations on these studies. In Section 3, I will present the methodology of the investigation of the tone system conducted in this paper. Section 4 will give a phonetic analysis by showing some pitch contours and a phonological analysis of the tone system based on the findings. Section 5 is the conclusion of this paper.

2. Overview of Previous Studies

Four studies have discussed the tonology of Itoman: Nakasone (ms.), Hattori (1959), Oshiro (1963), and Hirayama et al. (1966). Let me summarize each of these studies.

First, using all logically possible tone patterns for monomoraic to septamoraic words, Nakasone mainly examines the tone patterns of nouns and verbs. His findings are illustrated in Table 1:

Table 1. Tone Patterns Found by Nakasone

# of Moras	Tone Patterns and Examples
1	(H=L) (*kwa=ga* 'child=NOM')[2, 3]
2	HL (*habu* 'snake'), HH (*fushi* 'star')
3	HHH (*tiira* 'sun'), HHL (*akaa* 'red'), HLH (*yumun* 'to read')
4	HHHH (*kooin* 'to buy'), HHLH (*fuutai* 'cheek'), HHLL (*hooin* 'to crawl'), HLLH (*tariin* 'to make sake')
5	HHLLH (*kusuriyubi* 'ring finger'), HHLLL (*uuiibi* 'thumb')
6	HHLLLH (*katajikiin* 'to clean up')
7	HHLLLLH (*harakashinnan* 'slug')

Although his work contains many intriguing examples, it also raises some crucial issues. One of them is that the work contains very little information about the researchers and the dates of the research. Since this manu-

[2] The symbol '=' stands for the boundary between a word and a clitic.

[3] An actual form exemplified in Nakasone is *kwa*, i.e., without a clitic =*ga* (ms.: 292). Also in some studies this word is regarded as bimoraic, i.e., *kkwa*.

script consists of the findings made of Nakasone and by his students, it is unclear when, where, and by whom data were collected. The other issue is that no distinction is made between simple and compound nouns when the tone patterns are presented. Examples like *kusuriyubi* 'ring finger' and *harakashinnan* 'slug' consist of more than one word (*kusuri* 'medicine'+ *yubi* 'finger' and *haraka* 'bareness'+ *shinnan* 'snail').

Second, Hattori (1959), using some nouns corresponding to those in the Classified Vocabulary by Kindaichi and Wada (Kokugo Gakkai 1988: 7-10), investigates the tone patterns in Itoman and tries to determine the typological status of its tone system. He concludes that Itoman does not distinguish any tone pattern among the target words, and that the system can be classified as Class IV (1959: 279).[4]

A few issues are seen in Hattori (1959), however. He gives no detailed tone patterns of the words in Itoman. Hence, according to his description, we never know what kinds of tones (i.e., plateau, HL, LH, etc.) were realized in those words. Another is that, as Oshiro argues, the pattern Hattori discovered is limited to the variation used by fishermen. The fact that no survey of non-fishermen's variation is included means that his account fails to depict the whole picture of the typological tone system in Itoman. Finally, his conclusion about the typological classification of Shuri differs from my results based on *Okinawago jiten* (Kokuritsu Kokugo Kenkyūjo 2001): Hattori's classification is Class I, whereas my results suggest Class II.

Oshiro (1963) also examines the tonology of Itoman. Following Hattori's methodology, he mainly surveys non-fishermen's variation. He finds that words are divided into two types: (a) words with a plateau tone, e.g., *hana* 'nose' and *kii* 'hair,' and (b) those with a final H-tone (i.e., L...H or M...H), e.g., *hana* 'flower' and *kii* 'tree.' As a native speaker, Oshiro states that he tends to pronounce the words in (a) as HL (1963: 389). In addition, he mentions a tone shift whereby the H-tone of noun roots with a final H migrates to the final mora when a nominative clitic *=ga* is added, i.e., *hana* 'flower' (LH/MH) to *hana=ga* 'flower=NOM' (ML=H).

His study, however, includes some inconsistencies. According to his argument, only the final mora can be realized as a H-tone in words in (b) above (1963: 389). However, he illustrates the tone pattern of the tetramoraic trisyllabic word *furusan* 'old' as LLHH and the trimoraic disyllabic word *kakun* 'to write' as LLH (1963: 391). In the former case, the final two moras have H-tones, whereas a H-tone is located on only the final mora (i.e., a coda of the final syllable) in the latter. The other issue is the setting up of a M-tone in Itoman. In his estimation, in the case of *hana=ga* 'flower=NOM,' the initial mora has a phonetically higher tone than the second

[4] For more discussion about the classes, see Hattori (1959: 278-279)

mora and a lower tone than the final mora. However, he does not pursue the relationship between this phonetic realization and its phonological recognition. In other words, it is unclear whether native Itoman speakers really care about such a three-way acoustic difference phonologically.

The last study is Hirayama et al. (1966). According to their fieldwork with five native speakers, they conclude that in bimoraic nouns there are three tone patterns: HL (e.g., *hana* 'nose,' *haa* 'leaf'), LH (e.g., *hana* 'flower,' *haa* 'tooth'), and HH (e.g., *hai* 'needle'). In trimoraic verbs, two patterns are observed: HLL (e.g., *tubun* 'to fly') and HHH (e.g., *kakun* 'to write'). In tetramoraic adjectives, the patterns observed are three: LHLL (e.g., *achisan* 'thick'), HHHH (e.g., *takasan* 'high, tall'), and HLLL (e.g., *gassan* 'light') when the peninitial mora is nonsyllabic. They also point out that both ages and areas of their domicile are associated with different tone patterns.

In summary, although crucial observations about the tonology of Itoman have been made in the literature, there are some limitations on their studies. First, studies disagree in their accounts, leaving uncertainty about which analysis (if any) is correct. Second, particularly in Oshiro (1963), the necessity of a M-tone is unclear. Third, the relationship between the phonological analysis and the phonetic realization of the tones is not explicit in previous accounts. Taking these limitations into consideration, I will investigate the tonology of Itoman in the following sections.

3. Methodology

3.1. Data and Speakers

My data for this study were collected during three fieldwork trips to Okinawa between 2007 and 2010. The main focus was on the tonology of nouns, as well as pronouns and numerals.[5]

The number of target words, which consists of both monomorphemic and polymorphemic nouns, was 422. These words consist of the Classified Vocabulary (*Ruibetu goi* in Japanese), words listed in Oshiro (1963), and indigenous words with which the subjects were familiar. Each word was pronounced and recorded in the following contexts: (i) as a bare form, (ii) with a nominative case clitic *=ga*, (iii) with a topic marker *=ya*, and (iv) with a dative case clitic *=Nkai*. In this paper I focus on the first two contexts of the monomorphemic nouns.

Nine speakers (five male and four female) participated in this study. The range of ages was from fifty-eight through eighty-two. All participants were bilingual in Itoman and Japanese.

---

[5] The tonology of verbs and adjectives will be investigated in future research.

Usage of Itoman by these speakers is actually limited in that they choose Itoman only when they talk with the same or older generations. When talking with younger generations, they prefer to use standard Japanese. The situation they are placed in is also another crucial factor: they tend to speak Itoman in informal situations such as at lunch and dinner with close friends or at the local store, but tend to speak standard Japanese in formal situations such as at a town meeting or a lecture.

3.2. Methodology of Investigation of Tone Patterns

In this study I adopted two different methods to investigate tone patterns: impressionistic and acoustic work. To find out the impressionistic tone patterns, I asked each subject to pronounce bimoraic, trimoraic, and tetramoraic words. The patterns used by the subject were assessed by other subjects and by myself. After this assessment, I pronounced the same token with several tone patterns and the subjects chose the pattern they felt was closest to their pronunciation. This method sequence was applied to both bare forms and nouns with a clitic *=ga*.

To find out the phonetic realization as well as tone patterns in Itoman, 382 words for both bare and *=ga* forms pronounced by six subjects (three male and three female) were examined in this paper.

For the measurement of each mora, I used Praat 5.1.17 (Paul Boersma and David Weenink; www.praat.org). The pitch range was 75.0 to 500.0 Hz; the voicing threshold setting was 0.45. Three pitch measurements were taken: the pitch maximum, the pitch minimum, and average pitch. To avoid the influence of the preceding consonant, a twenty-millisecond window at the beginning of each mora was excluded from the measurements.

When a visible pitch trace showed a clear error, that part was excluded from the measurement. After the first measurement of each word, I changed the value of the voicing threshold to see whether errors were resolved; in cases where such errors were corrected, I re-measured the pitch of the mora in question.

As the final stage, the results of the measurements of different speakers were compared, and the tone patterns of the words were determined.

4. Phonological Analysis of Tonology in Itoman

4.1. Results of Tone Patterns

The patterns illustrated in Table 2 below were observed in bimoraic through tetramoraic nouns: [6]

[6] Some unexpected cases such as HL → HH=H or HHL (instead of HHH) → HHL=L were observed as phonetic realizations. It is common that only one word can be regarded as an independent utterance; a declarative clause tends to have a lower pitch at the end than non-final

Table 2. Observed Surface Tone Patterns

	Bimoraic		Trimoraic		Tetramoraic	
Bare form	*a.*	HL	*e.*	HLL	*h.*	HHLL
	b.	HH	*f.*	HHH	*i.*	HHHH
	c.	LH	*g.*	HLH	*j.*	HHLH
	d.	H				
ga-form	*a'.*	HL=L	*e'.*	HHL=L	*h'.*	HHLL=L
	b'.	HL=L or HH=H	*f'.*	HHL=L or HHH=H	*i'.*	HHLL=L
					j'.	HHLL=H
	c'.	HL=H	*g'.*	HHL=H		
	d'.	HL				

Figures 1 and 2 below illustrate the pitch contours of both bare forms and *ga*-forms. Because of space limitation, only the following bimoraic words are shown: *chii* 'blood,' *funi* 'boat,' *naa* 'you (formal),' and *mami* 'beans':

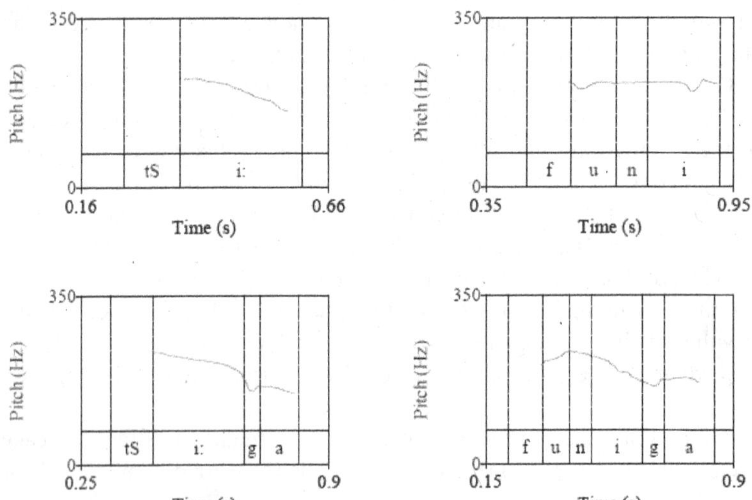

chii 'blood' (F3) *funi* 'boat' (F2)

Figure 1. Pitch Contours of chii 'blood' and funi 'boat'

---

position. Therefore, the lower pitch value in unexpected patterns can be considered a phrasal tone attributed to a boundary tone rules. Since in this paper I focus on only tone patterns of words, not phrases, I leave this issue to future study.

For *chii* 'blood,' both bare and *ga*-forms have a falling pitch trace. For *funi* 'boat', on the other hand, a pitch contour of a bare form is almost flat but that of a *ga*-form falls from the second mora. Therefore, the tone patterns of each word can be characterized as HL → HLL (for *chii*) and HH → HLL (for *funi*).

Figure 2 illustrates pitch traces of both bare and *ga*-form of *naa* 'you (formal)' and *mami* 'beans':

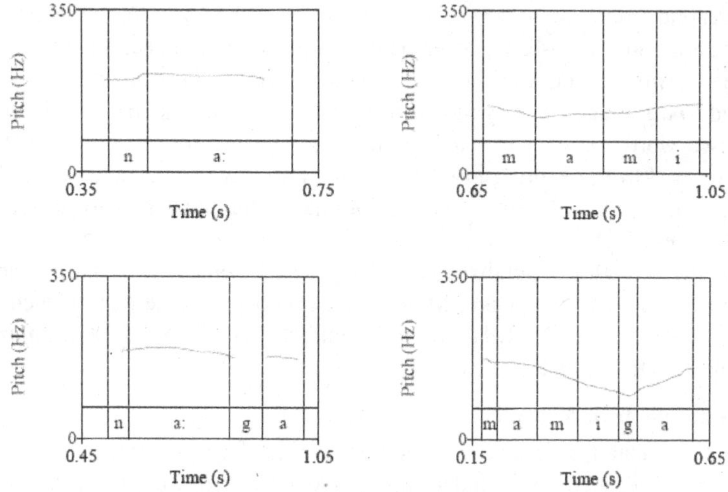

naa 'you (formal)' (F1) *mami* 'beans' (M4)

Figure 2. Pitch Contours of naa 'you (formal)' and mami 'beans'

For *naa* 'you (formal),' the pitch contours of both bare and *ga*-forms are flat. As for *mami* 'beans,' in the bare form the pitch contour of the final mora is rising and higher than that of the initial mora; in a *ga*-form, the pitch of the second mora is falling and lower than that of the initial mora, and the final mora is rising. Therefore, the tone patterns of each noun can be characterized as HH → HHH (for *naa*) and LH → HLH (for *mami*).

Interestingly, all six speakers do not necessarily have the same tone pattern for each word. For instance, although all speakers have the tone pattern HL → HLL for *chii* 'blood,' for *mami* 'beans,' on the other hand, only speaker M4 has the pattern LH → HLH whereas other speakers tend to have the pattern HH → HLL. One of the possibilities to account for this discrepancy is a historical change of the tone patterns among particular speakers/groups. Another might be related to idiolects. As space is limited, I will concentrate on the phonological analysis of the dominant tone patterns and leave examination of the minority patterns to future research.

Several intriguing features are observed in the tone patterns presented in Table 2. First, when adding a nominative clitic =*ga* to nouns, the tone shape within a noun root can be changed in some words. In the case of *chii* 'blood,' for instance, the tone shape of the bare form is HL; adding =*ga* does not affect the tone shape of the root, resulting in HLL. In the case of *chii* 'fishing hook,' which has HH in a bare form, the final mora of the root changes from H to L when adding =*ga*; finally the tone pattern of the *ga*-form turns into HLL.

Second, some nouns with a plateau tone in bare form are realized as a falling tone in the *ga*-form, whereas others preserve a plateau tone even in the *ga*-form. For instance, the tone pattern of the bare forms of *kumu* 'cloud,' *naa* 'name,' *naa* 'you (formal),' and *uta* 'song' is HH. For the former two words (*kumu* and *naa*), adding =*ga* changes the final mora of the root from H to L, resulting in HLL. For the latter two (*naa* and *uta*), on the other hand, adding a clitic =*ga* does not change the tone shape of the root, resulting in HHH.

Third, though the number is relatively small, some words (particularly in words produced by speaker Male 4) have a concave tone pattern such as *mami* 'beans' (LH → HLH), *hadaka* 'nudity' (HLH → HHLH), *saaruu* 'monkey' (HHLH → HHLLH), etc.

4.2. Phonological Analysis[7]

First, I postulate that Itoman has one lexical accent, which is presented as an asterisk '*.' This accent is underlyingly associated with a particular mora of the certain words. Words are classified into two categories: (i) words with an accent and (ii) words with no accent. Itoman also has two tonemes in (1), each of which is associated with nouns in different groups:

(1)Tonemes in Itoman
a.Toneme 1: HL; this is associated with nouns in Group 1
b.Toneme 2: LH; this is associated with nouns in Group 2; an accent with this toneme occurs on the penultimate mora of bare forms

Here I propose that the leftmost tone in each toneme (i.e., *H* in HL and *L* in LH) is linked to the accent. The location of the accent on the word also plays a crucial role in distinguishing the contrast between a falling tone (e.g., *chii* 'blood') and plateau tone (e.g., *chii* "fishing hook'): the former has an accent with HL on the initial mora, and the latter has it on the final mora.

[7] The analysis in this paper is slightly different from what was presented at the conference itself.

I also assume a rule of rightward tone spread and a default H-tone assigned to all tonally unspecified moras, i.e., those neither associated with an accent underlyingly nor receiving a tone through tone spreading.

The final ingredient in the analysis is the metrical foot. I propose that Itoman has mora-based foot construction: regardless of the syllable structure moras are parsed into feet. The direction of foot construction is right-to-left; the type of foot is iamb. In addition, I assume Weak Local Parsing as discussed in Hayes (1995: 308). That is, the initial three unparsed moras are footed based on Weak Local Parsing, which allows the leftmost two moras to be parsed into one foot.

To account for the change of the tone shape within a root when a clitic =*ga* is added, I propose a Accent Shift rule: when a nominative clitic =*ga* is added to the noun root, the accent can migrate to the leftmost foot head. Based on Accent Shift when =*ga* is added to the root, an accent with a LH-tone migrates to (a) an initial mora in bimoraic nouns, and (b) a peninitial mora in both trimoraic and tetramoraic nouns. However, the resulting patterns LHH, HLHH, and HLHHH do not correspond to the actual surface forms. Hence, I propose a Tone Flipping rule: when more than one H-tone follows a L-tone, the L-tone and the following H-tone(s) metathesize. To complete the analysis, a standard meta-constraint, Universal Tone Association Convention, presented in (2), is assumed to govern all representations:

(2) Universal Tone Association (from Haraguchi 1977: 11)
No association lines should cross.

The summary of these proposals and other required rules is illustrated and ordered in (3) overleaf.

Figure 3 (following page) demonstrates the autosegmental analysis of both bare forms and *ga*-forms of bimoraic nouns employing the rules shown in (3): (a) *chii* 'blood,' (b) *funi* 'boat,' (c) *naa* 'you (formal),' *mami* 'beans,' and *kkwa* 'child.'

(3) Summary of Rules

a. Foot Construction [FC]

i. right-to-left iambic mora-based foot with Weak Local Parsing, which creates a foot spanning the first two moras of a pentamoraic, septamoraic, and enneamoraic words to the exclusion of the third mora.

ii. A degenerate foot is allowed in Itoman.

iii. Alternative Trochaic Footing

- Trochaic footing triggered by a lexical accent can override the default iambic foot.

b. Accent Shift [AS]

- When a nominative enclitic =*ga* is added to the noun root, the accent migrates to the leftmost foot head.

c. Re-footing [RF] [8]

i. When the accent is located on a word-*initial* moraic obstruent, the accent moves to the following mora and the whole word is re-footed to make the mora bearing the shifted accent a head of the foot.

ii. When a moraic obstruent, which has a lexical accent or receives a shifted accent, is located in *non-initial* position of the word, progressive accent shift and re-footing is optional.

d. Leftmost Tone Linking [LTL]

- Link the leftmost tone of the toneme (i.e., *H* in HL and *L* in LH) to the accented mora.

e. Tone Association [TA]

- Associate the unassociated tone of the toneme to the toneless mora next to the accented mora.

f. Rightward Tone Spread [RTS]

- The rightmost tone of the toneme (i.e., *L* in HL and *H* in LH) spreads to toneless mora.

g. Tone Flipping [TF]

i. A sequence of H-tones after a L-tone is prohibited; instead, the L- and H-tones of a LH toneme metathesize.

ii. When the switched L-tone is still followed by two or mora H-tones (i.e., the H-tones derived by the Rightward Tone Spread rule), all but the final H-tones following the L-tone are deleted and the L-tone spreads, instead.

h. Tone Simplification [TS]

- Unlinked tones because of the Universal Tone Association Convention are simplified.

b. Default H-tone [DH]

- Assign a H-tone to the leftmost toneless mora.

---

[8] As space is limited, I do not present the application of the second subrule in this paper.

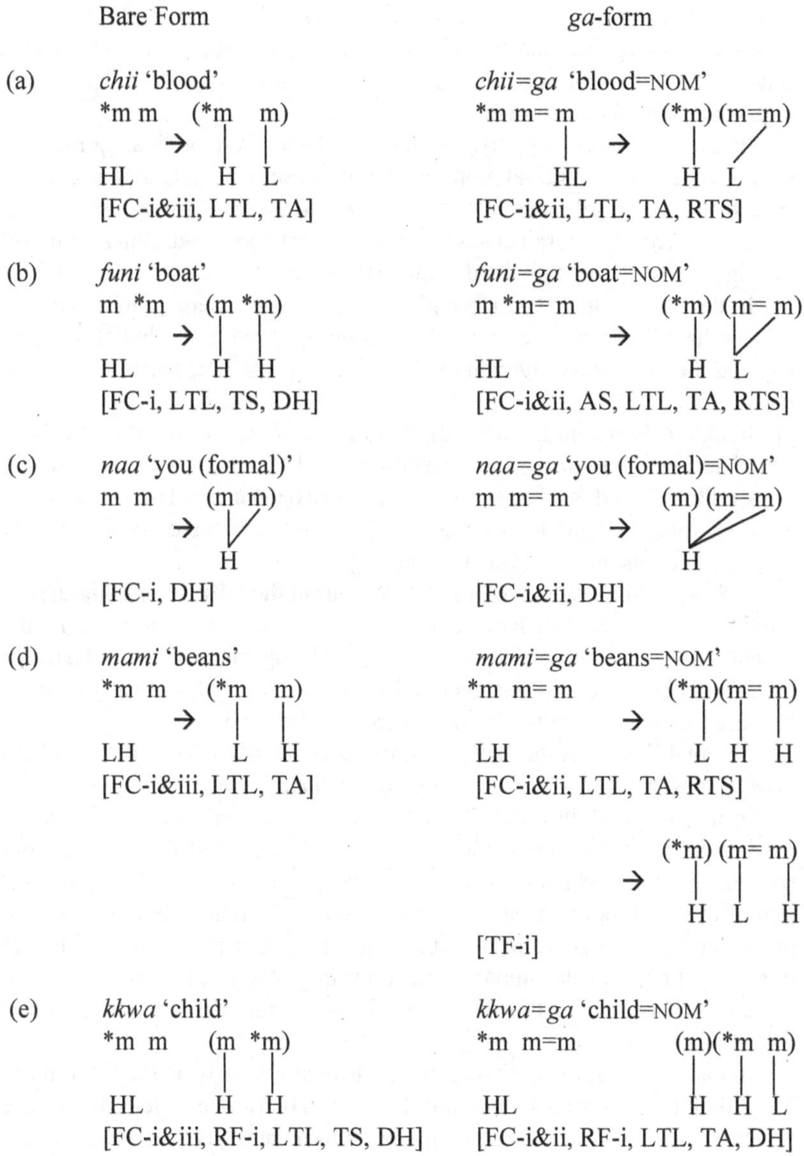

Figure 3. Autosegmental Analysis of Bimoraic Nouns

In *chii* 'blood' in Figure 3(a), a lexical accent with a HL-tone is on the initial mora. To eliminate the possibility of degenerate feet, these moras are parsed into a trochaic rather than an iambic foot. As a result, the whole word is realized as HL. In the case of *chii=ga* 'blood=NOM,' the final two moras forms one foot and the initial mora forms another foot. The accent stays on the initial mora because it belongs to the leftmost foot. Hence, the tone pattern in this form is realized as HLL.

In *funi* 'boat' in Figure 3(b), an accent is located on the final mora. A H-tone is assigned to an initial mora by DH; because of TS a L-tone is deleted. As a result, the word has a HH tone pattern. In the *ga*-form, the accent migrates to the initial mora because it is a leftmost foot head. Finally, the resulting tone pattern in this word is thus HLL.

In the case of *naa* 'you (formal)' in Figure 3(c), there is no lexical accent in the bare form. Therefore, the H-tone assigned to the initial mora by DH and the tone pattern turns into HH. Likewise, the tone pattern of the *ga*-form becomes HHH.

In *mami* 'beans' in Figure 3(d), there is a lexical accent with a LH-tone associated with the initial mora, resulting in a LH pattern. For the *ga*-form, rules LTL, TA and RTS apply, resulting in LHH. Since a H-tone sequence after a L-tone is prohibited in Itoman, TF(i) applies to the derived form and the expected tone pattern HLH is produced.

In *kkwa* 'child' in Figure 3(e), the accent on the initial mora migrates to the final mora by the rule RF, resulting in HH, Likewise, in the *ga*-form, the accent shifts to the second mora and the resulting tone pattern is HHL. In this word, phonologically assigned initial H-tone is not phonetically realized because the initial mora is a moraic voiceless obstruent.

Figure 4 illustrates the analysis of trimoraic words, (a) *wikiga* 'man,' (b) *takara* 'treasure,' (c) *unai* 'sister,' and (d) *hadaka* 'nudity.'

In *wikiga* 'man' in Figure 4(a), an accent with a HL-tone is located on the initial mora. The initial mora receives a H-tone and the second mora receives a L-tone, which spreads to the final mora. As a result, the tone pattern of this form becomes HLL. In the *ga*-form, the final two moras and the preceding two moras are parsed into separate feet. The accent, which was originally linked to the initial mora, now migrates to the peninitial mora since this mora is the leftmost foot head. As a result, the tone pattern turns into HHLL.

In *takara* 'treasure' in Figure 4(b), a lexical accent is on the final mora. The first three moras receive default H-tones. The L-tone is deleted because of TS. Hence, the tone pattern in this word turns into HHH. In the *ga*-form, since the peninitial mora is the leftmost foot head, the accent migrates to the peninitial mora. Hence, the resultant tone pattern is HHLL.

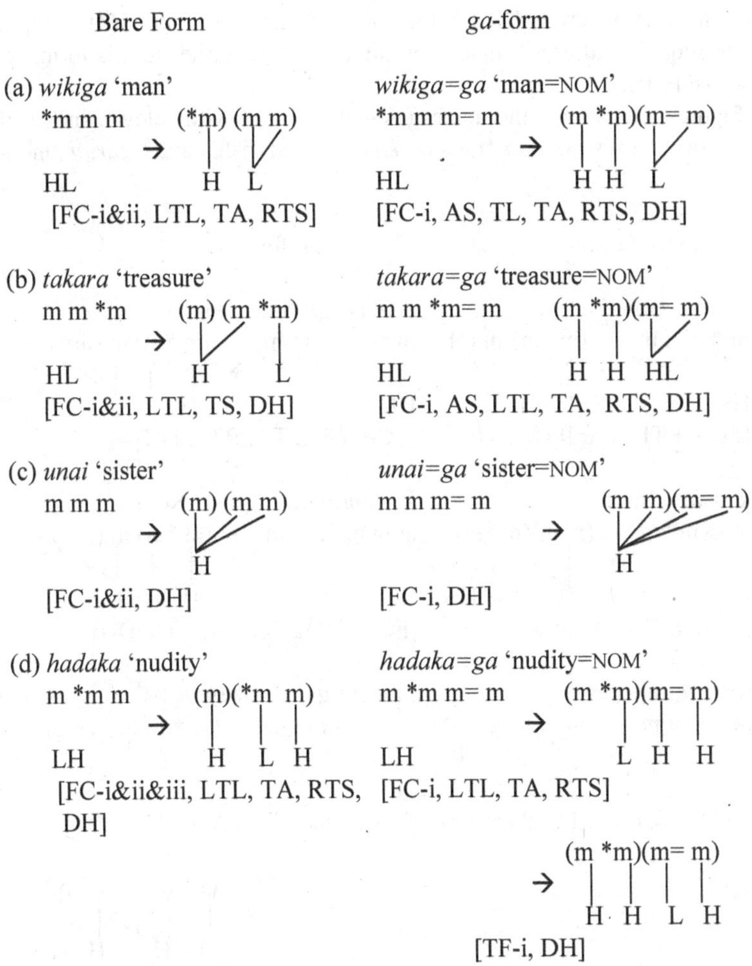

Figure 4. Autosegmental Analysis of Trimoraic Nouns

In *unai* 'sister' in Figure 4(c), there is no lexical accent. Hence, all the moras receive default H-tones, resulting in HHH. Likewise, in the *ga*-form, the tone pattern is realized as HHHH.

The last example in Figure 4 is *hadaka* 'nudity.' This word has an accent with a LH-tone on the penultimate mora. The final two moras are parsed into a trochaic foot and the penultimate and final moras are linked to L- and H-tones, respectively. The initial mora receives a default H-tone. Hence, the tone pattern of this form becomes HLH. In the *ga*-form, the accent stays on the same mora since the mora is the leftmost foot head. At this point, the tone pattern is HLHH. Like *mami* 'beans' in Figure 3(d) above, a H-tone sequence after a L-tone is prohibited, TF(i) applies to this form, resulting in HHLH.

Figure 5 illustrates the autosegmental analysis with relevant rules of tetramoraic words: *suutaa* 'father,' *kamanta* 'rayfish,' and *saaruu* 'monkey.'

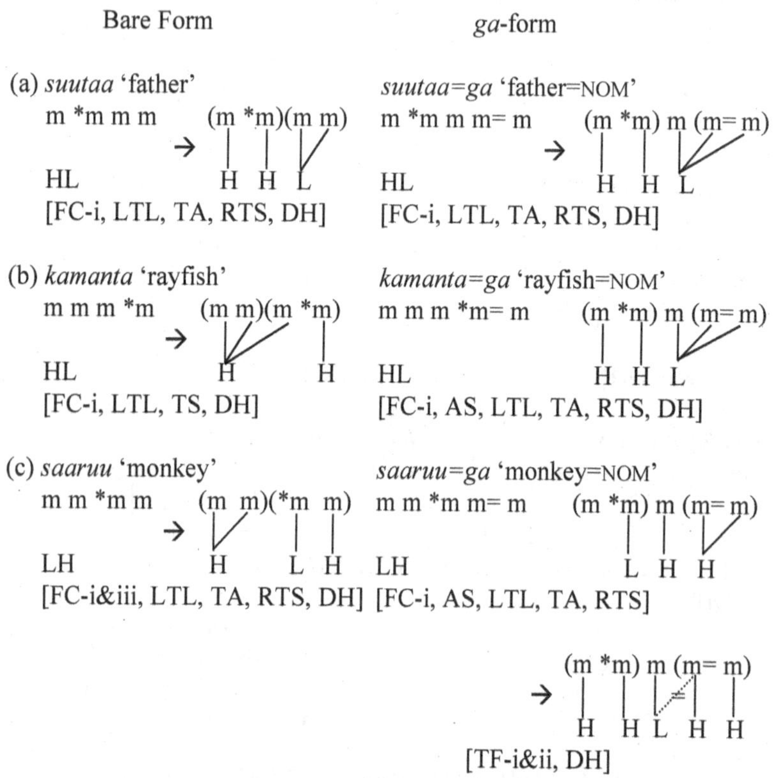

Figure 5. Autosegmental Analysis of Tetramoraic Nouns

In *suutaa* 'father,' a lexical accent with a HL-tone is linked to the peninitial mora. The peninitial and penultimate moras receive H- and L-tones, respectively; the L-tone on the penultimate mora also spreads to the final mora. The initial mora receives a H-tone by default. Therefore, the tonal shape of the whole word is HHLL. In the *ga*-form, the final two moras are parsed into a foot; Weak Local Parsing applies to the remaining three moras so that the initial two moras are parsed into a foot. The accent stays on the peninitial mora. Therefore, the tone pattern in this form turns out to be HHLLL.

The second example in Figure 5 is *kamanta* 'rayfish.' A lexical accent is linked to the final mora. Again, the L-tone is deleted by TS. Like *takara* 'treasure' in Figure 4(b), the initial three moras receive default H-tone. Hence, the tone pattern in this word becomes HHHH. In the *ga*-form, on the other hand, the accent migrates to the peninitial mora /N/ since this is the head of the leftmost foot. Therefore, this form is realized as HHLLL.

The last example is *saaruu* 'monkey' in Figure 5(c). In the bare form, a lexical accent with a LH-tone is linked to the penultimate mora; the final two moras are parsed as a trochaic foot to minimize degenerate foot formation. The tone pattern in this form surfaces as HHLH. In the *ga*-form, the accent migrates to the peninitial mora (i.e., the leftmost foot head), producing the tone pattern HLHHH. Again, the H-tone sequence after a L-tone is prohibited, TF(i) applies to this form, flip the L- and H-tone of LH toneme with one another, and turn to HHLHH. This derived form, however, contains the H-tone sequence that is a result of the spreading of H-tone in a LH toneme. By the application of TF(ii) to the derived form, the H-tone associated penultimate mora is deleted and the L-tone spreads to the penultimate mora, resulting in the expected pattern, HHLLH.

5. Conclusion

In this paper, I have investigated the tonology of Itoman. I presented an overview of four previous studies of the tonology of Itoman. Although each of these studies included intriguing discussions about the tone patterns and their characteristics, they also had several limitations. One of the limitations is that the studies disagree in their accounts. Another is that the necessity of positing a M-tone is unclear. Finally, the relationship between the phonological analysis and the phonetic realization of the tones is not explicit in previous accounts.

In order to shed light on some of the issues raised by previous research, I investigated the tone patterns of nouns, employing both impressionistic and acoustic work. In this investigation, some important facts were discovered. First, the tone shapes in Itoman are (i) falling, (ii) rising (only in bimoraic words with LH-tone), (iii) plateau, and (iv) concave. Second, when adding a nominative case clitic =*ga*, the tonal shape of the noun root can be altered. Third, some words with a plateau tone are altered to a falling tone in the *ga*-form.

Based on these facts, I proposed a phonological analysis of the tone system in Itoman. I proposed nine phonological rules and their subrules and showed through an autosegmental analysis that this set of rules can account for the tone patterns found in Itoman. By presenting pitch contours for some nouns, I also provided phonetic evidence in support of the discovered tone patterns.

References

Haraguchi, S. 1977. *The tone pattern of Japanese: an autosegmental theory of tonology*. Tokyo: Kaitakusha.

Hattori, S. 1959. *Nihongo no keito (Genealogy of Japanese)*. Tokyo: Iwanami Shoten.

Hayes, B. 1995. *Metrical Stress Theory*. Chicago and London: The University of Chicago Press.

Hirayama, T., I. Oshima, and M. Nakamoto. 1966. *Ryūkyū hōgen no sōgō-teki kenkyū (Comprehensive study of Ryukyuan dialects)*. Tokyo: Meiji Shoin.

Kokugo Gakkai, ed. 1988. *Kokugogaku dai jiten (A dictionary of traditional Japanese linguistics)*. Tokyo: Tokyo Do Shuppan.

Kokuritsu Kokugo Kenkyūjo ed. 2001. *Okinawago jiten (Okinawan dictionary)*. Tokyo: Zaimushō Insatsukyoku.

Nakasone, S. Ms. *Nakasone Seizen gengo shiryo (Linguistic Data collected by Seizen Nakasone)*. Preserved in the University of the Ryukyus.

Oshiro, K. 1963. Itoman hōgen no akusento, bunpō, goi (The Accentuation, grammar and vocabulary in Itoman dialect). *Ryūdai-Bunri-gakubu Kiyō* Vol. 7, 387-402.

Transition to a Two-Type Accent System in Tokyo Japanese? The Behavior of Surnames

TIMOTHY J. VANCE, MANAMI HIRAYAMA, & MIKIO GIRIKO
National Institute for Japanese Language and Linguistics

1. Introduction[1]

In the Tokyo Japanese pitch-accent system, the accent on an accent phrase is realized as a steep drop from a relatively high pitch to a relatively low pitch. Accent phrases (also known as minor phrases) are the units that carry the characteristic LH(L) intonation contour of this dialect. An accent phrase can range from a single word (or even just part of a long word) to several words, and speakers often have some freedom as to how many accent phrases they divide an utterance into.[2] We mark the location of an accentual

[1]The research reported here was supported in part by a grant-in-aid from the Japan Society for the Promotion of Science to the first author (no. 22820085). Early versions of this paper were presented to audiences at the Chinese University of Hong Kong.

[2]There is a vast literature on the Tokyo Japanese accent system, and interested readers can find bibliographies in introductory treatments by Kubozono (2006), Vance (2008: 142–198), and many others.

Japanese/Korean Linguistics 20.
Edited by Bjarke Frellesvig and Peter Sells.

pitch drop in phonemic transcriptions with a downward-pointing arrow, as in /ma↓kura/ 枕 'pillow' (first-syllable accent) and /omo↓ča/ 玩具 'toy' (second-syllable accent). The syllable containing the mora followed by the arrow is commonly referred to as the accented syllable. There are words with an accented last syllable, like /takara↓/ 宝 'treasure', but there are also words with no accented syllable at all, like /sakana/ 魚 'fish', and if the final syllable is short and phrase-final, as in these last two examples, the distinction between final accent and no accent is neutralized for most Tokyo speakers (McCawley 1968: 139; Haraguchi 1999: 5).[3] The difference appears only when something like the topic particle /wa/ は follows within the same accent phrase, as in /takara↓ wa/ 宝は versus /sakana wa/ 魚は.[4]

A larger intonational unit, usually called a major phrase (or intermediate phrase), consists of one or more accent phrases (seldom more than three) and is the domain of downstep (also called catathesis). Downstep means that if there is more than one accented accent phrase (and thus more than one accentual pitch drop) within a major phrase, the peak pitch in each accentual phrase after the first is noticeably lower than the peak pitch in the preceding accent phrase (Pierrehumbert and Beckman 1988: 11–12; Kubozono 1993: 180–196; Venditti 2005: 175–177). For example, the phrase *Okayama no tamago wa* 岡山の卵は 'Okayama's eggs TOP' is typically pronounced as a single major phrase containing two accent phrases: /Oka↓yama no ¦ tama↓go wa/, with the break between the two accent phrases represented by a broken vertical line. Consequently, the highest pitch in /tama↓go wa/ is lower than the highest pitch in /oka↓yama no/.

Content words are lexically specified for accent in Tokyo Japanese. For a noun with *n* syllables, there are *n*+1 possibilities for accent location: it may be accented on any of the syllables, or it may be unaccented (Haraguchi 1999: 7; Kubozono 2006: 15). But for a verb or adjective form, there are generally at most two possibilities (accented on a predictable syllable or unaccented), regardless of the number of syllables. For instance, aside from a very small number of problematic items, the citation form of a verb is either unaccented, like /hareru/ 腫れる 'swell', or accented on the second syllable from the end, like /hare↓ru/ 晴れる 'clear up' (Martin 1952: 33; Tanaka and Kubozono 1999: 80). Furthermore, nouns with *n* syllables are

[3]Some Tokyo speakers seem to maintain a distinction between final accent and no accent even when no particle follows (Sugitō 1982; Uwano 1977: 289).

[4]Since a long syllable provides ample time for the steep drop in pitch that realizes an accent, an accented long syllable starts very high and ends very low, although the tradition is to mark the accent between the two moras. It is easy to tell the difference between final accent and no accent in phrases with long final syllables, as in final-accented /ǰi‸yu↓.H/ 自由 'freedom' versus unaccented /ri‸yu.H/ 理由 'reason' (using a caret to mark a boundary between syllables and a period to mark a boundary between moras within a syllable).

nowhere near evenly distributed among the *n*+1 possibilities (Kubozono 2006: 13–15). About half of all nouns in Tokyo Japanese are unaccented, and among accented nouns that contain at least two moras, the great majority have the default accent location (McCawley 1968: 133–134; Kubozono 1989: 250; Kubozono and Honma 2002: 36–38), that is, accent on the syllable containing the third mora from the end (the second mora from the end if there are only two moras).

It is not far-fetched to predict that Tokyo Japanese will eventually develop a simpler, two-type accent system, with accented versus unaccented as the only distinctive feature. In fact, southwestern Kyūshū dialects and many languages of the Ryūkyū islands (which are closely related to Japanese) already have such two-type accent systems (McCawley 1977: 282–285). In an eye-opening study of a Kagoshima dialect that has a two-type system, Kubozono (2007) describes how Tokyo "standard" Japanese has influenced the lexical accent of individual words. To summarize Kubozono's findings, some unaccented Kagoshima words have shifted to the accented type when the corresponding Tokyo word is accented, and some accented Kagoshima words have shifted to the unaccented type when the corresponding Tokyo word is unaccented. The basic Kagoshima system is unchanged, and the actual pitch patterns on the shifted vocabulary items are often quite unlike the pitch patterns on the Tokyo items that have influenced them. It thus appears that the abstract distinction between accented and unaccented is highly salient for native speakers of this dialect. Is there any support for the notion that this same accented-versus-unaccented distinction is salient in something like the same way for native speakers of the Tokyo dialect?

2. Surnames

Japanese surnames are a subclass of nouns, and for all practical purposes, they already conform to the simpler accented-versus-unaccented system in the Tokyo dialect (Akinaga 1998: 184–185; Kindaichi and Akinaga 2001 [appendix]: 30–31). If a surname is accented, the accent almost always has the default location. For example, given the three-syllable surname *Fujita* 藤田, a speaker who does not know its accentuation only has to consider two possibilities: accented /fu↓ǰita/ or unaccented /fuǰita/. The former is correct in this case.

A few surnames are exceptional, i.e., they are accented but not on the default syllable. For example, some Tokyo speakers pronounce the surname *Maekawa* 前川 as /mae↓kawa/, with default accent, but others pronounce it /ma↓ekawa/. This variation is presumably due to the instability of the sequence /ae/.[5] For a minority of Tokyo speakers, a surname can be accented somewhere other than the default location if the default location is a syllable with a devoiced vowel. For example, some speakers treat the surname *Kita* 北 as final-accented /kita↓/ rather than initial accented /ki↓ta/ (the default), presumably because the vowel /i/ is typically devoiced.[6]

Some surnames, although only a small minority, are based on native monomorphemic nouns. Only two such surnames are among the fifty most common surnames in Japan: *Hayashi* 林 (ranked 19th) and *Mori* 森 (ranked 26th).[7] Surnames of this type are especially interesting in terms of accent. In some cases, the accentuation of the surname matches the accentuation of the common noun, but there are also many cases where the accentuation of the surname and the accentuation of the common noun do not match. Some examples are shown in (1).

(1)

COMMON NOUN	SURNAME	COMMON NOUN	SURNAME
/mori/ 森 'forest'	/mori/	/tani↓/ 谷 'valley'	/ta↓ni/
/ma↓cu/ 松 'pine'	/ma↓cu/	/tokoro↓/ 所 'place'	/to↓koro/
/hayaši/ 林 'woods'	/hayaši/		
/a↓raši/ 嵐 'storm'	/a↓raši/		

In the four examples on the left in (1), each unaccented surname corresponds to an unaccented common noun, and each accented surnames corresponds to an accented common noun with the same accent location. In the two examples on the right, however, each surname is accented and corresponds to an accented common noun, but the accent location differs.

The examples in (1) suggest the generalization in (2).

(2) PROPOSED GENERALIZATION

A surname based on a common noun is unaccented when the related noun is unaccented and accented when the related noun is accented, but an accented surname has the default accent location regardless of the accent location on the related common noun.

---

[5]For example, comprehensive dictionaries list /hai/ as an alternative pronunciation for /hae/ 蠅 'fly', and /kairu/ is a historically attested alternative pronunciation for /kaeru/ 蛙 'frog'. Present-day Tōkyō speakers seem to feel that there is a syllable boundary between the two vowels in /ae/, but they arguably treat many instances of /ai/ as a diphthong (Vance 2008: 133–138).

[6]Vance (2008: 206–214) provides an introduction to vowel devoicing in Tokyo Japanese, and Hirayama (2009) provides a comprehensive look at the theoretical issues that the phenomenon raises. The tendency to shift accent when it would fall on a syllable with a devoiced vowel has all but disappeared in recent years (Nihon Onsei Gakkai 1976: 748; Tsuchida 1997: 23–27; Hibiya 1999: 120), but two participants in the survey reported below in Section 3 said that the surname *Kita* has final accent.

[7]These are the rankings in the table provided by Niwa (2002: 19).

The pattern proposed in (2) is like the pattern of Tokyo influence on the Kagoshima dialect described in Section 1. Unfortunately, there are obvious exceptions to this appealing generalization, including the examples in (3).

(3) COMMON NOUN SURNAME
/hoši/ 星 'star' /ho↓ši/
/ho↓ri/ 堀 'moat' /hori/

3. Survey

The results of a survey conducted in the summer of 2010 indicate that the proposed generalization in (2) holds as a statistical tendency, although the exceptions are far too numerous to ignore. The first step in the survey was to compile a list of existing surnames based on monomorphemic nouns. We did this by going through a name dictionary organized by kanji (O'Neill 1972) and noting down each surname written with a single kanji if that kanji at least arguably can represent a monomorphemic common noun with the same segmental form. There were 113 items on our list, including 13 Sino-Japanese items (e.g., /se↓N/ 千).

We then recruited eleven native speakers of Japanese who grew up in the Tokyo area and asked each person to provide two sets of accent judgments. For the first set of judgments, we asked for the accent on each of our 113 items as a common noun. And for the second set, we asked for the accent on each item as a surname. Some of the participants were linguists, and we simply provided them with two printed lists, one for common noun judgments and one for surname judgments, and had them mark accent locations on their own. For example, the common noun *tani* 谷 'valley' and the corresponding surname *Tani* appeared on the lists as in (4).

(4) COMMON NOUN LIST SURNAME LIST
谷は ○ ○ ○ 谷さん ○ ○ ○ ○

Each circle represents a mora, and the participant's task was to mark the accent location (if any) in each case. The topic particle /wa/ was appended to each common noun, since, as we noted in Section 1, the distinction between final accent and no accent is neutralized for most Tokyo speakers when the last syllable of a word is short and utterance-final. The suffix /saN/ 'Mr/Ms' was appended to each surname for the same reason, since /saN/ does not alter the accent pattern that the name has in isolation (Kindaichi and Akinaga 2001[appendix]: 98). The suffix also served as a reminder that the item of interest was a surname and not the corresponding common noun. We used the same printed lists for non-linguist participants, but one of the researchers recorded each person's judgments.

When the common noun of interest was not in the participant's active vocabulary, no judgment was recorded. For example, six participants said that they did not use *hara* 原 'field' as a common noun (although all eleven participants knew the surname *Hara*). Similarly, when a participant did not know the surname of interest, no judgment was recorded. For example, only one participant claimed to know the surname *Tera* 寺, and this participant's judgments are dubious, since he or she claimed to know 98 of the 100 native Japanese items on the list as surnames. The number of surname judgments provided for these 100 items by the other ten participants ranged from a low of 22 to a high of 69 (with an average of 44.6). Of course, all eleven participants knew the common noun *tera* 'temple'.

There was broad agreement among our eleven participants for only a minority of the 100 native Japanese items, and there was unanimity for only six items. For 31 of the 100 items, at least six of our eleven participants knew both the common noun and the surname and agreed with each other on the accent judgments for both. We used this kind of consensus among six participants (a bare majority) as our working definition of broad agreement.

There were six items that at least six of the eleven participants judged to be unaccented both as a common noun and as a surname. These six items appear in (5), with the number at the left of each row indicating the number of participants who shared the accent judgments shown.[8]

(5)	PARTICIPANTS	COMMON NOUN	SURNAME
	11	/mori/ 森 'forest'	/mori/
	10	/cuǰi/ 辻 'crossroads'	/cuǰi/
	10	/hayaši/ 林 'woods'	/hayaši/
	10	/akebono/ 曙 'dawn'	/akebono/
	10	/minamoto/ 源 'source'	/minamoto/
	6	/miyako/ 都 'capital'	/miyako/

The top row in (5) shows that all eleven participants know both the common noun *mori* and the surname *Mori* and agree that both are unaccented, while the bottom row shows that six of the participants know both the common noun *miyako* and the surname *Miyako* and agree that both are unaccented. The items in (5) conform to the proposed generalization in (2) above.

[8]The common nouns corresponding to many of the surnames we chose are etymologically compounds or phrases, including /akebono/ and /minamoto/ in (5). As noted earlier, we restricted our survey items to cases involving "arguably" monomorphemic common nouns, and the two native-speaking authors were comfortable including /akebono/ and /minamoto/ in this category. The customary use of single kanji for these words in present-day orthography undoubtedly has an influence on native-speaker intuitions.

There were five items that at least six of the eleven participants judged to have the default accent location both as a common noun and as a surname. These five items appear in (6).

(6)	PARTICIPANTS	COMMON NOUN	SURNAME
	10	/ma↓cu/ 松 'pine'	/ma↓cu/
	10	/a↓raši/ 嵐 'storm'	/a↓raši/
	9	/se↓ki/ 関 'barrier'	/se↓ki/
	7	/na↓ka/ 仲 'relationship'	/na↓ka/
	6	/mi↓ne/ 峰 'peak'	/mi↓ne/

The items in (6) conform to the proposed generalization in (2).

There were seven items that at least six of the eleven participants judged to have a non-default accent location as a common noun but the default location as a surname. These seven items are shown in (7).

(7)	PARTICIPANTS	COMMON NOUN	SURNAME
	11	/tani↓/ 谷 'valley'	/ta↓ni/
	11	/tokoro↓/ 所 'place'	/to↓koro/
	10	/kiši↓/ 岸 'shore'	/ki↓ši/
	9	/šima↓/ 島 'island'	/ši↓ma/
	8	/haši↓/ 橋 'bridge'	/ha↓ši/
	7	/numa↓/ 沼 'marsh'	/nu↓ma/
	7	/hama↓/ 浜 'beach'	/ha↓ma/

The items in (7), like those in (5) and (6), conform to the proposed generalization in (2).

There were twelve items that at least six of the eleven participants judged to be unaccented as a common noun but accented as a surname. These items are shown in (8).

(8)	PARTICIPANTS	COMMON NOUN	SURNAME
	11	/niši/ 西 'west'	/ni↓ši/
	11	/hoši/ 星 'star'	/ho↓ši/
	11	/higaši/ 東 'east'	/hi↓gaši/
	10	/izumi/ 泉 'spring'	/i↓zumi/
	10	/minami/ 南 'south'	/mi↓nami/
	9	/oka/ 丘 'hill'	/o↓ka/
	9	/sugi/ 杉 'cedar'	/su↓gi/
	9	/taira/ 平 'level'	/ta↓ira/
	8	/kita/ 北 'north'	/ki↓ta/
	7	/oki/ 沖 'offing'	/o↓ki/
	7	/tawara/ 俵 'bale'	/ta↓wara/
	6	/taki/ 滝 'waterfall'	/ta↓ki/

The items in (8) contradict the proposed generalization in (2).

There was only one item that at least six of the eleven participants judged to be accented as a common noun but unaccented as a surname. This item is shown in (9).

(9) PARTICIPANTS	COMMON NOUN	SURNAME
8	/ho↓ri/ 堀 'moat'	/hori/

The item in (9), like those in (8), contradicts the proposed generalization in (2).

To summarize the items on which our participants showed broad agreement (though seldom unanimity), most conform to the proposed generalization in (2), but many do not. Almost all the items that contradict the generalization are cases where the common noun is unaccented but the surname is accented, i.e. those listed in (8).

In most cases where there was a lack of consensus, the cause was simply that most of our participants did not know the item as a surname. For example, six of our eleven participants did not know the surname *Ike* 池, but all eleven agreed that the common noun *ike* 'pond' has final accent (/ike↓/), and the five who did know the surname all agreed that it has default accent (/i↓ke/). However, there was also considerable disagreement on many items. One example is *miya* 宮 'shrine'. As shown in (10), the eight participants who knew the surname all agreed that it has initial (i.e. default) accent, but there was no consensus about the accent on the common noun, and two participants said that they do not know or do not use the common noun.

(10) PARTICIPANTS	COMMON NOUN	SURNAME
3	/mi↓ya/	/mi↓ya/
3	/miya↓/	/mi↓ya/
1	/miya/	/mi↓ya/
1	—	/mi↓ya/
1	/miya↓/	—
1	/miya/	—
1	—	—

To give just one more example of disagreement, all eleven participants said that the common noun *miyako* 都 'capital' is unaccented. As shown in (5) above, six participants said that the surname *Miyako* is also unaccented, but three participants said that it is accented, as in (11).

(11) PARTICIPANTS	COMMON NOUN	SURNAME
6	/miyako/	/mi↓yako/
3	/miyako/	/mi↓yako/
2	/miyako/	—

Moving on to a statistical analysis of the data from all eleven participants, we tabulated every case in which a participant gave an accent judgment both for the common noun and for the related surname. These responses can be displayed as the 2×3 contingency table in (12).

(12)

COMMON NOUN	SURNAME: UNACCENTED	SURNAME: DEFAULT	TOTAL
UNACCENTED	74	165	239
NONDEFAULT	21	144	165
DEFAULT	0	111	111
TOTAL	95	420	515

The result of applying chi-square to this table is significant: $\chi^2(2)=53.581$, $p<.001$. The results of residual analysis (adjusted residuals) were also significant: (1) an unaccented judgment for a common noun significantly increased the likelihood of an unaccented judgment for the related surname ($Z=6.814$, $p<.001$); (2) a nondefault accent judgment for a common noun significantly increased the likelihood of an accented judgment for the related surname ($Z=2.298$, $p<.05$); and (3) a default accent judgment for a common noun significantly increased the likelihood of an accented judgment for the related surname ($Z=5.657$, $p<.001$). In short, the responses reported in (12) conform to the proposed generalization in (2) to a statistically significant degree.

Notice, however, that an even simpler generalization than the one proposed above predicts the response data more accurately. To make comparison more convenient, we repeat the earlier generalization in (13) and state the alternative in (14).

(13) PROPOSED GENERALIZATION=(2)
A surname based on a common noun is unaccented when the related noun is unaccented and accented when the related noun is accented, but an accented surname has the default accent location regardless of the accent location on the related common noun.

(14) ALTERNATIVE GENERALIZATION
A surname based on a common noun is accented and has the default accent location.[9]

[9]Since so few of the relevant surnames are longer than three moras, default almost always means initial. The only four-mora surnames listed above are *Akebono* and *Minamoto* in (5), and since both are unaccented, they do not bear on the question of whether (14) should specify initial accent rather than default accent. A similar question arises below in Section 4.

As (15) shows, the proposed generalization in (13) correctly predicts 329 (64%) of the 515 judgments reported in (12): 74 cases of an unaccented surname corresponding to an unaccented common noun, 144 cases of a default-accented surname corresponding to a nondefault-accented common noun, and 111 cases of a default-accented surname corresponding to a default-accented common noun (74+144+111=329).

(15)

		SURNAME		
		UNACCENTED	DEFAULT	TOTAL
COMMON NOUN	UNACCENTED	**74**	165	239
	NONDEFAULT	21	**144**	165
	DEFAULT	0	**111**	111
	TOTAL	95	420	515

And as (16) shows, the simpler alternative generalization in (14) correctly predicts 420 (82%) of the 515 judgments reported in (12), i.e. all cases of an accented surname. The corresponding common noun is unaccented in 165 cases, nondefault-accented in 144 cases, and default-accented in 111 cases (165+144+111=420).

(16)

		SURNAME		
		UNACCENTED	DEFAULT	TOTAL
COMMON NOUN	UNACCENTED	74	**165**	239
	NONDEFAULT	21	**144**	165
	DEFAULT	0	**111**	111
	TOTAL	95	420	515

4. Pseudonyms

Despite the many exceptions to the proposed generalization in (2)/(13), it seems possible that it might be a productive pattern when common nouns are used as surnames that are nicknames or pseudonyms. Writers and entertainers often adopt pseudonym surnames that are based on monomorphemic common nouns. In some cases, the pseudonym is an existing surname. For example, the television personality Tokoro Jōji 所ジョージ (real name Haga Takayuki 芳賀隆之) was born in the city of Tokorozawa 所沢 in Saitama Prefecture, so his adopted surname is a tribute to his hometown. As shown in (1) and (7) above, the surname /to$^{\downarrow}$koro/ is based on the common noun /tokoro$^{\downarrow}$/ 'place'.

There is a complication with the names of famous people that requires mention here. In general, when a person has an accented surname, that person's full name is pronounced as two accent phrases within a single major phrase (see Section 1), as in (17).

(17) /yama↓zaki ¦ ma↓sako/ 山崎雅子
surname: /yama↓zaki/; given name: /ma↓sako/

However, even though the surname /toku↓gawa/ 徳川 is accented, the name of the famous historical figure Tokugawa Ieyasu is usually unified into a single accent phrase: /tokugawa ie↓yasu/ 徳川家康 (Kindaichi and Akinaga 2001[appendix]: 36). The same sort of unification is possible for /tokoro ǰo↓Hǰi/ 所ジョージ, but when one refers to Tokoro Jōji as just *Tokoro-san* 所さん 'Mr. Tokoro', the accent on the surname appears as expected: /to↓koro+saN/.

As a way of investigating whether the proposed generalization in (2) and (13) represents a productive pattern, we have contemplated asking native speakers of Tokyo Japanese to use appropriate common nouns as novel (nickname or pseudonym) surnames. But the intuitions of native-speaking linguists strongly suggest that such an endeavor would be fruitless. As an illustration, imagine that a person by the name of Suzuki Tarō becomes a television personality. If Mr. Suzuki is an entomologist specializing in praying mantises, he might adopt the word /ka↓makiri/ 蟷螂 'praying mantis' as a pseudonym surname, and if he is the president of a toy company, he might adopt the word /omo↓ča/ 玩具 'toy'. The proposed generalization predicts that these pseudonyms would have default accent (/kama↓kiri+saN/ 'Mr. Kamakiri' and /o↓moča+saN/ 'Mr. Omocha'), but our preliminary inquiries have given us no reason to believe ordinary native speakers would actually respond to such a scenario by shifting the accent in this way. Instead, speakers just retain the accentuation of the common noun: /ka↓makiri+saN/ and /omo↓ča+saN/. Notice, incidentally, that this retention is also inconsistent with an alternative to (2)/(13) that specfies initial accent rather than default accent. Since the common noun /ka↓makiri/ is initial-accented, retention in the pseudonym is consistent with the claim that all accented pseudonyms have initial accent, but the accent location in /omo↓ča/ is neither initial nor default.[10]

Before moving on to our conclusion, we should mention one other dead end. There is a common nickname pattern that involves shortening a surname to its first two moras, which often constitute a morpheme, and adding the hypocoristic suffix /čaN/. As it turns out, a nickname of this kind is initial-accented regardless of its source, as the examples in (18) show.

[10]See note 9 above.

(18)

COMMON NOUN	SURNAME	NICKNAME
/haꜜto/ 鳩 'dove'	/hato+yama/ 鳩山	/haꜜto+čaN/ 鳩ちゃん
/muraꜜ/ 村 'village'	/mura+kami/ 村上	/muꜜra+čaN/ 村ちゃん
/tori/ 鳥 'bird'	/tori+tani/ 鳥谷	/toꜜri+čaN/ 鳥ちゃん

There is no connection between the accent on the nickname and the accent on the corresponding common noun in these cases.

5. Conclusion

To recap, the generalization suggested in (2)/(13) is that a surname based on a monomorphemic common noun is unaccented when the related noun is unaccented and default-accented when the related noun is accented. We saw in Section 3 that existing surnames of the relevant type conform to this generalization to a statistically significant degree, but we also saw that there are many exceptions. The upshot of the discussion in Section 4 is that we cannot expect pseudonym surnames to conform to this generalization, except in those uninteresting cases where the pseudonym is just an existing surname that someone has adopted. About all we can reasonably say is that surnames based on monomorphemic nouns provide some weak support for the salience of the accented-versus-unaccented distinction in Tokyo Japanese.

In some cases, there is a diachronic explanation for a deviation from the proposed generalization in (2)/(13). For example, for all eleven of our survey participants the surname *Higashi* 東 is accented /hiꜜgaši/, while the corresponding common noun is unaccented /higaši/ 'east', as in (8). However, a well-known pronunciation dictionary (Kindaichi and Akinaga 2001) lists the common noun as final-accented /higašiꜜ/ and gives unaccented /higaši/ as a newer alternative. This dictionary entry suggests that the surname was based on the older (accented) version of the common noun and actually conformed to the proposed generalization when it was first adopted.

The same dictionary (Kindaichi and Akinaga 2001) also has an entry for the surname *Mori* 森, which appears above in (1) and (5). For all eleven of the survey participants, this surname and the corresponding common noun *mori* 'forest' are both unaccented /mori/, but the dictionary gives accented /moꜜri/ as a newer alternative for the surname. This accented version of the surname conforms to the simpler alternative generalization in (14), which just says that all surnames based on monomorphemic common nouns are default-accented. Incidentally, we also collected data from one speaker who was over 80 years old, although we did not include these responses in the results reported in Section 3. Unlike any of the eleven survey participants, who were all more than twenty years younger, this elderly speaker said that the surname *Mori* is accented, which leaves us wondering what to make of the characterization "newer" in the dictionary entry.

In any case, what these examples show is that once a common noun becomes a surname, the surname takes on a life of its own, independent of its source noun. The opaque spelling (with *x*) of the English surname *Nixon* (< *Nick's son*) indicates a similar loss of connection between a surname and its etymological source. Given the prodigious memory that ordinary speakers seem to have for the details of pronunciation, Tokyo speakers probably just memorize the accent pattern on each surname they encounter, one by one. It is not necessary to extract any regularities concerning surnames and corresponding common nouns. For non-native learners of Japanese, this is just one more instance of frustrating behavior in the Tokyo accent system, but for native speakers, this kind of thing is entirely trivial.

References

Akinaga, K. 1998. Kyōtsūgo no Akusento. *Nihongo Hatsuon Akusento Jiten*, ed. NHK Hōsō Bunka Kenkyūjo, 174–221. Tokyo: Nihon Hōsō Shuppankai.

Haraguchi, S. 1999. Accent. *The Handbook of Japanese Linguistics*, ed. N. Tsujimura, 1–30. Oxford: Blackwell.

Hibiya, J. 1999. Variationist Sociolinguistics. *The Handbook of Japanese Linguistics*, ed. N. Tsujimura, 101–120. Oxford: Blackwell.

Hirayama, M. 2009. Postlexical Prosodic Structure and Vowel Devoicing in Japanese. Doctoral dissertation, University of Toronto.

Kindaichi, H., and K. Akinaga, eds. 2001. *Shin Meikai Nihongo Akusento Jiten.* Tokyo: Sanseidō.

Kubozono, H. 1989. The Mora and Syllable Structure in Japanese: Evidence from Speech Errors. *Language and Speech* 32:249–278.

Kubozono, H. 1993. *The Organization of Japanese Prosody.* Tokyo: Kurosio.

Kubozono, H. 2006. *Akusento no Hōsoku.* Tokyo: Iwanami Shoten.

Kubozono, H. 2007. Tonal Change in Language Contact: Evidence from Kagoshima Japanese. *Tones and Tunes Volume 1: Typological Studies in Word and Sentence Prosody*, ed. T. Riad and C. Gussenhoven, 323–351. Berlin: Mouton de Gruyter.

Kubozono, H., and T. Honma. 2002. *Onsetsu to Mōra.* Tokyo: Kenkyūsha.

Martin, S. E. 1952. *Morphophonemics of Standard Colloquial Japanese.* Supplement to *Language* (*Language* Dissertation No. 47).

McCawley, J. D. 1968. *The Phonological Component of a Grammar of Japanese.* The Hague: Mouton.

McCawley, J. D. 1977. Accent in Japanese. *Studies in Stress and Accent* (Southern California Occasional Papers in Linguistics, 4), ed. L. M. Hyman, 261–302. Los Angeles: Department of Linguistics, University of Southern California.

Nihon Onsei Gakkai, ed. 1976. *Onseigaku Daijiten.* Tokyo: Sanshūsha.

Niwa, M. 2002. *Nihonjin no Myōji.* Tokyo: Kōbunsha.

O'Neill, P. G. 1972. *Japanese Names: A Comprehensive Index by Characters and Readings.* New York: Weatherhill.

Pierrehumbert, J., and M. Beckman. 1988. *Japanese Tone Structure.* Cambridge: MIT Press.

Sugitō, M. 1982. Tōkyō Akusento ni okeru "Hana" to "Hana" no Seisei to Chikaku. *Onsei Gakkai Kaihō* 129:1–4.

Tanaka, S., and H. Kubozono. 1999. *Nihongo no Hatsuon Kyōshitsu.* Tokyo: Kuroshio Shuppan.

Tsuchida, A. 1997. Phonetics and Phonology of Japanese Vowel Devoicing. Doctoral dissertation, Cornell University.

Uwano, Z. 1977. Nihongo no Akusento. *Iwanami Kōza Nihongo 5: On'in*, ed. S. Ōno and T. Shibata, 281–321. Tokyo: Iwanami Shoten.

Vance, T. J. 2008. *The Sounds of Japanese.* Cambridge: Cambridge University Press.

Venditti, J. 2005. The J_ToBI Model of Japanese Intonation. *Prosodic Typology: The Phonology of Intonation and Phrasing*, ed. Sun-Ah Jun, 172–200. Cambridge: Cambridge University Press.

Part IV

Experimental Linguistics

Japanese and Korean Speakers' Production of Mimetic Words*

NORIKO IWASAKI, LUCIEN BROWN
School of Oriental and African Studies, University of London

SOTARO KITA
University of Birmingham

DAVID VINSON
University College London

Both Japanese and Korean ('J' and 'K' henceforth) have similarly extensive mimetic or sound symbolic systems (Cho 2006). A comprehensive J mimetic dictionary written in English by Kakehi, Tamori, and Schourup (1996) consists of over 1,400 pages of mimetic words' meanings and examples. Recent mimetic dictionaries such as Yamaguchi (2003) and Ono (2007) have as many as 2,000 entries and 4,500 entries, respectively. Yet, according to Noma (1998) and E-A. Lee (2001), K has a more extensive repertoire

* This study was funded by a British Academy Small Grant and by a SOAS Seedcorn Grant. We would like to express our sincere gratitude to Professor Deok-Jae Park, Professor Yayoi Oshima, and Miss Sunhwa Kim, whose help in data collection was indispensable for this research. We are also very grateful for the audience at JK20 who provided us with many valuable comments and to Professor Bjarke Frellesvig and Professor Peter Sells for making JK20 and this volume possible and for their kindness and patience in editing our paper.

Japanese/Korean Linguistics 20.
Edited by Bjarke Frellesvig and Peter Sells.

of mimetic words. A dictionary written by Aoyama (1972), for example, contains about 8,800 entries.[1] J and K both have rich repertoires of phonomimes (auditory mimetics), phenomimes (visual or tactile mimetics) and psychomimes (mimetics referring to inner feelings). But it is not the sheer number of the mimetic words that make the place of mimetics significant in these two languages. Their sound-symbolic systems are highly developed (Garrigues 1995, Hamano 1998) and they are also indispensible in vivid and rich descriptions and narratives both in spoken and written languages (including literary works) (Song 2005, Yamaguchi 2002).

With both J and K mimetics having similarly highly developed sound-symbolic systems, comparing the two systems has been a popular topic for previous research (e.g. Garrigues 1995, Kang 1993, E-A. Lee 2001, Shibasaki 2002). A number of both similarities and differences are identified. We will first summarize findings related to the sound-symbolism of mimetic words in past research and discus some methodological concerns about these previous studies. We will then present the current study, in which we use auditory and pictorial experiments to assess how J and K speakers use mimetic words to describe identical stimuli.

1. Previous Studies

1.1. Findings on Similarities and Differences

Having compared the phonology and morphology of J and K mimetic words, Garrigues (1995) concludes that sound-symbolic systems in the two languages are strikingly parallel in their use of similar mechanisms of symbolic sound alternation, suffixation and reduplications. There are also a number of possible J-K cognates such as *kara-kara* vs. *k^hal-k^hal* for loud laughter, *tobo-tobo* vs. *t^həpək-t^həpək* 'plodding, trudging', *noro-noro* vs. *nɯlək-nɯlək* 'slowly' (Garrigues 1995: 393).[2]

In both languages, base forms (roots) of mimetic words can be altered by changing vowels or consonants, by reduplicating, vowel lengthening, or by adding extenders such as *–ri,* moraic /N/, and /Q/[3] in J and *–ək, -ətək, and –əng, ətəng, -ɯtəng* in K (Garrigues 1995: 363).[4] These alterations result in important changes in meaning.

Vowel alternation is meaningful in both languages but according to patterns that are at times claimed to be contradictory. For example, the J vowel

[1] But as Lee (2001) noted, the numbers of dictionary entries vary by such factors as how mimetic words are defined and whether to list different words involving sound alternations as separate entries. Hence, we cannot claim conclusively that Korean has more mimetic words.

[2] The words in text are all shown in phonemic transcriptions adopted by the current authors.

[3] /Q/ stands for the first half of geminate cluster (Hamano 1998:2), or what Vance (2008: 106) refers to as a 'mora obstruent'.

[4] These K suffixes may not be as pervasive as the J suffixes.

alternation is in accord with oft-cited 'universal' sound symbolism (see, for example, Nuckolls 1999) in that the low back vowel /a/ is augmentative (connoting largeness) and high front /i/ is diminutive (connoting smallness). The K counterparts are reported to connote the opposite: /a/ smallness and /i/ largeness (Kim 1977), similarly to Bahnar, a Mon-Khmer language of Vietnam, in which /i/ is augmentative (Diffloth 1994).

In K, there are distinctive classes of vowels, bright vowels (e.g. /a/, /o/ and /ɛ/), dark vowels (e.g. /u/, /e/ and /ə/), and neutral vowels (e.g. /i/ and /ɯ/ (or /ɨ/)). The bright vowels are said to symbolize smallness along with lightness, sharpness, brightness, and quickness, and the dark vowels their opposites (see Sohn 1999, for example). In J, some researchers attempted to rank all five vowels in terms of their size symbolism such as /a/ > /e/ > /u/ > /o/ > /i/ though the placement of /e/ and /u/ were reported to be unstable (e.g., Kobayashi 1933 cited by Hamano 1998, Otsubo 1989). However, Hamano (1998) considers it 'futile to try to place the five vowels in a linear order' (101). She only considers /a/ as symbolizing 'large area' and /u/ and /o/ as symbolizing 'small protruded opening' and 'small area', respectively, and regards /e/ as not participating in size-shape symbolism at all (Hamano 1998: 100). Besides the shape-size symbolism, the vowel /i/ symbolizes 'straightness, high-pitched sound' (Hamano 1998: 100) and quickness (Asano, 1978: 19), /o/ 'inconspicuousness and modestness', and /a/ 'totality of the object and conspicuousness', and /e/ 'vulgarity' (Hamano 1998:100).

Consonant alternation is also meaningful in both languages. In J, the consonant alternation of voiced vs. voiceless obstruents (/b/, /d/, /g/. /z/ vs. /p/, /t/, /k/, /s/) symbolizes 'heavy/large/coarse/thick' vs. 'light/small/ fine/thin'. In K the three-way alternation between the plain/lax /p, t, k, č/, their tense counterparts /p', t', k', č'/ and the aspirated forms /p^h, t^h, k^h, $č^h$/ is said to symbolize the degree of intensity with the plain consonants the least intense (Garrigues 1995). Because both vowel alternation and consonant alternation are related to the size of the signified in J whereas K vowel and consonant alternation appear to have distinctive functions, Garrigues concludes that whereas K has a clear distinction between the functions of vowel alternation and consonant alternation, it is not so clear-cut in J.

However, Hamano (1998) makes a distinction between the two types of alternations in J by assigning vowel alternation primarily to 'shape symbolism' and only secondarily to 'size symbolism' while voiced-voiceless alternation defines the mass of objects (130). Moreover, voiced-voiceless alternation appears to be more pervasive than vowel alternation (e.g. Shibasaki 2002). On the other side, the K three-way alternation may not be as clearly distinguished from the size symbolism of vowel alternation as Garrigues (1995) claims. According to Sohn (1999), the plain/lax consonants tend to connote 'slowness, gentleness, heaviness, and bigness', their tense counterparts 'compactness, tightness, hardness, smallness, and extra swiftness', and the aspirated forms 'flexibility, elasticity, crispness' (97).

Although descriptive comparisons of J and K mimetics abound, there is little in the way of experimental research. One exception is Shibasaki (2002), although this experimental study only features one informant from each language. He examined whether a K-speaking informant can understand the meaning of J mimetic words (phonomimes, phenomimes, and psychomimes) and whether a J-speaking informant can understand the meaning of the K counterparts. The informants could understand the meanings of phonomimes more easily than phenomimes, followed by psychomimes. He concluded that phonomimes in J and K are similar to each other while psychomimes are language-specific. He noted that some sounds, particularly animal noises, are perceived as being relatively "fixed." He also made an observation that J may have more psychomimes than K does.

Across languages, sound symbolism such as discussed above is generally explained by 'iconicity', namely resemblance between the symbol (word) and the signified (what it refers to). From this view, the informant's ease of understanding K and J phonomimes in Shibasaki's (2002) study is due to a higher degree of iconicity observed in phonomimes as compared to phenomimes and psychomimes. Fischer (1999) identifies three types of iconicity: 'Auditory iconicity' (seen in phonomimes), 'articulatory iconicity' (manner of articulation or position/shape of articulatory organs resemble the signified), and 'associative iconicity' (speakers associate sound or sound combination with certain meanings). Auditory iconicity appears to be the most iconic followed by articulatory and associative iconicity represented in phenomimes and psychomimes. Iwasaki, Vinson, and Vigliocco's (2007) work on English speakers' interpretation of J phonomimes and phenomimes also supports this.

Extent of iconicity is also said to be manifested in the forms of mimetic words in J and K. Hamano (1998) classified J mimetic words based on the type of roots: CV-based (e.g. *piQ, piN, pipi*) and CVCV-based (e.g. *pikuQ, pikuN, piku-piku*). She regards CV-based mimetic words as more iconic and found that sound symbolism is realized somewhat differently depending on which type of word and where the consonant or vowel occurs. M. Lee (2003) found that K sound-symbolic system is similar to the J system that Hamano (1998) identified in that monosyllabic CV(C)-based words are more iconic than disyllabic CV(C)VC-based words.

1.2. Problems

The comparisons of the J and K sound-symbolic systems in the studies above have relied upon examination of minimum pairs or triplets, their translation equivalents, and the judgments of the authors themselves. At times, particularly in earlier research, the impression is that the authors may have selected only the examples that are compatible with their pre-held beliefs. Although Shibasaki (2002) represents an isolated experimental work, the sample size is very limited.

Furthermore, translation equivalents may not always capture the kind of sensation (aural, visual, or tactile images) that speakers intend to convey by the mimetic words. For example, an imagined aural image of a dog's barking/crying may vary between cultures and among individuals; thus, individuals may select different mimetic expressions depending on their aural image. Interestingly, Yamaguchi (2002) found the mimetic word associated with dogs before the Edo Period was *biyo*, strikingly different from the modern *wanwan*. She attributed this difference to the fact that dogs described in early literature were wild dogs, and people heard them howl. According to Yamaguchi, in the Edo period both of these expressions were used but to refer either to howling or barking, respectively.

Due to these problems, the data in previous literature has only captured the most commonly believed stereotypical features of J and K mimesis. There has, to this point, been no way to ascertain how these claims relate to the way that J and K speakers actually describe sounds, states, and manners of the same value by using mimetic words.

2. Current Study

2.1. Objective

The current study uses two sets of experiments (an auditory experiment and a pictorial experiment for each language group) in which J and K speakers were asked to respond to the same auditory and pictorial stimuli. By using the same stimuli for both language groups, we are able to investigate similarities and differences between the actual mimetic words produced to describe the same sounds and the same (or nearly the same) events in the two languages. In so doing, we empirically evaluate the claims made in previous studies and provide (counter-)evidence for them.

2.2. Participants, Materials and Procedures

The auditory stimuli were selected from .wav files downloaded from several sound-effect websites[5]. The pictorial stimuli were selected from three publications on J mimetics (a pictorial dictionary by Gomi 2004, pictorial teaching materials by Tomikawa 1997, and a pictorial reference book for J learners by Akutsu 1994). The auditory stimuli were used to elicit the production of phonomimes while the pictorial stimuli were primarily used to elicit the production of phenomimes and psychomimes.

---

[5]The websites included www.freesound.org and www.freesfx.co.uk/soundeffects/.

Prior to the main study, we conducted a pilot study to select experimental stimuli and to refine the experimental method. We asked 27 J speakers studying at a university in Tokyo (18 women and 9 men) aged 18-43 (average 20) to describe the auditory stimuli and pictorial stimuli by using mimetic words.[6] Based on the participants' responses, stimuli that were relatively easily understood were selected, resulting in 20 audio stimuli (all targeting phonomimes including 10 artifacts noises, 2 water noises, 5 animal noises, and 3 human noises) and 19 pictorial stimuli (targeting 5 mimetic words for laughter, 5 for manner of walking, 5 mimetic words for pain, and 4 mimetic words for emotion). Table 1 summarizes the auditory stimuli; due to space restrictions, we do not provide the same summary for the pictorial stimuli.[7]

Table 1. Auditory Stimuli

Type	Description
Artifacts (10)	door bell, gong, small bell, sword, dishes, knocking, door creaking, door closing (louder and softer), stapler
Water (2)	water drop and splash
Animal (5)	dog, cat, rooster, crow, bee
Human (3)	noodle slurp, laughter (female voice), loud laughter (male)

In the main study, 23 J speakers (12 men and 11 women) studying at a university in Tokyo aged 18-22 (average 19) participated. They were all non-language majors who had never studied K. Likewise, 20 K speakers studying at a university in Seoul (19 men and 1 woman) aged 21-28 (average 24) participated. They were also all non-language majors who had never studied J.

Both the J and K groups participated in the experiments in two group sessions. One group were given the audio stimuli first and the other pictorial. Each audio stimulus was played twice. Both audio and pictorial stimuli were embedded in PowerPoint slides, and each sound or picture was presented with a sentential frame with a blank such as shown in 1a-b and 2a-b:

1 a. _____という音が聞こえた。 ____ to iu oto-ga kikoeta.
QT say sound-NOM hear-PAST
'A sound that goes ____ was heard'

---

[6] Since we did not conduct a pilot study with K speakers, we acknowledge the possibility that the sounds and pictures may have been more easily recognizable for J speakers.

[7] The written descriptions of manners of laughing and walking and the types of pain depicted in the pictorial stimuli would require substantive space. For this reason, we will only provide descriptions of those that are pertinent to the discussion.

b. ___ 하는 소리가 들린다. ____ ha-nun soli-ka tul-li-nta.
do-REL sound-NOM hear-PASS-PRS
'A sound that goes ___ was heard'

2 a. 男の人____あるいている。 otokonohito-ga ____ aruite iru
man-NOM walking is
'The man is walking ______'

b. 남자가 _______ 걷고 있다. namca-ka _____ ket-ko iss-ta
man-NOM _____ walking is
'The man is walking _____.'

The participants wrote their responses in the blanks in the sentences given on data sheets that had been distributed prior to the PowerPoint presentations. For the animal noises and laughter, *nakigoe* (crying voice) and *waraigoe* (laughter) were used in place of *oto* 'sound' in J since *oto* does not refer to animate noises.[8] These choices of words minimally gave out information about the type of sounds (i.e. animate or inanimate) for the J participants, but no other information about the stimuli (such as the information given in Table 1) was given. This was to avoid evoking aural images among the participants by prior knowledge of what they will hear (e.g., if participants know that they will hear a water splash, a specific aural image or a mimetic word may occur to their mind without hearing the actual sound). The sentence frame was provided for each stimulus to encourage the participants to produce linguistic expressions for the auditory stimuli rather than non-linguistic, precise imitations of what they hear ('wild' end of onomatopoeia, Rhodes 1999). This frame is similar to what Rhodes used to determine semi-wild onomatopoeia (1999:281). The choice of modality (writing task) was also to encourage the production of linguistic expressions.

3. Results

3.1. Auditory Experiment (Production of Phonomimes)

3.1.1. Root forms

Of the 20 stimuli, 12 were described by CV-based mimetic words and 6 by CVCV-based words with a doorbell and rooster being exceptional in J. Though K responses were not as clear-cut, K speakers largely used CV(C)-based words for 10 of the stimuli and CV(C)CV-based words for 3 stimuli, and the rest were found to be hard to classify (e.g., *k'ok'io* for rooster, *huluk* for slurping). Interestingly, the 3 stimuli largely expressed by CV(C)CV-based words by K speakers (door closing, stapler) were also all expressed by CVCV-based words by J speakers.

[8] The K word *soli* refers to both animate sounds (voices) and inanimate noises.

3.1.2. Variability

Phonomimes varied considerably even for animal sounds for which stereotypical 'fixed' forms are available. For each item, we tallied a 'conservative count' of the number of types of mimetic word. Under this system, sequences containing repetitions and sequence-internal vowel lengthening (regardless of the type of orthography used) were considered as variants of the same type unless the words were listed separately in a dictionary such as Kakehi et al. (1996).[9] In the case of J, sequence-internal intensifier /Q/ was also ignored for tallying types. For the 10 artifacts noises, the 23 J speakers produced 1 (i.e. *piNpo(:)N* for a doorbell) to 19 types (i.e. for a gong noise), averaging 11.2 for artifacts. The 20 K speakers produced 3 (doorbell) to 17 types (dishes), averaging 9. For the 5 animal noises, J speakers produced 5 (dog, rooster) to 12 types (cat), averaging 7.8. Likewise, the K speakers produced 3 (rooster) to 10 types (crow), averaging 7.4. Considering the number of participants (3 more for J), the extent of variability in the two groups is nearly identical.

3.1.3. Innovation vs. Convention

Rather than using conventional mimetic words (i.e. for J, those listed in Kakehi et al. 1996; for K, those listed in the Standard K Dictionary (Kwuklipkwukeyenkwuwen 2000) and/or recognized as conventional by two K informants), participants frequently made use of innovative phonomimes (26% for J speakers, 34% for K speakers). The K speakers showed the creative use of the plain/tense/aspirated distinction. For example, for the doorbell sound, which is conventionally *tiŋ-toŋ,* some participants substituted the lax /t/ with the tense /t'/ in both syllables (*t'iŋ-t'oŋ*) or just the first syllable (*t'iŋ-toŋ*). The mimetic words for animals and human voices which are said to be more 'fixed' were equally or more open to innovation than artifact/water noises (J speakers 35% vs. 20%; K speakers 34% vs. 34%). Examples in (3a-b) show the phonemic transcriptions of the participants'

---

[9] For example, for J *čiN* and *či:N* for a small bell were counted as two since Kakehi et al. (1996) has separate entries for these two sequences. Likewise, for K, in the case of the crow crowing, *k'aak* and *k'a:ak* were counted as two since they are listed as separate entries in the Standard K Dictionary. However, differential orthographies such as かあ, カア and カー (all /ka:/) for a crow in J were considered to be the same type. Similarly, lengthening by repetition of the vowel symbol (e.g. 끼이익 *k'i::k* for a door opening) or by the inclusion of a dash (e.g.꼬끼오~옥 *k'ok'io:ok*) were treated as being the same devices for lengthening in K, although it never happened that different speakers used both devices for the same word.

responses for the stimulus of a dog barking.[10] Note J speakers used innovative orthography such as ヴ (vu) and *dakuten* (traditionally used to indicate voicing) for such characters as ワ(wa)[11], which cannot readily be phonemically transcribed since the exact segmental values are not known.[12]

3a. J responses for a dog barking (5 types):
waNwaN(9), waNwaNwaN (3), waNwaNwaNwaN(6), waN(1), buN-buN(1), w"aN waN, waN(1), oN oN oN (1), vuoN woNwoN(1)

3b. K responses for a dog barking (6 types):
wəl-wəl(6), məŋ-məŋ(4), wal-wal(4), wəl-wəl-wəl(2), məŋ-məŋ-məŋ(1), pək-ək-ək-ttək(1), waŋ-məŋ-məŋ-məŋ (1), waŋ-waŋ(1).

It is interesting to note that only five K participants used the stereotypical K mimetic word for dog's barking, *məŋ-məŋ(-məŋ)*, underscoring the importance of empirical investigation of actual use. The phonomimes produced by the J and K are similar in the choice of the onset /w/ and the nasal coda /N/ or /ŋ/ (both are said to express resounding or reverberating sound). The empirical observation of J and K speakers' choices of mimetic words revealed substantive similarities that have not been apparent in previous comparisons of dictionary equivalents.

3.1.4. Vowels

The vowels used by J and K speakers were strikingly similar for many of the stimuli (Tables 2 and 3). The tables show the vowels used by the majority of speakers. If there were more than one vowel used frequently, they are shown with their frequency of use indicated in parentheses. For some stimuli, vowels used were somewhat different; yet, they did not diverge greatly between the two languages (Table 4). Tables 2-4 together show the vowels used for all 20 auditory stimuli. Clearly, there were substantial similarities between the two languages.

When comparing the vowels used in the phonomimes of artifacts for events differing in size-related aspects, the alleged differences of size symbolism are only modestly recognized. In K, among the stimuli for which more differences were evident (Table 4), the loud door closing was described using the dark vowels /ə/ and /u/ (14 of 20) (although there was no

[10] The J transcription in this article largely adopts the system used by Vance (2008); for K, we follow Sohn (1994).

[11] There was also one instance of *dakuten* for あ, describing a crow's cry.

[12] Instances of innovative orthography occurred in the K data as well, although not for this particular item. For instance, some participants placed final Hangul consonants outside of syllable blocks (such as 꼬끼오ㄱ for the sound of a rooster). Interestingly, one participant used a non-existent Hangul character combining "ㅗ" with "ㅒ" and which would presumably be pronounced as /wjɛ/.

use of /i/) slightly more often than the quieter door closing (11 of 20), and the sharp sword noise was often described by words containing the bright vowel /ɛ/ though the vowel /i/ was also used.

Table 2. Vowels used to describe artifact noises

	Japanese	Korean
doorbell	i-o	i-o
small bell	i(:)	i (8), ɛ (8)
gong	(u)(w)a:N	w(u)aŋ
door creak	i(:)	i (8), ɯ (7)
knocking	o	o
stapler	a-a	a-a

Table 3. Vowels used to describe animal and human noises

	Japanese	Korean
crow	a	a
rooster	o-e-o-o	o-i-o
cat	a	a
bee	ɯ	ɯ
slurp	ɯ	ɯ
laughter (female)	ɯ	ɯ
laughter (male)	a	a

Table 4. Stimuli for which vowels used were different.

	Japanese	Korean
door close (loud)	a-a	ə-ə (8), a/a-a(6), u, u-u(4)
sword	i	ɛ (13), i (7)
door close	a-a	ə-ə (11), a-a (7)
dishes & cutlery	a-a	ə-ə
splash	i-a	ə-ə (6), a, a-a(6)
splash (longer)	i-a (12), a-a (4)	a, a-a(4), ə-(u/ə)-ə (5)
dog barking	a	ə

There is also evidence that the use of vowels in K, as well as in J, is in accord with alleged 'universal' size symbolism. For instance, the noise of a gong is quite consistently expressed by the low back vowel /a/, and a sharp, high-pitched clear noise of a small bell was expressed by the high front /i/ (and also by open mid front vowel /ɛ/ in K), all instances are shown in (4a-b) in 3.1.5. below.

3.1.5. Consonants

For many of the stimuli (e.g. door creaking, knocking, small bell), the consonants used were also very similar between J and K speakers even in relatively fixed conventional phonomimes such as a rooster's crowing (i.e. /k/). However, the differences between the two languages were more salient in their use of consonants than in vowels as shown in Table 5. The differences are mostly observed in less iconic CVCV(C)-based words (e.g. describing a door closing or a splash).

Table 5. Consonants used to describe artifact noises

	Japanese	Korean
doorbell	p	t, t’
gong	b (13), v(3), d(3), g(2)	č’(3), k’(4), k^{h} (4), t (4), p (2)
door slam	g(10), b(5), d(3), k(5)	č^{h}(4), t(4), t^{h}(4), t’(3), k^{h}(3),
door close	k-(č/š/t) (16)	t’-k’(6), t-k^{h}(7), č^{h}-k^{h}(5)
Splash1	p-(č/š) (10), b-(č/š) (6)	č^{h}-l-s’(3), t^{h}, t’, t, k^{h}, s
Splash 2	p-(č/š) (12), b-(č/š)(6)	č^{h}(9)

The fact that C1VC2V-based or C1V(C)C2VC-based words show more differences corroborate the claim that these are more conventional. Due to fundamentally different phonological systems and inventories in the two languages, the use of different consonants is obviously expected (e.g. phonemically voiced consonants are not expected in K.) However, the place and/or manner of articulation for which the equivalents are available in the two languages are found to be quite different for the mimetic words produced for some of the stimuli. For a doorbell, for example, J speakers often used the bilabial stop /p/, but the K speakers used the alveolar stops /t/ and /t’/. For a gong, while J speakers used the bilabial stop /b/ often, K speakers used the velar stops /k/ and /k’/ or the alveolar stop /t/ or the affricate /č/.

Below, (4a-b) illustrates the words used for a small bell, for which J and K speakers' choices of vowels and consonants were very similar and (5a-b) illustrates the words for a gong, for which the difference is salient. Both are expressed by iconic CV(C)-based mimetic words.

4a. J responses for a small bell
či:N (11), čiN (5), pi:N (3), ki:N (3), t^{s}iN:

4b. K responses for a small bell
t’ɛŋ(8), t’iŋ(6), t’i-mjəŋ(1), t’iŋ-t’oŋ(1), t’iŋ-tiŋ(1), t^{h}iŋ(1), p’iŋ(1), t’aŋ-a-ti-iŋ(1)

5a. J responses for a gong
ba:N(3), bua:N(1), buwa:N(2), buo:N(1), bu:(1), bowa:N(2), boa:N(1), bio:N(1), bo:N(1), va:N, (1), vuwa:N(1), vyua:N(1), gua:N(1), guwa:N(1), dowa:N(1), doa:N(1), doša:N(1), ža:N(1), ua:n(1)

5b. K responses for a gong
č'i-iŋ(3), k'waŋ(3), pu-aŋ(2), k^hu-aŋ(1), kwe-eŋ(1), k^hwaaŋ(1), k^hu-ɛ-eŋ(1), k^hu-a-aŋ(1), k'wa-taŋ(1), u-wa-waŋ(1), pu-a-a-a(1), teŋ(1), tɛŋ(1), t'eŋ(1), teŋ-eŋ(1)

Moreover, while J speakers tend to agree among each other whether to use voiced or voiced consonants, K speakers' choice of the plain/tense/aspirated appears to vary. For each of the 10 artifact noises, the J speakers' choice of voiced/voiceless was in agreement at a rate of at least 70% (average 90%). But K speakers' agreement of plain/tense/aspirated reached more than 50% for only 6 stimuli.

Interestingly, however, the apparent differences for words for a door closing and for a splash are mostly positional. For a door closing, the segments used in C1 and C2 appear to be reversed in the two languages. For example, alveolar stops and affricates often used in the onset of the first syllable in K phonomimes for a splash are often used in the second syllable of the J counterparts.

3.2. Pictorial Experiment (Production of Phenomimes and Psychomimes)

3.2.1. Root forms

Most of the J phenomimes and psychomimes used for 14 of 19 pictorial stimuli were CVCV-based words, reflecting the less iconic, more conventionalized nature of phenomimes and psychomimes.[13] K speakers rarely used psychomimes, but CV(C)CVC-based words were favored for 10 of the 15 pictorial stimuli for phenomimes, again reflecting the conventionalized nature of phenomimes.

For the 4 pictorial stimuli targeting psychomimes, K speakers used 0, 2, 3, 4 mimetic words, respectively. K speakers mostly relied on non-mimetic words (e.g. *ansim-hada* 'to be relieved' was used for the psychological state of a thief hiding in a corner who has just seen a security guard passing by without noticing him, for which the J speakers often used the mimetic *hoQ).* Whether this can be attributed to the selection of the stimuli or to the limited repertoire of psychomimes in K (Shibasaki 2002) is not clear in this exper-

---

[13] The words elicited by the pictures of laughing can be considered as phonomimes as well as phenomimes since they describe the manner and sound of laughing at the same time.

iment. J speakers produced the most consistent responses *ira-ira* (21 of 23) for a picture of a man's frustration and annoyance caused by a traffic jam, but none of the K speakers produced any mimetic words for this item, despite the fact that Shibasaki lists *swulleng-swulleng* as the K counterpart for J *ira-ira*/*sowa-sowa* (83).

3.2.2. Variability

As expected, phenomimes and psychomimes used by the participants reflected convention more than for the phonomimes. Yet, substantive variability was observed. For manner of laughing/smiling, J speakers used 3 to 8 types of forms (average 5.8) and K speakers used 3 to 10 types (average 7.3). For manner of walking, J speakers used 3 to 9 types (average 7.2) and K speakers 2 to 6 types (average 3.8). For pain, J speakers used 5 to 7 types (average 6), and K speakers 3 to 8 types (average 5). Below, (6a-b) shows the actual forms used by both groups for plodding (for which similar, cognate forms exist in the two languages).[14]

6a. J responses for plodding
tobo-tobo(13), šonbori(1), šobo-šobo(1), noro-noro(1), koQsori(1), pot^{s}uri(1), šiNmiri to (1), šuN to(1), hiQsori to(1),

6b. K responses for plodding
t^{h}əpək-t^{h}əpək (4), t'upək-t'upək(1), t^{h}ətəl-t^{h}ətəl(1), č^{h}uk(1)

For *tobo-tobo* most often used by J speakers (13 of 23 participants), only 4 K speakers used the 'cognate' counterpart *t^{h}əpək-t^{h}əpək*. Instead, 13 of 20 K speakers used non-mimetic words such as *himəpsi* 'weakly' (3 speakers) and *mɛkəpsi* 'exhaustedly' (2 speakers).

As mentioned, K speakers produced very few psychomimes, but psychomimes used by J speakers also varied greatly for 3 of 4 items.

4. Discussions and Conclusion

The auditory experiment revealed striking similarities in the use of consonants and vowels in the production of phonomimes despite the significant differences between the J and K phonological systems and inventories. In particular, vowels used often reflected commonly suggested 'universal' sound symbolism, most notably with augmentative /a/ despite its alleged diminutive function. Even if the diminutive function of /a/ is evident in certain existing vocabulary, its sound symbolism does not seem to be available to creative, spontaneous production. This can be further supported by exper-

[14] The total numbers of mimetic words used are smaller than the total number of responses since some participants used non-mimetic words (e.g. *kanashisoo-ni* 'looking sad').

iments conducted by Shinohara and Kawahara (2011), who used novel written sequences varying in vowels (i, u, e, o, a) and voiced/voiceless consonants as stimuli to speakers of J, K, English, and Chinese, who were asked to judge the size of the referent. They found the general trend that the lower the vowel, the larger the image. Of most importance, K speakers rated the sequences containing /a/ as larger than sequences containing any other vowels.

More differences were found between J and K speakers' use of consonants. While J speakers consistently agree with each other as to whether to use voiced/voiceless consonants to describe given sounds/events, K speakers' choices of plain/tense/aspirated were more variable. In Shinohara and Kawahara's (2011) experiments, K speakers were different from the other three groups in their interpretation of the voiced-voiceless contrast. While all other speakers rated sequences containing voiced consonants as referring to larger referent, K speakers did not distinguish between sequences containing voiced and voiceless consonants. It appears that the plain/tense/aspirated distinction in K, rather than being a device used to systematically encode intensity or size, is rather used in creative or expressive ways by individual speakers.

Studying the J and K mimetic words produced in response to the same auditory and pictorial stimuli showed J and K speakers' rich expressivity utilizing both (arguably) universal and language-specific sound symbolism.

References

Akutsu, S. 1994. *E de wakaru Giongo Gitaigo: Nihongo no Hyōgenryoku ga mi ni tsuku Handobukku* [Mimetics through Pictures: Handbook for Developing Expressive Japanese]. Tokyo: Arc.

Aoyama, H. 1972. *Gendai Chōsengo no Giseigo* [The Mimetic Words of Modern Korean Language]. Tenri: Chōsen Gakkai.

Asano, C. (ed.) 1978. *Giongo Gitaigo Jiten* [Mimetic Word Dictionary]. Tokyo: Kadokawa Shoten.

Ҫho, Y.Y. 2006. Sound symbolism in Korean. *Korean Language in Culture and Society*, ed. H-M Sohn, 65-73. Honolulu: University of Hawai'i Press.

Diffloth, G. 1994. I: big, a: small. *Sound Symbolism*, eds. L. Hinton, J. Nichols, & J.J. Ohara, 107-114. Cambridge: Cambridge University Press.

Fischer, A. 1999. What, if anything is phonological iconicity? *Form Miming Meaning: Iconicity in Language and Literature*, eds. M. Nänny & O. Fischer, 123-134. Amsterdam/Philadelphia: John Benjamins.

Garrigues, S. 1995. Mimetic parallels in Korean and Japanese. *Studies in Language* 19(2): 359-398.

Gomi, T. 2004. *Nihongo Gitaigo Jiten* [Japanese Mimetic Dictionary]. Tokyo: Kōdansha.

Hamano, S. 1998. *Sound-symbolic System of Japanese*. Tokyo: Kurosio Publishers.

Iwasaki, N., D.P. Vinson, & G. Vigliocco 2007. What English speakers know about *gera-gera* and *yota-yota*? Cross-linguistics investigation of mimetic words of laughing and walking. *Japanese-Language Education around the Globe* 17: 53-78.

Kakehi, H., I. Tamori, & L. Schourup (eds.) 1996. *Dictionary of Iconic Expressions in Japanese*. Berlin: Mouton de Gruyter.

Kobayashi, H. 1933. *Kokugo Shōchō-on-no Kenkyū* [Study of Japanese Sound Symbolism]. *Bungaku* 1: 1-47.

Kang, B-J. 1993. A Contrastive Study on Onomatopoeia between Korean and Japanese. Unpublished Masters Dissertation. Konkuk University.

Kim, K-O. 1977. Sound symbolism in Korean. *Journal of Linguistics* 13(1): 67-75.

Kwuklipkwukeyenkwuwen [National Institute of the Korean Language] 2000. *Phyocwun kwukǒ taysacen* [Standard Korean Dictionary]. Seoul: Tusan Tonga.

Lee, E-A. 2001. A Contrastive Study on Japanese and Korean Onomatopoeia. Unpublished Doctoral Dissertation, Nagoya University.

Lee, M. 2003. Topics in Korean Mimetic Expressions. Unpublished MA Thesis, Cornell University.

Noma, H. 1998. Mottomo onomatope ga hōfu na gengo [The language that has the largest number of mimetic words]. *Gekkan Gengo*, 27(5): 30-34.

Nuckolls, J.B. 1999. The case for sound symbolism. *Annu. Rev. Anthropol.* 28: 225-252.

Rhodes, R. 1999. Aural images. *Sound Symbolism*, eds. L. Hinton, J. Nichols, & J.J. Ohara, 276-292. Cambridge: Cambridge University Press.

Shibasaki, R. 2002. On sound symbolism in Japanese and Korean. *Japanese/Korean Linguistics*, Volume 10, eds. N. Akatsuka and S. Strauss, 76-89. Stanford: CSLI.

Shinohara, K. & S. Kawahara (2011). A cross-linguistic study of sound symbolism: The Images of the size. *The Proceedings of BLS 36*. Berkeley Linguistic Society.

Sohn, H-M. 1994. *Korean*. London/New York: Routledge.

Sohn, H-M. 1999. *The Korean Language*. Cambridge: Cambridge University Press.

Song, J-J. 2005. *The Korean Language*. London: Routledge.

Ono, M. 2007. *Giongo Gitaigo 4500 Nihongo Onomatope Jiten* [4500 Mimetic Words: Japanese Onomatopoeia Dictionary]. Tokyo: Shōgakkan.

Otsubo, H. 1989. *Giseigo no Kenkyū* [Study of Phonomimes]. Tokyo: Meiji Shoin.

Tomikawa, K. 1997. *Rakuraku oboete dondon tsukaō: E de manabu Giongo Gitaigo kādo. Nihongo Kyōzai* [Let's learn fast and use them a lot: Giongo gitaigo learning through pictures]. Tokyo: Three A Network.

Vance, T.J. 2008. *The Sounds of Japanese*. Cambridge: Cambridge University Press.

Yamaguchi, N. 2002. *Inu wa 'biyo' to naite ita: Nihongo wa giongo gitaigo ga omoshiroi* [Dogs used to cry 'biyo']. Tokyo: Kōbunsha.

Yamaguchi, N. 2003. Kurashi no kotoba: giongo gitaigo jiten [Words of Daily Life: Mimetic Word Dictionary]. Tokyo: Kōdansha.

Seoul Korean Subjects' Perception of Japanese Pitch-Accent: Evidence for the absence of tonogenesis in Korean*

HYUNSOON KIM
Hongik University

The purpose of the present study is to examine whether native speakers of Seoul Korean are sensitive to pitch variation in vowels after Japanese voiced and voiceless consonants, given the tonogenesis account that the tone difference -H and L in vowels after aspirated and fortis consonants and after lenis ones, respectively, in word-initial position- is lexically specified in Korean (e.g., M.-R. Kim & Duanmu 2004).

According to Jun (2006), Seoul Korean has three tonally defined prosodic units above the Word: Intonation Phrase (IP) > Intermediate Phrase

* I would like to express my sincere thanks to Takeki Kamiyama for his help with recordings and his attestation of pitch manipulations. I am also grateful to the audience for their feedback at the Japanese-Korean linguistics 20 held at the University of Oxford in October 2010. Any errors remain my own.

Japanese/Korean Linguistics 20.
Edited by Bjarke Frellesvig and Peter Sells.

(ip) > Accentual Phrase (AP). Among the three prosodic units, AP, "a unit slightly larger than a Word" (Jun 2006:15) is motivated, because pitch range can change in Korean depending on the segmental property at the beginning of AP. For example, as pointed out by Jun (1993, 1998, 2006), APs beginning with fortis or aspirated stops (i.e., plosives and affricates) as in /s'/, /s/ or /h/ have a higher pitch range than those beginning with lenis stops. Thus, in AP-initial position which usually corresponds to word-initial position, H is expected in vowels after fortis or aspirated stops like /s'/, /s/ or /h/ and L after lenis stops and sonorants. Recently Jun's (1993, 1998, 2006) view that pitch range in AP-initial position is closely associated with the segmental property in Korean has led some linguists to further suggest that Korean is a tonogenesis languages (e.g., M.-R. Kim & Duanmu 2004). It has been assumed in a standard tonogenesis model that vowels after voiceless consonants are assigned to H and those after voiced ones to L due to the difference in F0. In line with this, M.-R. Kim & Duanmu (2004:78) have proposed that "the consonant-tone interaction in Korean is a standard case of voiceless-H and voiced-L, which is found in many other languages." That is, vowels after lenis stops are lexically marked as L because Korean lenis stops are underlyingly voiced with the specification of the features [+voice, -aspirated]. Vowels after aspirated and fortis stops are proposed to be lexically marked as H because aspirated and fortis ones are voiceless with the specification of [-voice, +aspirated] and [-voice, -aspirated], respectively. When lenis stops are in word-initial or in AP-initial position, they are assumed to be devoiced with the original feature value [+voice] changed into [-voice], but the underlying lexical tone L remains unchanged in following vowels. Therefore, according to M.-R. Kim & Duanmu (2004), lenis and fortis stops are identical in their feature specification of [-voice, -aspirated] in word-initial position due to the devoicing of lenis stops, and it is the tone specification that differentiates lenis stops from fortis ones. The tonogeneis account is different from Jun (1993, 1998, 2006) in that "there is no need to assume that Korean tones are unpredictable or assigned by prosodic rules" because tones are lexically specified in word-initial position (M.-R. Kim & Duanmu 2004:61). Silva (2006) has also suggested that it is only by tonal information of following vowels that lenis and aspirated stops in Korean are differentiated based on his sociolinguistic experiment where young Korean subjects do not have any difference in VOT (i.e., voice onset time) between lenis and aspirated consonants.

Given this brief literature review, we raise the question of whether native speakers of Seoul Korean are sensitive to the H/L distinction, if F0 plays the primary role in the three-way phonation contrast in Korean consonants. This question arises because assumptions within the tonogenesis account in Korean are not in agreement with recent articulatory and loanword adaptation data or with the past literature. According to H. Kim et al. (2005, 2010a, 2011), the difference in F0 between lenis vs. aspirated/fortis consonants is a phonetic effect caused by different glottal height during oral closure or constriction of Korean consonants. In addition, H. Kim (2008:338) has pointed that, though the Japanese word *kami* means 'god' with HL and 'paper' with LH, "both are borrowed as /ka.mi/ with no difference in pitch-accent, indicating that Japanese pitch-accent is ignored by Korean speakers." Moreover, the overlapping of VOT between lenis and aspirated consonants has already been reported in the literature (e.g., Lisker & Abramson 1964; C.-W. Kim 1965). For example, C.-W. Kim (1965) reported that VOT between /t/ and /t^h/ is overlapped though the range of VOT is much higher after the aspirated consonant than after the lenis one. According to C.-W. Kim (1970), it is not VOT but glottal opening that is invariant for the three-way phonation contrast in word-initial Korean plosives: it varies from small to large in the order of fortis < lenis < aspirated. The results of C.-W. Kim's (1970) cineradiographic study were confirmed by Kagaya's (1974) fiberscopic study. Recent MRI studies (H. Kim et al. 2005, 2010a, 2011) provide further data that glottal opening is invariant not only in word-initial position but also in word-medial position, such that the glottis opens wider in aspirated than in lenis and fortis consonants.

In order to answer the question of whether tones H and L are lexically specified in word-initial position in Korean, we investigate, in the present study, how native speakers of Seoul Korean perceive pitch variation in vowels after Japanese voiced and voiceless consonants in word-initial and word-medial position. If the consonant-tone interaction is lexically specified in word-initial position, as in the tonogensis account, then native speakers of Seoul Korean would be sensitive to F0 difference in vowels after Japanese voiceless and voiced plosives. Thus, native speakers of Seoul Korean would be more likely to perceive word-initial Japanese voiceless plosives with a H vowel as either aspirated or fortis consonants than those with a L vowel, and word-initial Japanese voiced plosives with a L vowel as lenis than those with a H vowel. This is because F0 of vowels after Japanese voiceless consonants is higher than that of vowels after voiced counterparts, as in other languages which have phonemic voicing contrast. In addition, if word-medial consonants do not affect tone because the tonal pattern of a word is determined solely by an initial consonant, native speakers of Seoul Korean would not perceive the pitch differences between Japanese voiced and voiceless plosives in word-medial position. Thus, native speakers of Seoul Korean would perceive a vowel after a word-medial Japanese plosive as either H or L and therefore, the Japanese plosive as either aspirated/fortis or lenis, no matter whether the plosive is followed by a H or L vowel and no matter whether it is voiced or voiceless.

The present paper is structured as follows: In Section 1, the method and results of our perception experiment are given, in Section 2 we discuss the results of the experiment, and Section 3 is a brief conclusion.

1. Experiment

1.1. Method

We used two-, three- and four-syllable Japanese words as test words, as shown in (1). Words with an accent are marked with '' over an accented vowel, as in *magó*. Words with no accent marking are all unaccented. In both word-initial and word-medial positions, the test words have the consonants /b, d, g, t, k/.[1] Note that no test word begins with the voiceless plosive /p/ or has the consonant in word-medial position in (1), because there are few Japanese words with /p/ in word-initial and word-medial positions except for loanwords.[2]

(1) Japanese words used in the present experiment

a. two-syllable words

bate	LH	'being done in'
Date	LH	'(family name, place name)'
gaka	LH	'painter'
kabe	LH	'wall'
Tada	LH	'(family name, place name)'
magó	LH	'grandchild'

b. three-syllable words

bakéru	LHL	'to transform oneself'
dokuga	LHH	'poisonous moth'
gogaku	LHH	'study of languages'
kotobá	LHH	'word, language'
tadami	LHH	'watching a game, etc. without paying the fee'
nakabá	LHH	'middle, half'

---

[1] The perception experiment in the present study is newly done, thus not the same as that in H. Kim (2010). This is because the Japanese test words in H. Kim (2010) were not controlled such that there were no Japanese three- and four-syllable test words beginning with /b/, /d/ and /g/ and no Japanese two-syllable words beginning with /b/. Even in word-medial position, there were no /g/ in two- and three-syllable Japanese words and no /b/ and /g/ in four-syllable words. In addition, pitch manipulations were not consistent.

[2] Japanese has initial /p/ in mimetics such as *pikapika*, yet this mimetics was not considered because it is one of the most frequently-used Japanese loans in Korean.

c. four-syllable words

bakamono	LHHH	'idiot'
botebote	LHHH	'(onomatopoeia representing a heavy manner)'
dakareru	LHHH	'to be embraced'
gatagata	LHHH	'(onomatopoeia representing a rattling noise)'
katagami	LHHH	'(paper) pattern (for a dress)'
todokéru	LHHL	'to deliver, to report'

The test words were put in /korewa __desu/ 'This is ___' and randomized. A male native speaker of Tokyo Japanese in his early 30s recorded the test words five times at a sound-proof recording room at the Laboratory of Phonetics and Phonology, CNRS/Sorbonne-Nouvelle (University of Paris 3). The best recorded test words were selected, and then pitches were manipulated in two ways, as follows: HL and LH for the two-syllable words; HLL and LHH for the three-syllable words; and HLLL and LHHH for the four-syllable words. The manipulated pitch patterns in the present study are among the pitch variation in Tokyo Japanese, as in (2). According to Shibatani (1990), Tokyo Japanese has HL and LH for two-syllable words; LHH, HLL and LHL for three-syllable words; and LHHH, HLLL, LHLL and LHHL for four-syllable words.

(2) Pitch variation in Tokyo Japanese (Shibatani 1990)

a. two-syllable words

ame	LH	'candy'
ame	HL	'rain'

b. three-syllable words

sakura	LHH	'cherry'
zakuro	HLL	'pomegranate'
kokoro	LHL	'heart'

c. four-syllable words

sirakaba	LHHH	'white birch'
kamakiri	HLLL	'mantis'
irogami	LHLL	'color paper'
kagaribi	LHHL	'torch'

In addition, the pitch manipulations - HL and LH for the two-syllable words; HLL and LHH for the three-syllable words; and HLLL and LHHH for the four-syllable words -were examined and attested by the Japanese speaker who recorded the test words in (1) and who is a trained phonetician. In our pitch manipulations, the average pitch differences between H and L, H and H, and L and L vowels were 30.9 Hz, 4.6 Hz and 6.2 Hz, respectively, when F0 was measured in the middle of each vowel. The total number of stimuli was 36 (18 test words x 2 pitch manipulations), and two repetitions of the stimuli were randomized at a 4 ms interval for one session. The seventy two tokens (36 stimuli x 2 repetitions) were presented three times to each participant in three sessions at a one-minute interval. One participant thus received a total of 216 trials (36 stimuli x 6 repetitions). Eighty native speakers of Seoul Korean (40 male and 40 female) participated in this perception experiment. All of the Korean subjects were in their 20s as university students and had no any hearing impairments. They had never learned Japanese. In a quiet room, each subject was asked to listen to the prepared stimuli, using a headphone (HD 202 SENNHEISER or Shure SRH440) and to write them down in the Korean orthography. The perception experiment was run using Praat's ExperimentMFC facility. After the perception experiment, all the responses of the subjects were stored in excel for data analyses.

1.2. Results

Table 1 presents how our subjects perceived the word-initial Japanese voiced consonants [b], [d] and [g] as /p/, /t/ and /k/, respectively, in pitch variation.[3] Regardless of pitch variation, the word-initial Japanese voiced plosives were mostly perceived as the lenis consonants. Paired samples two-tailed t-tests show that the difference in H and L does not have a significant effect on our subjects' perception of the word-initial Japanese voiced consonants [b], [d] and [g] as /p/, /t/ and /k/, respectively (**H**L vs. **L**H in ***b**ate*, **D***ate* and ***g**aka*: $t(2) = .4$, $p = .7105$; **H**LL vs. **L**HH in ***b**akeru*, ***d**okuga* and ***g**ogaku*: $t(2) = -1.3$, $p = .3206$; **H**LLL vs. **L**HHH in ***b**akamono*, ***b**otebote*, ***d**akareru* and ***g**atagata*: $t(3) = -1.2$, $p = .3256$).

Table 1. Responses for the word-initial Japanese voiced consonants [b], [d] and [g] as /p/, /t/ and /k/, respectively, in pitch manipulations in (a) the two-syllable words ***b**ate*, **D***ate* and ***g**aka*; (b) the three-syllable words ***b**akeru*, ***d**okuga* and ***g**ogaku*; and (c) the four-syllable words ***b**akamono*, ***b**otebote*, ***d**akareru* and ***g**atagata*.

a.	HL	1336 (/1440 = 93%)
	LH	1320 (/1440 = 92%)
b.	HLL	1319 (/1440 = 92%)
	LHH	1331 (/1440 = 92%)
c.	HLLL	1607 (/1920 = 84%)
	LHHH	1700 (/1920 = 89%)

[3] See H. Kim (2008) for Korean adaptation of voiced and voiceless Japanese consonants.

Our subjects' tendency to perceive the word-medial Japanese voiced consonants [b], [d] and [g] as /p/, /t/ and /k/, respectively, also shows that it has nothing to do with the difference in H and L in following vowels, as shown in Table 2. Regardless of H and L differences, our subjects are the most likely to perceive the word-medial Japanese voiced consonants [b], [d] and [g] as the lenis consonants. Also, paired samples two-tailed *t*-tests reveal that the difference in H and L in following vowels does not have a significant effect on our subjects' perception of the word-medial Japanese voiced consonants (HL vs. LH in *kabe*, *Tada* and *mago*: $t(2) = -2.9$, $p = .0998$; HLL vs. LHH in *kotoba, nakaba, tadami, dokuga* and *gogaku*: $t(4) = -.3$, $p = .7523$; HLLL vs. LHHH in *botebote, todokeru, katagami* and *gatagata*: $t(3) = -1.5$, $p = .2203$).

Table 2. Responses for the word-medial Japanese voiced consonants [b], [d] and [g] as /p/, /t/ and /k/, respectively, in pitch manipulations in (a) the two-syllable words *kabe*, *Tada* and *mago*; (b) the three-syllable words *kotoba*, *nakaba*, *tadami*, *dokuga* and *gogaku*; and (c) the four-syllable words *botebote*, *todokeru*, *katagami* and *gatagata*.

a.	**HL**	1310 (/1440 = 91%)
	LH	1349 (/1440 = 94%)
b.	**HLL**	2112 (/2400 = 88%)
	LHH	2121 (/2400 = 88%)
c.	**HLLL**	1772 (/1920 = 92%)
	LHHH	1814 (/1920 = 94%)

In Table 3, we can note that our subjects largely tended to perceive the word-initial Japanese voiceless consonants [k] and [t] in the test words as $/k^h/$ and $/t^h/$, respectively, regardless of pitch manipulations. Paired samples two-tailed *t*-tests show that there are no significant effects in all the comparisons (HL vs. LH in *kabe* and *Tada*: $t(1)=2.4$, $p = .2543$; HLL vs. LHH in *kotoba* and *tadami*: $t(1) = 2.7$, $p = .2228$; HLLL vs. LHHH in *katagami* and *todokeru*: $t(1) = .9$, $p = .5289$). Thus, this indicate that our subjects are likely to perceive the word-initial Japanese voiceless consonants as $/k^h/$ and $/t^h/$, no matter whether the source consonants are followed by a vowel in H or L.

Table 3. Responses for the word-initial Japanese voiceless consonants [k] and [t] as /k^h/ and /t^h/, respectively, in pitch manipulations in (a) the two-syllable ***kabe*** and ***Tada***; (b) the three-syllable words ***koto-ba*** and ***tadami***; and (c) the four-syllable words ***katagami*** and ***todokeru***.

a.	**HL**	887 (/960 = 92%)
	LH	842 (/960 = 88%)
b.	**HLL**	899 (/960 = 94%)
	LHH	836 (/960 = 87%)
c.	**HLLL**	895 (/960 = 84%)
	LHHH	853 (/960 = 89%)

On the other hand, the word-medial Japanese voiceless consonants [k] and [t] were mostly perceived as /k^h/ or /k'/ and /t^h/ or /t'/, respectively, regardless of whether following vowels have H or L, as shown in Table 4. Paired samples two-tailed *t*-tests show that the difference in H and L in following vowels does not have a significant effect on our subjects' perception of the word-medial Japanese voiceless consonants (H**L** vs. L**H** in *ga**ka**, ba**te*** and *Da**te***: $t(2) = .9$, $p = .4778$; H**LL** vs. L**HH** in *ba**ke**ru, do**ku**ga, go**ga**ku, na**ka**ba* and *ko**to**ba*: $t(4) = -2.5$, $p = .0669$; H**LLL** vs. L**HHH** in *ba**ka**mono, bo**te**bote, da**ka**reru, ga**ta**gata, ka**ta**gami* and *to**do**keru*: $t(7) = -3.4$, $p = .0562$).

Table 4. Responses for the word-medial Japanese voiceless consonants [k] and [t] as /k^h/ or /k'/ and /t^h/ or /t'/, respectively, in pitch manipulations in (a) the two-syllable words *ga**ka**, ba**te*** and *Da**te***; (b) the three-syllable words *ba**ke**ru, do**ku**ga, go**ga**ku, na**ka**ba* and *ko**to**ba*; and (c) the four-syllable words *ba**ka**mono, bo**te**bote, da**ka**reru, ga**ta**gata, ka**ta**gami* and *to**do**keru*.

a.	H**L**	1400 (/1440 = 97%)
	L**H**	1397 (/1440 = 97%)
b.	H**LL**	2314 (/2400 = 96%)
	L**HH**	2330 (/2400 = 97%)
c.	H**LLL**	3620 (/3840 = 94%)
	L**HHH**	3651 (/3840 = 95%)

2. Discussion

Based on the results of the present perception experiment, we suggest that F0 does not play a role in our subjects' perception of Japanese voicing contrast in word-initial position and also in word-medial position. If the consonant-tone interaction is lexically specified in word-initial position, as in the tonogensis account (M.-R. Kim & Duanmu 2004), then native speakers of Seoul Korean would be more likely to perceive word-initial Japanese voiceless plosives with a H vowel as either aspirated or fortis consonants than those with a L vowel, and word-initial Japanese voiced plosives with a L vowel as lenis than those with a H vowel. However, as shown in the above, the difference in H and L has no significant effect on our subjects' perception of the word-initial Japanese voiced plosives [b], [d] and [g] as /p/, /t/ and /k/, respectively. The same is true of our subjects' perception of the word-initial Japanese voiceless plosives [k] and [t]. The word-initial voiceless consonants were mostly perceived as aspirated, that is, /k^h/ and /t^h/, regardless of pitch manipulations (Table 3), and there are no significant effects in all the comparisons. This indicates that F0 does not play a role in our subjects' perception of word-initial Japanese voiced and voiceless plosives. Not only in word-initial position but also in word-medial position, F0 does not play a role. As shown in Table 2, our subjects' tendency to perceive the word-medial Japanese voiced consonants [b], [d] and [g] as /p/, /t/ and /k/, respectively, has nothing to do with the difference in H and L in following vowels. This is also true of the word-medial Japanese voiceless consonants [k] and [t]. Our subjects mostly perceived them as /k^h/ or /k'/ and /t^h/ or /t'/, respectively, regardless of whether following vowels have H or L (Table 4), and the difference in H and L in following vowels does not have a significant effect on our subjects' perception. Therefore, the results of the present perception experiment show that Seoul Korean speakers are not sensitive at all to pitch variation in vowels after Japanese voiced and voiceless consonants in word-initial and also in word-medial position like Kyungsang Korean speakers (H. Kim 2011b). This leads us to say that the lexical specification of the H/L distinctions in word-initial position in Korean is not empirically supported by the present perception experiment.

In addition, the assumption that F0 plays the primary role in the three-way phonation contrast of Korean consonants in the tonogenesis account (M.-R. Kim & Duanmu 2004) is not supported by recent articulatory studies, either. According to recent MRI studies of the Korean obstruents (H. Kim et al. 2005, 2010a, 2011), glottal position varies from low to high in the order lenis < aspirated (<) fortis consonants and closure/constriction duration also varies from short to long in the same order word-initially and word-medially. Based on the MRI finding, H. Kim et al. (2010a, 2011) have proposed that both glottal raising and closure/constriction duration result from the tensing of the parimary articlator and the vocal folds and the tensing is encoded by the feature [tense] in Korean. Given that glottal raising is associated with glottal tension, that is, stiffening and slackening of the vocal folds which is acoustically reflected by F0 rises (e.g., Honda 1995), glottal tension is part of the articulatory bases of the proposed feature [tense] in Korean. Systematic F0 difference in vowels after Korean consonants – F0 is higher in vowels after aspirated and fortis than after lenis consonants (e.g., C.-W. Kim 1965; Han & Weitzman 1970; Hardcastle 1973; Kagaya 1974; Cho et al. 2002) – is one of the phonetic correlates of the feature [tense] in Korean. Therefore, F0 does not play the primary role in the three-way phonation contrast of word-initial Korean consonants, as assumed in the tonogenesis account.

Given the results of our perception experiment and that F0 does not play the primary role in the three-way phonation contrast in Korean, we may reconsider the underlying specification of the feature [voice] in the tonogenesis account. By assuming that Korean lenis stops are underlyingly specified for the feature [+voice] and aspirated and fortis ones for [-voice] in line with Kingston & Diehl (1994), M.-R. Kim & Duanmu (2004:68) have proposed that fortis and lenis stops contrast in [voice] word-medially, whereas "the contrast is shifted to tone on the vowel" in word-initial position because lenis stops get devoiced, thus specified as [-voice, -aspirated] just like fortis ones. In word-initial position, vowels after fortis consonants have L and those after lenis have H. However, the assumption that Korean lenis stops are underlyingly voiced is neither phonetically nor phonologically supported. According to Jun (1993, 1994), it is in the phonetics that Korean lenis consonants get voiced in intervocalic position. This is, the voicing of lenis consonants in intervocalic position is not complete but partial. In addition, vocal fold vibrations were not always observed during the oral closure of word-medial lenis consonants in the MRI coronal data taken from two subjects in H. Kim et al. (2005, 2010a, 2011). For example, the average glottal width of the word-medial lenis plosive /k/ in the context /_a_a/ taken from the female subject in H. Kim et al. (2010a) is wider than that of the fortis counterpart.

The feature [±voice] is not motivated, either, in the Korean phonology. For example, the intensification of lenis consonants into fortis in word-initial position, to the exclusion of aspirated ones, as in (3), cannot be accounted for by the feature [±voice], because consonants are all voiceless in word-initial position, regardless of whether they are lenis, aspirated or fortis. The difference in tone cannot account for the sound pattern in (3), either, because vowels are H after not only fortis but also aspirated consonants in word-initial position in the tonogenesis account.

(3) The alternation of the lenis and fortis stops in native Korean words intensified expressions

pʌn.tɛ.ki	~	p'ʌn.tɛ.ki	* p^hʌn.tɛ.ki	'chrysalis, pupa'
po.k'ɨm.pap	~	p'o.k'ɨm.pap	* p^hok'.ɨm.pap	'fried rice'
taŋ.ki.ta	~	t'aŋ.ki.ta	* t^haŋ.ki.ta	'to pull'
tsuŋ.kuk	~	ts'uŋ.kuk	*ts^huŋ.kuk	'China'
tsal.li.ta	~	ts'al.li.ta	*ts^hal.li.ta	'to be laid off'
tsa.sik	~	ts'a.sik	*ts^ha.sik	'chap'
kop.p'æ.ki	~	k'op.p'æ.ki	*k^hop.p'æ.ki	'double'
ka.si	~	k'a.si	*k^ha.si	'thorn'

Rather, based on recent MRI, acoustic and aerodynamic studies of the Korean obstruents /p, p^h, p', t, t^h, t', ts, ts^h, ts', s, s', k, k^h, k'/ (H. Kim et al. 2010a, b, 2011a) as well as the sound patterns of the obstruents (H. Kim 2003, 2005, 2011a), it has been proposed that aspirated and fortis consonants are specified as [+tense] and lenis as [-tense]; lenis and fortis as [-spread glottis] and aspirated as [+spread glottis] (henceforth, [s.g.]) in underlying representations. Under this feature specification of Korean obstruents, the sound pattern in (3) can be given an account by virtue of the features [tense] and [s.g.]. To the exclusion of aspirated consonants which are specified as [+tense, +s.g.], lenis consonants ([-tense]) are intensified as fortis ([+tense]), though lenis and fortis consonants group together as natural class by virtue of the feature [-s.g.].

Moreover, Silva (2006: 299) has proposed that H and L are specified at surface for aspirated and lenis plosives, respectively, because "VOT differences have been neutralized and F0 appears to have assumed a primary role in marking the lax vs. aspirated distinction" in the case of younger speakers born after 1982. In his account, "the aspiration feature (here [spread]) no longer functions phonemically" for Korean young speakers. Yet, this is not supported, either, by the results of the present perception experiment and also phonetic studies in the literature. First, VOT overlapping in Korean plosives have already been found in the past literature (e.g., Lisker & Abramson 1964; C.-W. Kim 1965), as mentioned in the introduction. Instead of VOT, the glottal opening/closing in Korean consonants has been incorporated into the feature [±s.g.] (e.g., Halle & Stevens 1971; Kagaya 1974; H. Kim et al. 2005, 2010a, 2011). Second, all the subjects (40 male and 40 female) in the present study were in their 20s, most of whom were born in early 1990s except that six subjects were born between 1982 and 1984 and three in 1981, but they do not distinguish L and H at surface for lenis and aspirated consonants, respectively, in the present experiment. For example, as shown in Table 1, the word-initial Japanese voiced consonants [b, d, g] are mostly perceived as lenis /p, t, k/, regardless of pitch variation. The word-initial Japanese voiceless consonants [k, t] are also largely perceived as aspirated /k^h, t^h/, regardless of pitch variation, as in Table 3. Third, our subjects' perception of the word-initial Japanese [k, t] as the aspirated /k^h, t^h/ indicates that our subjects are sensitive to the difference in VOT. According to H. Kim (2008), the word-initial Japanese voiceless plosives have been borrowed as lenis, like word-initial Japanese voiced [b, d, g], as in (4).

(4) Korean adaptation of Japanese voicing contrast in word-initial position

a.	[**t**a.ra.i]	**t**a.la.i	'washing basin'
	[**t**oo.kjoo]	**t**o.k'jo ~ **t**o.k^{h}jo	'Tokyo'
	[**k**a.na]	**k**a.na	'Kana'
	[**k**i.mo.no]	**k**i.mo.no	'kimono'
	[**k**joo.to]	**k**jo.t'o ~ **k**jo.t^{h}o	'Kyoto'
b.	[**b**a.ku.ɸu]	**p**a.k^{h}u.hu	'government in Shogun period'
	[**d**a. ʃi]	**t**a.si	'seasoning, soup stock'
	[**g**ee. ʃa]	**k**ɛi.sja	'Geisha'

However, Table 5 shows that our subjects mostly tended to perceive the word-initial Japanese voiceless [k, t] as aspirated rather than lenis, contradictory to H. Kim (2008).

Table 5. Responses for the word-initial Japanese voiceless consonants [k] and [t] as (i) /k^h/ and /t^h/ and as (ii) /k/ and /t/ for (a) the two-syllable words, (b) the three-syllable words and (c) the four-syllable words, and (iii) the sum of responses in (i) and (ii).

		i.	ii.	iii
a.	HL	887	15	902 (/960 = 94%)
	LH	842	66	908 (/960 = 95%)
b.	HLL	899	52	951 (/960 = 99%)
	LHH	836	115	951 (/960 = 99%)
c.	HLLL	895	57	952 (/960 = 99%)
	LHHH	853	100	953 (/960 = 99%)

The contradictory results of our perception experiment would be attributed to the presence/absence of the lexicalization of Japanese words into the Korean vocabulary. When Japanese words beginning with voiced and voiceless plosives are borrowed and thus lexicalized in Korean, the word-initial voicing contrast of the source language is constrained to be neutralized, as in (4). By contrast, we assume that the absence of the lexicalization of the Japanese test words in (1) led our subjects to be sensitive to the phonetic difference in VOT between the word-initial Japanse voiced and voiceless plosives, given that the average VOT of the word-initial voiced plosives in our test words is 15 ms and that of the word-initial voiceless ones is 50 ms.

Before closing this section, we suggest some implications of the present study. First, the results of our perception experiment support an L1-feature driven perception of L2 sounds (H. Kim 2008, 2009). More specifically, our Korean young subjects' perception of Japanese voiced and voiceless plosives is driven by the Korean laryngeal features [tense] and [s.g.] in support of H. Kim (2008). Our measurements of closure duration and VOT in the test words in (1) showed that the difference in VOT between word-initial Japanese voiced (15 ms) and voiceless (50 ms) plosives is 35 ms, whereas that in closure duration between word-initial voiced (77 ms) and voiceless (80 ms) is 3 ms. By contrast, in word-medial position, the difference in closure duration between Japanese voiced (56 ms) and voiceless (76 ms) plosives is 20 ms, whereas that in VOT between voiced (28 ms) and voiceless (22 ms) plosives is 6 ms. Given that the difference in closure duration is incorporated into the feature [tense] in Korean, it is suggested that the difference in closure duration between word-medial Japanese voiceless and voiced plosives is parsed by the Korean laryngeal feature [tense], as shown in (5a). Thus, word-medial Japanese voiceless plosives are perceived as either aspirated or fortis ([+tense]), and word-medial Japanese voiced ones as lenis ([-tense]). On the other hand, in word-initial position (5b), the difference in VOT between Japanese voiceless and voiced plosives is parsed by the Korean laryngeal feature [s.g]. As a result, Japanese voiceless plosives are perceived as aspirated ([+s.g., +tense]) and voiced ones as lenis ([-s.g., -tense]).

(5)	Japanese (L2)		cue		Korean (L1)
a.	[-voice]	↔	long closure duration	↔	[+tense]
	[+voice]	↔	short closure duration	↔	[-tense]
b.	[-voice]	↔	long VOT	↔	[+s.g., +tense]
	[+voice]	↔	short VOT	↔	[-s.g., -tense]

Second, our present study supports the view that speech perception is greatly affected by the grammar of the native language (e.g., Polivanov 1974; Trubetzkoy 1939; Hyman 1970). As shown in (5), the Korean laryngeal features [tense] and [s.g.] play a role in our subjects' perception of Japanese voiced and voiceless plosives in word-initial and word-medial positions, regardless of pitch variation or Japanese phonological voicing contrast ([voice]).

3. Conclusion

In the present study, we have conducted the perception experiment of eighty young native speakers of Seoul Korean (40 male and 40 female) in order to investigate whether they are sensitive to the H/L distinctions in vowels after Japanese voiced and voiceless plosives in word-initial and word-medial positions, given the tonogenesis account (M.-R. Kim & Duanmu 2004). We have found that our subjects' perception of Japanese voiced and voiceless plosives has nothing to do with pitch variation in both word-initial and -medial positions. We have also found that, regardless of pitch variation, our subjects are sensitive to the difference in VOT between word-initial Japanese voiced and voiceless plosives and to the difference in closure duration in word-medial position. Therefore, the consonant-tone interaction in Seoul Korean is not empirically supported, as in Kyungsang Korean (H. Kim 2011b). Instead of tones H and L, the Korean laryngeal features [tense] and [s.g.] are at play in our subjects' perception of Japanese voiced and voiceless plosives in both word-initial and word-medial positions, as shown in (5), supporting an L1 feature-driven perception of L2 sounds (H. Kim 2008, 2009).

References

Cho, T., Jun, S.-A., & Ladefoged, P. 2002. Acoustic and Aerodynamic Correlates of Korean Stops and Fricatives. *Journal of Phonetics* 30: 193-228.

Halle, M. & K. N. Stevens. 1971. A note on laryngeal features. *Quarterly progress report* 101: 198-212. Cambridge, MA: Research Laboratory of Electronics, MIT.

Han, M. S. & R. S. Weitzman. 1970. Acoustic Features of Korean /P, T, K/, /p, t, k/ and /ph, th, kh/. *Phonetica* 22: 112-128.

Hardcastle, W. J. 1973. Some Observations on the Tense-lax Distinction in Initial Stops in Korean. *Journal of Phonetics* 1: 263-272.

Honda, K. 1995. Laryngeal and Extralaryngeal Mechanisms of F0 Control. *Producing speech: Contemporary issues*, ed. F. Bell-Berti & J. H. Abbs, 215-232. New York: American Institute of Physics.

Hyman, L. 1970. The Role of Borrowing in the Justification of Phonological Grammars. *Studies in African Linguistics* 1: 1-48.

Jun, S.-A. 1993. *The Phonetics and Phonology of Korean Prosody*. Doctoral dissertation, The Ohio State University.

Jun, S.-A. 1994. The Status of the Lenis Stop Voicing Rule. *Theoretical Issues in Korean Linguistics*, ed. Y.-K. Kim-Renaud, 101-114. Stanford: CSLI.

Jun, S.-A. 1998. The Accentual Phrase in the Korean Prosodic Hierarchy. *Phonology* 15: 189-226.

Jun, S.-A. 2006. Intonational Phonology of Seoul Korean Revisited. *Japanese-Korean Linguistics* 14: 15-26. Stanford: CSLI.

Kagaya, R. 1974. A Fiberscopic and Acoustic Study of the Korean Stops, Affricates and Fricatives. *Journal of Phonetics* 2: 161-180.

Kim, C.-W. 1965. On the Autonomy of the Tensity Feature in Stop Classification (with the Special Reference to Korean Stops). *Word* 21: 339-359.

Kim, C.-W. 1970. A Theory of Aspiration. *Phonetica* 21: 107-16.

Kim, H. 2003. The Feature [tense] Revisited: the Case of Korean Consonants. *NELS* 34: 319-332.

Kim, H. 2005. The Representation of the Three-way Laryngeal Contrast in Korean Consonants. *The Internal Organization of Phonological Segments*, ed. M. van Oostendorp & J. van de Weijer, 263-293. Berlin/New York: Mouton de Gruyter.

Kim, H. 2008. Loanword Adaptation between Japanese and Korean: Evidence for L1 Feature-driven Perception. *Journal of East Asian Linguistics* 17: 331-346.

Kim, H. 2009. Korean Adaptation of English Affricates and Fricatives in a Feature-driven Model of Loanword Adaptation. *Loan Phonology*, ed. Andrea Calabrese and W. Leo Wetzel, 155-180. Amsterdam/Philadelphia: John Benjamins.

Kim, H. 2010. A Non-native Perception of Japanese Pitch-accents: A Case of Native Speakers of Seoul Korean. *Phonological Studies*, ed. The Phonological Society of Japan, 13, 75-86. Tokyo: Kaitakusha.

Kim, H. 2011a. What features Underline the /s/ vs. /s'/ Contrast in Korean? Phonetic and Phonological Evidence. *Where do phonological contrasts come from? Cognitive, physical and developmental basis of distinctive speech categories*, ed. G. Nick Clements and Racid Ridouane, 99-130. Amsterdam/Philadelphia: John Benjamins.

Kim, H. 2011b. Kyungsang Korean subjects' perception of Japanese pitch-accent. *Proceedings of ICPhS* 17: 1058-1061. Hong Kong.

Kim, H., K. Honda and S. Maeda. 2005. Stroboscopic-cine MRI Study of the Phasing Between the Tongue and the Larynx in the Korean Three-way Phonation Contrast. *Journal of Phonetics* 33: 1-26.

Kim, H., S. Maeda and K. Honda 2010a. Invariant Articulatory Bases of the Features [tense] and [spread glottis] in Korean: New Stroboscopic cine-MRI Data. *Journal of Phonetics* 38: 90-108.

Kim, H., S. Maeda, K. Honda and S. Hans 2010b. The Laryngeal Characterization of Korean Fricatives: Acoustic and Aerodynamic Data. *Turbulent sounds: An interdisciplinary guide*, ed. Susanne Fuchs, Martine Toda and Marzena Zygis, 143-166. Berlin/New York: Mouton de Gruyter.

Kim, H., S. Maeda and K. Honda 2011. The Laryngeal Characterization of Korean Fricatives: Stroboscopic cine-MRI data. *Journal of Phonetics*, doi : 10.1016/j.wocn2011.06.001.

Kim, M.-R. and S. Duanmu 2004. Tense and Lax Stops in Korean. *Journal of East Asian Linguistics* 13: 59-104.

Kingston, J. and R. L. Diehl. 1994. Phonetic Knowledge. *Language* 70: 419-454.

Lisker, L. and A. S. Abramson 1964. Cross-Language Study of Voicing in Initial Stops: Acoustical Measurements. *Word* 20: 384-422.

Polivanov, E. D. 1974. The Subjective Nature of the Perceptions of Language Sounds. *Selected Works: Articles on General Linguistics*, ed. A. Leont'ev, 223-237. The Hague: Mouton.

Shibatani, M. 1990. *The Languages of Japan*. Cambridge: Cambridge University Press.

Silva, D. 2006. Acoustic Evidence for the Emergence of Tonal Contrast in Contemporary Korean. *Phonology* 23: 287-308.

Trubetzkoy, N. S. 1939. *Grundzüge der Phonologie*. Göttingen: Vandenhoeck & Ruprecht. (English edition: *Principles of Phonology*. tr. C.A.M. Baltaxe. Berkeley and Los Angeles: University of California, 1969.)

Comprehension of VP-Ellipsis and Null Object Constructions in Korean

JINSOOK KIM
University of Hawai'i at Mānoa

1. Introduction

A number of studies have extensively examined the linguistic characteristics of VP-ellipsis (1a) and null object constructions (1b) in order to elucidate similarities and differences between these constructions (Goldberg 2005; Hoji 1997, 1998; Huang 1991; Kim 1999; Lee 2005; Li 2002; Otani and Whitman 1991; Pan 2002; Park 1997; Xu 2003).

(1) a. VP-ellipsis (English)
John ate an apple and Bill did too.
b. Null object construction (Korean)
Chelswu-ka sakwa-lul mek-ess-e. Yenghuy-to mek-ess-e.
Chelswu-NOM apple-ACC eat-PST-DECL Yenghuy-also eat-PST-DECL
(lit.) 'Chelswu ate an apple. And Yenghuy ate too.'

In some previous studies, it has been claimed that the null object construction in Chinese, Japanese, and Korean structurally corresponds to VP-

Japanese/Korean Linguistics 20.
Edited by Bjarke Frellesvig and Peter Sells.

ellipsis in English since both constructions can yield sloppy readings (Huang 1991; Otani and Whitman 1991). Consider the following sentence in (2a), which is ambiguous and leads to several possible interpretations:

(2) English
   a. John washed his car and Bill did too.
   b. John$_i$ washed his$_i$ car and Bill$_j$ washed his$_j$ car too.
   c. John$_i$ washed his$_i$ car and Bill$_j$ washed his$_i$ car too.
   d. John$_i$ washed his$_k$ car and Bill$_j$ washed his$_k$ car too.
   e. *John$_i$ washed his$_k$ car and Bill$_j$ washed his$_m$ car too.

In example (2a), the auxiliary verb did replaces the elided verb phrase in the second conjunct. This elided verb phrase can be interpreted in several different ways, as indicated by the coindexing relation between the phrase's pronoun and its referent. For instance, the second clause Bill did too can mean that 'Bill washed his own car' (2b), which is traditionally called the "sloppy" reading, also known as the "bound variable" interpretation because a pronoun is treated as a variable bound to a local noun phrase. Sentence (2a) can also be interpreted as either 'Bill washed John's car' (2c), or 'John washed a third person's car and Bill washed the same person's car'(2d). The interpretations in (2c) and (2d) are both called "strict" readings. Sentence (2c) illustrates the typical strict reading, which is often referred to as the "coreference interpretation," while (2d) is the "deictic" interpretation. In the coreference interpretation (2c) and the deictic interpretation (2d), the pronouns in both the first clause and the second clause refer to the same referent. In contrast to (2c), (2d) contains a pronoun, hisk, whose referent can only be known from the discourse context, rather than from the sentence itself. Finally, the interpretation offered in (2e) is called "free reference" and is grammatically impossible.

Like the VP-ellipsis illustrated in (2), the null object construction containing a pronoun can also yield multiple interpretations. In example (3a), the second clause Yenghuy-to takk-ass-e 'Yenghuy washed too (lit.)' can mean that 'Yenghuy washed her own car' (3b), which is the sloppy reading. It can also mean that 'Yenghuy washed Chelswu's car' (3c), which is the strict reading.

(3) Korean

a. Chelswu-ka caki cha-lul takk-ass-e. Yenghuy-to takk-ass-e.
Chelswu-NOM self car-ACC wash-PST-DECL Yenghuy-also wash-PST-DECL
(lit.)'Chelswu washed self's car. Yenghuy washed too.'

b. Chelswu$_i$ washed self's$_i$ car and Yenghuy$_j$ washed self's$_j$ car too.

c. Chelswu$_i$ washed self's$_i$ car and Yenghuy$_j$ washed Chelswu's$_i$ car too.

As exemplified in (2) and (3), when the antecedent clause contains pronouns, both VP-ellipsis and the null object construction can result in multiple interpretations, such as the strict reading and the sloppy reading. This similarity supports the argument that the null object construction is a construction equivalent to VP-ellipsis.

However, Hoji (1997) observes that null object constructions in Japanese and VP-ellipsis in English cannot be considered comparable due to the unavailability of sloppy readings in Japanese. Consider examples (4)-(5):

(4) Japanese (Hoji 1998, (12))

a. John$_i$-wa zibun(zisin)$_i$-o nagusameta.
John-TOP self-ACC consoled
'John$_i$ consoled himself$_i$.'

b. Bill-mo *ec* nagusameta.
Bill-also consoled
'Bill consoled *ec* too.'

c. *Bill$_j$-mo zibun(zisin)$_j$-o nagusameta
Bill-also self-ACC consoled
'Bill$_j$ consoled himself$_j$ too.'

(5) English (Hoji 1998, (13))

a. John consoled himself.

b. Bill did too.

If the null object construction in (4) corresponds to the VP-ellipsis pattern in (5), it should allow the same sloppy reading that VP-ellipsis does. In example (4a), the reflexive pronoun *zibun(zisin)* 'self' obligatorily refers to the subject of its containing clause, yielding the meaning "John consoled himself." If the null object construction corresponded to VP-ellipsis, the phonetic string *Bill-mo nagusameta* 'Bill consoled too' (4b) would yield the sloppy reading, *Bill-mo zibun(zisin)-o nagusameta* 'Bill consoled himself, too' (4c). The null object construction in Japanese (4b), however, cannot yield the sloppy interpretation (4c). The unavailability of this reading leads Hoji (1998) to claim that the null object construction cannot be analyzed as corresponding to VP-ellipsis.

Supporting Hoji (1998), other studies have explored the differences between these two constructions (Goldberg 2005; Li 2002; Xu 2003). For instance, Xu (2003) provides evidence suggesting that, with respect to adverbial recovery, Chinese VP-ellipsis is equivalent to English VP-ellipsis but Chinese null object constructions are not. Consider example (6):

(6) Chinese (Xu 2003, (8) and (9))
  a. John hui zixide shua ya, Peter ye hui.
   John will carefully brush teeth Peter also will
   'John will brush his teeth carefully and Peter will too.'
  b. John zixide shua-le ya, Peter ye shua-le.
   John carefully brushed teeth Peter also brushed
   (lit.) 'John carefully brushed his teeth and Peter brushed too.'

In Chinese VP-ellipsis, the copular verb *shi* 'to be' and some modal verbs, such as *hui* 'will' in (6a), can be used in the elided verb phrase to replace the verb phrase used in the first clause. In (6a), the second conjunct *Peter ye hui* 'Peter also will' is interpreted as 'Peter will brush his teeth carefully too' although the adverbial *zixide* 'carefully' does not appear in the second conjunct. That is, the adverbial is phonetically null in the second conjunct in VP-ellipsis, but it is recovered at the elided site when readers/listeners comprehend the second conjunct. For the null object construction (6b), the adverbial *zixide* 'carefully' in the first conjunct does not appear in the second conjunct either. In contrast to VP-ellipsis, the adverbial in the null object construction is not obligatorily recovered in the second conjunct by comprehenders. The second conjunct in (6b) is acceptable not only when it is interpreted as 'Peter will brush his teeth carefully,' but also when it is understood as 'Peter will brush his teeth carelessly.' The differences between VP-ellipsis and the null object construction in terms of adverbial recovery led Xu (2003) to conclude that these two elliptical constructions cannot be treated as the same.

2. The current study

Based on the previous studies, this study experimentally investigates whether null object constructions can be considered comparable to VP-ellipsis in Korean. In particular, this study explores how native Korean speakers interpret elliptical constructions with respect to recovery of adverbials, focusing on their sensitivity to the differences between VP-ellipsis and null object constructions in Korean. This section describes two experiments, each exploring VP-ellipsis and null object constructions containing different types of adverbial modifier: Experiment 1 involves manner and temporal adverbials, and Experiment 2 uses reason and locative adverbials. Finally, I propose an adverbial hierarchy on the basis of the findings of this study.

2.1. Experiment 1

Participants

Twenty adult native speakers of Korean participated in this study. They included seven males and thirteen females, all of whom were college students in Korea.

Materials

Each target item consists of two sentences. The first sentence includes an adverbial phrase, which is located between the direct object and the verb. In the second sentence, the verb phrase is elided, creating VP-ellipsis or the null object construction. With respect to context, there were two different storylines—a parallel condition and a non-parallel condition. In the story that tests manner adverbial recovery, for instance, two main characters behave in the same manner in the parallel condition, whereas in the non-parallel condition, they perform the same action but in different manners. Here are examples of a manner adverbial recovery context:

<Manner adverbial recovery context>

Parallel condition

Context story (English translation):
Pooh, Piglet, and Tigger went shopping. After shopping, it was time for lunch. Tigger bought a pizza for them all to share for lunch. Because Pooh was very hungry, he ate his part of the pizza quickly. Piglet was also hungry, but he wanted to read books at the bookstore instead of eating. <u>However, Tigger suggested going to the bookstore after lunch, so Piglet ate the pizza quickly.</u>

Non-parallel condition

Context story (English translation):
Pooh, Piglet, and Tigger went shopping. After shopping, it was time for lunch. Tigger bought a pizza for them all to share for lunch. Because Pooh was very hungry, he ate his part of the pizza quickly. Piglet was also hungry, but he wanted to read books at the bookstore instead of eat-

ing. However, when Piglet saw the pizza, he thought that it looked very delicious and smelled so good. Forgetting about the bookstore, Piglet ate the pizza slowly, chewing it well.

Target sentences

a. VP-ellipsis

Pooh-ka pizza-lul ppalli mek-ess-eyo. Piglet-to-e-yo.
Pooh-NOM pizza-ACC quickly eat-PST-POL Piglet-also-be-POL
'Pooh ate the pizza quickly. Piglet did too.'

b. Null object construction

Pooh-ka pizza-lul ppalli mek-ess-eyo. Piglet-to mek-ess-eyo.
Pooh-NOM pizza-ACC quickly eat-PST-POL Piglet-also eat-PST-POL
(lit.) 'Pooh ate the pizza quickly. Piglet ate too.'

Procedure

The experiment consisted of two sessions—a practice session and a main test session. Each participant was asked to listen to stories, which were presented with animated pictures on a laptop computer screen, using Microsoft Office PowerPoint slides. At the end of each story, a written statement about what happened in the story was presented on the computer screen. Participants were asked to judge whether the statement was correct by marking 'True' or 'False' on an answer sheet. When participants mark the 'True' column, it indicates that the statement matches the story. If the 'False' column is marked, it signals that the statement does not match the story. Participants were also asked to briefly outline the reason why they marked the answer they did. The whole task took about 20 minutes for each participant to complete.

Results

As shown in figure 1, the results reveal that Korean speakers comprehended VP-ellipsis and the null object construction differently overall. In VP-ellipsis containing manner adverbials, Korean participants accepted the parallel condition 95% of the time, whereas they totally rejected the non-parallel condition. In VP-ellipsis containing temporal adverbials, similarly, they accepted the parallel condition 100% of the time, but most of them rejected the non-parallel condition.

For the null object construction, participants answered 'TRUE' to 100% of both manner and temporal adverbial recovery patterns in the parallel conditions. In the non-parallel conditions, however, they responded differently to manner versus temporal adverbial recovery. For manner adverbials, they gave 70% 'TRUE' responses. For temporal adverbials, on the other hand, participants gave only 10% 'TRUE' responses.

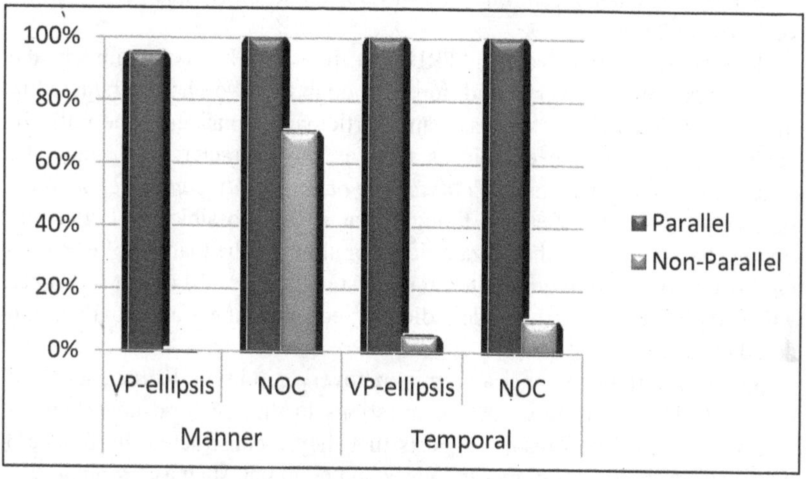

Figure 1. Acceptance rates of manner and temporal adverbial recovery in VP-ellipsis and null object constructions

VP-ellipsis

When Korean participants comprehended elided verb phrases in VP-ellipsis, they reconstructed the entire verb phrase from the first conjunct at the elided site in the second conjunct, regardless of adverbial classes. In the parallel condition, for example, Korean speakers answered 'TRUE' to the statements presented at the end of the stories, suggesting that they reconstructed the full verb phrases from the first conjunct in the second conjunct because the two main characters performed the same action in the same manner or at the same time. In the VP-ellipsis non-parallel condition, Korean speakers also reconstructed the full verb phrases from the first conjunct in the second conjunct, and in doing so they found that the statements did not match the stories, in which the two main characters did not act in the same manner or during the same time. Therefore, they did not accept the statements.

The null object construction

In the parallel condition, Korean speakers gave the response 'TRUE' to 100% of the manner and temporal adverbial conditions. That is, the two main characters in the parallel condition did the same thing in the same manner or during the same time, and Korean speakers considered the statements true. In the non-parallel condition, however, Korean speakers reconstructed the verb phrases in the second conjunct in different ways, depending on the adverbial class. That is, they tended to reconstruct the full verb phrases from the first conjunct in the second conjunct in the temporal adverbial recovery condition, but they did not do so in the manner adverbial recovery condition.

Korean speakers gave the 'TRUE' response 70% of the time in the manner adverbial recovery condition. Although the two characters acted in different manners in the stories, many participants considered the null object target sentences acceptable as long as the characters performed the same action. In the sentence, '*Pooh ate the pizza quickly and Piglet ate too*,' for example, Korean speakers thought that it was possible for Piglet, the second character, to eat the pizza quickly or slowly. The manner of eating—quickly or slowly—did not matter in understanding the null object sentences, which implies that comprehenders did not recover manner adverbials in the elided clause.

In contrast to the manner adverbial recovery condition, Korean speakers answered 'TRUE' to only 10% of questions in the temporal adverbial recovery condition. This result suggests that they reconstructed the full verb phrases from the first conjunct in the second conjunct, such as '*Pooh ate the pizza last night and Piglet ate the pizza last night too*,' and they found that the statements did not match the stories where the two main characters did the same thing but at different times. Although the two characters did the same thing, most participants considered the statements incorrect because they acted at different times. This result implies that comprehenders recovered temporal adverbials in the second conjunct.

In sum, the results of Experiment 1 show that Korean speakers were sensitive to the differences between VP-ellipsis and the null object construction in terms of adverbial recovery. In VP-ellipsis, they reconstructed the entire VP of the first conjunct at the elided site in the second conjunct. By contrast, in the null object construction, they comprehended the elided VP of the second conjunct in different ways, depending on the type of adverbial modifier.

2.2. Experiment 2

Participants

Twenty adult native speakers of Korean who participated in Experiment 1 were also tested in Experiment 2.

Materials

As in Experiment 1, there were two storylines—a parallel condition and a non-parallel condition. In the story that tests reason adverbial recovery, the two main characters perform the same action motivated by the same reason in the parallel condition, whereas in the non-parallel condition they perform the same action but are motivated by different reasons. In the story that tests locative adverbial recovery, the two main characters perform the same action in the same place in the parallel condition, and they perform the same action in different places in the non-parallel condition.

Each target item consisted of two sentences. Either a reason or a locative adverbial phrase was included in the first conjunct, located between a direct object and a verb. In the second sentence, the verb phrase was elided, creating either VP-ellipsis or the null object construction. In VP-ellipsis, -*eyo* 'to be' was used with a polite ending form. In the null object construction, the verb used in the first conjunct was repeated in the second conjunct.

Here are examples of a reason adverbial recovery context and a locative adverbial recovery context:

<Reason adverbial recovery context>

Parallel condition

> **Context story (English translation):**
> Mickey and Donald played at a playground and came home. Mickey enjoyed playing with his friends very pleasantly. When he came back home, he felt very hungry so Mickey ate the leftover pizza. <u>However, Donald didn't like pizza. He didn't want to eat pizza, but Donald was very hungry so Donald also ate the pizza.</u>

Non-parallel condition

> **Context story (English translation):**
> Mickey and Donald played at a playground and came home. Mickey enjoyed playing with his friends very pleasantly. When he came back home, he felt very hungry so Mickey ate the leftover pizza. <u>However, Donald didn't feel hungry because he had eaten a large lunch. But when Donald saw Mickey eating pizza, it looked very delicious, so Donald also ate the pizza.</u>

Target sentences

a. VP-ellipsis

Mickey-ka pizza-lul paykakop-ase mek-ess-eyo. Donald-to-e-yo.
Mickey-NOM pizza-ACC hungry-due to eat-PST-POL Donald-also-be-POL
'Mickey ate the pizza due to hunger. Donald did too.'

b. Null object construction
Mickey-ka pizza-lul paykakop-ase mek-ess-eyo. Donald-to mek-ess-eyo.
Mickey-NOM pizza-ACC hungry-due to eat-PST-POL Donald-also eat-PST-POL
'Mickey ate the pizza due to hunger. Donald ate too.'

Procedure

Experiment 2 was conducted, using the same procedure as in Experiment 1.

Results

For the data analysis, the percentages of 'True' and 'False' responses to the statements were calculated. As shown in figure 2, the results show that, overall, Korean participants comprehended the two elliptical constructions containing reason and locative adverbials differently. In the VP-ellipsis condition, Korean participants treated reason and locative adverbials in the same way, but they treated them in different way in the null object construction condition, depending on the type of context (i.e., parallel condition versus non-parallel condition).

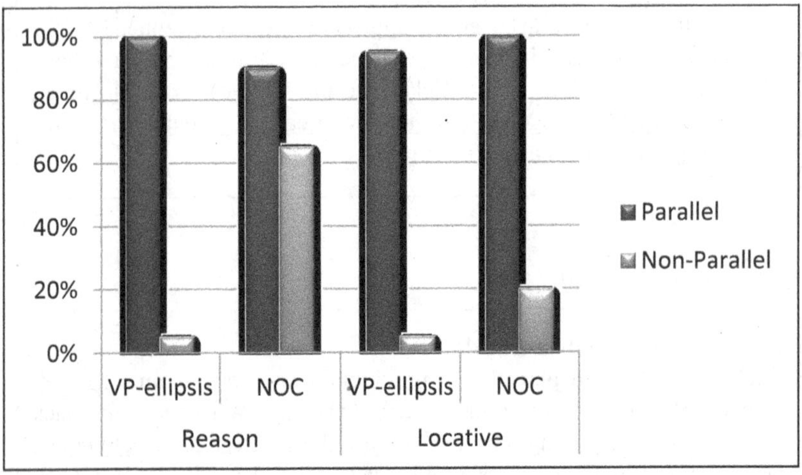

Figure 2. Acceptance rates of reason and locative adverbial recovery in VP-ellipsis and null object constructions

Looking at the details, in the VP-ellipsis condition, Korean participants answered 'TRUE' 100% of the time to the reason adverbial parallel condition, whereas most of them rejected the test items in the reason adverbial non-parallel condition. In the case of locative adverbial recovery, they gave 95% 'TRUE' responses in the parallel condition and only 5% 'TRUE' responses in the non-parallel condition, respectively.

In the null object constructions, they gave 90% and 65% 'TRUE' responses to the reason adverbial recovery parallel and non-parallel conditions, respectively. On the other hand, they answered 'TRUE' 100% of the time in the locative adverbial recovery parallel condition and 'TRUE' 20% of the time in the locative adverbial recovery non-parallel condition.

VP-ellipsis

In the reason adverbial recovery condition, Korean participants answered with 100% 'TRUE' responses in the parallel condition, suggesting that they reconstructed the full verb phrases from the first conjunct in the second conjunct (e.g., *Mickey ate the pizza due to hunger and Donald ate the pizza due to hunger, too*) and they matched the story where the two main characters did the same thing motivated by the same reason. In contrast, they answered with only 5% 'TRUE' responses to the non-parallel condition because they reconstructed the same verb phases in the first and second conjuncts as well, but the reconstructed statements did not match the story where the two main characters did the same thing motivated by different reasons. Therefore, they rejected the target statements in the reason adverbial recovery non-parallel condition by answering 'FALSE.'

In the locative adverbial recovery conditions, as the results suggest, most Korean participants reconstructed the same verb phrases in the first and the second conjuncts in both parallel and non-parallel conditions (e.g., *Mickey ate the pizza at school and Minnie ate the pizza at school, too*). As a result, there were 95% 'TRUE' responses in the parallel condition, which indicates that the statement they reconstructed matched the stories where the two main characters did the same thing during the same time. In contrast, there were only 5% 'TRUE' responses in the non-parallel condition, which indicates that the statement did not match the story where the two main characters did the same thing at different times.

The null object construction

For the null object construction, Korean participants answered 90% and 100% 'TRUE' to the reason and the locative adverbial recovery parallel conditions, respectively, which suggests that they reconstructed the full verb phrases from the first conjunct in the second conjuncts. That is, in the parallel condition, the two main characters did the same thing motivated by the same reason in the reason adverbial condition, and they did the same thing in the same place in the locative adverbial condition. Therefore, the statements that Korean participants reconstructed were considered true, matching the stories in the parallel condition.

In the non-parallel condition, however, Korean participants reconstructed verb phrases in the second conjunct in a different way, depending on the adverbial classes. That is, they tended to reconstruct the full verb phrases from the first conjunct in the second conjunct in the locative adverbial recovery condition, whereas they tended not to do so in the reason adverbial recovery condition.

In the reason adverbial recovery condition, Korean participants answered 'TRUE' in 65% of responses. Although the two characters did something for different reasons in the stories, many participants considered the null object target sentences acceptable as long as the two characters carried out the same action. In the sentence, '*Mickey ate the pizza due to hunger and Donald ate too,*' for example, Korean speakers thought that it was possible for Donald, the second character, to eat the pizza because he was hungry or because the pizza smelled very good. This suggests that comprehenders did not recover reason adverbials in the elided clause.

On the other hand, there were only 20% of 'TRUE' responses in the locative adverbial recovery condition, indicating that Korean participants reconstructed the full verb phrases from the first conjunct in the second conjunct, such as '*Mickey ate the pizza at school and Minnie ate the pizza at school, too,*' and they found that the statements they reconstructed did not match the stories where the two main characters did the same things but in different places. Although the two characters did the same things, most participants considered the statements false because the characters acted in different locations. This result implies that comprehenders recovered locative adverbials in the elided clause.

In sum, the results of Experiment 2 show that Korean speakers consistently recovered reason and locative adverbials from the first clause at the elided site in the second conjunct in VP-ellipsis construction, regardless of the type of context (i.e., parallel condition and non-parallel condition). In the null object constructions, however, they recovered reason and locative adverbials in different ways, depending on the type of context.

3. Concluding Remarks

The purpose of this study was to experimentally investigate the recovery of adverbials in elliptical constructions. Although previous studies have pointed out that VP-ellipsis and null object constructions have different reconstruction patterns at the elided site depending on the type of adverbial modifier, there have been very few empirical studies of this phenomenon. Concerning Chinese elliptical constructions, for instance, Cheung (2007) conducted an experiment to explore Chinese-speaking children's comprehension of VP-ellipsis and null object constructions with respect to manner adverbial recovery. Adapting Cheung's method, this study examined Korean adult speakers' comprehension of VP-ellipsis and null object constructions containing four different types of adverbial phrases (i.e., manner, reason, time, and location).

Then, why do manner/reason and temporal/locative adverbials behave in different ways? And why are the adverbials recovered in the second clause differently depending on elliptical construction type? One possibility is that verbs, particularly action verbs, generate time and location argument positions by virtue of the fact that the events they denote occur at particular points/periods of time or at a particular point in space. Indeed, in languages such as English, many verbs (e.g., *place*, *put*, *dash*, etc.) require overt location arguments. If this is on the right track, then a time phrase and location phrase are always present, either covertly or overtly. Where they are covert, as in the null object constructions under consideration, they can be retrieved contextually, with the help of something that was mentioned in the previous discourse.

In contrast, manner and reason adverbial positions are not obligatory, presumably because information about an event's manner and reason is more peripheral to an event's conceptual structure than information about its time and location. As a result, null manner and reason adverbial phrases are unlikely to be generated and comprehenders will make no effort to retrieve them from the antecedent phrase in the null object constructions.

Based on the findings of this study, I also propose that there is an adverbial hierarchy with relation to verbal semantics. Although it has been generally considered that manner and reason adverbials behave in the same way, comprehenders tend to reconstruct manner adverbials at the elided site less, as compared to reason adverbials. Note that, in Experiments 1 and 2, comprehenders gave 'TRUE' responses to the non-parallel manner adverbial condition more than to the non-parallel reason adverbial condition in the null object constructions. To a certain extent, the temporal and locative adverbials in Experiments 1 and 2 showed similar reconstruction patterns in the non-parallel conditions of null object constructions. However, comprehenders are likely to reconstruct temporal adverbials at the elided site more often than locative adverbials. As a result, they gave 'FALSE' responses to the temporal adverbial contexts more often than to the locative adverbial contexts in the non-parallel conditions of the null object constructions. Given the different frequency of recovery of adverbials in the null object constructions, it is observed that not all adverbial modifiers have the same reconstruction patterns.

That is, as suggested in figure 3, temporal adverbials are the most strongly implied by verbs, and therefore comprehenders can easily retrieve them by means of verbal semantics even when they are elided in the sentence. Locative adverbials can also be frequently recovered by verbs, although they are not as strongly implied as temporal adverbials. Compared to these adverbials, reason adverbials are less strongly implied by verbs and manner adverbials even less so. Therefore, manner adverbials are the least frequently recovered by comprehenders.

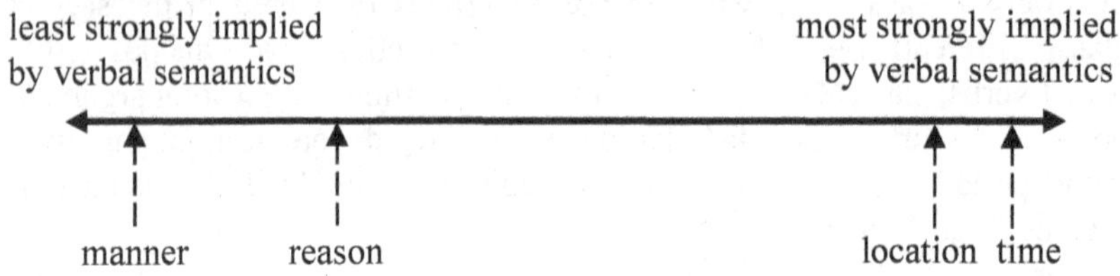

Figure 3. Adverbial hierarchy with relation to verbal semantics

Concerning Korean speakers' sensitivity to the differences between these two elliptical constructions containing adverbial phrases, I suggest that comprehenders use syntactic knowledge as well as discourse information to reconstruct null arguments in null object constructions, whereas they are more sensitive to syntactic constraints when they comprehend VP-ellipsis. Regarding the interaction between syntactic knowledge and discourse information, we need further investigation in future studies.

Acknowledgements

I would like to thank Professor William O'Grady and Professor Kamil Deen for their comments and great support. I am also grateful to the University of Hawai'i at Mānoa Linguistics Department Language Acquisition Group, the audience at the 20th Japanese/Korean Linguistics Conference, and reviewers for their valuable questions and comments.This work was supported by a University of Hawai'i at Mānoa Graduate Student Organization grant.

References

Cheung, L. Y.-L. 2008. First Language Acquisition of elliptical structures in Cantonese. Retrieved December 8, 2010, from http://www.linguistics.ucla.edu/people/grads/yllc/pdf/Cheung_2008_VPE_Acquisition(BUCLD).pdf

Goldberg, L. M. 2005. *Verb-stranding VP-ellipsis: A cross-linguistic study*. Ph.D. Dissertation. McGill University.

Hoji, H. 1997. Sloppy identity and formal dependency. *WCCFL*, 15:209–271. Stanford: CSLI.

Hoji, H. 1998. Null object and sloppy identity in Japanese. *Linguistic Inquiry*, 29:127–152.

Huang, C.-T. J. 1991. Remarks on the status of the null object. In R. Freidin (Ed.) *Principles and parameters in comparative grammar* (pp. 56–76). Cambridge: MIT Press.

Kim, S. 1999. Sloppy/strict identity, empty objects, and NP ellipsis. *Journal of East Asian Linguistics*, 8:255–284.

Lee, E. 2005. The status of the null object in the VP ellipsis context. *Studies in Generative Grammar*, 15:609–629.

Li, H. G. 2002. *Ellipsis constructions in Chinese*. Ph.D. Dissertation. University of Southern California.

Otani, K. and J. Whitman. 1991. Remarks and replies. *Linguistic Inquiry*, 22:345–358.

Pan, H. 2002. Null object constructions, focus, VP-ellipsis, and sentence interpretation. The 2nd International Conference on Formal Linguistics. Changsha, Hunan, China. Retrieved December 8, 2010, from http://www.zas.gwz-berlin.de/fileadmin/material/webfest-for-dieter-gasde/Pan.PDF

Park, M.-K. 1997. The syntax of VP ellipsis in Korean. *Language Research*, 33, 629–648.

Xu, L. 2003. Remarks on VP-ellipsis in disguise. *Linguistic Inquiry*, 34:163–171.

Korean L2 Speakers' Phonological Representation of the English /l/-/r/ Contrast

LUCY KYOUNGSOOK KIM & ELSI KAISER
University of Southern California

1. Introduction[1]

The current study investigates how phonemic contrasts that are specific to a second language (L2) are represented in learners' abstract knowledge. Prior work has shown that L2 learners face challenges in accurately perceiving and pronouncing sounds that are present only in the second language (e.g. Best et al. 2001; Ingram & Park 1998; Ota et al. 2009; Pallier et al. 2001). Studies have demonstrated that even highly proficient bilingual speakers, who appear to have no foreign accent, are still not quite native-like in distinguishing L2-specific sounds (Pallier et al. 2001; Weber & Cutler 2004 among others). For example, Pallier et al. (2001) found that highly fluent Catalan-Spanish bilinguals, whose dominant language is Spanish, were un-

[1] We thank Mitsuhiko Ota, Robert Hartsuiker, and Sarah Haywood, who generously allowed us to use their design and stimuli. Many thanks also to JK 20 participants for useful feedback.

Japanese/Korean Linguistics 20.
Edited by Bjarke Frellesvig and Peter Sells.

able to discriminate the Catalan-specific distinction between the vowels /e/ and /ɛ/ given that their dominant language, Spanish, has only /e/, and lacks /ɛ/. However, Catalan-dominant bilinguals were able to tell the sounds apart. Another well-known example of L2 speakers' challenges with L2-specific sounds is the English /l/-/r/[2] contrast for speakers whose native languages (L1s) do not distinguish them, such as Korean and Japanese. L1 Korean and L1 Japanese speakers have difficulties in accurately pronouncing and distinguishing these English sounds (e.g. Goto 1971; Ingram & Park 1998).

As a whole, adult L2 speakers' perception of speech contrasts is argued to be influenced greatly by the experiences they have with their native language phonology (see also Abramson & Lisker 1970; Best et al. 2001). Furthermore, Finn and Kam (2008) argue that learners' knowledge of first language phonology influences and even impairs the ability to use statistical patterns to segment words in a novel language. More recently, Ota et al. (2009) showed that recognition of non-native words and, by implication, their lexical representations, is influenced by L1 phonological representations. Ota et al. showed that even when issues regarding auditory perception are eliminated, the nature of L1 phonology influences the representations that learners construct for L2 words.

In the experiment presented in this paper, we build on the research conducted by Ota et al. Their findings suggest that L1 speakers of Japanese – a language with only one liquid phoneme – map the English liquids /l/ and /r/ onto a single category. We investigated Korean, which has a more complex system: a syllable-final liquid is realized as an alveolar lateral [l], whereas an intervocalic liquid is realized as an alveolar flap [ɾ]. In essence, although Korean does not exhibit multiple liquid phonemes as English does (e.g. /l/ and /r/), its single liquid phoneme (i.e. /L/ following Ingram & Park 1998) has different phonetic variations, such as [l] and [ɾ]. To further our understanding of the effects of L1 phonemic categories, as well as their phonological realizations on L2 phoneme representations, we tested how Korean speakers represent syllable-initial /l/ and /r/ in English, given that Korean—unlike Japanese—distinguishes different liquids in other syllable positions.

In Section 2, we review Ota et al.'s research and work on Korean liquids. In Sections 3 and 4, we present our experiment and results. We discuss the implications of the results in Section 5, and Section 6 is the conclusion.

[2] We use /r/ to indicate the alveolar approximant /ɹ/. Forward slashes / / represent phonemic-level representations and square brackets [ ] represent phonetic realizations.

2. Prior Work: Ota, Hartsuiker, & Haywood (2009)

Because our experiment is based largely on Ota et al.'s research paradigm, in this section we summarize their work. To test the effects of native language phonology on the lexical representation of L2 words, Ota et al. tested L1 speakers of Japanese and Arabic who were L2 speakers of English. Japanese speakers were expected to have difficulty accurately encoding the English-specific contrast between /l/ and /r/. Their native language is reported to have one liquid, an alveolar flap /ɾ/, which is pronounced somewhat in-between English /l/ and English /r/ (Goto 1971; Mochizuki 1981). L1 Arabic speakers were expected to have difficulty encoding the contrast between English /p/ and /b/, given that Modern Standard Arabic has only a voiced bilabial plosive (/b/) and lacks a voiceless bilabial plosive (/p/).

Ota et al. were interested in learners' abstract mental representations of words and sounds, i.e. how well learners are able to *encode/represent* different sounds, and not in how well learners are able to *perceive* the distinctions between various sounds.[3] Thus, they made sure that all participants were able to *hear* the difference between /l/ vs. /r/ and /p/ vs. /b/. Their main experiment used a written task – discussed in more detail below – which allowed them to probe perception-independent questions regarding the mental representations that language learners construct for words in the L2.

A crucial observation underlying Ota et al.'s design is the finding that access to the meaning of visually-presented words is mediated by phonology. This is evident from homophone effects with monolingual speakers: In a semantic-relatedness decision task, readers make more false positive errors for homophones than for spelling controls. For example, people are more likely to incorrectly say that ROWS belongs to the 'flower' category than they are to say that ROBS does (e.g. Van Orden 1987; Van Orden et al. 1988), even though neither ROWS nor ROBS is a flower. ROWS-FLOWER is an example of a homophone condition as ROWS is a homophone of ROSE, and ROBS-FLOWER is the spelling control condition.

Building on these prior studies, Ota et al. hypothesized that if a lack of contrast in L1 renders L2 words functionally homophonous, the same kind of homophone effects that had been found in monolingual visual word recognition (e.g. ROWS-FLOWER) should be found in L2 minimal pairs with non-native contrasts. That is to say, words such as LOCK and ROCK would function as homophones for Japanese L2 speakers of English if both /l/ and /r/ are mapped onto a single Japanese phoneme /ɾ/.

---

3 The question of perception is also very interesting, and has been investigated by many researchers, including Best & Strange (1992), Ingram & Park (1998).

2.1 Design of Ota et al.

To test this, Ota et al. used a written semantic-relatedness decision task. As mentioned above, they avoided using a task that involves spoken stimuli because any task that deals with auditory perception poses a compound effect between learners' inability to perceive the contrast and their inability to correctly categorize the sounds in abstract representation. In Ota et al.'s experiment, participants saw words on a screen and indicated whether the words in the pair were related in meaning. The target items included: (i) 20 real homophone pairs (e.g. SON-MOON, SUN-DAUGHTER), (ii) 20 /l-r/ near-homophone pairs (e.g. LOCK-HARD, ROCK-KEY), and (iii) 20 /p-b/ near-homophone pairs (e.g. PEACH-SAND, BEACH-APRICOT). Each target word (e.g. LOCK) was paired with a semantic associate (e.g. HARD) of its competing phoneme-counterpart (e.g. ROCK). As illustrated in Table 1, each (near)-homophone pair had a corresponding spelling-control pair.

Table 1. Ota et al.'s experimental and spelling control conditions

(Near)-Homophones	Experimental	Spelling Control
real	SON-MOON	SIN-MOON
	SUN-DAUGHTER	SIN-DAUGHTER
/l-r/	LOCK-HARD	SOCK-HARD
	ROCK-KEY	SOCK-KEY
/p-b/	PEACH-SAND	REACH-SAND
	BEACH-APRICOT	REACH-APRICOT

The researchers compared participants' error rates and response times (RTs) for the target pairs to those of the corresponding spelling controls. They used the term 'near-homophones' for the /l/-items in relation to the /r/-items (e.g. LOCK vs. ROCK) and vice versa, and we adopt this terminology.

2.2 Ota et al.'s Predictions and Results

Ota et al. predicted that all participants – L1 English speakers, as well as L1 Japanese and L1 Arabic speakers – should produce more false positive errors and slower reaction times with the real homophones (e.g. ROWS-FLOWER) than their spelling controls (e.g. ROBS-FLOWER). With regard to the near-homophones, for Japanese speakers, Ota et al. expected more false positives and slower RTs with the /l-r/ near-homophones (LOCK-HARD, ROCK-KEY) than the corresponding spelling controls (SOCK-HARD, SOCK-KEY). For the L1 Arabic group, more false positives and slower RTs were expected for /p-b/ near-homophones.

As predicted, all three groups produced more false positive errors in the real homophone condition than in the corresponding spelling control condition. Furthermore, only Japanese speakers (and not native English speakers or Arabic speakers) produced more false positive errors with /l-r/ near-homophones when compared to the spelling controls. That is, Japanese speakers were more likely to say that LOCK-HARD (or ROCK-KEY) are related than they were to say that SOCK-HARD (or SOCK-KEY) are related. This suggests that the /l/-words and the /r/-words were processed as homophones by L1 Japanese speakers. More specifically, Ota et al. hypothesized that when Japanese speakers read LOCK, its (near)-homophone ROCK is also activated, making the LOCK-HARD pair seemingly related because HARD is a semantic associate of ROCK (see McNamara 2005 for a review of the large body of work on semantic priming). This results in an increased rate of 'yes' responses (false positives). Likewise, only Arabic speakers produced more false positives in the /p-b/ near-homophone condition compared to its spelling control condition. These findings suggest that near-homophones produce homophone-like effects for non-native speakers. Ota et al. propose that transfer of L1 phonology occurs not only in the perception and articulation of L2 sounds, but also *in the phonological encoding of L2 lexical entries.* They conclude that late bilinguals cannot completely separate L2 lexical entries that involve non-native phonological contrasts.

2.3 Korean Liquids

The English /l/ and /r/ contrast poses a challenge for L1 Korean speakers, as well as L1 Japanese speakers (Ingram & Park 1998). However, Korean liquid consonants differ in interesting ways from their Japanese counterparts: Korean reportedly has only one liquid phoneme (Ingram & Park 1998; Iverson & Sohn 1994). However, researchers do not agree as to what the underlying representation of the Korean liquid consonant is. Some have suggested that /l/ is the underlying form (Kim-Renaud 1974; Ahn 1985), but others argue that the phonemic representation of the liquid is neutral with respect to the phonetic differences between [l] and [r] (Iverson & Sohn 1994). For instance, if /l/ is considered the phonemic representation, it is realized as [r] in onset position. However, if /r/ is the base form, it is realized as [l] in coda position.

Ingram and Park (1998) note that the Korean liquid phoneme has a range of phonetic variations similar to those of the Japanese liquid. Japanese has a syllable initial liquid, which has different phonetic variants, including an alveolar flap, a retroflexed flap, a combination of an alveolar lateral and a retroflexed flap, a lax alveolar stop, and an alveolar lateral. In Japanese, these liquids appear in word-initial or syllable-initial position, but *not* in syllable-final (coda) position. Importantly, in contrast to Japanese, liquids in Korean *can* occur in both syllable-initial and syllable-final position. What is of particular importance for us is that *Korean liquids are realized differently depending on syllable position* (Ingram & Park 1998): (i) Syllable-initial and intervocalic liquids are realized as an alveolar flap [ɾ], though word-initial liquids are rare (occurring mainly in loan words, such as *radio* and *lasik*), but (ii) liquids in coda position are realized as an alveolar lateral [l]. On the basis of this distributional asymmetry between Korean and Japanese, Ingram and Park propose that Korean speakers (unlike Japanese speakers) have a phonetic model available to them for the English /l-r/ contrast as long as the liquid is not in word initial position.

This difference is crucial for our study. Ota et al. did not look separately at /l/- and /r/-pairs, treating them as a single condition. However, because we are interested in potential asymmetries in L1 Korean speakers' encoding of English /l/ and /r/, we investigated these two phonemes separately.

3. Experiment

In light of Ota et al. (2009)'s finding that speakers whose L1 has only one liquid phoneme (e.g. /ɾ/ in Japanese) map English /l/ and /r/ onto the single L1 liquid category in lexical encoding, we wanted to find out what happens with Korean speakers, whose L1 has phonetic variants of a single liquid phoneme available in specific syllable positions. More broadly, this research has implications for our understanding of how L1 phonology influences the abstract representation of L2 phonemes.

3.1 Participants

Thirty-two people participated: Sixteen were native Korean speakers who speak English as their second language, and sixteen were native English speakers (control group). All participants were between the ages of eighteen and thirty-five and had normal or corrected-to-normal vision and hearing. The Korean participants' average length of residence in English-speaking countries was two years and four months (range 1;2-7;0 years). Participants received $10.

3.2 Materials and Procedure

Participants completed (i) a semantic-relatedness decision task, (ii) a phoneme identification task, (iii) a cloze test[4], and (iv) a lexical knowledge test.

3.2.1 Semantic-relatedness Decision Task

In the semantic-relatedness decision task, participants saw two words on the computer screen and indicated whether they were related. We used the /l-r/ materials and fillers from Ota et al. Thus, the experimental stimuli for the semantic-relatedness decision task were twenty /l/-/r/ near-homophone pairs

---

[4] We included the cloze test as a means of evaluating the Korean L2 speakers' English proficiency. However, because English proficiency was not taken into consideration for the current report of the study, we will not comment on it further.

(e.g. LOCK-HARD and ROCK-KEY) and twenty spelling-control pairs (e.g. SOCK-HARD and SOCK-KEY). As in Ota et al.'s design, the target words involving /l/ and /r/ were paired with the semantic associates of their competing phoneme-counterpart. For example, LOCK was paired with HARD because HARD is a semantic associate of LOCK'S competing counterpart, ROCK. Sample items are in Table 2. All experimental words were semantically *unrelated* to the words with which they were paired – in other words, LOCK is not related to HARD, and ROCK is not related to KEY.

Targets were controlled for frequency (based on the word-form frequency in CELEX; Baayen et al. 1993) and the number of orthographic and phonological neighbors (based on The English Lexicon Project; Balota et al. 2007). Eighteen of the twenty experimental items had the target phonemes (/l/ or /r/) in word-initial position.[5] The target phonemes in two additional items were part of an onset cluster (CLAP/CRAP and CLOUD/CROWD). The study also included twenty practice pairs and 120 filler pairs. Overall, half of the pairs in the experiment consisted of semantically unrelated words, and the other half related. We constructed four lists and four reverse lists. Each list had two blocks. A critical word (e.g. LOCK) and its spelling control (e.g. SOCK) appeared in the same list but never in the same block.

Table 2. Sample experimental pairs and their spelling controls

/l/-item	/l/-spelling control	/r/-item	/r/-spelling control
LOCK-HARD *(HARD is a semantic associate of ROCK.)*	SOCK-HARD	ROCK-KEY *(KEY is a semantic associate of LOCK.)*	SOCK-KEY

Each trial began with a fixation point at the center of the screen for 1000ms, followed by the test words (e.g. LOCK-HARD) in 24-point bold Arial font, juxtaposed horizontally and center-aligned. The words remained on the screen until the participant pressed a button to indicate whether they were related in meaning. E-Prime software was used to run the experiment.

3.2.2 Phoneme Identification Task

We included a phoneme identification task to ensure that the L1 Korean speakers were able to differentiate /l/ and /r/ perceptually, following Ota et al.'s procedure. This was a two-alternative forced-choice matching task involving auditory and visual nonsense syllables. Half of the critical items

[5] Two items had non-initial target phonemes: ELECT/ERECT, COLLECT/ CORRECT.

were adopted from Ota et al. ([lɑ], [rɑ], [lɛnk], [rɛnk]). Four additional nonsense syllables were created for the current study ([li], [ri], [loʊf], [roʊf]). Participants saw two nonsense syllables on the computer screen for 1000 ms, and then heard one of the two words presented auditorily. They were asked to indicate which of the two written syllables they had heard. The phoneme identification task included thirty-two targets and 100 fillers, presented in a random order.

3.2.3 Lexical Knowledge Test

Following Ota et al., we tested participants' lexical knowledge of the words used as targets and spelling control. For each word, participants were asked to choose a synonym or a definition out of three choices. This test was included to ensure that participants are able to make decisions as to whether each pair of words was related in meaning. Only the items that participants answered correctly were included in the accuracy analysis (Section 4.2.1).

3.4 Predictions

We predicted that Korean speakers' L1 phonology, particularly the fact that syllable-initial and intervocalic liquids are realized as a flap [ɾ], not an alveolar lateral [l], influences their ability to categorize word-initial /l/ and /r/ in English to different extents, resulting in more accurate performance with /r/ than /l/. Given that [l] does not appear word-initially in Korean, we expected that the encoding of English words involving /l/, such as LOCK, would be interrupted by access to the competing liquid phoneme /r/.[6] The interference from /r/ during the encoding of /l/ may result in L1 Korean speakers' judging pairs such as LOCK-HARD to be related because R̲OCK is semantically related to HARD. So, our prediction was that L1 Korean speakers would be more likely to say that LOCK-HARD is related than to say that SOCK-HARD (spelling control) is related. However, we predicted /r/-initial words to pattern differently: Because there is no phonetic model for onset /l/ in Korean, we predicted that encoding of word-initial /r/ as in ROCK would not be hampered by /l/: A pair such as ROCK-KEY would not trigger more false positives than the spelling control pair SOCK-KEY.

4. Results

We first report on the screening tasks (phoneme identification and lexical knowledge), and then the main semantic-relatedness decision task.

---

[6] This prediction is based on the assumption that the realization of the Korean word-initial [ɾ] might be more closely related to English /r/ than /l/. This could be due to the articulatory gestures in [ɾ] being more similar to those of /r/ than /l/ (i.e. /ɾ/ and /r/ both involve the tongue tip gesture without tongue dorsum gestures as in /l/, Browman & Goldstein 1995; Gick et al. 2001; Oh & Gick 2002).

4.1 Phoneme Identification Task and Lexical Knowledge Test

All Korean participants scored above 50% (16/32) on the phoneme identification task. Following Ota et al., we take this as an indication that they can perceive the difference between English /l/ and /r/ at the phonetic level. Following Ota et al., items on which participants made errors in the lexical knowledge test were excluded from subsequent analyses (L1 Korean: 77/640 (12.03%) excluded; L1 English: 6/640 (0.9%) excluded).

4.2 Semantic-relatedness Decision Task

We report the following three types of data from the semantic-relatedness task: (i) 'YES-NO' response accuracy, (ii) response latencies for correct 'NO' responses; and (iii) response latencies for incorrect 'YES' responses.

4.2.1 Response Accuracy

Response accuracy indicates how often participants correctly answered 'NO' (see Table 3 and Figure 1 overleaf). To test effects of *Phoneme* (/l/ vs. /r/) and *Condition* (Experimental vs. Spelling control), mixed ANOVAs of the mean accuracy rates were conducted for each group. There was an overall effect of *Condition* in the L1 Korean group (F1(1,15)=8.74, *p*=.01; F2(1,19)=3.41, *p*=.081: marginal by item[7]) and the L1 English group (F1(1,15)=8.17, *p*=.012; F2(1,19)=1.29, *p*=.269: n.s. by item).

We then compared the experimental condition and the spelling control condition separately for /l/ and /r/. Planned paired-samples t-tests showed that the Korean speakers' accuracy rate was lower in the experimental condition than in the spelling control condition for both the /l/-items (t1(15)=-2.935, *p*=.01; t2(19)=1.658, *p*=.114: n.s. by item) and the /r/-items (t1(15)=-2.688, *p*=.017, t2(19)=1.318, *p*=.203: n.s. by item[8]). Thus, L1 Korean speakers were more likely to give an incorrect 'yes' response to LOCK-HARD and ROCK-KEY than to SOCK-HARD or SOCK-KEY. In contrast, L1 English speakers showed no differences between the experimental and the spelling control conditions for the /l/-items (t1(15)=1.509, *p*=.152; t2(19)=-.971, *p*=.344) or the /r/-items (t1(15)=1.941, *p*=.071: marginal by subjects; t2(19)=-.807, *p*=.430).

---

[7] The marginal effect of *Condition* in the items analysis for the L1 Korean group seems to have been caused by one of the spelling control pairs (CHAP-APPLAUD, a spelling control for CRAP-APPLAUD). Those L1 Korean speakers who passed the lexical knowledge test on this item (n=3) all incorrectly responded that this pair was *related*. When we ran a statistical analysis after excluding this item (and the corresponding pairs from the other conditions, i.e. CLAP-GARBAGE, CHAP-GARBAGE, CRAP-APPLAUD), the effect of *Condition* reached significance by the items analysis as well: F2(1,18)=11.830, *p*=.003).

[8] The items analyses reached significance after the above-mentioned CLAP-based items were excluded: t2(18)=2.191, *p*=.042 for the /l/-items; t2(18)=2.786, *p*=.012 for the /r/-items.

Table 3. Accuracy rates from the semantic-relatedness decision task

Condition	Sample item	Correct ('NO') responses (%)	
		Korean	English
/l/ experimental	LOCK-HARD	74.95	96.25
/l/ spelling control	SOCK-HARD	85.74	93.68
/r/ experimental	ROCK-KEY	79.66	97.5
/r/ spelling control	SOCK-KEY	90.07	95.56

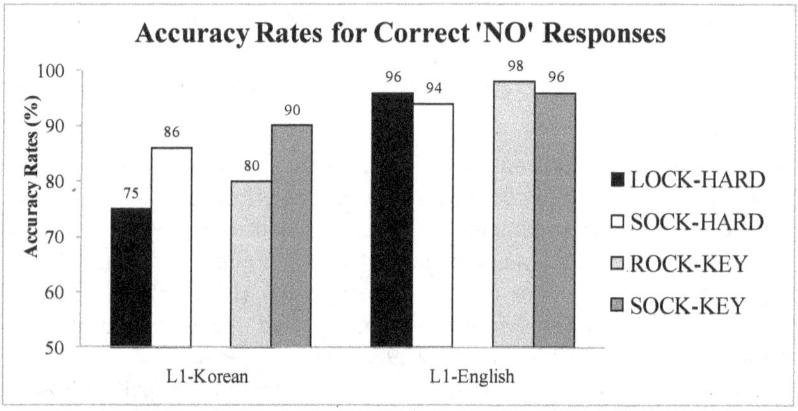

Figure 1. Mean 'YES-NO' response accuracy rates

4.2.2 Response Latencies for Correct 'NO' Responses

Now, we turn to the response latencies, the time taken to correctly respond that the experimental and spelling control pairs were unrelated (see Table 4, and Figure 2). Following Ota et al., we excluded errors ('YES' responses) and outliers (RTs>10,000 ms): 4.42% of the L1 English data and 17.76% of the L1 Korean data were excluded. In addition, following Ota et al., we used the median RTs to reduce the impact of extreme reaction times.

Table 4. Median response latencies for correct 'NO' responses

Condition	Sample item	Median response latencies (ms)	
		Korean	English
/l/ experimental	LOCK-HARD	2452	1143
/l/ spelling control	SOCK-HARD	2039	1193
/r/ experimental	ROCK-KEY	2189	1145
/r/ spelling control	SOCK-KEY	2173	1127

When analyzing response latencies, we conducted *Phoneme* x *Condition* mixed ANOVAs of the median RTs. In the L1 Korean group, there was a main effect of *Condition* (F1(1,15)=4.985, *p*=.041; F2(1,19)=.159, *p*=.695: n.s. by item). That is, L1 Korean speakers responded slower in the /l-r/ experimental condition (2320 ms) than in the spelling control condition (2106 ms). There was also an interaction between *Phoneme* and *Condition* (F1(1,15)=8.517, *p*=.011; F2(1,19)=2.638, *p*=.121: n.s. by item). That is, the RT difference between the experimental condition and the spelling control condition was greater in the /l/-items than in the /r/-items. Planned paired-samples t-tests showed that the RT in the experimental condition (LOCK-HARD) was longer compared to the spelling control condition (SOCK-HARD) only in the /l/-items (t1(15)=-3.045, *p*=.008; t2(19)=-1.082, *p*=.293: n.s. by item[9]), and not in the /r/-items. RTs for the native English speakers revealed no significant effects.

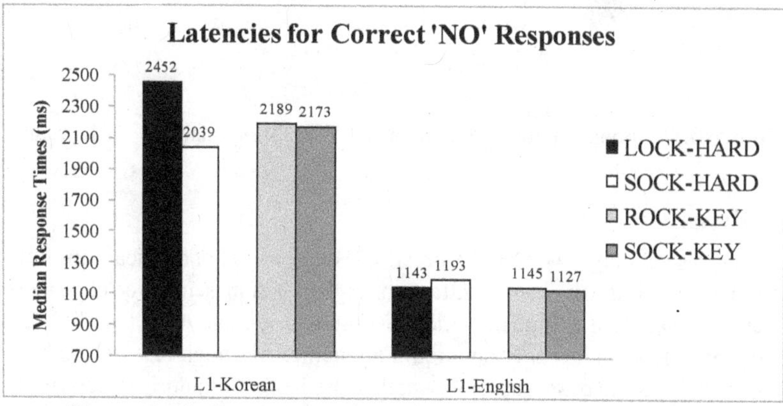

Figure 2. Median response latencies for correct 'NO' responses

4.2.3 Response Latencies for Incorrect 'YES' Responses

With correct 'NO' responses, L1 Korean speakers exhibited a slowdown with /l/-pairs, such as LOCK-HARD, but not with /r/-items, such as ROCK-KEY. In light of this asymmetry, it would be helpful to examine how rapidly L1 Korean speakers *incorrectly* judge /l/- and /r/-items to be related. Figure 3 shows the outcomes. (Due to the small and unbalanced nature of the dataset, statistical analyses could not be conducted.)

As shown in Figure 3, when L1 Korean speaking participants incorrectly responded that an /l/-item such as LOCK-HARD was related, the time it took to make this incorrect decision was noticeably shorter than the time it took participants to incorrectly decide that a spelling control pair such as

---

[9] The non-significant *p*-values from the items analyses for response latency seem to have been caused by a large amount of variance in RTs among the items across the four conditions.

SOCK-HARD was related. In other words, with /l/-items, the incorrect decisions are made rapidly. In contrast, /r/-items such as ROCK-KEY show no speed-up relative to the spelling control SOCK-KEY.

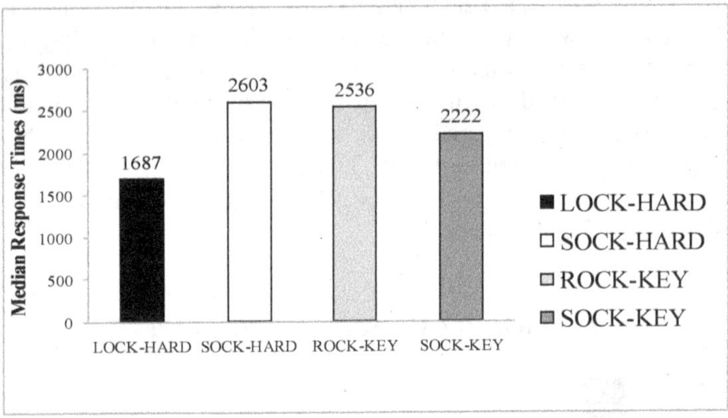

Figure 3. Response latencies for incorrect 'YES' responses by L1 Koreans

5. Discussion

In the present study, we tested Korean L2 speakers' phonological representation of the English /l/-/r/ contrast through a visual semantic-relatedness decision task. Unlike English, which distinguishes /l/ and /r/ as two different phonemes, Korean has only one liquid phoneme. Although researchers have not yet reached a consensus as to whether the Korean liquid is underlyingly /l/ or /ɾ/, what is of interest for us here is that it is realized differently depending on syllable position: an alveolar flap [ɾ] syllable-initially and an alveolar lateral [l] syllable-finally. Thus, we wanted to find out whether this variance facilitates Korean speakers' ability to encode the /l/ vs. /r/ distinction in English. This question was triggered by prior work by Ota et al. (2009) showing that native Japanese speakers, whose L1 does not show positional effects in liquid realization, encode English /l/ and /r/ as homophonous. Ota et al. found that L1 Japanese speakers tend to map both English /l/ and /r/ onto a single Japanese category of an alveolar flap [ɾ]. However, Ota et al. did not consider /l/ and /r/ separately and treated both phonemes as a single experimental condition. In the present study, we analyzed the two phonemes separately to see whether the two L2 phonemes differ in how they are mapped onto the L1 category, if at all.

The *YES-NO response accuracy results* showed that L1 Korean speakers, but not the native English controls, had lower accuracy rates in both the /l/- and the /r/-experimental conditions with respect to their spelling control conditions. Thus, we found a symmetric effect in that both /l/ and /r/ triggered an increased number of false positives: L1 Korean speakers were more likely to incorrectly answer that /l/-items such as LOCK-HARD and /r/-items such as ROCK-KEY are related when compared to their spelling controls (e.g. SOCK-HARD, SOCK-KEY). This suggests that at the point when the YES/NO relatedness decision is made, processing LOCK triggers access to its phonemic counterpart ROCK, which consequently makes the LOCK-HARD pair seemingly related. Likewise, processing ROCK seems to trigger access to LOCK, which in turn makes the ROCK-KEY pair seemingly related. This pattern seems to suggest that L1 Korean speakers cannot completely separate word-initial /l/ and /r/ at the point when the relatedness decision is made. Thus, it appears that Korean speakers may be mapping syllable-initial liquids in English onto a single Korean category.

It is important to keep in mind that the offline results show speakers' behavior at the final stage of processing. What about the processing that occurs before this final stage? We can make inferences about the real-time encoding of the L2 phonemes by looking closely at the time taken to reach the final decision. For instance, comparatively *shorter* response latencies would indicate that reaching the end-point was relatively easy, whereas *longer* response latencies would suggest that it took greater effort to reach the final 'YES' or 'NO' response.

When we examined the *response latencies,* the symmetric interference from both /l/ and /r/, found in the offline results, did not occur. L1 Korean speakers took significantly *longer* to correctly respond that /l/-items such as LOCK-HARD are unrelated when compared to spelling controls (SOCK-HARD). Furthermore, when they incorrectly responded that an item such as LOCK-HARD was *related*, their response time was noticeably shorter than that of the spelling control pair. In contrast, the time taken to correctly answer that an /r/-item such as ROCK-KEY is unrelated did not differ from the time taken to respond that the spelling control (SOCK-KEY) is unrelated. This suggests that in online processing, the /r/-initial representation (e.g. ROCK) gets in the way of encoding /l/-initial words (e.g. LOCK), making it difficult to decide whether LOCK-HARD is related. We take this as an indication that reaching the correct representation of /l/ takes more processing effort, while reaching the correct form of /r/ seems to be easier. The fact that /r/ interfered with /l/ when encoding LOCK suggests that the phonetic realizations of Korean word-initial liquid consonants are more closely related to English /r/ than English /l/.

6. Conclusions

The present investigation aimed to shed light on how the /l/-/r/ phonemic contrast in English is encoded in Korean speakers' abstract knowledge, whose L1 has only one liquid phoneme. We employed a semantic-relatedness decision task in which participants were asked to decide whether pairs of visually-presented words (e.g. LOCK-HARD, SOCK-HARD, ROCK-KEY, and SOCK-KEY) were related in meaning. The YES-NO response accuracies indicated that both /l/ and /r/ interfered with each other in L1 Korean speakers' lexical encoding of the target words when their offline final decision was considered. However, a close look at the online response latencies revealed that the degree of interference is not symmetric between the two phonemes. More specifically, reaching the correct representation of /r/ occurs faster – which we interpret as an indication of greater processing ease – than reaching the correct representation of /l/. This suggests that, in word-initial position, the realization of the Korean liquid phoneme is more closely related to that of English /r/ than /l/ (cf. Aoyama et al. 2004 for a review of Japanese /ɾ/ being perceived and pronounced more like English /l/ than /r/). Overall, our study supports the view that L1 phonology can influence L2 lexical representations independently of perception (as shown in Ota et al. 2009). Furthermore, our findings also suggest that the experiences L2 speakers have with their L1 phonology influences the representation of L2 phonemes even in a language that exhibits more than one allophonic variant of a liquid phoneme in other linguistic environments.

References

Abramson, A. & L. Lisker. 1970. Discriminability Along the Voicing Continuum: Cross-language Tests. *Proceedings of the 6th International Congress of Phonetic Sciences*, eds. B. Hala, M. Romportl, & P. Janota, 569–573. Prague: Academia.

Ahn, S.-C. 1985. The Interplay of Phonology and Morphology in Korean. Doctoral dissertation, University of Illinois.

Aoyama, K., J. E. Flege, S. G. Guionc, R. Akahane-Yamadad, & T. Yamada. 2004. Perceived Phonetic Dissimilarity and L2 Speech Learning: the Case of Japanese /r/ and English /l/ and /r/. *Journal of Phonetics*, 32: 233-250.

Baayen, R. H., R. Piepenbrock, & H. Van Rijn. 1993. *The CELEX Lexical Database*. Philadelphia: Linguistic Data Consortium.

Balota, D. A. et al. 2007. The English Lexicon Project. *Behavior Research Methods*, 39: 445–459.

Best, C. T., G. McRoberts, & E. Goodell. 2001. Discrimination of Non-native Consonant Contrasts Varying in Perceptual Assimilation to the Listener's Native Phonological System. *Journal of Acoustic Society of America*, 109 (2): 775-794.

Best, C. T., & W. Strange, 1992. Effects of Phonological and Phonetic Factors on Cross-language Perception of Approximants. *Journal of Phonetics*, 20: 305–330.

Browman, C. & L. Goldstein. 1995. Dynamics and Articulatory Phonology. *Mind as Motion: Explorations in the Dynamics of Cognition*, eds. Port & Van Gelder, 175-193. MIT Press.

Finn, A., & C. L. H. Kam. 2008. The Curse of Knowledge: First Language Knowledge Impairs Adult Learners' Use of Novel Statistics for Word Segmentation. *Cognition*, 108: 477-499.

Gick, B., F. Campbell, & S. Oh. 2001. A Cross-linguistic Study of Articulatory Timing in Liquids. Poster Presented at 142nd Meeting of Acoustical Society of America. *JASA* 110 (5), Pt. 2: 2656.

Goto, H. 1971. Auditory Perception by Normal Japanese Subjects of the Sounds "L" and "R". *Neuropsychologia*, 9: 317-323.

Ingram, J. C. L., & S.-G. Park. 1998. Language, Context, and Speaker Effects in the Identification and Discrimination of English /r/ and /l/ by Japanese and Korean Listeners. *Journal of Acoustic Society of America*, 103 (2): 1161-1366.

Iverson, G., & H.-S. Sohn. 1994. Liquid Representation in Korean. *Theoretical Issues in Korean Linguistics*, ed. Y. Kim-Renaud, 77–100. CSLI, Stanford.

Kim-Renaud, Y.-K. 1974. Korean Consonantal Phonology. Doctoral dissertation, University of Hawai'i.

McNamara, T. P. 2005. *Semantic Priming: Perspectives from Memory and Word Recognition*. Psychology press: New York.

Mochizuki, M. 1981. The Identification of /r/ and /l/ in Natural and Synthesized Speech. *Journal of Phonetics*, 9: 283-303.

Oh, S. & B. Gick. 2002. An Ultrasound Study of Articulatory Gestures of Korean Liquids. *Proceedings of International Conference on Speech Sciences*, 1: 236-242. Seoul.

Ota, M., R. Hartsuiker, & S. L. Haywood. 2009. The KEY to the ROCK: Near-Homophony in Nonnative Visual Word Recognition. *Cognition*, 111: 263-269.

Pallier, C., A. Colomé, N. Sebastián-Gallés. 2001. The Influence of Native-language Phonology on Lexical Access: Exemplar-based Versus Abstract Lexical Entries. *Psychological Science*, 12(6): 445-449.

Van Orden, G. C. 1987. A Rows is a Rose: Spelling, Sound, and Reading. *Memory and Cognition*, 15: 181-198.

Van Orden, G. C., J. C. Johnston, & B. L. Hale. 1988. Word Identification in Reading Proceeds from Spelling to Sound to Meaning. *Journal of Experimental Psychology: Learning, Memory, and Cognition*, 14: 371-386.

Weber, A., & A. Cutler. 2004. Lexical Competition in Non-native Spoken-Word Recognition. *Journal of Memory and Language*, 50: 1-25.

Three Types of 'Root Infinitives': Theoretical Implications from Child Japanese*

KEIKO MURASUGI & TOMOMI NAKATANI
Nanzan University / University of Connecticut & Nanzan University

1. Introduction

The early verbal forms in child languages reflect the core properties of the adult grammar. It is well known that very young children, at around two years old, produce nonfinite verbs or Root Infinitives (RIs) in a root clause, as shown in (1).

*The authors would like to express their gratitude to Mamoru Saito, Kamil Deen, Chisato Fuji, Tomoko Hashimoto, and the members of Center for Linguistics at Nanzan University for helpful discussions, and to the Bjarke Frellesvig, Peter Sells, participants and the anonymous reviewers of JK 20 for valuable comments. The research presented here was supported in part by the Nanzan International Research Project on Comparative Syntax and Language Acquisition (Japanese Ministry of Education and Science), Pache Research Grant I-A (Nanzan University, 2011), Open Research Project on First Language Acquisition (NINJAL), and JSPS Grant-in-Aid (Principal Investigator: Keiko Murasugi).

Japanese/Korean Linguistics 20.
Edited by Bjarke Frellesvig and Peter Sells.

(1) a. mama radio aan doen (Dutch)(2;0) (Wijnen et al. 2001)
mummy radio on do-Inf [1] 'Mummy switch on radio.'
b. Thorsten Caesar haben (German) (2;1) (Poeppel & Wexler 1993)
Thorsten Caesar have-Inf 'Thorsten has [the doll] Caesar.'

The infinitive form is used in a root clause in child Dutch and child German, while it is not allowed in the adult grammar. There are some salient morpho-syntactic and semantic properties of RIs/ Root Infinitive Analogues (RIAs).

(2) Properties common among Root Infinitives/ Root Infinitive Analogues
a. At the RI stage, no T-related/ C-related items are found.
b. RIs occur in modal contexts (Modal Reference Effects).
c. RIs occur in aspect contexts (Aspect Effects).
d. RIs are restricted to event-denoting predicates (Eventivity Constraint).
e. Head Merger is not available during the RI(A) stage.
(Cf. Deen 2002, Murasugi, Fuji & Hashimoto 2007, among others)

As listed in (2), at the RI(A) stage, C-related elements such as *wh*-questions and Complementizer (Haegeman 1995) and T-related elements are not found. RIs are used in a modal context, expressing volition or request, which is termed the Modal Reference Effects (MREs) (Hoekstra and Hyams 1998), and they are also used in aspect contexts, which we term the Aspect Effects. In addition, RIs, in general, are largely restricted to the eventive predicates (Hoekestra and Hyams 1998). Phillips (1995, 1996) and Murasugi and Fuji (2009) argue that the head merger between V and T is not available in English and Japanese, respectively, at the stage of RI(A)s.

However, there is a clear cross-linguistic variation in the form of RIs. Salustri and Hyams (2003, 2006) observe that Italian, which has been considered to have no RIs (Guasti 1993/1994), has, in fact, RIAs.

(3) Italian RIAs: Imperative form (Salustri & Hyams 2003, 2006)
dammi! (1;10)
give-to me$_{cl}$ 'give it to me.'

Italian speaking children use the imperative forms as in (3) as the RIAs.

[1] Abbreviations used in this paper are as follows: Inf=Infinitive, SA=subject agreement, 1s=1st singular, pres=present, IND=Indicative, OA=object agreement, 2s=2nd singular, cl=clitics, Decl=Declarative, Imp=Imperative, Acc=Accusative, OP=onomatopoeia, Nom=Nominative, 3s=3rd singular, VZ=verbalizer, INFL=inflection, PST=past, AT=Actor Trigger, STR=strong.

Deen (2002) argues that Swahili has a RIA, whose form is a bare verb. He argues that Swahili-speaking children omit prefixes in a pattern consistent with Schütze and Wexler's (1996) Agreement and Tense Omission Model (ATOM). According to ATOM, tense and agreement have distinct properties and play distinct roles in licensing the subjects and inflection. Table 1 summarizes a possible combination of the features of INFL. When agreement is fully specified in English, nominative Case must be assigned. When agreement is underspecified, nominative Case cannot be assigned, and hence, a default case, accusative Case, may arise. When Tense is underspecified, a verb appears with a bare verb. When tense and agreement are both underspecified, subject is marked with genitive Case with a bare verb.

Table 1. Summary of possible features of INFL (Schütze & Wexler 1996)

INFL features	Subject	Examples
+Tense, +agreement	NOM	he cries
+Tense, - agreement	ACC	him cry, him cried
- Tense, +agreement	NOM	he cry
- Tense, - agreement	GEN	his cry

Accordingly, the very young children speaking Swahili omit functional elements such as tense and subject agreement, as shown in (4).

(4) Swahili RIAs: Bare Verbs (Deen 2002)

a. Child: mimi	Ø	-na	-ruk	-a (2;10)		
Adult: mimi	ni	-na	-ruk	-a (present tense)		
I	SA1s	-pres	-jump	-IND		
'I am jump down.'						
b. Child:ni	-Ø	-kw	-ambi	-a (1;10)		
Adult: ni	-na	-kw	-ambi	-a		
SA1s	-pres	-OA2s	-tell	-IND		
'I am telling you.'						
c. Child: Ø	-Ø	-tak	-a	tuwadh	-a	(2;6)
Adult: ni	-na	-tak	-a	tuwadh	-a	
SA1s	-pres	-want	-IND	bathe	-IND	
'I want to bathe.'						

(4a) is a clause which lacks subject agreement. (4b) is a clause which lacks tense, and (4c) indicates the bare stem of the verb which lacks both subject agreement and tense.

Furthermore, Deen (2002) typologically classifies child languages into three types: languages that allow "true" RIs such as German and French, languages that has no RI phenomenon such as Italian and Japanese, and languages like Swahili whose very early nonfinite verb forms appear with bare verbs.

Table 2. Typology of Root Infinitives (Deen 2002)

True RI Languages		Non-RI Languages		Bare Verb Languages	
German	Swedish	Italian	Japanese	English	Quechua
French	Icelandic	Spanish		Sesotho	Inuktitut
Dutch	Russian	Catalan		Siswati	Swahili

This paper is concerned with the reanalysis of Deen's typology of RIs. Based on the corpus analysis of CHILDES (Noji 1973-77) and a longitudinal study with a Japanese-speaking child, we propose that RIs are not a phenomenon specific to European languages: Children universally go through a very early nonfinite verb stage when tense features are not yet fully specified. Crucially, we propose that there are RIAs in Japanese and Korean, and hence, three types of very early nonfinite verb forms in child languages that Deen (2002) proposed can be reanalyzed as shown in Table 3: RIs found with Dutch and German as in (1), Surrogate Infinitives like Italian, Japanese and Korean as in (3), and Bare Verbs like Swahili as in (4).

Table 3. Our proposal of the typology of the very early nonfinite verbs

Root Infinitives [-bare stem]		Surrogate Infinitives [-bare stem]		Bare Verbs [+bare stem]	
German	Swedish	Italian	Turkish	English	Inuktitut
French	Icelandic	Spanish	Greek	Sesotho	Swahili
Dutch		Catalan	Romanian	Siswati	Malagasy
		K'iche' Maya		Quechua	
		Kuwaiti Arabic		(Japanese onomatopoeia)	
		Korean	Japanese		

We argue that what decides the type of the RIs is a verbal morphology related to whether or not the verb stem can stand by itself as a word, but not language *per se*. Hence, two types of RI forms may coexist in a language depending on the verbal form, and we argue that this hypothesis is borne out. There are two types of RIAs in child Japanese: Surrogate Infinitives and Bare-Verb-Type RIA's appearing with (bare) onomatopoeia.

2. Surrogate Infinitives in Child Japanese: Verb+*ta* form

It has been widely accepted that there are no RIs in *pro*-drop languages (Guasti 1993/1994) and hence, there is no RIs in child Japanese (Sano 1995, Kato et al. 2003) either. However, Murasugi, Fuji and Hashimoto (2007)(=MFH), Murasugi and Fuji (2009)(=M&F) and Murasugi, Nakatani and Fuji (2009)(=MNF), among others, propose that Japanese has, in fact, RIAs, and that the form of Japanese RIAs is Verb+*ta* (past morpheme) form. *Ta*-forms produced by one-year-old Japanese-speaking children show the typical properties of RIs as listed in (2). Examples shown in (5) indicate that the Japanese RIAs appearing with *ta*-form is "erroneously" used for volition and request (MREs), and for the resultative aspects (Aspect Effects).

(5) a. Ai-ta. Ai-ta (Yuta: 1;7) (adult: *ake-ru/ake-te*) [MREs]
open-Past open-Past
'(I) want to open (the cabinet)/(You) open (the cabinet).' (MNF)
b. Baba tui-ta (Sumihare: 1;6) (adult: *tui-te-iru*) [Aspect Effects]
thread stick-Past 'The thread stuck (to my finger).' (M&F)

In (5a), the child used *ta*-form, *ai-ta* 'opened', when he wanted to ask his grandmother to open the cabinet. In this context, adults use the present form *ake-ru* or the imperative form *ake-te*. Thus, the past-tense marker *ta* is "erroneously" employed for volition and request (MREs). In (5b), the child used *ta*-form, instead of an aspectual form, *tui-te-iru*, in order to tell his mother that a thread was on his finger (Aspect Effects).

As for the reason why the *ta*-form is employed for the RIAs, Murasugi (2009) and MNF propose that Verb+*ta* is the default infinitive form for both child and adult Japanese. They argue that in the languages where the bare stem of the verb cannot stand by itself ([-stem]), there are "surrogate" verbs that look like finite verbs, but are, actually, nonfinite, in both child and adult grammar. Surrogate Infinitives are chosen as RIAs in the languages that take the value of [-Stem] for the Stem Parameter (Hyams 1986 and 2008).

(6) The Stem Parameter: A verbal stem does/does not constitute a well-formed word. (Hyams 1986, 2008) [2]

Children acquiring [-bare stem] languages undergo the Surrogate-Infinitive RIA stage. This analysis is consistent with Cinque's (2004) analysis that in adult Salentino and Serbo-Croatian, verb particle + stem followed by person or number agreement is treated as a surrogate form to make the

2 For example, in English, a verbal stem *speak* is a well-formed word in the language, while in Italian, **parl-* is ill-formed. (Hyams 1986, 2008)

verbal stem a well-formed morphological word.[3] Murasugi (2009) presents some evidence for the nonfinite status of *ta*-form. Just like Italian infinitives in root clause used as strong imperatives given in (7a) (Rizzi 1993/1994), *kaet-ta*, the *ta*-form, can be used to express the strong imperative force in Japanese as shown in (7b). [4]

(7) a. Partire Immediatamente! (Strong Imperatives in Italian)
go immediately
'Go back (somewhere) immediately!' (Rizzi 1993/1994)
b. Sassa to kaet-ta ! kaet-ta !
immediately go back-Past go back-Past
'Go back (somewhere) immediately.' (Murasugi 2009)

Thus, the *ta*-form would be a nonfinite form as well as a past-tensed form in adult Japanese. Children, without being taught by caretakers, even at one year old, choose the nonfinite V+*ta* form, attaching a "default" morpheme *ta* to the verb stem to make Surrogate Infinitives or RIAs, before they fully acquire the conjugation system of the verbs.

Then, would the analysis of Surrogate Infinitives proposed in this paper be supported cross-linguistically? The answer seems to be positive. There are a lot of important reports finding that very young children produce verbs which appear to be finite, but are, in fact, nonfinite, i.e., the Surrogate Infinitives in our term. For example, as in (8), Kim and Phillips (1998) find that Korean-speaking children, as early as two years, attach the mood marker *e*

---

[3] Kawai (2006) also argues that the Japanese RO (the subject raising to object) complement is a tenseless, aspectless clauses which is homophonic with the finite complement.

[4] Teramura (1982) and Abe (1993) argue that the past tense form V-*ta* displays not only ordinary past tense reading, but also result-state reading in certain relative clauses. Murasugi (2009) discusses the examples that indicate that nonfiniteness of V-*ta* form in adult Japanese. (See Svahn (2012; this volume) also for the discussion of the phenomenon in which an imperative is expressed with the markers of past tense *ta*.)

(i) V-*ta* form behave as nonfinite in adult Japanese
a. tabe-ta ri non-da ri su-ru/-ta
eat-Past drink-Past do-Pres/Past
'We eat/ate, and we drink/drank.'
b. it-ta ri ki-ta ri de taihen da/ dat-ta
go-Past come-Past by troublesome is/ was
'It is/was troublesome (of you) to go back and forth.'

(ii) V-*ta* form for nonrealized eventualities
Mosimo watasi-ga ie-o tate-ru/-ta nara
If I-Nom house-Acc build-pres/Past then
Tiisana ie-o tate-ru/-ta (deshoo)
small house-Acc build-pres/Past
'If I built a house, I would build a tiny one.'

and the form is used in the full range of environments almost 100 percent, just like Japanese *ta*. According to Kim and Phillips, in adult Korean, *e* functions as a default mood marker, while the child uses Verb+*e* in contexts which are not allowed in adult Korean.[5]

(8) Korean RIAs: Stem + Mood particle *–e(/a)* form

a. mek-e	emma (2 yrs) (adult form: *mek-ca* (eat-Propositive))
eat-Decl	mommy 'Let's eat, Mommy.'
b. ayki	pwo-a (2 yrs)
	(adult form: *pwo-l-kkeya* (look-Presumptive))
baby	look-Decl 'Baby (I) will look at it.'

(Kim & Phillips 1998)

In (8a), instead of the propositive morpheme, and in (8b), instead of the presumptive morpheme, *e* is used.

Table 4 summarizes child languages that have "Surrogate Infinitives".

Table 4. Child Languages that have Surrogate Infinitives

	±bare stem	Forms	Source
Italian	–	Imperative form	Salustri & Hyams (2003, 2006)
Kuwaiti Arabic	–	Masculine imperative form	Aljenaie (2000)
Spanish	–	3rd person singular form	Grinstead (1994), Pratt & Grinstead (2007)
Catalan	–	3rd person singular form	Grinstead (1994), Torrens (1995)
Roma-nian	–	Verb+Past participle form	Sava (2006)
Greek	–	Bare perfective form	Varlokosta, Vainikka & Rohrbacher (1996), Hyams (2005)
Turkish	–	Verb+-*di* (Past tense marker)	Aksu-Koç & Ketrez (2003)
K'iche' Maya	–	Stem+*ch/ik* (sen-tence terminator)	Pye (2001)
Korean	–	Stem+Mood par-ticle *e(/a)* form	Kim and Phillips (1998)

[5] Kim and Phillips (1998) argue that *e* is used by Korean-speaking children as a suffix that closes off the sentence to satisfy "Morphological Closure", using Kang's (1988) term.

For example, Arabic is a synthetic language with rich bound morphology. As shown in (9), Aljenaie (2000) finds that Kuwaiti Arabic-speaking children at one to two typically produce verbs which lack present and past tense, and mark the stem with another inflection.

(9) Kuwaiti Arabic ([-bare stem]) RIAs: Masculine imperative form
    Eh xalis (1;11-2;5) (adult form: *xalis-at* (finish-3f))
    yes, finished 'Yes, it is finished.' (Aljenaie 2000)

Children never leave the form uninflected as it does not constitute a well-formed word in Kuwaiti Arabic, but alternatively, children choose another default infix, masculine imperative form, the Surrogate Infinitive form.

Many children speaking the [-bare stem] languages produce a Surrogate Infinitive at around late one or early two years old. These children consistently use the default "conjugated" infinitive form during the period.

3. Two Types of Very Early Nonfinite Verbs in Japanese

3.1. Two types of Very Early Nonfinite verbs in a Language

Given the discussion so far, the Stem Parameter (Hyams 1986, 2008) is responsible for the possible form of the very early nonfinite verbs. If a language L selects the parametric value of [-bare stem] of the verb, children produce Surrogate Infinitives or Infinitives. On the other hand, if a language L selects the parametric value of [+bare stem] of the verb, then, children would omit the functional elements and produce bare verbs as RIAs.

However, a close examination of the previous findings reveals that RI phenomenon is not so simple. There are cases where two types of RI forms are observed in a single language as RIs. For instance, Bar-Shalom and Snyder (2001) report that children speaking Russian, a [-bare stem] language, produce two forms of RIs: infinitives in a root clause as in (10a), and imperative forms or the surrogate form in our term as in (10b).

(10) Russian [-bare stem] RIAs
   a. Tosiki [=trusiki] adet'. (1;6-2;4) [request]
      panties to-put-on (Bar-Shalom & Snyder 1999)
   b. Oden' <zakolku> (1;8) [on-going-action]
      put-on (Imp.) pin (Bar-Shalom & Snyder 2001)

In (10b), an imperative form *oden* 'put-on' describes on-going action and shows the Aspect Effects. From our point of view, Russian-speaking children produce two types of the nonfinite verbs: RIs and Surrogate Infinitives.

Salustri and Hyams (2003) also observe that the proportion of imperatives or the Surrogate Infinitives is significantly higher than that of RIs, but Italian-speaking children do produce infinitive forms as well, as in Table 5.

Table 5. Proportion of Imperative & RIs (Bilingual (Italian/German) Child)

	Imperative		Root Infinitives	
Stage	Tokens	%	Tokens	%
2;0-2;4	25/45	55.5	1/45	2
2;6-2;7	10/29	34.4	2/29	7

(Salustri & Hyams 2003)

Dutch has been considered to be a typical RI language, but still, there are some mysterious descriptions found. As shown in (11), Wijnen, Kempen and Gillis (2001) report that verbal forms resembling imperatives are found, in addition to the Infinitive forms, at the early two-word stage. If it is the case, then, Dutch-speaking children produce the imperative forms as the Surrogate Infinitives as well as the infinitive forms as their first verbs.

(11) "...Starting with the early two-word stage, forms resembling imperatives were discarded from the analyses, as it is unclear whether they are finite or nonfinite." (Wijnen, Kempen & Gillis 2001)

The findings independently obtained from Russian, Italian and Dutch may not be labeled coincidental. The very early nonfinite verbs do not necessarily appear in a single form per language.

Then, how about Japanese? Do Japanese-speaking children produce another type of "infinitive" form besides *ta*-forms? Based on the descriptive analysis, we argue that the answer is positive. The very young Japanese-speaking children produce onomatopoeic verbs just at the time when surrogate *ta*-forms are produced at around late one year old. In what follows, we argue that the onomatopoeic verbs and *ta*-forms are both RIAs in Japanese.

3. 2. Onomatopoeic/Mimetic Verbs in Adult Japanese

Japanese is rich in onomatopoeia and mimetic words. They can be used as verbs, nouns and adverbs in adult Japanese as shown in (12).

(12) a. Onomatopoeic verbs: *giragira* *suru* (do) 'glare'
b. Onomatopoeic nouns: *wanwan* 'a dog'
c. Onomatopoeic adverbs: *suyasuya* *nemuru* (sleep) 'sleep peacefully'

The onomatopoeic verbs are typically followed by the light verb *suru* 'do'. For example, mimetic verb *burabura* is followed by a light verb *suru* as in

(13a). In the structure, *suru* describes an event to walk aimlessly. Tense and aspect are marked on the light verb as shown in (13b).

(13) Onomatopoeic verbs followed by the light verb, *suru* 'do'
   a. Koen-o burabura-suru.
      park-Acc OP-do-Present '(I) walk aimlessly in the park.'
   b. Mune-ga dokidoki-si-tei-ta.
      heart-Nom OP-do-Asp-Past '(My) heart was pounding fast.'

Tsujimura (2009) points out that Bare Onomatopoteia, the onomatopoeia without being associated with the light verb *suru,* can be also used as a verb in Japanese. Bare Onomatopoeia, *pisyari* 'shut out' and *syan* 'straighten the back' in (14a) and (14b) are verbs.

(14) Bare Onomatopoeia (without the light verb *suru*) (Tsujimura 2009)
   a. Sasaki oosama-ga pisyari kanpuu riree
      Sasaki king-Nom OP shutout relay
      'The king, Sasaki, shutout a game and he let his team prevent the opposing team from scoring after several changes of pitchers.'
   b. Sesuji-ga syan
      back-Nom OP '(He) straightens (his) back.'

In fact, adult Bare Onomatopoeia shows the Modal Reference Effects, which is one of the typical properties of RIs.

(15) a. *Shi!*:'Silence!' (Strong Imperative)
   b. *Shi!*: 'Go away!' (Strong Imperative with derogatory connotation)
   c. *Sesuji-o Syan!*: 'Straighten your back!' (Strong Imperative)

Onomatopoeia *shi* in (15a) and (15b) can be the strong imperatives, meaning 'Silence!' or 'Go away', respectively. *Syan* in (15c) can also used for an imperative, meaning 'Straighten your back!' This is exactly parallel with the Italian infinitives and the Japanese *ta*-forms that we discussed in (7).

Thus, RIs may appear in two forms in adult Japanese, and two parametric values of the verb morphology may coexist: [+inflected, -stem] verbs such as V+*ta* form, and [-inflected, +stem] verbs such as Bare Onomatopoeia.

3.3. Bare Onomatopoeia as RIAs

Then, do Japanese-speaking children produce two types of RIAs? In this section, based on the corpus analysis of CHILDES (Sumihare (0;0～6;0 (Noji 1973-1977))) and our longitudinal study with a Japanese-speaking child, Yuta (0;1~3;5), we argue that the children do produce Bare Onomatopoeia, in addition to Verb+*ta*, as the very early nonfinite verbs.

Our subjects produced the onomatopoeic verbs and V+*ta* form during the same period when T-related elements such as nominative *ga* and C-related elements such as Complementizer and *wh*-phrases were not found.

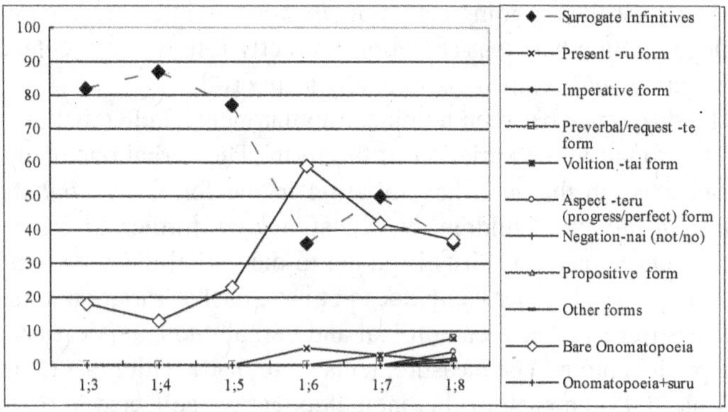

Figure 1. Proportion of Verbal Forms (Yuta)

They were predominantly produced until 1;8, until the fully conjugated verb forms are used as shown in Figure 1. These facts naturally lead us to construct a hypothesis that if the Bare Onomatopoeia show the typical properties of RI(A)s, the Bare Onomatopoeias produced along with *ta*-forms are RIAs as well.

To begin with, it is questioned if the children use "nominal" and "verbal" onomatopoeia distinctively just like adults do. Examples in (16) show that our subjects, in fact, distinctively used the onomatopoeia.

(16) a. buu itta. Atti itta (S:1;5) [nominal OP]
OP go-past there go-past
'A three-wheeler went by that way.'

b. tittyai buu buu, tittyai buu buu (Y:1;8) [nominal OP]
small OP small OP
'a small car'

c. dadadadadadadada (Y:1;6) [looking at *shinkansen*] [verbal OP]
OP
'Shinkansen, a bullet train, is running extremely fast.'

d. toon -naa (S:1;7) [S falls down and hits the head.] [verbal OP]
OP -mood
'(I) fell down.'

“Nominal” onomatopoeia are exemplified in (16a) and (16b). An onomatopoeia *buu* in (16a) refers to a three-wheeler, which is the subject of a verb *it-ta* ‘went’. *Buu buu* in (16b) modified by an adjective *tittyai* ‘small’ refers to a car. In contrast, in (16c), Yuta produced *dadadadadadadada* when he saw a bullet train, *shinkansen,* which runs very fast. Note here that at the stage, he named *shinkansen* ‘*shinkantan’* always; he used ‘*dadadadadadadada’* only for the on-going action of *shinkansen.* In contrast, onomatopoeia produced by Sumihare was sometimes directly followed by sentence-ending mood marker *na* to emphasize empathy as in (16d).

The difference between nominal onomatopoeia and verbal onomatopoeia is also found in the variation of the form. The verbal onomatopoeia *buu,* meaning “to run the car”, has variation in the form, e.g., *bubuu, buu bubuu buu buu* etc. Children, by repeating *buu,* further adverbial meaning (e.g., to run the car very fast) is added to the verbal meaning. Nominal onomatopoeia, on the other hand, does not have such a variation in the form.

The difference between nominal and verbal onomatopoeia is also found in the pitch contour. The measurements were made with Praat (Boersma and Weekink 2005) on each of the onomatopoeia we collected in the longitudinal study. Figure 2 and Figure 3 show that the nominal *buubuu* and the verbal *buu* are distinct in the pitch accent. A marked fall in pitch is obtained with the nominal *buubuu,* while the verbal *buu* has flat or rising intonation. Such patterns are also obtained from the contrast between the nominal *byuu* and the verbal *byuu*, as shown in Figure 4 and Figure 5.

Figure 2. The Pitch Contour of Nominal Onomatopoeia: *buu* (Y:1;8)

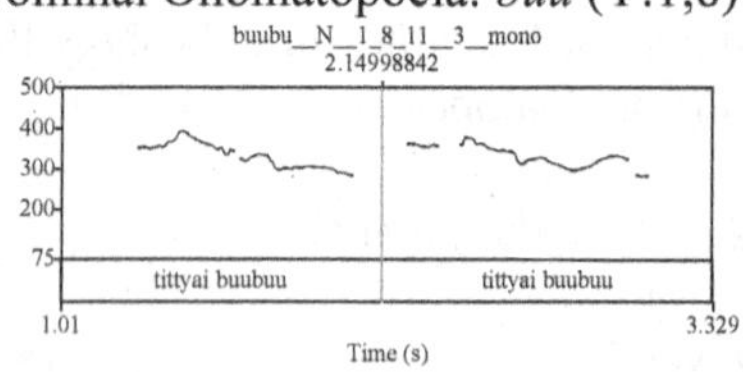

Figure 3. The Pitch Contour of Verbal Onomatopoeia:*buu* (Y:1;6)

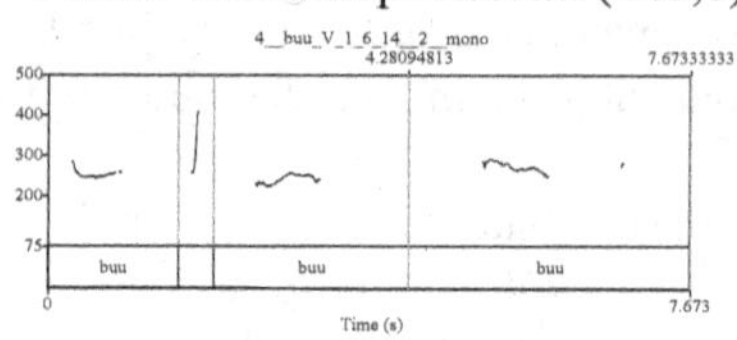

Figure 4. The Pitch Contour of Nominal Onomatopoeia: *byuu* (Y:1;7)

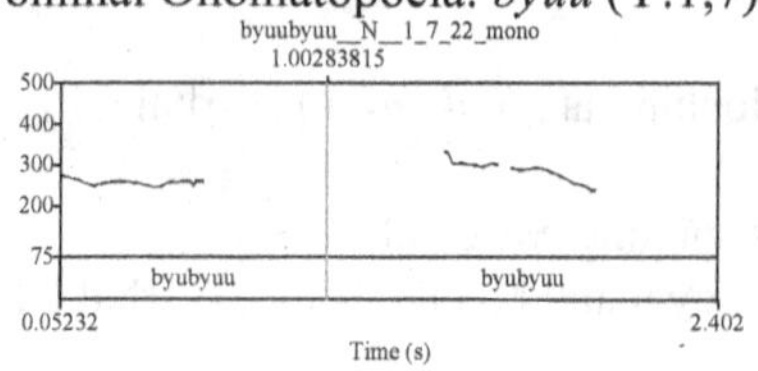

Figure 5. The Pitch Contour of Verbal Onomatopoeia:*byuu* (Y:1;8)

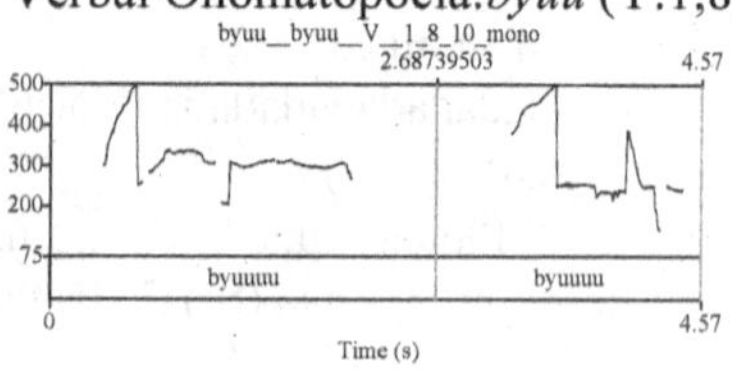

Then, are the Bare Onomaopoeia associated with the typical properties of RI(A)s given in (2)? First, Modal Reference Effects are, in fact, found with Bare Onomatopeia as shown in (18), just like the typical RI(A)s.

(18) Modal Reference Effects of Onomatopoeic RIAs

a. baba pai -ta (S:1;8)
[S wants mother to remove the dirt on a potato.]
dirt OP -past '(You) remove the dirt.'

b. odenti pai -na (S:1:10) [trying to take off his gown]
gown OP -mood '(I want to) take off (my) gown.'

c. buu, buu, buu (Y:1;6) [Y wants grandmother to move the chair that he was sitting on.]
OP '(You) move (the chair).'

d. byuuuu, byuuuu (Y:1;8) [Yuta wants his mother to draw a picture.]
OP '(You) draw a picture.'

In (18a), Sumihare produced *baba pai-ta* (onomatopoeia *pai* followed by past tense morpheme *ta*) to ask his mother to remove dirt on a potato. This expression expresses volition and request, but not the past event. (18c) also indicates that *buu buu buu* is produced to order someone to move the chair.

Aspect effects are also found. Bare Onomatopoeia were used for progressive and resultative aspect.

(19) Aspect Effects of Onomatopoeic RIAs

a. tonton tonton (S:1;6) [running after children trotting happily]
OP '(I) am running.' (progressive)

b. omoti tonton-naa (S:1;9) [watching rice-cake making]
rice-cake OP -mood '(They are) making rice-cake.' (progressive)

c. Gasyaan (Y:1;6) [looking at the broken bowl]
OP 'This bowl is broken.' (result state)

d. Pooi (Y:1;6) [looking at grandfather taking out the trash]
OP 'Grandpa is taking out the trash.' (progressive)

(19a) shows that Sumihare produced *tonton tonton* to express the progressive aspect, and (19c) shows that Yuta produced *gasyaan* to express the resultative aspect of a broken bowl, but not the bowl itself. The bowl itself was never referred to as *gasyaan* by the subject in our longitudinal study.

Just like typical RIs, Bare Onomatopoeia used as verbs are eventive. 100 percent of Bare Onomatopoeia produced by Yuta (1;3～1;8) were eventive.

(20) Eventive Constraint of Onomatopoeic RIAs

a. Bare Onomatopoeia (Sumihare): *pai* 'remove/take off', *sii* 'pee', *maimai* 'screw', *toon* 'fall down/drop', *tonton* 'hit/run'

b. Bare Onomatopoeia (Yuta): *buu* 'move', *poi* 'throw a thing', *byuu* 'draw', *jaa* 'pour', *dada* 'run fast', *biribiri* 'tear', *bibi* 'zip'

Thus, Bare Onomatopoeia in child Japanese show the MREs, the Aspect Effects and Eventivity Constraint. The analysis given above naturally leads us to conclude that there are RIAs in Japanese. Bare Onomatopoeia are, unlike Surrogate Infinitives, followed by no functional elements. Bare Onomatopoeia are, rather, like the bare verbs without functional elements that Swahili-speaking children produce as RIAs as given in (21).

(21) RIAs in Swahili (Deen 2002)

Child:	Ø	-Ø	-ka	-a	hapa	(2;3)
Adult:	a	-na	-ka	-a	hapa	
	SA3s	-pres	live	IND	here	'She lives here.'

Bare verbs as RIAs are also observed in other [+bare stem] languages. Inuktitut-speaking children produce bare verbs which are ungrammatical in their target language, as shown in (22).

(22) RIAs in Inuktitut (Swift & Allen 2002)

a. Kuapaliarumapaa. (Elijah 2;0)

kuapa	-liaq	-guma	-paaq
coop	-VZ.GO.TO	-MODAL.SIFFOX	-OH.HOW.I

'Oh, how I want to go to the co-op.'

b. Kuapalia. (Elijah 2;0)

kuapa	-liaq	- ϕ	
coop	-VZ.GO.TO	-NO.INFL	'(I want to) go to the co-op.'

Swift and Allen (2002) observe that MREs are found when inflection drops. The subject, who could produce the full form in (22a), produced bare verbs omitting the verbal inflection in (22b) when he expressed his strong volition. The parallel phenomenon is found in Malagasy as well. In (23), the subject omitted a morpheme of past tense and "actor trigger" *ni* which is obligatory in adult Malagasy.

(23) RIAs in Malagasy (Ntelitheos&Manorohanta 2004)

a.	Tomany	za	(Tsiorisoa 2;7)	
	cry	1SG NOM STR		'I cried.'
b.	Ni	tomany	aho (adult form)	
	PST AT	cry	1SG NOM STR	

The nonfinite verbs appear with Bare Onomatopoeia and V+*ta* form in Japanese. Onomatopoeia and V+*ta* form can be nonfinite in adult and child Japanese. Even one-year-old children naturally acquire the two parametric values possible in the target language, i.e., [+bare stem] and [-bare stem], and produce the two types of RIAs as their first verbs.

4. Conclusion

To conclude, whether or not the target language is *pro*-drop, children go through the very early nonfinite verb stage, where features in inflection are underspecified. What children tell us is that there are at least three types of possible nonfinite verb forms in human languages, and it is the Stem Parameter, or a parameter related to the verbal morphology that determines the form of the very early nonfinite verbs.

References

Abe, Y. 1993. Dethematized Subjects and Property Ascription in Japanese. *Language, Information and Computation, Proceedings of Asian Conference*:132-144. Seoul: Thaehakea.

Aksu-Koç, A. and F. N. Ketrez. 2003. Early Verbal Morphology in Turkish: Emergence of Inflections. *Mini-paradigms and the Emergence of Verb Morphology*, eds. D. Bittner, W. U. Dressler and M. Kilani-Schoch, 27-52. Berlin: Mouton de Gruyter.

Aljenaie, K. 2000. The Emergence of Tense and Agreement in Kuwaiti Children Speaking Arabic. *Reading Working Paper in Linguistics* vol.4. eds. R. Ingham and P. Kerswill:1-24.

Bar-Shalom, E. and W. Snyder. 1999. On the Relationship Between Root Infinitives and Imperatives in Early Child Russian. *BUCLD 23*:56-67.

Bar-Shalom, E. and W. Snyder. 2001. Desciptive Imperatives in Child Russian and Early Correct Use of Verbal Morphology. *BUCLD 25*:94-101.

Boersma, P. and D. Weenink. 2005. Praat: Doing Phonetics by Computer. [Computer program]. Retrieved from http://www.praat.org/

Cinque, G. 2004. "Restructuring" and Functional Structure. *Structures and Beyond: The Cartography of syntactic structures* vol. 3, ed. A. Belletti, 132-191. New York: Oxford University Press.

Deen, K. U. 2002. The Acquisition of Nairobi Swahili: The Morphosyntax of Inflectional Prefixes and Subjects. Ph.D. dissertation, UCLA.

Grinstead, J. 1994. The Emergence of Nominative Case Assignment in Child Catalan and Spanish. MA thesis, UCLA.

Guasti, M. T. 1993/1994. Verb Syntax in Italian Child Grammar: Finite and Nonfinite Forms. *Language Acquisition* 3:1-40.

Haegeman, L. 1995. Root Infinitives, Tense, and Truncated Structures in Dutch. *Language Acquisition* 4:205-255.

Hoekstra, T. and N. Hyams. 1998. Aspects of Root Infinitives. *Lingua* 106:91-112.

Hyams, N. 1986. Language Acquisition and the Theory of Parameters. Dordrecht: D. Reidel Publishing Co.

Hyams, N. 2005. Child Non-Finite Clauses and the Mood-Aspect Connection: Evidence from Child Greek. *The Syntax, Semantics and Acquisition of Aspect*, eds. P. Kempchinsky & R. Slabakova, 293-316. Dordrecht: Kluwer.

Hyams, N. 2008. The Acquisition of Inflection: A Parameter-Setting Approach. *Language Acquisition 15*:192-209.

Kang, M-Y. 1988. Topics in Korean Syntax: Phrase Structure, Variable Binding and Movement. Ph.D. dissertation, MIT.

Kato, S., Y. Sato, Y. Chikuda, R. Miyoshi, Y. Sakai & M. Koizumi. 2003. "Root Infinitives": Nihongo karano Kensho [Root Infinitives: From the Perspectives of Japanese]. *Tohoku University Linguistics Journal* 12:113-127

Kawai, M. 2006. Raising to Object in Japanese: Small Clause Analysis. *Linguistic Inquiry* 37:329-339.

Kim, M. and C. Phillips. 1998. Complex Verb Construction in Child Korean: Overt Markers of Covert Functional Structure. *BUCLD 22*:430-441.

Murasugi, K. 2009. What Japanese-Speaking Children's Errors Tell Us about Syntax. Paper presented at Asian Glow VII. English and Foreign Languages University. Hyderabad, India, February 28th.

Murasugi, K. and C. Fuji. 2009. Root Infinitives in Japanese and the Late Acquisition of Head-Movement. *BUCLD 33 Proceedings supplement.* http://www.bu.edu/linguistics/BUCLD/supplement33/Murasugi.pdf

Murasugi, K., C. Fuji and T. Hashimoto. 2007. What Acquired Later in an Agglutinative Language. Paper presented at the Asian GLOW VI. Chinese University of Hong Kong. December 27th.

Murasugi, K., T. Nakatani and C. Fuji. 2009. The Roots of Root Infinitive Analogues: the Surrogate Verb Forms Common in Adult and Child Grammars. Poster-presented at BUCLD 34. Boston University. November 7th.

Noji, J. 1973-1977. *Youzino Gengoseikatuno Zittai* [The Language Use in Child Age] I-IV. Tokyo: Bunka Hyoron Shuppan.

Ntelitheos, D. and C. Manorohanta. 2006. Default Pronouns and Root Infinitives in Malagasy Acquisition. *The Inaugural Conference on Generative Approaches to Language Acquisition in North America (GALANA)*:249-260.

Phillips, C. 1995. Syntax at Age Two: Cross-Linguistic Differences. *MITWPL* 26: 325-382.

Phillips, C. 1996. Root Infinitives are Finite. *BUCLD* 20:588-599.

Poeppel, D. and K. Wexler, 1993. The Full Competence Hypothesis of Clause Structure in Early German, *Language* 69:1-33.

Pratt, A. and J. Grinstead. 2007. Optional Infinitives in Child Spanish. *The 2nd Conference on Generative Approaches to Language Acquisition in North America (GALANA)*:351-362.

Pye, C. 2001. The Acquisition of Finiteness in K'iche'Maya. *BUCLD* 25:645-656.

Rizzi, L. 1993/1994. Some Notes on Linguistic Theory and Language Development: The Case of Root Infinitives. *Language Acquisition* 3:371-393.

Salustri, M. and N. Hyams. 2003. Is There an Analogue to the RI Stage in the Null Subject Languages? *BUCLD* 27:692-703.

Salustri, M. and N. Hyams. 2006. Looking for the Universal Core of the RI Stage. *The Acquisition of Syntax in Romance Languages*, eds. V. Torrens and L. Escobar, 159-182. Amsterdam: John Benjamins.

Sano, T. 1995. Roots in Language Acquisition: A Comparative Study of Japanese and European Languages. Ph.D. dissertation, UCLA.

Sava, N. 2006. Towards an Adult-Like Verbal Paradigm: The Optional Infinitive Stage in Romanian. *Analele Ştiinţifice ale Universităţii Ovidius Constanţa Seria Filologie*. [The Annals of Ovidius University Constanta Philology] 17. 255-268. Constanta: "Ovidius" University Press. Central and Eastern European Online Library.

Schütze, C. and K. Wexler. 1996. Subject Case Licensing and English Root Infinitives. *BUCLD* 20:670-681.

Svahn, A. 2012. The Perfective Imperative in Japanese. In B. Frellesvig and P. Sells (eds.) *Proceedings of the 20th Japanese/Korean Linguistics conference*. Stanford, CSLI Publications.

Swift, M. D. and S. E. M. Allen. 2002. Contexts of Verbal Inflection Dropping in Inuktitut Child Speech. *BUCLD* 20:670-681.

Teramura, H. 1982. *Nihongo no Sintakkusu to Imi* [Japanese Syntax and Meanings]. Tokyo: Kuroshio Shuppan.

Torrens, V. 1995. The Acquisition of the Functional Category Inflection in Spanish and Catalan. *MIT Working Papers in Linguistics* 26:451-472.

Tsujimura, N. 2009. Onomatope Dousi no Imi・Koukouzou no Iti Kousatu [Examination of the Meaning and Argument Structure of Mimetic Verbs]. *KLS 29; Proceedings of the Thirty-Third Annual Meeting, Kansai Linguistics Society*: 334-343.

Varlokosta, S., A. Vainikka and B. Rohrbacher. 1996. Root Infinitives without Infinitives. *BUCLD 20*:816-827.

Wijnen, F., M. Kempen, and S. Gillis. 2001. Root Infinitives in Dutch Early Child Language: an Effect of Input? *Journal of Child Language* 28:629-660.

The Acquisition of the Japanese Imperfective Aspect Marker: Universal Predisposition or Input Frequency?*

YASUHIRO SHIRAI & YOKO SUZUKI
University of Pittsburgh & University of Tokyo/JSPS

In crosslinguistic research on the acquisition of tense-aspect marking, it has been observed that children associate past-perfective marking with telic verbs, general imperfective marking with atelic verbs, and progressive marking with activity verbs at the early stages of development (for example, Bloom, Lifter & Hafiz 1980 in English, Antinucci & Miller 1976 in Italian, Stephany 1981 in Greek, Aksu-Koç 1988 in Turkish). Although researchers generally agree on this empirical observation (for example, Shirai, Slobin & Weist 1998), its explanation has been controversial. One major hypothesis appeals to a universal predisposition (e.g. Bickerton 1981, 1984); this hypothesis presupposes that children have a bias in mapping tense-aspect

* This research is supported by grants from the Japan Iron and Steel Federation and Mitsubishi Endowments at the University of Pittsburgh to Shirai, and by JSPS (Japan Society for the Promotion of Science) Research Fellowship for Young Scientists to Suzuki. We thank Kevin Gregg for his valuable comments on the paper.

Japanese/Korean Linguistics 20.
Edited by Bjarke Frellesvig and Peter Sells.

markers to particular semantic content; namely, they look for punctuality/telicity on the one hand, and durativity/atelicity on the other, on which to map morphology. Another major hypothesis appeals to input (the Distributional Bias Hypothesis, e.g. Andersen 1993, Shirai & Andersen 1995); this argues that children make particular associations based on input frequency; that is, associations in acquisition are driven by skewed input. Shirai & Andersen supported this position by analyzing input data in mother-child interaction in English. In this paper, we will report on a study that looked at Japanese data to test which of these competing hypotheses is more tenable.

1. Lexical Aspect Categories

Here, we briefly summarize Vendler's (1957) lexical aspect categories, which will be the basis for the issues addressed in this paper. Vendler's semantic categories of verb (phrase) are state, activity, accomplishment, and achievement. These are schematically represented below (Andersen 1990):

State	________________	*love, contain, know*
Activity	~~~~~~~~~~~~	*run, walk, play*
Accomplishment	~~~~~~~~~~~x	*make a chair, walk to school*
Achievement	x	*die, drop, win the race*

State terms (e.g. *love*) describe a situation that is viewed as continuing to exist unless some outside situation makes it change. Activity terms (e.g. *run*) describe a dynamic and durative situation that has an arbitrary endpoint, i.e., it can be terminated at any time. In contrast, accomplishment terms (e.g. *make a chair*) describe a situation that is dynamic and durative, but has a natural endpoint after which the particular action cannot continue. Finally, achievement terms describe a situation that can be reduced to a point on a time axis, i.e., one that is instantaneous and punctual. In the above schematization, the solid line is used to represent state, which is to last timelessly, without beginning point or endpoint in its focus. The wavy lines for activity and accomplishment indicate dynamic duration of an action, while x for accomplishment and achievement represents punctual point of change of state, signaling telicity. This verb type classification based on temporal schemata of the situation described by the verb nicely predicts the aspectual meanings that aspectual markers (e.g. *be -ing*) carry.

2. The Acquisition of Tense and Aspect

At least since the 1970s, first language acquisition researchers have observed interesting correlations between tense-aspect markers and temporal semantics of verbs to which the grammatical markers are attached. This semantic bias can be summarized as follows, which is often called the Aspect Hypothesis (Andersen & Shirai 1994), or by various other names.

1. Learners first use past marking (e.g. English) or perfective marking (Chinese, Spanish, etc.) on achievement and accomplishment verbs, eventually extending its use to activities and stative verbs.
2. In languages that encode the perfective/imperfective distinction, imperfective past appears later than perfective past, and imperfective past marking begins with stative verbs, then extending to accomplishments and activity verbs.
3. In languages that have progressive aspect, progressive marking begins with activity verbs, then extends to accomplishment or achievement verbs.
4. Progressive markings are not incorrectly overextended to stative verbs. (Andersen & Shirai 1996: 533)

Various explanations have been offered for this observation, including children's cognitive deficit (Antinucci & Miller 1976), primacy of aspect over tense (Bloom et al. 1980), the verb island hypothesis (Tomasello 1992); see Shirai (2009) for an overview. Although all these factors may be at work at some level, a theoretically important question concerns whether there is an innate basis in such a semantic bias.

Bickerton (1981, 1984) attributed such an observation to his proposed bioprogram. Assuming that children's language acquisition is influenced by his proposed bioprogram, he argued that children use past tense marking to denote punctuality, or telicity in aspectology, and progressive/imperfective marking to mark lack of telicity, because PNPD, the Punctual-NonPunctual Distinction is the distinction that has a special status in his bioprogram hypothesis.

Shirai & Andersen (1995) proposed an alternative account for the phenomena, which they called the Distributional Bias Hypothesis. Based on the analysis of child-directed speech in English, they showed that speech addressed to children also has a similar bias, though not to the same extent as in children's language. For example, about sixty percent of past tense markings are attached to achievement verbs in child-directed speech, while children's past tense markings are almost exclusively on achievement verbs at the earliest stages of past tense development.

These two competing hypotheses, however, cannot easily be tested because for most languages, they make the same prediction. This is because the telic-perfective/past, atelic-imperfective, and activity-progressive associations are highly frequent universal prototypes or defaults, coming from discourse motivations of conveying temporal information in real time (Andersen & Shirai 1994, Bohenmeyer & Swift 2004, Wu 2002). For example, when one talks about a state, one is more likely to talk about the present state, rather than the past state. (We are more likely to say *She is beautiful* rather than *She was beautiful.*) When one talks about ongoing action, it is more natural to use activity verbs with duration in present tense rather than achievement verbs, where the action is almost over with when one wants to comment on it, and thus is more often commented on in the past tense. This kind of naturalness of combination (Comrie 1976) is reflected in the frequency bias of tense-aspect marking in discourse crosslinguistically, as reviewed in Andersen & Shirai (1996).

Most of the languages in which semantic bias in tense-aspect marking is observed in language acquisition naturally follow this pattern, and thus both the bioprogram account and the input frequency account make the same prediction. Therefore, it is essential to investigate a language where the two forces compete. Japanese is one such language.

The Japanese imperfective marker *-te i-(ru)* is unusual in that it combines imperfective/progressive and perfective/resultative meanings in one form. That is, when used with durative verbs (namely, accomplishment, activity, and state verbs), it denotes progressive meaning, which is dynamic imperfective, but when used with achievement verbs, it denotes resultative meaning, which is closely associated with perfective aspect. Bickerton (1981) argued that for English, learners first map atelic verbs with progressive marking, and then (irregular) past marking to telic verbs. This is because children look for notions specified in their bioprogram –in this case, the PNPD, the punctual-nonpunctual distinction, which in aspectology roughly corresponds to the telic-atelic distinction and thus look for such notions to be mapped onto grammatical morphology.

If we follow this line of argument, Bickerton's prediction for Japanese would be as follows: Children first map telic verbs to past tense *-ta*; and then map atelic verbs to imperfective marker *-te i-(ru)*. The order is different from English because in Japanese past tense *-ta* develops much faster than imperfective *-te i-(ru)* (Shirai 1998).

The Distributional Bias Hypothesis makes a different prediction. It predicts the same association for past tense *-ta* with telic verbs, but for imperfective *-te i-(ru)*, it does not predict association with atelic verbs because as noted above, *-te i-(ru)* in the input is used with both achievement and activities very frequently. In fact, in adult-to-adult discourse, achievement verbs are more frequently used with *-te i-(ru)* than with activity verbs (Shirai & Kurono 1998, Shirai & Nishi 2005). Therefore, the input frequency account does not predict a clear association between *-te i-(ru)* and activity verbs as would be predicted by the bioprogram account.

There are two studies that looked at input frequency to Japanese children in the domain of tense-aspect (Shirai 1993, 1998). Shirai (1993) showed that Sumihare's (Noji 1976, 1977) use of *-te i-(ru)* is skewed toward activity verbs at the early stages, and indeed input he received was also skewed in the same direction (i.e. more activity verbs with *-te i-(ru)*), which may support the Distributional Bias Hypothesis. Shirai (1998) analyzed Aki's (Miyata 1995) mother's speech, in which the mother's use of *-te i-(ru)* was somewhat skewed toward activity. These studies indicate that caregivers may use *-te i-(ru)* more frequently with activity verbs. However, both corpora have limitation in that they recorded adult input only selectively. Thus, at this point we do not know the relationship between input language and children's speech in the use of *-te i-(ru)* in Japanese, which we test in this study. The present study used newly available data on CHILDES database (MacWhinney 2000) from four boys: Taro (Hamasaki 2002), Jun (Ishii 2004), Ryo (Miyata 2004) and Tai (Miyata 2000) to investigate how children and their caretakers use imperfective *-te i-(ru)*.

The research questions addressed are:

(1) Is children's use of *-te i-(ru)* associated more with activity verbs than with achievement verbs?

(2) Is caretakers' use of *-te i-(ru)* associated more with activity verbs than with achievement verbs?

(3) How does caretakers' use of *-te i-(ru)* correspond to their child's use?

(4) How does the use of *-te i-(ru)* by children and caretakers change over time?

To recap, the bioprogram hypothesis predicts that children's use of *-te i-(ru)* is associated with activity verbs, while the distributional bias hypothesis predicts that children's use follows the frequency in caretaker speech.

3. Data Analysis and Results

All tokens of *-te i-(ru)* in caretakers' and children's speech were extracted, and were coded for lexical aspect (Vendler 1957), using the linguistic tests used in Shirai (1998, see Appendix). The CLAN program (MacWhinney 2000) was used for frequency analysis. 2,517 tokens of *-te i-(ru)* were coded for lexical aspect. Table 1 is a summary of tokens produced by children and caretakers. Caretakers here include all adults engaged in the conversation. Other children, such as older siblings, are not included.

Table 1. Tokens of *-te i-(ru)* Produced by Children and Caretakers

	Child	Caretakers
Hamasaki-Taro	23	578
Ishii-Jun	144	445
Miyata-Ryo	185	134
Miyata-Tai	317	706

Here we report the results in the order of research questions (RQs).

3.1. RQ 1: Children's Use of *-te i-(ru)*

The results indicate that there is no preponderance of activity verbs and thus progressive meaning. Figure 1 summarizes overall results from children's and caretakers' speech. Since states and accomplishments are very infrequent (3.5% and 6.4% respectively), the following discussions will focus on activities and achievements. For all three children, *-te i-(ru)* is used with achievements much more frequently than with activities (average 65.5% vs. 31%).

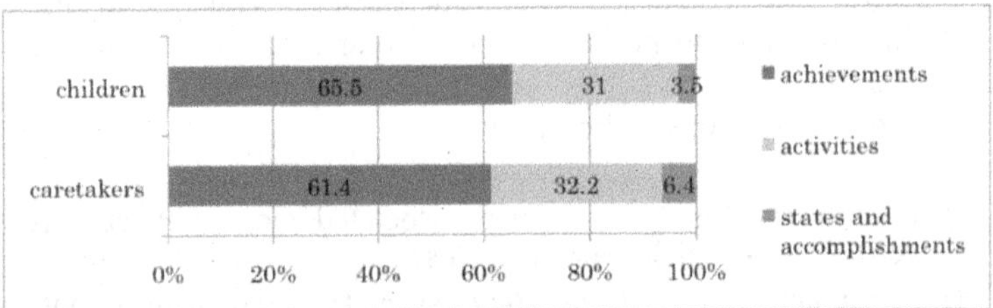

Figure 1. Children's and Caretakers' Use of Aspect Marker *-te i-(ru)*

3.2. RQ 2: Caretakers' Use of *-te i-(ru)*

Caretaker speech also showed the same tendency as that of children, exhibiting more frequent use of achievements with *-te i-(ru)* (average 61.4% vs. 32.2%). Note that children's use roughly mirrors caretakers' use in average numerical terms.

3.3. RQ 3: Relationship Between Caretakers and Their Children

Table 2 shows the percentages of achievement verbs used with *-te i-(ru)*. For Ishii's Jun and Miyata's Tai, children closely reflect the frequency of their caretakers, while one child increases the frequency of activities (Hamasaki's Taro), and one inflated the frequency of achievements (Miyata's Ryo). Thus, there is no evidence that children associate *-te i-(ru)* to activity verbs disregarding input distribution.

3.4. RQ 4: Change over Time

Altough there is no preponderance of activity verbs overall, there still is a possibility that children's early use of *-te i-(ru)* is associated with activities (and thus progressive meaning), as in the case of Sumihare (Shirai 1993) and Aki (Shirai 1998). So, let us look at Table 2, which shows the longitudinal development of *-te i-(ru)* over time. Since states and accomplishments are very infrequent, by looking at achievements, we can tell its ratio vis-à-vis activities. First, children's use of *-te i-(ru)* is very sporadic at the early stages, and therefore it is hard to observe clear trends. Still, we cannot find any evidence that children prefer activities at the early stages. During the first three months after the emergence of *-te i-(ru)*, there was only two months when activities was more frequent than achievements (Miyata's Ryo at 2;2 and Tai at 1;9). In some cases children show very high percentages of achievements, such as 90% to 100% (Hamasaki's Taro at 3;0, Miyata's Ryo at 2;1 and 2;3, Miyata's Tai at 1;7). Here again, no preponderance of activities with *-te i-(ru)* is observed.

Table 2. The Percentage of Achievement Verbs Used with *-te i-(ru)* by the Children and Caretakers (token count)

Hamasaki	pre-emergence	post-emergence						average
Age	2;2-2;10	2;11	3;0	3;1	3;2	3;3	3;4	
child	N/A	0(0)	100(1)	50(2)	88.9(8)	71.4(5)	0(0)	51.7
caretakers	61.8(222)	57.8(37)	62.5(10)	69.2(9)	60.6(20)	78.3(18)	63.2(43)	65.3

Ishii	pre-emergence	post-emergence				average
Age	1;5-2;1	2;2	2;3	2;4	2;5	
child	N/A	50.0 (2)	57.1 (8)	62.5 (20)	68.8 (64)	59.6
caretakers	52.6 (121)	66.7 (14)	50.0 (14)	57.6 (19)	64.3 (81)	59.7

Miyata-Ryo	pre-emergence	post-emergence												average
Age	1;3-2;0	2;1	2;2	2;3	2;4	2;5	2;6	2;7	2;8	2;9	2;10	2;11	3;0	
child	N/A	100(3)	40(2)	93.3(14)	75(6)	88.9(8)	100(8)	81.8(9)	60.4(29)	66.7(12)	83.3(20)	48.3(14)	85.7(6)	77.0
caretakers	86.7(11)	43(3)	50(3)	82.4(14)	70(7)	40(2)	90.9(10)	37.5(3)	38.9(7)	71.4(5)	71.4(10)	81.3(13)	100(2)	63.1

Miyata-Tai	pre-emergence	post-emergence										average
Age	1;5 -1;6	1;7	1;8	1;9	1;10	1;11	2;0	2;1	2;2	2;3	2;4	
child	N/A	100(2)	0(0)	39.1(9)	64.7(22)	69.2(18)	78.7(37)	63(17)	63.3(19)	80.5(33)	75.4(43)	63.4
caretakers	78.2(48)	40.0(22)	70(14)	42.1(32)	71.7(43)	72.2(26)	61.4(35)	57.1(40)	71.4(45)	52.8(38)	64.8(57)	60.4

Now let us look at the caretakers. The data prior to children's use of *-te i-(ru)* is analyzed separately as pre-emergence stage. This is because it is reported in the literature that caretakers change their speech depending on children's level of language development (Cross 1977). However, it turned out that there was no preponderance of activities in caretakers' speech before emergence of *-te i-(ru)*; the ratio of achievement verbs is higher than activity used with *-te i-(ru)* verbs for all caretakers (52.6% to 86.7%) at pre-emergence stage. The overall data that include both pre- and post-emergence did not show preponderance of activity verbs, either. The percentages of achievements used with *-te i-(ru)* range from 59.7 to 65.3. The comparison of overall trend and pre-emergence is interesting in that two children that Miyata investigated received much higher concentration of achievements with *-te i-(ru)* prior to emergence than after emergence.

4. Discussion

The results can be summarized as follows, according to the research questions stated earlier.

(1) Children's use of *-te i-(ru)* is more strongly associated with achievement verbs than with activity verbs.

(2) Caretaker's use of *-te i-(ru)* is more strongly associated with achievement verbs than with activity verbs.

(3) Two children showed distribution of *-te i-(ru)* similar to their caretakers, one child using more activity verbs, and one child more achievements, than their caretakers.

(4) No evidence that children (or caretakers) use *-te i-(ru)* more with activity verbs than achievement verbs at early stages.

These results suggest that contra the universalist prediction that early use of *-te i-(ru)* is associated with activity verbs to mark non-punctuality, children's use of *-te i-(ru)* is more strongly associated with achievements. Frequency in the input appears to be more important than universal predisposition in the acquisition of tense-aspect markers, thus supporting the Distribution Bias Hypothesis.

How, then can we account for some previous studies that showed preference for activity-progressive *-te i-(ru)*. Table 3 summarizes previous studies, and then the present study on children's and their caretakers' use of *-te i-(ru)*. NA indicates that in these studies input was not investigated, while ? shows that the input corpora were not adequate for the analysis. The children happen to be all boys.

If we look at all these cases, the only two children who showed some preference for activity-progressive were Sumihare and Aki, and for both children, the analysis of input showed some indication that input was skewed in the direction of activities, even though the input data were not suited for frequency analysis as discussed above. However, if they were indeed skewed in terms of overall distribution, the picture becomes clear — children follow the distributional pattern observed in the input. This is reminiscent of Shirai (1994) where one out of three children produced many stative progressives, including ungrammatical ones, contra Bicketon's (1981) state-process hypothesis, which predicts that children do not overuse progressive marking with stative verbs. This was in fact a reflection of the mothers' speech addressed to children since the mother of the child who produced many stative progressives (Naomi) also produced similar percentages of stative progressives, while the other two mothers produced none, despite the fact that stative progressives are quite common in native discourse (e.g., *I'm feeling OK. I'm living in Tokyo.)*

Table 3. Preference of Verb Semantics in the Use of *-te i-(ru)* by Children and Caregivers

	Children's speech	Input
Hiroki (Rispoli 1981)	No preference	NA
H (Horiguchi 1981)	Progressive	NA
Sumihare (Noji 1976)	Progressive-Activity	Progressive-Activity?
Taachan (Okubo 1982)	Resultative-Achievement	NA
Aki (Miyata 1995)	Progressive-Activity	Progressive-Activity?
Taro (Hamasaki 2002)	Resultative-Achievement	Resultative-Achievement
Jun (Ishii 2004)	Slight preference for Achievement	Slight preference for Achievement
Ryo (Miyata 2004)	Resultative-Achievement	Resultative-Achievement
Tai (Miyata 2000)	Resultative-Achievement	Resultative-Achievement

5. Conclusion

In conclusion, this paper investigated the acquisition of imperfective aspect marker *-te i-(ru)* in Japanese to address the issue of whether universal tendencies in tense-aspect acquisition (i.e. past-perfective marking with telic verbs, and progressive marking with activities) can be attributed to universal predisposition or input. Although teasing out these two forces has been difficult, Japanese makes it possible since the two theories make different predictions for Japanese. The results clearly indicate that contra the bioprogram hypothesis, *-te i-(ru)* was not associated with activities, and it is argued that children follow the pattern in the input language. We conclude that the results support the Distributional Bias Hypothesis in the domain of tense-aspect acquisition (Andersen 1993, Shirai & Andersen 1995), and more broadly the usage-based model of language acquisition (Tomasello 2003, Lieven & Tomasello 2008).

References

Aksu-Koç, A. 1988. *The Acquisition of Aspect and Modality: The Case of Past Reference in Turkish.* Cambridge: Cambridge University Press.

Andersen, R. W. 1990. Unpublished lecture, Applied Linguistics, University of California, Los Angeles.

Andersen, R. W. 1993. Four Operating Principles and Input Distribution as Explanations for Underdeveloped and Mature Morphological Systems. *Progression and Regression in Language*, eds. K. Hyltenstam & A. Viborg, 309-339. New York: Cambridge University Press.

Andersen, R. W., & Shirai, Y. 1994. Discourse Motivations for Some Cognitive Acquisition Principles. *Studies in Second Language Acquisition* 16:133-156.

Andersen, R. W., & Shirai, Y. 1996. Primacy of Aspect in First and Second Language Acquisition: The Pidgin/Creole Connection. *Handbook of Second Language Acquisition*, eds. W. C. Ritchie & T. K. Bhatia, 527-570. San Diego, CA: Academic Press.

Antinucci, F., & Miller, R. 1976. How Children Talk about What Happened. *Journal of Child Language* 3:169-189.

Bickerton, D. 1981. *Roots of Language*. Ann Arbor, MI: Karoma Publishers.

Bickerton, D. 1984. The Language Bioprogram Hypothesis. *The Behavioral and Brain Sciences* 7:173-188.

Bloom, L., Lifter, K., & Hafitz, J. 1980. Semantics of Verbs and the Development of Verb Inflection in Child Language. *Language* 56:386-412.

Bohnemeyer, J., & Swift, M. 2004. Event Realization and Default Aspect. *Linguistics and Philosophy* 27:263-296.

Comrie, B. 1976. *Aspect*. Cambridge: Cambridge University Press.

Cross, T. G. 1977. Mothers' Speech Adjustments: The Contribution of Selected Child Listener Variables. *Talking to Children: Language Input and Acquisition*, eds. C. E. Snow & C. A. Ferguson, 151-188. Cambridge: Cambridge University Press.

Hamasaki, N. 2002. The Timing Shift of Two-year-olds' Responses to Caretakers' Yes/No Questions. *Studies in Language Sciences*, vol. 2, eds. Y. Shirai, H. Kobayashi, S. Miyata, K. Nakamura, T. Ogura & H. Sirai, 193-206. Tokyo: Kurosio Publishers.

Horiguchi, S. 1981. Nensyoozi no Asupekuto [Aspect in Young Children]. *Gengo Syuutoku no Syosoo* [Aspects of Language Acquisition], eds. M. Hori & F. Peng. Hiroshima: Bunka Hyooron.

Ishii, T. 2004. Ishii-Corpus. Pittsburgh, PA: TalkBank. ISBN 1-59642-054-5.

Lieven, E., & Tomasello, M. 2008. Children's First Language Acquisition from a Usage-Based Perspective. *Handbook of Cognitive Linguistics and Second Language Acquisition*, eds. P. Robinson & N. Ellis, 168-196. London: Routledge.

MacWhinney, B. 2000. *The CHILDES Project: Tools for Analyzing Talk*. Mahwah, NJ: Erlbaum.

Miyata, S. 1995. The Aki Corpus: Longitudinal Speech Data of a Japanese Boy Aged 1;5.7-3;0.0. *The Bulletin of Aichi Shukutoku Junior College* 34:183-191.

Miyata, S. 2000. The Tai Corpus: Longitudinal Speech Data of a Japanese Boy Aged 1;5.20-3;1.1. *The Bulletin of Shukutoku Junior College* 39:77-85.

Miyata, S. 2004. Ryo-Corpus. Pittsburgh, PA: TalkBank. 1-59642-056-1.

Noji, J. 1976. *Yooziki no Gengo Seikatu no Zittai (II)* [The Language Development of a Child, 2] Hiroshima: Bunka Hyoron.

Noji, J. 1977. *Yooziki no Gengo Seikatu no Zittai (I)* [The Language Development of a Child, 1] Hiroshima: Bunka Hyoron.

Okubo, A. (Kokuritu Kokugo Kenkyuuzyo) 1982. *Yoozi no Kotoba Siryoo: Issaizi no Kotoba no Kiroku* [Child Language Data: A Record of Language by a One-Year-Old]. Tokyo: Shuei Shuppan.

Rispoli, M. J. V. 1981. The Emergence of Verb and Adjective Tense-Aspect Inflections in Japanese. Unpublished MA thesis, University of Pennsylvania.

Shirai, Y. 1993. Inherent Aspect and the Acquisition of Tense/Aspect Morphology in Japanese. *Argument Structure: Its Syntax and Acquisition*, eds. H. Nakajima & Y. Otsu, 185-211. Tokyo: Kaitakusha.

Shirai, Y. 1994. On the Overgeneralization of Progressive Marking on Stative Verbs: Bioprogram or Input? *First Language* 14:67-82.

Shirai, Y. 1998. The Emergence of Tense-Aspect Morphology in Japanese: Universal Disposition? *First Language* 18:281-310.

Shirai, Y. 2009. Temporality in First and Second Language Acquisition. *The Expression of Time*, eds. W. Klein & P. Li, 167-193. Berlin and New York: Mouton de Gruyter.

Shirai, Y., & Andersen, R. W. 1995. The Acquisition of Tense-aspect Morphology: A Prototype Account. *Language* 71:743-762.

Shirai, Y., & Kurono, A. 1998. The Acquisition of Tense-Aspect Marking in Japanese as a Second Language. *Language Learning* 48:245-279.

Shirai, Y., & Nishi, Y. 2005. How What We Mean Impacts How We Talk: The Japanese Imperfective Aspect Marker *-teiru* in Conversation. *The Power of Context in Language Learning and Teaching*, eds. J. Frodesen & C. Holten, 39-48. Boston, MA: Thomson Heinle.

Shirai, Y., Slobin, D., & Weist, R. M. 1998. Introduction: The Acquisition of Tense-Aspect Morphology. *First Language* 18:245-253.

Stephany, U. 1981. Verbal Grammar in Modern Greek Early Child Language. *Child Language: An International Perspective*, eds. P. S. Dale & D. Ingram, 45-57. Baltimore, MD: University Park Press.

Tomasello, M. 1992. *First Verbs: A Case Study of Early Grammatical Development.* New York: Cambridge University Press.

Tomasello, M. 2003. *Constructing a Language: A Usage-Based Theory of Language Acquisition.* Cambridge, MA: Harvard University Press.

Vendler, Z. 1957. Verbs and Times. *The Philosophical Review* 66:143-160

Wu, R-J. R. 2002. Discourse-pragmatic Principles for Temporal Reference in Mandarin Chinese Conversation. *Studies in Language* 26:513-541.

Appendix: Tests for Lexical Aspect for Japanese (Shirai 1998)

Each test is used only on the clauses remaining after the preceding test.

Step 1: State or Non-state?

Can the predicate refer to present state in simple present tense without having a habitual or vivid-present interpretation?

If **yes** → State, e.g., *Tukue no ue ni hon ga aru.* 'There is a book on the table.'

If **no** → Non-state, e.g., *Boku wa gohan o taberu.* 'I will eat rice.'

→ Go to Step 2

Step 2: Activity or Non-activity? (telic or atelic)

If you stop in the middle of the action, does that entail that you did it?

If **yes** → Activity, e.g. aruku 'walk'

If **no** → Non-activity, e.g. eki made aruku 'walk to the station'

→ Go to Step 3

If it is difficult to distinguish between 'punctual verbs denoting resultative state' and 'activity verbs denoting action in progress', use the following tests (a), (b), (c) and/or (d).

(a) Is it possible to say X wa Y (Y = time, e.g. ten minutes) V-ta without iteration involved?

If yes, activity, e.g., *John wa sanzyuppun hanasita.* 'John talked for thirty minutes.'

If no, resultative state, e.g., **John wa sanzyuppun sinda.* 'John died for thirty minutes.'

(b) Is it possible to say *X wa Y (= place) de V-teiru*, and if so, is it more natural than to say *X wa Y ni V-teiru*?

If yes, to both questions, activity, e.g., *John wa soko de neteiru*. 'John is sleeping there.'

If no, resultative state (and therefore the verb is achievement), e.g., *John wa soko ni/?de taoreteiru*. 'John fell down and is lying there.'

(c) Is it possible to say *V-hazimeru* without iteration involved?

If yes, activity, e.g. *hanasi-hazimeru* 'start talking'

If no, resultative state, e.g. **suwari-hazimeru* 'start sitting'

(d) Does the predicate have a 'simultaneous activity' reading in the frame *V-nagara*?

If yes, activity, e.g. *hanasi nagara* 'while talking'

If no, may be resultative state *siri nagara* 'although knowing'

- but not necessarily, since this test also involves 'agency'.

Step 3: Accomplishment or Achievement? (punctual or non-punctual)
If test (a) does not work, apply test (b), and possibly (c).

(a) Does *X wa Y de V-ta* (Y = time, e.g. ten minutes), entail that X was involved in Ving (i.e. *V-teita*) during that time?

If **yes** → Accomplishment, e.g., *Kare wa zyuppun de itimai no e o kaita*. 'He painted a picture in ten minutes.'

If **no** → Achievement, e.g., *Kare wa zyuppun de itimai no e ni kizuita*. 'He noticed a picture in ten minutes.'

(b) Can *V-teiru* have the sense of 'action-in-progress'?

If **yes** → Accomplishmen, e.g., *Kare wa oyu o wakasiteiru*. 'He is heating water till it is hot.'

If **no** → Achievement, e.g., *Kare wa sono e ni kizuiteiru*. 'He has noticed the picture.'

(c) *X wa Yde V-daroo* (Y = time, e.g., ten minutes) = *X wa Y-go-ni V-daroo*

If **no** → Accomplishment, e.g., *Kare wa itizikan de e o ka ku daroo*. 'He will paint a picture in an hour.' is different from *Kare wa itizikan go ni e o kaku daroo* (He will paint a picture after an hour), because the former can mean he will spend an hour painting a picture, whereas the latter does not.

If **yes** → Achievement, e.g., *Kare wa nihun de utai hazimeru daroo*. 'He will start singing after two minutes', with no other reading possible.

Children's Interpretations of Quantifier Scope Interactions in Japanese*

KYOKO YAMAKOSHI
Senshu University / Harvard University

1. Introduction

The issue of quantifier scope interactions has received much attention in language acquisition studies in recent years (Musolino 1998, 2006, Musoli-

* I would like to thank C.-T. James Huang, Noriko Imanishi, Miwa Isobe, Shigeru Miyagawa, Keiko Murasugi, Barbara Lust, Tom Roeper, Tetsuya Sano, Yasuhiro Shirai, Akira Watanabe, Ken Wexler, John Whitman and the members of TPL for their support and discussions on the earlier versions of this paper. I thank Bjarke Frellesvig, Peter Sells, the organizers and the audience at the 20th Japanese/Korean conference. The earlier versions of this paper were presented at the 6th International Conference on Language Acquisition, *GALANA*4 and Shigeru Miyagawa's seminar at MIT in Fall 2010. I thank the audience at the conferences and the seminar for their valuable comments. I am grateful to Chiaki Komatsu, the staff and the children at Zoshigaya Hoikuen in Tokyo, Japan, for their great help with the experiments. I thank Melissa Towne for the editorial help. This study is supported by the grant from Senshu University for the study of first language acquisition. All remaining errors are my own.

Japanese/Korean Linguistics 20.
Edited by Bjarke Frellesvig and Peter Sells.

no, Crain and Thornton 2000, Lidz and Musolino 2002, 2006, Musolino and Lidz 2003, 2006, Papafragou and Musolino 2003, Musolino and Gualmini 2004, Gualmini 2003, 2004, 2005/2006, Hulsey, Hacquard, Fox and Gualmini 2004, Conroy, Lidz and Musolino 2009, Zhou and Crain 2009, Terunuma 2010, etc.). The recent discussions began with Musolino (1998), in which he examined the scope interaction between *every* and negation, among other interactions, as in (1):

(1) Every horse didn't jump over the fence.

For (1), both the surface scope reading (*every>not*) and the inverse scope reading (*not>every*) are possible for English-speaking adults. Musolino found that the children accepted only the surface scope readings (*every>not*) and rejected the inverse scope readings (*not>every*), unlike adults. Musolino named this 'the observation of Isomorphism' as follows:

(2) The Observation of Isomorphism
Unlike adults, young children systematically interpret negation and quantified NPs on the basis of their position in overt syntax. (Musolino 1998, Musolino, Crain &Thornton 2000, etc.)

Since then various explanations have been proposed to explain why children interpret quantifier scope interactions differently from adults. Several studies have shown that children could accept the inverse scope readings like adults if the contexts in the experiments were carefully designed and pragmatically felicitous (e.g. Gualmini 2003, 2004, Musolino and Lidz 2003, Musolino 2006, Hulsey, Hacquard, Fox and Gualmini 2004, Zhou and Crain 2009).

This paper reports the results of our experiment on a quantifier scope interaction in Japanese which show the reverse of the Isomorphism effect. We will show that Japanese children accept both surface and inverse scope readings in the cases where adults accept only a surface scope reading. This paper focuses on the acquisition of *some/every* interaction, particularly with negation, in Japanese.

2. *Some/Every* Interaction in Japanese and Previous Acquisition Studies

First let us consider (3) in English:

(3) Someone loves everyone. (^{ok} some>every, ^{ok} every>some)

When *some* and *every* are in a simple clause as in (3), the sentence is ambiguous in English (May 1977, 1985, Huang 1982, Hornstein 1995, etc.). One reading is the surface scope reading in which *some* takes scope over *every*. Let us call this a collective reading since only one person loves everyone. The other reading is the inverse scope reading in which *every* takes scope over *some*. This means that for everyone, there is someone who loves that person, so it has a one-to-one correspondence between the person who loves and the person who is loved. Let us call this a distributive reading.

A corresponding example in Japanese is given in (4):

(4) Dareka-ga daremo-o aisiteiru.
someone-Nom everyone-Acc love
'Someone loves everyone.' (^{ok} some>every, *every>some)

When *some* and *every* are in a canonical word order as in (4) in Japanese, only the collective reading is allowed. However, when the object is scrambled as in (5), both collective and distributive readings become possible for adults (Kuroda 1970, Hoji 1985).

(5) Daremo-o dareka-ga aisiteiru.
everyone-Acc someone-Nom love
'Everyone, someone loves.' (^{ok} some>every, ^{ok} every>some)

Regarding the acquisition studies in Japanese, Sano (2004) and Goro (2007) tested Japanese children on the *some/every* interaction. Sano (2004) examined 20 children from 4;1 (i.e. four-year one-month old) to 6;5 using the Truth Value Judgment Task (Crain and Thornton 1998.) In the experiment, the experimenter told stories which included several pictures to the child. At the end of the story, the puppet who was played by another experimenter gave a test sentence as the description of what happened at the end, such as (6) and (7):

(6) Dareka-ga dono-neko-mo tukamae-ta. (Canonical SOV)
someone-Nom every-cat catch-Past
'Someone caught every cat.' (^{ok} some>every, *every>some)

(7) Dono-neko-mo dareka-ga tukamae-ta. (Scrambled OSV)
every-cat someone-Nom catch-Past
'Every cat, someone caught.' (^{ok} some>every, ^{ok} every>some)

Each test sentence was given either in a collective context or a distributive context. The child was asked to judge whether the description of the puppet given in the test sentence was right or wrong according to the given context. Table 1 shows the results of Sano (2004). With canonical word order, as shown in the highlighted part of the table, the children rejected the distributive reading correctly only 30% of the time, which means that they accepted the distributive readings 70% of the time. Adults, on the other hand, rejected the distributive reading 80% of the time. So Sano's results show that children accepted both the collective and distributive readings for canonical and scrambled word orders, unlike adults. Goro (2007) also gives similar results.

Table 1. Correct response rates for *some/every* interaction in Sano (2004)

	canonical word order (SOV)		scrambled word order (OSV)	
Situation	∃>∀	∀>∃	∃>∀	∀>∃
right answer	accept	reject	accept	accept
Children (4;1-6;5)	18/20 (90%)	6/20 (30%)	15/20 (75%)	14/20 (70%)
Adult Control	10/10 (100%)	8/10 (80%)	10/10 (100%)	10/10 (100%)

Furthermore, Yamakoshi and Sano (2007) tested children's interpretations of the *some/every* interaction in bi-clausal structures as shown in (8):

(8) Dareka-ga dono-ringo-mo oisii-to it-tayo.
someone-Nom every-apple delicious-Comp say-Past
'Someone said that every apple was delicious.'
(ok some>every, *every>some)

We examined 28 children from 4;3 to 6;9 using the Truth Value Judgment Task. In the stories, there were three boys and Snow White. Snow White asked the boys to choose the most tasty apple and bring it to her. Each test sentence was given either in a collective context (i.e. the matched context) or a distributive context (i.e. the mismatched context). In this bi-clausal structure, Japanese adults allow only the collective reading, and not the distributive reading. The results are shown in Table 2.

Table 2. Correct response rates for *some/every* interaction in bi-clausal Structures in Yamakoshi and Sano (2007)

	Children	Adults
Accepting collective reading (∃>∀)	94.6% (53/56)	95.5% (21/22)
Rejecting distributive reading (∀>∃)	51.8% (29/56)	95.5% (21/22)

As shown in the highlighted part, the children rejected the distributive readings 51.8% of the time, whereas adults rejected the distributive readings 95.5% of the time. So the studies we have seen so far show that Japanese children accept distributive readings for *some/every* interaction in both mono-clausal and bi-clausal structures.

Recently Sano (2009) examined another type of interaction, between the numeral *two* and *every* as shown in (9):

(9) Nihiki-no buta-ga dono-koppu-mo kosut-tayo.
two-Gen pig-Nom every-cup brush-Past
'Two pigs brushed every cup.' (^{ok} two>every, *every>two)

What Sano found was that, although the percentages are relatively low (42.5%), children still accepted both collective and distributive readings for both canonical and scrambled sentences.

Furthermore, Sano (2010) tested the interaction between the numeral *two* and *every* with negation as shown in (10). Sano reported that this time children successfully rejected the inverse scope readings 100% of the time.

(10) Nihiki-no risu-ga dono-yasai-mo kazira-na-kattayo.
two-Gen squirrel-Nom every-vegetable bite-Neg-Past
'Two squirrels did not bite every vegetable.'

The results of Sano's (2010) experiment show that the children were sensitive to negation and rejected distributive readings for the *numeral/every* interaction with negation. This paper extends Sano's research by investigating the interaction between *some* and *every* with negation to see if Japanese children could reject distributive readings.

First, let us compare *some/every* interaction with negation between adult English and adult Japanese. We have seen that in English *some* and *every* interaction allows both collective and distributive readings without negation in (1) at the beginning. In contrast, it has been reported that *some/every* interaction with negation allows only the collective reading in adult English (Aoun and Li 1993, Hornstein 1995, etc.). The presence of negation in (11) blocks *every* taking scope over *some*, and thus only the collective reading is allowed. The scope taking order in (11) is *some>not>every*:

(11) Someone doesn't love everyone.

The corresponding Japanese sentence in (12) also allows only the collective reading as in English.

(12) Dareka-ga daremo-o aisitei-nai.
someone-Nom everyone-Acc love-Neg
'Someone did not love everyone.' (^{ok} some>every, *every>some)

In Japanese, however, negation does not take scope over *every* and the scope taking order needs to be *some>every>neg*. Thus the quantifier *every* may be higher than negation, and the absence of distributive readings might not be due to the presence of negation. Although the position of negation in Japanese is controversial, I assume that negation in Japanese has its own projection NegP under TP as shown in (13), following Pollock (1989), Aoyagi and Ishii (1994), Kato (2000), Miyagawa (2001), Kataoka (2006):

(13) $[_{TP}\ [_{NegP}\ [_{vP}\ [_{VP}\ V\ ]\ v\ ]\ Neg\ ]\ T\ ]$

The positions of *some* and *every* in Japanese may not be the same as those in English, but in Sano (2010), it seems that negation plays a role when children rejected distributive readings in the *numeral/every* interaction. Therefore, by building on Sano's research, we examine the acquisition of *some* and *every* with negation in canonical and scrambled word orders in Japanese. An example of a scrambled sentence with negation in Japanese is (14):

(14) Daremo-o dareka-ga aisitei-nai.
everyone-Acc someone-Nom love-Neg
'Everyone, someone does not love.' (^{ok} some>every, ^{ok} every>some)

When the object is scrambled, both collective and distributive readings become possible in adult speech.

3. Experiment

In the experiment the subjects were twenty-eight monolingual Japanese children from 4;2 to 6;7. We also tested seven adults as a control. The children were tested individually in a quiet room in a nursery school in Tokyo, Japan.

The method was the Truth Value Judgment Task (Crain and Thornton 1998). The specific method of the experiment is as follows. First, the child heard stories about elephants and Mr. Doraemon (a famous cartoon character in Japan), acted out by the experimenter using stuffed animals. The puppet Miffy, who was played by the other experimenter, watched the stories together with the child. After the story, Mr. Doraemon asked the puppet Miffy what happened in the story. The child was asked to judge whether Miffy's response was right or wrong. If the child thought Miffy was right, the child was told to give a candy to Miffy as a reward, and if the child thought Miffy was wrong, the child was told to give Miffy a piece of plastic corn which would make Miffy smarter.

The stories were acted out in Japanese. The translation of a sample story in English is as follows. At the beginning, three elephants appear in front of Mr. Doraemon. The Elephants say, "Hello, Mr. Doraemon!" Mr. Doraemon replies, "Hello! Today I would like to ask you to color some pictures. Would that be ok with you?" The Elephants say, "OK!" Then Mr. Doraemon says, "In the room behind the curtain, there are some pictures like this. I am going to tell you how to color them. Could you go to the room and color them? Here is a red pen, a blue pen and a green pen. Each of you pick one color and do not change your color. You will see these three pictures with no color. Please color them like this and bring them to me." (A picture of a ship colored with red, blue and green pens is shown.) The Elephants say, "Ok!" Then the Elephants go behind the screen. This setting of the first part of the experiment is shown in Picture 1 below:

Picture 1

After a short while, they bring the pictures of ships in front of the screen without their pens. Thus the subjects cannot tell which elephant did not color the ships. The Elephants say, "Here they are!" Then Mr. Doraemon says, "OK! Miffy, what happened in this story?" Then the puppet Miffy, who is played by the other experimenter, answers giving one test sentence at the end of the each story. In this scenario, the test sentence was 'Dareka-ga dono-fune-mo nura-na-katta. (Someone did not color every ship.)' Then the child gives Miffy a candy or a piece of corn. The pictures of the end of the experiment are given in Pictures 2 and 3.

Picture 2. Collective context

Picture 3. Distributive context

The types of test sentences are as follows. In the main session after the practice session, three sentences with canonical word order were presented with one collective reading context, which was true, and two distributive reading contexts, which were false. In the collective context (e.g. Picture 2), one elephant who had a blue pen did not color the half of the sails of all the ships. In the distributive context (e.g. Picture 3), each elephant did not color a part of one ship. That is, one elephant did not color the half of the sail of one ship with a blue pen. Another elephant did not color the half of the sail of another ship with a green pen, and the last elephant did not color the body of another ship with a red pen. Three scrambled sentences were given with one collective reading context, which was true, and two distributive reading contexts which were also true. One sentence with *every* and negation was also included. I also included three practice sentences in the practice session and five fillers, which were false, to avoid yes-bias. The results are given in the next section.

4. Results

The results are given in Table 3.

Table 3. Results of *some/every* interaction with negation

	Word Order			
	Canonical (SOV)		Scrambled (OSV)	
Reading	∃>∀	∀>∃	∃>∀	∀>∃
Correct answer	accept	reject	accept	accept
Age 4 (N=12)	90.9% (10/11)	25.0% (6/24)	81.8% (9/11)	83.3% (20/24)
Age 5 (N=7)	85.7% (6/7)	21.4% (3/14)	85.7% (6/7)	100% (14/14)
Age 6 (N=9)	88.9% (8/9)	27.8% (5/18)	77.8% (7/9)	77.8% (14/18)
Total (N=28)	88.9% (24/27)	25.0% (14/56)	81.5% (22/27)	85.7% (48/56)
Adult control	100% (7/7)	71.4% (10/14)	71.4% [1] (10/14)	71.4% (10/14)

Regarding the sentences with the canonical word order, the correct response for the distributive reading is rejection (i.e. the highlighted part.) In total the children rejected the distributive readings only 25% of the time, which means that they accepted the readings 75% of the time. This is the reverse of the results of the adults since the adults rejected the distributive readings 71.4% of the time. In the canonical word order, the children accepted the collective readings 88.9% of the time. For the scrambled word order, the

[1] There were two adults who consistently did not like scrambled sentences with this quantifier scope interaction. The two adults rejected the scrambled sentences all the time. The adults who accepted distributive readings for the canonical word order and the adults who did not like scrambled sentences were different groups.

children accepted the collective reading 81.5% of the time and accepted the distributive readings 85.7% of the time.

Considering these results together with the results of Sano (2004) and Goro (2007), which I noted at the beginning, the children accepted both collective and distributive readings for canonical and scrambled sentences regarding the *some/every* interactions with and without negation.

5. Discussion

Although there may be several ways to explain these results, I would like to suggest that there is a correlation between the acquisition of scope interaction and scrambling. Miyagawa (to appear) proposes that Quantifier Raising and scrambling in Japanese are the same scope shifting operations based on their same properties regarding scope change and locality. The difference between the two is that Quantifier Raising is covert whereas scrambling is overt.

In Japanese, as we have seen at the beginning, when the word order is canonical (SOV), only the surface scope readings are allowed for quantifier scope interactions, i.e. the subject taking scope over the object. When the word order is scrambled (OSV), the sentence becomes ambiguous: the object can take scope over the subject, and the subject can take scope over the object, too. Therefore scrambling changes the quantifier scope relations, and this is why Miyagawa called scrambling as a scope shifting operation. Johnson (2000) comes to a similar conclusion regarding Quantifier Raising and scrambling by analyzing the data in German and Dutch. Similarly, Bobaljik and Wurmbrand (2008) propose that,the reason that Japanese does not allow Quantifier Raising to get distributive readings is because Japanese has scrambling. If these analyses are on the right track, they will give clues towards explaining our acquisition results.

As we have seen, unlike Japanese adults, the children accepted both collective and distributive readings for canonical and scrambled sentences for *some/every* interaction with and without negation. These results suggest that Japanese children are using Quantifier Raising to interpret *some/every* interaction. It is possible that the children raise the quantifier *every* to a higher position than *some* and negation, and thus the children accept distributive readings, unlike adults. If so, why do Japanese children use Quantifier Raising for *some/every* interaction, unlike adults? My hypothesis is that children do not acquire scrambling as a scope shifting operation until a later stage. Since Japanese adults know that scrambling is the scope shifting operation, they do not use Quantifier Raising to get distributive readings.

There are some acquisition studies which show that Japanese children have difficulty in scrambling. Although it is not clear yet what aspect of scrambling is particularly difficult for children, I review some previous studies which suggest the problems that children might have.

First, Hayashibe (1975) conducted an experiment using the act-out task. In that task, children act out the scrambled sentences they heard by moving stuffed animals. Hayashibe tested twenty-three children from 3;1 to 5;10. Among the children, he reported that ten children (average 4;9, youngest 3;4, oldest 5;10) relied on the word order strategy (Agent-Patient-Verb) and misunderstood the OSV sentences as SOV sentences. This result shows that some children at 5;10 still had problems to act out scrambled sentences.

Later, Otsu (1994) showed that Japanese three-year-old children could act out scrambled sentences correctly when the discourse contexts are given before the scrambled sentence. However, the children who were tested without these contexts still had difficulty in acting out the scrambled sentences. The sentences Otsu used in his experiment are in (15) and (16).

(15) Without contexts

Ahirusan-o	kamesan-ga	osi-masi-ta.
duck-Acc	turtle-Nom	push-Polite-Past

'A/The turtle pushed a/the duck.'

(16) With contexts

Kooen-ni	ahirusan-ga	i-masi-ta.	
Park in	duck-Nom	is-Polite-Past	
Sono	ahirusan-o	kamesan-ga	osi-masi-ta.
The	duck-Acc	turtle-Nom	push-Polite-Past

'There was a duck in the park. A turtle pushed the duck.'

(15) was given without a context. (16) was given with a discourse context: 'There was a duck in a park.' Then a scrambled sentence was given with the definite marker *sono*.

Otsu used the act-out task as Hayashibe did. He tested 24 children (3;1 – 4;11), and he divided the children into two groups of twelve children: Group 1 was given scrambled sentences without contexts, and Group 2 was given scrambled sentences with contexts. Otsu's results are shown in Table 4.

Table 4. Results of Otsu (1994) regarding scrambling

Group 1 (without contexts)	Group 2 (with contexts)
45.8% (22/48)	89.6% (43/48)

The correct response rate for Group 1 without contexts was only 45.8% of the time, whereas the rate for Group 2 was 89.6% of the time. This shows that the presence of the discourse contexts changes children's interpretation of scrambled sentences dramatically.[2]

Next, Sano (2005) has shown similar results regarding topicalization in Japanese. He showed that Japanese children needed a topicalizing discourse and the definite marker with the preposed phrase, unlike adults. He had two conditions for the topicalized sentences: one without a topicalizing discourse and the definite marker as in (17); the other condition is a topicalizing discourse with the definite marker *sono* in (18).

(17) Simple introduction of names of participants and without the definite marker *sono*

Zou,	kaeru,	buta-ga	i-masi-ta.
elephant	frog	pig-Nom	be-Polite-Past

Sosite,	buta-wa	zou-ga	ketobasi-masi-ta.
And	pig-Top	elephant-Nom	kick- Polite-Past

'There were an elephant, a frog, and a pig. And, the pig, the elephant kicked.'

(18) The topicalizing discourse and the definite marker *sono*

Zou,	kaeru-ga	i-masi-ta.	Soko-e	buta-ga
elephant,	frog-Nom	be-Polite-Past	There	pig-Nom

yatteki-masi-ta.	Sono	buta-wa	zou-ga
come-Polite-Past	The	pig-Top	elephant-Nom

ketobasi-masi-ta.
kick-Polite-Past

'There were an elephant and a frog, and there came a pig. The pig, the elephant kicked.'

Sano's experiment used the act-out task as Otsu did. The subjects were 50 children from three-year-olds to six-year-olds, and the children were divid-

---

2 Murasugi and Kawamura (2004) examined the acquisition of scrambling in Japanese and has shown that children could act out scrambled sentences like adults without any discourse context. She tested two two-year-olds, six, three-year-olds, six four-year-olds, six five-year-olds and two six-year-olds. The test sentences included active, passive, scrambled sentences, seven for each type. The correct response rates for each age group are as follows: 74.5% for two-year-olds, 83.0% for three-year-olds, 100% for four, five and six-year-olds. There results contrast with the response rates of the groups without discourse contexts and the definite marker in Otsu (1994) and Sano (2005). Murasugi and Kawamura speculate that the inclusion of passives made the children pay more attention to the relation between Case particles and theta-roles. The reason for the high correct response rates in Murasugi and Kawamura (2004) is still not clear and further investigation is necessary to clarify whether children have problems with Japanese scrambling or not.

ed into two groups: Group A was given the sentences like (17), and Group B was given the sentences like (18). The results are in Table 5.

Table 5. Results of Sano (2005) regarding topicalization and scrambling

	Group A (w/o *Sono*)	Group B (with *Sono*)
Canonical	90.9% (90/99)	95.0% (95/100)
Scrambled	66.7% (66/99)	92.0% (92/100)
Topicalization	49.0% (49/100)	93.0% (93/100)

You can see that Group A did poorly with scrambling and topicalization, whereas Group B acted out the test sentences correctly more than 90% of the time. So Sano concluded that marking the object phrase with the topic marker *–wa* is not sufficient for children's comprehension of OSV topicalization.

Furthermore, Mizumoto (2007) examined the acquisition of Japanese scrambling regarding the presence the definite marker *sono*, using the picture selection task. Each test sentence was read with two pictures in front of the subject and the subject was asked to choose which picture matched the test sentence. Among the various contexts he tested, we focus on the results of the following test sentences:

(19) Kooen-ni ahirusan-ga i-masi-ta.
Park in duck-Nom is-Polite-Past
Ahirusan-o kamesan-ga osi-masi-ta.
Duck-Acc turtle-Nom push-Polite-Past
'There was a duck in the park. A turtle pushed (the) duck.'

(20) Kooen-ni ahirusan-ga i-masi-ta.
Park in duck-Nom is-Polite-Past
Sono ahirusan-o kamesan-ga osi-masi-ta.
The duck-Acc turtle-Nom push-Polite-Past
'There was a duck in the park. A turtle pushed the duck.'

In (19), the scrambled object is given without the definite marker *sono*, whereas the scrambled object in (20) is introduced with the definite marker *sono*. The subjects were 61 children (4;6 – 6;6). The results show that the children responded correctly 63.75% of the time for (19) and 92.57% of the time for (20). (The percentages are taken from the slide of Mizumoto (2007)). Mizumoto concluded that the presence of the definite marker *sono* played a crucial role for the children's comprehension of scrambled sentences.

These studies suggest that the acquisition of scrambling as a scope shifting operation is not very early. Therefore children acquiring Japanese use

Quantifier Raising instead of scrambling to interpret *some/every* interaction in Japanese, with or without negation.

6. Conclusion

This paper examined Japanese children's acquisition of *some/every* interaction with negation. The results of the experiment have shown that Japanese children accepted not only collective readings but also distributive readings for the sentences with canonical word order and scrambled word order. I have suggested that Japanese children use Quantifier Raising instead of scrambling for *some/every* interaction because of the late acquisition of scrambling as a scope shifting operation.

References

Aoun, J. and Y.-H. A. Li. 1993. *Syntax of Scope*. Cambridge, Mass.: MIT Press.

Aoyagi, H. and T. Ishii. 1994. On NPI Licensing in Japanese. *Japanese/Korean Linguistics 4*, ed. Noriko Akatsuka, 295-311. Chicago: The University of Chicago Press.

Bobaljik, J. and S. Wurmbrand. 2008. Word Order and Scope: Transparent Interfaces and The ¾ Signature. Ms., University of Connecticut.

Crain, S. and R. Thornton. 1998. *Investigations in Universal Grammar: A Guide to Experiments in the Acquisition of Syntax and Semantics*. Cambridge, Mass.: MIT Press.

Conroy, A., J. Lidz, and J. Musolino. 2009. The fleeting Isomorphism Effect. *Language Acquisition*, 16(2): 106-117.

Goro, T. 2007. Language-specific Constraints on Scope Interpretation in First Language Acquisition. Doctoral Dissertation, University of Maryland, College Park.

Gualmini, A. 2003. The Ups and Downs of Child Language. Doctoral dissertation, University of Maryland, College Park.

Gualmini, A. 2004. Some Knowledge Children Don't Lack. *Linguistics* 42 (5): 957-982.

Gualmini, A. 2005/2006. Some Facts about Quantification and Negation One Simply Cannot Deny: A Reply to Gennari and MacDonald. *Language Acquisition* 13: 363-370.

Hayashibe, H. 1975. Word Order and Particles: A developmental study in Japanese. Descriptive and Applied Linguistics 8: 1-18.

Hoji, H. 1985. Logical Form constraints and configurational structures in Japanese. Doctoral dissertation, University of Washington, Seattle.

Hornstein, N. 1995. *Logical Form: From GB to Minimalism*. Oxford: Blackwell.

Huang, C. –T. J. 1982. Logical Relations in Chinese and the Theory of Grammar. Doctoral dissertation, MIT.

Hulsey, S., V. Hacquard, D. Fox and A. Gualmini. 2004. The Question-Answer requirement and scope assignment. *Plato's Problem: Problems in Language Ac-*

quisition. MIT Working Papers in Linguistics 48. ed. A. Csirmaz, A. Gualmini, and A. Nevins. 71-90. Cambridge, Mass.: MITWPL.

Johnson, K. 2000. How Far Will Quantifiers Go? *Step by Step: Essays on Minimalist Syntax in Honor of Howard Lasnik*, ed. Roger Martin, David Michaels, Juan Uriagereka, 187-210. Cambridge, Mass.: MIT Press.

Kataoka, K. 2006. *Nihongo Hiteibun no Kouzou*. Tokyo: Kuroshio Publisher.

Kato, Y. 2000. Interpretive Asymmetries of Negation. *Negation and Polarity. ed.* L. Horn and Y. Kato, 62-87. Oxford: Oxford University Press.

Kuroda, S.-Y. 1970. Remarks on the notion of subject with reference to words like *also, even,* or *only*. Part 2. *Annual Bulletin* 4. 127-152. Research Institute of Logopedics and Phoniatrics, University of Tokyo. Reprinted in *Papers in Japanese Linguistics* 11: 121-152.

Lidz, J. and J. Musolino. 2002. Children's command of quantification. *Cognition* 84-2: 113-154.

Lidz, J. and J. Musolino, 2006. On the quantificational status of indefinites: the view from child language. *Language Acquisition*, 13(2): 73-102.

May, R. 1977. The Grammar of Quantification. Doctoral dissertation, MIT.

May, R. 1985. *Logical Form.* Cambridge, Mass.: MIT Press.

Miyagawa, S. 2001. The EPP, Scrambling, and wh-in-situ. *Ken Hale: A Life in Language.* ed. M. Kenstowicz, 293-338. Cambridge, Mass.: MIT Press.

Miyagawa, S. to appear. Optionality. *The Oxford Handbook of Linguistic Minimalism,* ed. Cedrix Boeckx. Oxford: Oxford University Press.

Mizumoto, G. 2007. Yoji no tanbun rikai ni okeru bunmyaku ni yoru rikai sokushin koka to sadoukioku – toku ni kakimazebun no rikai ni tuite (The comprehension promoting effect and working memory by discourse contexts in the comprehension of simple clauses by young children – On the comprehension of scrambled sentences). Paper and powerpoint slides presented at The 13th Gengo Shori Gakkai, Ryutani University, Seta, Japan.

Murasugi, K. and T. Kawamura. 2004. On the Acquisition of Scrambling in Japanese. *Language and Linguistics* 5: 131 – 151.

Musolino, J. 1998. Universal Grammar and the Acquisition of Semantic Knowledge: An Experimental Investigation into the Acquisition of Quantifier-Negation Interaction in English. Doctoral dissertation, University of Maryland at College Park.

Musolino, J. 2006. Structure and Meaning in the Acquisition of Scope. *Semantics in Acquisition*, ed. V. Van Geenhoven. 141-166. Dordrecht: Springer.

Musolino, J., S. Crain and R.Thornton. 2000. Navigating Negative Quantificational Space. *Linguistics* 38(1): 1-32.

Musolino, J. and A. Gualmini, 2004. The role of partitivity in Child Language. *Language Acquisition* 12(1): 97-107

Musolino, J. and J. Lidz, 2003. The scope of Isomorphism: Turning Adults into Children. *Language Acquisition* 11(4): 277-291.

Musolino, J. and J. Lidz, 2006. Why Children aren't universally successful with Quantification. *Linguistics* 44(4): 817-852.

Otsu, Y. 1994. Early Acquisition of Scrambling in Japanese. *Language Acquisition Studies in Generative Grammar*, ed. T. Hoekstra and B. Schwartz, 253-264. Amsterdam: John Benjamins.

Papafragou, A. and Musolino, J. 2003. Scalar implicatures: Experiments at the semantics-pragmatics interface. *Cognition*, 86-3: 253-282.

Pollock, J. –Y. 1989. Verb movement, Universal grammar, and the structure of IP. *Linguistic Inquiry* 20: 365-424.

Sano, T. 2004. Scope Relations of QP's and Scrambling in the Acquisition of Japanese. In *the Proceedings of GALA2003, Volume 2, LOT Occasional Series 3*, ed. J. van Kampen and S. Baauw. Utrecht: LOT.

Sano, T. 2005. The Acquisition of Japanese Topicalization and the Role of Discourse Context. *BUCLD Proceedings Supplement,* ed. Alejna Brugos, Manuella R. Clark-Cotton and Seungwan Ha. Boston: Boston University.

Sano, T. 2009. Some Notes on Cross-linguistics variation and Children's Acquisition of Japanese. Powerpoint presentation at GLOW in Asia VII.

Sano, T. 2010. More observations on the scope interactions in L1 acquisition of Japanese. Poster presentation at *GALANA*4.

Terunuma, A. 2010. The Acquisition of Negative Sentences Containing a Quantified Noun Phrase: Relative Scope and Implicatures in Child Grammar. Doctoral dissertation, University of Tokyo.

Yamakoshi, K. and T. Sano. 2007. Children's Interpretations of Some/Every Interactions in Mono-clausal and Bi-clausal Structures in Japanese. *The Proceedings of GALANA2*, ed. Alyona Belikova, Luisa Meroni, and Mari Umeda, 471-482. Somerville: Cascadilla Press.

Zhou, P. and S. Crain. 2009. Scope assignment in child language: Evidence from the acquisition of Chinese. *Lingua* 119: 973-988.

Part V

Syntax and Semantics

Semantic Realization of the Layered TP: Evidence from the ambiguity of the sentential *koto*-nominal

YURIE HARA
City University of Hong Kong

YOUNGJU KIM
Hiroshima University

HIROMU SAKAI
Hiroshima University

SANAE TAMURA
Kyoto University

1. Introduction

This paper is concerned with one kind of sentential nominalization in Japanese. In (1), a sentence or a clause can be nominalized by attaching the so-called formal noun *koto* at the end of a sentence/clause.

(1) [akuseru-pedaru-ga koshoo-shita] koto
gas.pedal-NOM break-did KOTO
'(the fact) that the gas pedal broke.'

Japanese/Korean Linguistics 20.
Edited by Bjarke Frellesvig and Peter Sells.

In the previous literature, the *koto*-nominalized clause (hereafter, *koto*-nominal) is argued to denote a fact (Kuno 1973), an event, or a proposition (Masuoka 2007). This paper reconsiders the status of the *koto*-nominal by looking at causal statements. In particular, (1) can be the subject of a causal statement as in (2) and (3).

(2) [akuserupedaru-ga koshoo-shita koto]-ga
gas.pedal-NOM break-did KOTO-NOM
shoohisha-no toyota-banare-o hikiokoshita.
consumers-GEN Toyota-leave-ACC caused
'The fact that the gas pedal broke caused the consumers to leave Toyota.'

(3) [akuserupedaru-ga koshoo-shita koto]-ga
gas.pedal-NOM break-did KOTO-NOM
jiko-o hikiokoshita.
accident-ACC caused
'That the gas pedal broke caused the accident.'

These statements represent two kinds of causal relations. First, we consider (2) as an instance of volitional causation since it involves a decision made by a volitional agent (Degand 2000). That is, in (2), the *koto*-nominal represents the *fact/proposition* that the gas pedal broke and the consumers, the cognitive agent, recognized the fact, and this recognition leads them to decide to leave Toyota.

On the other hand, (3) represents an instance of non-volitional causation, since it does not involve any intervention of a cognitive agent. The *event* that the gas pedal broke directly causes the accident.

The difference between the two kinds of caution seems to correlate with the availability of a modal expression. For instance, *kamoshirenai* 'maybe' can be embedded within *koto*-nominal if the whole sentence denotes a volitional causation as in (4).

(4) [akuserupedaru-ga koshoo-shita kamoshirenai koto]-ga
gas.pedal-NOM break-did maybe KOTO-NOM
shoohisha-no toyota-banare-o hikiokoshita.
consumers-GEN Toyota-leave-ACC caused
'The fact that the gas pedal might have broke caused the consumers to leave Toyota.' (Volitional)

However, the same *koto*-nominal is not available for non-volitional causation as in (5). The same pattern obtains with other modal expressions such as *nichigainai* 'must' and *osoraku* 'probably'.

(5) *[akuserupedaru-ga koshoo-shita kamoshirenai koto]-ga
gas.pedal-NOM break-did maybe KOTO-NOM
jiko-o hikiokoshita.
accident-ACC caused
'That the gas pedal might have broke caused the accident.'
(Non-volitional)

The data presented so far can be summarized as follows. In some contexts, the *koto*-nominal refers to a fact/proposition and it can embed a modal. In other contexts, it refers to an event and it cannot embed a modal. The goal of this paper is to build an analysis that derives the two interpretations of the *koto*-nominal and explains the asymmetry of the distribution and the corre-lation between the types of causation and the availability of a modal. More specifically, we will propose the semantics of the formal nou n *koto*, and show how we can derive two different semantic objects (proposition on one hand and event on the other) from the same string of words. We argue that the difference between the semantic objects is syntactically manifested. Finally, we explain the (un)availability of a modal.

2. Problems of the previous studies

In previous analyses, *koto*-nominals have been considered to refer to abstract objects. For instance, Kuno (1973) claimed that the *koto*-nominal denotes a fact. His proposal is motivated by "the factive presupposition" of the *koto*-nominal. He observes that compared to the complementizer clause (6-b), the *koto*-nominal in (6-a) gives an impression that the embedded proposition 'Mary was stupid' is assumed to be true.

(6) a. John-wa Mary-ga baka-na koto-o nageita.
John-TOP Mary-NOM stupid-is KOTO-ACC deplored
'John deplored that Mary was stupid (she was stupid).'

b. John-wa Mary-ga baka-da-to nageita.
John-TOP Mary-NOM stupid-is-COMP deplored
'(Lit.) John deplored that Mary was stupid (she might or might not have been stupid).'
(Kuno 1973, 216–217)

Masuoka (2007), however, provides the following data to argue against Kuno's observation. In (7-a), the *koto*-nominal does not refer to a particular fact, but it refers to a general state of affairs, and the proposition embedded under the *koto*-nominal in (7-b) is a mere possibility and not a fact.

(7) a. Hayaku okiru koto-wa kenkoo-ni yoi.
early get.up KOTO-TOP health-DAT good
'Getting up early is good for your health.'

b. Tantoosha-ga gyoosha-kara wairo-o
person.in.charge-NOM trader-from bribe-ACC
moratta koto-wa machigainai.
received KOTO-TOP no.doubt
'There is no doubt that the person in charge received a bribe from the trader.' (Masuoka 2007)

Instead, Masuoka (2007) claims that a *koto*-nominal denotes "a conceptually constructed state of affairs" in his terms. He also states that it is "a sentence that is deprived of its modality, in particular, its truth-value". In other words, in Masuoka's analysis, the *koto*-nominal seems to denote a propositionalized sentence.

The data presented in section 1 is a problem for either analysis. First of all, if the sentential *koto*-nominal always denoted the same abstract concept, why do we have the asymmetry regarding the modal expression? Second, as observed by many philosophers and linguists (Davidson 1967; Lewis 1973), the non-volitional causal relation requires concrete objects as its arguments. Therefore, the abstract 'fact/proposition' cannot be an argument of non-volitional causation. Hence, the *koto*-nominal in non-volitional causation is predicted to be ungrammatical even without a modal. Contrary to this prediction, however, (3) is grammatical.

(3) [akuserupedaru-ga koshoo-shita koto]-ga
gas.pedal-NOM break-did KOTO-NOM
jiko-o hikiokoshita.
accident-ACC caused
'That the gas pedal broke caused the accident.' (Non-volitional)

Given this new data, we have to conclude that the *koto*-nominal is not semantically homogeneous. In other words, we need to derive two distinct semantic objects, proposition and event. In order to achieve this goal, we will first propose a uniform semantics of *koto* as a maximality operator. Second, we show that the ambiguity of the *koto*-nominal stems from the different syntactic structures attached to *koto*. An inflectional category such as TP has a layered structure, and each syntactic representation in the layer has a semantic counterpart. In a nutshell, the *koto*-nominal is syntactically ambiguous between TP-*koto* vs. AspP-*koto*. As a result, its denotation is semantically ambiguous between a proposition (i.e., the denotation of TP-*koto*) and an event (i.e., the denotation of AspP-*koto*).

3. *Koto* as a Max operator

Before going into the analysis of the sentential *koto*-nominal, we will define the semantic function of the formal noun *koto*. We argue that *koto* functions as a Max operator. The formal noun *koto* can attach not only to sentences/clauses but also to noun phrases. It has been observed that when it attaches to a noun phrase, the whole construction NP-*no koto* gives rise to a definiteness effect (Kurafuji 1998).[1] Let us see how this effect is obtained. Since Japanese does not have a definite article, a bare NP can be ambiguous between the indefinite and the definite reading as in (8).

(8) Taroo-wa kyooju-o mitsuketa.
Taroo-TOP professor-ACC found
a. 'Taroo has found the professor.'
b. 'Taroo has found a professor'

Attaching *koto* disambiguates the sentence into the definite reading as in (9).[2]

(9) Taroo-wa kyooju-no-koto-o mitsuketa
Taroo-TOP professor-GEN-KOTO-ACC found
a. Only 'Taroo has found the professor.'
b. Not 'Taroo has found a professor.'

Now, a brief introduction of the semantics of the English defi nite article *the* is in order. Based on Sharvy's (1980) analysis on the definite plural, Schwarzschild (1991, 1992) treats the definite article as a m aximality opera-tor with a uniqueness condition (10-a). That is, the definite article takes a set of things and returns the largest one within the set (10-b).[3]

---

[1] Takubo (2007) discusses a similar set of data, but he treats the NP in the NP-*no koto* construction as referential rather than definite, since *koto* can be attached to a specific indefinite as in (i).

(i) Watasi-wa aru inu-no koto-o mikake-ta.
I-TOP certain dog-GEN FN-ACC SEE-PAST
I saw a certain dog yesterday. (Takubo 2007)

[2] We assume the genitive *no* is required for syntactic reasons and makes no semantic contribution.

[3] The term *maximal* used in this paper and in the linguistic literature of the definite article is different from the one in mathematics. In mathematics, the *maximal* element of a set is an element which is not smaller than any other element in the set, while the greatest element of a set is an element which is greater than or equal to any other element of the set. Following the linguistic convention, we use the term *maximal* to refer to the greatest element of a set.

(10) a. $[\![\textbf{the}]\!] \in D_{\langle\langle\alpha,t\rangle,\alpha\rangle} = \lambda\chi.\,\mathrm{Max}(\chi)$
b. $\mathrm{Max}(\chi) := \iota X[X \in \chi \,\&\, \forall Y[Y \in \chi \rightarrow Y \subseteq X]]$

This treatment of the definite article allows us to interpret the singular definite and the plural definite in a uniform way. In the case of a singular noun, for instance, the extension of the bare noun *professor* contains a single individual $\{a\}$ (due to the uniqueness condition, it would be undefined if there were more than one individual).[4] The definite article *the* picks out the largest one within the set, namely $\{a\}$.

(11) a. $[\![\textbf{professor}]\!] = \{\{a\}\}$
b. $[\![\textbf{the professor}]\!] = \mathrm{Max}(\{\{a\}\}) = \{a\}$

In the case of plural definite, the extension of the bare noun contains an identifiable set of individuals $\{a, b, c\}$ as in (12-a). The plural morpheme *-s* generates a powerset of the set minus the empty set (Link 1983) as in (12-b)-(12-d). Finally, in (12-e), the definite article returns the largest one within the set, namely $\{a, b, c\}$.

(12) a. $[\![\textbf{professor}]\!] = \{a, b, c\}$
b. $[\![\textbf{−s}]\!] \in D_{\langle\langle e,t\rangle,\langle e,t\rangle,t\rangle} = \lambda X.\,\mathrm{Pow}(\chi)$
c. $\mathrm{Pow}(A) := \wp(A) - \{\emptyset\}$
d. $[\![\textbf{professors}]\!] = \mathrm{Pow}(\{a, b, c\})$
$= \{\{a\}, \{b\}, \{c\}, \{a, b\}, \{b, c\}, \{c, a\}, \{a, b, c\}\}$
e. $[\![\textbf{the professors}]\!] = \mathrm{Max}(\mathrm{Pow}\{\{a, b, c\}\}) = \{a, b, c\}$

Let us go back to the Japanese NP-*no-koto*. We define *koto* has the same function as the English article *the*. That is, it functions as a maximality operator. Hence, *kyooju-no-koto* in (9) can denote a single salient individual as in (13-a). Furthermore, since Japanese has no number distinction, the same string of words *kyooju-no-koto* can denote a plural definite, i.e., a salient set of individuals as in (13-b).

(13) a. $[\![\textbf{kyooju}_s\textbf{ no koto}]\!] = \mathrm{Max}(\{\{a\}\}) = \{a\}$
b. $[\![\textbf{kyooju}_p\textbf{ no koto}]\!] = \mathrm{Max}(\mathrm{Pow}(\{a, b, c\})) = \{a, b, c\}$

A use of the plural definite can be found in the following example:

[4] We assume with Quine (1969) and Schwarzschild (1992) that a singleton set of an individual is identical to the individual, i.e., $a = \{a\}$. As Schwarzschild (1992) notes, this assumption allows Max to uniformly operate over a set of sets.

(14) Taroo-wa kyooju-no-koto-o katappashikara nagutta.
Taro-TOP professor-GEN-KOTO-ACC left-and-right hit
'Taro hit every one of the professors.'

In short, the analysis of the English definite article *the* can be extended to the Japanese *koto* in NP-*no-koto*. In the case of singular noun phrase, it takes an individual property of type $\langle e,t \rangle$ and returns an individual of type **e**. However, we show below that this function of *koto* as a maximality operator can be extended to other kinds of properties, i.e., a world property $\langle s,t \rangle$ (an intensionalized proposition) and an event property $\langle v,t \rangle$. Therefore, we claim that the semantics of *koto* can be uniformly defined as follows:

(15) $[\![\textbf{koto}]\!] \in D_{\langle\langle \alpha,t\rangle,\alpha\rangle} = \lambda\phi.\,\mathrm{Max}(\phi)$,
where α can be:
a. *e*, s, or v in the case of singular; or
b. $\langle e,t \rangle$, $\langle s,t \rangle$, or $\langle v,t \rangle$ in the case of plural.

4. The Sentential Nominal and the Layered TP

Let us go back to the sentential *koto*-nominal. We claim that the ambiguity of the sentential *koto*-nominal is a byproduct of the layered structure of TP. Since Pollock's (1989) split INFL hypothesis, it has been argued by many linguists that there could be a series of functional categories in a sentence. In particular, some functional categories are argued to be syntactic representations of events (Travis 1994; Kratzer 1998; Rosen 1999; Ritter and Rosen 2000; Borer 2005).[5] For instance, Kratzer (1998) has shown that TP consists of tense/aspect combination as in (16).

(16)

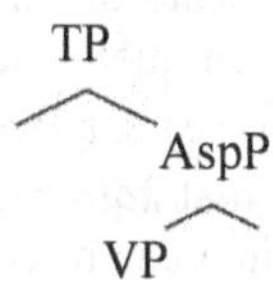

Following Kratzer's hypothesis, we hypothesize that the clause to the left of *koto* in (1) can be either AspP or TP.

(1) [akuseru-pedaru-ga koshoo-shita] koto
gas.pedal-NOM break-did KOTO
'(the fact) that the gas pedal broke.'

[5] See Rosen (1999) for a review of works on the syntactic representation of events.

Let us start with the structure which only contains a reduced inflectional phrase, i.e., AspP. Note that we treat *-ta* as an aspectual marker not as a tense morpheme (see Ogihara 1999 for the controversy of the status of *-ta*).

(17)

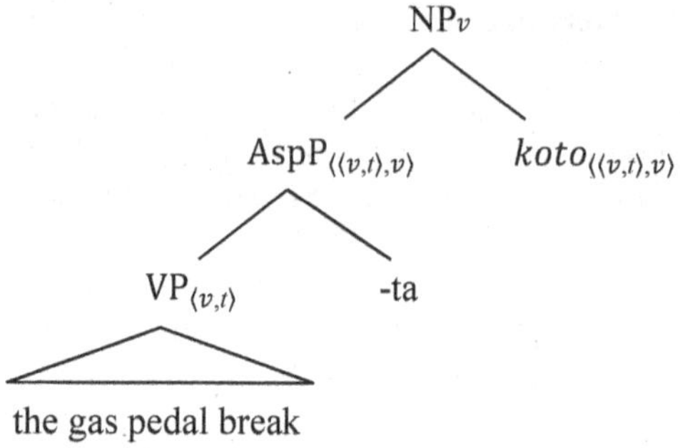

In this construction, the verb phrase denotes a set of events (Parsons, 1990; Kratzer, 1996; Pylkkänen, 2008, among others). (18-a) and-*ta* adds an aspectual description and restricts the set of the events into the culminated events (18-c).

(18) a. $[\![$**akuseru-pedaru-ga koshoo-shi**$]\!] \in D_{\langle v,t\rangle}$
$= \lambda e.\left[\text{THEME}(e, \text{g-p}) \; \& \; \text{BREAK}(e)\right]$

b. $[\![$**-ta**$]\!] \in D_{\langle\langle v,t\rangle,\langle v,t\rangle\rangle}$
$= \lambda P \in D_{\langle v,t\rangle}. \lambda e. \exists t. [P(e) \; \& \; t < now \; \& \; \text{Cul}(e,t)]$

c. $[\![$**akuseru-pedaru-ga koshoo-shi-ta**$]\!] \in D_{\langle v,t\rangle}$
$= \lambda e. \exists t. \left[\text{THEME}(e, \text{g-p}) \; \& \; \text{BREAK}(e) \; \& \; t < now \; \& \; \text{Cul}(e,t)\right]$

In (17), the event predicate directly becomes the argument of *koto* the Max operator, yielding a uniquely identifiable maximal event *e* such that $\exists t.\left[\text{THEME}(e, \text{g-p}) \; \& \; \text{BREAK}(e) \; \& \; t < now \; \& \; \text{Cul}(e,t)\right]$.

Recall from section 3 that *koto* can attach to a plural noun. Hence, it is predicted that a *koto*-nominal can refer to a set of plural events. Indeed, Masuoka (2007) provides an example where AspP can also denote a set of plural events. In (19), it is clear that the *koto*-nominal is not referring to a particular single event of getting up early but some generalization about getting up early.

(19) Hayaku okiru koto-wa kenkoo-ni yoi.
early get.up KOTO-TOP health-DAT good
'Getting up early is good for your health.' (Masuoka 2007)

Hence, we assume that there is a covert pluralization process involved in the construction above as in (20-b) and *koto* returns a salient set of the getting-up-early events (20-c).

(20) a. $[\![\textbf{hayaku okiru}]\!] \in D_{\langle v,t\rangle} = \lambda e.[\text{GET.UP}(e)\ \&\ \text{EARLY}(e)]$

b. $[\![\textbf{hayaku okiru}_{\text{p}}]\!] \in D_{\langle\langle v,t\rangle,t\rangle}$
$= \text{Pow}(\lambda e.[\text{GET.UP}(e)\ \&\ \text{EARLY}(e)])$
$= \{\{e_1\},\{e_2\},\{e_3\},\ldots,\{e_1,e_2,e_3,\ldots\}\}$

c. $[\![\textbf{hayaku okiru}_{\text{p}}\ \textbf{koto}]\!] \in D_{\langle v,t\rangle}$
$= \text{Max}\{\{e_1\},\{e_2\},\{e_3\},\ldots,\{e_1,e_2,e_3,\ldots\}\}$
$= \{e_1,e_2,e_3,\ldots\}$

Now, let us turn to the other structure where koto attaches to a full-fledged TP as in (21).

(21)

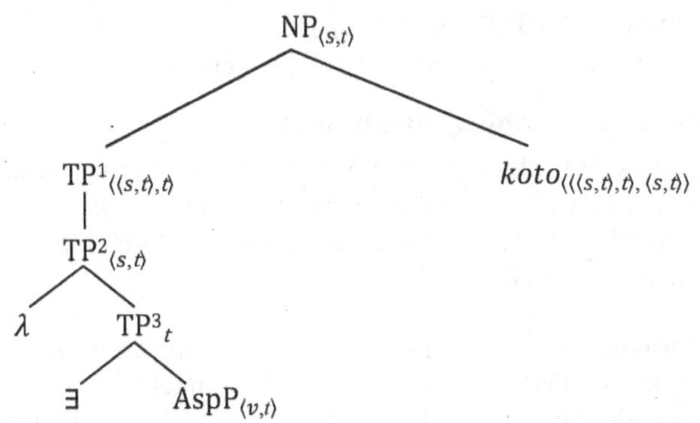

Let us look at the semantic composition bottom-up. First, as before, the AspP denotes a set of culminated events (22-a). Next, at the level of TP, the event argument of the logical form is existentially closed, yielding a proposition of type t (22-b). Third, the proposition is intensionalized (22-c). Fourth, the intensionalized proposition is pluralized (22-d). Finally, *koto*, the maximal-ity operator, takes this pluralized propositions and returns a maximal set of worlds where it is true that the gas pedal broke (22-f).[6]

[6] One might feel uneasy about operating Pow or Max over a proposition or a set of propositions, since a proposition is an *infinite* set of possible worlds. Although it might be counter-intuitive to consider a powerset of an infinite set, there is nothing mathematically wrong about these operations. Since the ordered set is defined in terms of the inclusion relation, we can

(22) a. $[\![\text{AspP}]\!]$
$= \lambda e. \exists t. [\text{THEME}(e, \text{g-p}) \; \& \; \text{BREAK}(e) \; \& \; t < now \; \& \; \text{Cul}(e, t)]$
b. $[\![\text{TP}^3]\!]$
$= \exists e. \exists t. [\text{THEME}(e, \text{g-p}) \; \& \; \text{BREAK}(e) \; \& \; t < now \; \& \; \text{Cul}(e, t)]$
c. $[\![\text{TP}^2]\!] = \lambda w. {}^\wedge\exists e. \exists t.$
$[\text{THEME}(e, \text{g-p}) \; \& \; \text{BREAK}(e) \; \& \; t < now \; \& \; \text{Cul}(e, t)](w)$
d. $[\![\text{TP}^1]\!] = \text{Pow}(\lambda w. {}^\wedge\exists e. \exists t. [\text{THEME}(e, \text{g-p}) \; \&\text{BREAK}(e) \; \& \; t <$
$now \; \& \; \text{Cul}(e, t)](w))$
e. $[\![\textbf{koto}]\!] = \lambda \phi. \text{Max}(\phi)$
f. $[\![\text{NP}]\!] = \text{Max}(\text{Pow}(\lambda w. {}^\wedge\exists e. \exists t.$
$[\text{THEME}(e, \text{g-p}) \; \& \; \text{BREAK}(e) \; \& \; t < now \; \& \; \text{Cul}(e, t)](w)))$

A set of worlds is a proposition. Hence, the *koto*-nominal denotes a propo-sition that the gas pedal broke.

To summarize this section, by assuming the two syntactic possibilities, we can derive two distinct semantic objects. AspP-*koto* denotes a maximal event e such that $\exists t. [\text{THEME}(e, \text{g-p}) \; \& \; \text{BREAK}(e) \; \& \; t < now \; \& \; \text{Cul}(e, t)]$, while TP-*koto* denotes a maximal set of worlds (i.e., a proposition), namely: $\text{Max}(\text{Pow}(\lambda w.^{\exists e}. \exists t. [\text{THEME}(e, \text{g-p}) \; \&$ $\text{BREAK}(e) \; \& \; t < now \; \& \; \text{Cul}(e, t)](w))) = \{w_1, w_2, w_3, \ldots\}$.

5. The (un)availability of a modal

Now, let us go back to the asymmetry between the two causal statements in terms of the availability of a modal. The modal expression *kamoshirenai* 'maybe/might' can occur in the volitional causation (4), while it cannot in the non-volitional one (5):

(4) [akuserupedaru-ga koshoo-shita kamoshirenai koto]-ga
gas.pedal-NOM break-did maybe KOTO-NOM
shoohisha-no toyota-banare-o hikiokoshita.
consumers-GEN Toyota-leave-ACC caused
'The fact that the gas pedal might have broken caused the consumers to leave Toyota.' (Volitional)

---

obtain the original proposition as the maximal set among the powerset. To see this, let W be the set of all possible worlds and A a proposition. Now, $\text{Pow}([\![A]\!]) = \{X \subseteq W : X \subseteq [\![A]\!]\}$. Hence, $[\![A]\!]$ is the unique X such that $X \in \text{Pow}([\![A]\!]) \; \& \; \forall Y. Y \in \text{Pow}([\![A]\!])$. Therefore, $[\![A]\!]$ is *the* maximal element of $\langle \text{Pow}([\![A]\!]), \subseteq \rangle$.

(5) *[akuserupedaru-ga koshoo-shita kamoshirenai
gas.pedal-NOM break-did maybe
koto]-ga jiko-o hikiokoshita.
KOTO-NOM accident-ACC caused
'That the gas pedal might have broken caused the accident.'
(Non-volitional)

Given the discussion in section 4, there are two structures for the *koto*-nominal as in (23). The question now pertains as to which node *kamoshire-nai* can merge with.

(23) a. High merger of *koto*

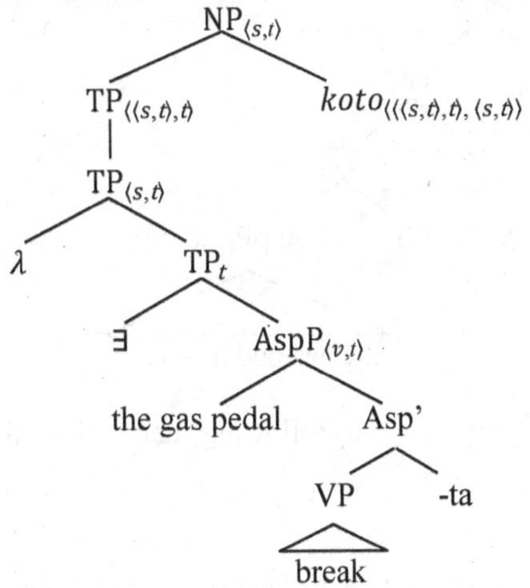

b. Low merger of *koto*

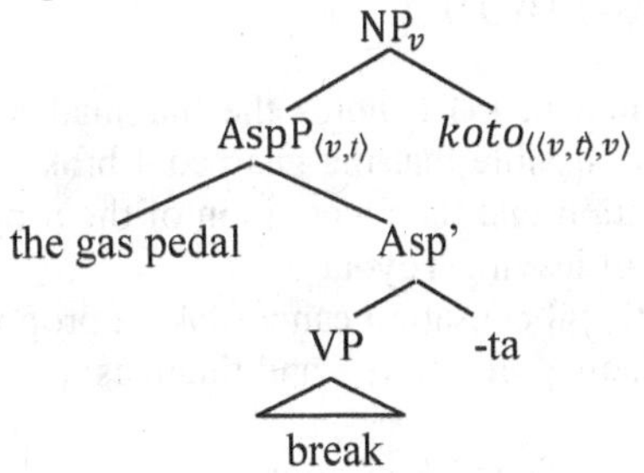

Now, *kamosirenai* 'maybe/might' is a ◊-operator, which takes an intensionalized proposition and returns a proposition, 'it is possible that ^*p*' (24). Hence, *kamosirenai* is of type ⟨⟨*s*,*t*⟩,*t*⟩.

(24) ⟦**kamoshirenai**⟧ $\in D_{\langle\langle s,t\rangle,t\rangle} = \lambda{}^\wedge p.\Diamond{}^\wedge p$

Therefore, the only node with which *kamosirenai* can be merged is the $\mathrm{TP}_{\langle s,t\rangle}$ in (23-a) yielding the following structure:

(25)

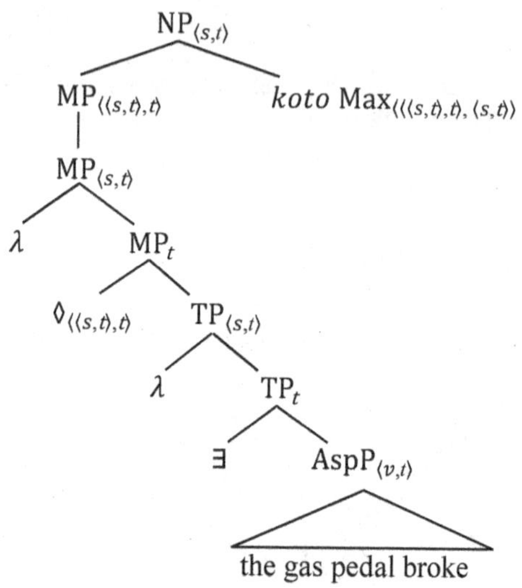

The composition gives us the following denotation for the *koto*-nominal:

(26)
⟦**NP**⟧ $= \mathrm{Max}(\mathrm{Pow}(\lambda w'.{}^\wedge \Diamond\, [\lambda w.{}^\wedge\exists e.\exists t.[\textsc{theme}(e, \text{g-p})\ \&\ \textsc{break}(e)\ \&\ t < now\ \&\ \mathrm{Cul}(e,t)](w)](w')))$

In words, the *koto*-nominal in (4) denotes the maximal set of worlds in which it is true that it is possible that the gas pedal broke. Hence, (4) expresses a volitional causation that the recognition of the proposition caused the con-sumers' decision of leaving Toyota.

In contrast, non-volitional causation cannot take a proposition as its argument as observed by many philosophers and linguists:

(27) Constraint on (Non-volitional) Causation
Non-volitional causation is a relation between two concrete objects. (Davidson 1967; Lewis 1973; Bennett 1988; Asher 1993; Degand 2000; Hara et al. 2010, among others)

In particular, events and individuals, which can be spatio-temporally located, are concrete objects which can be causal relata, while propositions are abstract objects and cannot be connected by causal relations without invoking volitionality.

This constraint on non-volitional causation leads us to conclude that the TP-*koto* cannot appear in the construction of the non-volitional causation. As discussed above, if a sentential nominal headed by *koto* contains a modal, it must be the TP-*koto*. The TP-*koto* does not denote an event but it denotes a set of worlds (i.e., a proposition). A proposition is not a legitimate argument for the non-volitional causation. Therefore, (5) with the modal is ungrammatical.

In sum, there are two possible syntactic candidates for the *koto*-nominal, AspP-*koto* and TP-*koto*. The volitional causation can host a TP-*koto*, which in tern can host *kamoshirenai*, while the non-volitional causation can host only an AspP-*koto* which cannot host *kamoshirenai*.

6. Conclusion

We have presented a novel set of data which show that the sentential *koto* can denote not only an abstract proposition but also a concrete event. This semantic ambiguity of the *koto*-nominal stems from its syntactic ambiguity. To see this, we have hypothesized that *koto* serves as a maximality operator not only for NPs but also for clauses. That is, *koto* has a uniform semantic function from a set of α to a maximal α. The sentential *koto* is syntactically ambiguous depending on the structure with which *koto* merges. If *koto* merges with a full-fledged clausal projection TP, the *koto*-nominal denotes a maximal set of worlds (= a proposition) and can host a modal. Furthermore, the TP-*koto* cannot be an argument of non-volitional causation because it denotes an abstract object, i.e., a proposition. On the other hand, if *koto* merges with a reduced clausal projection AspP, the *koto*-nominal denotes a maximal event (or a set of events) and cannot host a modal. Since an event is a concrete object, the AspP-*koto* can be an argument of non-volitional causation. Our analysis evidences that the layered structure for TP is crucial since each syntactic structure gives us a distinct semantic object.

Acknowledgments

We would like to thank Makoto Kanazawa, Christopher Kennedy, Katsuhiko Sano, Yukinori Takubo, Satoshi Tomioka, and the audience at the 20th con-ference on Japanese/Korean Linguistics (October 2010), Semantics Research Group (July 2010), Kaken workshop at Kyoto (July 2010) as well as the Sakura workshop in Paris (September 2010) for valuable comments and discussions. The fourth author is supported by JSPS Japan-France Integrated Action Program (SAKURA). All remaining errors are our own.

References

Asher, N. (1993). *Reference to Abstract Objects in Discourse*. Springer.

Bennett, J. F. (1988). *Events and Their Names*. Clarendon.

Borer, H. (2005). *The Normal Course of Events*, Volume II of *Structuring Sense*. Oxford: Oxford University Press.

Davidson, D. (1967). Causal relations. *Journal of Philosophy 64*(21), 691–703.

Degand, L. (2000). Causal connectives or causal prepositions?: Discursive constraints. *Journal of Pragmatics 32*, 687–707.

Hara, Y., Y. Kim, H. Sakai, and S. Tamura (2010). Japanese sentential nominalization and different kinds of causation. In *7th Workshop on Altaic Formal Linguistics*, Los Angeles. University of Southern California.

Kratzer, A. (1996). Severing the external argument from its verb. In J. Rooryck and L. Zaring (Eds.), *Phrase Structure and the Lexicon*. Dordrecht: Kluwer.

Kratzer, A. (1998). More structural analogies between pronouns and tenses. In *Semantics and Linguistic Theory 8*, Cornell. CLC Publications.

Kuno, S. (1973). *The Structure of the Japanese Language*. MIT Press.

Kurafuji, T. (1998). Definiteness of koto in Japanese and its nullification. In *RuLing Papers*, pp. 169–184. Rutgers University.

Lewis, D. K. (1973). Causation. *The Journal of Philosophy 70*(17), 556–567.

Link, G. (1983). The logical analysis of plurals and mass terms: a lattice-theoretical approach. In R. Bauerle, C. Schwarze, and A. von Stechov (Eds.), *Meaning, Use and Interpretation of Language*, pp. 250–209. Berlin: de Gruyter.

Masuoka, T. (2007). Nihongo Modaritii Tankyuu [The investigation into Japanese Modality]. Tokyo: Kuroshio Shuppan.

Ogihara, T. (1999). The semantics of tense and aspect in Japanese. In N. Tsujimura (Ed.), *The Handbook of Japanese Linguistics*, pp. 326–348. Blackwell.

Parsons, T. (1990). *Events in the Semantics of English: A Study of Subatomic Seman-tics*. Cambridge, MA: MIT Press.

Pollock, J.-Y. (1989). Verb movement, universal grammar, and the structure of IP. *Linguistic Inquiry 20*, 365–424.

Pylkk¨anen, L. (2008). *Introducing Arguments*. Cambridge, MA: MIT Press.

Quine, W. V. O. (1969). *Set Theory and Its Logic*. Cambridge: Harvard University Press.

Ritter, E. and S. Rosen (2000). Event structure and ergativity. In C. Tenny and J. Puste-jovsky (Eds.), *Events as Grammatical Objects*, pp. 187–238. Stanford: CSLI.

Rosen, S. (1999). The syntactic representation of linguistic events. *Glot International 4*, 3–10. A Stateof-the-Article.

Schwarzschild, R. (1991). *On the meaning of definite plural noun phrases*. Ph. D. thesis, University of Massachusetts at Amherst.

Schwarzschild, R. (1992). Types of plural individuals. *Linguistics and Philoso-phy 15*(6), 641–675.

Sharvy, R. (1980). A more general theory of definite descript ions. *The Philosophical Review 89*(4), 607–624.

Takubo, Y. (2007). An overt marker for individual sublimation in Japanese. In B. Frellesvig, M. Shibatani, and J. Smith (Eds.), *The History and the Structure of Japanese*, pp. 135–151. Tokyo: Kuroshio Shuppan.

Travis, L. (1994). Event phrase and a theory of functional categories. In P. Koskinen (Ed.), *Proceedings of the 1994 Annual Conference of the Canadian Linguistic Association, Toronto Working Papers in Linguistics*, Toronto, pp. 559–570.

Kuroda's Left-Headedness and Linkers*

KEN HIRAIWA
Meiji Gakuin University

1. Introduction

Japanese has a peculiar type of relative clause —prima facie a "left-headed" relative clause construction that Kuroda (1977, 1992) called a *no*-introduced relative (hereafter *No*-RC). Given that Japanese is an SOV language, the existence of left-headed relative clauses is typologically not so typical.

(1) [**negi-no** komakaku kizan-da no]-o tukat-ta.
scallion-NO_1 finely cut-Pst NO_2-Acc use-Pst
'I used the scallions that were cut finely.' (*No*-RC)

* The project reported here is partially funded by the Grant-in-Aid for Young Scientists (B) (No. 22720168) for which I am very grateful. Thanks to Edith Aldridge, Tomohiro Fujii, Satoshi Kinsui, Akira Watanabe, and John Whitman, as well as participants in my graduate seminar. Parts of this article have been presented at the TCP Workshop 2010 held at Keio University and the 20th Japanese/Korean Linguistics held at University of Oxford. I would like to thank Chung-hye Han and Heejeong Ko for Korean data and Feng-Fan Hshie for Chinese and Taiwanese data.

Japanese/Korean Linguistics 20.
Edited by Bjarke Frellesvig and Peter Sells.

In this example, the head of the relative clause is a thematic object of the transitive verb. However, the head of the relative clause *negi* 'scallions' is located at the left periphery and marked by *no*, which is homophonous with the genitive Case particle. I will call the DP headed by no_1 a *no*-introduced NP. The element no_2 at the end of the relative clause will be called a *post-relative no*. These two instances of *no* will be glossed as NO_1 and NO_2, respectively, to avoid an a priori conclusion about the nature of these elements for the moment.

(2) [NP-no_1 . . . V no_2] (The schematic structure of *No*-RCs)

Since Kuroda's initial work, this phenomenon has not been extensively addressed. The main aim of this paper is to unveil the syntax of this type of relative clause and the nature of *no* associated with it. Furthermore, I will also investigate a parameter governing the absence of corresponding relative clauses in Korean and Chinese.

(3) *[**tomato-uy** calu-n kes]-ul mek-ess-ta.
tomato-Gen slice-Rel thing-Acc east-Pst-Decl
'I ate tomatoes that were sliced.' (Korean)

(4) ***fanqie-de** qie-le-de
tomato-Gen slice-Perf-Nml
'tomatoes that were sliced' (Chinese)

2. *no* as a Linker

In this article, I will demonstrate, with ample empirical evidence, that no_1 in *No*-RCs is a genitive *linker*.[1]

(5) no_1 is a genitive linker.
(neither a genitive Case marker nor a copula)

It should be stressed that my claim is that *no*, despite its appearance, comes in (at least) two varieties: a genitive Case marker and a genitive linker.

Unlike some previous work (Martin 1975 and Kitagawa 1977), no_1 is not an adnominal form of the copula *da*. This can be confirmed straightfor-

---

[1] See Hiraiwa (to appear) for full discussions and a detailed comparision with *de*-introduced relative clauses.

wardly by the fact that another adnominal form *de-aru* cannot be used instead of *no*.

(6) *[**negi-dearu** komakaku kizan-da no]-o
scallion-Cop finely cut-Pst NO_2-Acc
tukat-ta.
use-Pst
'I used the scallions that were cut finely.'

2.1. Connective *'katu'*

Another piece of supporting evidence for *de* being a continuative form of copula comes from the insertion of the sentential conjunction marker *katu* 'and'. (7) shows that *No*-RCs disallow *katu* to intervene between the left-edge head NP and the rest of the relative clause.

(7) ookina ringo-no (***katu**) oisisoona no-o
big apple-NO_1 and tasty-looking NO_2-Acc
tabe-ta.
eat-Pst
'I ate the big apple that looked tasty.' (*No*-RC)

The fact that the copula *de* is compatible with the connective *katu* shows that *no* is not a copula. In (8), two copula phrases are conjoined and the first copula takes the form *de(-atte)* and the connective *katu* is licit.

(8) Naomi-wa insei-de(-atte) **katu** nihonzin da.
Naomi-Top student-Cop(-exist) and Japanese Cop
'Naomi is a grad student and a Japanese (at the same time).'

On the other hand, usually two genitive phrases cannot be coordinated in this way as shown in (9a). Although bare NPs can be coordinated, then *katu* is obligatory as in (9b). In contrast, *katu* is only optional with the copula *de* as in (9c).

(9) a.*kono hito-wa [Ken-no **(katu)** Naomi]-no
this person-Top Ken-Gen and Naomi-Gen
sensei da.
teacher Cop
'This person is Ken's and Naomi's teacher.'

b. kono hito-wa [Ken-no sensei *(**katu**)
this person-Top Ken-Gen teacher and
Naomi-no sensei] da.
Naomi-Gen teacher Cop
'This person is Ken's and Naomi's teacher.'

c. kono hito-wa [Ken-no sensei] de(-atte)
this person-Top Ken-Gen teacher Cop
(**katu**) [Naomi-no sensei] da.
and Naomi-Gen teacher Cop
'This person is Ken's and Naomi's teacher.'

2.2. Predicates and HIRCs

The next piece of evidence is based on a restriction on HIRCs. Since Kuroda (1999), it is well known that HIRCs cannot appear as a predicate nominal. (10) shows that the HIRC cannot appear in this position.

(10) *ano otoko-ga [$_{\text{HIRC}}$ gootoo-ga ginkoo-kara
Dem man-Nom robber-Nom bank-from
dete-ki-ta no] **desu**.
out-come-Pst NO$_2$ Cop
'That man is the robber who just came out of the bank.'
(HIRC)

Applying this to the *No*-RCs reveals that an entire HIRC is felicitous in the *no*-introduced position, as shown in (11).

(11) [$_{\text{HIRC}}$ teeburu-no ue ni negi-ga oiteat-ta
table-Gen on at scallion-Nom put-be-Pst
no]-**no** komakaku kizan-da no-o tukat-ta.
NO$_2$-NO$_1$ finely cut-Pst NO$_2$-Acc use-Pst
'I used the scallions that were on the table and that were cut finely.'
(*No*-RC and HIRC)

3. Linker and the Structure of *No*-RCs

In this section, I will investigate the nature of *no*$_1$ in *No*-RCs in detail and propose that it is related to the linking function that is one of the various functions of the genitive particle *no* in Japanese. Building on this observation, I will further argue that *No*-RCs are derived by inversion from HERCs.

3.1. Linker and inversion

In the previous section, I have claimed that the no_1 in the *No*-RCs is a genitive linker. It is analogous to the appositive use found in the examples like (12). In (12), NP_1 and NP_2 are in an appositive relation and in this environment, *de* cannot be used.

(12) *NP_1-no NP_2*

a. [kasa-**no**	sinsimono]-o	kat-ta.
umbrella-NO_1	for.men-Acc	buy-Pst
'I bought a men's umbrella.'		

b. [iPhone-**no**	32GB]-o	kat-ta.
iPhone-NO_1	32GB-Acc	buy-Pst
'I bought a 32GB iPhone.'		

Now let us compare (12) and (13). Interestingly, NP_1 and NP_2 in (12) can be switched around, as shown in (13). It is quite significant to observe that (12) and (13) are semantically equivalent. Given this semantic identity, I argue that (12) is derived by syntactic inversion from the underlying 'NP_2-Gen NP_1' construction (13), where NP_2 is a modifier and NP_1 is a modifiee. Therefore, the semantic interpretation is maintained even after inversion.

(13) *NP_2-no NP_1*

a. [mizingiri-**no**	negi]-o	maze-ta.
mince.cut-Gen	scallion-Acc	mix-Pst
'I mixed minced scallions.'		

b. [32GB-**no**	iPhone]-o	kat-ta.
32GB-Gen	iPhone-Acc	buy-Pst
'I bought a 32GB iPhone.'		

The 'NP_2-no NP_1' in (13) is in a modifier-modifiee relation. In other words, 'NP_2-no' is a modifying predicate for NP_1. I assume that the genitive Case-marking *no* is assigned by D whenever two NPs are adjacent (see Kitagawa and Ross 1982 and others).

Now I propose that the appositive genitive no_1 in (12) and no_1 of *No*-RCs is an instance of a *Linker* (Lk) and this Linker Phrase (LkP) mediates *inversion*, as stated in (14).[2]

[2] Theoretical studies on linkers are only recently done by Richards (1999) for Tagalog, Baker and Collins (2006) for Kinande and Khoisan languages, and den Dikken (2006) for English and several other languages. The properties of the linkers are not completely uniform crosslinguis-

(14) The appositive genitive no_1 in Japanese is licensed by a linker head Lk.

In his series of papers in the 1970's, S.-Y. Kuroda investigated *No*-RCs for the first time in a generative framework. To the best of my know ledge, there is no other detailed work on these constructions in other frameworks and his work still remains to be virtually the only extensive study to date.

Kuroda (1965, 121) suggested an possibility of inversion very briefly but it was not fully developed subsequently.

(15) a. [ringo-no aka-i no]-o tabe-ta.
apple-NO_1 red-Pres NO_2 eat-Pst
'I ate a red apple.' (No-RC)

b. [aka-i ringo]-o tabe-ta.
red-Pres apple-Acc eat-Pst
'I ate a red apple.' (HERC)

He wrote "the above form (KH: (15a)) has an inverted order and is clearly related to the normal form (KH: (15b))". However, details were not explicated unfortunately, and the analysis was never developed further in his subsequent work.

Thus, in (12), the modified noun phrase NP *negi* 'scallions' moves to [Spec, LkP]. After movement, the NP is marked by the genitive assigned by the linker head, and the genitive on the lower NP *mizingiri* 'mince.cut' disappears in the absence of any noun following it.[3]

With this in mind, let us consider the *No*-RC again.

(16) a. [[e_i mizingirini-si-ta] **negi**$_i$]-o tukat-ta.
mince.cut-do-Pst scallions use-Pst
'I used the scallions that were minced.' (HERC)

b. [**negi-no** mizingirini-si-ta no]-o tukat-ta.
scallion-NO_1 mince.cut-do-Pst NO_2-Acc eat-Pst
'I used the scallions that were minced.' (*No*-RC)

---

tically, but one of the important functions is that they mediate inversion by providing a specifier, as discussed in the latter two articles.

[3] The possessive type NP_1-*Gen* NP_2 constructions and other types do not permit inversion.

(i) a. Naomi-no hon
Naomi-Gen book
Naomi's book'

b. *hon-no Naomi
book-NO1 Naomi

I propose that exactly the same mechanism of inversion derives *No*-RCs. Specifically, I argue that the *No*-RC (16b) has the HERC (16a) as an underlying structure. Let us consider first the structure of HE RCs in (17).

(17) HERC

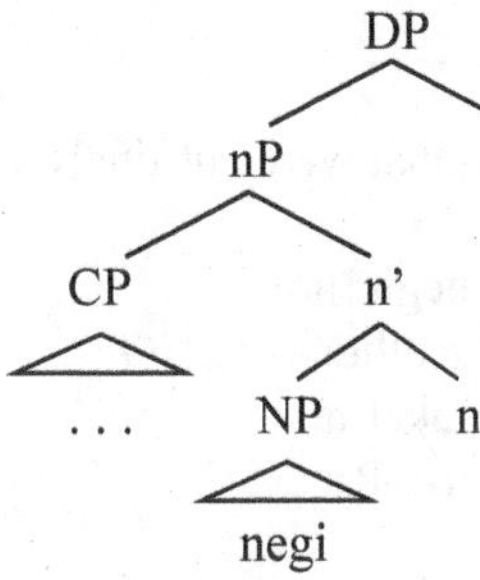

In (17), the external head noun *negi* 'scallions' is modified by the relative clause CP. Now, it undergoes inversion to [Spec, LkP]. The inverted NP is assigned genitive marking by the linker head, and the n head is realized as *no*. This derives the surface structure of *No*-RCs as represented in (18).[4]

(18) *No*-RCs

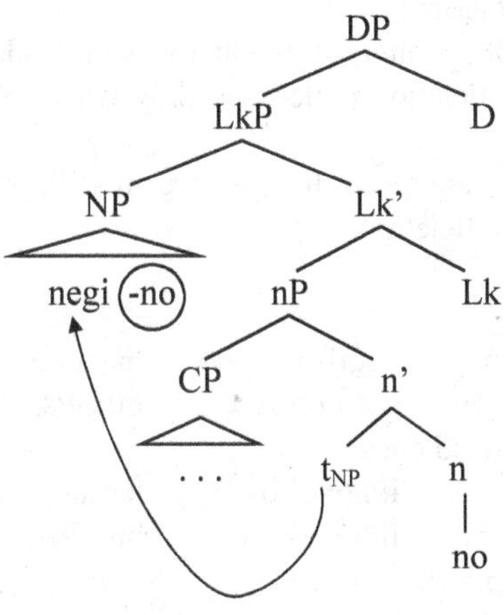

This analysis makes a correct prediction that the *no*-introduced NP should not be preceded by a material within a relative clause. Syntactically, as briefly noted by Kuroda (1977), the *no*-introduced NPs cannot remain in their orig-inal positions (see also Kuroda 1977 for some observations on

---

[4] Note that it is also supported by the diachronic evidence mentioned much earlier that *No*-RCs and HERCs existed earlier than HIRCs.

Classical Japanese). As shown in (19), none of the elements internal to the relative clause can precede the *no*/*de*-introduced NPs.

(19) a. [negi-no **komakaku** kizan-da no]-o
scallion-Acc/NO_1 finely cut-Pst NO_2-Acc
tukat-ta.
use-Pst
'I used the scallions that were cut finely.' (*No*-RC)

b. [**komakaku** negi-*no kizan-da
finely scallion-Acc/NO_1 cut-Pst
no]-o tukat-ta.
NO_2-Acc use-Pst

3.2. N'-deletion

So-called N'-deletion provides corroborating evidence that the element *no* that introduces a head noun in *No*-RCs is not a genitive Case marker. It is well known that a genitive modifier licenses N'-deletion. Saito and Murasugi (1990) and Lobeck (1995) convincingly argue that N'-deletion is licensed under spec-head agreement between D and its specifier and is reformulated as NP-deletion.

Saito et al. (2008) reinterpret the analysis of N'-deletion in Japanese in such a way that the deletion is licensed only when [Spec, DP] is occupied by a phrase with *no*.

Thus, under this analysis, the genitive modifiers in NP_2*-no* NP_1 construc-tions license N'-deletion.

(20) NP_2*-no* NP_1
a. [mizingiri-**no** ~~negi~~]-o maze-ta.
mince.cut-Gen scallion-Acc mix-Pst
'I mixed minced ones.'
b. [32GB-**no** ~~iPhone~~]-o kat-ta.
32GB-Gen iPhone-Acc buy-Pst
'I bought a 32GB iPhone.'

Then, it is predicted that *No*-RCs should not allow "N'-deletion" because *no* in *NP-no*$_1$ is not a genitive Case assigned by D and the entire phrase is not in [Spec, DP] but in [Spec, LkP]. (21) shows that N'-deletion is in fact ungrammatical in such cases.

(21) *NP$_1$-no NP$_2$*

a. *[negi-**no** ~~mizingiri~~]-o maze-ta.
scallion-NO$_1$/DE mince.cut-Acc mix-Pst
'minced scallion.'

b. *[iPhone-**no** ~~32GB~~]-o kat-ta.
iPhone-NO$_1$/DE 32GB-Acc buy-Pst
'I bought a 32GB iPhone.'

Then, the proposed mechanism of inverted relativization predicts that *No*-RCs should not allow N'-deletion either. The prediction is indeed borne out. The *no*-introduced NP does not allow N'-deletion. As shown by the example in (22), N'-deletion is indeed blocked.

(22) *Mazu [**negi-no** komakaku kizan-da
first scallion-NO$_1$ finely cut-Pst
no]-o irete, sonoato-ni [**syooga-no** ~~komakaku~~
NO$_2$-Acc put then-at ginger-Nom finely
~~kizan-da~~ ~~no~~]-o irete.
cut-Pst NO$_2$-Acc put.Imp
'First put the scallions that are cut finely and then put the ginger that are cut finely.'

Summarizing the discussions so far, I have argued that *No*-RCs are derived from HERCs by "inverting" the head noun NP to [Spec, LkP]. This analysis captures the parallelism between *NP-no NP* constructions and *No*-RCs. I have further supported the proposed analysis with the N'-deletion test.

4. A Comparative Syntax

As I mentioned at the beginning of the article, *No*-RCs are, to the best of my knowledge, typologically peculiar.[5] For example, *No*-RCs are not observed in East Asian languages, even those geographically close to Japanese such as Korean, Chinese, and Taiwanese. Thus, such an asymmetry implies an existence of a parameter.

4.1. Japanese, Korean, and Chinese

In Korean, the relativized head of a relative clause cannot be marked by the genitive Case, as shown in (23a), while the HIRC counterpart is grammatical as shown in (23b). Chinese, on the other hand, lacks not only HIRCs but also a counterpart of *No*-RCs as (24) indicates.

[5] Typological surveys on relative clauses such as Keenan (1985), de Vries (2002), and Andrews (2007) do not record any possible counterparts of this peculiar type of relative clause.

(23) a. *[**tomato-uy** calu-n kes]-ul mek-ess-ta.
tomato-Gen slice-Rel thing-Acc east-Pst-Decl
'I ate tomatoes that were sliced.' (Korean)

b. [**tomato-lul** calu-n kes]-ul mek-ess-ta.
tomato-Acc slice-Rel thing-Acc east-Pst-Decl
'I ate tomatoes that were sliced.' (Korean)

(24) *[fanqie-de qie-le-de]
tomato-Gen slice-Perf-Nml
'tomatoes that were sliced' (Chinese)

This is expected under the analysis suggested above, however. For despite their functional similarities with *no*, genitive markers in Korean and Chinese crucially do not have a use as an appositive linker that triggers inversion, as shown below.[6]

(25) a. John-i [32GB-**uy** iPhone]-lul sa-ss-ta.
John-Nom 32GB-Gen iPhone-Acc buy-Pst-Decl
'John bought a 32GB iPhone.' (Korean)

b. *John-i [iPhone-**uy** 32GB]-lul sa-ss-ta.
John-Nom iPhone-Gen 32GB-Acc buy-Pst-Decl
'John bought a 32GB iPhone.' (Korean)

(26) a. 32GB **de** iPhone
32GB Gen iPhone
'a 32GB iPhone' (Chinese)

b. *iPhone **de** 32GB
iPhone Gen 32GB
'a 32GB iPhone' who is an idiot' (Chinese)

Given that a linker plays a crucial role in inversion in *NP-Gen NP* constructions as well as in *No*-RCs, the ungrammaticality of the counterparts of *No*-RCs in Korean and Chinese follow, providing further cross-linguistic ev-idence for the proposed inversion analysis of *No*-RCs in Japanese.

Naturally, there are further differences. The genitive *no* in Japanese is multifunctional and marks arguments (subjects/objects) within nominals,

[6] Saito et al. (2008) argue that *de* in Chinese is actually a determiner head D.

possessors, adjuncts, numerals, and so on. According to Seo (2009), both genitives in Japanese and Korean co-occur with arguments and adjuncts, but in Korean, genitives marking arguments can be dropped, which is never possible in Japanese. In addition, An (2009) and Seo (2009) observe that Korean does not allow N'-ellipsis unlike Japanese and Chinese.

(27) a. Chelswu(-**uy**) cha
Chelswu-Gen car
'Chelswu's car' (Korean: An 2009)

b. tol-lo*(-**uy**) kongkyek
stone-with-Gen attack
'an attack with stones' (Korean: An 2009)

(28) *Chelswu-uy ~~cha~~
Chelswu-Gen car
'Chelswu's' (Korean)

However, perhaps the most important difference for us is that Korean genitives do not function as a copula. According to John Whitman (p.c.), Korean genitive marker *-uy* crucially lacks a copula use unlike *no* in Japanese.

(29) sensei-**no** hito
teacher-Gen man
'a man who is a teacher' (Japanese)

Similarly, Chinese *de* also lacks a copula use.

(30) laoshi **de** nuren
teacher DE woman
'*a woman who is a teacher'
'^{ok}the teacher's woman' (Chinese)

Very interestingly, Edith Aldridge (p.c.) informed me that Old Chinese had a relative clause that looks quite similar to the *No*-RC in Japanese. Notice that in (31a), the left-most DP headed by *zhi* is the head of the relative clause. Old Chinese also had a prenominal relative clause like Japanese as shown in (31b).

(31) a. ma zhi si zhe yi guo ban yi.
horse Gen die ZHE Asp surpass half Asp
'The horses which have died are more than half.'
(Old Chinese: Aldridge 2008)

b. qi ruo cong [[bi shi] **zhi** shi] zai.
how like follow escape world Gen scholar Excl
'How could that compare to following a scholar who escapes from the world?' (Old Chinese: Aldridge 2008)

Notice that *zhi* is a genitive marker in Old Chinese, as shown in the following example.

(32) [Wen wang **zhi** you] fang qishi li.
Wen king Gen park square 70 neighborhood
'King Wen's park was as big as 70 neighborhoods (70 square li).'
(Old Chinese: Aldridge 2008)

A natural hypothesis is that Chinese has undergone a syntactic change from a linker language to non-linker language (a *reverse ezafe* language in Larson's terms; see below). It should be noted that Old Chinese had case-distinctions while Modern Chinese has lost case-distinctions.[7]

The properties of genitive elements are summarized below.

(33)

	Japanese	Korean	Chinese
drop	*	ok	ok
N'-ellipsis	yes	no	yes
copula	yes	no	no
linker	yes	no	no

It seems to be plausible, then, to think that a copula function and a linker function have something in common, although it is left for future research.

[7] Another interesting contrast between Japanese and Korean/Chinese is that the Japanese genitive can, but the Korean and Chinese genitives cannot, mark the adjunct noun 'rain' according to the data observed in Seo (2009). This is possibly explained by the lack of the appositive use of the genitives in the latter two languages.

(i) ame-no hi
rain-Gen day
'rainy day'

(ii) pi(*-uy) nal
rain-Gen day

(iii) yu(*de) tian
rain Gen day

As a passing note, the fact that classifiers cannot be followe d by *de* in Chinese and classifiers do not allow *-uy*-drop in Korean suggests that genitive elements accompanying classifiers might be different from the other instances.

(34) sey-kwen-*(**-uy**) chayk
three-Cl-Gen book
'three books' (Korean: An 2009)

(35) san ge (***de**) ren
3 Cl Gen people
'three people' (Chinese: Watanabe 2006)

In this respect, my approach is sympathetic to Watanabe (2010), who argues that the genitive *no* that appears with numeral classifiers is what he calls a linker. Watanabe's point is precisely that numeral classifiers do not allow N'-ellipsis in Japanese, because *no* that follows a numeral classifier is not a genitive Case particle but a linker. While his linker here does not mediate inversion, I leave it open whether this instance of *no* can be subsumed under the analysis proposed in this article.

The idea that a linker is case-related is further confirmed by indeterminates in Japanese. As shown in (36a), indeterminates in Japanese cannot be directly modified by adjectives and instead, they have to be modified indirectly through a constructions comparable to *something spicy* in English as in (36b) (see Hiraiwa 2010 for a detailed discussion). Now, the fact that a linker cannot be attached to the indeterminate *nanika* 'something' in (36c) makes sense if a linker is case-related and indeterminates are not nouns (see Watanabe 2006 for a relevant idea).

(36) a?*asita.-wa karai **nanika-o** tabe-yoo.
tomorrow-Top spicy something-Acc eat-Fut
'I will have something spicy tomorrow.'

b. asita-wa **nanika** karai no-o tabe-yoo.
tomorrow-Top something spicy Ln eat-Fut
'I will have something spicy tomorrow.'

c. *asita-wa **nanika-no** karai no-o tabe-yoo.
tomorrow-Top something-NO_1 spicy Ln eat-Fut
'I will have something spicy tomorrow.'
(*No*-RC)

4.2. Japanese as an Ezafe and Reverse Ezafe Language

Larson and Yamakido (2008) and Larson (2009) present detailed discussions about the nature of *ezafe* in Iranian languages and argue that it is case-related.

Ezafe (EZ) is an element that appears between XP and YP where the latter modifies the former. By contrast, what Larson (2009) calls a *reverse ezafe* (REZ) appears between YP and XP where the former modifies the l atter

(37) a. XP-*e* YP (EZ)
b. YP-*e* XP (REZ)

According to Larson and Yamakido (2008) and Larson (2009), *ezafe* con-structions are found in Modern Persian (Farsi), in Kurdish (Kurmanji and Sorani) and in Zazaki. Let take an *ezafe* language Farsi and briefly draw a parallel between the linker in Japanese and the *ezafe* in Farsi. The *ezafe* morpheme does not appear in prenominal constructions in Farsi (38), but it appear in postnominal constructions (39). Note also the nonfinite relative clause in (39b) also takes an *ezafe*. Thus, the surface form (39a) (and (39b)) is reminiscent of *No*-RCs in Japanese.

(38) a.

kûechektarin	mive
smallest	fruit

'the smallest fruit' (Farsi: Larson and Yamakido 2008)

b.

on	mard
that	man

'that man' (Farsi: Larson and Yamakido 2008)

c.

sé	tá	dokhtar
three	NM	daughters

'three daughters' (Farsi: Larson and Yamakido 2008)

(39) a.

otâq- **é**	besyar	kucik
room-EZ	very	small

'very small room' (Farsi: Larson 2009)

b.

ask-**e**	[čâp	šode	dar	ruznâme]
photo-EZ	publication	become	in	newspaper

'the photo published in the newspaper' (Farsi: Larson 2009)

Thus, the behavior of *ezafe* is quite similar to the linker *no* in Japanese. It is interesting to note that even though a linker does not appear with a finite relative clause in Farsi, it does appear with a non-finite relative clause. Relevant to this is that in *No*-RCs, the relative clause is semantically parallel to participial/adjectival relatives in English.

(40) a. marde [ke Nanazo mibine]
the.man REL Nanaz see
'the man who sees Nanaz' (Farsi: Larson 2009)

b. aks-**e** [čâp šode dar ruznâme]
photo-EZ publication become in newspaper
'the photo published in the news paper' (Farsi: Larson 2009)

In contrast, Larson (2009) points out that there are languages that show a mirror image of those *ezafe* languages.

(41) a. John- **é** xowne
John-REZ house
'John's house' (Gilaki: Larson 2009)

b. surx-ə gul
red-REZ flower
'red flower' (Gilaki: Larson 2009)

Finally, there are languages that show no sign of *ezafe*, such as Pashto (see Larson 2009).

(42) a. pindz ə pəghle
five girls
'five girls' (Pashto: Larson 2009)

b. wəgay alək
hungry boy
'hungry boy' (Pashto: Larson 2009)

Putting my proposal in the cross-linguistic context, it amounts to saying that Japanese is a language that possesses an *ezafe* and a *reverse ezafe* element within a single language. Furthermore, to make the picture a little more complicated, these two elements happen to be morpho-phonologically identical. In other words, Japanese is diametrically opposite to what Larson

(2009) calls *no ezafe languages* such as Pashto. In contrast, Chinese and Korean are of the same type as Gilaki in that they lack linkers.[8]

(43)

	EZ	REZ
Japanese	*no* (=linker)	*no* (Case particle)
Farsi	*-e*	—
Korean & Chinese	—	*-uyl-de*
Gilaki	—	*-e*
Pashto	—	—

References

An, D.-H. (2009). A note on genitive drop in Korean. In *Nanzan Linguistics 5*, pp. 1–16. Nagoya, Japan: Nanzan University.

Andrews, A. (2007). Relative clauses. In T. Shopen (Ed.), *Language Typology and Syntactic Description (Vol. 2): Complex Constructions (2nd edition)*, pp. 206–236. Cambridge, UK: Cambridge University Press.

Baker, M. and C. Collins (2006). Linkers and the internal structure of *v*P. *Natural Language & Linguistic Theory 24*, 307–354.

de Vries, M. (2002). *The Syntax of Relativization.* Utrecht, Netherlands: LOT. den Dikken, M. (2006). *Linkers and Relators*. Cambridge, MA: MIT Press.

Hiraiwa, K. (2010). The syntax of light nouns and indeterminates in Japanese. Ms., Meiji Gakuin University.

Hiraiwa, K. (2011). The mechanism of inverted relativization in Japanese: A silent linker and inversion. *Journal of Linguistics*.

Keenan, E. (1985). Relative clauses. In T. Shopen (Ed.), *Language Typology and Syntactic Description (Vol. 2): Complex Constructions*, pp. 141–170. Cambridge: Cambridge University Press.

Kinsui, S. (1994). Rentaisyuusyoku no "ta" ni tuite. In Y. Ta kubo (Ed.), *Nihongo no meisisyuusyoku hyooogen*, pp. 19–65. Tokyo: Kurosio Publishers.

Kitagawa, C. (1977). No-introduced relative clauses. *Journal of the Association of Teachers of Japanese XII*(2&3), 229–247.

Kitagawa, C. and C. Ross (1982). Prenominal modification in C hinese and Japanese. *Linguistic Analysis 9(1)*, 19–53.

Kuroda, S.-Y. (1965). *Generative Grammatical Studies in the Japanese Language*. Ph.D. dissertation, MIT.

Kuroda, S.-Y. (1974-1977). Pivot-independent relativization in Japanese i, ii, iii. *Papers in Japanese Linguistics 3–5* , 59–93, 85–96, 157–179.

[8] Larson (2009) argues that in those Iranian languages, *ezafe* forms a constituent with the following element. This is in contrast with Japanese, Korean, and Chinese, in which the genitives form a constituent with the preceding element.

Kuroda, S.-Y. (1992). *Japanese Syntax and Semantics: Collected Papers*. Dordrecht: Kluwer Academic Publishers.

Kuroda, S.-Y. (1999). Syubunaizai kankeisetu. In S.-Y. Kuroda and M. Nakamura (Eds.), *Gengo no naizai to gaizai*, pp. 27–103. Tokyo: Kurosio Publishers.

Larson, R. K. (2009). Chinese as a reverse Ezafe language. *Yuyanxue Luncong (Jour-nal of Linguistics)*, 30–85. Pekin University.

Larson, R. K. and H. Yamakido (2008). Ezafe and the deep position of nominal mod-ifiers. In L. McNally and C. Kennedy (Eds.), *Adjectives and Adverbs: Syntax, Semantics, and Discourse*, pp. 43–70. New York, NY: Oxford University Press.

Lobeck, A. (1995). *Ellipsis: Functional Heads, Licensing, and Identification* . New York, NY: Oxford University Press.

Martin, S. E. (1975). *A Reference Grammar of Japanese*. New Haven and London: Yale University Press.

Richards, N. (1999). Complementizer cliticization in Tagalog and English. In Smallwood and C. Kitto (Eds.), *Proceedings of AFLA 6*, pp. 297–312. Toronto: University of Toronto Working Papers in Linguistics.

Saito, M., H.-H. Lin, and K. Murasugi (2008). N'-ellipsis and the structure of noun phrases in Chinese and Japanese. *Journal of East Asian Linguistics 17*, 247–271.

Saito, M. and K. Murasugi (1990). N'-deletion in Japanese: A preliminary study. In *Japanese/Korean Linguistics 1*, Number 258–301. Stanford, CA: CSLI Publications.

Seo, S. (2009). Constraints on NP-ellispsis and DP-internal movement.

Watanabe, A. (2006). Functional projections of nominals in Japanese: Syntax of clas-sifiers. *Natural Language & Linguistic Theory 24(1)*, 241–306.

Watanabe, A. (2010). Notes on nominal ellipsis and the nature of *no* and classifiers in Japanese. *Journal of East Asian Linguistics 19*, 61–74.

On Japanese Indirect Passives*

HIDEHITO HOSHI
Doshisha University

1. Introduction

This paper aims to provide a new way of looking at the syntactic structure of the so-called indirect passives in Japanese, exploring the differences between *ni* and *ni yotte*, both of which are markers for the logical subject of passive verbs (verbs followed by the passive morpheme -(*r*)*are*).

Japanese indirect passives have two peculiar properties: (i) the internal argument of transitive passive verbs can be retained in the original position (= (1a)) and (ii) intransitive verbs can be passivized (= (1b)). Thus, unlike direct passives, indirect passives cannot have their active counterparts.

(1) a. Jiroo-ga doroboo-ni saifu-o nusum-are-ta
-Nom thief-Dat wallet-Acc steal-Pass-Past
'Jiroo was affected by a thief's stealing his wallet.'

* For comments, questions, and criticisms, I am grateful to Jim Huang, Toru Ishii, Shen Li, Shigeru Miyagawa, Akira Watanabe, and Ken Wexler. All errors and oversights are my own. This research was supported by Doshisha University Overseas Research Grant 2009-2010.

Japanese/Korean Linguistics 20.
Edited by Bjarke Frellesvig and Peter Sells.

b. Jiroo-ga kodomo-ni nak-are-ta
-Nom child-Dat cry-Pass-Past
'Jiroo was affected by a child's crying.'

In (1) the logical subject of the passive verb is the dative NP (i.e., NP-*ni*). Although the logical subject can also be marked by *ni yotte* as shown in (2), *ni* cannot be replaced by *ni yotte* when intransitive verbs are passivized (Inoue 1976, Kuno 1973, Kuroda 1979). This suggests, contra Kuno (1983), that *ni yotte* is not a stylistic variant of *ni*.

(2) a. Jiroo-ga doroboo-ni yotte saifu-o nusum-are-ta
-Nom thief-by wallet-Acc steal-Pass-Past
'Jiroo was affected by a thief's stealing his wallet.'

b. *Jiroo-ga kodomo-ni yotte nak-are-ta
-Nom child-by cry-Pass-Past
'Jiroo was affected by a child's crying.'

In what follows, I will argue that the above "transitive-intransitive asymmetry" can be ascribed to the properties of the event interpretation denoted by passive verbs. On the assumption that the event interpretation is expressed by eventuality predicates that occur as light verbs (= *v*) (Hale and Keyser 1991, Huang 1997), I claim that two different types of indirect passives (*ni* indirect passives and *ni yotte* indirect passives) exist in Japanese, demonstrating that the postpositional phrase NP-*ni yotte* is adjoined only to *v*P denoting a causing event.

2. Two Types of Indirect Passives in Japanese

Assuming that there are three types of passives in Japanese (*ni* direct passives, *ni* indirect passives, and *ni yotte* passives), Hoshi (1999) claims that the ungrammaticality of (2b) is attributed to the properties of *ni yotte* passives. In *ni yotte* passives, -(*r*)*are* suppresses an external θ-role ("subject demotion") and absorbs accusative Case, so that the internal argument of a passive verb must move to the surface subject position (SpecTP) in order to receive Case ("object promotion").[1] It thus follows that -(*r*)*are* in *ni yotte* passives is inconsistent with intransitive verbs: intransitive verbs do not take any accusative Case-marked NP. However, if Case absorption is always required for *ni yotte* passives, we have to explain why (2a) is possible. Hoshi (1999) maintains, following Kuroda (1979)'s observation, that such

[1] The terms "demotion" and "promotion" are based on the idea that there is a hierarchy of syntactic relations. For more detailed discussion, see Perlmutter and Postal 1977, 1984, Comrie 1977.

apparent counterexamples are derived from the structure of multiple object NPs. Thus, (2a) is no longer regarded as indirect passives because its active counterpart actually exists. Consider the following example discussed by Kuroda (1979):

(4) John-ga kokumusyoo-ni yotte ryoken-o toriager-are-ta
-Nom State Department-by passport-Acc take away-Pass-Past
'John was affected by the State department's revoking his passport.'

The active counterpart of (4) would be represented as in (5) on the assumption that the verb *toriage* 'take away' takes multiple object NPs.

(5) kokumusyoo-ga [$_{NP}$ John] [$_{NP}$ ryoken] toriage-ta
State department-Nom passport take away-Past

The possible surface form of (5) would be (6a), where the first NP (indirect object) *John* in (5) appears with the postposition *kara* 'from' but not (6b) with the accusative Case marker *-o*. The ungrammaticality of (6b) is due to the "double-*o* constraint" (Harada 1973): double accusative NPs are prohibited in Japanese.

(6) a. kokumusyoo-ga John-kara ryoken-o toriage-ta
State department-Nom -from passport-Acc take away-Past
'The State Department revoked John's passport.'

b. *kokumusyoo-ga John-o ryoken-o toriage-ta
State department-Nom -Acc passport-Acc take away-Past

However, it is not always the case that *ni yotte* passives with a retained object can be derived from the structure with multiple object NPs. Consider the following example of the indirect passive involving the verb *satsugais* 'murder':

(7) Jiroo-ga nanimonoka-ni yotte hahaoya-o satsugais-are-ta
-Nom someone-by mother-Acc murder-Pass-Past
'Jiroo was affected by someone's murdering his mother.'

According to Hoshi's analysis, (7) must have multiple object NPs in its underlying structure, as depicted in (8).

(8) nanimonoka-ga [$_{NP}$ Jiroo] [$_{NP}$ hahaoya] satsugaisi-ta
someone-Nom mother murder-Past

However, it is quite dubious to assume that *satsugais* 'murder' can take multiple object NPs since no surface form is allowed with any type of postpositions, as indicated in (9).

(9) *nanimonoka-ga Jiroo-kara/ni/e/de hahaoya-o satsugaisi-ta
someone-Nom -from/to/to/in mother-Acc murder-Past
'Someone murdered Jiroo's mother.'

The only possible surface form is (10), where instead of postpositions, the genitive Case marker *no* '-Gen' appears with *Jiroo*.

(10) nanimonoka-ga Jiroo-no hahaoya-o satsugaisi-ta
someone-Nom -Gen mother-Acc murder-Past

This suggests that the underlying structure of (10) is not (8), but (11), in which *satsugais* 'murder' takes a single NP as its complement and the genitive Case is assigned to *Jiroo* within the NP.

(11) nanimonoka-ga [$_{NP}$ Jiroo hahaoya] satsugaisi-ta
someone-Nom mother murder-Past

We are thus led to conclude that Case absorption is not always required for *ni yotte* passives. Notice, however, that we can still derive *ni yotte* passives as in (7) by NP-movement: "possessor raising" may be another option (cf. Kubo 1990, Pylkkänen 2008). Consider (12). (12b) is derived by possessor raising from the underlying structure (12a) with a single object NP.

(12) a. [$_{TP}$ [$_{vP}$ nanimonoka-ni yotte [$_{NP}$ Jiroo hahaoya] satsugais-are-ta]]
someone-by mother murder-Pass-Past

b. [$_{TP}$ Jiroo$_1$-ga [$_{vP}$ nanimonoka-ni yotte [$_{NP}$ t_1 hahaoya]-o
-Nom someone-by mother-Acc
satsugais-are-ta
murder-Pass-Past

However, such a possessor-possessee relation is not needed for *ni yotte* passives. Consider the following gapless *ni yotte* passive:

(13) gakusei-ga gattkootookyoku-ni yotte Suzuki-kyoojyu-no
student-Nom school authorities-by Suzuki-Prof.-Gen
meiyo-o kizutsuker-are-ta
honor-Acc sully-Pass-Past
'The students were affected by the school authorities' sullying Prof. Suzuki's honor.'

In (13) no possessor-possessee relation can be established between the surface subject and the object, as the ill-formedness of (14) indicates, although pragmatically speaking, there may be some relationship between *gakusei* 'student' and *Suzuki-kyoojyu no meiyo* 'Prof. Suzuki's honor', for example, in the sense that the students respect Prof. Suzuki and are very proud of his honor.

(14) *[$_{NP}$ gakusei-no Suzuki-kyoojyu no meiyo]
student-Gen Suzuki-Prof.-Gen honor

Since there is no possessor-possessee relation in (13), the surface subject NP must be base-generated in a θ-position without inducing any NP-movement.

To confirm that the *ni yotte* passive in (13) is really gapless, examine the example involving numeral quantifier (NQ) floating in (15). *San-nin* 'three Cl' cannot be separated from the surface subject in (15b). This indicates that no "trace" (or "copy") is created by NP-movement, so that the floating NQ in (15b) cannot be associated with the surface subject.

(15) a. san-nin-no gakusei-ga gattkootookyoku-ni yotte
three-Cl-Gen student-Nom school authorities-by
Suzuki-kyoojyu-no meiyo-o kizutsuker-are-ta
Suzuki-Prof.-Gen honor-Acc sully-Pass-Past
'Three student were affected by the school authorities' sullying Prof. Suzuki's honor.'

b. *gakusei$_1$-ga gattkootookyoku-ni yotte san-nin$_1$
student-Nom school authorities-by three-Cl
Suzuki-kyoojyu-no meiyo-o kizutsuker-are-ta
Suzuki-Prof.-Gen honor-Acc sully-Pass-Past

This sharply contrasts with the *ni yotte* direct passive in (16) (Miyagawa 1989), where *san-nin* can be associated with the "trace" created by NP-movement.

(16) a. san-nin-no gakusei-ga nanimonoka-ni yotte satsugais-are-ta
three-Cl-Gen student-Nom somebody-by murder-Pass-Past
'Three students were murdered by someone.'

b. gakusei$_1$-ga nanimonoka-ni yotte t_1 san-nin$_1$ satsugais-are-ta
student-Nom somebody-by three-CL murder-Pass-Past

Furthermore, consider (17). In (17a) the subject-oriented adverb *orokanimo* 'stupidly' can be associated with the surface subject in the gapless *ni yotte* passive. This shows that the surface subject NP can be assigned an external θ-role in the matrix clause (cf. Hoshi 1999, Kuroda 1979). (17a) is in sharp contrast with (17b), where the surface subject in the *ni yotte* direct passive cannot be modified by the subject-oriented adverb. This is because the surface subject is assigned a patient θ-role by the passive verb in the original position.

(17) a. gakusei-ga orokanimo keisatsu-ni yotte Suzuki-kyoojyu-no
student-Nom stupidly police-by Suzuki-Prof.-Gen
migara-o koosokus-are-ta
person-Acc place-Pass-Past
'It was stupid of students to have Prof. Suzuki placed in custody by the police.'

b. ?*gakusei$_1$-ga orokanimo keisatsu-ni yotte t_1 taihos-are-ta
student-Nom stupidly police-by arrest-Pass-Past
'It was stupid of students to be punished by the school authorities.'

Summarizing, we have shown that there is a case of *ni yotte* passives, in which no object promotion takes place and no gap is created. That is, neither absorption of accusative Case nor possessor raising is required for *ni yotte* passives. This suggests that "*ni yotte* indirect passives" exist in Japanese.[2] However, it remains to be seen why *ni yotte* indirect passives are incompatible with intransitive verbs. In the following section, I will attempt to elucidate why intransitive verbs cannot be passivized in *ni yotte* indirect passives in terms of the event interpretation of indirect passives.

2 Thus, it follows that there are four types of passives in Japanese. A detailed explication of *ni* and *ni yotte* direct passives is beyond the scope of this paper. For extensive discussion of direct passives in Japanese, see Hoshi 2011.

3. Proposal

3.1 Event Structure of Japanese Indirect Passives

I propose that the interpretation of events plays a crucial role in generating the structure of indirect passives. Let us first examine the *ni* indirect passive in (18).

(18) Jiroo-ga Hanako-ni musuko-o homer-are-ta
-Nom -Dat son-Acc praise-Pass-Past
'Jiroo was affected by Hanako's praising his son.'

Notice that (18) contains two events (Washio 1993). There is an event (= E_1) such that Hanako praised Jiroo's son. In addition to E_1, there is another event (= E_2) such that Jiroo was affected by E_1. The fact that two distinct events are involved in indirect passives can be straightforwardly captured by assuming that the structure of indirect passives is bi-clausal: -(*r*)*are* behaves as a verb that selects TP as its complement (cf. Hoshi 1999, Howard and Niyekawa-Howard 1976, Kuroda 1965, 1979, Shibatani 1978).[3] That is, the embedded and matrix TP correspond to E_1 and E_2, respectively. Since the surface subject NP *Jiroo*, which is base-generated in the matrix Spec*v*P, is an affected element, an affectee (or experience) θ-role is assigned to *Jiroo* via the matrix *v*. On the basis of the fact that every clause has a specific eventuality (a causing, an action, a state, an experience, a becoming, and so on), let us assume that the eventuality is expressed as an eventuality predicate such as CAUSE, DO, BE, HAVE, BECOME (cf. Hale and Keyser 1991), each of which occurs as *v* (Huang 1997). Thus, HAVE appears as the matrix *v* (= v_{HAVE}) in indirect passives and the amalgam of the matrix V (i.e., -(*r*)*are*) and v_{HAVE} assigns an affectee (or experience) θ-role to the subject in the Spec of *v*P denoting an affecting (or an experiencing) event. On the other hand, various types of events can occur in the embedded clause of *ni* indirect passives as shown in (19).

(19) a. Jiroo-ga nanimonaka-ni hahaoya-o koros-are-ta (cause)
-Nom someone-Dat mother-Acc kill-Pass-Past
'Jiroo was affected by someone's killing his mother.'

---

3 Kitagawa and Kuroda (1992) argue that -(*r*)*are* in indirect passives takes a VP complement. See also Washio 1989-1990 for the VP complement analysis. However, we maintain here that events are interpreted through TP dominating *v*P with a specific eventuality predicate.

b. Jiroo-ga siranaihito-ni tegami-o yom-are-ta (action)
-Nom stranger-Dat letter-Acc read-Pass-Past
'Jiroo was affected by a stranger's reading his letter.'

c. Jiroo-ga Hanako-ni toire-no naka-ni ir-are-ta (state)
-Nom -Dat rest room-Gen inside-in be-Pass-Past
'Jiroo was affected by Hanako's being in the restroom.'

d. Jiroo-ga hahaoya-ni sin-are-ta (change of state)
-Nom mother-Dat die-Pass-Past
'Jiroo was affected by his mother's dying.'

Given the eventuality predicate hypothesis, the structure of *ni* indirect passives can be represented as in (20).

(20) $[_{TP}$ NP$_1$-*ga* $[_{T'}$ $[_{vP}$ t$_1$ $[_{v'}$ $[_{VP}$ $[_{TP}$ NP$_2$-*ni* $[_{T'}$ $[_{vP}$ t$_2$ $[_{v'}$ $[_{VP}$ (NP-*o*) V] $v_{CAUSE/DO/BE/BECOME}$]] T]] $[_V$ (*r*)*are*]] v_{HAVE}]] $[_T$ *ru*/*ta*]]]

In (20) the dative NP is generated in Spec*v*P in the embedded clause for θ-role assignment. Let us assume that the dative Case marker *ni* is licensed by v_{HAVE} in the matrix clause (Hoshi 2007): the dative NP escapes out of the embedded *v*P and raises to the embedded SpecTP for Case assignment.[4] Therefore, the dative NP can syntactically behave as a subject. This is empirically true. Consider (21), in which NP-*ni* as well as the surface subject can be the antecedent of the subject-oriented anaphora *zibun* 'self', whereas the *ni yotte*-marked NP cannot (McCawley 1972, Kuno 1973).

(21) a. Jiroo$_1$-ga Hanako$_2$-ni zibun$_{1/2}$-no heya-de hahaoya-o
-Nom -Dat self-Gen room-in mother-Acc
satsugais-are-ta
murder-Pass-Past
'Jiroo was affected by Hanako's murdering his mother in his/her room.'

---

[4] Another possibility is that the dative NP stays outside the embedded TP: NP-*ni* is further moved out of the embedded TP and adjoined to *v*P$_{HAVE}$. See Kuroda 1965, 1978 and Hoshi 2007 for the subject *ni* raising hypothesis. See also Shibatani 1978, in which the logical subject (i.e., the dative NP) is base-generated in the matrix complement position and the identical NP in the embedded subject position is deleted via "Equi-NP deletion".

b. Jiroo$_1$-ga Hanako$_2$-ni yotte zibun$_{1/*2}$-no heya-de hahaoya-o
-Nom -by self-Gen room-in mother-Acc
satsugais-are-ta
murder-Pass-Past

The same asymmetry holds of the interpretation of the empty pronoun (*pro*) within NP: *pro* must be c-commanded by its appropriate antecedent.

(22) a. Jiroo$_1$-ga Hanako$_2$-ni [$_{NP}$ pro$_{1/2}$ kaminoke]-o kir-are-ta
-Nom -Dat hair-Acc cut-Pass-Past
'Jiroo was affected by Hanako's cutting his/her hair.'

b. Jiroo$_1$-ga Hanako$_2$-ni yotte [$_{NP}$ pro$_{1/*2}$ kaminoke]-o kir-are-ta
-Nom -by hair-Acc cut-Pass-Past

Furthermore, a floated NQ is possible if the associated NP is the dative NP, but not if it is marked by *ni yotte*. This is because the antecedent NP within PP cannot c-command the NQ (Miyagawa 1989).

(23) a. Jiroo-ga san-nin-no sensei-ni/ni yotte ronbun-o
-Nom three-Cl-Gen teacher-Dat/-by paper-Acc
kyakkas-are-ta
reject-Pass-Past
'Jiroo was affected by three teachers rejecting his paper.'

b. Jiroo-ga sensei$_1$-ni/*ni yotte san-nin$_1$ ronbun-o
-Nom teacher-Dat/by three-Cl paper-Acc
kyakkas-are-ta
reject-Pass-Past

By contrast, *ni yotte* indirect passives have a syntactic structure slightly different from (19), although the bi-clausality of -(*r*)*are* is the same: two distinct events are also involved in *ni yotte* indirect passives. Notice that *ni yotte* originally comes from the verb *yoru* 'cause', to which the gerundive morpheme *-te* 'Te' is attached, yielding the form *yotte*. Thus, *ni yotte* is regarded as a complex postposition involving *ni* (the dative Case marker) followed by *yotte* 'cause-Te'. Consider the example involving the verb *yoru*, where the dative NP (*insyu unten* 'drunken driving') indicates a causer, and the nominative NP (*kootsuuziko* 'traffic accident'), an effect brought about by the causer.

(24) keisatsu-wa [sono kootsuuziko-ga kare-no
police-Top that traffic accident-Nom he-Gen
insyu unten-ni yoru to] syutyoosi-ta
drunken driving-Dat cause Comp claim-Past
'The police claimed that his drunken driving causes the traffic accident.'

Since *yotte* means 'cause' (cf. Kinsui 1997), it is natural to assume that NP-*ni yotte* modifies *v*P denoting a "causing event" (= $v\mathrm{P_{CAUSE}}$). I claim that the structure of *ni yotte* indirect passives is represented as in (25), where NP-*ni yotte* is adjoined to $v\mathrm{P_{CAUSE}}$.

(25) $[_{\mathrm{TP}}$ $\mathrm{NP_1}$-ga $[_{\mathrm{T'}}$ $[_{v\mathrm{P}}$ t_1 $[_{v'}$ $[_{\mathrm{VP}}$ $[_{\mathrm{TP}}$ $[_{\mathrm{T'}}$ $[_{v\mathrm{P}}$ $[_{\mathrm{PP}}$ NP-ni yotte$]$ $[_{v\mathrm{P}}$ $[_{v'}$ $[_{\mathrm{VP}}$ NP-o V$]$ $v_{\mathrm{CAUSE}}]]]$ T$]]$ $[_{\mathrm{V}}$ *(r)are*$]]$ $v_{\mathrm{HAVE}}]]$ $[_{\mathrm{T}}$ *ru/ta*$]]]$

Given (25), we can straightforwardly explain why intransitive verbs such as *nak* 'cry', *fur* 'fall', and *sin* 'die', is incompatible with *ni yotte* indirect passives.

(26) a. Jiroo-ga kodomo-ni/*ni yotte nak-are-ta
-Nom child-Dat/by cry-Pass-Past
'Jiroo was affected by a child's crying'.

b. boku-wa ame-ni/*ni yotte fur-are-ta
I-Top rain-Dat/by fall-Pass-Past
'Jiroo was affected by raining.'

c. Jiroo-ga hahaoya-ni/*ni yotte sin-are-ta
-Nom mother-Dat/by die-Pass-Past
'Jiroo was affected by his mother's dying.'

Notice that *nak* 'cry' and *fur* 'fall' denote an action while *sin* 'die', a change of state. Those *v*P structures do not contain CAUSE as *v*, but instead have DO (= action) for *nak* 'cry' and *fur* 'fall', and BECOME (= change of state) for *sin* 'die'. Thus, *ni yotte* indirect passives cannot be licensed by such light verbs. This is also true of transitive verbs denoting an action or a state. Consider the examples of (27). (27a) denotes an action, and (27b), a state. If *ni yotte* occurs instead of *ni,* the sentences become ill-formed.

(27) a. Jiroo-ga siranaihito-ni/*ni yotte tegami-o yom-are-ta
-Nom stranger-Dat/by letter-Acc read-Pass-Past
'Jiroo was affected by a stranger's reading his letter.'

b. Jiroo-ga Hanako-ni/*ni yotte toire-no naka-ni
 -Nom -Dat/by restroom-Gen inside-in
ir-are-ta
be-Pass-Past
'Jiroo was affected by Hanako's being in the restroom.'

To recapitulate, we have argued that the crucial difference between *ni* and *ni yotte* indirect passives lies in the specification of the eventuality predicate in the embedded clause: NP-*ni* occurs in the Spec of *v*P denoting various types of events, whereas NP-*ni yotte* must be adjoined only to *v*P denoting a causing event. Now, a question immediately arises. When NP-*ni yotte* is adjoined to vP_{CAUSE}, the Spec of vP_{CAUSE} becomes empty. Then under what condition can the Spec of vP_{CAUSE} be empty? Just stipulating that the external θ-role is automatically suppressed sounds untenable: there must be a principled mechanism by which the external θ-role is suppressed. We will deal with this issue in the next subsection, arguing that subject demotion in *ni yotte* indirect passives has to do with whether overt V-to-*v* movement takes place.

3.2 Spontaneous Demotion and Optional V-to-*v* movement

Let us first consider how the English *be*-passive can be derived (cf. Jaeggli 1986). The English *be*-passive is the "canonical" passive in the sense that it involves both subject demotion and object promotion. That is, the external θ-role of a passive verb (*be*+V-*en*) is suppressed and the logical subject is changed into an oblique object (*by* NP), while the accusative Case of the passive verb is absorbed, forcing the object NP to move to the vacant subject position. The question to be asked is how far removed Japanese indirect passives are from the "canonical" passive. In order to answer the question, let us examine the impersonal passive with "spontaneous" demotion (Comrie 1977): the external θ-role is suppressed without object promotion. This type of "less canonical" passives can be observed in Welsh. Consider the following examples:

(28) a. Lladdodd draig ddyn
 killed dragon man
 'A dragon killed a man.'

b. Lladdwyd dyn (gan ddraig)
 was-killed man by dragon
 'A man was killed (by a dragon).'

Since the basic word order of Welsh is VOS, one might wonder whether *dyn* 'man' in (28b) stays in the object position or in the subject position as in (28a). However, there is a reason to assume that no object promotion is involved in (28b).[5] First, passive verbs in Welsh impersonal passives exhibit no agreement, although passive verbs in personal passives agree with the following (pronominal) subject. This suggests that no element occupies the subject position of impersonal passive sentences. Secondly, consider (29), where the particle *fe* is followed by the clitic form *i* of the pronoun, which occurs only when the pronoun is in the position of direct object.

(29) a. Fe'i lladdwyd (gan ddraig)
him was-killed by dragon
'He was killed (by a dragon).'

b. Fe'i lladdodd draig
him killed dragon
'A dragon killed him.'

Thus, the above Welsh data demonstrate that spontaneous demotion is a possible option permitted in UG, which suggests that subject demotion and object promotion are independent processes.[6] Here I would like to suggest that spontaneous demotion is also involved in Japanese *ni yotte* indirect passives. Recall that the structure of Japanese indirect passives is bi-clausal and two "subject" positions are available for external θ-role. Putting aside the matrix subject to which the affectee θ-role is always assigned, we can say that spontaneous demotion occurs in the embedded clause of *ni yotte* indirect passives: the external θ-role of a passive verb is suppressed, although the accusative Case can be assigned to the internal argument. That is, the logical subject within the embedded clause is "demoted" to the postpositional phrase (NP-*ni yotte*) without inducing object promotion.

By contrast, in *ni* indirect passives, NP-*ni* syntactically behaves as a subject, which indicates that no subject demotion takes place. Although the nominative Case is not assigned to the NP in the non-finite embedded

---

5 I will leave open the issue of how exactly passive verbs in Welsh impersonal passives can contribute to suppressing an external θ-role, while retaining the accusative Case.

6 See Perlmutter and Postal 1984 for the argument against spontaneous demotion in Welsh impersonal passives. However, Roberts (2005) argues that in Welsh the EPP requirement need not be satisfied and the subject position in finite clauses can be vacant, resulting in a "subject-less" sentence. Note, incidentally, that spontaneous demotion is clearly inconsistent with Burzio's (1986) generalization. Woolford (2003) argues that Burzio's generalization can be replaced by a new descriptive generalization, suggesting that the linkage between the external θ-role and the accusative Case is not so robust. Fore more detailed discussion, see Woolford 2003 and references cited therein.

SpecTP, the dative Case can be licensed by v_{HAVE} in the matrix clause.[7] Thus, *ni* indirect passives are much less "canonical" than *ni yotte* indirect passives in the sense that neither subject demotion nor object promotion is involved in *ni* indirect passives. This amounts to saying that *ni* indirect passives are no longer passives: -(*r*)*are* is just a two place predicate. However, the amalgam of -(*r*)*are* and v_{HAVE} assigns an affectee θ-role to the surface subject, so that a "passive sense" can be expressed to a certain degree.

The next question to be considered is how spontaneous demotion occurs in *ni yotte* indirect passives. That is, we have to explain how the external θ-role of a passive verb is suppressed in *ni yotte* indirect passives, but not in *ni* indirect passives. Notice that -(*r*)*are* can play no role in subject demotion because the syntactic relation between -(*r*)*are* and *v* (or V) is not local: the non-finite T intervenes between them. I propose that the lack of V-to-*v* movement is relevant to suppression of an external θ-role. The idea is that external θ-role assignment is activated via V-to-*v* movement. Since an eventuality predicate in *v* is an abstract entity, the substantial element, namely, V must be associated with it for θ-role assignment. If V does not move to *v*, no argument can be generated in Spec*v*P because *v* cannot assign any external θ-role, with the result that the dative subject is "demoted" to NP-*ni yotte* and the subject position (i.e., Spec of *v*) becomes empty. It should be noted here that our analysis implies that V-to-*v* movement may be optional in overt syntax.[8] However, once overt V-to-*v* movement is allowed to be optional, "subjectless" sentences involving NP-*ni yotte* as in (30b) would be overgenerated: spontaneous subject demotion could freely occur since V-to-*v* movement need not be triggered in overt syntax.[9]

(30) a. keikenhoofuna gekai-ga moochoo-o zyokyosi-ta
experienced surgeon-Nom appendix-Acc remove-Past
'An experienced surgeon removed the appendix.'

b. *keikenhoofuna gekai-ni yotte moochoo-o zyokyosi-ta
experienced surgeon -by appendix-Acc remove-Past

---

[7] I assume that when the logical subject of a passive verb is "deleted", but not "demoted", *pro* is generated in the Spec of *v*P, so that the external θ-role of the passive verb can be assigned to *pro*.

[8] Accusative Case assignment is not affected by V-to-*v* movement on the assumption that unlike θ-role assignment, Case is licensed by feature valuation through Agree (Chomsky 2001).

[9] I assume that V-to-*v* movement can take place in LF on the assumption that θ-role must be somehow discharged to NP-*ni yotte* adjoined to $v\text{P}_{\text{CAUSE}}$ in LF. However, since lexical items can no longer be selected from the lexicon in LF, external Merge can never apply in LF, so that the Spec of *v*P remains vacant if no V-to-*v* movement is triggered in overt syntax.

However, as long as the "subjectless" clause is tolerable, V-to-*v* movement may be optional in overt syntax. Let us assume that the EPP-feature is pertinent to whether or not the subject NP is required in a clause (Chomsky 1995). Then the EPP-requirement must be satisfied on the assumption that finite T has the EPP-feature in Japanese. Notice that *pro* cannot be base-generated in SpecTP because it cannot be assigned any theta-role. Expletive *pro* cannot be generated in SpecTP, either. This is because expletive *pro* has neither PF nor LF property, so that its existence can never be justified externally (Roberts 2005). Therefore, the "subjectless" sentence in (30b) is intolerable and thus excluded. By contrast, let us assume that no EPP-feature is specified in non-finite T in Japanese. Then the "subjectless" clause may be licensed unless it is ruled out by another principle, which is exactly the case in *ni yotte* indirect passives in Japanese.

The proposed analysis predicts that spontaneous subject demotion can occur without -(*r*)*are* because -(*r*)*are* in indirect passives does not play any role in subject demotion. As long as the EPP-requirement in the matrix finite T is satisfied, the dative subject in the non-finite embedded clause can be "demoted" to NP-*ni yotte* due to the absence of overt V-to-*v* movement. This prediction actually holds. Consider the benefactive construction V-*te-moraw* 'V-Te-receive' in (31), where the non-finite TP is selected as the complement of *te-moraw* and v_{HAVE} also occurs in the matrix clause for dative Case assignment. (31) demonstrates that *ni yotte* as well as *ni* can occur in the embedded clause of V-*te-moraw* construction. The alternation between *ni* and *ni yotte* in V-*te-moraw* construction can be explicated in the same way as we have argued for indirect passives: overt V-to-*v* movement is not required in non-finite clause in Japanese.

(31) Hanako-ga [$_{TP}$ keikenhoofuna gekai-ni/ni yotte moochoo-o
-Nom experienced surgeon-Dat/by appendix-Acc
zyokyosi]- te-morat-ta
remove- te-receive-Past
'Hanako received a favor of removing the appendix from an experienced surgeon.'

4. Conclusion

In this paper, I have argued that there are two types of indirect passives in Japanese, namely, *ni* and *ni yotte* indirect passives. They are similar in that both contain -(*r*)*are*, which is a verb taking a nonfinite TP as its complement, so that two distinct events are involved in both types of indirect passives. I have also argued that *ni* and *ni yotte* indirect passives differ in terms of whether V-to-*v* movement takes place in overt syntax. When overt V-to-*v* movement occurs, *v* can assign an external theta-role and the Spec of *v*P is occupied by the subject NP, which eventually moves up to the embedded SpecTP for dative Case assignment. By contrast, if V-to-*v* movement does not take place in overt syntax, no external theta-role is assigned and thus the Spec of *v*P is vacant. Thus, the dative subject is "demoted" to NP-*ni yotte* without object promotion. Furthermore, the eventuality predicate in the embedded *v* is specified in a different way: in *ni* indirect passives various types of eventuality predicates occur in the embedded *v*, whereas *ni yotte* indirect passives allow only v_{CAUSE} to occur, which is due to the property of the complex postposition *ni yotte*. The difference concerning the specification of the eventuality predicate thus enables us to explain why intransitive verbs cannot be passivized in *ni yotte* indirect passives: NP-*ni yotte* must be adjoined to *v*P denoting a causing event.

References

Burzio, L. 1986. *Italian Syntax*. Dordrecht: Reidel.

Chomsky, N. 1995. *The minimalist program*. Cambridge, Massachusetts: MIT Press.

Chomsky, N. 2001. Derivation by phase. In Michael J. Kenstowicz (ed.), *Ken Hale: A life in language*, 1-52. Cambridge, Massachusetts: MIT Press.

Comrie, B. 1977. In defense of spontaneous demotion: The impersonal passive. In P. Cole and J. M. Sadock (eds.), *Syntax and semantics Vol.8: Grammatical relations*, 47-58. New York: Academic Press.

Hale, K. and J. Keyser. 1991. On the syntax of argument structure. *Lexicon Project Working Papers* 34. MIT, Center for Cognitive Science.

Harada, S.I. 1973. Counter Equi NP deletion. In Vol. 7 of *Annual Bulletin*, 113–147. University of Tokyo, Research Institute of Logopedics and Phoniatrics.

Hoshi, Hidehito. 2007. Kansetsuukemibun ni okeru yokakumeisiku no toogoteki seisitu ni tuite [On the syntactic status of the marked dative NP in indirect passives]. *Koobe-si gaikokugo daigaku gaikokugaku kenkyuu* [Foreign Studies in Kobe city university of foreign studies] 67: *Gengo intaafeisu eno rirongengogakuteki siten* [Theoretical linguistic perspectives on language interfaces], 19-43.

Hoshi, Hidehito. 2011. Four types of passives in Japanese. Ms., MIT/Doshisha University.

Hoshi, Hiroto. 1999. Passives. In Natsuko Tsujimura (ed.), *The handbook of Japanese linguistics*, 191-235. Oxford: Blackwell.

Howard, I. and A. M. Niyekawa-Howard. 1976. Passivization. In M. Shibatani (ed.), *Japanese Generative Grammar, Syntax and Semantics* 5, 201-237. New York: Academic Press.

Huang, C.-T. J. 1997. On lexical structure and syntactic projection. *Chinese Languages and Linguistics* 3: 45-89.

Inoue, K. 1976. *Henkei bunpoo to nihongo, joo* [Transformational grammar and Japanese, Vol. 1]. Tokyo: Taishukan.

Jaeggli, O. 1986. Passive. *Linguistic Inquiry* 17: 587-622.

Kinsui, S. 1997. The influence of translation on the historical development of the Japanese passive construction. *Journal of Pragmatics* 28: 759-779.

Kitagawa, Y. and S.-Y. Kuroda. 1992. Passive in Japanese. Ms., Indiana University and UC San Diego.

Kubo, M. 1990. Japanese passives. Ms., MIT.

Kuno, S. 1973. *The structure of the Japanese language*. Cambridge, Massachusetts: MIT Press.

Kuno, S. 1983. S*in nihonbunpoo kenkyuu* [A new study of Japanese grammar]. Tokyo: Taishukan.

Kuroda, S.-Y. 1965. *Generative grammatical studies in the Japanese language*. Doctoral dissertation, MIT.

Kuroda, S.-Y. 1978. Case-marking, canonical sentence patterns and counter Equi in Japanese (A preliminary survey). In John Hinds and Irwin Howard (eds.), *Problems in Japanese syntax and semantics*, 30-51. Tokyo: Kaitakusha.

Kuroda, S.-Y. 1979. On Japanese passives, in G. Bedell, E. Kobayashi and M. Muraki (eds.), *Exploration in linguistics: Papers in honor of Kazuko Inoue*, 305-347. Tokyo: Kenkyusha.

McCawley, N. A. 1972. On the treatment of Japanese passives. *Papers from the Eighth Regional Meeting of the Chicago Linguistics Society* 8, 256-270.

Miyagawa, S. 1989. *Syntax and Semantics 22: Structure and Case Marking in Japanese*. New York: Academic Press.

Perlmutter, D. and P. M Postal. 1977. Toward a universal characterization of passivization. *Proceedings of the 3rd Annual Meeting of the Berkeley Linguistics Society*, 394-417.

Perlmutter, D. and P. Postal. 1984. Impersonal passives and some relational laws. In D. Perlmutter and C. G. Rosen (eds.), *Studies in Relational Grammar* 2, 126-170. Chicago: University of Chicago Press.

Pylkkänen, L. 2008. *Introducing arguments*. Cambridge, Massachusetts: MIT Press.

Roberts, I. 2005. *Principles and parameters in a VSO language, A case study in Welsh*. Oxford: Oxford University Press.

Shibatani, M. 1978. *Nihongo no bunseki : seisei bunpoo no hoohoo* [An analysis of Japanese language: the methodology of generative grammar]. Tokyo: Taishukan.

Washio, R. 1990. The Japanese passive. *The Linguistic Review* 6: 227-263.

Washio, R. 1993. When causative means passive: A cross-linguistic perspective. *Journal of East Asian Linguistics* 2: 45-90.

Woolford, E. 2003. Burzio's generalization, markedness, and constraints on nominative objects. In E. Brandner and H. Zinsmeister (eds.), *New perspectives on Case theory*, 301-329. Stanford, California: CSLI.

Postsyntactic Compounds and Semantic Head-marking in Japanese

TARO KAGEYAMA
National Institute for Japanese Language and Linguistics

1. Introduction

More than 20 years ago, when Noun Incorporation [NI] in polysynthetic languages was hotly debated, Shibatani and Kageyama (1988) introduced a new type of compounding in Japanese, called post-syntactic compounding, which turns a clausal structure into a compound structure, as in (1).[1]

(1) Clausal structure:
gakusei-ga erebeetaa-o siyoo no toki
student-NOM elevator-ACC use GEN when
'when students use the/an elevator'

---

[1] This paper elaborates on the first half of my keynote presentation "Distorted Argument Realization in Agent Compounding" at the 20th J/K Conference. The second half addressed descriptive and theoretical issues of agent incorporation is to be published in a separate paper. I am grateful to Yile Yu for helping me with Chinese examples, and to Sung-yeo Chung and especially Alan H.-O. Kim for discussing Korean data with me. This work is funded by my Collaborative Research Project at the National Institute for Japanese Language and Linguistics.

Japanese/Korean Linguistics 20.
Edited by Bjarke Frellesvig and Peter Sells.

→ Compound structure:
gakusei-ga **[*erebeetaa* | *siyoo*]** *no* *toki*
student-NOM [elevator | use] GEN when

In the clause structure of (1), the predicate *siyoo* 'use' takes the accusative-marked object *erebeetaa-o*, whereas in the compound structure, the two words are combined into one unit [*erebeetaa* | *siyoo*] (elevator | use) with drop of the accusative marker. Evidence of lexical integrity proves the combined unit to be a 'word'. The compounding is fully productive, with absolutely no difference in conceptual meaning between the clausal and compound structures, though stylistically, the compound form sounds a bit more formal or elevated than the clausal form, presumably because of the nature of Sino-Japanese words. Thus, postsyntactic compounding shares syntactic, semantic, and morphological properties with NI in Native American and other polysynthetic languages, the sole difference being in the degree of phonological integration of complex predicates. That is, the noun+verb combinations in NI languages have phonological solidarity as a single word, whereas the post-syntactic compounds in Japanese, as in [*erebeetaa* | *siyoo*] 'use an elevator' in (1), are accompanied with a short pause indicated by the symbol '|' in (1) or by a colon (:) in Shibatani and Kageyama (1988) and are pronounced with an accentual prominences on each member. Because of this phonological peculiarity, the modifier 'postsyntactic' is added to imply that the compounding takes place after the syntax in which lexical accentuation is completed. And because of this idiosyncrasy, textbooks such as Spencer (1991) and Fabb (1998) have described postsyntactic compounding as a special phenomenon unique to Japanese and distinct from NI.

The present paper will argue that the phonological non-integration, which makes postsyntactic compounding look unique, should be dissociated from the morphosyntactic properties of the compounding itself; instead it should be attributed to the general characteristic of what Kageyama (2001) calls 'Word plus' (W^{+}) — a morphological category which is bigger than a simple word because of its phraselike phonology but nonetheless makes up a 'word' because of its lexical integrity or syntactic atomicity. By divorcing the apparently extraneous phonological behavior from the intrinsic morphosyntactic properties, we can maintain that postsyntactic compounding is really a case of Noun Incorporation that takes place on syntactic structure.

At first blush, the demonstration that Japanese, an agglutinative language, has a syntactic NI appears to be problematic for Baker's (1996) polysynthesis parameter, which characterizes NI as a unique feature of polysynthetic languages that have a rich agreement system of verbs. Actually, the exact status of NI in grammar still remains controversial. Many instances of NI which Sadock (1991) and Baker (1988) assumed to be syntactic are better analyzed as lexical on empirical grounds (Mithun 1984, Rosen 1989, Spencer 1995), and Chomsky (2001) argues on theoretical grounds that there should be no head movement in syntax. On the other hand, Baker (1996, 2009) and Roberts (2010) contend that head movement in syntax is still valid. In the present paper I will suggest that Japanese postsyntactic compounding will be given a proper status as NI if the verb's morphological agreement system on which Baker's polysynthesis parameter is built is relaxed so that semantic agreement (i.e. semantic head-marking) can count as a factor to license NI.

The distinction between head-marking and dependent-marking was discussed in great detail by Nichols (1986), who was also concerned with syntactically and morphologically overt markings. As far as overt markings are concerned, Japanese is duly classified as a dependent-marking language, with the arguments of a verb designated by case particles. However, if we broaden the scope of head/dependent-marking to semantic selection, then Japanese turns out to have a propensity to head-mark the semantic properties of grammatical arguments on the main verb. I suggest that such morphosemantic head-marking lays the foundation for motivating syntactic incorporation in Japanese.

The discussion in this paper proceeds through a crosslinguistic comparison of postsyntactic compounds and related phenomena in Japanese, Chinese, and Korean. The comparative approach to the origin of postsyntactic compounding is feasible because the Verbal Nouns [VNs] that serve as host predicates are, in principle, Sino-Japanese [S-J] words borrowed from Chinese. It is universally recognized (e.g. Yamada 1940, Schmidt 2009) that Chinese loan words have contributed immensely to deepening, widening, and enriching the Japanese vocabulary in much the same way as French loan words have enormously benefited the English lexicon in all fields of life. But that is a matter of the permanent lexicon, and it is little known in what way and to what extent the Chinese loan lexemes participated in the dynamic change of word formation processes in Japanese. The present paper thus has a secondary purpose of exploring 'loan morphology' or borrowing of abstract word formation processes. Loan morphology in this sense presents a theoretical issue of how abstract morphological rules, as opposed to concrete words, are borrowed through language contact. Just because postsyntactic compounding pivots on S-J words, does it follow that the compounding process itself was also borrowed from Chinese? If so, what kind of tangible trigger was there that motivated the borrowing? On the other hand, if it was not borrowed, how was the compounding created in Japanese? The answer to these questions will be provided by comparison of Japanese with contemporary Chinese and Korean.

2. The Morphological Category of Word Plus

The key to the dissociation of the idiosyncratic accentual pattern from the other properties of postsyntactic compounds resides in a special set of Sino-Japanese prefixes, exemplified in (2) (Kageyama 2001, Poser 1990).[2]

(2) a. *zen* 'ex-, immediately preceding': *zen* | *daitooryoo* 'ex-President'
  b. *gen* 'current': *gen* | *kaityoo* 'the current president'
  c. *kaku* 'each': *kaku* | *daigaku* 'each university'
  d. *boo* 'a certain': *boo* | *tyomei-sakka* 'a certain famous writer'
  e. *doo* 'above-mentioned': *doo* | *daigaku* 'the above-mentioned university'
  f. *hon* 'this, the present': *hon* | *koo* 'this school'
  g. *ryoo* 'both': *ryoo* | *koku* 'both countries'
  h. *ko* 'deceased': *ko* | *Tanaka Kakuei* 'late Kakuei Tanaka'
  i. *hi* 'non': *hi* | *kyoosansyugi* 'non communism'
  j. *han* 'anti': *han* | *kyoosansyugi* 'anti communism'
  k. *kyuu* 'formerly': *kyuu* | *teikokudaigaku* 'former imperial universities'

A conspicuous trait of these prefixes is that they involve a slight phonological break after them at the point symbolized by ' | ', whereby such a prefix and its base word are pronounced with their own separate accents-, without being integrated into one accentual unit. This phraselike pronunciation is correlated with the syntactic and semantic peculiarities of these prefixes. Semantically, most of them are characterized by determinerlike meanings that make reference to external entities, such as 'former' (2a), 'current' (2b), 'each' (2c), 'a certain' (2d), 'the abovementioned' (2e), 'this' (2f), and 'both' (2g). In particular, *doo* 'above-mentioned' (2e) has the function of creating a syntactic anaphor that refers to an antecedent in the preceding linguistic context (Kageyama 2001), thus directly violating Postal's (1968) anaphoric island constraint.

A glance at the list in (2) makes it clear that the phonological length of the base nouns the prefixes are attached to has no bearing on the phraselike pronunciation. In (2f), for example, *koo* 'school' is a short bound morpheme (represented by a single Chinese character) that cannot be used alone, and yet it can freely make up phraselike complexes with the aid of special pre-

[2] Poser (1990) dubs these prefixes 'Aoyagi prefixes' after the name of the Japanese phonetician whose work he cites (Aoyagi 1969). I find several infelicities with Aoyagi's descriptions of the relevant prefixes, the most problematic one being his claim that all the prefixes of this sort are followed by a glottal stop, which is clearly false in the standard pronunciation.

fixes, as in *ryoo* | *koo* 'both schools', *kaku* | *koo* 'each school', and *doo* | *koo* 'the said school'.

Based on these and other observations, Kageyama (2001) proposes that the S-J prefixes illustrated in (2) bear a special morphological category called 'Word plus' or 'W^+', which constitutes the maximal category above Root and Word in morphological structure. W^+ is likely to be part of the universal inventory of morphological categories, as suggested by such English prefixes as *ex*- and *non*- which exhibit similar phonological behavior. (3) shows the hierarchy of morphological and syntactic categories.

(3) Root < Word < **Word$^+$** < Phrase < Sentence

domain of morphology (Root < Word < Word$^+$) *domain of syntax* (Phrase < Sentence)

Although W^+ thus involves a loose boundary (represented by the symbol '##' in Kageyama (1982)), it nonetheless belongs to the realm of morphology because complex expressions bearing that category are identified as words by testing their lexical integrity (Bresnan and Mchombo 1995) or syntactic atomicity (Di Sciullo and Williams 1987). Precisely speaking, lexical integrity or syntactic atomicity should be decomposed into two elements (Kageyama 2009): (i) 'syntactic indeformability' (also called 'non-interruptability' by Booij 2009), which means that the internal structure of a word cannot be destroyed or impaired by syntactic means; and (ii) 'syntactic unanalyzability' (also called 'non-accessibility' by Booij 2009), which means that part of a word may not be directly utilized for interpretations of syntactic structures. Of these, syntactic unanalyzability, which subsumes what is known as 'anaphoric islandhood' (Postal 1968), is not entirely reliable as a diagnosis for wordhood, as pointed out earlier. This leaves syntactic indeformability or non-interruptability as the only valid way to identify the wordhood of a given expression. And this property follows from the general architecture of grammar in which morphology and syntax constitute separate components (Di Sciullo 2005, Kageyama 2009). The examples in (4) demonstrate that complex expressions with W^+ prefixes are identified as 'words' because they reject intrusion of syntactic elements: the genitive particles *–no* (4a) and the inflection *–na* (4b).

(4) a. [*zen-* | *huransu(*-**no**)* *daitooryoo*]$_{W+}$
ex- | France(*-GEN) president 'the former President of France'
b. [*kaku* | *kyodai(*-**na**)* *tosi*]$_{W+}$
each | gigantic(*-INFL) city 'each megalopolis'

It is necessary that each S-J prefix be lexically specified as to the category it belongs to. For example, prefix *doo-* 'same' has two possibilities as a W-level prefix (as in *doo-nen* 'the same age', with phonological integration) and a W^+-level prefix (as in *doo* | *nen* 'the abovementioned year', with no phonological integration), whereas prefix *go-* 'wrong, wrongly' is unambiguously a W-level prefix (e.g. *go-doosa* 'mal-operation, with phonological integration) and cannot be W^+-level (e.g. **go* | *doosa*, with no phonological integration).

It should now be noted that the characteristic phraselike accentuation is not a prerogative of S-J prefixes but is also observed with compounds involving S-J words whose members have particular semantic relationships with each other, such as a whole-part relation as in (5a) and a designator-designatum relation as in (5b) (cf. Kubozono 1993).

Compounds at W^+ level

(5) a. [*booeki-gaisya* | *syatyoo*]$_{W+}$
　　trade-company | president　　'president of a trading company'
　b. [*dai-nijukkai* | *JK konfaransu*]$_{W+}$
　　the 20th　| JK conference　　'the 20th J/K conference'

Not all S-J compounds are pronounced like this, however. Relatively short S-J compounds are integrated into a single unit with a native lexical accent.

(6) a. integrated: [*Pari-ryokooo*]$_W$　non-integrated: *[*Pari* | *ryokoo*]$_{W+}$
　　Paris-trip　'a trip to Paris'
　b. integrated: [*nihonzin-ryokoosya*]$_W$　non-integrated: *[*nihonzin* | *ryokoosya*]$_{W+}$
　　Japanese-traveler

It is also possible to mix W^+ prefixes with W^+ compounds to build more and more complex words.

(7) a. [*Amerika-gassyuukoku*　| [*zen* | *daitooryoo*]$_{W+}$]$_{W+}$
　　United States of America　| ex- | president
　　'the ex-President of the United States of America'
　b. [*zen* | [*Amerika-gassyuukoku*　| *daitooryoo*]$_{W+}$]$_{W+}$
　　ex- | United States of America | president
　　'the ex-US President'

To summarize so far, regular lexical accentuation applies to both native and Sino-Japanese words of the W category, whereas the phrase-like accentuation occurs with S-J words of the W^+ category involving a loose boundary. Since Root and Word are indigenous to the native Japanese stratum, all native prefixes and suffixes that induce phonological integration fall under them. It is therefore legitimate to conjecture that the W^{+} category was transplanted to Japanese through a special group of Chinese prefixes[3] and extended to certain types of S-J compounds.

This conjecture proves correct. Chinese as well as Korean has more or less the same set of determinerlike prefixes that are pronounced with a slight pause after them.[4] Although it is generally difficult in Chinese to determine whether a given morpheme is a prefix or a syntactic modifier, the test on syntactic non-interruptability shows that the expressions involving such prefixes are really qualified as words.

(8) Chinese

a. *[qián | měiguó zǒngtǒng]*$_{W+}$
ex | U.S.A. president 'the ex-President of the U.S.A.'

b. *[*qián* | [*měiguózǒng de zǒngtǒng*]$_{NP}$]$_{W+}$
ex | U.S.A. GEN president
lit. 'the ex USA's President'

(9) a. *[gè | dìfāng chéngshì]*$_{W+}$
each | region town 'each local town'

b. *[*gè* | [*dìfāng de chéngshì*]$_{NP}$]$_{W+}$
each | region GEN city
(This is acceptable only if it means 'the cities in each region'.)

Interestingly, however, Chinese does not seem to have compounds of the W^{+} category. Compare thus the Japanese examples in (10), where the genitive particle *no-* is disallowed inside the compounds, with the Chinese

---

[3] The only exception that I am aware of is the native Japanese prefix *moto-* 'former, ex-, erstwhile', used as in (ia). However, it violates the lexical integrity constraint because it can not only take a phrasal base as in (ib) and (ic) but also be separated from the base as in (id).

(i) a. *moto* | *sooridaizin* 'a one-time Prime Minister'

b. *moto* | [*kyozingun no kantoku*]$_{NP}$ 'an ex-manager of the Giants'

c. *moto* | [*yuumei-na myuuzisyan*]$_{NP}$ 'a person who was formerly a famous musician'

d. *Kare-wa kyozingun no kantoku da yo, {moto/*zen}.* 'He was a manager of the Giants formerly.'

Such idiosyncratic behavior strongly suggests that *moto-* is a prefix-like determiner made on analogy with the genuine S-J prefix *zen-* 'ex-, immediately preceding'.

[4] It seems that native speakers of Chinese are not so aware of the pause as Japanese speakers feel about the same prefixes; many Japanese speakers of younger generations also fail to perceive the difference between W and W^{+} accentuation patterns.

counterparts in (11), where the genitive maker can intrude into the complex expression.

(10) a. [*kaki* | [*kissabu(*-no)* *eigyoozikan*]]$_{W+}$
summer-time | coffee-shop(*-GEN) business.hours
'the coffee shop's business hours during the summer'
b. [*Koobe-daigaku* | [*gakutyoo(*-no)* *hosa*]]$_{W+}$
Kobe-university | president(*-GEN) assistant
'the President's assistant at Kobe University'

(11) a. *xiàjì* *cháshè* *yíngyèshíjiān*
summer-time coffee-shop business.hours
b. *xiàjì* *cháshè* *de* *yíngyèshíjiān*
summer-time coffee-shop GEN business.hours

The expression in (11) is thus not a word but a phrase. More generally, it appears that Chinese does not have compound words of the W^+ level. Although this point needs more extensive examination, at present I tentatively conclude that Japanese generalized the novel category of W^+ found with a particular set of prefixes to relatively long compound words involving Sino-Japanese words arranged in whole-part and other semantic relations.

Turning to Korean, we find virtually the same situation as in Japanese. Namely, Korean has both prefixes and compounds of the W^+ category.

(12) a. [*cen* | *mikwuk* *taythonglyeng*]$_{W+}$
ex | America president 'the ex-U.S. president'
b. [*cenkwuk* | [*kak* | *cipangtosi*]$_{W+}$]$_{W+}$
all-country | each | local.town
'each local town of the whole country'

These complex expressions in Korean qualify as words because no syntactic elements can intrude into them to interrupt their sequence.

(13) a. [*kak* | [*cipang(*-uy)* *tosi*]]$_{W+}$
each | region(*-GEN) town
b. [*cen* | [*mikwuk(?*-uy)* *taythonglyeng*]]$_{W+}$
ex | America(?*-GEN) president
c. [*hakyey* | [*kkiktapu(*-uy)* *yeng'ep sikan*]]$_{W+}$
summer | coffee.shop(-*GEN) business-hours

The fact that the prefixes with a loose boundary are common to all of Chinese, Japanese, and Korean strongly indicates that they have the same origin; namely, Japanese and Korean borrowed them from Chinese. This fact alone is not surprising at all because the borrowing pertains to a set of designated lexical prefixes. The important upshot of the borrowing of the W^+ category lies at a more abstract level. The introduction of a novel category changed the organization of the Japanese (and Korean) word formation system, which supposedly used to have only Root- and Word-level lexemes that are phonologically integrated into an accentual unit. The result is that both Japanese and Korean generalized the W^+ category from prefixes to compounding in the lexicon.

The preceding discussion strongly indicates that the source of the phonological non-integration that appeared to characterize postsyntactic compounds should be reduced to the general accentuation pattern of the W^+ category rather than to the 'postsyntactic' or phonological component in which they were originally believed to be formed. Observe thus the parallel accentuation pattern in (14), where capital letters stand for high pitches.

(14) a. W^+ prefix: [*ZEn* | *aMERIKA-DAITOoryoo*]$_{W+}$
ex- | America-president
W^+ compound noun: [*boOEKI-GAisya* | *syaTYOO*]$_{W+}$
trade-company | president
b. Sino-Japanese compound: [*eREBEetaa* | *siYOO*]$_{W+}$ no sai
elevator | use GEN time

Once the seemingly idiosyncratic property of phonological non-integration is disentangled from the other regular properties and attributed to the morphological W^+ category, postsyntactic compounding is not 'postsyntactic' any more but is simply 'syntactic'. However, we will continue to employ the modifier 'postsyntactic' in quotes to avoid unnecessary confusions.

3. Postsyntactic Compounds in Japanese and Korean

Baker (1996: 19) gives four criteria for identifying a word formation process as 'robust' NI in a language: (a) it is reasonably productive, (b) the noun is fully integrated with the verb morphologically, (c) the noun is referentially active in the discourse, and (d) both the noun and the verb can in general be used independently. Of these, criterion (b) is not satisfied by 'postsyntactic' compounds, but the deviance is ascribed to an independent factor as explained in Section 2. The other criteria in (a), (c), and (d) are fully met (see Shibatani and Kageyama (1988)). Besides, additional evidence is available to justify the syntactic nature of Japanese 'postsyntactic' compounding.

First, the prefix *go-* for subject honorification can be attached directly to the head VNs, as shown in (15).

(15) *okyakusama-ga menzeihin-o* ***go**-koonyuu no toki*
customer-NOM duty.free.goods-ACC HON-purchase GEN time
'when a customer purchases/purchased duty free goods'
COMPOUNDING →
*okyakusama-ga [menzeihin | **go**-koonyuu]*$_{W+}$ *no toki*
customer-NOM [duty.free.goods | HON-purchase] GEN time

The grammaticality of (15) presents a marked contrast to lexical compounds, which cannot accommodate the subject honorific prefix inside them.

(16) a. Word-level lexical compounds
[*kaigai (***go**-)ryokoo*]$_W$
[overseas (***HON**)-travel] 'overseas travel'
b. W$^+$-level lexical compounds
[*menzeihin | (***go**-)koonyuu-kyaku*]$_{W+}$
[duty.free.goods | (***HON**-)purchase-customer]
'customers who purchase duty-free goods'

Particularly striking is the disparity in acceptability between (15) and (16b). Despite their superficial resemblance in accent patterns, the 'postsyntactic' compound in (15) and the W$^+$-level lexical compound in (16b) differ in the syntactic functions: the former is a predicate, and the latter a simple NP. Since incorporation is a process whereby an argument is incorporated with a predicate, it cannot take place in a lexical compound noun like (16b) where *koonyuu-kyaku* 'customer' is not a predicate. The contrast between (15) and (16b) thus reinforces our claim that W$^+$-level compounding/incorporation takes place both in the lexicon and in the syntax, as does W-level compounding/incorporation like Verb+Verb compounding (Kageyama 1989).

Second, the application of 'postsyntactic' compounding is rigorously constrained by structural relations, whereby only the complements of predicates — the objects of transitive VNs (17a), subjects of unaccusative VNs (17b), and dative complements of motion VNs (17c) — can be incorporated whereas the subjects of transitive VNs (18a), unergative VNs (18b), and most importantly adjuncts (18c) are excluded.

(17) a. *gakusei-ga erebeetaa-o siyoo no toki*
student-NOM elevator-ACC use GEN time
'when students use the/an elevator'
COMPOUNDING →
gakusei-ga [***erebeetaa*** | ***siyoo***]$_{W+}$ *no toki*
student-NOM [elevator | use] GEN time

b. *Tookyoo-de daizisin-ga hassei no toki*
Tokyo-LOC big.earthquake-NOM occur GEN time
'if a big earthquake occurs in Tokyo'
COMPOUNDING →
Tookyoo-de [***daizisin*** | ***hassei***]$_{W+}$ *no toki*
Tokyo-LOC [big.earthquake | occur] GEN time

c. *hikooki-ga Narita-kuukoo-ni tyakuriku no sai*
plane-NOM Narita-airport-DAT land GEN when
'when the plane landed at Narita Airport'
COMPOUNDING →
hikooki-ga [***Narita-kuukoo*** | ***tyakuriku***]$_{W+}$ *no sai*
plane-NOM [Narita-airport | land] GEN when

(18) a. **erebeetaa-o* [***gakusei*** | ***siyoo***]$_{W+}$ *no toki*
elevator-ACC [student | use] GEN time
'when students use the/an elevator'

b. **tennai-de* [***kaimonokyaku*** | ***kituen***]$_{W+}$ *no toki*
store.inside-LOC [shopper | smoke] GEN time
'if customers smoke in the shop'

c. **kookoosei-ga* [***zitensya*** | ***tuugaku***]$_{W+}$ *no toki*
high.school.student-NOM [bicycle | go.to.school] GEN time
'when a high-school student went to school by bicycle'

With this much background in mind, we turn to Chinese and Korean. Informant work suggests that Chinese does not have 'postsyntactic' compounds. Given that the object follows the verb in the normal word order of Chinese, as in (19a), the object cannot be moved to the front of the verb except in the *ba*- topicalization construction. In the V+O order, the object may involve a phrase, as in (19b), so that the whole string cannot be a compound word. Also the head may consist of a phrase, as in (19c), thereby violating the restriction that the head of a word must not be a phrase, although the modifier may involve a phrase, as in phrasal compounds.

(19) Chinese

a. *xuésheng shǐyòng diàntī de shíhou*
student use elevator GEN time
'when students use the elevator'

b. *xuésheng shǐyòng jiàozhíyuángōng zhuānyòng (?de) diàntī*
student use teacher-staff-for GEN elevator
de shíhou
GEN when
'when students use the elevator for teachers and staff'

c. *xuésheng shǐyòng huòzhě pòhuài diàntī de shíhou*
students use or break elevator GEN when
'if students use or break the elevator'

From these observations, it is concluded that Chinese does not have 'postsyntactic' compounds. More generally, it seems that Chinese compound verbs are limited to lexically formed compounds consisting of two morphemes (V+V or V+N).

On the other hand, Korean provides examples that are very much similar to Japanese 'postsyntactic' compounds. In particular, the structural constraints match up closely in the two languages.

(20) a. Objects of transitive VNs cf. (17a)
haksayng-i [***eyllipeyithe* | *sayong***] *si-ey-nun*
student-NOM [**elevator | use**] time-DAT-TOP

b. Subjects of unaccusative VNs cf. (17b)
Tongkyeng-eyse [***taycicin*** | ***palsayng***] *si-ey-nun*
Tokyo-LOC [big.earthquake | occur] time-DAT-TOP

c. Dative complements of motion VNs cf. (17c)
pihayngki-ka [***Nalithakonghang*** | ***chaklyuk***] *si-ey-nun*
plane-NOM [Narita-airport | land] time-DAT-TOP

d. Subjects of transitive VNs cf. (18a)
eyllipeyithe-lul* [*haksayng*** | ***sayong***] *si-ey-nun*
elevator-ACC [student | use] time- DAT-TOP

It is questionable, however, whether compounds like those in (20a, b, c) are derived directly from the corresponding syntactic structures, because the case-marked constructions that are supposed to underlie them are hardly acceptable in Korean, as my informants told me.

(21) a. Transitive objects in the accusative (cf. 20a)
?**haksayng-i eyllipeyithe-**lul** sayong si-ey-nun*
student-NOM elevator-ACC use time- DAT-TOP

b. Unaccusative subjects in the nominative (cf. 20b)
?**Tongkyeng-eyse taycicin-**i** palsayng si-ey-nun*
Tokyo-LOC big.earthquake-**NOM** occur time-DAT-TOP

c. Dative complements marked in the dative (cf. 20c)
?**pihayngki-ka Nalithakonghang-**ey** chaklyuk si-ey-nun*
plane- NOM Narita-airport-**DAT** land time-DAT-TOP

The fundamental motivation for the syntactic derivation of compounds is that the noun element and the verb element are used independently in a syntactic structure with the same meaning as a compound. The low acceptability of (21), as contrasted with the perfect acceptability of the Japanese examples in (17a, b, c), raises a serious question as to the formation of Korean compounds in (20a, b, c) directly from the corresponding syntactic structures. Before probing into the cause for this crosslinguistic disparity, we will observe another type of compound, agent compounding, that exhibits parallel differences in Japanese and Korean.

4. Agent Compounds in Japanese and Korean

The preceding section established that Japanese 'postsyntactic' compounding (as well as its Korean counterpart) obeys the universal constraint that the subjects of transitive verbs cannot be incorporated/compounded (Mithun 1984, Baker 1988). In contradiction to this robust constraint, however, it is discovered that Japanese has a fairly productive process of compounding agent nouns (subjects of transitive verbs) with Sino-Japanese transitive VNs. Interestingly enough, such agent-incorporating compounds are also pronounced with two accentual prominences, thus displaying exactly the same phonological pattern as W^{+} prefixes and 'postsyntactic' compounds.

(22) a. [***daitooryoo* | *syusai***]$_{W+}$ *no paatii*
[President | host] GEN party
'a/the party/parties the President hosts/hosted'

b. [***Spielberg-kantoku* | *seisaku***]$_{W+}$ *no eiga*
[Spielberg-director | produce] GEN movie
'a/the movie(s) Spielberg produces/produced'

Despite the phonological non-integration, such agent-incorporating compounds qualify themselves as 'words', as shown by the impossibility of inserting a syntactic phrase inside them in (23).

(23) a. *[***daitooryoo*** | *kyonen* | ***syusai***] *no paatii*
[president last.year host] GEN party
'the/a party/parties that the President hosted last year'

b. *[***Spielberg*** | *Hollywood-de* | ***seisaku***] *no eiga*
[Spielberg Hollywood-in produce] GEN movie
'a/the movie(s) that Spielberg produced/produces in Hollywood'

The similarity of agent compounds with 'postsyntactic' compounds is enhanced by the stratum restriction on the predicates, whereby Sino-Japanese VNs are permitted as incorporation hosts, but not native Japanese verbs.

(24) a. *[***daitooryoo*** | ***moyoosi***]$_{W+}$ *no paatii*
[President | hold (native v.)] GEN party (cf. 22a)
b. *[***Spielberg-kantoku*** | ***tukuri***]$_{W+}$ *no eiga*
[Spielberg-director | make (native v.)] GEN movie (cf. 22b)

Korean presents apparently the same kind of agent compounds, as exemplified by (25a). The ungrammaticality of (25b) shows that they are indeed qualified as words.

(25) a. [*Taythonglyeng* | *cwuchoy*]-*uy phathi*
[president | host]-GEN party cf. Japanese (22a)
b. *[*Taythonglyeng* | *caknyen* | *cwuchoy*]-*uy phathi*
[president last.year host]-GEN party cf. Japanese (23a)

Intriguingly enough, Japanese and Korean again exhibit distinct behavior as to the availability of case-marked paraphrases. The Japanese example in (22b) can be paraphrased as (26a) with the agent noun marked in the nominative, whereas the Korean counterpart does not accept the nominative marking on the agent noun, as shown by (26b).

(26) a. *Spielberg-kantoku-**ga** seisaku no eiga*
Spielberg-director-NOM produce GEN movie
b. **Suphilpekukamtok-**i** ceycak uy yenghwa*
Spielberg-director-NOM produce GEN movie

This contrast in the availability of case marking with Japanese and Korean VNs is exactly parallel to the one observed with 'postsyntactic' compounds in the last section, and it is actually spread across other syntactic environments as well. Observe the relative clause construction in (27) and the purposive motion construction in (28):

(27) a. Japanese
*erebeetaa-**o*** *siyoo no* *gakusei-wa*
elevator-**ACC** use GEN student-TOP
'students who use the elevator'

b. Korean
eyllibeyithe-lul*** *sayong-uy* *haksayng-nun*
elevator-**ACC** use-GEN student-TOP

(28) a. Japanese
Kanozyo-wa Hokkaidoo-ni Ainugo-o tyoosa-ni itta.
she- TOP Hokkaido-LOC Ainu-**ACC** investigate-DAT went
'She went to Hokkaido to do research on Ainu.'

b. Korean
**Kunye-nun Pukhayto-ey Ainumal-ul cosa-lo kassta.*
she- TOP Hokkaido-LOC Ainu-**ACC** investigate-DAT went

I suggest that the disparities in all these constructions could be systematically attributed to the way they borrowed verbs from Chinese. In line with the general propensity of language to import foreign words as nouns, Korean borrowed Chinese verbs as simple nouns ([+N]) that can theta-mark their arguments but are not capable of case assignment. By contrast, Japanese presumably adopted them as a hybrid category of Noun and Verb ([+N, +V] in Kageyama's (1982) notation) that can both theta-mark and case-mark their arguments on their own in the same way as native verbs, the difference being that native verbs are directly inflected in tense whereas Sino-Japanese VNs require a light verb to carry tense. As Yamada (1940: 487) points out, a few Sino-Japanese VNs can even be used as predicates in the imperative or request construction, as in *Ano yama-o go-ran.* 'Look at that mountain.' and *Gohoobi-o tyoodai.* 'Give me a reward.' with the object arguments marked in the accusative. Japanese has another hybrid category of Adjectival Noun ([+A, +N]) which is closely associated with Chinese loan adjectivals. Like VNs, Adjectival Nouns can also trigger 'postsyntactic' compounding, as in *nihongo-ni tokuyuu* 'peculiar to Japanese' → [*nihongo* | *tokuyuu*] (Kageyama 1993). These two hybrid categories are known to display idiosyncratic behavior outside compounding as well (Kageyama 2010).

Given the verblike properties of Japanese VNs, it is not surprising that Japanese has developed NI in the syntax (i.e. 'postsyntactic' compounding and agent compounding on syntactic structure). On the other hand, Korean VNs, which are nouns, are unable to license the syntactic configuration necessary for incorporation and consequently, Korean compounds that appear to correspond to Japanese 'postsyntactic' and agent compounds should be analyzed as lexically formed. In a nutshell, the small difference in the lexical treatment of verbs borrowed from Chinese as either simple nouns or verblike nouns brought about a seemingly big difference in Korean and Japanese syntax.

Regardless of the syntax/lexicon distinction, we encounter an obvious contradiction. The agent compounds introduced in this section directly contradict the universal constraint that Noun Incorporation applies only to the complement of a verb, thereby excluding agent nouns, especially subjects of transitive verbs. In my presentation at the 20th J/K Conference, I proposed that a special mechanism is at work that creates individual-level predicates by incorporating agent arguments. Because of space limitations, the full demonstration of this point must be put off for another paper.

5. Syntactic Incorporation and Semantic Head-marking

In the foregoing sections, I endeavored to explicate the syntactic nature of Japanese 'postsyntactic' compounding, firstly by removing the peculiar phonological property from the compounding process itself, and secondly by comparing it with the Korean counterpart. The remaining question is how Japanese was able to develop compounding in syntactic structure.

At first blush, it looks plausible to seek the answer in the 'agglutinative' nature of Japanese. Presumably well before the creation of Sino-Japanese 'postsyntactic' compounding, Japanese had already possessed a relatively productive rule of compounding nouns with finite verbs of the native Japanese stratum. Compound verbs of this sort, still found rather commonly in contemporary Japanese (e.g. *tema-doru* (time-take) 'take time', where the verb *doru* (lexical entry *toru*) has undergone *rendaku*), appear to have been more abundant in Old Japanese (Sakakura 1966, Kinuhata 2010), although it is not clear as yet whether those Old Japanese compounds were lexical or syntactic. It is highly conceivable that such N+V compounds motivated the creation of 'postsyntactic' compounding at least partially. This account, however, is not sufficient to explain the relatively high productivity of syntactic compounding in Japanese, as compared with Korean, which also has compound verbs of the form 'noun + native Korean verb' like *ay-ssuta* (effort-use) 'make efforts' (Sohn 1999: 253). The active implementation of syntactic incorporation in Japanese is further illustrated by Verb+Verb compound verbs. As demonstrated by Kageyama (1989), Japanese has a solid distinction between lexical and syntactic Verb+Verb compounds, but Korean is rather impoverished in this domain, lacking syntactic V+V compound verbs.

I would suggest that the essential reason for why Japanese is rich in syntactic compounding can be sought in the way languages mark their arguments. Some languages specify the arguments of a verb by case markers or case inflections on the dependents (namely the argument NPs themselves), while others mark argument relations as affixes attached to heads (namely, verbs), with actual argument NPs optionally showing up in the clause. Nichols (1986) shows that this distinction between 'head-marking' and 'dependent-marking' provides a basic criterion for language typology, although this distinction is not strictly dichotomous but gradient. Nichols (1986) summarizes the typical differences between head-marking and dependent-marking as in (29). The importance of head-marking is echoed by part of Baker's (1996) polysynthesis parameter for syntactic incorporation (also called 'the Morphological Visibility Condition') in (30). Baker assumes that the true polysynthetic languages satisfy both (30i) and (30ii).

(29) a. Dependent-marking
- case
- adnominal genitive
- non-finite verbs
- agreement in adjectives
- uninflected adpositions which govern cases

b. Head-marking
- verbal agreement or cross-reference with nominal arguments
- incorporation
  - instrumental, directional (etc.) affixes on verbs
- inflected adpositions
- pronominal (possessive) affixes on nouns
- polysynthesis

(Nichols 1986: 64)

(30) The Morphological Visibility Condition

A phrase X is visible for theta-role assignment from a head Y only if it is coindexed with a morpheme in the word containing Y via:

(i) an agreement relationship, or

(ii) a movement relationship. (Baker 1996: 17)

It is commonly assumed that Japanese is a purely dependent-marking language, inasmuch as its syntax marks the verb's arguments exclusively by case particles while the verbs lack complicated agreement affixes like those found in polysynthetic languages. If Japanese is 100% dependent-marking, however, there should be no intrinsic motivation for syntactic incorporation. I would suggest that there are morphosemantic phenomena that hint at the head-marking character of Japanese.

First, a good example is the well-known rule of Subject Honorification, which attaches the prefix *o-* to a native verb or *go-* to an S-J predicate, as in *(Sensei-ga) o-kaeri/go-tootyaku desu.* '(Our teacher) has returned/arrived', where the verb, with or without the pro-drop of the subject phrase, conveys that the subject is an honorable person. The object honorification, as in *Wa-*

tasi-ga (sensei-o) o-tasuke simasu. 'I will help (the teacher).', serves the same purpose for identifiying the status of the object referent, which may or may not be pro-dropped. Korean lacks such systematic honorification rules for non-subjects.

Second, many Japanese verbs contain selectional information on the referents of their arguments either overtly or covertly. The lexical verbs of giving and receiving (*yaru* 'give', *ageru* 'give', *kureru* 'give', *kudasaru* 'give', *sasiageru* 'give', *morau* 'receive', *itadaku* 'receive', *tamawaru* 'receive'), which are distinguished by the social relations of the giver and receiver, encode the information on subject and object lexically. Such semantic agreements are found, albeit not systematically, with verbs in a variety of semantic fields. For example, *hiku* 'play', when applied to musical instruments, selects only those object nouns that have strings such as 'violin', 'cello', 'guitar', and 'piano', but not 'trumpet', 'flute', or 'timpani'. The verbs of wearing specify the body part on which a garment is put, for example, *kaburu* 'put on one's head', *haku* 'put on one's feet or legs', and *kiru* 'put on one's torso'. Plentiful examples of this sort are found in Miyajima (1972) and Kageyama (1980). All these examples can be subsumed under the rubric of 'semantic head-marking'.

Third, lexical head-marking is abundantly found with morphologically complex verbs of both native and Sino-Japanese strata. Sino-Japanese compound VNs that consist of a noun element and a verb element basically mark an argument or adjunct by the noun element. Thus, the predicate *sensya* (wash-car), used as in *zibun-no kuruma-o sensya(suru)* 'to wash one's car', necessarily refers to a car as its object, and *nyuu-in* (enter-hospital), used as in *genti-no byooin-ni nyuu-in(suru)* 'to be admitted to a local hospital', necessarily designates a hospital as its locative complement. Such morpholexical marking of the information on arguments and adjuncts is also common among native verbs which are etymologically looked upon as N+V compounds, as in *na-noru* (name-tell) 'give one's name', used as in *zibun-no na-o na-noru* 'give one's name', where the morpheme *na-* 'name' in the verb agrees with the object NP *zibun-no na-o* 'one's own name (accusative)', *tuma-biku* (nail-play) 'play (a musical instrument) with one's fingertips', used as in *gitaa-o ippon-no yubi-de tumabiku* 'to play the guitar with one finger', where the morpheme *tuma-* 'finger nail', the bound allomorph of *tune*, agrees with the adjunct *ippon-no yubi-de* 'with one finger', and *to-gireru* (path-be.broken) 'be interrupted', used as in *miti-ga to-gireru* 'the road comes to an end', where the morpheme *to-* 'path' in the verb semantically agrees with the unaccusative subject *miti-ga* 'the road'.

All the three phenomena presented above are construed as morphosemantic versions of 'verbal agreement with arguments' in Nichols' list of head-marking properties in (29b).

Fourth, despite its extensive use of adpositions for arguments and adjuncts, Japanese lacks adpositions like English *along*, *across*, *over*, and *through* that represent traversal paths. Instead, all those notions of traversal paths are encoded in motion verbs themselves, as in *koeru* 'go over', *wataru* 'go across', *sugiru* 'go past', *tutau* 'go along', and *yokogiru* 'go across'. These semantic notions contained in the motion verbs correspond to 'directional affixes on verbs' in Nichols' list (29b).

These and many other phenomena, taken together, strongly suggest that Japanese has a head-marking character from the viewpoint of morphosemantics, despite its common classification as a syntactically dependent-marking language (Nichols 1986). Because morphosemantic head-marking means that a verb contains the lexical information on its arguments either overtly or covertly, it is considered to be harmonious, in spirit, with what the condition (30i) of Baker's Morphological Visibility Condition aims at. It will be reasonable to hypothesize that this predilection for morphosemantic head-marking enhanced the development of 'postsyntactic' compounding and other syntactic incorporation in Japanese.

References

Aoyagi, S. 1969. A Demarcative Pitch of Some Prefix-Stem Sequences. *The Study of Sounds* 12: 241-247. [Journal of the Phonetic Society of Japan]

Baker, M. 1988. *Incorporation*. Chicago: University of Chicago Press.

Baker, M. 1996. *The Polysynthesis Parameter*. Oxford: Oxford University Press.

Baker, M. 2009. Is Head Movement Still Needed for Noun Incorporation? *Lingua* 119: 148–165.

Booij, G. 2008. Lexical Integrity as a Formal Universal. *Universals of Language Today*, ed. S. Scalise, E. Magni, and A. Bisetto, 83–100. Dordrecht: Springer.

Bresnan, J. and S.A. Mchombo. 1995. The lexical integrity principle: Evidence from Bantu. *Natural Language & Linguistic Theory* 13: 181–254.

Chomsky, N. 2001. Derivation by Phase. *Ken Hale: A Life in Language*, ed. M. Kenstowicz, 1–52. Cambridge, MA: MIT Press.

Di Sciullo, M.A. 2005. *Asymmetry in Morphology*. Cambridge, MA: MIT Press.

Di Sciullo, M.A. and E. Williams. 1987. *On the Definition of Word*. Cambridge, MA: MIT Press.

Fabb, N. 1998. Compounding. *The Handbook of Morphology*, ed. A. Spencer and A. Zwicky, 66–83. Oxford: Blackwell.

Kageyama, T. 1980. *Goi no Koozoo [Lexical Structures]*. Tokyo: Shohakusha.

Kageyama, T. 1982. Word Formation in Japanese. *Lingua* 57: 215–258.

Kageyama, T. 1989. The Place of Morphology in the Grammar: Verb-Verb Compounds in Japanese. *Yearbook of Morphology* 2, ed. G. Booij and J. van Marle, 73–94. Dordrecht: Foris.

Kageyama, T. 1993. *Bunpoo to Gokeisei [Grammar and Word Formation]*. Tokyo: Hituzi Syobo.

Kageyama, T. 1999. Word Formation. *The Handbook of Japanese Linguistics*, ed. N. Tsujimura, 297–325. Oxford: Blackwell.

Kageyama, T. 2001. Word Plus. *Issues in Japanese Phonology and Morphology*, ed. Jeroen van de Weijer and Tetsuo Nishihara, 245–276. Berlin: Mouton de Gruyter.

Kageyama, T. 2009. *Isolate*: Japanese. *The Oxford Handbook of Compounding*, ed. R. Lieber and P. Štekauer, 512–526. Oxford: Oxford University Press.

Kageyama, T. 2010. Variation between Endocentric and Exocentric Word Structures. *Lingua* 120: 2405–2423.

Kinuhata, T. 2010. Joodai no Meishi-hoogoo nit suite [On Noun Incorporation in Old Japanese]. *Gobun* 92/93: 34–44. Osaka University.

Kubozono, H. 1993. *The Organization of Japanese Prosody*. Tokyo : Kurosio.

Mithun, M. 1984. The Evolution of Noun Incorporation. *Language* 60: 847–893.

Miyajima, T. 1972. *Dooshi no Imi-Yoohoo no Kijututeki Kenkyuu [A Descriptive Study on the Meaning and Uses of Japanese Verbs]*. Tokyo: Kokuritsu Kokugo Kenkyujo/Shuei Shuppan.

Nichols, J. 1986. Head-marking and Dependent-marking Grammar. *Language* 62: 56–119.

Poser, W. 1990. Word-internal Phrase Boundary in Japanese. *The Phonology–Syntax Connection*, ed. S. Inkelas and D. Zec, 279-288. Chicago: University of Chicago Press.

Postal. P.M. 1968. Anaphoric Islands. *Chicago Linguistic Society* 5: 205–239.

Roberts, I. 2010. *Agree and Head Movement*. Cambridge, MA: MIT Press.

Rosen, S. 1989. Two Types of Noun Incorporation. *Language* 65: 294-317.

Sadock, J. 1991. *Autolexical Syntax*. Chicago: University of Chicago Press.

Sakakura, A. 1966. *Gokoosei no Kenkyuu [A Study of Word Composition]*. Tokyo: Kadokawa Shoten.

Schmidt, C.K. 2009. Loanwords in Japanese. *Loanwords in the World's Languages*, ed. M. Haspelmath and U. Tadmor, 545–569. Berlin: Mouton de Gruyeter.

Shibatani, M. 1990. *The Languages of Japan*. Cambridge: Cambridge University Press.

Shibatani, M. and T. Kageyama. 1988. Word Formation in a Modular Theory of Grammar. *Language* 64: 451–484.

Sohn, H.-M. 1999. *The Korean Language*. Cambridge: Cambridge University Press.

Spencer, A. 1991. *Morphological Theory*. Oxford: Blackwell.

Spencer, A. 1995. Incorporation in Chukchi. *Language* 71: 439-489.

Yamada, Y. 1940. *Kokugo no naka ni okeru Kango no Kenkyu [A Study of Chinese Words in the Japanese Language]*. Tokyo: Hobunkan.

Ani 'No'-Prefaced Responses to WH-Questions as Challenges in Korean Conversation

HYE RI STEPHANIE KIM
University of California, Los Angeles

1. Introduction

The present study revisits the Korean negative response particle *ani* in naturally occurring interaction by using Conversation Analysis. While the most commonly noted vernacular usage of *ani* is negating the proposition of a yes/no question (as does *no* in English), in other sequential environments, *ani* poses an analytic puzzle. One environment in which *ani* becomes particularly puzzling is when it is in response to WH-questions. Consider the following case (example 1 overleaf), in which Hee and Jil, two friends in their late 20s, are talking on the telephone about Jil's move.

Japanese/Korean Linguistics 20.
Edited by Bjarke Frellesvig and Peter Sells.

(1) [jenme060907_0:00:40][1]

01 Jil: a:: ecekkey ton toy:key manhi sse-ss-e kulayse,
VOC yesterday money very much spend-ANT-IE so
02 mak isacim seyntha pwulu-ko mak ile-kwu.
DM moving center call-and DM like:that-and
Ah:: so {I} spent so much money yesterday calling the moving company and things like that.
03 Hee: e:: com to-wa tal-la kule-ci kulay-ss-e,
yes little help-CONN give-QT like:that-NML say-ANT-INTERR
Ye::ah {you} should have asked for help,
04 (0.2)
05 Jil: nwukwu-hanthey?
who-to
From who?
06 Hee: **a↑ni::** mwe, namca-tul manh-cahn-a.
DM men-PL many-you:know-IE
a↑ni:: *well, there are many guys you know.*
07 (.)
08 Hee: ta pappu-n-ka?
all busy-ATTR-INTERR
Is everyone's busy {perhaps}?

In response to Jil's complaint about the money spent on the move, Hee, rather than sympathizing with Jil, provides a possible remedy that could have taken place (line 3). This prompts Jil to produce the rising intoned

---

[1] All data are transcribed according to the conventions adapted from Jefferson (2004):

[ ]	overlapping or simultaneous talk	↑↓	mark sharper rises or falls in pitch
=	contiguous utterances (with no break or gap)	°	the following talk is markedly quiet or soft
(0.5)	length of silence between utterances in tenths of seconds	:::	prolongation or stretching of the preceding sound
(.)	micro-pause	hhh	laughter
?	rising intonation, not necessarily a question	(hh)	laughter inside the boundaries of a word
,	continuing intonation	.hhh	inhalation
.	downward, period intonation	-	a cut-off or self-interruption
¿	a rise stronger than a comma but weaker than a question mark	___	(underline) stress and emphasis, either by increased loudness or higher pitch
<	the immediately following talk is "jump-started," i.e., sounds as if it starts with a rush	(( ))	transcriber's description of event
		{}	unsaid words necessary for smooth translation
><	the talk between them is compressed or rushed.	( )	uncertainty on the transcriber's part

question, *nwukwu-hanthey?* 'from who?' (line 5), to which Hee begins responding, *a↑ni::* (line 6).

This *ani* cannot be interpreted as negating the proposition of the WH-question. Then, what is *ani* negating? Or, *is* it deployed to negate? This article aims to solve this puzzle by describing the ways in which *ani* is used when it prefaces responses to WH-questions used as challenges. The analysis demonstrates that the speakers deploy *ani* in this environment to resist responding to a challenge, registering the challenge as unexpected or unwarranted at the first opportunity possible. This analysis is substantiated by focusing on 'action' as a unit of analysis and by analyzing a broader context in which the target practice occurs.

I begin by discussing previous research on *ani* as a discourse particle and on responses to questions, followed by a description of the study's data and analytical framework. Then, in Sections 3 and 4, I analyze representative data extracts and give a conclusion.

2. Background

2.1. Previous studies on *ani* as a discourse marker

The possibility of *ani* as a discourse marker was first noted by Martin (1992) in his comprehensive reference grammar book of Korean. There have since been three studies on *ani* as a discourse marker. Among them, Kim (1997) is most comprehensive in its account of *ani*'s conversational usages. Using data from natural as well as overheard/invented conversations, she viewed the marker within the framework of the turn-taking system (Sacks et al. 1974) and stated that it is used to 1) express an unacceptable attitude, 2) call one's attention to something, and 3) repair an error.

Some of these functions are further explicated from a diachronic perspective by Koo (2008). Comparing written data from the 15th-18th centuries to spoken/written data from the 21st century, she demonstrates that the negation marker *ani* observed in Middle and Early Modern Korean slowly became replaced by a shorter negation marker, *an* (as in *an ha-ta* NEG do-DECL). During this process, *an* became specialized as a negation marker and *ani* obtained discourse functions. Also shown in Koo's study are *ani*'s modern conversational usages marking 1) a repair/correction, 2) a topic shift, and 3) a negative attitude. These usages show that *ani*, despite its new discourse functions, has maintained its negating function in a broader sense. In other words, according to Koo (2008), initiating a repair is negating some aspect of a previous utterance, shifting to a new topic is negating a previous topic, and indexing a negative attitude is connected to the speaker's negative attitude towards the recipient's utterance. However, what it means to "negate" needs to be further clarified because of the term's broad and ambiguous nature. Also, the functions mentioned in Koo (2008), for example repairing and shifting to a new topic, do not necessarily "negate" prior talk in social interaction (cf. Schegloff 1992, 2001).

Although Kim (1997) and Koo (2008) showed quite diverse functions of *ani*, Yang (2002), who approached the marker from a discourse-pragmatic perspective, demonstrated just how varied *ani*'s uses can be in discourse. The functions included correcting and monitoring prior talk, initiating turns, and marking politeness, uncertainty, sarcasm, commitment avoidance, and topic shifts.

All of these studies agree that *ani* does not always serve as a negative-polarity marker that negates the truth-conditional meaning of prior talk. However, although they have contributed much to an understanding of *ani* in spoken discourse, they are less clear about what speakers are *doing* by producing *ani*. The present study aims to complement the previous works by providing a conversation analytic account of which social action(s) speakers project with *ani* (Sacks et al. 1974, Heritage 1984a).

Since *ani* is observed in a wide range of sequential contexts, thereby carrying varied local interactional functions, a necessary first step was to restrict its environment and study how *ani* is used in a particular local context. As Schgeloff (2007: 20-21) argues, "the action which some talk is doing can be grounded in its *position*, not just its *composition* – not just the words that compose it, but its placement." The reason for selecting responses to WH-questions as the study's environment was due to its strikingly frequent occurrences in that context as well as to eliminate the alternative understanding of *ani* as a negative response particle.

2.2. Responding to challenges formulated as WH-questions

Challenges in interaction can be formulated in a variety of ways, but the most common format discussed is using questions, WH-questions in particular (Schegloff 1984, Koshik 2003, Heinemann 2008, Steensig and Drew 2008, cf. Yoon 2006). It should be noted that there is a functional distinction between interrogatively formatted utterances that purely request information and those that use the format as a vehicle to do other actions, such as complaining, accusing and challenging (e.g. Schegloff 1984, Koshik 2003). This function of question is clearly shown in Schegloff (1984), in which he analyzes questions such as 'for whom?' and 'by what standard?' not as information-seeking questions, but attacks (and thereby siding with the recipient in the case he examines). As English WH-questions, Korean WH-questions are also used as a vehicle to initiate repair, challenge and complain (Yoon 2006, 2010).

The earliest studies of question and response in naturally occurring interaction note that it is an adjacency pair, a series of adjacently placed, type-related turns produced by two different speakers (Schegloff 1968, Schegloff and Sacks 1973). In an example of an adjacency pair, a current turn (e.g. a greeting, *hello*) requires a reciprocal action (e.g. *hello*) at the first possible opportunity after the completion of the first; if such a reciprocal action does not occur, the next action is treated as "noticeably absent" (Schegloff 1968). One of the basic adjacency pairs is question-response. When a question is asked, the next relevant turn normatively projected is a response from the selected speaker.

One of the most important findings of questioning and responding of the last decade has been that of Raymond (2003) on type-conformity of response turns. Type-conforming answers are those that "conform" to the type of question; simply put, 'yes' or 'no' answers are type-conforming answers to yes/no questions. Raymond (2003) has demonstrated for English that there is a strong preference for type-conforming answers to yes/no questions and that non-type conforming answers (such as repeats; e.g. A: *Has Mia arrived?* B: *She's arrived*) are involved in showing more agency or authority of the response speaker (Heritage and Raymond frth.). Yes/no questions in Korean also show a preference for type-conforming answers (Yoon 2010), similar to the other nine languages studied (cf. Enfield et al. 2010). Such strict type-conformity is not expected of a response to a WH-question; however, a Q-word in the WH-question (e.g. *what, where*) constrains the type of response that a recipient is expected to provide. In other words, by asking *where?* the question speaker is expecting to receive as an answer "a place" (cf. Schegloff and Lerner 2009).

Challenge WH-questions, as a first pair part, make an answer relevant, but also imply that there is not really a defensible account (cf. Clayman and Heritage 2002, Heinemann 2008). Such characteristics of challenge questions present a dilemma to the recipients, placing question recipients in the position of responding to the challenge in some way, regardless of whether a defensible account is available.[2] *Ani* in these contexts becomes deployed to undercut the question speaker's claim.

3. Data and Methodology

The data collected for the study included approximately 15 hours of audio-recorded telephone and video-recorded face-to-face everyday conversations. The participants included both genders; ages ranged from 20s to 50s. As

---

2 Although WH-question is a vehicle with which many challenges and accusations are implemented, polar questions can also do similar work depending on how they are formulated and where they are placed in a sequence. Sometimes, challenge polar questions can put the question recipients in even more serious dilemma because neither confirming nor disconfirming (as requested) is an adequate response (Heinemann 2008). See Kim (2011) for the analyses of Korean polar questions as challenges.

mentioned earlier, the methodology adopted is Conversation Analysis (CA), which from its inception has focused on the 'activity' and 'action' of an utterance rather than its propositional content (Sacks et al. 1974, Heritage 1984a, Schegloff 1984). As Schegloff (2007: 1-3) writes,

> ...it is important to register that a great deal of talk-in-interaction [ ] is better examined with respect to action, [ ] more for what it is doing than for what it is about. . . [ ] parties to talk-in-interaction [ ] monitor and analyze [talk-in-a-turn] for what action or actions its speaker might be doing with it...because the action that a speaker might be doing in or with an utterance may have implications for what action should or might be done in the next turn as a response to it.

Such an approach to language by scholars interested in describing pragmatic and interactional functions of a grammatical or lexical token has met with much success (e.g. see Kim and Suh 1994, Park 1998, Hayashi 2004, Kim 2004, 2010, for the application of CA to Japanese and Korean).

Following the research tradition of CA, I focus on the action(s) questioning speakers undertake by asking a WH-question, and the action(s) responding speakers undertake by prefacing their response turn with *ani*. To understand the ways *ani* prefacing is deployed in each conversational exchange, the target turn's prior and subsequent turns are also included in the analyses.

3. Analysis

I begin with a case in point below. Present in this face-to-face conversation are: Min and Ria, a couple who got married earlier on the day of recording, as well as Ria's girlfriends, Ara and Joo. As the couple is only in their early 20's, the idea of getting married early has been the topic of conversation. Ara and Joo are for the idea of getting married early (lines 1-4), with which Min weakly disagrees (line 5). This Min's statement about 'missing single life' becomes the subject of challenge in lines 8 and 10 by the bride's friend, Ara.

(2) [wednight1_00:47:10][3]

01 Joo(F):	com ppalli:: anceng-ul:: chac-nun kes-to
	little early stability-ACC find-ATTR thing-ADD
02	>koaynchanh-ul ke< [kath-untey:
	okay-ATTR thing seem-but
	Having a stable life a little early sounds like a good idea.

[3] (M) denotes male, and (F) female.

03 Ara(F): [°kòaynchanh-un ke kath-ay.
okay-ATTR thing seem-IE
{It} sounds good.
04 Joo(F): ppalli ay-tul kil-lese nacwungey nohwu-lul:=
early child-PL raise-after afterwards retirement-OBJ
After raising children early on, life after retirement
05 Min(M): =<kuntey aswuiwun myen-to iss-nuntey,
but lacking aspect-also exist-but
But there's an aspect {you} miss
06 (0.1)
07 Joo(F): cang-[tan-cem[-i iss-keyss-ci.]
pros-cons-thing-NOM exist-DCT:RE-COMM
There must be pros and cons.
08 Ara(F): [m(h)we(h),
w(h)hat(h),
09 Min(M): [kamanha-ko ha-nun] ke-- e(h)?
consider-CONN do-ATTR thing- huh
{You} do {it} taking {it} into consideration- huh(h)?
10 Ara(F): aswuiwun ke mwe=
lacking thing what
Missing what
11 Min(M): =**ani** (.) a: kunyang nay-ka, single-lo sal-ass-eto
oh just I-NOM single-as live-PST-even:though
12 caymisskey sal-ass-ul [swu-to iss-ul ke kath-ki-n ha-ta,=
entertainingly live-PST-ATTR can-also exist-ATTR thing seem-NML-TOP do-DECL
***ani** (.) o:h just if I lived single, {it} seems it too could have been fun.*
13 Min(M): =°mwe kule-n ke.
what like:that-ATTR thing
something like that.

Although Min's disagreement with Joo and Ara's idea in line 5 is mitigated (with *-to* 'also' and *-nuntey* 'but'), as a statement, it presents Min as someone who has lived through and owns the experience. However, as Min has been married only for a few hours at the time of conversation, his opinion becomes questioned by Ara in lines 8 and 10, asking to name a specific aspect he misses. The potential challenge is clear: Is Min yet entitled to make such judgment, having been married only for a few hours?

Min responds to the question but not to the specifics of the challenge that the question implemented. In other words, he elides what the question was getting at, specifically the challenge that was embedded in the WH-question to name the aspect(s) he misses. This response by Min is prefaced by *ani*.

Another related case is in (1) presented at the beginning as a puzzling case of the practice. As mentioned earlier, Jil has been complaining about the money she spent on her recent move, for which Hee suggests in line 3 '{you} should have asked for help'. This advice becomes the subject of challenge in line 5 by Jil, formatted as a WH-question. Jil's question could be understood to be plainly asking for clarification, i.e. initiation of repair due to trouble in understanding (Schegloff 2000), because whom Jil could have asked for help was not mentioned in Hee's remedy. This repair initiator, however, has an alternative understanding: challenging Hee regarding the remedy she provided.[4] Regardless of how the 'from who' question is intended or received, however, the question implies that the prior talk presupposed someone specific available to help and treats the presupposition accountable and requiring it to be given an account. It is this potentially challenging question Hee has to deal with in her response and for which she uses *ani*-prefacing in line 6.

Here are the features the two excerpts share. A speaker takes some position and describes the world in a given way. This is challenged by the other speaker with a WH-question. Then, the first speaker uses *ani* in responding to the challenge. This can schematically be represented as below:

A: 'takes a position about the world'
B: WH-question that challenges A
A: *ani*-prefaced response

I will explain how this is exhibited in the examples above. In (1), Hee provides a potential remedy for Hee's complaint (line 3). This remedy becomes challenged by Jil (line 5) in the format of WH-question. Then, Hee responds to the challenge by prefacing the turn with *ani* and referring to indefinite 'many guys' as possible helpers, explaining that she did not refer to particular person(s) in her remedy. In (2), Min's statement that there is an aspect he misses by being married is challenged by Ara in the WH-question format. The challenge is responded to by Min by prefacing the turn with *ani* and explicating his prior opinion in a more general way, focusing on a favorable aspect about being single, rather than addressing a specific aspect he misses

[4] Which of the understandings the recipient takes can be shown by the response the recipient provides in the next turn (Heritage 1984a). The ways in which the response is formulated in lines 11-12 demonstrate that Hee understood the question as a challenge, which she needs to try to account her prior action for.

about being single. And, Min further weakens his position by adding 'something like that' (line 13).

In having to respond to the question as well as to the action of challenge, the question recipients use (almost instinctively and reflexively) *ani* in beginning to respond. *Ani* is deployed here to block the challenge. It should, however, be noted that *ani* does not index the response speakers' evasion to respond to the challenge (which could be an even more disaffiliative move). In other words, *ani* indexes the speaker's resistance to the challenge, but also that the speaker is going to somehow respond to it even if there may be no account given. In fact, using *ani* enables the response speakers to mark the challenge as unwarranted and/or unexpected (cf. Kim 1997), and then respond to the attack by providing the best-possible account or re-positioning their previous position. For example, in (1), Hee attempts to defend herself by minimizing her remedy with the discourse particle *mwe* and invoking the knowledge they share (i.e. that 'many guys' are available to help her with the move) using *canh-a* 'you know.' Hee further retracts her remedy by raising the possibility that 'many guys' may not be available and thus that her suggestion may have been an implausible one (line 8). A very similar practice is observed in (2). Min displays his vulnerability to the challenge by mitigations and back-downs infused throughout his response turn, such as *kunyang* 'just', *swu* 'could' *-to* 'also', and *kath-* 'seem'. More significantly, framing the response with an 'oh' (Heritage 1984b) and formulating it as a noticing with the sentence-ender *-ta* in low boundary tone (Kim 2004, 2010), Min displays the disagreement as having been a thought that just occurred to him in passing, not what he had been contemplating all along. These responses address the challenge, providing defensible accounts. It is this kind of response that is commonly prefaced with *ani*.

In summary thus far, *ani* is a resource for speakers to 1) resist the challenge implemented by the question and mark the challenge as unwarranted or unexpected, and 2) reposition themselves from their prior action in beginning to respond to the challenge. With the practice of *ani*-prefacing, response speakers are able to more efficiently convey from the beginning of their response that the challenge is inappropriate and is thus being blocked. Such a resource at the beginning of a turn "provides a coloring or propositional attitude for the entire turn constructional unit that follows (Heritage 1998: 327)." In other words, the resistance to the challenge becomes a springboard for an incipient defense. This is more explicitly illustrated in the two examples below, in which response speakers do indeed have a defensible account.

(3) is from a telephone conversation recorded in December between two men in late 50's. C and R are part of a group who goes to play golf regularly, and thus 'having a gathering' implies 'playing golf'. When C suggests R

that it is about time that they have their regular group gathering (line 8) and that R discuss this proposal with other group members who are with R at the time of conversation (line 16), the proposal of playing golf becomes the subject of challenge in lines 20-21.

(3) [DEC08 DM100053 0:02:13]

05 C: ani hoycang (0.2) hoy:cang-i aphu-ko nanikka mal-i-ya::
DM president president-NOM sick-CONN after word-be-IE
After the president (0.2) the president is sick

06 R: ey
Yes

07 C: macimak han pen twutulki-ko, (.2) ike: ceki: mwe-ya,
last one time hit-and this that what-IE

08 mangnyenhoy-n-ci songnyenhoy-n-ci hay-ya toy-nun ke ani-nya::
year:end:party-ATTR-or year:end:party-ATTR-or do-must be
come-ATTR thing NEG-INTERR
After {we} hit once last time, (0.2) Um: uh: whatsmacallit,
Shouldn't we have mangnyenhoy or songnyenhoy?[5]

09 R: a
Oh

((4 irrelevant lines cut))

14 C: hh kunikka:
hh So

15 R: yey
Yeah

16 C: kekise sangui-tul cal ha-sye-kaciko
there discussion-PL well do-SH:IE-after
Have some discussion there, and

17 R: yey
Yeah

18 (0.5)

19 R: [i nalssi chwuwu-ntey mwe eti ka-se
this weather cold-CIRCUM what where go-CONN

20 ay mek-ul il iss-e-yo:: cikum eti-l ka-se ttwutu-lye_?
hardship eat-ACC work exist-IE-POL now where-ACC go-CONN hit:INTERR
[In this cold weather, {where} would {you} want to go and
suffer. Where would {you/we} hit {a ball} now?

---

[5] *Songnyenhoy* and *mangnyenhoy* both mean 'year-end party', which is very common in Korea among a group of friends or co-workers in December.

21 C: **ani::** kulayto yeng-sang-tay-nun: (.) toy-ci anh-na?
but zero-above-zone-TOP be-NML NEG-NCOMM
ani:: *but isn't {it} above zero?*
22 R: um:: ani ta el-ese an-toy-ci:: [tachye-yo.
uh no all freeze-because NEG-become-COMM hurt:IE-POL
Uh no {it}'s all frozen so {it}'s not okay:: [{we/you'll} get hurt.
23 C: [yeng-sang toy-l ttay.
zero-above be-ATTR time
When {it}'s above zero.

R challenges C's proposal to play golf under the premise that the current temperature is too cold and unsafe for playing golf (lines 19-20). This challenge is resisted in C's response turn (line 21), as C prefaces the turn with *ani* to register the challenge as unwarranted and refuse to accept the challenge's premise. C's account is that he had thought that the temperature was above freezing. At the same time, however, C's response, constructed with the post-verbal negation *-ci ahn-*, displays that the speaker is also backing down from his previous proposal by being open to negotiate the statement with the recipient (Noh 2009). This stance is further carried through by C's adding a phrase that makes the proposal contingent on the temperature, 'when {it}'s above zero' (line 23).

A similar practice of blocking the challenge with *ani* and then providing a defensible account is demonstrated in (4). Sol and Ari, women in their late 50's living in Korea, are on the phone. Ari has a daughter, who is visiting from the U.S. and has health conditions that may require her to take a leave of absence from her studies and return to Korea for medical treatment. The decision for the daughter, however, is 'not to return' (line 7), which becomes the source of challenge in line 8 by Sol.

(4) [DM100072 0:23:14]
01 Sol: ayu Heeju-nun kulem kass-ta uncey wa?
VOC NAME-TOP then go:PST-after when come:INTERR
Ayu when is Heeju, after leaving, coming back then?
02 (.)
03 Ari: mwe-ka, kass-taka, (.) [i il-nal.
what- go:PST-after two date-day
What, after leaving, (.) {On} the 2nd.
04 Sol: a[ni kass-taka incey Sewul-
no go:ANT-after now PLACE
N[o after leaving, now Seoul-
05 >ani:::_ (.) kass-taka Sewul tasi wa kaciko
no go:PST-after PLACE again come:CONN and:then

06 han hakki tongan iss-nun-ta-may: ay:: ceki=
one quarter during stay-IMPFV-DC-HEARSAY baby that
No:::_ (.) after leaving Seoul, {you} said {she}'s coming back and staying for a semester . Baby:: uh

07 Ari: =aaa:: an kule-ki-lo hay-ss-e.
oh NEG like:that-NML-as do-PST-IE
Oh:: {she/we} decided not to do that.

08 Sol: ↑WA::y_ ((surprised))
Why ((surprised))

09 Ari: **ani:** tto-- talun hanuiwen-ey ka-ss-nuntey:[:=
again other oriental:medicine:hospital-LOC go-PST-CIRCUM
***ani**: {she/we} went to another oriental medical clinic again=*

10 Sol: [e:
Yeah

11 Ari: =mwe kulehkey pyello kulay yayki-n an ha-te-la-ko,
DM like:that not:really like:that story-TOP NEG do-RT-INTROS-QT
and {he/they} didn't really say {it} in that way (i.e. Heeju has a serious condition that requires treatment).

12 Sol: °e: [kekise com opa-hay-ss-na-po-ta.
yes there a:little over-do-PST-NCOMM-seem-DECL
°Yea:h {it} must've been that {they} overreacted there.

Sol's WH-question, 'why?', in line 8 expresses surprise with a sudden increase in volume and elongation of the word, which displays that Sol had understood the treatment to be necessary for Ari's daughter. This challenge is resisted by *ani* in Ari's response (line 9). Then, in the same turn, Ari explains the updated circumstance, i.e. a conflicting diagnosis that led them to make the new decision, as an account for the challenge.

4. Discussions and Conclusion

I began the paper by proposing, if the goal is to understand *ani*'s interactional functions in conversation, that it should be studied in a more restricted sequential environment with more attention on action. Following this perspective, I have analyzed the practice of prefacing a response with *ani* to a WH-question used as a challenge, with a focus on what the utterances are 'doing' in interaction. As illustrated in this study, one of the most common forms through which challenges are formulated is with questions. Use of questions for these actions is also noted in Steensig and Drew (2008), who find that questions, contrary to the common belief, are almost never asked solely for the purpose of requesting information or confirmation; they are employed to do other actions, commonly for disaffiliative moves such as criticizing, complaining, challenging, accusing, reproaching, disagreeing, etc. *Ani*, I suggest, is a turn preface that is strategically employed to respond to such challenge.

On the one hand, responding to questions conveys that the response speakers are also accepting the terms of the question (i.e. presupposition, action/topic agenda, and preference) (Heritage 2002b). Thus, when responding to the challenge-implemented questions, the speakers run the risk of accepting all terms of the challenge implemented by the question. On the other, questions implemented as challenges are not really answerable since challenging implies that there is no defensible account from the recipient (Clayman and Heritage 2002, Heinemann 2008).

These complex interactional consequences are handled with *ani* in beginning to respond to a challenge. It is an interactionally strategic move for the challenged speakers to resist accepting the terms in order to respond to the challenge and defend themselves, if possible, but at the same time to align with the challenger by being an accountable responder to the challenge (for alignment/affiliation, see Stivers 2008). In other words, the speakers of *ani*-prefaced responses to challenges, despite their resistance to the act of challenging, are oriented to providing an account, taking the responsibility on themselves to mend the interactional trouble (rather than counter-attacking or completely evading any response). Thus, the speakers of *ani*-prefaced responses to a challenge, despite their resistance to the challenge, are oriented to providing an account and restoring the social relationship with challengers.

Response speakers need a way to responsibly and accountably respond to challenges. In Korean, *ani* affords response speakers a resource for blocking the challenge and then using this as a springboard to defend their position against the challenge.

Turn-prefaces in other languages have also been observed to carry pragmatic functions, indexing from the outset how the turn is related to the prior talk and what the turn sets out to do (e.g. Heritage 1984b, 1998, Bolden 2009, Hayashi 2009, Schegloff and Lerner 2009). In responding turns, in particular, turn-beginnings can be a crucial place where the respondents show whether and/or how they have understood the prior action, and whether and/or how they will respond to it. For example, *well* prefacing to WH-questions is found to alert the recipient of a response's unstraightforwardness (Schegloff and Lerner 2009), and *oh* prefacing to questions to index the inappositeness of the question's presupposition (Heritage 1998). Unlike these turn-initial tokens, however, *ani* is not completely wiped of its semantic meaning. As Koo (2008) argues, *ani* seems to still retain the broader sense of negating. Nevertheless, as has been demonstrated in this paper, "negating (or rejecting)" is not an adequate description of the interactional work *no* does in many places in conversation.[6]

It is possible that *ani* does a similar job in other interactional contexts (see Kim 2011). However, before one can start connecting the dots, the local interactional functions of this response particle should be identified by rigorously analyzing its use in each environment. I hope to have shown in this study one piece of the big picture.

References

Bolden, G. B. 2009. Implementing Incipient Actions: The Discourse Marker *So* in English Conversation. *Journal of Pragmatics* 41.5: 974-998.

Clayman, Steven and John Heritage. 2002. *The News Interview: Journalists and Public Figures on the Air*. Cambridge: Cambridge University Press.

Enfield N. J., T. Stivers and S. C. Levinson. 2010. Question-Response Sequences in Conversation across Ten Languages: An Introduction. *Journal of Pragmatics* 42.10: 2615-2619.

Hayashi, M. 2004. Projection and Grammar: Notes on the 'Action-Projecting' Use of the Distal Demonstrative *Are* in Japanese. *Journal of Pragmatics* 36: 1337-1374.

Heinemann, T. 2008. Questions of accountability: Yes-No interrogatives that are unanswerable. *Discourse Studies* 10.1: 55-71.

Heritage, J. 1984a. *Garfinkel and Ethnomethodology*. Cambridge: Polity press.

Heritage, J. 1984b. A Change-of-State Token and Aspects of its Sequential Placement. *Structures of Social Action*, eds. J. M. Atkinson and J. Heritage, 299-345. Cambridge: Cambridge University Press.

Heritage, J. 1998. *Oh*-Prefaced Responses to Inquiry. *Language in Society* 27: 291-334.

Heritage, J. 2002b. Designing Questions and Setting Agendas in the News Interview. *Studies in Language and Social Interaction*, eds. P. Glenn, C. LeBaron and J. Madelbaum pp. 57-90. Mahwah, NJ: Erlbaum.

Heritage, J. and G. Raymond (forthcoming). Navigating Epistemic Landscapes: Acquiescence, Agency and Resistance in Responses to Polar Questions. *Questions: Formal, Functional and Interactional Perspectives*, ed. J. P. de Ruiter. Cambridge: Cambridge University Press.

Jefferson, G. 2002. Is 'No' an Acknowledgment Token? Comparing American and British Uses of (+)/(-) Tokens. *Journal of Pragmatics* 34: 1345-1383.

Jefferson, G. 2004. Glossary of Transcript Symbols with an Introduction. *Conversation Analysis: Studies From the First Generation*, ed. G. H. Lerner, 13-31. Philadelphia: John Benjamins.

---

[6] Also refer to the analyses of the English *no* (Schegloff 2001, Jefferson 2002); note that the *no*'s in third-position repairs (Schegloff 1992) are not to be confused with rejecting the prior turn, according to Schegloff (2001).

Kim, H. R. S. 2010. A High Boundary Tone as a Resource for a Social Action: The Korean Sentence-Ender *-Ta*. *Journal of Pragmatics* 42: 3055-3077.

Kim, H. R. S. 2011. Beginning an Action in English and Korean: Turn Design and Action Projection. Unpublished Doctoral Dissertation, UCLA.

Kim, K.-H. and K.-H. Suh. 1994. The Discourse Connective *Nikka* in Korean Conversation. *Japanese/Korean Linguistics*: 113-129.

Kim, K.-H. 2004. A Conversation Analysis of Korean Sentence-Ending Modal Suffixes *-ney*, *-kwun(a)*, and *-ta*: Noticing as a Social Action. *Sociolinguistic Journal of Korea* 12: 1-35.

Kim, M.-S. 1997. Tayhwakwucho-lo pon 'ani'-ui kinung (Some Functions of 'ani' in a Conversational Structure of Korean). *Discourse and Cognition* 4: 77-101.

Koo, H. J. 2008. Grammaticalization of Negation Markers in Korean. *Discourse and Cognition* 15.3: 1-27.

Koshik, I. 2003. Wh-Questions Used as Challenges. *Discourse Studies*, 5: 51-77.

Martin, S. E. 1992. *A Reference Grammar of Korean: A Complete Guide to the Grammar and History of the Korean Language.* Rutland: C.E. Tuttle.

Noh, J. 2009. The Development of Korean Negative Interrogatives in Conversational Discourse: A Sign-Based Approach. *Japanese/Korean Linguistics* 16: 304-318.

Park, Y.-Y. 1998. A Discourse Analysis of Contrastive Connectives in English, Korean, and Japanese Conversations: With Special Reference to the Context of Dispreferred Responses. *Discourse Markers: Descriptions and Theory*. eds. A. H. Jucker & Y. Ziv, 277-300. Philadelphia: John Benjamins.

Raymond, G. 2003. Grammar and Social Organization: Yes/no Interrogatives and the Structure of Responding. *American Sociological Review* 68: 939-967.

Sacks, H., E. A. Schegloff and G. Jefferson. 1974. A Simplest Systematics for the Organization of Turn-taking for Conversation. *Language* 50: 696-735.

Schegloff, E. A. 1968. Sequencing in Conversational Openings. *American Anthropologist* 70: 1075–1095.

Schegloff, E. A. and H. Sacks. 1973. Opening Up Closings. *Semiotica* 8: 289-327.

Schegloff, E. A. 1984. On Some Questions and Ambiguities in Conversation. *Structures of Social Action*, eds. J. M. Atkinson and J. Heritage, 266-298. Cambridge: Cambridge University Press.

Schegloff, E. A. 1992. Repair After Next Turn: The Last Structurally Provided Defense of Intersubjectivity in Conversation. *American Journal of Sociology* 97.5: 1295-1345.

Schegloff, E. A. 2000. When 'Others' Initiate Repair. *Applied Linguistics* 21.2: 205–243.

Schegloff, E. A. 2001. Getting Serious: 'Joke - > Serious No'. *Journal of Pragmatics* 33.12: 1947-55.

Schegloff, E. A. 2007. *A Primer in Conversation Analysis*. Cambridge: Cambridge University Press.

Schegloff, E. A. and G. H. Lerner. 2009. Beginning to Respond: *Well*-Prefaced Responses to WH-Questions. *Research on Language and Social Interaction* 42: 91-115.

Steensig, Jakob and Paul Drew. 2008. Introduction: Questioning and affiliation/disaffiliation in interaction. *Discourse Studies* 10.1: 5-15.

Stivers, T. 2008. Stance, Alignment and Affiliation During Story Telling: When Nodding is a Token of Affiliation. *Research on Language in Social Interaction* 41: 29-55.

Yang, C. 2002. *Ani* 'No': It Doesn't Always Mean 'No' in Korean. *Discourse and Cognition* 9: 101-119.

Yoon, K.-E. 2006. Interrogatives with Question Words as Complaint Utterances in Korean Conversation. *Japanese/Korean Linguistics, Vol. 14*. eds. T. J. Vance and K. Jones, 423-434. Stanford: Stanford University.

Yoon, K.-E. 2010. Questions and Responses in Korean Conversation. *Journal of Pragmatics* 42.10: 2782-2798.

Forward and Backward Feature Agreement: Evidence from Korean Numeral Classifier Constructions

ON-SOON LEE
University of Hawai'i at Mānoa

1. Introduction

Previous studies in psycholinguistic research have shown that semantically associated information facilitates parsing of upcoming words, while it hinders processing of unexpected words (Federmeier & Kutas 1999, Kamide, Scheepers, & Altmann 2003, Schwanenflugel & LaCount 1988). Kamide et al. (2003), for example, found that syntactic and semantic information was used to predict the subsequent input. The approach taken by these studies is similar to several information theoretical perspectives on sentence processing, including the *surprisal* hypothesis and expectation-based accounts (Gennari & MacDonald 2008, Levy 2008, Nakatani & Gibson 2010); highly expected material is read more quickly than less expected material. In particular, Levy (2008) proposed the *surprisal* hypothesis, a theory of expectations based on frequent structures. Under this hypothesis, because object relative clauses are relatively infrequent, they are harder to process than subject relative clauses. Findings from Gennari and MacDonald (2008) and Nakatani and Gibson (2010) showed that, on frequent structures, expecta-

Japanese/Korean Linguistics 20.
Edited by Bjarke Frellesvig and Peter Sells.

tion facilitated processing of upcoming words, but uncertainty on infrequent structures caused comprehension difficulty. Many studies have tested the expectation-based accounts in syntactically complex but unambiguous structures (e.g., object relative clauses), but few studies have tested different unambiguous structures (e.g., numeral classifier constructions). This paper attempts to fill the gap in the literature on expectation-based accounts by employing Korean numeral classifier constructions that include semantic feature agreement between numeral classifiers and the associated nouns. Two experiments were conducted. First, an off-line judgment task investigated the acceptability of classifiers and associated noun pairs. Although there are different degrees of expectation from the two types of classifiers, each predicts the semantic class of nouns, thus highly expected words are read quickly. Next, a self-paced reading experiment was conducted to confirm the results of the off-line judgment task.

The paper is organized as follows. Section 2 describes the phenomenon focused on in this paper in terms of semantic and syntactic properties. Sections 3 and 4 present results from the two experiments. Section 5 discusses the implications of the experimental results. Section 6 is the conclusion.

2. Numeral classifier constructions in Korean

This section will describe two types of classifiers from a semantic perspective and two types of constructions from a syntactic perspective.

According to Unterbeck (1994), Korean has several classifiers, which are divided into several semantic subgroups; the choice of classifier depends on the semantic class of the noun. That is, the classifier that is used depends on semantic feature agreement with associated nouns. For example,

(1) a. sey **myeng**-uy **haksayng**-i sakwa-lul mek-nun-ta.
three **CL**$_{\textbf{people}}$-GEN student-NOM apple-ACC eat-PRES-DECL
'Three students eat apples.'

b. * sey **pel**-uy **haksayng-i** sakwa-lul mek-nun-ta.
three **CL**$_{\textbf{clothing}}$-GEN student-NOM apple-ACC eat-PRES-DECL
*'Three students eat apples.'

The classifier *myeng* (a classifier for people) in (1a) is used only to classify people, while the classifier *pel* (a classifier for clothing) in (1b) is used only to classify clothing. Therefore, the sentence in (1b) is ungrammatical because the classifier *pel* cannot occur with the associated noun ('student'). The examples in (1) thus shows that there is semantic agreement between classifiers and associated nouns.

Korean classifiers can be divided into two types according to the degree of semantic relatedness between the classifiers and associated nouns: specific classifiers and a general classifier. The sentence in (2) provides an example of each type:

(2) a. haksayng-i twu **kwen**-uy **chayk-ul** sass-ta.
student-NOM two **CL**$_{specific}$-GEN book-ACC bought-DECL
'A student bought two books.'

b. haksayng-i twu **kay**-uy **chayk-ul** sass-ta.
student-NOM two **CL**$_{general}$-GEN book-ACC bought-DECL
'A student bought two books.'

As seen in (2a), *kwen* (a classifier for books) is a specific classifier, which can be used only for the semantically associated noun ('book'), whereas *kay* (a classifier for inanimate entities), which appears in (2b) as a substitute for the specific classifier, is a general classifier. To summarize, Korean classifiers semantically agree with associated nouns, and the semantic relatedness between specific classifiers and associated nouns is much closer than that between a general classifier and associated nouns. Specific classifiers easily predict the semantic class of nouns, whereas a general classifier offers relatively little information about the semantic class of nouns.

From the syntactic perspective, there are two types of Korean numeral classifier constructions depending on the position of the numeral classifier: prenominal constructions and postnominal constructions. In the examples in (3), a numeral classifier ('two'), with the genitive marker *-uy* appears before the associated noun ('book'); this is called the prenominal construction. In the examples in (4), the numeral classifier ('two'), with no genitive marking follows the associated noun ('book'); this is called the postnominal construction (Sohn, 1999).

Prenominal Constructions [Numeral + Classifier] + (GEN) + Noun	Postnominal Constructions Noun + [Numeral + Classifier]
(3) a. twu kwen-uy chayk two CL$_{book}$-GEN book 'two books'	(4) a. chayk twu kwen book two CL$_{book}$ 'two books'
b. sey myeng-uy haksayng three CL$_{people}$-GEN student 'three students'	b. haksayng sey myeng student three CL$_{people}$ 'three students'

Prenominal constructions optionally have the genitive marker *uy* between the numeral classifier and the associated noun; there is no discernable semantic difference in meaning between sentences with or without the genitive marker. Also, as examples (5a) and (5b) show, modifiers (e.g., adjectives) such as 'pretty' can intervene between numeral classifiers and associated nouns. However, a numeral classifier sequence such as *twu myeng* ('two') in either of the two constructions cannot be split by an intervening word, as seen in (5c) and 5(d).

(5) a. **twu myeng-uy** yeyppun haksayng
two CL_{people}-GEN pretty student

b. yeyppun haksayng **twu myeng**
pretty student two CL_{people}

c. *yeyppun **twu** haksayng **myeng**
pretty two student CL_{people}
'*Two pretty students'

d. ***twu** yeyppun haksayng **myeng**
two pretty student CL_{people}
'*Two pretty students'

In (3), the numeral classifier directly modifies the associated noun *chayk* ('book'), whereas in (4), the numeral classifier *twu kwen* ('two') is floated—that is, it appears after the associated noun ('book'). There remain many unresolved theoretical issues about how prenominal constructions differ structurally from postnominal constructions, but these matters are beyond the scope of this paper.

3. Experiment 1: An off-line judgment experiment

To test the degree of expectation created by the two types of classifiers, two experiments were conducted. First, an off-line judgment experiment was designed to investigate how natural the choice of specific classifiers and associated nouns is, compared to the choice of a general classifier and associated nouns. Results indicate that semantic information provided by specific classifier is enough to trigger an expectation for particular nouns.

3.1 Method

Twenty native speakers of Korean participated in the off-line judgment experiment. The design of this task used two types of classifiers (specific vs. general) × one type of condition (prenominal). Two lists in a Latin square design were presented to participants. This task was conducted by using a web-based judgment task. It consisted of twenty-four noun phrases with no filler phrases. Participants were asked to sit in front of a computer, and then to rate the naturalness of each phrase (n=24) containing classifiers and associated nouns on a scale of 1 (very unnatural) to 5 (very natural). The task lasted less than fifteen minutes. An example set of experimental conditions used in Experiment 1 is shown in (6):

(6) a. sey calwu-uy kitalan nolan-sayk yenphil
three $CL_{specific}$-GEN long yellow-color pencil
b. sey kay-uy kitalan nolan-sayk yenphil
three $CL_{general}$-GEN long yellow-color pencil
'three long, yellow pencils'

3.2 Results

Table 1 shows the average ratings for the naturalness of the classifiers and associated nouns. Average ratings for twelve specific classifiers with associated nouns range from 3.9 to 2.9 out of 5. The total average rating in the condition with specific classifiers is 3.44 out of 5, while the total average rating in the condition with a general classifier is 2.82 out of 5. This task shows that even though the naturalness rating for all patterns with classifiers is low, the choice of specific classifiers and associated nouns seems to be relatively natural compared to that of a general classifier and nouns. A paired *t*-test shows a significant difference between conditions: $t(19) = -3.834$, $p < .001$ by subject analysis; $t(23) = -6.351$, $p < .001$ by item analysis. If it is true that specific classifiers sound more natural with particular head nouns than a general classifier does, as the ratings in Table 1 indicate, it makes sense to think that they will more strongly evoke or activate those nouns as well.

Table 1. Average rating for the naturalness of classifiers with nouns

Classifier	Type (CL-NPs)	Rating: Mean	Rating: *SD*
Specific	kok (song)	3.9	1.02
	phyen (film)	3.85	1.04
	calwu (pencil)	3.7	0.98
	tay (car)	3.75	1.02
	pyeng (beer)	3.6	1.1
	kwen (book)	3.6	1.1
	cang (paper)	3.5	1.15
	pel (shirt)	3.35	1.14
	can (coffee)	3.15	1.14
	kulwu (tree)	3.05	1.23
	songi (flower)	2.95	1
	thong (bucket)	2.9	0.97
	Total	3.44	
General	kay	2.82	1.14

The semantic expectation triggered by specific classifiers should quickly predict the following associated nouns; therefore, upcoming words, such as associated nouns, should be read quickly. To confirm the effect of expectation depending on types of classifiers, a self-paced reading experiment was conducted.

4. Experiment 2: A self-paced reading experiment

Based on the results from Experiment 1, a self-paced reading experiment was designed to test the role of semantically related information in processing the two different types of constructions. When native speakers are processing phrases of numeral classifiers and associated nouns, the expectation from the different types of classifiers leads to different effects on the comprehension of the sentences. In the case of forward prediction in prenominal constructions, highly expected information should facilitate parsing of associated nouns. Interference appears in postnominal constructions due to a working memory limitation when the previous information needs to be retrieved, but highly expected information from specific classifiers should help the backward retrieval.

4.1 Predictions

The differences in expectations generated by the two types of classifiers lead to two different predictions. Table 2 shows a sample set of prenominal constructions.

Table 2. A sample set of experimental conditions in prenominal constructions

A. Prenominal, Specific classifier					
sonyen-i/1	ecey/2	**sey**	**calwu-uy/3**	kitalan nolan-sayk/4	**yenphil-ul/5**
boy-NOM	yesterday	three	$CL_{specific}$-GEN	long,yellow-color	pencil-ACC
mwunpangkwu-eyse/6			sass-ta/7.		
stationery store-LOC			bought.		
B. Prenominal, General classifier					
sonyen-i/1	ecey/2	**sey**	**kay-uy/3**	kitalan nolan-sayk/4	**yenphil-ul/5**
boy-NOM	yesterday	three	$CL_{general}$-GEN	long,yellow-color	pencil-ACC
mwunpangkwu-eyse/6			sass-ta/7.		
stationery store-LOC			bought.		

'A boy bought three long, yellow pencils at a stationery store yesterday.'

At region 3, the reading times in the condition with a specific classifier should be faster than those in the condition with a general classifier, because a specific classifier triggers a few specific associated nouns, whereas a general classifier, lacking particular associations, expects relatively more non-specific associated nouns due to a lower degree of expectation. The first prediction for this experiment is that when participants encounter an associated noun (e.g., 'pencil') after passing the numeral classifier, the reading time for region 5 (e.g., 'pencil') in the condition with a specific classifier will be faster than the reading time in the condition with a general classifier, because the expectation that originates at the specific classifier (region 3) facilitates the processing of the upcoming associated noun. Due to the comprehenders' prediction of a particular head noun after the specific classifier, but not after the general classifier, the activation of target nouns is faster in the condition with a specific classifier than in the condition with a general classifier.

The second prediction for this experiment is that in postnominal constructions, as seen in Table 3, the reading time for region 5 (e.g., 'three') in the condition with a specific classifier will be faster than that in the condition with a general classifier, because the specific classifier is much more strongly related with an associated noun (e.g., 'pencil') than the general classifier is. That is, semantically related information that originates at the specific classifier (region 5) triggers the retrieval of the preceding associated nouns (region 3), so the reactivation of previous information should be faster in the condition with a specific classifier than in the condition with a general classifier. A self-paced reading task was conducted in order to test these two predictions.

Table 3. A sample set of experimental conditions in postnominal constructions

A. Postnominal, Specific classifier			
sonyen-i/1	kitalan nolan-sayk/2	**yenphil-ul/3**	ciwukay-wa hamkkey/4
boy-NOM	long,yellow-color	pencil-ACC	eraser-and together
sey calwu-lul /5	mwunpangkwu-eyse/6	sass-ta/7.	
three $CL_{specifc}$-ACC	stationery store-LOC	bought.	
B. Postnominal, General classifier			
sonyen-i/1	kitalan nolan-sayk/2	**yenphil-ul/3**	ciwukay-wa hamkkey/4
boy-NOM	long, yellow-color	pencil-ACC	eraser-and together
sey kay-lul /5	mwunpangkwu-eyse/6	sass-ta/7.	
three $CL_{specifc}$-ACC	stationery store-LOC	bought.	

'A boy bought three long, yellow pencils with an eraser at a stationery store.'

4.2 Method

Forty-three native speakers of Korean participated in the self-paced reading experiment. They were paid five dollars each for their participation in the experiment.

The design of the experiment used two types of classifiers (specific vs. general) × two types of constructions (prenominal vs. postnominal). Four lists in a Latin square design were presented to participants. Tables 2 and 3 show one set of the four conditions used in this experiment. The results of a pilot study showed that there was no difference in reading times for prenominal and postnominal constructions for sentences in which the classifiers were closely adjacent to the associated nouns. This indicates the possibility that readers do not have enough time to predict or retrieve the semantic feature agreement between the classifier and the noun. That is, readers easily ignore this agreement in real time. Therefore, test sentences manipulated the distance between the classifiers and associated nouns across the two constructions.

As shown in Table 2, while the direct object (region 5) remains the same in the conditions with a specific and with a general classifier, the numeral classifiers (region 3) vary in the degree of their semantic relatedness to the direct object. Adjectives intervene between numeral classifiers and associated nouns to increase the distance between them. In Table 3, the choice of numeral classifiers and associated nouns is the same as in Table 2, but the associated nouns occur before the numeral classifiers. As Table 3 shows, sentences with the postnominal construction included local nouns (e.g., 'eraser') as distractors intervening between nouns and classifiers. The reason for this manipulation is that, as explained by the dependent locality theory (Gibson 1998) or the theory of working memory retrieval (Lewis & Vasishth 2005), the retrieval process in postnominal constructions is harder to trigger than the prediction process in prenominal constructions due to processing loads. The local nouns (e.g., 'eraser') inserted in the postnominal constructions belong to the same semantic group as the preceding associated nouns (e.g., 'pencil'), but do not match categorically with the following specific classifiers. This triggers the retrieval process for checking semantic agreement of classifiers with the preceding associated nouns—that is, the two nouns in the postnominal constructions compete to agree with classifiers in terms of semantic feature agreement between specific classifiers and associated nouns.

In this experiment, twelve different types of specific classifiers and one general classifier, *kay*, were employed; each specific classifier appears twice in each list, while the general classifier appears twelve times.[1] Each list includes twenty-four target sentences with forty-eight filler sentences. Filler sentences do not include any numeral classifiers. The experiment was conducted on a computer running E-prime (Version 2.0) at the University of Hawai'i. Each sentence was presented one region at a time on the computer

[1] All specific classifiers used are counters for inanimate entities.

screen, left to right, in a noncumulative, moving-window manner as a participant pushed the space bar (Just, Carpenter, & Woolley 1982). Participants were asked to read as naturally as possible, and then to answer a *yes/no* comprehensive question in order to ensure that they attended to the stimuli. All reading times for each region were recorded, along with responses to comprehensive questions. The entire experiment lasted less than 30 minutes.

4.3 Results

Analyses were conducted on comprehension task response accuracy and reading times as dependent measures. All data from participants whose accuracy was less than 70% were excluded. Three participants (7%) were excluded, leaving 40 participants' data to be included in the analysis. Reading times more than 2.5 standard deviations above or below the mean were removed; this affected 8.07% of the data. The analyses presented below are based on the remaining items. Among participants included in the analysis, the average comprehension accuracy is 86%. The average correct response percentage does not differ significantly in postnominal constructions, but average comprehension accuracy differs significantly in prenominal constructions.[2] Results of reading times in prenominal and postnominal constructions will be reported in order.

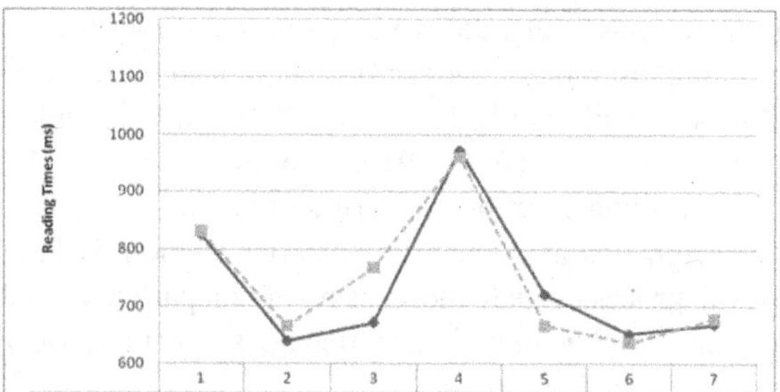

	1	2	3	4	5	6	7
Specific CL	825.38	639.82	672.05	972.11	721.63	652.21	668.75
General CL	831.16	666.58	767.99	959.26	666.91	636.80	679.02

Sub-NOM1/ Adverb2/ Num+CL-GEN3/ Adjective 4/ Associated NP-ACC5/ Loc-DAT6/ Verb7

Figure 1a. Reading times for prenominal constructions

2 In the prenominal construction, the average correct response percentage is 67% in the condition with the general classifier, compared to an average correct response percentage of 98% in the condition with a specific classifier. This indicates that participants might be less sensitive to general classifiers.

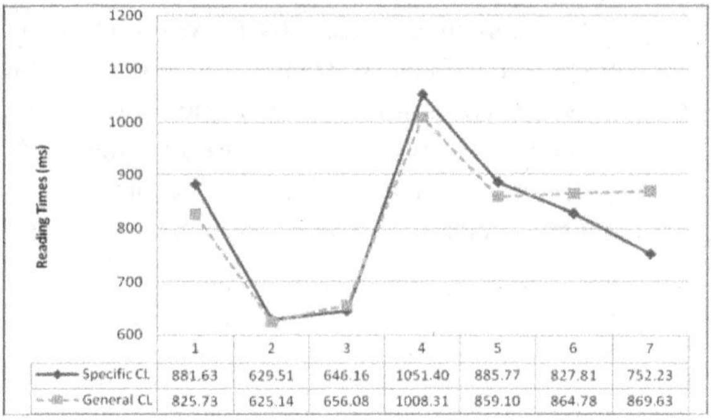

Sub-NOM1/ Adjective2/ AssociatedNP-ACC3/LocalNP4/ Num+CL-ACC5/ Loc-DAT6/ Verb7

Figure 1b. Reading times for postnominal constructions

Reading times for prenominal constructions are shown in Figure 1a. At region 3 (numeral classifier sequence), reading times in the condition with a general classifier are numerically slower than those in the condition with a specific classifier. At region 5 (associated nouns), the reading times in the condition with a specific classifier are numerically slower than those in the condition with a general classifier (F_1 (1,36) = 9.641, $p < .004$; F_2 (1,21) = 1.415, $p < .2$). This is not consistent with the first prediction, regarding prenominal constructions, but rather is the opposite effect than what was predicted. Reading times for postnominal constructions are shown in Figure 1b. At region 5 (numeral classifier), the reading times did not differ in the two conditions, but the reading times for region 7 (verb) in the condition with a specific classifier are significantly faster than those in the condition with a general classifier, as predicted (F_1 (1,39) = 5.863, $p < .02$; F_2(1,23) = 4.739, $p < .05$). The main finding from this experiment is that semantically related information that originates at a specific classifier (region 5) facilitates the backward retrieval process much more easily than partially related information that originates at the general classifier does when a retrieval process is needed.

5. General discussion

It is clear that semantic feature agreement between classifiers and associated nouns occurs in real time. Results from the off-line judgment task provide evidence that the degree of expectation created by specific classifiers is stronger than that created by general classifier. This finding was confirmed by the results of the self-paced reading experiment. In the backward retrieval process, semantically related expectation that originates at specific classifiers facilitates the retrieval process. This is consistent with the expectation-based accounts, in that the highly expected information helps in reading the associated words quickly.

The results of the self-paced reading experiment raise the question of why semantically related information facilitates access to the preceding nouns in a backward retrieval process. One factor is expectation on based on frequency of co-occurrence. A corpus study was conducted, using data from one general corpus, the *Sejong Corpus* (2,050,000 spoken words).[3] Table 4 summarizes the distributional pattern of specific and general classifiers across the two constructions. It shows that sentences containing numeral classifiers in the direct object occur rarely across the two constructions—that is, most classifiers appear in postnominal constructions, and in particular, all the specific classifiers that were used in Experiment 2 occur only in postnominal constructions. These findings suggest that postnominal constructions with specific classifiers are comprehended more easily, due to their frequent use, than prenominal constructions with specific classifiers. This is consistent with results from Experiment 2.

Table 4. Frequency of specific/general classifiers in two constructions

Classifier		Prenominal	Postnominal
Specific	kok (song)	0	2
	phyen (film)	0	23
	calwu (pencil)	0	11
	tay (car)	0	14
	pyeng (beer)	0	15
	kwen (book)	0	2
	cang (paper)	0	9
	pel (shirt)	0	11
	can (coffee)	0	23
	kulwu (tree)	0	0
	songi (flower)	0	34
	thong (bucket)	0	0
General	kay	122	308

6. Concluding remarks

In this paper, I report on a test of Korean numeral classifier constructions. An on-line experiment found that the presence of the specific classifiers facilitates the processing of semantic feature agreement in postnominal con-

3 Since 1998, a national project has aimed at building an information technology system for the Korean language. This has produced the *Sejong Corpus*, the largest corpus of Korean language data as of 2004 (Bley-Vroman & Ko, 2005, p. 258).

structions, in support of expectation-based theories. However, a question remains as to why a specific classifier does not facilitate forward prediction in the prenominal pattern any more than the general classifier does. One possible answer has to do with the effect of frequency. As the corpus study shows, specific classifiers rarely occur in prenominal constructions, whereas the general classifier *kay* frequently occurs in these constructions. When native speakers process the specific classifier in prenominal patterns, its infrequency hinders and limits its potential value. Hopefully, future research will shed light on this matter.

Acknowledgement

I would like to thank William O'Grady for his valuable comments and discussions at every stage of this study. I am also grateful to Amy J. Schafer, Kamil Ud Deen, and Bonnie D. Schwartz for their comments. I also acknowledge with thanks the financial support provided by the Linguistics Department Endowment Fund.

References

Bley-Vroman, R. and Ko, H. 2005. *Corpus linguistics for Korean language learning and teaching*. Honolulu: University of Hawai'i Press.

Federmeier, K. and Kutas, M. 1999. A rose by any other name: Long-term memory structure and sentence processing. *Journal of Memory and Language*, 41, 469-495.

Gennari, S. and MacDoanld, M. 2008. Semantic indeterminacy in object relative clauses. *Journal of Memory and Language,* 58, 161-187.

Gibson, E. 1998. Linguistic complexity: Locality of syntactic dependency. *Cognition,* 68, 1-76.

Just, M.A. and Carpenter, P.A., Wooley, J.D. 1982. Paradigms and processing in reading comprehension. *Journal of Experimental Psychology: General*, 111, 228-238.

Kaiser, E., Runner, J., Sussman, R., and Tanenhaus, M. 2009. Structural and semantic constraints on the resolution of pronouns and reflexives. *Cognition,* 112, 55-80.

Kamide, Y., Scheepers, C., and Altmann, G. 2003. Integration of syntactic and semantic information in predictive processing: Cross-linguistic evidence from German and English. *Journal of Psycholinguistic Research*, 32, 37-55.

Levy, R. 2008. Expectation-based syntactic comprehension. *Cognition,* 106, 1126-1177.

Lewis, R. and Vasishth, S. 2005. An activation-based model of sentence processing as skilled memory retrieval. *Cognitive Science*, 29 (3), 375-419.

Nakatani, K. and Gibson, E. 2010. An on-line study of Japanese nesting complexity. *Cognitive Science*, 34, 94-112.

Sohn, H. 1999. *The Korean Language*. Cambridge: Cambridge University Press.

Schwanenflugel, P. J. and LaCount, K. L. 1988. Semantic relatedness and scope of facilitation for upcoming words in sentences. *Journal of Experimental Psychology: Learning, Memory, and Cognition*, 14, 344-254.

Unterbeck, B. 1994. Korean classifiers. In *Theoretical Issues in Korean Linguistics*, ed. by Young-Key Kim-Renaud, 367-386. Stanford: CSLI Publications.

Two Modes of Argument Selection in Nominals

NAOYUKI ONO
Tohoku University

Verbs are a prototypical argument-taking category. They need to select proper arguments because the event denoted by a verb is represented in terms of semantic roles that the arguments bear in relation with each other. Thus, the argument selection of verbs is in a substantial sense a linguistic manifestation of eventiveness. Is this the case in other argument-taking categories? Obviously nouns are an argument-taking category, but the expression of eventiveness is not as self-evident as with verbs because they denote individuals as well as events. Consequently, do they select arguments in a manner substantially different from verbs? If so, how is eventiveness concerned with the syntactic or lexical realization of semantic relations associated with the arguments of nouns?

In this article I argue that there are two distinct modes of argument selection in nominals depending on how the denotation of the head noun is determined with reference to ontological relations encoded in lexical structure. Along with Pustejovsky's (1995) basic idea that the distinction between individual-level predicates (e.g. *Firemen are intelligent*) and stage-level predicates (e.g. *Firemen are available*) can be extended to the distinction in nominals, I assume that nominals generally fall into two semantic

Japanese/Korean Linguistics 20.
Edited by Bjarke Frellesvig and Peter Sells.

categories in terms of eventiveness: individual-level and stage-level nominals.

Japanese has a wide variety of noun-forming affixes that refer to this distinction (Miyajima 1997, Kageyama 1999; 2002, Ogawa 2001, Nishiyama 2003[1]). For instance, complex nouns with affixes such as *-sya* (-者) and *-te* (-手) are stage-level (e.g. *hokoosya* 'pedestrian' and *utaite* 'singer') whereas those affixed *-syu* (-手) and *-ka* (-家) (e.g. *untensyu* 'driver' and *syoosetuka* 'novelist') are individual-level. Through an extensive survey of noun-forming affixes in Japanese, I will discuss how the semantic distinction in question is implemented in the argument selection of nominals. Specifically I propose that there are two different modes of argument selection in nominals, which I will call the eventive mode and the relational mode, and selection of arguments by stage-level nominals is conducted via the eventive mode whereas selection of arguments by individual-level nominals is done in the relational mode.

1. Individual-level vs. stage-level nominals

Pustejovsky (1995) proposes that nouns fall into two categories: individual-level and stage-level. For example, *violinist* and *pedestrian* are different in this respect, as the former may refer to a person who is not engaged in the activity of playing the violin at the time of reference. The noun *violinist* is thus not eventive because we need not assume a particular situation that determines the proper denotation of the noun. In contrast, the noun *pedestrian* is eventive, i.e. a stage-level nominal, because it properly denotes an entity only if the entity is identified as being involved in the walking event. The difference in eventiveness shows up in the contrasts in (1) :

(1) a. Watch out, there is a pedestrian on the crosswalk!
    b. Watch out, there is a violinist on the crosswalk!

The sentence in (1a) implies that the person referred to as a pedestrian is walking on the crosswalk at the time of the utterance whereas the sentence in (1b) lacks this implication.

Within the framework of the Generative Lexicon (GL), Pustejovsky further proposes that the distinction in question follows from different values of qualia roles in the Qualia Structure of each lexical representation. The distinction is represented as follows:

[1] Nishiyama draws a related distinction between saturated and unsaturated nominals.

(2) a. violinist Qualia = FORMAL = x
TELIC = play_act (x, y: violin)
...

b. pedestrian Qualia = FORMAL = x
AGENTIVE = walk_act(x)
...

Thus, in this framework, the distinction in the event interpretations implicated by the two types of nominals follows from different lexical-semantic representations.[2]

In terms of the stage-level/individual-level distinction, English agentive *-er* nominals exhibit ambiguity in many cases. For example, *driver* may refer to a person whose job is to drive a vehicle (individual level) or to a person who is engaged in driving at the time of reference (stage level). This would lead one to assume that *driver* has the following lexical representation:

(3) driver Qualia = FORMAL = human (x)
TELIC = drive (x, y)
AGENTIVE = drive (x, y)

Thus, the ambiguity of agentive *-er* nominals in English follows from a generative mechanism of GL, where selection of different qualia gives rise to the polysemic nature of words.

In contrast with English agentive nominals, Japanese makes a relevant distinction by affixing different morphemes with the same base. For *driver*, for instance, the Japanese counterpart has two forms *untensya* and *untensyu*, where *-sya* and *-syu* attach to the base *unten* 'drive'. *Untensya* is a stage-level noun, whereas *untensyu* is an individual-level noun.Thus, unlike English, the Japanese lexicon involves distinct lexical entries for stage/individual interpretations of agentive nominals. This is illustrated in (4):

(4) a. untensyu (DRIVE-syu) 'driver' Qualia = TELIC = drive (x, y)
b. untensya (DRIVE-sya) 'driver' Qualia = AGENTIVE = drive (x, y)

---

[2] GL assumes four qualia roles. CONSTITUTIVE: the relation between an object and its constituent parts or between an object and what that object is logically part of; FORMAL: that which distinguishes it within a larger domain; TELIC: its purpose and function; AGENTIVE; factors involved in its origin or "bringing it about", Pustejovsky (1995: 76, 85-86, 98). See also Vikner and Jensen (2002: 198).

The interpretation of *untensyu* is associated with the value in the Telic quale and that of *untensya* is associated with the value of the Agentive quale.

As observed by Miyajima (1997) and Kageyama (1999, 2002), Japanese has a large set of affixes that implement the semantic distinction in question. The following are a partial list of examples:

(5) a. Individual-level
untensyu (DRIVE-*syu*) 'driver', ensooka (PERFORM-*ka*) 'performer', odoriko (DANCE-*ko*) 'dancer', sakka (CREATE-ka) 'writer', kaisyain (COMPANY-*in*) 'office worker', kangosi (NURSING-*si*) 'nurse'

b. Stage-level
untensya (DRIVE-*sya*)'driver', ensoosya (PERFORM-*sya*) 'performer', odorite (DANCE-*te*) 'dancer', sakusya (CREATE-*sya*) 'author', syain (COMPANY-*in*) 'employee', kangonin (NURSING-*nin*) 'nurse'

Japanese has plenty of noun-forming affixes that make an individual/stage-level distinction (e.g. *-syu* (-手) and *-ka* (-家) vs. *-sya* (-者) and *-te* (手) in (5)) but morphological markers do not always make a clear distinction.

Both Miyajima's and Kageyama's arguments for the distinctive classes of deverbal nominals are mainly centered around agentive nominals; however, the same distinction can be observed in regard to object-denoting nominals. Japanese also has a wide variety of noun-forming affixes such as *-mono* (-物), *-butu* (-物), *-hin* (-品) that denote an object. See some of the examples below:

(6) -mono 'thing' (-物);

a. individual level
hakimono (WEAR-ON-FOOT-*mono*) 'footwear', norimono (RIDE-*mono*) 'vehicle', kazarimono (DECORATE-*mono*) 'decoration', nisemono (FAKE-*mono*) 'fake (thing)'

b. stage level
otosimono (LOSE-*mono*) 'lost item', wasuremono (LEAVE-*mono*) 'lost item', okurimono (GIVE-*mono*) 'gift', todokemono (DELIVER-*mono*) 'delivered item'

(7) -butu 'thing' (-物)

a. Individual-level
kikenbutu (DANGER-*butu*), kobutu (OLD-*butu*) 'antique',
kanenbutu (INFLAME-*butu*) 'inflammables'

b. Stage-level
haikibutu (WASTE-*butu*) 'wastes', yuubinbutu (POSTAL-*butu*)
'postal parcel', tinretubutu (EXHIBIT-*butu*) 'exhibition'

Thus, the distinction between event vs. non-event, or stage-level vs. individual-level, is more pervasive in the Japanese nominal lexicon than is assumed by Miyajima and Kageyama.

It is important to note there is one striking systematic difference between stage-level and individual-level nominals. Kageyama (1999, 2002) notes that *novelist* in (8a), an individual-level nominal, does not take a complement. But *author* and *writer* are stage-level nominals, licensing a complement as shown in (8b).

(8) a. *the novelist of this best-seller (individual-level)
b. the author/writer of children's books (stage-level)

The same is true in Japanese. In (9a) *sakka* 'writer', which is an individual-level noun, does not take a complement. In (9b), on the other hand, the stage-level counterpart, *sakusya* 'writer', takes a complement:

(9) a. *doowa no sakka (individual-level)
fairy tale GEN writer
'a writer of fairy tales'

b. (sono) doowa no sakusya (stage-level)
(the) fairy tale GEN writer
'the writer of fairy tales'

The relevant semantic distinction parallels a distinction between event and nonevent nominals in Rappaport Hovav and Levin's (1992) analysis of *–er* nominals. Stage-level nominals correspond to event nominals and individual-level nominals correspond to nonevent nominals. They claim that there is a correlation between the presence of complements and an event interpretation of nominals. In our terms, it means that the presence of complements correlates with stage-level nominals. Compare the examples in (10). If the head noun takes a complement as in (10a), it receives an event interpretation, where the noun denotes a person who has actually participated in an event of grinding imported coffees, i.e. it is taken to be a stage-level noun; whereas, if the noun lacks a complement as in (10b) or if it appears in a compound form as in (10c), it receives nonevent interpretation, namely, it refers to a machine which is designed to grind coffee but need not have been used for that purpose, i.e. an individual-level noun:

(10) a. a grinder of imported coffees
b. a grinder
c. a coffee grinder

Rappaport Hovav and Levin (1992: 140) attribute the event interpretation of the nominals to the existence of an event position [e] in argument structure. The nominal in (10a) has an event position while those in (10b) and (10c) lack it.

In light of the argument realization patterns in (10), we see that the agentive nominals in Japanese exhibit parallels. The individual-level nominal can have a compound form as in (11a) but the stage-level counterpart does not as in (11b):

(11) a. doowa sakka (individual-level)
fairy-tale writer
'a fairy-tale writer'

b. *doowa sakusya (stage-level)
fairy-tale writer
'a writer of fairy tales'

On the basis of these observations concerning the difference in argument selection between the two types of nominals, and the assumption that the source of the relevant semantic difference lies in the distinct values of qualia in the lexicon, we suggest that Agent qualia roles are associated with argument structure in the lexical representation of a stage-level nominal, and that the argument structure gives rise to the presence of complements in syntax. On the other hand, Telic qualia roles are not associated with argument structure, and thus, individual-level nominals do not select complements.

My account of argument selection based on Qualia roles predicts that the stage-level nominal *untensya* 'driver' and its individual-level counterpart *untensyu* 'driver' exhibit the same patterns as the *sakka*/*sakusya* examples in (9) and (11). This prediction is partially borne out as in (12) where the compound form of the individual-level nominal is rejected:

(12) a. torakku untensyu (individual-level)
truck driver
'a truck driver'

b. *zikosya untensya (stage-level)
crashed-car driver
'a crashed-car driver'

However, as shown in (13a), the individual level noun *untensyu* can appear with a genitive phrase *torakku no* 'of a truck', in parallel with the stage-level nominal *untensya* in (13b). If the genitive phrase in (13a) is a complement of the head noun, then we would expect that (13a) is ruled out:

(13) a. torakku-no untensyu (individual-level)
truck GEN driver
'a driver of a truck'

b. zikosya no unten sya (stage-level)
crashed car GEN driver
'a driver of a crashed car'

A closer look at the example, however, would reveal that the phrase 'of a truck' is a restrictive modifier in (13a). The modifier serves to pick out a set of drivers in contrast with *basu no* 'of a bus', *densya no* 'of a train', etc. Thus, it is not a syntactic manifestation of the Telic role that the lexical item specifies in the lexicon.[3]

2. Eventive mode of argument selection

As we have seen in the previous section, Rappaport Hovav and Levin (1992) assume that the correlation manifested by deverbal nominals between the presence of complement structure and the event interpretation follows from the existence of an event position in the base verb's argument structure.

The idea of dividing nouns into stage-level and individual-level is extensively discussed by Ogawa (2001), who claims that the relevant distinc-

[3] Along the same lines, the genitive phrases in *Nagoya no sityoo* 'the mayor of Nagoya', *ryokakki no pairotto* 'the pilot of an airliner' are not arguments but restrictive modifiers. Kageyama (2002: 50) notes *suirisyoosetu no sakka* 'a writer of detective stories' is acceptable in contrast with *doowa no sakka* 'a writer of fairy tales' in (9a), because *suirisyoosetu no* 'of detective stories' denotes a particular genre of stories that restrict the set of writers; hence, it is a restrictive modifier.

tion is made between event nominals and inalienable possession (IAP) nominals on the one hand, and simple nouns on the other. In (14) some examples of each class of noun are shown:

(14) a. Event nominals
tyuukoku 'advice', *teian* 'proposal', *kensa* 'examination'
b. Inalienable possession nominals
te 'hand', *kao* 'face', *kami* 'hair', *tume* 'nail', *asi* 'leg'
c. Simple nominals
kuruma 'car', *hon* 'book', *tukue* 'desk', *koppu* 'glass'

Ogawa adopts an idea which is similar to the one proposed by Rappaport Hovav and Levin (1992) to explain the semantic distinction in question. He proposes that event nominals and IAP nominals contain an event position whereas simple nominals do not.

I agree with Ogawa in saying that the relevant distinction is attributed to the presence or absence of an event position in the semantics of nominals; however, my claim crucially differs from his in that I do not assume that the IAP nominals are stage-level nominals. I will return to his analysis of the IAP nominals shortly, after reviewing his arguments for the distinction between event nominals and simple nominals, i.e. stage-level nominals and individual-level nominals.

One piece of evidence that motivated his proposal is what he calls the multiple genitive construction in Japanese. Let us first take a look at his examples. In (15), the event noun *kooen* 'speech' is modified by two genitive phrases *Oosaka-de no* 'in Osaka' and *John no* 'John's'. It is possible for the spatio-temporal modifier 'in Osaka' to modify the nominal head if it is on the left edge of the noun phrase, or if it is moved to the position between the possessor and the head. This flexibility of the spatio-temporal modifier is, according to Ogawa, due to the presence of an event position which licenses the modifier.

(15) a. [Oosaka-de no John no kooen] wa totemo omosirokatta.
Osaka-in GEN John GEN speech TOP very was-interesting
'John's speech in Osaka was very interesting.'

b. [John no Oosaka-de no kooen]
John GEN Osaka-in GEN speech

However, this is not true with simple nouns. As shown in (16), the locative phrase is licensed on the left edge of the NP, but it is ruled out "deep inside" the NP because the individual-level noun 'dog' does not have an event position.

(16) a. [Kooen-de no Taroo no inu] wa totemo genki-ga-ii.
park-in GEN Taro GEN dog TOP very is-active
'Taro's dog is very active in the park.'

b. *[Taroo no kooen-de no inu]
Taro GEN park-in GEN dog

Given that the distinction between event nouns and simple nouns is, in effect, a distinction between stage-level and individual-level, or event and nonevent, nominals, we may well make use of the contrast in (15) and (16) as supporting evidence for the distinction we have made so far. Let us see if *untensyu* 'driver' (stage-level) and *untensya* 'driver' (individual-level) show any difference if the modifier changes its position. In (17b) and (18b), the locative modifiers intervene between the head and their complement phrase. The stage-level nominal in (17b) licenses the modifier in that position but the individual-level nominal in (18b) does not:

(17) a. [koosaten-de no zikosya no untensya] wa isikihumei-da.
intersection-at GEN crashed car GEN driver TOP coma-COP
'The driver of the crashed car at the intersection is in coma.'

b. [zikosya no koosaten-de no untensya]
crashed car GEN intersection-at GEN driver

(18) a. [koosokudooro no torakku no untensyu] wa inemuri o sigati-da.
freeway GEN truck GEN driver TOP sleep ACC do-be-likely
'The driver of the truck on the freeway'

b. *[torakku no koosokudooro no untensyu]
truck GEN freeway GEN driver

If interchangeability of arguments and adjuncts serves as evidence for the presence of an event position in the nominal, as Ogawa claims, then (17) and (18) show that the former contains an event position, but the latter lacks it.

The contrast in question is observed in object-denoting nominals as well. In (19), with a stage-level noun as the head, the location modifier may intervene between the head and its complement as illustrated in (19b). Yet it is impossible to put a locative modifier between an individual-level head and its complement as shown in (20b):

(19) a. eki de no kyaku no otosimono (stage level)
station at GEN passenger GEN lost-thing
'a lost article of a passenger at the station'

b. kyaku no eki de no otosimono
station at GEN passenger GEN lost-thing
'a lost article of a passenger at the station'

(20) a. sokubaikai de no Louis Vuitton no nisemono (individual level)
sales exhibition at GEN L. V. GEN imitation
'an imitation of a Louis Vuitton at a sales exhibition'

b. *Louis Vuitton no sokubaikai de no nisemono
L. V. GEN sales exhibition at GEN imitation
'an imitation of a Louis Vuitton at a sales exhibition'

Thus, the fact that both agent nominals and object-denoting nominals exhibit the same patterns in terms of the stage-level and individual-level distinction supports the idea that stage-level nominals are in parallel with event nominals as far as the presence of an event position is concerned.

3. IAP nominals revisited

Let us return to Ogawa's claim that inalienable possession (IAP) nominals such as *te* 'hand', *kao* 'face', *kami* 'hair', *tume* 'nail', and *asi* 'leg' are stage-level. Evidence in support of his claim includes the fact that the modifiers in the IAP nominal in (21) and (22) can modify the heads.

(21) a. [Butai-de no Taroo no koe] wa yoku tooru.
stage-on GEN Taroo no koe TOP well carry
'Taro's voice on a stage carries well.'

b. [Taroo no butai-de no koe]
Taroo no stage-on GEN koe

(22) a. [Kinoo-no Mary no kami] wa totemo ii kaori ga sita.
yesterday GEN Mary GEN hair TOP very nice flavor NOM did
'Mary's hair was very fragrant yesterday.'

b. [Mary no kinoo-no kami]
Mary GEN yesterday GEN hair

If we assume that the spatio-temporal modifiers in (21) and (22) are licensed because they are associated with an event position, as Ogawa does, then it follows that the nominal heads, *koe* 'voice' and *kami* 'hair' have to have an event position; hence, they are stage-level nominals. However, this analysis poses an empirical problem. Notice that not all IAP nominals have adverbial modification. In contrast with *koe* 'voice' and *kami* 'hair' in (23 a, b), *sintyoo* 'height' and *aoi me* 'blue eyes' do not license spatio-temporal modifiers as shown in (24).

(23) a. [Butai-de no Taroo no koe]
stage-on GEN Taroo GEN voice
'Taro's voice on a stage'

b. [Kinoo no Mary no kami]
yesterday GEN Mary GEN hair
'Mary's hair yesterday.'

(24) a. *[Butai-de no Taroo no sintyoo]
stage-on GEN Taro GEN height
'Taro's height on a stage'

b. *[Kinoo no Mary no aoi me]
yesterday GEN Mary GEN blue eyes
'Mary's blue eyes yesterday'

What is crucial here is not just whether the head noun implies an event interpretation, but whether the denotation of the head noun subsumes a variable property.

With regard to the contrast between (23) and (24), Kageyama (2008) notes that the body-part nouns are divided into two types, according to the variability of the property that a given IAP noun denotes. While voice and hair change from time to time, height and the color of one's eyes do not change. Kageyama claims that the former type is a "semi-property nouns", which contain a suppressed or unactivated event variable [$e^{\wedge}$]. This event variable is 'activated' when the noun is modified by a spatio-temporal adverb.

4. Qualia and the interpretation of relational nouns

We have so far argued that in the eventive mode, Agent qualia roles are associated with argument structure in the lexical representation of a stage-level nominal, and that the argument structure gives rise to the presence of complements in syntax. In contrast with the argument selection by stage-level nominals, we propose that individual-level nominals select arguments in a different manner. They select arguments that denote individuals which are in particular lexical-semantic relations with the denotation of the head noun.

I would like to claim that a subset of individual-level nominals fall into a class of nominals which are often dubbed "relational nouns" (Barker and Dowty 1993 among others). For instance, *wife, friend, top, hand* are typical relational nouns whose argument selection is based on such ontological relations as the *wife-of* (x, y) relation for *wife* or the *part-of* (x, y) relation for *hand.* We propose that individual-level nominals which are relational in nature select arguments associated with Qualia roles. In the rest of this article, I will present evidence in support of our claim that individual-level nominals systematically differ in the selection of arguments. My arguments are mainly based on the genitive construction in Japanese.

The genitive construction in Japanese [X-*no* Y] 'X's Y' expresses various semantic relations between X and Y, as is the case in English genitive construction. As a default value of interpretation of the relation, it is a Possessor-Possessee relation with a wide range of its pragmatic extension (Nishiyama 2003). Vikner and Jensen (2002) propose that the lexical interpretations of relational nouns in the English genitive construction are predictable from the information contained in the qualia roles. Extending their analysis to apply to the genitive construction in Japanese, we assume that the semantic relations between X and Y in the [X-*no* Y] 'X's Y' construction follow from the qualia structure.

As we have discussed so far, Agentive roles are responsible for associating argument structures of stage-level nominals with their complement structures. Telic roles are relevant to representing the semantics of individual-level nominals but they are not linked to argument structure. Therefore, we need to explain how the Formal role and Constitutive role are relevant to selection of arguments in individual-level nominals. Let us see the representations below:

(25) Formal role (Inherent relation)

Taroo no tuma   wife_of (x, y)
Taro GEN wife
'Taro's wife'

(26) Constitutive role (Part-whole relation)
kuruma no enzin part_of (x, y)
car GEN engine
'the engine of a car'

In the next section, I will present some evidence that Formal and Constitutive roles comprise argument structures of individual-level nominals. Individual-level nominals, thus, select arguments on the basis of semantic relations specified in Formal and Constitutive qualia. My claim is based on an existential construction in Japanese.

5. Relational mode of argument selection

Muromatsu (1997) observes that there are two types of existential sentences in Japanese: one expresses a part-whole relation between the denotation of the nominative subject and that of the locative *ni* phrase arguments and the other expresses a spatial relation between them. The sentence in (27) is ambiguous in this respect.

(27) Kuruma ni enzin ga aru.
car LOC engine NOM be
'There is an engine in the car.'

In one reading, it expresses a part-whole relation between 'the car' and 'an engine', which may be translated into 'The car has an engine.'; in another reading, it expresses a locative relation between them, i.e. 'In the car is an engine.' But if we topicalize the *ni* phrase in (27), the sentence is disambiguated, allowing the part-whole interpretation only, as in (28a). And if we change the word order as in (28b), we obtain the spatial interpretation only:

(28) a. Kuruma (ni) wa enzin ga aru.
car LOC TOP engine NOM be
'The car has an engine.'

b. Enzin ga kuruma ni aru.
engine NOM car LOC be
'An engine is in the car.'

Notice that this ambiguity does not hold if there is no appropriate ontological relation between the nouns. If we replace 'an engine' with 'groceries' in (29), then the sentence will exhibit a spatial sense only. The topicalized counterpart is thus ruled out as shown in (29a) since we do not normally assume any ontological relation between 'the car' and 'groceries'. The locative counterpart is ruled in.

(29) a. *Kuruma wa syokuryoohin ga aru.
car TOP groceries NOM be
'Lit. The car has groceries.'

b. Syokuryoohin ga kuruma ni aru.
groceries NOM car LOC be
'There are groceries in the car.'

Given that this construction is sensitive to the ontological relation of the subject and the *ni* phrase, we can test the argumenthood of X in relation with Y. As it turns out, individual-level nouns that have a relational sense can occur in this construction.[4]

(30) a. Taroo (ni) wa musuko ga aru.
Taro LOC TOP son NOM be
'Taro has a son.'

b. Taroo (ni) wa tuma to ko ga aru.
Taro LOC TOP wife and children NOM be
'Taro has a wife and children.'

However stage-level nominals are rejected from this construction.[5]

(31) a. *zikosya (ni) wa untensya ga aru.
crashed car (in) TOP driver NOM be
'Lit. The crashed car has a driver.'

---

[4] Notice that not all relational nouns fit in this construction: e.g. *Sono robotto wa nagai ude ga aru* (the robot TOP long arms be) 'That robot has long arms.' is OK, but **Mary wa aoi me ga aru* (Mary TOP blue eyes be) 'Mary has blue eyes.' is out. The latter can be expressed as *Mary wa aoi me o siteiru* (Mary TOP blue eyes ACC do ASP) 'Mary has blue eyes', where the aspect marker *teiru* gives rise to a property reading. See Kageyama (2008) for more discussion.

[5] Stage-level nominals may appear in a similar construction. For example, *Sono syoosetu ni wa sakusya ga iru* (that novel LOC TOP writer NOM be) 'Lit. That novel has an author.' *Otosimono ni wa otosinusi ga iru* (lost articles LOC TOP owner NOM be) '(Every) lost article has an ower (who lost it).' But in this construction, the locative marker *ni* is not omissible and the verb *iru*, instead of *aru*, should be used. Moreover, sentences such as *Tosyokan ni wa ookuno riyoosya ga iru/aru* (library LOC TOP many users NOM be) 'There are many users in the library.' should be distinguished because they have an event reading.

b. *doowa (ni) wa sakusya ga aru.
fairy tale in TOP writer NOM be
'Lit. The fairy tale has a writer.'

Individual-level nominals associated with Telic roles are rejected too.

(32) a. *Doowa (ni) wa sakka ga aru.
fairy tale in TOP writer NOM be
'Lit. The fairy tale has a writer.'

b. *Torakku (ni) wa untensyu ga aru.
truck in TOP driver NOM be
'Lit. The truck has a driver.'

Thus, we have seen that argument selection of individual-level nominals is conducted via relational mode in which Formal and Constitutive roles comprise argument structures of nominals. In other words, individual-level nominals also select arguments on the basis of semantic relations specified in Qualia structure.

6. Conclusion

I hope to have shown that there are two distinct modes of argument selection at work in nominals. I have claimed that argument-taking nominals are either eventive or relational, depending on how the denotation of the head noun is determined with reference to ontological relations encoded in lexical structure.

This article has important theoretical implications for the argument structure of nominals. My analysis develops Barker and Dowty's (1993) idea that "nominal proto-roles" govern the argument selection of nominals in a parallel fashion that "verbal proto-roles" govern the argument selection of verbal predicates. Also, it raises a question concerning a recent proposal by Baker and Vinokurova (2009) that maintains a simple dichotomy of agent-denoting nominals and event-denoting nominals. We have shown that agent-denoting nominals, as well as object-denoting nominals, fall into two categories in terms of eventiveness.

References

Baker, M. C. and N. Vinokurova. 2009. On Agent Nominalizations and Why They Are Not Like Event Nominalizations. *Language* 85:517-556.

Barker, C. and D. Dowty. 1993. Non-verbal Thematic Proto-roles. *Northeastern Linguistic Society* 23: 49-62.

Kageyama, T. 1999. *Keitairon to Imi.* [Morphology and Meaning], Tokyo: Kurosio publishers.

Kageyama, T. 2002. Doosasyumeisi ni okeru goi to toogo no kyookai. [The Boundary between Lexicon and Syntax in Agentive Nominals]. *Kokugogaku* 53, 44-55.

Kageyama, T. 2008. *Zokuseizyozyutu to gokeisei* [Property Predication and Word Formation], Masuoka ed. *Zyozyutu ruikeiron.* Kurosio.

Miyajima, T. 1997. Hitomeisi no imi to asupekuto/tensu. [The Semantics of Human Nouns and Aspect/Tense]. *Nihongobunpoo taikei to hoohoo.* [The Japanese Grammar: System and Methodology]. ed. Y. Kawabata and Y. Nitta, 157-171. Tokyo: Hitsuzi Syoboo.

Muromatsu, K. 1997. Two Types of Existentials: Evidence from Japanese. *Lingua* 101: 245-269.

Nishiyama, Y. 2003. *Nihongomeisi no imiron to goyooron.* [The Semantics and Pragmatics of Nouns in Japanese]. Tokyo: Hitsuzi Syoboo.

Ogawa, Y. 2001. The Stage/Individual Distinction and (In)alienable Possession. *Language* 77: 1-25.

Pustejovsky, J. 1995. *Generative Lexicon.* Cambridge, Massachusetts: The MIT Press.

Rappaport Hovav, M. and B. Levin. 1992. -ER Nominals: Implications for the Theory of Argument Structure. *Syntax and Semantics 24, Syntax and the lexicon*, ed. T. Stowell and E. Wehrli, 127-53. New York: Academic Press.

Vikner, C. and P. A. Jensen. 2002. A Semantic Analysis of the English Genitive: Interaction of Lexical and Formal Semantics. *Studia Linguistica* 56, 191-226.

What can Japanese dialects tell us about the function and development of the nominalization particle *no*?

MASAYOSHI SHIBATANI
Rice University

1. Introduction

One of the most contentious issues in Japanese historical linguistics is concerned with the function and development of the nominalization particle (or *zyuntai-zyosi* 'quasi-nominal particle') *no* developed in the 16th century in the then central dialect of Japanese. This paper examines the problem in light of dialect data, which I believe provide a window with a clearer view to the relevant issues than what is afforded by the available philological evidence. The title of this paper calls for two qualifications. First by "Japanese dialects" I am referring to various dialects found in Japan including the local varieties of Ryukyuan spoken in the Ryukyu archipelago stretching over the two prefectures of Okinawa and Kagoshima. Secondly, the term "nominalization particle *no*" used in the title does not necessarily imply that the function of this particle is to derive a nominalized form. Indeed, this is one of the issues to be resolved below, where arguments are advanced for two different *no*'s in Standard Japanese that qualify as "nominalization particles" but whose functions and development differ—one is a true nominal-

Japanese/Korean Linguistics 20.
Edited by Bjarke Frellesvig and Peter Sells.

izer, which derives nominal-based nominalizations, and the other is simply a nominalization marker, which indicates nominalizations in NP-use. A great advantage of looking at dialects is a revealing picture that they afford in distinguishing these two types of nominalization particles, which are phonologically identical in Standard Japanese. Before venturing into the discussion of dialect forms, however, a brief introduction to a theory of nominalization is in order.[1]

2. What is nominalization?

Nominalization creates linguistic units which are associated with a denotation comprised of entity-concepts characterized in terms of a state-of-affairs in which the relevant concept has crucial relevance, e.g., participates in them as an agent or patient. Nominalizations, as products of this process, are similar to regular nouns by virtue of their having an entity-concept denotation, as opposed to verbs that are associated with a relational concept. Lexical nominalization (e.g., the formation of *employment* from the verb *employ*) produces nouns (e.g., $[\text{employment}]_{\text{N}}$), whereas grammatical nominalization forms units larger than nouns such as *John's employing Bill* and *that John is employing Bill*, which are labeled NMZN as $[\text{John's employing Bill}]_{\text{NMZN}}$ and $[\text{that John is employing Bill}]_{\text{NMZN}}$.[2] Both lexical nominalization *employment* and grammatical nominalization *John's employing Bill* denote states-of-affairs or events and are therefore event nominalizations. On the other hand, lexical nominalizations *employer/employee* and grammatical nominalizations *what was hanging on the wall* and *what I bought* denote event participants and are argument nominalizations.

---

[1] The preparation of this work has been supported in part by a short-term research fellowship of the Japan Foundation for the year 2010. I am also grateful to the following individuals, who have been very helpful in providing me with valuable data as specialists of the dialects indicated and in assisting my brief fieldwork in Yamaguchi, Okinawa and Hachijōjima in the summer of 2010. While not all the data provided by these experts are used in this paper, they have played a very important role in developing my ideas reported here. Takanori Hirano (Fukuoka and Yamaguchi), Takeru Koguma (Kanazawa and Toyama), Yuka Hayashi (Ikema Ryukyuan), Michinori Shimoji (Irabu Ryukyuan), Thomas Pellard (Ōgami Ryukyuan), Shinshō Miyara (Shuri Ryukyuan), Shigehisa Karimata (Jana and Agena Ryukyuan), Yūto Ṇiinaga (Amami Ryukyuan), Hiromi Shigeno (Amami Ryukyuan), Hiromitsu Machi (Yoron Ryukyuan), Tetsuo Nitta (Hachijō). Thanks are also due to Naonori Nagaya for reading and commenting on a draft of this paper. Abbreviations used in glosses are: ADN=adnominal, COP=copula, DIM=diminutive, FOC=focus marker, IMPF=imperfective, NM=nominalization marker, NMZR=nominalizer, NOM=nominative, NPST=non-past, TOP=topic, QP=quotation particle.

[2] Be aware that, contrary to the widely-held belief reflected in the term "clausal nominalization", these nominalizations are not clauses. While clauses predicate (say something about the referent of a subject NP), NMZNs do not; they instead have a denotation providing a basis for the referential function of an NP which they may head.

With the understanding of nominalization above, we recognize two types of nominalization in Japanese (and elsewhere). Because of the variety and clarity in nominalization morphology, we first use Classical Japanese to illustrate the two relevant types of nominalization.[3] The first, nominal-based, type of nominalization derives forms such as *Kakinomoto Hitomaro=**ga*** 'Kakinomoto Hiromaro's' and *Yamato=**no*** 'Japan's', where particles *ga* and *no* derive nominalization units [Kakinomoto Hitomaro=ga]$_{NMZN}$ and [Yamato=no]$_{NMZN}$ that denote entities having crucial relevance to Kakinomoto Hitomaro or to Japan such as poems by the former or those composed in the Japanese style, or any such entities.

Just as regular nouns can head an NP or can modify another noun (in a compound like [[inu]$_N$ [koya]$_N$]$_N$ 'dog house'), nominal-based NMZNs display two usage patterns. As the head of a noun phrase, a NMZN, based on its denotation property, provides content to the referential property of the NP it heads, just a noun heading an NP does. The other use of NMZNs is as modifiers of another nominal, where they play the function of restricting the denotation of the head nominal, perhaps an N′. These usage patterns of nominal-based NMZNs were already found in Classical Japanese as seen in the following examples:

(1) NP-use of nominal-based NMZNs[4]

a. Kono uta aru hito iwaku [[**Kakinomoto Hitomaro=ga**]$_{\mathbf{NMZN}}$]$_{\mathbf{NP}}$ nari. (*Kokinshū*)

'This poem, a certain person says, is Kakinomoto Hitomaro's.'

b. [[**Kara=no**]$_{NMZN}$]$_{NP}$=mo [[**Yamato=no**]$_{NMZN}$]$_{NP}$=mo kakikegasi. (*Genji Monogatari*)

'writing and disgracing China's as well as Japan's (poems)'

(2) Modification-use of nominal-based NMZNs

a. [[**Kakinomoto Hitomaro=ga**]$_{\mathbf{NMZN}}$ [uta]$_{N'}$]$_{NP}$

'Kakinomoto Hitomaro's poem'

b. [[**Yamato=no**]$_{\mathbf{NMZN}}$ [uta]$_{N'}$]$_{NP}$

'poems of Japan'

Verbal-based nominalization, dealing with verbs and adjectives, calls for the so-called *rentaikei* (adnominal) verbal endings, which were distinct

---

[3] The expression "Classical Japanese" is used here as a cover term for both Old (8th C) and Middle Japanese (9th-16th C).

[4] Japanese examples and grammatical terms are rendered in the modern reading and are transliterated in the Kunreishiki Romanization system, while the Hepburn system is used in rendering proper nouns.

in form (at least in adjectives and some verbs) from the *syuusikei* (conclusive/finite) verbal endings in Classical Japanese. Just like nominal-based NMZNs, verbal-based ones allow the two usage patterns of NP- and modification-use, as in the following Classical Japanese forms:

(3) NP-use of verbal-based NMZNs[5]
  a. [[**mizu=no nagaru-*ru***]$_{\mathrm{NMZN}}$]$_{\mathrm{NP}}$=o miru (verb-based)
    'see the flowing of the water'
  b. [[**tuki=no kiyo-*ki***]$_{\mathrm{NMZN}}$]$_{\mathrm{NP}}$=o mederu (adjective-based)
    'appreciate the moon's being clear and beautiful'

(4) Modification-use of verbal-based NMZNs
  a. [[**nagaru-*ru***]$_{\mathrm{NMZN}}$ [mizu]$_{\mathrm{N'}}$]$_{\mathrm{NP}}$
    'flowing water'
  b. [[**kiyo-*ki***]$_{\mathrm{NMZN}}$ [tuki]$_{\mathrm{N'}}$]$_{\mathrm{NP}}$
    'clear and beautiful moon'

The Classical Japanese particles *ga* and *no* and the so-called *rentaikei* (adnominal) verbal endings (*-ru* and *-ki*) are nominalizers par excellence, respectively deriving nominal- and verbal-based nominalizations, both associated with an entity-concept denotation. The proposed theory of nominalization obviates the so-called genitive particles (*no* and *ga* in Classical Japanese and Modern Japanese dialects). The so-called genitive noun forms are nothing but nominal-based NMZNs in modification-use, as in (2). It also offers a natural and uniform account of the *no* found in (1) and (2) without resorting to a deletion- or a pro-analysis often proposed for (1).[6]

3. Two types of nominalization particles

The analysis proposed above straightforwardly extends to Modern Japanese, which has lost the morphological distinction between the adnominal and the conclusive verbal form—hence the inflectional morphology marking verbal-based NMNZs—except for the copula forms *na* (adnominal) and *da* (conclusive). The other difference between Classical Japanese and Modern Japanese dialects is that the latter typically require an additional marker for NMZNs in NP-use. This marker is *no* in Standard Japanese, as seen in the NP-use of modern forms of verbal-based NMZNs (compare (3) and (5a)). Importantly, the new nominalization marker does not occur in the modification-use of NMZNs, as seen in (5b):

[5] The internal structures of these grammatical event nominalizations deserve a detailed study.

[6] See Kinsui (1995) for various proposals for the analysis of the forms in (1) and related ones.

(5) a. NP-use

[[mizu=no nagareru]$_{\mathrm{NMZN}}$]$_{\mathrm{NP}}$=**no**=o miru
'see the flowing of the water'
[[tuki=no kiyoi]$_{\mathrm{NMZN}}$]$_{\mathrm{NP}}$=**no**=o mederu
'appreciate the moon's being beautiful and clear'

b. Modification-use

[[nagareru]$_{\mathrm{NMZN}}$ [mizu]$_{\mathrm{N'}}$]$_{\mathrm{NP}}$
'the water that flows'
[[kiyoi]$_{\mathrm{NMZN}}$ [tuki]$_{\mathrm{N'}}$]$_{\mathrm{NP}}$
'the clear and beautiful moon'

While there is an obvious resemblance between the *no* particle above and the nominalizer *no* for nominal-based NMZNs discussed above—the so-called genitive particle *no*—the two relevant *no*'s are actually different historically and dialectally, as well as functionally. As noted above, the nominalizing *no* (or genitive *no*) seen in (1) existed in Old Japanese, whereas the particle *no* seen in (5a), known as *zyuntai-zyosi*, started to appear toward the end of the 16th century.

In various dialects of Japanese, the markers corresponding to this newly introduced *no* differ in form from the particles used in the genitive construction.[7] In western Japan, we find dialects in parts of Kumamoto prefecture where genitive forms have *ga* and *no/n*, while the equivalent of Standard Japanese *no* seen in (5a) is *tu*, which is obviously related to the Fukuoka form *to* and perhaps also to *so* seen Yamaguchi as in (7b) below:

(6) Kumamoto dialect

a. oru=**ga** megane
'my glasses'
sensei=**no** sikona
'teacher's nickname'
anta=**n** me
'your eyes'

b. akaka=**tu**
'a/the red one'
yonda=**tu**
'the one (I) have read'

[7]For the sake of simplicity and because of the familiarity, we continue to use the traditional term "genitive" in reference to the particles involved in nominal-based nominalizations.

(7) Yamaguchi dialect (courtesy of Takanori Hirano)[8]

a. ore=**no/n** hon
'my book'

b. akai=**so**
'a/the red one'
Hanako=ga kootyoru =**so**
'the one Hanako is keeping' (speaking about a pet cat)

Some other notable dialect particles corresponding to Standard Japanese *no* in (5a) are *ga* (Kōchi, Kanazawa, Toyama), *gan* (Niigata), and the Akita form *na* illustrated below:

(8) Akita Honjō City dialect (Ōno 1983:47-48)

a. ore (=**no**) ko
'my child'
Taroo (=**no**) hon
'Taro's book'

b. Ii=**na** mo arusu, warii=**na**=mo assu
'There are good ones and bad ones as well.'
Hon min=**na**=mo, terebi min=**na**=mo ii
'Reading books and watching TV is also O.K.'

Dialect forms, thus, provide compelling evidence for distinguishing the two types of particles involved in nominalization. In the traditional terms, the first type of particles is called *zokkaku-zyosi* "genitive particles" (*no* in (8a)) and the second type *zyuntai-zyosi* "nominalization particles" (*na* in (8b)). The theory of nominalization advocated in Section 2 treats these two types of particles as nominalization particles but possibly with two different functions. The former is a true nominalizer that derives nominal-based NMZNs, while the function and development of the latter is controversial and is the main topic of this paper dealt with below. In order to make the relevant distinction clearer, we distinguish the two types of particles as "nominalizers" (NMZRs) and "nominalization markers" (NMs). Summarizing the findings so far, we have the following two types of particles to contend with:

[8] The examples without mention of the source are those collected by the author.

Table 1. Nominalization particles across some Japanese dialects

	NOMINALIZATION PARTICLES	
	Nominalizers (aka *zokkaku-zyosi*)	**Nominalization markers** (aka *zyuntai-zyosi*)
Classical Japanese	*no, ga*	*Ø, no* (Late Middle Japanese)
Standard Japanese	*no/n*	*no*
Kumamoto	*no/n, ga*	*tu*
Yamaguchi	*no/n*	*so*
Akita Honjō City	(*no*)	*na*

4. Prevailing views on the function of nominalization markers

The most widely-held views on the function and the development of the nominalization marker *no* in Late Middle Japanese relate them to the merger of the *rentaikei* (adnominal) and the *syuusikei* (conclusive) endings, which started at the end of the 12th century. Kinsui (1995), for example, tells us that:

> In Classical Japanese, nominalized clauses can be said to face a cognitive crisis in distinguishing themselves from independent sentences [due to the *rentai-syuusi* merger]. This risk increases as the time progresses, whereby a possibility emerges for the development of a means of indicating that nominalized clauses are subordinate clauses. (169; my translation)[9]
>
> Upon the progress of the merger of the *syuusikei* to the *rentaikei* during the Muromachi period, the function of the *rentaikei* as a complement marker has essentially been lost. It can be entertained that the nominalization particle *no* developed in response to the need for a new clause boundary [marker]. (174; my translation)

Another view on the functional correlation between the *no* particle in question and the *rentai-syuusi* merger is expressed in an oblique way in a recently published book by Frellesvig (2010) as below:

> [N]ominalizing *no* took over the nominalizing functions of the OJ/EMJ [Old Japanese/Early Middle Japanese] adnominal and came to be used in all contexts where the OJ/EMJ formed headless nominalizations [i.e., nominalizations in NP-use as in (3)]...(364)

One of the difficulties with these explanations is the huge time lag between the time when the *rentai-syuusi* merger started (the end of the 12th century) and the time of the emergence of the nominalization marker (the end of the 16th century). Why did it take 400 years to attend the "cognitive crisis" that Middle Japanese nominalizations were apparently facing? Despite this

[9] In my view nominalizations are neither clausal nor subordinated (see Section 2 and Shibatani 2009).

doubt, the possibility of a connection between the development of the nominalization marker(s) and the *rentai-syuusi* merger remains a long-standing question in Japanese historical linguistics, which we address in the final section of this paper in the light of dialectal data.

A second problem with the prevailing views is: Why "*no* took over the nominalizing functions of the OJ/EMJ adnominal" only in the NMZNs in NP-use and not in those in modification-use, i.e., relative clause contexts, when OJ/EMJ adnominal endings were involved in all verbal-based NMZNs regardless of their use (see (3)-(4) above)? Thirdly, the accounts above have no ready answer to a likely connection between the nominalization marker in question and the one that marks nominal-based NMZNs in NP-use seen in the following examples, whose full appearance started toward the end of the 16th century, when the nominalization marker *no* also appeared.[10]

(9) a. kokin=no tyooka, Ise=ga=**no**=ga
old.new=NMZR long poems Ise=NMZR=NM=NOM
sugurete omosiroi=to yuu nari. (*Jiteiki* 1598-1602)
particularly interesting=QP say COP
'As for long poems of old and new, Ise's are said to be particularly interesting.'

b. kore=wa mi=ga=**no** zya. (*Ōkura Toraakira-bon* 1642)
this=TOP I=NMZR=NM COP
'This is mine.'

Notice that the context in which *no* occurs in the examples above is exactly the same as that where nominalization marker *no* occurs, namely where NMZNs are used as the head of a noun phrase. If our claim, based on the dialect data below, that the nominalization marker originated in the *no*-marking of nominal-based NMZNs in NP-use seen in (9) is correct, then the motivation and function of this particle, at least in its origin, had nothing to do with the *rentai-syuusi* merger or the marking of subordinate clauses. Moreover, the said *no* does not take on the nominalizing function. The forms *mi=ga* 'mine' and *Ise=ga* 'Ise's' in (9) are already nominalized with denotations comprising entity-concepts having crucial relevance to the speaker and the *Ise Monogatari*, and attaching *no* to them does not derive new nominalizations with different denotations.

What then was the function of the *no* particle marking the nominal-based NMZNs in NP-use as found in examples such as (9)? A hint to this question can be sought in those dialects in which the marking analogous to

[10]The earliest, and the sole, instance of the forms like (9) is attested in the 10th century.

the present case is still optional as in the Hachijō dialects, where *me* optionally marks nominalizations in NP-use, as in the following example:

(10) Hachijō Sueyoshi dialect
Sono akaake kutu=wa a=ga (=**me**) dara
that red shoe=TOP I=NMZR=NM COP
'Those red shoes are mine.'

According to the consultants, the *me* form would be used when someone were about to mistake their shoes for hers, indicating that the *me*-marking underscores the referential function of the nominalization heading an NP with the effect of contrasting the referent of this NP with some other entity. This understanding of the original function of the nominalization marker is consistent with the fact that many main-island dialects recycle the Old Japanese nominalizer particles (genitive *no* and *ga*) for this purpose.

If the original function of the *no*-marking of nominal-based nominalizations in NP-use were similar to that of the *me*-marking in the Hachijō dialects (and there is no contrary evidence), then its extension to verbal-based nominalizations in NP-use must have had the same functional motivation. This assumption naturally accounts for the fact that the nominalization marker *no* and its dialectal variants (see the next section) only mark NMZNs in NP-use and never those in modification-use (i.e., genitive and relative clause contexts) whether they are nominal- or verbal-based.

Based on these observations and assumptions, our conjectures about the nominalization marker (or *zyuntai-zyosi*) *no* at this point are as follows:

(11) a. Its origin lies in the marking of nominal-based NMZNs in NP-use (see (9)).[11]
b. Its function is to mark the NP-use of NMZNs or to indicate the referential function of the NMZNs heading an NP.
c. It is **not** a nominalizing particle or nominalizer; it does not derive a new NMZN with a new denotation.
d. What it marks has already been nominalized in both Classical and Modern Japanese. In most dialectal varieties of the latter, adnominal inflectional forms have replaced conclusive forms in effect obliterating nominalization morphology in verbal-based NMZNs.

[11] See Hashimoto (1969:216) for a similar view on the origin of the nominalization marker.

5. Dialect forms

Let us now turn to dialect forms that support the above view on the nominalization markers. The dialect data presented in Section 3 are incomplete. A fuller picture is presented below for several dialects, where the NP-use of both nominal- and verbal-based NMZNs is marked the same by a particle equivalent to the Standard Japanese nominalization particle *no*.

(12) Kumamoto dialect

Nominal-based NMZNs	**Verbal-based NMZNs**
a. *NP-use*	
oru=ga=**tu**	akaka=**tu**
'mine'	'a/the red one'
	yonda=**tu**
	'the one that (I) have read'
b. *Modification-use*	
[oru=ga] megane	[akaka] hana
'my glasses'	'a/the red flower'
	[yonda] hon
	'the book (I) read'

(13) Yamaguchi dialect (courtesy of Takanori Hirano)

Nominal-based NMZNs	**Verbal-based NMZNs**
a. *NP-use*	
ore=no/n=**so**	akai=**so**
'mine'	'a/the red one'
	Hanako=ga kootyoru=**so**
	'the one that Hanako is keeping'
b. *Modification-use*	
[ore=no/n] hon	[akai] kuruma
'my book'	'a/the red car'
	[Hanako=ga kootyoru] neko
	'the cat that Hanako is keeping'

(14) Toyama dialect

Nominal-based NMZNs	**Verbal-based NMZNs**
a. *NP-use*	
anta=no=**ga**	hurui=**ga**
'yours'	'an/the old one'
	nita=**ga**
	'the one that (I) have cooked'

b. *Modification-use*

[anta=no] hon
'your book'

[hurui] kuruma
'an/the old car'

[nita] nasubi
'the egg plants that (I) have cooked'

(15) Akita Honjō City dialect (Ōno 1983:47-48)

Nominal-based NMZNs

a. *NP-use*

Taroo=**na**=mo Hanako=**na**=mo hitotu da.
'Taro's and also Hanako's are the same.'

b. *Modification-use*

Taroo (=no) hon
'Taro's book'

Verbal-based NMZNs

a. *NP-use*

Ii=**na** mo arusu, warii=**na**=mo assu.
'There are good ones and bad ones as well.'
Hon min=**na**=mo, terebi min=**na**=mo ii
'Reading books and watching TV is also O.K.'

b. *Modification-use*

(Data unavailable)

(16) Hachijō Sueyoshi dialect

Nominal-based NMZNs

a. *NP-use*

a=ga (=**me**)[12]
'mine'

b. *Modification-use*

[a=ga] kutu
'my shoes'

Verbal-based NMZNs

a. *NP-use*

wakake (=**me**)=ga uku=ni arozya.
'A/The young one is there.'
Yamada-san=ga yomo (=**me**)=wa Asahi Shinbun dara.
'What Mr. Yamada reads is Asahi Newspaper.'

---

[12]The origin of *me* is unclear. It attaches obligatorily to animal names and a few other kinds of nouns; e.g., *nekko-me* 'cat', *inu-me* 'dog', *usi-me* 'cow', *doongo-me* 'a fool'.

b. *Modification-use*
[wakake] gakusei
'a/the young student'
[Yamada-san=ga yomo] sinbun=wa Asahi dara.
'The newspaper that Mr. Yamada reads is Asahi.'

(17) Miyako Ikema Ryukyuan (courtesy of Yuka Hayashi)
Nominal-based NMZNs
a. *NP-use*
ba=ga=**munu**
'mine'
b. *Modification-use*
[ba=ga] yaa
'my house'
Verbal-based NMZNs
a. *NP-use*
baka=**munu** nu=du uman ui
young=NM NOM=FOC there be
'A/The young one is there.'
Yamada-san=ga yun=**munu**=u Miyako Mainichi
read=NM=TOP
'What Mr. Yamada reads is Miyako Mainichi.'
b. *Modification-use*
[baka] gakusei
'a/the young student'
[Yamada-san=ga yun] sinbun
'the newspaper that Mr. Yamada reads'

It is clear from the above that what corresponds to the Standard Japanese nominalization marker *no* occurs systematically across different dialects in the NMZNs in NP-use regardless whether they are nominal-based or verbal-based. This very fact, that the same marker is used for both nominal- and verbal-based NMZNs, supports our analysis that the so-called genitive forms are nominalizations equivalent in function to verbal-based nominalizations expressed by the so-called adnominal endings in Classical Japanese.[13]

When we compare the dialect patterns above with the Standard Japanese paradigm, we recognize a gap in this variety of Japanese.

---

[13]Other languages supporting this analysis are Korean, various Chinese dialects, Lahu, and Nepali, all of which use the same marker for nominal- and verbal-based NMZNs.

(18) Standard Japanese

Nominal-based NMZNs	**Verbal-based NMZNs**
a. *NP-use*	
ore=no (< ore=no=**no**)	akai=**no**
'mine'	'a/the red one'
	kirei-na=**no**
	'a/the pretty one'
	kinoo katta=**no**
	'the one that (I) bought yesterday'
b. *Modification-use*	
[ore=no] megane	[akai] ringo
'my glasses'	'a/the red apple'
	[kirei-na] ringo
	'a/the pretty apple'
	[kinoo katta] ringo
	'the apple that (I) bought yesterday'

The nominalization marker *no* that marks verbal-based NMZNs in NP-use is missing in nominal-based NMZNs in Standard Japanese, where *ore=no=**no*** 'mine' is expected. The particle *no* of *ore=no* is the nominalizing *no* (so-called genitive *no*) that remains in the modification-use, as in *ore=no megane* 'my glasses'. This gap is due to a historical development of the nominalization marker *no* in the speech of the Tokyo area. Matsushita (1930: 246) notes that the speech along the old Tōkaidō road (once) had a form such as *zibun=no=**no*** (=wa nai) 'Mine (does not exist)'. The most recent such forms in Tokyo speech that I was able to find are expressions such as *ore=no=**no*** 'mine' and *Fujishima-san=no=**no*** 'Mr. Fujishima's' in the memoir of Natsume Sōseki by his wife first published in 1928.[14]

Thus, it appears that Tokyo speech also had a complete paradigm of NMZN usage patterns, where *no* was indeed used as a marker of the NP-use of both nominal- and verbal-based NMZNs, as in other contemporary dialects. What seems to have happened to Tokyo speech and Standard Japanese is the loss of the second *no* turning such a form as *ore=no=**no*** 'mine' into *ore=no* (cf. the Osaka form *ore=no=**n*** 'mine').

The following table summarizes the correspondence pattern of nominalizers and nominalization markers across a number of Japanese and Ryukyuan dialects:

[14] *Sōseki=no Omoide* (1928), narrated by Kyōko Natsume and transcribed by Yuzuru Matsuoka. Tokyo: Kaizōsha. Newer editions, published by Iwanami Shoten, are readily available.

Table 2: Correspondence pattern of NMZRs (nominalizers) and NMs (nominalization markers) across some dialects

		NOMINALIZATIONS	
		Nominal-based	**Verbal-based**
Classical Japanese	NMZR	*no, ga*	*-ru; -ki* (adnominal)
	NM	no (10th C?)	no (16th C)
Standard Japanese	NMZR	*no/n*	Ø
	NM	Ø (<*no*)	*no*
Kumamoto dialect	NMZR	*no/n, ga*	Ø
	NM	*tu*	*tu*
Toyama dialect	NMZR	*no*	Ø
	NM	*ga*	*ga*
Hachijō dialects	NMZR	*no, ga*	*-o* (adnominal)
	NM	(*me*)	(*me*)
Amami Yuwan Ryukyuan	NMZR	*Ø, nu*	*-n* (adnominal)
	NM	*-sï, mun*	*-sï*
Okinawa Agena Ryukyuan	NMZR	*Ø, ga*	*-ru* (adnominal)
	NM	*mun*	*-sï*
Miyako Ikema Ryukyuan	NMZR	*nu, ga*	Ø
	NM	*munu*	*munu*[15]

A final issue addressed here is whether dialect data support our hypothesis that the nominalization markers develop from the markers of the NP-use of nominal-based NMZNs (e.g., *ore=no=**no*** 'mine') extending their use to the NP-use of verbal-based NMZNs (e.g., *akai=**no*** 'a/the red one', *kirei-na=**no*** 'a/the pretty one', *katta=**no*** 'the one that (I) bought'). Support comes from Ryukyuan dialects, where varying degrees of the development of *mun(u)* as a nominalization marker are seen across different dialects. The dialects of the Okinawa Island generally seem to use *mun(u)* only for nominal-based NMZNs in NP-use, as below. But it has not spread to verbal-based NMZNs, which, in a dialect like Agena Ryukyuan overleaf, can be expressed by the adnominal inflection as in Classical Japanese:

[15] See below on the restriction on the use of this marker in this dialect.

(19) Agena Ryukyuan (courtesy of Shigehisa Karimata)

Nominal-based NMZNs

a. *NP-use*

ʔure: wa:=**mun** do:.
that I=NM COP
'That is mine.'
ʔure: sinsi:=ga=**mun** do:.
'That is the teacher's.'

b. *Modification-use*

[wa:] kkwa
I child
'my child'
[sinsi:=ga] kkwa
'teacher's child'

Verbal-based NMZNs

a. *NP-use* (*mun* not used)

ʔama=nkai tattʃo:-ru wa: ikigangwa.
there=at standing-ADN I son
'The one standing there is my son.'
ʔama=nkai tattʃo:-**së:** wa: ikigangwa. (-së: = sï+ya)
there=at standing-NM.TOP I son
'The one standing there is my son.'

b. *Modification-use*

[ʔama=nkai tattʃo:-**ru**] ttʃo: wa: sinsi:.
there=at standing-ADN person I teacher
'The person standing there is my teacher.'
*[ʔama=nkai tattʃo:-**sï**] ttʃo: wa: sinsi:.
there=at standing-NM person I teacher
'The person standing there is my teacher.'

Compare the NP-use of the verbal-based NMZNs above with the patterns exhibited by the dialects belonging to the Miyako group southwest of the Okinawa Island—the Ikema pattern in (17) above and the Irabu pattern below, where *munu* is also used in the NP-use of verbal-based NMZNs.

(20) Miyako Irabu Ryukyuan (courtesy of Michinori Shimoji)

Nominal-based NMZNs

a. *NP-use*

uri=a ba=ga=**munu**.
that=TOP I=NMZR=NM
'That is mine.'

b. *Modification-use*
[ba=ga] biki-vva
I=NMZR male-child
'my son'

Verbal-based NMZNs

a. *NP-use*
kama=n taci-ur=**munu**=u ba=ga biki-vva.[16]
there=at stand-IMPF=NM=TOP I=NMZR male-child
'The one standing there is my son.'

b. *Modification-use*
[kama=n taci-ur] ba=ga biki-vva.
there=at stand-IMPF I=NMZR male-child
'my son(,) who is standing there'

Naturally a question can be raised whether or not the Miyako pattern is more recent than the one shown by Agena Rykyuan from the Okinawa Island. One may very well argue that the Agena pattern is more progressive and that the dialect has lost the *mun*-marking from verbal-based NMZNs. This position, however, is not tenable since the loss of nominalization markers seems to progress from nominal-based NMZNs to verbal-based NMZNs, rather than the other way around. This is seen from both Ryukyuan and Yamaguchi scenes.

The pan-Ryukyuan NMZN marker, also seen in Omorosōshi (1531-1623), is /si/, which presumably once marked both nominal- and verbal-based NMZNs in NP-use. This form is still widely used from southern Amami to Yonaguni marking verbal-based NMZNs in NP-use. However, its use in nominal-based NMZNs is now found only in the dialects north of the Okinawa Island, including the Kumejima Island due west of the Okinawa Island. Compare the Yuwan Amami forms and the Agena forms in (19) above:

(21) Amami Yuwan Ryukyuan (courtesy of Yūto Niinaga)

Nominal-based NMZNs

a. *NP-use*
waa=**sï**=ya dïru
I=NM=TOP which.one
'Mine is which one?'

[16]In addition to this form with *munu*, Irabu permits ones with the adnominal ending as well as those with the NMZN marker /si/, seen widely in central and northern Ryukyuan dialects (see below). On the various functions of Irabu *munu*, see Shimoji (2008).

b. *Modification-use*
[waa] hon
'my book'

Verbal-based NMZNs

a. *NP-use*
yum-yu-**sï**=ya dïru
read-IMPF-NM=TOP which.one
'the one that (I) read is which one?'

b. *Modification-use*
[yum-yu-n] hon
read-IMPF-ADN book
'the book which (I) read'

While the Yuwan dialect still has /si/ in both nominal- and verbal-based NMZNs in NP-use, the Agana dialect has replaced the /si/ form in nominal-based NMZNs with *mun*. But this dialect and others still retains its use in verbal-based NMZNs.

That this is a case of loss and replacement of /si/ by the newer *mun(u)* marker in central and southern Ryukyuan is seen from the on-going replacement pattern in southern Amami dialects. While nominal-based NMZNs in NP-use are freely marked by /si/ in Yuwan Amami as seen in (21) above, the use of /si/ in this function is more restricted in Sokari, Katsu'ura, Atetsu and other villages, where the use of the relevant forms is recalled only when asked if such forms exist in the dialects or where such forms are said to be heard only in "men's rough speech".

A similar pattern of loss is observed in the Yamaguchi dialect, where the marker *so* has been lost in nominal-based NMZNs (e.g., *ore=no/n=**so*** > *ore=no/n* 'mine') among younger speakers, who would still use it in verbal-based NMZNs (e.g., *akai-**so*** 'a/the red one'), while older speakers use *so* in both contexts (see (13) above).

6. Correlation with the *rentai-syuusi* merger

Let us finally discuss the possible functional link between the rise of nominalization markers and the *rentai-syuusi* merger, the correlation that has frequently been invoked in the explanation for the emergence of the nominalization marker *no* in Late Middle Japanese (see Section 4). We will look at the Ryukyuan situation first and then turn to the Hachijō dialects.

Compared to the Miyako group, the dialects of the Okinawa Island and those from further north have restored and maintain the *rentai-syuusi* distinction analogous to that found in Classical Japanese. For example, the Agena dialect of the Okinawa Island shows the following morphological contrast between the adnominal (*rentai*) and the conclusive (*syuusi*) form:

(22) Agena Ryukyuan (courtesy of Shigehisa Karimata)

a. Conclusive form (*-N*)

Midʒi nage:ri:**N**.

'The water flows.'

b. Adnominal form (*-ru*)

[nage:ri:**ru**] midʒi

'the water that flows'

c. Midʒi=nu=**du** nage:ri:**ru**.

water=NOM=FOC flow=ADN

'It is the water that flows.'

As shown in (22c) above, Agena Ryukyuan also maintains the phenomenon analogous to *kakari-musubi* of Classical Japanese, where *du*, corresponding to the Japanese adverbial particle (or *kakari-zyosi*) *zo,* calls for the adnominal (*rentai*) form of a verb.

Despite this *rentai-syuusi* distinction, the nominalization marker /si/ and its renewal by the marker *mun(u)* are widespread in both north and south of the Okinawa Island. When we compare the two alternative verbal-based NMZNs in NP-use of Agena Ryukyuan, the /si/ marker looks as if it is taking over the nominalization function of the adnominal *-ru* ending, as it is the case in other dialects that use /si/.

(23) Agena Ryukyuan verbal-based NMZNs in NP-use

a. ʔama=nkai tattʃo:-**ru** wa: ikigangwa.

there=at standing-ADN I son

'The one standing there is my son.'

b. ʔama=nkai tattʃo:-**së:** wa: ikigangwa. (-së: = sï+ya)

there=at standing-NM.TOP I son

'The one standing there is my son.'

This replacement by /si/ or its spread to verbal-based NMZNs, however, does not really take over the nominalization function of the adnominal ending, for /si/ forms cannot modify an N′ (see (19b) under the modification-use of verbal-based NMZNs).

Now, that the development of a nominalization marker has no direct correlation with the *rentai-syuusi* distinction is seen from the replacement pattern of /si/ by *mun(u)* in Miyako and Yaeyama. As mentioned above, many Miyako dialects have started using *mun(u)* as a nominalization marker for the NP-use of verbal-based NMZNs (see (20) above), which has not taken place on the Okinawa Island. It is tempting to attribute this difference between Miyako and Okinawan dialects to the difference between the absence of the *rentai-syuusi* distinction in the former and its presence in the latter. This explanation, however, is not tenable. If we compare the development of *mun(u)* marking in Miyako and Yaeyama (Ishigaki dialect, in particular), we recognize that *mun(u)* marking is more developed in the latter, where the *rentai-syuusi* distinction, similar to the contrast seen in the Agena dialect in (22), is robust, than in the former, where this distinction is quite obscure as it is seen only in the existential verbs.

In Miyako Ikema Ryukyuan *munu* cannot be used when the NMZNs denote an animate being. In Miyako Irabu Ryukyuan, *munu* can denote animate beings, including a human, but not a respectable person, while in the Ishigaki dialect, *munu* is fully established as a general nominalization marker and can denote all these.[17]

(24) Miyako Ikema Ryukyuan

a. kura=a ba=ga umyasI,
this=TOP 1SG=GEN chopstick
vva=ga muci+cc-ya=a **munu**=u ara-n
2SG=NOM bring+come=RES NM=TOP COP-NEG.NPST
'These are my chopsticks, not what you have brought.'

b. *kama=n nivv-yu=ui **munu**=u banti=ga mayu
over.there=DAT sleep-CVB=PROG.NPST NM=TOP 1PL=GEN cat
'The one sleeing over there is my cat.'

(25) Miyako Irabu Ryukyuan (Courtesy of Michinori Shomoji)

a. kama=n taciur **munu**=u ba=ga biki-vva
there=at standing NM=TOP I=GEN male-child
'The one standing there is my son.'

b. *kama=n taciur **munu**=u ba=ga sinsii
there=at standing NM=TOP I=GEN teacher
'The one standing over there is my teacher.'

(26) Yaeyama Ishigaki Ryukyuan (Courtesy of Yukinori Takubo)

a. kamaNga taciuru **munu**=ya baa Faa du yaru
there standing NM=TOP we child FOC COP
'The one standing there is our child.'

b. kamaNga tiacooru **munu**=ya baa sinsii du yaru
there standing NM=TOP we teacher FOC COP
'The one standing there is my teacher.'

Hachijō dialects are another dialect group that is said to maintain the *rentai-syuusi* distinction. This is indeed the case, but the contrast is not in

---

17 In all these dialects munu can mark the NP-use of event nominalizations.

terms of the traditional *rentai* and *syuusi* forms. The present-day contrast in verbs is as follows:

(27) Hachijō Sueyoshi dialect
  a. Conclusive
    Yamada-san=wa sinbun=o **yomo-wa/zya**.
    'Mr. Yamada reads newspaper.'
  b. Adnominal
    [Yamada-san=ga **yomo**] sinbun=wa Asahi dara.
    'The newspaper which Mr. Yamada reads is Asahi.'

The present-day conclusive form consists of the old adnominal form of a verb (*yomo* 'read.ADN') and the final particle *wa* or *zya*. These particles are now grammaticalized and are obligatory in ending a sentence, and the forms without them are ungrammatical. Thus, it appears that the *rentai-syuusi* merger has taken place once but that the contrast has been restored in terms of the ADN vs. ADN-*wa/zya* formal opposition.[18]

Without available evidence about the time of the old *rentai-syuusi* merger, it is hard to determine whether the rise of the nominalization marker *me* (see (16) above) had anything to do with it. But it is at least clear that the restoration of the *rentai-syuusi* contrast took place earlier than the use of *me*. As noted above, the use of the *wa/zya*-conclusive ending is now obligatory, whereas the use of *me* is still largely optional. In elicitation sessions, *me* typically does not occur in initial responses. It is only when asked if *me* is usable that native speakers give *me* forms. This was generally the case across different Hachijō dialects, except for a couple of younger speakers of the Kashidate dialect in the early 60s and the late 50s, who produced *me* forms rather readily. Kaneda (2001), describing the speech of much older speakers than our consultants in great detail, makes only a passing remark on *me* forms in his grammar, and the fair-size narrative and folktale texts at the end of the book yield only a very few instances (two) of *me*-marked nominalizations. It, thus, appears safe to conclude that the development of *me* started after the *rentai-syuusi* distinction had been restored. The above are cases in which (new) nominalization markers (or *zyuntai zyosi*) have developed despite there is the *rentai-syuusi* distinction. There is also an "opposite" case, where a nominalization marker has not developed despite the loss of the *rentai-syuusi* distinction. The case in point is the Izumo dialect, a variety of the so-called Unpaku dialects, spoken in the Shimane Prefecture.

---

[18]The old conclusive verb forms are seen in forms like the conjectural form ***nomu**-nou-wa* (Kaneda 2001:113).

The Izumo dialect, like the central dialects, have lost the rentai-syuusi distinction, as seen in (a)-(b) forms below:

(28) a. Okaka=ga sakana **yaita**
mother=NOM fish broiled
'Mother broiled the fish.'
b. Otottsan=ga **yaita** sakana kutta
father=NOM broiled fish ate
'Father ate the broiled fish.'
c. Ora=mo sakana=no **yaita**=o kuitai
I=also fish=NMZR broiled=ACC want.to.eat
'(Lit.) I also want to eat the broiled of the fish.'

(29) a. Kono sao **nagee**
this pole long
'This pole is long.'
b. **Nagee** sao(=o) kaitai
long pole(=ACC) want.to.buy
'(I) want to buy a long pole.'
c. Motto sao=no **nagee**(=ga) hosï
more pole=NMZR long(=NOM) want
'(Lit.) (I) want a long one of the pole.'

(30) a. Ora=no/ga kutu=wa **okkena**
I=NMZR/NMZR shoe=TOP big
'My shoes are big.'
b. Sono **okkena** kutu=wa ora=na yatsu da
that big shoe=TOP I=NMZR NM COP
'Those big shoes are mine.'
c. Sono **okkena**=wa sensei=no kutu da
that big=TOP teacher=NMZR shoe COP
'Those big ones are the teacher's shoes.'

As can be clearly seen in (c) forms above, the elder speakers (those above 80-years old) use the *rentai/syuusi* forms as nominalizations without an additional nominalization marker equivalent of the *zyntai-zyosi* in the central dialects. Those in the 70's and anyone younger, on the other hand, are likely to use *no* in marking nominalizations in NP-use. Judging from other speech traits of these younger speakers, this is due to the influence of Standard Japanese.

The development of a nominalization particle in those dialects maintaining the *rentai-syuusi* distinction in southern Okinawa and Hachijōjima, and the absence of such a particle in the Izumo dialect, where the *rentai-syuusi* distinction has also been lost jointly point to the conclusion that there is no necessary connection between the *rentai-syuusi* merger and the development of a nominalization marker or *zyntai-zyosi*. This is consistent with our view that the so-called *zyntai-zyosi* first arises in the marking of nominal-based nominalizations in NP-use, where the notion of *rentai-syuusi* distinction is irrelevant.

7. Conclusion

Japanese dialects have a lot to tell us about the function and development of the nominalization marker *no* in Standard Japanese. While a fair number of dialects recruiting Old Japanese genitive *no* and *ga* as a nominalization marker intimate a direct connection between the genitive and nominalization particles, there is a sufficient number of dialects showing that the link is indirect at best since they use different markers reflecting the difference in the historical development of these particles and the difference in function between the two. The theory of nominalization briefly summarized in Section 2 recognizes the Old Japanese genitive particles *no* and *ga* as nominalizers deriving nominal-based nominalizations (e.g., *Yamato=no* 'Japan's'). So-called genitive constructions (e.g., *Yamato=no uta* 'Japan's poems') are simply the modification-use of these nominalizations, which also occur as the heads of noun phrases, where they play a vital role in the referential function of NP's. The *no* particle generally recognized as a nominalization marker (*zyuntai-zyosi*) in the field (e.g., *akai=**no*** 'a/the red one', *kinoo katta=**no*** 'the one (I) bought yesterday) arose in the 16th century in the central dialect of Late Middle Japanese. Dialect evidence suggests that the rise of nominalization markers starts in the marking of the NP-use of nominal-based nominalizations (e.g., Toyama form *anta=no=**ga*** 'yours') and then they are extended to the NP-use of verbal-based nominalizations (*akai=**ga*** 'a/the red one', *kinoo katta=**ga*** 'the one that (I) bought yesterday'). Since these markers, like the *zyuntai-zyosi* in Standard Japanese, occur only in the NP-use of both nominal- and verbal-based NMZNs, they (along with the Standard Japanese *zyuntai-zyosi*) are not true nominalizers. They mark what is already nominalized, and their function is to mark the NP-use of NMZNs or to indicate clearly the referential function played by the NMZNs as the head of a noun phrase. The extension of nominalization markers from nominal-based to verbal-based NMZNs supports the theory of nominalization that recognizes these two types of constructions as nominalizations.

Japanese dialects also tell us that the rise and spread of nominalization markers have little to do with the *rentai-syuusi* merger, contrary to the views widely-held in the field. There are dialects where new nominalization markers have developed despite the *rentai-syuusi* contrast has been restored and maintained in a new pattern (many Ryukyuan dialects and the Hachijō dialects). In addition, there are main-island dialects (the so-called Unpaku dialects in Shimane and Tottori prefectures), where the *rentai-syuusi* merger has taken place, but where the equivalent of the Standard Japanese nominalization marker has not developed.

References

Frellesvig, B. 2010. *A History of the Japanese Language*. Cambridge: Cambridge University Press.

Kaneda, A. 2001. *Hachijō-hōgen Dōshi no Kisokenkyū*. Tokyo: Kasama Shoin.

Kinsui, S. 1995. Nihongo no iwayuru N' sakujo ni tsuite. *Dai 3 kai Nanzan Daigaku Nihongo-kyōiku Nihongo-gaku Kokusai Shinpojiumu Hōkokusyo, ed.* Y. Abe, T. Sakamoto, and M. Soga , 153-176.

Hashimoto, S. 1969. *Joshi Jodōshi no Kenkyū*. Tokyo: Iwanami Shoten.

Matsushita, D. 1930. *Kaisen Hyōjun Nihon Bunpō.* Tokyo: Chūbunkan Shoten.

Ōno, S. 1983. Gendai nihongo ni okeru rentai kaku-joshi to juntai-joshi. *Ōsaka University Nihongaku-hō* 2: 27-66.

Shibatani, M. 2009. Elements of complex structures, where recursion isn't: the case of relativization. *Syntactic Complexity*. Amsterdam: John Benjamins, ed. T. Givón and M. Shibatani, 163-198.

Shimoji, M. 2008. *A Grammar of Irabu, a Southern Ryukyuan Language*. Doctoral thesis, Australian National University.

The Perfective Imperative in Japanese

AXEL SVAHN
Lund University

1. Introduction

This article focuses on a phenomenon in Japanese in which an imperative is expressed through the use of the markers of tense and aspect, *-ta* and *-tari*.

(1) Doi-ta, doi-ta!
move.away-PAST move.away-PAST
'Get out of my way!' (lit.) 'You got out of my way!'

(2) Saa saa, it-tari it-tari!
Well well go-TARI go-TARI
'Go on, scram!' (lit.) '[You] have gone!'

The constructions shall here be termed imperative *-ta* and imperative *-tari*. Their use has been remarked on by scholars, but a detailed account of the phenomenon, its diachrony, and its place in a cross-linguistic context has not previously been given.

The relation between aspect and utterances of command seen in imperative *-ta* and *-tari* is discussed, focusing on their connection to perfective aspect. The discussion also touches on the occurrence of past tense and per-

Japanese/Korean Linguistics 20.
Edited by Bjarke Frellesvig and Peter Sells.

fective imperatives cross-linguistically, comparing the Japanese construction to similar phenomena in other languages.

The history and development of the perfective imperative in Japanese is then outlined, establishing the facts currently available as to the possible origins of the construction and enumerating some of the hypotheses that the data allows us to put forward. The goal is to take the analysis of the diachrony of the perfective imperative as far as it can be taken. We shall see what explanations are available for the emergence of imperative *-tari* and *-ta*. A number of alternate hypotheses as to this development, all with their consequences in interpreting the diachronic evolution as well as the synchronic function of the constructions, are presented.[1]

2. General properties of imperative *-ta*

The discussion will first focus on the synchronically more common imperative *-ta*. Its fundamental characteristics include the following:

1. It functions as a highly informal imperative.
2. It is associated with a feeling of urgency and/or anger on the part of the speaker.
3. It is not a phonetic alteration of another existing imperative construction, but instead originally derived from the suffix *-ta*(*ri*).

These characteristics are shared in part by imperative *-tari*. Hirata (1987:56) describes the distinction between imperative *-ta* and other constructions as follows:

> […] *ta* command sentences would be used when the speaker wants to very impolitely command the hearer, and/or he wants to show his power over the hearer, and/or he wants to express his anger toward the hearer. It also implies that the event is very urgent so that the speaker wants an immediate reaction and a result from the hearer.

Imperative *-ta* might first be introduced to the nonnative speaker through the cry of the *yaoya* or grocery salesman, encouraging potential customers to buy his goods:

(3) Saa, banana kat-ta, kat-ta!
well banana buy-PAST buy-PAST
'Bananas for sale!'

[1] For those interested in a more thorough account, my Master's thesis on the same topic is available at http://www.lunduniversity.lu.se/o.o.i.s?id=24923&postid=1579617.

Alternatively, through the traditional shout of the sumo judge or *gyoozi,* encouraging the wrestlers to fight hard and stay in the ring:

(4) Nokot-ta nokot-ta!
remain-PAST remain-PAST
'Hang in there!'

Or (as most probably seen in a gangster- or samurai movie) through the cry of the *tyoohan*[2] dealer, informing the gamblers that the time has come to make a bet:

(5) Saa, hat-ta hat-ta!
well place-PAST place-PAST
'Place your bets!'

Although these stylized expressions are possibly the most striking uses of imperative *-ta*, the construction is also used in everyday speech. However, it may, excepting the stylized expressions which require its use, always be replaced by an imperative construction using the *-te* or *-e* (*ro*) verbal suffixes.

(6) Tyotto mat-te/ mat-ta!
little wait-IMP/wait-PAST
'Wait a little!'

The verbs used tend towards basic vocabulary describing everyday actions, such as *miru* 'see', *doku* 'move over', *yameru* 'stop' *kau* 'buy' *matu* 'wait' and the like. The limited range of vocabulary employed may be regarded as a consequence of the informal contexts in which imperative *-ta* is normally used rather than a restriction inherent to the construction itself.

Iteration of the verb is exceedingly common in imperative -ta, somewhat less so when the verb is paired with adverbs. The phenomenon is not exclusive to imperative -ta, being seen in imperatives employing the suffixes -e (ro) and -te as well, although not as consistently as with -ta.

(7) Hora, damar-e damar-e/ damat-ta damat-ta!
hey be.quiet-IMP be.quiet-IMP /be.quiet-PAST be.quiet-PAST
'Shut up! Shut up!'

2 A form of gambling involving dice.

In the case of *suru* verbs, only the verb itself is repeated, not the noun.

(8) Moo anta ossan da kara, intai si-ta si-ta!
Already you old man COP because retirement do-PAST do-PAST
'You're an old man now! Go retire!'

Some of the sociolinguistic properties of imperative *-ta* are also worth mentioning. While Hirata states that it is the least polite of all imperative constructions, both Shirota (1998:34) and my informant confirm that imperative *-ta* may, as with the *-e* (*ro*) imperative, be used not only as a rude way of giving an order, but also as a way of displaying intimacy among close friends.

Imperative *-ta* is not as often used as other imperative constructions. On the occasions in which imperative *-ta* is used by younger people, it is often employed in an ironic manner to make an order or request seem comical. However, there are still instances in which imperative *-ta* is used by people of younger generations with none of this comical intent. Among older speakers the 'serious' use of imperative *-ta* seems to be more prevalent, and it is used by middle aged people towards younger people with no humorous undertones.

As previously mentioned, there are generally no circumstances under which a *-ta* imperative may not be replaced with another imperative construction. However, the inverse is not true. While the use of all imperative constructions in Japanese is governed by social factors, imperative *-ta* is also subject to restrictions in context of utterance and in the auxiliary verbs and particles which may be used with it. To exemplify, the *-ta* imperative can replace another imperative construction only in an utterance in which the following criteria are met.

1. The speaker in is a position to make an informal request of the hearer.
2. In the context of the utterance, the speaker desires that the action ordered be immediately carried out.
3. The hearer is capable of voluntarily and immediately performing said action.
4. The verb used expresses an instantaneous transition from one state to another, corresponding with the notion of perfective (or completive) aspect.

The requirement that the speaker be in a position to make an informal request of the hearer renders impossible the use of honorific verbs and expressions with imperative *-ta*.

(9) Mesiagare!/ *mesiagat-ta mesiagat-ta!
eat (HON)-IMP eat (HON)-PAST eat (HON)-PAST
'Eat!'

However, the sociolinguistic 'restrictions' on imperative *-ta* usage are probably less binding than the grammatical restrictions described below. For instance, the use of the form when speaking to superiors is not ungrammatical, but would appear strange under most circumstances.

The degree of urgency involved in the context of the sentence is crucial in determining whether the use of imperative *-ta* is acceptable. The following sentence (without any explicit context) would not typically merit the use of imperative *-ta*:

(10) Mado o ake-ro/ ?ake-ta!
window OBJ open-IMP/ open-PAST
'Open the window!'

However, if we supply a fitting context, imperative *-ta* can be used.

(11) Kusai! Mado o ake-ro/ ake-ta!
foul-smelling window OBJ open-IMP/open-PAST
'It stinks in here! Open the window!'

As pointed out by Hirata (1987:56) among others, imperative *-ta* cannot be negated, nor used to express a negative command.

(12) Yaru na/ *yar-anakat-ta!
do-NIMP/ do-NEG-PAST
'Don't do it!'

Soga (1983:67) explains the reason for this restriction thus:

> There is no negative form of the indirect command using the past tense form [...] The reason for this seems to be that the verb in the indirect command of the *-ta* form must be 'completive' in its underlying structure. However, a negative Japanese verb becomes adjectival and so imperfective, thus becoming irrelevant to the notion of completion.

The demand that the verb be 'completive' in nature is highly relevant to the overall function of imperative *-ta*. Because of this restriction, temporal adverbials expressing that the action ordered takes place over a period of time may not be used in an imperative *-ta* sentence.

(13) Go-hun ma-te/ *mat-ta!
five minutes wait-IMP/ wait-PAST
'Wait for five minutes!'

The imperfective (or progressive) auxiliary *-te iru* may also not be used.

(14) Mat-te i-ro/ *mat-te i-ta!
wait-GER be-IMP/ wait-GER be-PAST
'Wait!'

Finally, no sentence final particles may be used in an imperative *-ta* construction.

(15) Mate yo/ *mat-ta mat-ta yo
wait-IMP FP wait-PAST wait-PAST FP
'Wait!'

3. The issue of aspect

In Svahn (2007), the position was taken that *-tari* expressed perfect aspect and that, diachronically, the driving force behind imperative *-ta* was a remnant of this function, expressing a 'fossilized perfect' as modern *-ta* is mainly a past tense suffix. The terms 'perfective' and 'completive' were also used, especially when discussing the aspectual properties of the verbs used with the construction. However, in view of the discussion of imperative *-ta* in a more complex diachronic and cross-linguistic context (as outlined in the following sections), it is attractive to look upon the construction as being expressed through a 'perfective-completive' manifestation of fossilized aspect rather than through perfect aspect.

Soga (1983:25) states that perfective aspect is most often, but not always, associated with a notion of completion of the action described, citing examples from Japanese such as *Sinu tokoro da* 'He is about to die' and *Itu yomihazimeru ka* 'When will (you) start reading?' as demonstrating the use of perfective verbs in a noncompletive context. By adopting the moniker 'perfective-completive' we clarify what is meant by the use of the term 'perfective', while remaining terminologically compatible with most uses of the terms 'perfective' and 'completive' in the context of imperative constructions. This makes for a more coherent description of the phenomenon and allows for an easier integration into the abovementioned broader perspective.

My view is as follows: The aspectual context of imperative *-ta* is that of a 'perfective-completive'. An action is viewed as bounded and complete(d), but not necessarily relevant to a current event as in the case of the perfect.

Future references to the form as 'perfective' are to be interpreted in this sense. Whether we regard older *-tari* as expressing perfect (Sansom 1928), completive (Soga 1983), perfective (Shinzato 2005), or stative aspect (Frellesvig 2010), the modern *-ta* and *-tari* imperatives are contextually tied to the completion of an action, and this forms their aspectual basis.

4. Perfective imperatives crosslinguistically

Languages from various language families exhibit constructions similar to the Japanese perfective imperative. The study on which this article is based includes examples from (among others) German, Russian, Polish, Persian, Swedish, and Mandarin Chinese.

My attempt to identify perfective imperatives in other languages is in conjunction with the search for hortative and near-future uses of past tense or perfective markers, as the two constructions show many similarities in Japanese. Based on data from the languages examined, I posit a typological generalization: Languages that employ the past/perfective to express the certain future are more likely to also express the imperative through their use than languages that do not. Conversely, the use of a past/perfective marker as an imperative may often occur in tandem with uses of the past/perfective to express the certain future.

A fair amount has been written on the use of pasts in expressing vagueness, politeness and creating distancing effects (Fleischman 1989 is an example). Their use in expressing forcefulness and certainty is not as well explored. However, the concept of *deictic projection* as first advanced by Lyons (1977) has been used by Tavangar and Amouzadeh (2006) to account for related phenomena. In their article the term describes a shifting of the temporal deictic center.

> In sharp contrast to those cases where the projected past is used to express such concepts as supposition [or] tentativeness [...] the version under study is characterized by its implications of factivity. In other words, *future events, states or processes are envisaged as having already materialized* [my emphasis] [...] although the future as such is not observable, [...] we are enabled, through metaphorization, to observe it by attributing to it an intrinsic property associated with the past: certainty of occurrence. (Tavangar and Amouzadeh 2006:98).

Although their approach is interesting, the descriptive focus of their article is on Persian, and they do not provide a detailed account of constructions in other languages.

In my survey I have relied on a number of native informants in listing the basic properties of related phenomena crosslinguistically. This method takes as its starting point the distinctive features of the Japanese perfective imperative. Consequently constructions were compared based on their level of formality, circumstances of use, restrictions in lexical aspect and productivity, complexity of utterance, and expected emotional state in the speaker at time of utterance.

Three distinct categories of past tense or perfective uses appear. The first category is what I term the 'Let's go/I'm off' use. Verbs of movement are used in the first person plural or singular to announce one's imminent departure, or function as hortatives.

Swedish:

(16) (Kom) så gick vi.
come-IMP so go-PAST we
We are off now.' (lit. 'Come and we went.')

Persian:

(17) Mæn ræft-æm!
I go-PAST-1SG
'I'm going!' (lit. 'I went.')

Mandarin Chinese:

(18) Wǒ zǒu le.
I go LE
'I'm off.' (lit. 'I have gone.')

There are also the certain futures, expressing the speaker's belief that the realization of an event is absolutely assured.

Japanese:

(19) Make-ta, make-ta!
lose-PAST lose-PAST
'[We] are going to lose!' (lit. 'We lost!')

Persian:

(20) Ma bāxt-im!
we lose-PAST-1SG
'We are going to lose!' (lit. 'We lost!')

Finally there are the imperatives or commands.

German:
(21) Still ge-blieb-en!
Quiet PTCP-keep-PTCP
'Keep quiet!' (lit. '[Has] kept quiet!')

Russian:
(22) Poše-l!
go-PAST-2SG
'Go!' (lit. '[You] went!') (Shirota 1998:34)

Persian:
(23) Xor-di-yo zud umæ-di.
drink-PAST.2SG-and quickly come-PAST.2SG
'You may drink and come back quickly.'
(Tavangar and Amouzadeh 2009:868)

As is to be expected the constructions show variation in the particulars of usage among the different languages, but do seem to have the properties of hurried, informal, and emotionally loaded contexts in common. Some of the constructions may derive originally from markers of past tense, but there is also evidence for development from passives (German), subjunctives (Russian) and imperative forms (Swedish) (Svahn 2010). What unifies these phenomena is the perfective/completive aspect of the verbs in conjunction with an ostensible marker of past tense/perfective aspect.[3] Still, before declaring the perfective imperative a valid crosslinguistic category it should be noted that this aspectual tendency may perhaps be accounted for by other means.

The tendency for perfective verbs to occur together with the imperative use of past tense markers may be related to the general connection between pasts and perfectives (for more on this connection, see Dahl 1985:78). There is also the possibility that hurried orders tend towards perfective utterances ('Wait up!' as opposed to 'Wait one hour!') and that this apparent restriction has to do with a distribution of verbal aspect governed by context rather than factors inherent to the constructions. This can be compared with the case of imperative *-ta*, which in a strict sense lacks some of the restrictions (for instance, use only with action verbs) assumed by previous scholars, but requires specific contexts to appear in utterances that do not fulfil them.

[3] Or perfect in the case of German.

5. The diachrony of the perfective imperative in Japanese

A number of hypotheses as to the historical development of the perfective imperative can be postulated, all with their consequences in interpreting the diachronic evolution as well as synchronic function of the constructions.

Early Middle Japanese *-tari* survives today in the form of representative-*tari...-tari*, derived forms such as the conditional *-tara* and the discourse particle *-ttara*. To this list we can add imperative *-tari,* which is considerably more obscure than the others. It is a construction that to some extent exists today along with imperative *-ta*. However, it is no longer part of the native competence of most speakers. Imperative *-tari* and its historical connection to imperative *-ta* are at the center of the historical discussion.

Among others Yoshida (1971) and Shinzato (2005) have made interesting statements on imperative *-tari*. Yoshida gives perhaps the most complete account of imperative *-ta* and its historical development available. He provides the (to my knowledge) earliest potential attestation of the perfective imperative, the use of *Matta*! 'Wait!' in a kabuki play from 1715 (1971:240), although he notes that it it is not clear if it is a true example of the form. Nonetheless, if valid this attestation of the *-ta* imperative predates that of its *-tari* counterpart, first attested in *Ukiyoburo* (1809).

Several hypotheses can be made as to the emergence and function of imperative *-ta* and *-tari*. Among the more notable are Yoshida's suggestions that they are derived from *-tare*, the original imperative form of *-tari* (although he himself dismisses this idea) or that it originates in the imperative use of the *renyookei* of *-tari*. Another hypothesis is that their function lies in the use of *-tari* as a nominalizer, *Doitari*! being comparable to *Taizyoo*! 'Exit!' (Cho 2003).

Most promising, however, is the proposal that imperative *-ta*/*-tari* are ultimately derived from …*-tari* …*-tari*, as suggested by Shinzato Rumiko and independently by Bjarke Frellesvig (personal communication). In an unpublished conference paper (2005) kindly provided by Shinzato Rumiko, she traces the development of *-tari* from perfective suffix in Old Japanese (ca. 700 CE) to discourse particles in the modern language. Touching upon imperative *-tari* as one of the later evolved uses of the form, she theorizes that the use of *-tari* as a request is directly related to its perfectivity. Shinzato describes the use of …*-tari* …*-tari* in Middle Japanese (ca. 1300 CE) to relate the iterated occurrence of similar actions and states that the development of the request sense of the construction took place in Early Modern Japanese (1600 CE). Her view of the construction is thus that it originates in the precursor to modern representative ...-*tari*...-*tari*[4] and that the perfectivity of the -*tari* suffix is what forms the basis for its use as an imperative.

This view ties in with the previous discussion of perfective-completive aspect, providing a link between the historical development of -*tari*, -*ta*, and the perfective imperative as a cross-linguistic phenomenon. It is also helpful in explaining the phenomenon of iteration of the verb so often found in -*tari* and -*ta* imperatives, as it is a prominent feature of iterative -*tari*.

Having accepted the ...-*tari*...-*tari* hypothesis as the most plausible, a timeline of the development of the perfective imperative in Japanese can be presented thus:

1. From representative ...-*tari* ...-*tari* is derived a use as an imperative. This imperative is associated with the use of -*tari* in a perfective-completive context. At this stage, -*ta* has already replaced -*tari* as the main past tense suffix of Japanese.

2. From imperative -*tari* emerges the phonetically reduced form imperative -*ta*, possibly through analogy with past tense -*ta*. Both imperative -*tari* and -*ta* are used in the middle to late Edo period, perhaps with little to no difference in use.

3. Imperative -*tari* falls into disuse and becomes archaic and humorous in tone, while imperative -*ta* retains its function as a rude imperative.

4. Today few speakers use or even recognize the -*tari* imperative. Furthermore, the -*ta* imperative is regarded by my informant as old-fashioned and humorous, although it is still used seriously at times. It is probable that the -*ta* imperative will undergo the same process of attrition as imperative -*tari*.

---

[4] In Modern Japanese this construction examplifies different actions: *Hanbaagaa o tabetari, tabako o suttari suru koto ga suki desu* 'I like doing things like eating hamburgers and smoking'.

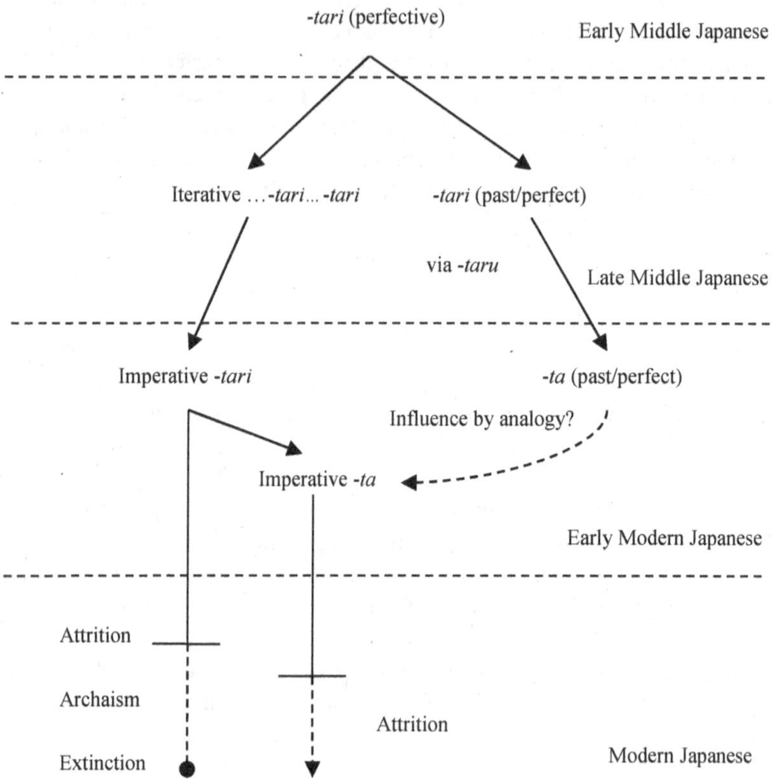

Figure 1. Hypothetical timeline of the Japanese perfective imperative

A clear time and place for the emergence of imperative *-tari* cannot be fixed, although my guess is the Kanto region, the reason being that the written sources available are from Edo and reflect the Edo vernacular. There is also anecdotal evidence that speakers of dialects other than Tokyo Japanese are especially unfamiliar with imperative *-tari.* It is possible that the construction existed for some time before being recorded in writing, giving us a period of no later than the first decade of the 1800s if we stick to *Ukiyoburo* as the first solid attestation.

There are some issues with the account presented above, particularly relating to the matter of aspect. Although this article has followed Shinzato (2005) in presenting the origin of the imperatives as a perfective there is a widely held view that *-tari* is a stative in earlier forms of Japanese (Sandness 1999:19, Frellesvig 2010:69).

Reconciling the view of *-tari* as a stative marker with its later development into an imperative restricted to completive or perfective contexts[5] seems to me a more complex task than outlining its hypothetical transition from perfective marker to perfective imperative, as has been done here. The viability of a 'stative to perfective' hypothesis is a fitting topic for future research.

A further task is to account for the featural differences between *...-tari...-tari* and the perfective imperative(s). As Kinuhata Tomohide and Murasugi Keiko (personal communication) respectively point out, modern *...-tari...-tari* (among other differences) requires the verbs involved to be different (as in for instance *tabetari* [...] *suttari*) and allows for negation both among the *-tari* verbs (*kitari konakattari sita* 'Did things like coming and not coming') and the final verb *suru* 'do' (*ittari kitari sinakatta* 'Did not do things like coming and going').[6]

6. Conclusion

This description of the origin and function of the perfective imperative in Japanese is not a definitive one, although it is probably the most complete account available on the topic. Still, an analysis of one or two constructions is not sufficient to understand the full range of 'nonmorphological' imperative uses in Japanese, and a detailed survey of the alternation between different constructions in the imperative system as a whole may prove rewarding. The search for perfective imperatives or similar peripheral constructions in Japanese and Ryukyuan dialects should also not be neglected as a topic for the future.

Beyond Japanese linguistics, a promising avenue of future research is the further exploring of uses of past tense and perfective-completive aspect as manifested in certain futures, hortatives and imperatives, through a contrastive and typological mapping out of their use in the languages of the world. Much has yet to be said about these kinds of constructions, and the very existence of the 'past tense imperative' as a valid category is still uncertain; the only common feature identified being a tendency towards the use of perfective-completive aspect. Still, it is probable that thousands of languages throughout human history have had past or perfective markers take on function of expressing a command. Hundreds of them are probably around today. What was viewed as a quirk of Japanese pragmatics may now

---

[5] For references to imperative *-ta* as being the latter, see Soga (1983), Hirata (1987), Svahn (2007, 2010).

[6] If one of the *-tari* verbs is negated then iteration is permissible.

be placed in a wider category, as a linguistic phenomenon shared in principle, if not in the details of usage and historical development, with many other languages.

References

Cho, M. 2003.'Ta' no mentaru supeesu rironteki kaishaku (An interpretation of *-ta* based on the mental space theory). *Journal of Human Environmental Studies* 1. 63-79.

Dahl, Ö. 1985. *Tense and Aspect Systems*. Oxford: Basil Blackwell. [Available at http://www.ling.su.se/staff/oesten/recycled/Tense&aspectsystems.pdf]

Fleischman, S. 1989. Temporal distance: A basic linguistic metaphor. *Studies in Language* 13: 1-50.

Frellesvig, B. 2010. *A History of the Japanese Language*. Cambridge: Cambridge University Press.

Hirata, K. 1987. *Temporal Properties in Japanese*. PhD dissertation, University of Arizona, Tucson.

Lyons, J. 1977. *Semantics*. Vol. 2. Cambridge: Cambridge University Press.

Sandness, K. 1999. *The Evolution of the Japanese Past and Perfective Suffixes* (Michigan Monograph Series in Japanese Studies, No. 26). Ann Arbor: Center for Japanese Studies, The University of Michigan.

Sansom, G. 1928. *A Historical Grammar of Japanese*. London: Oxford University Press.

Shinzato, R. 2005. *Perfective auxiliary to discourse markers: A case of Old Japanese* tari. Unpublished conference paper.

Shirota, S. 1998. *Nihongokeitairon* (Japanese Morphology). Tokyo: Hitsujishoboo.

Soga, M. 1983. *Tense and aspect in modern colloquial Japanese*. Vancouver: University of British Colombia Press.

Svahn, A. 2007. *Imperative -ta in colloquial Japanese: A descriptive analysis*. Bachelor's thesis, Lund University.

Svahn, A. 2010. *The perfective imperative in Japanese: A further analysis*. Master's thesis, Lund University.

Tavangar, M. & Amouzadeh, M. 2006. Deictic projection: An enquiry into the future-oriented past tense in Persian. *Studia Linguistica* 60: 97-120.

Tavangar, M. & Amouzadeh, M. 2009. Subjective modality and tense in Persian. *Language Sciences* 31: 853-873.

Yoshida, K. 1971. *Gendai jodooshi no shiteki kenkyuu* (Historical Research on Modern Auxiliaries). Tokyo: Meiji Shoin.

'Topic' and 'Contrast': A Comparative Approach to Japanese and Korean

REIKO VERMEULEN*
Ghent University

There is overwhelming evidence in the literature that [topic], [focus] and [contrast] are autonomous notions of information structure that syntax may target. Moreover, there is also some evidence that contrastive topic should be treated as a composite of [topic] and [contrast], and similarly, contrastive focus as a composite of [focus] and [contrast] (Vallduví & Vilkuna 1998, Molnár 2002). Based on these two ideas, Neeleman et al. (2009) propose the following syntactic typology of information structural notions:

*The research reported here has been funded by the FWO (No. G091409), the AHRC (No. 119403) and the British Academy (No. SG50500). I thank Ad Neeleman, Daniel Büring and Jieun Kim for many inspiring discussions. I also thank my informants for their patient help.

Japanese/Korean Linguistics 20.
Edited by Bjarke Frellesvig and Peter Sells.

Table 1. Syntactic typology of topic, focus and contrast

	Topic	**Focus**
	noncontrastive topic [topic]	information focus [focus]
Contrast	contrastive topic [topic] [contrast]	contrastive focus [focus] [contrast]

The main empirical motivation for the above typology comes from the observation that languages show crosscutting generalisations over the syntactic distribution of items sharing one of the three privative notions. Thus, in some languages contrastive items behave alike, whilst in other languages topics behave alike, for instance. One way to understand this observation is to propose that there are discrete mapping rules between syntax and information structure pertaining to each notion. Neeleman et al. provide Dutch, Russian and Japanese as example languages with mapping rules pertaining to [contrast], [focus] and [topic], respectively.

In this paper, I provide further support for the typology in 0 from Japanese and Korean. Nothing inherent in the typology prevents one language from having mapping rules relevant for more than one notion. However, if a language has a rule for [topic] and another rule for [contrast], for instance, it is not immediately clear which rule should be relevant for contrastive topics in that language. In such a situation, I argue that the language adopts one rule over the other. This predicts that a contrastive topic should systematically behave either like a contrastive focus or a noncontrastive topic in that language. My claim is that Japanese and Korean exemplify precisely these situations. Specifically, I argue that Japanese and Korean have the same rule pertaining to [topic] and also the same rule for [contrast]. For contrastive topics, however, Japanese adopts the rule for [topic], while Korean adopts the one relevant for [contrast].

In Section 1 I first clarify the notions [topic], [focus] and [contrast] that I adopt in this paper. Section 2 discusses the distribution of noncontrastive topics in Japanese and Korean and shows that the two languages share the same rule for [topic]. Section 3 examines the distribution of contrastive foci and show that the two languages have the same rule relevant for [contrast]. In Section 4 I show that contrastive topics in Japanese behave like noncontrastive topics with respect to the rule for [topic], while Korean contrastive topics behave like contrastive foci regarding the rule for [contrast]. Finally, there are some phrases marked by the so-called topic markers *wa* in Japanese and *nun* in Korean that do not fall under the category [topic] on the definition adopted in this paper. I show in Section 5 that the current proposal makes correct predictions concerning their syntactic distribution.

1. Terminologies

The notion of [topic] that this paper adopts is that of 'sentence topic' and not 'discourse topic' (Reinhart 1981). A sentence topic is a syntactic category that newly introduces a referent as what the rest of the sentence is about, while a discourse topic is what the whole discourse is about and can be much more abstract. A referent introduced by a sentence topic often also functions as a discourse topic. The distinction between a sentence topic and a discourse topic is widely recognised in the literature. A sentence topic is known variously as 'chain-initial topic' (Givón 1983), 'link' (Vallduví 1992), or 'aboutness topic' (Frascarelli & Hinterhölzl 2007).[1] I will use the term 'topic' to refer to a sentence topic whenever the distinction is clear.

A sentence topic can be identified as the item *X* in an answer to the request *tell me about X* (Reinhart 1981). Such a request explicitly instructs the hearer to introduce *X* as the discourse topic and make a statement about it. Thus, *John* in Speaker B's utterance below is a sentence topic.

(2) A: Tell me about John.
B: Well, John_{TOP} is a student from Canada.

Sentence topics must also be distinguished from discourse given items that simply refer back to them (Givón 1983, Chafe 1987, Lambrecht 1994, Vallduví & Engdahl 1996). Uttered discourse-initially, *Max* in the question in (3A) is a sentence topic: native speakers of English generally interpret this question as being about Max. However, the pronoun *he* in the reply by B is not a sentence topic. It does not newly introduce the referent as what the sentence is about. It is merely a discourse given item whose antecedent happens to be a sentence topic. Utterances such as (3B) can be analysed as consisting only of a comment, inheriting its discourse topic from the previous utterance (Vallduví 1992, Vallduví & Engdahl 1996).

(3) A: Who did Max_{TOP} see yesterday?
B: He saw Rosa yesterday.

Sentence topics are reported to have distinct grammatical effects in various languages, in comparison to discourse topics or items referring back to them, such as the directionality of dislocation (Vallduví 1992, Lambrecht 1994) and distinct prosodic properties (Frascarelli & Hinterhölzl 2007).

---

[1] 'Sentence topic' is similar to, but not identical to, Kuno's (1973) notion 'theme'. Kuno assumes that any phrase marked by *wa* without a contrastive interpretation is a theme. However, I have argued in Vermeulen (2010) that not all *wa*-marked phrases are sentence topics.

As for focus, I adopt the standard assumption that it is a new piece of information with respect to the rest of the sentence (Rooth 1992, Schwarzchild 1997). It can therefore be identified as the item answering the *wh*-expression of the preceding question. Thus, *Rosa* in (3B) is a focus.

Turning to contrast, I take 'contrast' to be a notion that can combine with focus or topic. In either case, I assume that a statement containing a contrastive item is associated with a set of alternatives out of which it is selected (É. Kiss 1998). There are differences in the implicature between contrastive topics and contrastive foci, deriving from the fact that focus is propositional, while a topic is an utterance-level notion (Tomioka 2010). In the simplest cases a statement with a contrastive item implies the rejection of at least one of the relevant alternatives. I will not go into the details of the precise meaning of 'contrast' due to lack of space (see Repp 2010 for an overview), but instead introduce discourse contexts that are widely adopted for contrastive foci and contrastive topics.

A typical context requiring a contrastive focus is a correction context, such as (4). *The Extended Phenotype* in B's utterance is a contrastive focus. By uttering the statement, B implies that the alternative proposition with a different object expressed by A is false. A contrastive focus carries the so-called A-accent in English (Jackendoff 1972):

(4) A: John read The Selfish Gene.
B: No, he read The Extended Phenotype$_{CF}$.
{[John read The Extended Phenotype],
~~[John read The Selfish Gene]~~,...}

A context which requires a contrastive topic is illustrated in (5) (see also Büring 1997, 2003, Tomioka 2010). The question by A is about Bill, but B's reply is about Maxine, shifting the topic of discourse from Bill to Maxine. *Maxine* is therefore a sentence topic that is interpreted contrastively. By uttering the sentence, B implies that an alternative assertion regarding Bill cannot be made. Unlike the case of contrastive focus, what is rejected here is an utterance, because topic is an utterance-level notion. The reason for this rejection could be pragmatic. It could be that the speaker does not know the truth value of the proposition expressed by the alternative utterance, as made explicit in (5B). It could also be the case that the speaker knows the truth value of the proposition expressed by an alternative utterance, but wishes not to communicate it. A contrastive topic in English carries the so-called B-accent (Jackendoff 1972, Büring 2003).

(5) A: Tell me about Bill. Did he read the Selfish Gene?
B: Well, I don't know about Bill, but Maxine$_{CT}$ read The Selfish Gene.
{Assert[Maxine read The Selfish Gene], ~~Assert[Bill read the Selfish Gene]~~, ...}

The exchanges in (4) and (5) illustrate the default interpretation of a contrastive focus and a contrastive topic, respectively. However, the negative implicature regarding at least one alternative in the set can be modified by particles such as *only*, *also* and *even*. *Only* implies that all relevant alternatives are false, *also* implies that there is at least one other alternative which is true or can be asserted, and *even* indicates that there are alternatives that are true, but less remarkable than the one selected. I take phrases marked by such particles to be contrastive items too and assume that they fall under the category 'contrast' for the purpose of the syntactic typology in (1) (See Neeleman & van de Koot 2008 for evidence from Dutch supporting this view). This last point will be relevant in Section 5, where I discuss the contrastive meaning of *wa* in Japanese and *nun* in Korean.

2. [Topic]: noncontrastive topics

In this section I demonstrate that Japanese and Korean have the same mapping rule pertaining to the notion [topic], informally stated as in (6).

(6) [Topic] is licensed in clause-initial position.

(6) is very much in line with what is generally assumed in the literature (Kuno 1973, Kuroda 2005, Heycock 2008 and references therein for Japanese; Choe 1995, Choi 1997, 1999, Han 1998, for Korean). The following data confirm (6) with a relevant discourse context discussed in Section 1.

(7) ano boosi-nituite nanika osiete-kudasai. (J)
'Tell me something about that hat.'

(8) a. ano boosi-wa$_{TOP\text{-}i}$	John-ga kinoo	e_i	kaimasita.[2]
b. #John-ga	ano boosi-wa$_{TOP}$	kinoo	kaimasita.
John-NOM	that hat-WA	yesterday	bought

'John bought that hat yesterday.'

---

[2] For reasons not entirely clear to me, *wa-* or *nun*-marked phrases sometimes prefer not to surface adjacent to the verb. I insert an adverbial to circumvent this effect. This does not affect the discussion in the main text. I also assume that an object preceding an adverbial, as in (8b) and (10b) can be base-generated in that position (Neeleman & Reinhart 1998).

(9) ku moca-eytayhayse mal-hay-po-a.[3] (K)
'Tell me about this hat.'

(10) a. ku moca-nun$_{TOP-i}$ John-i ecey e_i sasse.
b. #John-i ku moca-nun$_{TOP}$ ecey sasse.
John-NOM this hat-NUN yesterday bought
'John bought this hat yesterday.'

It has been reported on occasion that a noncontrastive *wa*-phrase in Japanese can appear elsewhere (Kuroda 1988, Watanabe 2003). I argue in Vermeulen (2010), however, that such *wa*-phrases are not sentence topics, but discourse given items referring back to topics, like the pronoun in (3B), with distinct grammatical effects. I will thus not discuss such cases here.[4]

With respect to what triggers the displacement, I argue that it is motivated by its effect at the interface. It creates a transparent mapping between the syntactic structure and the topic-comment structure at the level of information structure (for the nature of the empty category, see Saito 1985, Hoji 1985). I take this effect to be an instantiation of a mapping rule regarding [topic] (see Neeleman & van de Koot 2008), as illustrated in (11). For concreteness, I assume that the topic is adjoined to the highest maximal projection in the clause. I will return to the effects of (15) in Section 5.

(11) *Mapping rule for [topic]*
Syntax: $[_{TP}$ XP_i $[_{TP}$ (pro_i/t_i) $]]$
I.S.: Topic Comment

3. [Contrast]: contrastive focus

In this section, I demonstrate that Japanese and Korean have the same rule relevant for the notion [contrast], informally stated in (12).

(12) [Contrast] licenses scrambling.

In both Japanese and Korean, a contrastive focus in a correction context can remain in-situ, or undergo scrambling to a clause-medial or clause-initial position, as demonstrated by (13)/(14) and (15)/(16), respectively. (Here and below, SMALL CAPS indicate emphatic stress (raised F_0-peak).)

[3] In Korean, the nominative case marker is realised as *ka* after a vowel and as *i* elsewhere. Similarly, the accusative marker is *lul* if following a vowel and *ul* elsewhere, and the putative topic marker is *nun* after a vowel and *un* elsewhere.

[4] See Shimojo & Choi (2001) for differences between Japanese and Korean on the morphological marking of topics.

(13) John-wa Sue-ni CD-o agemasita. (J)
'John gave a CD to Sue.'

(14) a. Ie, John-wa Sue-ni ANO HON-O_{CF} agemasita.
b. Ie, John-wa ANO HON-$O_{CF\text{-}i}$ Sue-ni t_i agemasita.
c. Ie, ANO HON-$O_{CF\text{-}i}$ John-wa Sue-ni t_i agemasita.[5]
No, that book-ACC John-WA Sue-to gave
'No, John gave that book to Sue.'

(15) John-i Sue-eykey CD-ul cwuess-e. (K)
'John gave a CD to Sue.'

(16) a. Ani, John-i Sue-eykey KU CHAYK-UL_{CF} cwuess-e.
b. Ani, John-i KU CHAYK-$UL_{CF\text{-}i}$ Sue-eykey t_i cwuess-e.
c. Ani, KU CHAYK-$UL_{CF\text{-}i}$ John-i Sue-eykey t_i cwuess-e.
No, that book-ACC John-NOM Sue-to gave-DECL
'No, John gave that book to Sue.'

In both languages, a phrase answering a simple *wh*-question, such as 'what did John give to Sue?' can also undergo the same kind of scrambling as in (14) and (15). Thus, one may wonder whether the relevant notion in licensing the kind of scrambling above is [focus] rather than [contrast]. However, speakers report that scrambling of a focus in such a context clearly requires accommodation of an additional contrastive interpretation. I conclude therefore that it is the notion [contrast] that licenses optional scrambling of the above type by a contrastive focus.

For concreteness, I assume following Neeleman et al. (2009) that scrambling of a contrastive item is motivated by interface considerations, like the displacement of a topic discussed earlier. Specifically, Neeleman et al. argue that contrast is quantificational and therefore takes scope. The scope of contrast ('domain of contrast' in their terminology) is the sister constituent to the scrambled item, as illustrated by the mapping rule for [contrast] in 0 and determines the material to be included in the set of alternatives. In (14c)/(16c), the object scrambles to clause-initial position. Thus, all other material in the clause is included in the scope of contrast, yielding the set of alternative propositions of the form 'John gave x to Sue.' In (14b)/(16b), on the other hand, the subject is not included in the scope of contrast. Assuming that contrast operates minimally on the level of propositions (Schwarzchild 1999), existential closure applies to the VP, the sister

[5] This is an example of a noncontrastive *wa*-phrase in a position other than clause-initial position, mentioned at the end of the previous section. See Vermeulen (2010) for discussion.

constituent to the scrambled direct object, yielding a set of alternative propositions of the form 'someone gave x to Sue.' (See Neeleman et al. (2009) for further discussion.)

(17) *Mapping rule for [contrast]*

Syntax: $[_{YP}$ XP_i $[_{YP}$ t_i $]]$

I.S.: Contrastive Focus/Topic — Scope of Contrast

4. Contrastive Topics

Before examining the distribution of contrastive topics, a remark is in order regarding the particles *wa* in Japanese and *nun* in Korean. Contrastive topics are marked by the two particles in the respective languages, like their noncontrastive counterparts discussed in Section 2. However, it is often claimed that the particle that attaches to a noncontrastive topic and the one that attaches to a contrastive topic are two different lexical items (Kuroda 1965, 2005, Kuno 1973, Oshima 2008, Lee 2006, Hetland 2007). In both languages the particle appearing on a contrastive topic is associated with a distinct set of properties: it is emphatically stressed, shows much freer syntactic distribution and induces a contrastive interpretation. In line with this general view, I treat *wa* and *nun* that attach to contrastive topics as different lexical items from those that attach to noncontrastive topics and refer to them as 'contrastive *wa*' and 'contrastive *nun*', respectively. Their contrastive meaning will be discussed in the next section, where I show that they are also compatible with contrastive foci.

The following exchange shows that contrastive topics in Japanese must move to clause-initial position, like their noncontrastive counterpart, (7)/(8).

(18) Dare-ga Sue-ni ano CD-o ageta no? (J)
'Who gave that CD to Sue?'

(19) Hmm, ano CD-wa doo-da-ka siranai kedo ...
'Well, I don't know about that CD, but ...'
a. #JOHN-GA Sue-ni ANO HON-WA$_{CT}$ kinoo ageteita (yo).
b. ??JOHN-GA ANO HON-WA$_{CT\text{-}I}$ Sue-ni kinoo t_i ageteita (yo)
c. ANO HON-WA$_{CT\text{-}i}$ JOHN-GA Sue-ni kinoo t_i ageteita (yo)
that book-WA John-NOM Sue-to yesterday gave PRT
'as for that book, John gave it to Sue yesterday.'

On the other hand, contrastive topics in Korean behave like contrastive foci: they can be in-situ or scramble to a clause-medial or clause-initial position.

(20) John-I nwukwu-hanthey ku CD-lul ecey cwuesse? (K)
'To whom did John give this CD yesterday?'

(21) Hmm, ku CD-nun molu-keyss-ko
'Well, I don't know about this CD, but...'
a. John-i SUE-HANTHEY I CHAYK-UN$_{CT}$ ecey cwuesse
b. John-i I CHAYK-UN$_{CT\text{-}i}$ SUE-HANTHEY ecey t_i cwuesse
c. I CHAYK-UN$_{CT\text{-}i}$ John-i SUE-HANTHEY ecey t_i cwuesse
this book-NUN John-NOM Sue-to yesterday gave
'as for this book, John gave it to Sue yesterday.'

I conclude that Japanese contrastive topics are subject to the rule for [topic] in (11), while Korean ones are subject to the rule for [contrast] in (17).

The above data show patterns that differ from what is generally assumed in the literature. In Japanese, there are instances in which a contrastive *wa*-phrase can surface in a clause-medial position. The standard view is that a contrastive *wa*-marked phrase is a contrastive 'topic' regardless of its position in the clause (Tomioka 2010, Heycock 2008, Kishimoto 2009). In Korean, the standard description is that a contrastive *nun*-marked phrase is a contrastive 'topic' only in clause-initial position and is a contrastive 'focus' elsewhere (Choe 1995, Han 1998, Choi 1997, 1999, Gill & Tsoulas 2004). I provide below further interpretive and syntactic arguments that these standard descriptions are inaccurate.

5. Contrastive *wa*- and *nun*-phrases

5.1. The interpretation of contrastive *wa* and *nun*

There has recently been much work on the precise meaning of contrastive *wa* and *nun* (Kuroda 2005, Hara 2006, Hara & van Rooij 2007, Tomioka 2010, Oshima 2008 for Japanese; Choi 1999, Lee 1999, 2003, 2006, Hetland 2007 for Korean). For Japanese, Hara (2006), for instance, proposes that sentences containing contrastive *wa* presupposes that a scalar alternative stronger than the assertion exists and also implicates that the stronger alternative could be false. The following example, which contains a contrastive *wa*-phrase in-situ, illustrates the point. A stronger scalar alternative might contain a universal quantifier and the implicature is that this alternative could be false, i.e. John perhaps did not help everyone.

(22) John-ga NANNINKA-WA tasuketa. (J)
John-NOM some.people-WA helped
'John helped some people.' (Implicature: John did not help all)

The analysis extends to nonquantified DPs. Uttered in a context where Mary and Bill are the only salient individuals who can be helped by John, the stronger scalar alternative to (23) is that John helped both Mary and Bill. However, the speaker asserts that John helped Mary. The hearer can thus infer the intended implicature that John perhaps did not help Bill.

(23) John-ga MARY-WA tasuketa. (J)
John-NOM Mary-WA helped
'John helped Mary' (Implicature: John perhaps did not help Bill.)

There are clearly differences amongst the proposals mentioned above, but one idea shared by most is that contrastive *wa* encodes a particular implicature regarding the alternative(s) that is/are not selected. Importantly, there is nothing inherent in such a meaning of contrastive *wa* that makes the host phrase a contrastive 'topic'. (22) does not mean 'as for some people, John helped them', and (23) is not interpreted as a statement about Mary.

Accordingly, I propose that contrastive *wa* has the kind of contrastive interpretation proposed by Hara (2006). However, it only contributes a necessary element of the interpretation of a contrastive topic, and is not a sufficient one. A contrastive *wa*-phrase must additionally move to clause-initial position, if it is to function as a contrastive topic, where it can be interpreted as a topic via the mapping rule in (11). Thus, topicality and the contrastive interpretation are two independent aspects of a contrastive topic.

Some authors have proposed that contrastive *wa* does not mark contrastive 'topics', but is more akin to focal particles such as *dake* 'only', *sae* 'even' and *mo* 'also' (Kuorda 1965, 2005, Hara 2006, Oshima 2008). Indeed, as we will see in the next subsection, the implicature of *wa* is compatible also with focus, and a contrastive *wa*-phrase may function as a contrastive focus. Even so, these authors treat contrastive *wa*-phrases uniformly regardless of their clausal position. Thus, it is difficult to explain why they must occupy clause initial position in certain contexts, which we saw above.

For Korean, Lee (2006, 2008) proposes that contrastive *nun* implicates the denial of a stronger alternative, in a similar vein to Hara's proposal for contrastive *wa* (see also Hetland 2007). The examples in (24) (Choi 1999:168) and (25) have similar implicatures to the Japanese (22) and (23).

(24) John-i SEY-MYENG-NUN kwuha-yss-e. (K)
John-NOM three-CL-NUN helped
'John helped at least three people.' (Implicature: John did not help all)

(25) Swuni-ka INHO-NUN manna-ss-e. (K)
Swuni-NOM Inho-NUN meet-PAST-DECL
'Swuni met Inho.' (Implicature: Maybe Swuni did not meet others)

In a similar fashion to the claim regarding contrastive *wa* in Japanese, I argue that contrastive *nun* in Korean encodes the kind of scalar implicature proposed by Lee (2003). Whether a contrastive *nun*-phrase may function as a contrastive topic is determined independently by pragmatics.

As mentioned above, the standard view for Korean is that contrastive *nun*-phrases function as contrastive 'topics' only in clause-initial position and as contrastive 'foci' elsewhere (Choe 1995, Choi 1997, 1999, Han 1998, Gill & Tsoulas 2004). We saw in the previous section that a contrastive *nun*-phrase can function as a contrastive topic in a variety of positions and we will see below that the meaning of contrastive *nun* is also compatible with focus. In such cases a contrastive *nun*-phrase may move to clause-initial position, contrary to the standard view.

It is worth noting that when a contrastive *nun*-phrase is described as a contrastive 'focus' in the literature on Korean, the interpretation provided is rather different from one that the standard discourse and semantic literature adopts for 'contrastive focus', discussed in Section 1. For instance, Choi (1999:168), describes the example in (25) above as follows: "[(25)] implies that "Swuni met Inho, but she *probably* did not meet other people', or 'Swuni met Inho at least, but *we do not know whether* she met other people as well" (*emphasis* mine). In addition, Lee (2003, ex. (46)/(47)) shows that in a correction case such as *A: Yumi gave birth to a son. B: No, she gave birth to a daughter*, the contrastive focus, *daughter*, in B's reply in Korean must be case-marked and cannot be marked with *nun* (see also (15)/(16)). Thus, a contrastive *nun*-phrase may function as a contrastive focus, but it is loaded with the particular scalar implicature discussed above.

5.2. The distribution of contrastive *wa-/nun*-phrases

The current typological approach predicts a syntactic difference between contrastive *wa*-phrases and contrastive *nun*-phrases that are not topics. Recall that Japanese adopts for contrastive topics the rule relevant for [topic], provided in (11). This means that Japanese directly links the discourse function 'topic' with the relative position in the clause. Thus, from a functional perspective, one expects that this language would interpret any contrastive *wa*-phrase displaced to clause-initial position as a contrastive topic. In other words, if a contrastive *wa*-phrase appears in a non-initial position, moving it to clause-initial position should be disallowed. On the other hand, Korean adopts the rule relevant for [contrast] for contrastive topics, so the language does not rely on the position of a contrastive *nun*-phrase for determining its discourse function. Consequently, there should be no comparable restriction on contrastive *nun*-phrases that are not contrastive topics. The prediction is borne out in two discourse contexts.

First, a contrastive *wa-/nun*-phrase can answer the *wh*-part of the preceding question, with the implicature that an alternative utterance cannot be asserted. If we take seriously the ability to answer a *wh*-question as indicative of focushood, then the objects in (27)/(29) must be foci. As discussed above, the meaning of the particles itself does not make the host a contrastive 'topic'. Thus, like other focal particles such as *only*, *even* and *also*, nothing prevents contrastive *wa* or *nun* from attaching to a focus so long as their contrastive meaning is compatible with the discourse context given. As demonstrated by the (b)-examples, the *wa*-phrase in Japanese cannot move to clause-initial position, while the *nun*-phrase in Korean can.

(26) John-wa nani-o katta no? (J)
'What did John buy?'

(27)	a. John-wa	OSENBEE-WA$_{CF}$	tikaku-de	katta
	b. #OSEENBEE-WA$_{CF\text{-}i}$	John-wa t_i	tikaku-de	katta.
	rice.crackers-WA	John-WA	near-at	bought

'John bought rice crackers nearby.'
(Implicature: But he probably did not buy cookies.)

(28) Mary-ka nwukwu-lul poass-ni? (K)
'Who did Mary see?'

(29)	a. Mary-ka	JOHN-UN$_{CF}$	poass-ta.	
	b. JOHN-UN$_{CF\text{-}i}$	Mary-ka	t_i	poass-ta.
	John-NUN	Mary-NOM		saw-DECL

'Mary saw John' (Implicature: 'But perhaps, she did not see Bill.')

The second context exemplifies a peculiar property of contrastive *wa* and *nun*, namely that they can project the contrast to a larger constituent. In the (a)-examples of (30) and (31), contrastive *wa* and *nun* mark the subject *ame* and *pi* 'rain', respectively, in the first conjunct and the object *kasa* and *wusan* 'umbrella', respectively, in the second conjunct. The interpretation is not that the first conjunct is about rain and the second conjunct is about an umbrella, so the contrastive *wa*- and *nun*-phrases are not contrastive topics. It is also not that rain is contrasted with an umbrella. Rather, the targets of contrast are the events described by the two conjuncts. As the (b)-examples demonstrate, this context permits the Korean *nun*-phrase, but not the Japanese *wa*-phrase, to move to clause-initial position in the second conjunct. ((30a) is modified from Kuno (1973: 46) attributed to Minoru Nakau (p.c.).)

(30) [Seeing someone worried] *What's happened? / What's wrong?* (J)
a. [AME-WA hutteita-ga] [John-ga KASA-WA motte-ik-anakatta].
b. #[AME-WA hutteita-ga] [KASA-WA$_i$ John-ga *t*$_i$
rain-WA falling.was-but umbrella-WA John-NOM
motte-ik-anakatta].
bring-go-not.PAST
'It was raining, but John did not bring an umbrella.'

(31) [Seeing someone worried] *What's happened? / What's wrong?* (K)
a. [PI-NUN o-nuntey] [John-i WUSAN-UN kacyeo-ci an-hassta]
b. [PI-NUN o-nuntey] [WUSAN-UN$_i$ John-i t$_i$
rain-NUN come-but umbrella-NUN John-NOM
kacyeo-ci anh-assta]
bring-NEG NEG-PAST

At present, it is not entirely clear to me what the precise discourse function of the contrastive *wa-*/*nun*-phrases in the above examples is. The preceding question ensures that they are part of noncontrastive focus, and their interpretation suggests that they do not have the scalar implicature discussed in the previous subsection. Nonetheless, the crucial point here is the distinction in the movement possibility between the object contrastive *wa*-phrase in Japanese and the object contrastive *nun*-phrase in Korean. This is sufficient to show that the contrastive *wa*-phrase in 0 is not a contrastive topic and a contrastive *nun*-phrase that is not a contrastive topic can move to clause initial position, contrary to the standard descriptions.

6. Conclusion

In this paper, I examined the distribution of noncontrastive topics, contrastive focus and contrastive topics in Japanese and Korean and demonstrated that their syntactic patterns are predicted by the syntactic typology in 0. Specifically, I argued that the two languages have the same mapping rule for [topic] and the same one for [contrast], but for contrastive topics, Japanese adopts the rule for [topic], while Korean adopts the rule for [contrast]. The proposal also helps provide more accurate characterisations of phrases marked by contrastive *wa* and *nun*, which are not necessarily contrastive topics, both in terms of their interpretation and corresponding syntax.

References

Büring, D. 1997. *The Meaning of Topic and Focus*. London: Routledge.

Büring, D. 2003. On D-trees, beans, and B-accents. *Linguistics & Philosophy* 26: 511–545.

Chafe, W. 1987. Cognitive constraints on information flow. *Coherence and Grounding in Discourse: Typological Studies in Language Vol. XI*, ed. R. Tomlin, 21-52. Amsterdam: John Benjamins.

Choe, H. S. 1995. Focus and topic movement in Korean and licensing. *Discourse Configurational Languages*, ed. K. É. Kiss, 269-334. Oxford: OUP.

Choi, H.-W. 1997. Topic and focus in Korean: The information partition by phrase structure and morphology. *Japanese/Korean Linguistics* 6: 545-560. Stanford: CSLI.

Choi, H-W. 1999. *Optimizing Structure in Context: Scrambling and Information Structure*. Stanford: CSLI.

É. Kiss, K. 1998. Identificational focus versus information focus. *Language* 74: 245-273.

Frascarelli, M. & R. Hinterhölzl. 2007. Types of topics in German and Italian. *On Information Structure, Meaning and Form*, ed. K. Schwabe & S. Winkler, 87–116. Amsterdam: John Benjamins.

Gill, K.-H. & G. Tsoulas 2004. Peripheral Effects without Peripheral Syntax: The Left Periphery in Korean. *Peripheries*, ed. D. Adger, C. De Cat & G. Tsoulas, Kluwer: Dordrecht.

Givón, T. 1983. Introduction. *Topic Continuity in Discourse*, ed. T. Givón, 5-41. Amsterdam/Philadelphia: John Benjamins.

Han, C.-H. 1998. Asymmetry in the interpretation of *-(n)un* in Korean. *Japanese / Korean Linguistics* 7: 1-15. Stanford: CSLI.

Hara, Y. 2006. *Grammar of Knowledge Representation: Japanese Discourse Items at Interfaces*. Doctoral dissertation, University of Delaware.

Hara, Y. & R. van Rooij. 2007. Contrastive Topics Revisited: a Simpler Set of Topic-Alternatives. Talk given at *NELS* 38, University of Ottawa, Canada.

Hetland, J. 2007. The Korean particle *nun*, the English fall-rise accent and thetic/categorical judgements. *On Information Structure, Meaning and Form*, K. Schwabe & S. Winkler, 117-127. Amsterdam/Philadelphia: John Benjamins.

Heycock, C. 2008. Japanese *-wa*, *-ga*, and Information Structure. *Oxford Handbook of Japanese Linguistics,* ed. M. Saito & S. Miyagawa, 54-83. Oxford: OUP.

Hoji, H. 1985. *Logical Form Constraints and Configurational Structures in Japanese*. Doctoral dissertation, University of Washington.

Jackendoff, R. 1972. *Semantic Interpretation in Generative Grammar*. Cambridge, MA: MIT Press.

Kishimoto, H. 2009. Topic prominency in Japanese. *The Linguistic Review* 26: 465–513.

Krifka, M. 1999. Additive Particles under Stress. *Proceedings of SALT 8*: 111-128. Cornell: CLC Publications.

Kuno, S. 1973. *The Structure of the Japanese Language*. Cambridge, MA.: MIT Press.

Kuroda, S.-Y. 1965. Generative Grammatical Studies in the Japanese Language. Doctoral dissertation, MIT. [reproduced by Garland, New York, (1979)]

Kuroda, S.-Y. 1988. Whether we agree or not: A comparative syntax of English and Japanese. *Linguisticae Investigationes* 12: 1-47.

Kuroda, S.-Y. 1992. Judgment Forms and Sentence Forms. *Japanese Syntax and Semantics: Collected Papers*, 13-77. Dordrecht: Kluwer.

Kuroda, S.-Y. 2005. Focusing on the matter of topic: A study of *wa* and *ga* in Japanese. *Journal of East Asian Linguistics*, 14:1–58.

Lambrecht, K. 1994. *Information Structure and Sentence Form*. CUP.

Lee, C. 1999. Contrastive topic: A locus of the interface evidence from Korean and English. *The Semantics / Pragmatics Interface from Different Points of View*, ed. K. Turner, 317-342. Oxford: Elsevier Science.

Lee, C. 2003. Contrastive topic and/or contrastive focus. *Japanese/Korean Linguistics 12*. Stanford: CSLI.

Lee, C. 2006. Contrastive (Predicate) Topic, Intonation, and Scalar Meanings. *Topic and Focus: Crosslinguistic Perspectives on Meaning and Intonation*. ed. C. Lee, M. Gordon & D. Büring, 151-175. Dordrecht: Springer.

Molnár, V. 2002. Contrast — from a contrastive perspective. *Information Structure in a Cross-Linguistic Perspective*, H. Hallelgard, S. Johansson, B. Behrens, and C. Fabricius-Hansen, 147-161. Amsterdam/New York: Rodopi.

Neeleman, A. & T. Reinhart 1998. Scrambling and the PF interface. *The Projection of Arguments*. ed. M. Butt & W. Gueder, 309-353. Stanford: CSLI.

Neeleman, A. & H. van de Koot. 2008. Dutch scrambling and the Nature of Discourse Templates. *Journal of Comparative Germanic Linguistics* 11: 137-189.

Neeleman, A., E. Titov, H. van de Koot and R. Vermeulen. 2009. A syntactic typology of topic, focus and contrast. *Alternatives to Cartography*, ed. J. Van Craenenbroeck, 15-51. Berlin: Mouton de Gruyter.

Oshima, D. Y. 2008. Morphological vs. phonological contrastive topic marking. In *Proceedings of CLS* 41: 371-384.

Reinhart, T. 1981. Pragmatics and linguistics: An analysis of sentence topics. *Philosophica* 27: 53-94.

Repp, S. 2010. Defining 'contrast' as an information-structural notion in grammar. *Lingua* 120: 1333-1345.

Rooth, M. 1992. A theory of focus interpretation. *Natural Language Semantics* 1: 75-116.

Saito, M. 1985. *Some Asymmetries in Japanese and their Theoretical Implications*. Doctoral dissertation, MIT.

Schwarzchild, R. 1999. Givennes, AvoidF and other constraints on the placement of accent. *Natural Language Semantics* 7: 141–177

Shimojo, M. & H.-W. Choi 2001. On asymmetry in topic marking: The case of Japanese *wa* and Korean *nun*. *Proceedings of CLS* 36. eds. A. Okrent & J. Boyle, 454-467. Chicago: CLS.

Tomioka, S. 2010. Contrastive topics operate on Speech Acts. *Information Structure: Theoretical, Typological, and Experimental Perspectives*, ed. M. Zimmermann & C. Féry, 115-138. Oxford: OUP.

Vallduví, E. 1992. *The Informational Component.* New York / London: Garland.

Vallduví, E. & M. Vilkuna. 1998. On rheme and kontrast. On rheme and kontrast. *Syntax and semantics 29: The limits of syntax*, P. Culicover & L. McNally, 79-108. San Diego: Academic Press.

Vallduví E. & E. Engdahl. 1996. The linguistic realization of information packaging. *Linguistics* 34: 459-519.

Vermeulen, R. 2009. The Syntax of Topics in Japanese. Ms. Ghent University.

Vermeulen, R. 2010. Non-topical *wa*-phrases in Japanese. *Interfaces in Linguistics: New Research Perspectives*, ed. R. Folli & C. Ulbrich. Oxford: OUP

Watanabe, A. 2003. Wh and operator constructions in Japanese. *Lingua* 113: 519–558.

Measure Phrase Modification in the Extended Projection of Adjectives

AKIRA WATANABE
University of Tokyo

This paper deals with the Japanese counterparts of (1).

(1) This building is twenty meters tall.

The past literature (Hayashishita 2009 and Snyder, Wexler, and Das 1995) points to examples like (2), which only allow the comparative reading, and concludes that Japanese lacks the structure that associates a measure phrase (MP) with the neutral reading of dimensional adjectives.

(2) Kono biru-wa nijuu-meetoru takai.
This building-TOP twenty-meter tall
'This building is twenty meters taller.'
'*This building is twenty meters tall.'

The conclusion is premature, however, in view of examples like (3).

Japanese/Korean Linguistics 20.
Edited by Bjarke Frellesvig and Peter Sells.

(3) a. Kono biru-wa takasa nijuu-meetoru aru/dearu.
this building-TOP height twenty-meter is/is
'This building is twenty meters tall.'

b. Kono hako-wa omosa juk-kiro aru/dearu.
this box-TOP weight ten-kilogram is/is
'This box weighs ten kilograms.'

After all, Japanese has a way of expressing the same meaning as the English example in (1). At the same time, close investigation reveals that one of the variants in (3) exhibits an unusual additional semantic property that has significant implications for the syntax and semantics of adjectives. This paper explores issues surrounding the syntactic treatment of the two types of constructions in (3), which have not received proper attention in the past.

The organization is as follows. I will first show in section 1 that the structure we have in (3) is adjectival in nature. The semantic properties of the constructions in question are taken up in section 2. Section 3 provides a syntactic account of why the two constructions in (3) differ semantically. Section 4 concludes.

1. Adjectival Nature of the Constructions

The first task is to show that the structure in (3) is adjectival. At first sight, expressions like *takasa* and *omosa* look like nominalizations of adjectives with the suffix *-sa*. And indeed, they can be accompanied by case marking, as in (4).

(4) a. Kono biru-wa takasa-**ga** nijuu-meetoru aru/dearu.
this building-TOP height-NOM twenty-meter is/is

b. Kono hako-wa omosa-**ga** juk-kiro aru/dearu.
this box-TOP weight-NOM ten-kilogram is/is

The nominative marker is absent in (3), however. Crucially, it is impossible to drop the nominative marker in this context, as illustrated in (5).

(5) Taroo-wa musuko*(-**ga**) isha dearu.
Taro-TOP son-*(-NOM) doctor is
'As for Taro, his son is a medical doctor.'

Since case marking is a rather decisive indicator of the nominal status, its absence in (3) shows that expressions like *takasa* and *omosa* are not nouns there, despite the fact that they can act as nouns under other structural conditions. We are then led to say that the form with the suffix *-sa* is adjectival in (3). Though I continue to gloss the item in question with a nominalization throughout the paper, that is a matter of convenience and consistency.

2. Non-Neutral Interpretation under Measure Phrase Modification

Let us turn to the semantic properties of the constructions in (3).

It is well known (Lehrer 1985, Seuren 1978, Svenonius and Kennedy 2006, Winter 2005, among many others) that MP modification is based on the neutralized meaning of the adjective. In other words, the bare adjective is interpreted in such a way that its subject exceeds the contextually determined standard with respect to the degree specified by the adjective, whereas no such meaning is found in the case of MP modification. Thus, (6a) does not entail (6b).

(6) a. My son is five feet tall. —/—> (6b)
b. My son is tall.

The standard way of handling the interpretation of the bare adjective in (6b) since Cresswell (1976) is to posit a degree modifier *pos* as in (7).

(7) My son is **pos** tall.

If MP semantically competes with *pos* for combination with the adjective, the neutralized interpretation of (6a) is guaranteed.

One of the Japanese constructions behaves in the same as the English counterpart in this respect. (8a) does not entail (8b), which can be verified by the felicity of the continuation in (8c).

(8) a. Kono biru-wa takasa juu-meetoru dearu. —/—> (8b)
this building-TOP height ten-meter is
b. Kono biru-wa takai.
This building-TOP tall
c. Kono biru-wa takasa juu-meetoru dearu. Totemo hikui.
this building-TOP height ten-meter is very short

The other variant with the copular verb *ar*, however, is different. (9a) entails (8b), as demonstrated by the infelicity of the continuation in (9b).

(9) a. Kono biru-wa takasa juu-meetoru aru. ——> (8b)
this building-TOP height ten-meter is
b. Kono biru-wa takasa juu-meetoru aru. #Totemo hikui.
this building-TOP height ten-meter is very short

The same point can be illustrated in another way. A 170 cm tall basketball player does not count as tall, and for that reason, (10a) sounds strange, in contrast to (10b).

(10) a. #Sono basukettobooru senshu-wa shinchou 170-cm aru.
 that basketball player-TOP height 170-cm is
 b. Sono basukettobooru senshu-wa shinchou 170-cm dearu.
 that basketball player-TOP height 170-cm is

One may wonder whether *shinchou* in (10) is adjectival. Again, case considerations indicate that it is. In (11), where MP is removed, the nominative marker is obligatory with the verb *ar*, which shows that *shinchou* is a noun in this construction.

(11) John-wa shinchou*(-**ga**) aru.
 John-TOP height*(-NOM) is
 'John is tall.'

The absence of case marking in (10), therefore, should be taken as evidence that *shinchou* is a form of an adjective there.

A straightforward way of accommodating the Japanese data is to say that MP and *pos* are not incompatible in this language, unlike in English. It is probably related to this parametric variation that items like *shinchou*, which are not morphologically related to ordinary forms of adjectives, can serve as adjectives nevertheless. The rest of the paper is devoted to explaining why the co-occurrence of MP and *pos* is associated with *ar*.

3. Structural Basis for Interpretive Properties

To figure out why *pos* and MP are not always incompatible, we need to specify exactly where they are located in structure. In addition, the account should be able to explain why *ar*, but not *dear*, forces the non-neutral interpretation. I will start with the demonstration that syntax does matter, and then turn to structural details.

3.1. Characteristics of Measure Phrase Modification

A well-known important property of MP modification of dimensional adjectives is that only positive members of antonym pairs allow it, as illustrated in (12).

(12) a. The man is five feet tall/*short.
 b. The box is ten centimeters wide/*narrow.

The two constructions that concern us share this property, as the ill-formedness of the examples in (13) shows.

(13) a. *Kono biru-wa hikusa nijuu-meetoru aru/dearu.
this building-TOP shortness twenty-meter is/is
b. *Kono hako-wa karusa ni-kiro aru/dearu
this box-TOP lightness two kilogram is/is

Significantly, this asymmetry between positive and negative members of antonym pairs is not found in another construction that also features the form suffixed with *-sa*, given in (14), where both positive and negative members yield well-formed expressions.

(14) a. Kono biru-wa juu-meetoru-no takasa dearu/*aru.
this building-TOP ten-meter-link height is/is
'This building is as tall as ten meters.'
b. Kono biru-wa (takasa) juu-meetoru-no hikusa dearu/*aru.
this building-TOP height ten-meter-link shortness is/is
'This building is as short as ten meters.'
c. Kono hako-wa sanjuu-guramu-no omosa dearu/*aru.
this box-TOP thirty-gram-link weight is/is
'This box is as heavy as thirty grams.'
d. Kono hako-wa (omosa) sanjuu-guramu-no karusa dearu/*aru.
this box-TOP (weight) thirty-gram-link lightness is/is
'This box is as light as thirty grams.'

In this construction, where MP precedes the form with *sa*, the linker *no* must be attached to MP, which indicates that the form with *sa* is a noun (see Watanabe 2010 on the distinction between genitive case and the linker). Curiously, the positive member can appear in front of MP when the negative member follows, as in (14b, d). Note also that only *dearu* is allowed.

It is a topic for another paper to investigate the structure exemplified in (14). What is important for us is that the two constructions in (3) are indeed equivalent to the English counterpart in their limitation to positive dimensional adjectives and that syntactic configurations determine semantic properties of expressions involving the form with *sa*.

3.2. Internal Syntax

Turning now to the syntactic analysis of the constructions in (3), repeated below, notice that MP follows the adjective, unlike in the English counterpart.

(3) a. Kono biru-wa takasa nijuu-meetoru aru/dearu.
this building-TOP height twenty-meter is/is
'This building is twenty meters tall.'

b. Kono hako-wa omosa juk-kiro aru/dearu.
this box-TOP weight ten-kilogram is/is
'This box weighs ten kilograms.'

This word order, however, is an option allowed by UG. Corver (2009) provides an in-depth analysis of the Romance counterparts, illustrated in (15), where MP follows the adjective.

(15) a. La voiture est longue de deux mètres. French
the car is long of two meters

b. Gianni è alto due metri. Italian
Gianni is tall two meters

Thus, there is nothing unusual about the word order of the Japanese constructions in (3).

Corver's analysis is that there is an additional movement step involved in the derivation of the Romance structures, compared with the English counterpart. Watanabe (to appear) proposes a modification of Corver's analysis, retaining the idea that the Romance (and Japanese) word order requires an additional movement step. The structural basis of Watanabe's revised analysis is the layer of functional projections in (16a). To put it in the head-final order for Japanese, we have (16b).

(16) a. $[_{DegP}$ Deg° $[_{DimP}$ Dim° $[_{\#P}$ MP #° AP]]]

b.

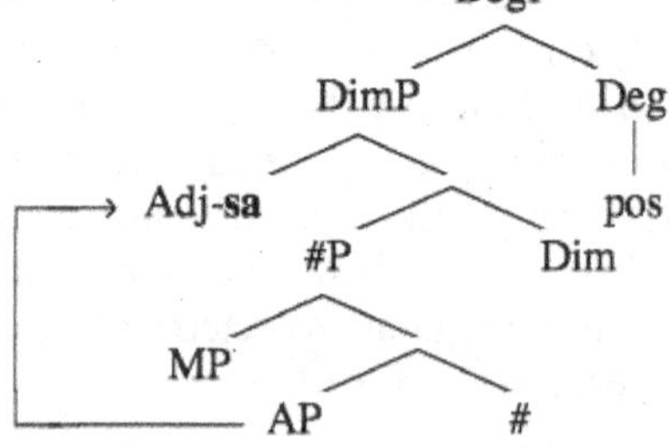

AP undergoes movement to Spec of DimP in Romance and Japanese, while no such movement is executed in English. It is also proposed in Watanabe (to appear) that the *sa*-suffix in Japanese is a reflection of agreement with the Dim head, which encodes information about dimension of measurement.

A major motivation for this analysis comes from comparison with PP syntax. Watanabe (2009) observes that MP can either precede or follow a noun-like P head, as in (17a, b).

(17) a. John-no ni-meetoru ushiro(-no-tokoro)-ni Bill-ga iru
John-gen two-meter behind-link-dim-loc Bill-NOM is
Bill is (in a place that is) two meters behind John.

b. John-no ushiro ni-meetoru*(-no-tokoro)-ni Bill-ga iru.
John-gen behind two-meter-link-dim-loc Bill-NOM is
Bill is two meters *(place) behind John.

The P head in question, *ushiro*, is characterized as noun-like, since its complement is genitive marked. This P head is categorized as P_n, to distinguish it from another type of P head, which is called P_o. When the P_n head precedes MP, P_nP is analyzed as being raised to Spec of DimP, which is headed by *tokoro*. The complement of P_nP itself is further raised to Spec of P_oP. The entire structure for (17b) is displayed in (18).

(18)

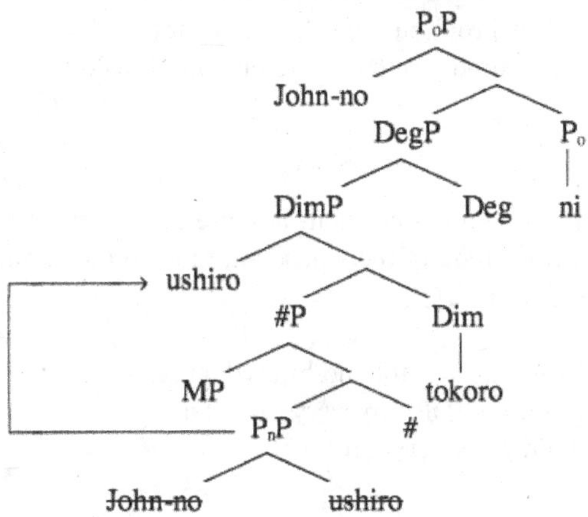

In this treatment, DimP plays a crucial role, regulating displacement of P_nP. The version of the Dim head that triggers movement of P_nP is obligatorily realized as *tokoro*, whereas the version that does not gets the shape *tokoro* only optionally. Furthermore, movement to Spec of DimP is restricted to the locational dimension. Thus, when the temporal relation is expressed, MP must come in front of P_nP, as illustrated in (19).

(19) a. John-wa jiken-no ni-jikan mae-/ato-ni Mary-ni atta.
John-TOP incident-gen two-hour before/after-loc Mary-dat met
'John met Mary two hours before/after the incident.'

b. *John-wa jiken-no mae-/ato ni-jikan(-no-toki/koro)-ni
John-TOP incident-gen before/after-loc two-hour-link-time/loc
Mary-ni atta.
Mary-dat met

Though movement to Spec of DimP is optional in the case of PP while obligatory for AP, essentially the same structural configuration is involved.

According to Watanabe's (2009) analysis, non-measure degree modifiers are located in Spec of DegP. This placement ensures that they will always precede P_nP, as shown in (20).

(20) a. John-no sugu/sukoshi/kanari ushiro(-no-tokoro)-ni Bill-ga iru.
John-gen right/a.little/a.lot behind-link-dim-loc Bill-NOM is
'Bill is found right/a little/far behind John.'

b. John-no ushiro ??sugu/*sukoshi/*kanari(-no-tokoro)-ni
John-gen behind right/a little/far-link-dim-loc
Bill-ga iru.
Bill-NOM is

In the adjectival projection, too, non-measure degree modifiers behave differently. They do not require the suffix *–sa*, nor do they come after the adjective, as illustrated in (21).

(21) Kono biru-wa totemo/hijouni takai.
this building-TOP very/very tall
'This building is very tall.'

Now, since *pos* is an instance of non-measure degree modifiers, we can safely conclude that it is not incompatible with MP, at least syntactically. I have placed it at the Deg head in (16b), but it may be hosted in Spec of DegP. I will leave the choice open.

To sum up, AP and PP utilize essentially the same structural resource for MP modification. In the case of AP, MP and *pos* are located in different positions. Thus, they can cooccur, as far as syntax is concerned.

3.3. External Syntax

Our next task is to explain why *ar*, but not *dear*, forces the non-neutral positive interpretation. To understand what is going on, it is necessary to look at the inflectional morphology associated with adjectives. For the purposes of this paper, I will adopt a modified version of Nishiyama's (1999) analysis.

Nakayama (1988) observes that adjectives are accompanied by the copular verb *ar*, which is visible in the past tense (22a) and in the presence of a focus particle (22b), even though it is not visible otherwise (22c).

(22) a. Sono biru-wa taka-k-atta.
that building-TOP tall-K-was
'That building was tall.'
b. Sono biru-wa taka-ku-mo aru.
that building-TOP tall-K-also is
'That building is also tall.'
c. Sono biru-wa taka-i.
that building-TOP tall-PRES
'That building is tall.'

These examples involve *pos*. Since the same copular verb induces the non-neutralized interpretation even in the presence of MP in (22), it seems reasonable to assume that *ar* is closely connected to the presence of *pos*. But the story is not that simple, for *dear* is decomposable into *de* and *ar*.

The environments for *dear* are heterogeneous. It can follow a predicate nominal (23a), a nominal adjective (23b), and a PP predicate (23c).

(23) a. Hanako-wa gakusei-dearu.
Hanako-TOP student-is
'Hanako is a student.'
b. Hanako-wa (totemo) kenkou-dearu.
Hanako-TOP very healthy-is
'Hanako is (very) healthy.'
c. Sono tegami-wa Hanako-kara-dearu.
that letter-TOP Hanako-from-is
'That letter is from Hanako.'

The fact that *dear* consists of *de* and *ar* can be seen clearly when a focus particle comes in between, as in (24).

(24) Hanako-wa gakusei-de-mo-aru.
Hanako-TOP student-DE-also-is
'Hanako is also a student.'

Thus, it is not *ar* itself but the structure below that makes a difference.

Nishiyama (1999) proposes that *k(u)* in (22a, b) and *de* in (23) head PredP, positing the structure in (25a) for (22a, b), (25b) for (22c), and (25c) for (23).

(25) a.

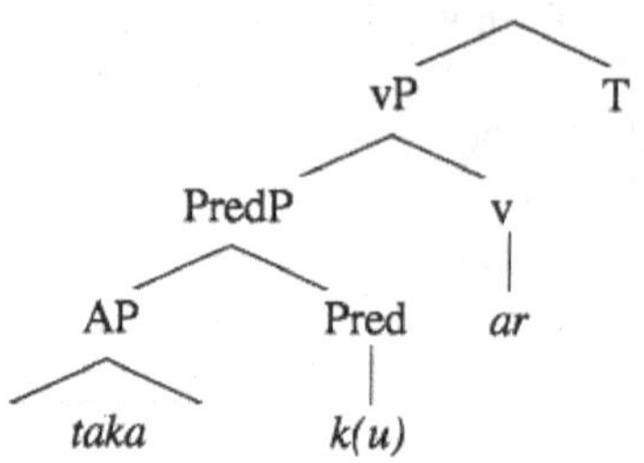

b.

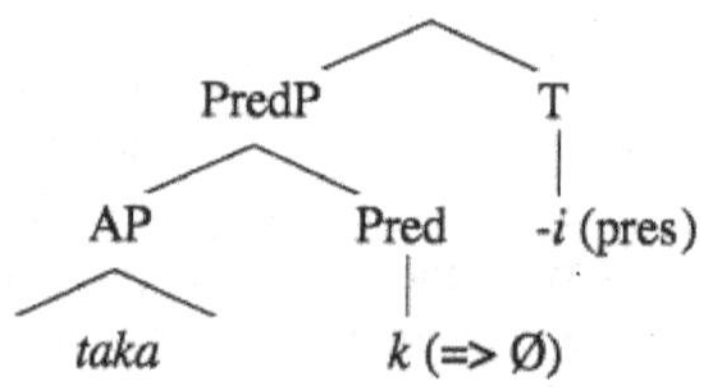

c.

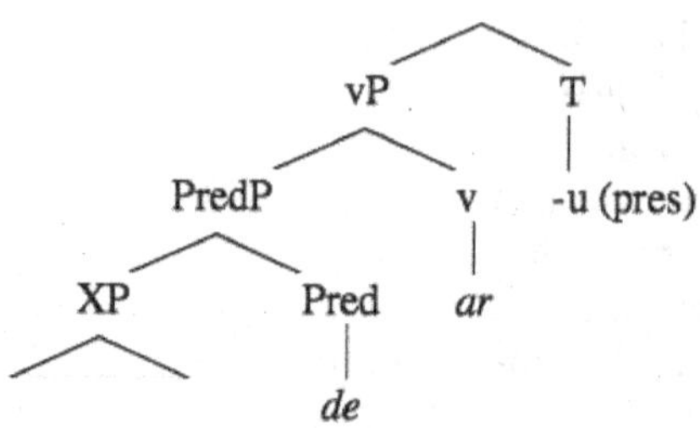

The absence of *k* in (22c) is accounted for by deleting it in the context of the following present tense suffix *i*.

The Pred head was introduced by Bowers (1993) to host an external argument in its Spec across categories. I will follow Baker (2003) in limiting the Pred head to non-verbal predication, though this decision does not affect the direction of analysis in this paper. I will abstract away from the exact position of the subject throughout this discussion. The original position of the subject vis-à-vis MP becomes extremely significant when number inflection of adjectives is taken into account. See Watanabe (to appear) on this.

Nishiyama's analysis needs to be modified in several respects. First, *k*(*u*) must be treated as part of the adjectival stem. This modification is necessary, because the two constructions that concern us, repeated below, lack the suffix *k*(*u*).

(3) a. Kono biru-wa takasa nijuu-meetoru aru/dearu.
this building-TOP height twenty-meter is/is
'This building is twenty meters tall.'

The status of *k*(*u*) is the default stem-forming suffix, used when the other stem-forming suffix *-sa* is not attached to the root. In both cases, the Pred head is phonologically null. Furthermore, the complement of the null Pred head must be DegP.

Nishiyama tries to justify the structure in (25b) by mentioning the cross-linguistic tendency that present tense does not require an overt form of the copula. If (25b) is allowed, however, it is not clear why (26) is impossible.

(26) a.

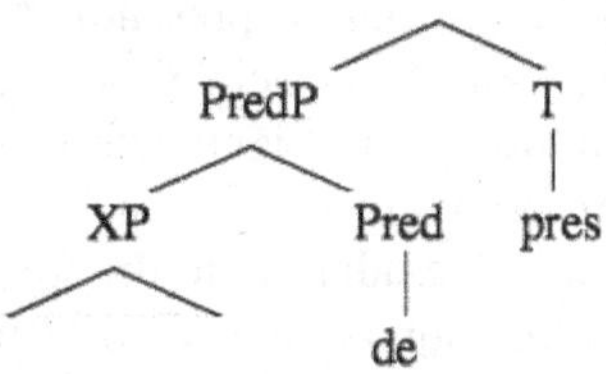

b. *Hanako-wa gakusei-de-(r)u/-i.
Hanako-TOP student-DE-PRES

Nishiyama rules out the structure (26a) by not giving tense any morphological realization in this syntactic context, restricting the present tense suffix (*r*)*u* to structures that contain a verb and requiring the suffix *i* to follow the Pred head *k(u)* directly. But this result is nothing more than an artifact of the proposed morphological analysis. It also fails to capture the fact that (*r*)*u* is the default present tense marker. I will instead adopt an alternative according to which the copular verb is syntactically present even in cases like (22c), attributing the alternation between the overt and null forms of the copula to the morpho-syntactically conditioned choice of vocabulary items in the manner of Distributed Morphology (Halle and Marantz 1993), the framework of which forms the basis of Nishiyama's analysis in other respects.

(27) shows the structural analysis shared by all the examples in (22).

(27)

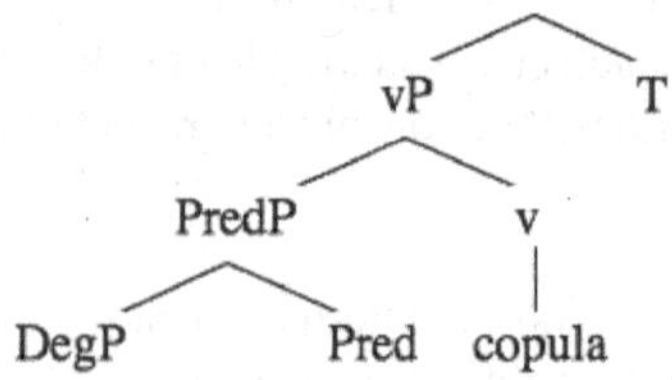

The relevant vocabulary items are those in (28).

(28) Vocabulary Items
  a. Ø ↔ copula / Adj ___ [indicative, –past]
  b. ar ↔ copula
  c. -i ↔ [–past] / Adj ___
  d. -(r)u ↔ [–past]

Suppose the T head in (27) contains [–past] in the indicative clause. When the copula is sandwiched by an adjective and the present indicative, (28a) is chosen over (28b) because of the Elsewhere Principle, since the former contains more specific structural information. Significantly, the functional heads within DegP and the Pred head in (27) are all phonologically empty, which guarantees that the copula is string-adjacent to the adjective. Similarly, (28c) is chosen over (28d) as the morphological realization of T, once the null version of the copula is chosen. Vocabulary insertion thus takes place cyclically as in (29), yielding (22c) after *k* is deleted (see Harbour 2008 and the references cited there for cyclic vocabulary insertion).

(29) Vocabulary Insertion
  i. takak-copula-Pres => takak-Pres
  ii. takak-Pres => takak-i (=> taka-i)

We need to restrict the null version of the copula to the indicative present context, in view of the following contrast, for which Nishiyama (1999: note 9) has no explanation:

(30) Yama-wa taka-ku-aru/??taka-i beki-dearu.
  mountain-TOP tall-K-is/tall-PRES should-is
  'Mountains should be high.'

Given the modal meaning, the complement of *beki* cannot be indicative. I therefore take it as subjunctive (see Watanabe 1996 for the distinction between indicative and subjunctive in Japanese). Thus, (28a) is inapplicable in (30). (28b) applies instead, destroying the environments for (28c). (28d), then, provides the morphological realization of T.

In (22b), repeated below, the copula is not string-adjacent to the adjective, due to the intervention of the focus particle.

(22) b. Sono biru-wa taka-ku-mo aru.
that building-TOP tall-K-also is

(28b) is therefore selected. (28b) is also chosen when T is [+past].

Now we are ready to specify how the choice between *ar* and *de-ar* affects semantic interpretation for examples like (3). Suppose that the null Pred head (call it $Pred_A$) always selects DegP. Then, the structure that contains MP is (31), where the copula is overtly realized because it is not adjacent to the adjective due to the presence of MP.

(31)

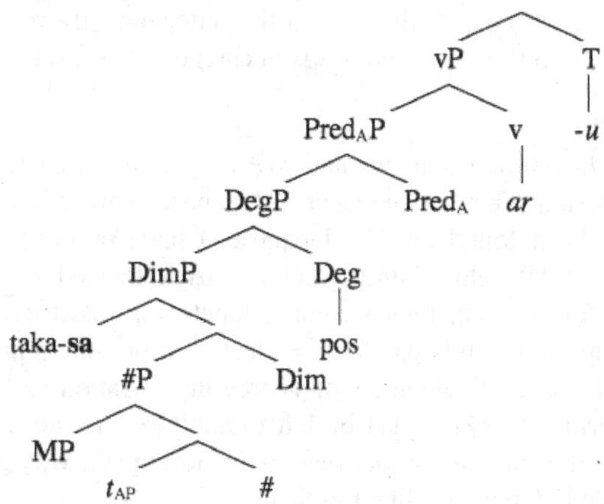

The DegP contains *pos*, giving rise to the non-neutral interpretation. The complement of the overt Pred head *de*, on the other hand, is heterogeneous in category. Thus, it can take DimP (without DegP) as its sister as in (32).

(32)

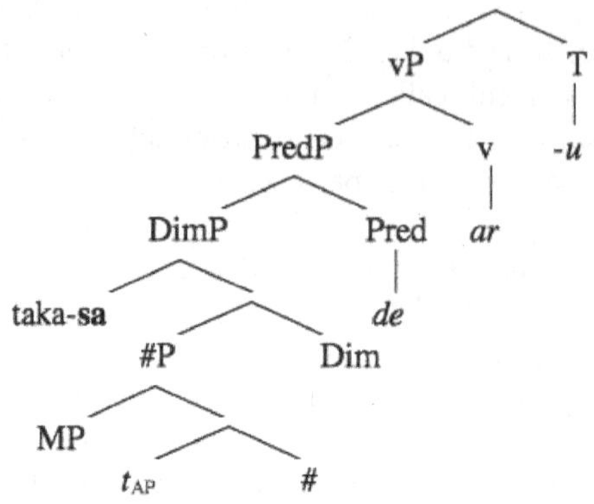

Since the structure does not contain *pos*, the neutral interpretation is obtained.

To summarize, we can attribute the presence or absence of the non-neutral interpretation of the adjective to the independently recognized difference between two types of Pred heads in category selection.

4. Conclusion

It has been demonstrated that *pos* and MP are not necessarily in complementary distribution. They can cooccur in Japanese. This striking phenomenon has so far been found only in Japanese. I have proposed that MP is hosted in Spec of #P below DimP whereas *pos* is located in DegP above DimP. It then follows that they do not compete for structural placement. The findings reported in this paper are expected to provide a precious window into the working of semantics of degree modification as well, though presenting a formal analysis must be left to another occasion due to space limitations. Another task for future research is to explain why *pos* and MP are incompatible in languages like English.

In the proposed syntactic analysis, Spec of DimP serves as the landing site of AP movement. Lying behind this movement is the agreement relation between Dim and AP, which triggers suffixation of *–sa* in Japanese. Thus, DimP is involved in MP modification syntactically and morphologically. Dimension of measurement has been considered to be an important ingredient of the degree semantics. Choice of measure words is influenced by which dimension of measurement is employed, for example. Our results show that it is hosted in a functional projection in syntax and affects morphology, too.

References

Baker, M. 2003. *Lexical Categories*. Cambridge: Cambridge University Press.

Bowers, J. 1993. The Syntax of Predication. *Linguistic Inquiry* 24:591–656.

Corver, N. 2009. Getting the (Syntactic) Measure of Measure Phrases. *The Linguistic Review* 26:67–134.

Cresswell, M. J. 1976. The Semantics of Degree. *Montague Grammar,* ed. B. Partee, 261–292. New York: Academic Press.

Halle, M. and A. Marantz. 1993. Distributed Morphology. *The View from Building 20,* ed. K. Hale and S. J. Keyser, 111–193. Cambridge, MA: MIT Press.

Harbour, D. 2008. Discontinuous Agreement and the Syntax-Morphology Interface. *Phi Theory,* ed. D. Harbour, D. Adger, and S. Béjar, 185–220. Oxford: Oxford University Press.

Hayashishita, J.-R. 2009. *Yori*-Comparatives: A Reply to Beck et al. (2004). *Journal of East Asian Linguistics* 18:65–100.

Lehrer, A. 1985. Markedness and Antonymy. *Journal of Linguistics* 21:397–429.

Nakayama, M. 1988. Empty Copulas. *Mita Working Papers in Psycholinguistics* 1, ed. Y. Otsu, 121–128. Keio University, Tokyo.

Nishiyama, K. 1999. Adjectives and the Copulas in Japanese. *Journal of East Asian Linguistics* 8:183–222.

Seuren, P. A. M. 1978. The Structure and Selection of Positive and Negative Gradable Adjectives. *Papers from the Parasession on the Lexicon, CLS* 14, ed. D. Farkas, W. M. Jacobsen, and K. W. Todrys, 336–346. Chicago: Chicago Linguistic Society.

Snyder, W., K. Wexler, and D. Das. 1995. The Syntactic Representation of Degree and Quantity: Perspectives from Japanese and Child English. *Proceedings of WCCFL* 13, ed. R. Aranovich, W. Byrne, S. Preuss, and M. Senturia, 581–596. Stanford: CSLI.

Svenonius, P. and C. Kennedy. 2006. Northern Norwegian Degree Questions and the Syntax of Measurement. *Phases of Interpretation,* ed. M. Frascarelli, 133–161. Berlin: Mouton de Gruyter.

Watanabe, A. 1996. Nominative-Genitive Conversion and Agreement in Japanese: A Cross-linguistic Perspective. *Journal of East Asian Linguistics* 5: 373–410.

Watanabe, A. 2009. Measure Phrases in PP. *The Proceedings of the Tenth Tokyo Conference on Psycholinguistics*, ed. Y. Otsu, 1–25. Tokyo: Hituzi Syobo.

Watanabe, A. 2010. Notes on Nominal Ellipsis and the Nature of *No* and Classifiers in Japanese. *Journal of East Asian Linguistics* 19:61–74.

Watanabe, A. to appear. Adjectival Inflection and the Position of Measure Phrases. *Linguistic Inquiry.*

Winter, Y. 2005. Cross-Categorial Restrictions on Measure Phrase Modification. *Linguistics and Philosophy* 28:233–267.

Index